WARNOCK

WARNOCK

MICHAEL DUGGAN
THE CONSUMING FIRE

WARNOCK

REV. MICHAEL DUGGAN

The Consuming Fire

A Christian Introduction
to the Old Testament

IGNATIUS PRESS   SAN FRANCISCO

Map design by:
Rabil & Associates
814 West Diamond Avenue
Gaithersburg, MD 20878

Cover art: *Elijah Taken up in a Chariot of Fire*
Giovanni Battista Piazzetta (Date c. 1745)
National Gallery of Art, Washington, D.C.
(Canvas; 1.746 x 2.648 [68¾ x 10.25 in.])

Cover design by Riz Boncan Marsella

In Memory of My Mother

"[F]or Yahweh your God is a consuming fire. . . . "

Deuteronomy 4:24

" 'Is my word not like fire,' Yahweh demands, 'is it not like a hammer shattering a rock?' "

Jeremiah 23:29

" 'Did not our hearts burn within us as he talked to us on the road and explained the scriptures to us?' "

Luke 24:32

CONTENTS

WRITINGS

DEUTEROCANONICAL BOOKS

ABBREVIATIONS

Old Testament

Genesis	Gn	Proverbs	Prv
Exodus	Ex	Qoheleth	Qo
Leviticus	Lv	Song of Songs	Sg
Numbers	Nm	Wisdom	Wis
Deuteronomy	Dt	Sirach	Sir
Joshua	Jos	Isaiah	Is
Judges	Jgs	Jeremiah	Jer
Ruth	Ru	Lamentations	Lam
1 Samuel	1 Sm	Baruch	Bar
2 Samuel	2 Sm	Ezekiel	Ez
1 Kings	1 Kgs	Daniel	Dn
2 Kings	2 Kgs	Hosea	Hos
1 Chronicles	1 Chr	Joel	Jl
2 Chronicles	2 Chr	Amos	Am
Ezra	Ezr	Obadiah	Ob
Nehemiah	Neh	Jonah	Jon
Tobit	Tb	Micah	Mi
Judith	Jdt	Nahum	Na
Esther	Est	Habakkuk	Hb
1 Maccabees	1 Mc	Zephaniah	Zep
2 Maccabees	2 Mc	Haggai	Hg
Job	Jb	Zechariah	Zec
Psalms	Ps(s)	Malachi	Mal

New Testament

Matthew	Mt	1 Corinthians	1 Cor
Mark	Mk	2 Corinthians	2 Cor
Luke	Lk	Galatians	Gal
John	Jn	Ephesians	Eph
Acts of the Apostles	Acts	Philippians	Phil
Romans	Rom	Colossians	Col

1 Thessalonians	1 Thes	1 Peter	1 Pt
2 Thessalonians	2 Thes	2 Peter	2 Pt
1 Timothy	1 Tm	1 John	1 Jn
2 Timothy	2 Tm	2 John	2 Jn
Titus	Ti	3 John	3 Jn
Philemon	Phlm	Jude	Jude
Hebrews	Heb	Revelation	Rv
James	Jas		

cf. = compare
c. = approximately
NAB = New American Bible
NJB = New Jerusalem Bible
NRSV = New Revised Standard Version

PREFACE

God teaches us his word within the setting of the Christian community. I would like to acknowledge my debt to the people of God who have instructed me in his word. While I assume responsibility for all the defects and inadequacies of this book, I attribute its virtues to the people who have influenced me by simply living their faith.

I have had the privilege of sharing in two expressions of Christian community. First, Bishop Paul O'Byrne and the priests and people of the Diocese of Calgary, who compose my diocesan family, exemplify for me the faith of the universal Church. Secondly, the men and women of the Mother of God Community have encouraged me to pursue the practical aspects of divine revelation in daily life.

In particular, I want to express my gratitude to Anthony Bosnick, the editor of *The Word among Us,* for encouraging me to persevere in writing this book, which originated in a series of articles that appeared in the publication. I thank Laura Millman for the hours of labor she expended on this book in formulating the study questions, checking the accuracy of the Scripture citations, composing the indices and bibliography, and especially for transforming my alternately ponderous and ornate prose into something more worthy of commenting on God's word.

GENERAL INTRODUCTION
THE OLD TESTAMENT IN OUR LIVES

Do you find reading the Old Testament difficult? Does it seem as if there are too many characters, too many conflicts, too many wars, prophets, and kings for you ever to get the point of what you are reading? Take heart. These frustrating thoughts indicate you have an interest, and that should encourage you. God's grace first affects us as a hunger for him in our soul. Pause for a moment and consider that your desire to read the Old Testament might derive from such a hunger.

A Guide to the Old Testament

This book is offered to you as a guide to help you find your way into the native soil of your faith. Rest assured that when you read the Old Testament, you are not entering an alien land, but you are going home to find the roots of your relationship to God and his people.

Hopefully, this book will introduce you more personally to individuals who might have seemed distant and unapproachable up to now. You will meet Abraham and Sarah, Isaac and Rebekah, Jacob and Rachel in their native surroundings and see in them how God works through the joys and tensions in marriage and family life to form a people. You might be impressed with Moses' humility, Jeremiah's sensitivity for people, and Ezekiel's genius—qualities that popular opinion does not usually associate with these individuals. The faith of the foreigner Ruth, the leadership skills of Deborah the judge, the devotion of Hannah the woman of prayer, and the zeal for reformation of Huldah the prophetess typify but a few characteristics of the remarkable women you will encounter in ancient Israel. A scribe at the royal court will tell you all about David and his family in a report that might astonish you because it so vividly reflects the king's weaknesses. But upon reflection, you will marvel not only at the honesty of the biblical author but also at the faithfulness of God to his servants when their frailty becomes evident.

When we come to know the great people of the Bible within the setting of their culture and times, we can identify with them as our brothers and sisters as well as our forebears in faith. The pages of Scripture welcome us into their lives devoid of all pretense. None of them was perfect, and all of them knew the struggle of surrendering their lives to God. They invite us to learn from their experiences as well as from their words so that we will have assurance of God's love in the face of our human limitations and know beyond all else that God is always faithful to his people in every situation.

The Word, Our Lives, and Community

Once we identify with God's people, we can experience God's action. God's word has a practical aspect. It does not stand outside time but rather relates to particular events that occur at specific moments within history. The more we learn about the historical setting of the Old Testament, the more we appreciate the texts as the word of God applied to concrete situations. As we appreciate how the Lord spoke to the specific circumstances of his people in the past, we will appreciate how he speaks to us in the confines of our daily existence. The word of God becomes an event that molds our lives here and now.

Under the power of God's word, we partake of the divine promises and journey in faith with Abraham. With Moses, we undertake our own exodus, leaving behind the slavery of our old life, passing through a sea of troubles by a miracle of God's grace, and finally entering into the security of God's embrace in the bond of the covenant. In the prophets, we experience the immediacy of the word touching the practical issues of our lives, calling us to conversion, faith, deeper love of God, and the practice of justice, especially for the oppressed. The Wisdom Literature teaches us how to use our minds in order to think about the great issues of life and death, good and evil, suffering and divine mercy, creation and the ultimate destiny of all that exists. In summary form, everything about creation, Abraham and Moses, the prophets, and wisdom comes together in the psalms, which raise our hearts in prayer to the God of all mercy. If we should doubt the benefits of reading the Old Testament, we need only consider that Jesus and every saint in the Church's history prayed the psalms.

Reading the Old Testament will lead us to community. The Old Testament breaks down our isolation and teaches us that we enter into the life of promise by joining ourselves to God's people. We learn very quickly that God redeems us in a most personal manner precisely by drawing us into the community of faith. As we appreciate that God saves a people and addresses his word to them as a body, we will develop a great love for the Church.

The word and the community belong together. The word forms community, and the community proclaims the word. Our study will demonstrate that God's action among his people throughout a period of almost two thousand years gave birth to the biblical text. The inspired word that has come from the heart of the community enters into the deep recesses of our hearts as we read it in union with the mind of the Church. Our reading will always bear fruit if our meditation on the word arises out of love for God and his people.

The General Design of This Guide to the Old Testament

This guide will take you through every book of the Old Testament. It presumes that you have never undertaken a systematic study of the Scriptures. Therefore the first three chapters provide you with a panorama of the Bible, first by describing the various traditional ways of listing the books (Chapter 1), then by offering a survey of biblical history and geography (Chapter 2), and finally by providing an overview of dating the composition of the individual texts (Chapter 3).

The Old Testament becomes manageable when we recognize how the texts relate to one another. We have grouped the texts under headings that represent a blend of Hebrew and Greek traditions: the Pentateuch, the Historical Books, the Prophets, Writings, and the Deuterocanonical Books (see Chapter 1). This arrangement brings together books that are similar in literary form. As a general rule, within each category, we study the books according to their chronological sequence from earliest to latest.

We have included introductory chapters that identify the distinguishing features of four major collections: the Pentateuch (Chapters 4–6), the Deuteronomic History (Chapter 13), the Prophets (Chapter 19), and Wisdom Literature (Chapter 30). Due to the wonderful intricacy of the Pentateuch, we subdivide its introduction into three chapters that provide a general overview of its contents (Chapter 4), a summary of the history of the Patriarchal period (Chapter 5), and an analysis of how the texts grew out of more than a thousand years of sacred tradition (Chapter 6).

Examining the texts in historical sequence enables us to note their interrelationships from a literary viewpoint. For example, when discussing the book of Deuteronomy, we point out its stylistic distinctiveness by comparison to Genesis, Exodus, Leviticus, and Numbers, and its affinity to Joshua, Judges, Samuel, and Kings, the compendium that makes up the Deuteronomic History. Studying the prophets according to their historical order offers us the advantage of perceiving both how the prophetic tradition developed and how these great servants of the Lord influenced one another.

Within the category of the Writings, our arrangement does not always follow the chronological sequence of publication. Although Ruth and Esther differ markedly in their history of composition, we treat them in the same chapter because they exhibit similarities in literary form and theme. Furthermore, in the ensuing chapter, we discuss Lamentations, Qoheleth, and the Song of Songs. These three texts are distinctive from each other in history and in literary form, but we group them together because they, along with Ruth and Esther, comprise the Hebrew collection of the *megilloth,* or scrolls for the great feasts. Finally, although we must read Daniel in light of the history narrated in 1 and 2 Maccabees, we treat this apocalyptic book first because it belongs to the Writings, while the accounts of the Maccabaean history belong to the Deuterocanonicals.

Our historical approach will allow us to appreciate the dynamic fluidity that characterizes God's word as it moves through history and shapes the life of his people. The divine word is symphonic; it echoes and resonates across the centuries with ever new and inspiring tones. The symphony of the word arises out of tradition, the inspired process by which God's people transmit God's word from one generation to the next. A sensitivity for history and tradition will enable us to pick up echoes of Deutero-Isaiah in the first chapter of Genesis, resonances of Ezekiel in Leviticus, and soundings of Deuteronomy in Jeremiah.

Great compositions come from times of great suffering. This principle comes to mind when we consider the wealth of inspired literature that emerged from the hands of the exiles in Babylon. Their words were forged in the fires of affliction resulting from the destruction of Jerusalem and the Temple. The final editions of the Deuteronomic History, Jeremiah, and Ezekiel represent some of the fruit of exilic labor. Even the dry rubrics of Leviticus take on a prophetic tone when we realize they are components of a blueprint for the reconstruction of Judah after the Exile. The Exile provided for a convergence and dynamic interaction of Israel's traditions evident in the rich texture of the Sacred Scriptures from that period.

The Design of Each Chapter

We have designed the individual chapters with the aim of allowing the text to speak most directly to you. Each chapter has six parts:

1. First, we describe the historical situation of Judah and the ancient Near East that provides the setting for the events related to the text.

2. Then we consider the historical situation of the author and his audience, which is often quite distant from the events themselves. For example, the Deuteronomists who labored in the Exile (587–538 B.C.) produced the

final edition of the story of David some four hundred years after the great king's reign (1010–971 B.C.).

3. After describing the historical context, first of the events and then of the book, we identify some of the major themes in the sacred text. What does this particular book say about God, his people, and the event of salvation? What did the text mean to the original author and his audience? How is this text related to other biblical texts? Furthermore, at the beginning of most chapters, we include a paragraph identifying an area of our own lives that will be affected by our reading of a particular book. These introductory reflections suggest a way of responding to our common concern, "How does the text apply to our situation today?"

4. A distinguishing feature of this guide to the Old Testament is its intent to illustrate how the contents of a particular biblical book foreshadow the coming of Christ. We contemplate the insights that Jesus and the New Testament authors bring to the text. We believe this is essential because Christ is both the fulfillment and the interpreter of Sacred Scripture for the Christian and the Church (see Lk 24:25–27, 32, 44–47). The symphony of the word reaches its crescendo in Christ. As we learn from the anointed New Testament writers how to read the Old Testament, we realize that Christ does not conform to the letter of the texts as if they were mere predictions about his coming; rather, he fulfills the Scriptures by breaking them open to expose a depth of revelation beyond the conceptual limitations of their original authors. When citing the New Testament texts, we generally follow the chronological order in which they were completed rather than the sequence in which they appear in the Bible. (Therefore, for example, we cite Mark before Matthew and Philippians before Ephesians.)

5. Each chapter contains a list of study questions designed to enhance personal comprehension and to stimulate group discussion.

6. At the end of the chapter, you will find an outline of the complete biblical book. This functions as a table of contents and thus offers you a perspective on the structure of the document so you can interpret a particular passage within its broader context.

For the sake of maintaining fluidity of style and freedom from technicalities, we have not used footnotes. The sources consulted in the composition of this book are listed in the bibliography. Readers who would like to pursue further study are directed to the auxiliary aids, particularly the bibliography.

Auxiliary Aids

We invite you to consult the historical charts and maps near the end of the book, as well as the bibliography, which follows. Furthermore, three indices will assist your research of more particular issues. The first two indices provide references to figures, places, and themes in the Old and New Testaments. The third index lists the New Testament verses to which we allude and which we discuss in the text.

All the quotations of Scripture come from *The New Jerusalem Bible.* The numbering of the verses in the biblical text follows the standard of *The New Jerusalem Bible,* which adheres to the Hebrew rather than the Greek convention. The cross-references and notes to *The New Jerusalem Bible* have established a standard of excellence unsurpassed among study editions of the Bible.

The Perspective of Vatican II

The "Dogmatic Constitution on Divine Revelation" (*Dei Verbum*) has inspired the approach to Scripture underlying the methodology of this book. This indispensable text of Vatican II teaches us that revelation is God's communication of his life to us in Jesus Christ. The substance of revelation is not simply divine words but divine life. Sacred Scripture is the servant of divine revelation insofar as it contains and mediates the very life of God to the Church and to the world. For this reason, the Church extends to Sacred Scripture the veneration she has for the Body of the Lord in the Eucharist. Word and sacrament together nurture and form the people of God in all liturgical celebrations.

Through Sacred Scripture, God makes his love and truth known to us and invites us into a participation in his divine life. Faith constitutes our response to this revelation. Faith itself is a gift of the Holy Spirit, who first opens our minds in conversion and then provides the charisms necessary for us to mature in ever-deeper union with God. By faith, we consent to God's love and respond by giving our lives to him in an obedience that is born out of gratitude for new life and reverence for truth. Sacred Scripture not only teaches us about God and his love but instructs us about our response. We read the Scriptures in order to know God ever more deeply by surrendering our lives to him in obedience. In our reading, we must allow the words of the text to lead us beyond superficial impressions and put us in touch with the deeper resources of divine life.

Sacred Scripture has reached its definitive and unalterable form in the Church's canon of inspired texts. We can be certain that in the Scripture we possess, God inerrantly teaches us the truth that is necessary for our salvation. Nevertheless, God's word always remains living and active, speaking afresh to each new generation. The Church's understanding of the revelation contained in the Scriptures develops over the course of the ages in the dynamic process of living and communicating the faith that we call tradition. As the Bride of Christ, the Church is always the hearer of the word who constantly integrates the Scriptures into her life. In more specific terms, the Church assimilates the word as the faithful devote themselves to contemplation and study, as individuals rightly discern the interior experience of divine grace, and as bishops teach according to the charism of truth that is theirs as successors to the apostles (*Dei Verbum* 8). The Magisterium of the Church fulfills its role as the servant of the word by caring for the authentic interpretation of the text.

What was the meaning of the text for the biblical author and his audience? This must be the foremost concern of anyone who wishes to interpret the Bible. What the text meant in its original setting governs what it means in our contemporary situation. Ever since the publication of Pope Pius XII's seminal encyclical *Divino afflante Spiritu* in 1942, the Magisterium has insisted that Catholic exegetes study the Bible in its original languages and decipher its message within its indigenous historical and cultural context. In order to determine the meaning intended by the inspired author, the interpreter must take account of the linguistic conventions and literary forms current at the time of composition.

Throughout the twentieth century, our understanding of the biblical world has advanced dramatically through an acceleration of archaeological discoveries, breakthroughs in linguistic research, and new developments in literary studies. In this book, we try to offer you the benefit of the best, most reliable, and up-to-date biblical research. In matters of scholarly debate, we tend to respect the reliability of traditional postures. Biblical scholarship has achieved a consensus on historical and critical issues that is basically trustworthy. However, we do realize that further research may refine, nuance, and modify some of our positions.

Uncovering the meaning of the text in its historical and cultural setting is essential but, by itself, inadequate to a genuine interpretation of Scripture as God's word. When we have ascertained what the text meant to the human author, we must still consider what it reveals about the mind of God. In order to comprehend the fullest implications of the text, we would have to study it in light of: (1) the whole of the Bible; (2) the Church's tradition, especially as represented in the teachings of the Fathers; (3) the development of theology; and (4) the statements of the Magisterium (*Dei Verbum* 12). Obviously, the present book cannot fulfill all these requirements, but it attempts to address the first one.

We study the text on the premise of the Bible's unity and coherence as the vehicle of divine revelation. The whole of Scripture points to Christ. *Dei Verbum* has motivated our reading the Old and New Testaments in view of one another. The Council opens vast horizons for us when it teaches us that "the books of the Old Testament, all of them caught up into the Gospel message, attain and show forth their full meaning in the New Testament (cf. Mt 5:17; Lk 24:27; Rom 16:25–26; 2 Cor 3:14–16) and, in their turn, shed light on it and explain it" (*Dei Verbum* 16).

By your life of prayer, you, the reader, will supply the primary aid to understanding the Old Testament. The word always remains God's, and we must hear him speak it to us in the innermost recesses of our personalities. When prayer accompanies our study of Sacred Scripture, we enter into a dialogue with the Lord in communion with the Church. The two disciples whom Jesus met on the road to Emmaus describe for all of us the experience of really understanding the Old Testament when they exclaim, "Did not our hearts burn within us as he talked to us on the road and explained the Scriptures to us?" (Lk 24:32). May we allow the risen Lord to instruct us in a similar manner as we receive the precious gift of the word he speaks to us in the community of faith.

PRELIMINARY SURVEY

I

THE OLD TESTAMENT LIBRARY

Look over the table of contents for the Old Testament (usually located at the beginning of the Bible). Have you ever wondered why the books are arranged in this order? Why are these books included and not others? Why are there thirty-nine books according to Jewish and Protestant traditions and forty-six according to Catholic tradition? The very fact that such questions come to mind suggests you already have a correct impression of what lies before you. Your Bible is not just a book; it is a library.

Our English word *Bible* comes from the Greek plural form *ta biblia,* meaning "the books". At the time of Jesus, the Scriptures were contained in scrolls of papyrus (a kind of paper made from reeds harvested in the shallow waters of the northern Nile) or parchment (fine leather made from sheep or calfskin). The texts were inscribed on sections of material that were sewn together side by side. Each scroll contained a distinct literary work. Thus, a synagogue or rabbinical school would not have a single text of Hebrew Scriptures but rather a collection of various scrolls—a library.

In part to distinguish themselves from the synagogues, but even more for the sake of convenience, early Christian scribes and scholars developed a new format for sacred manuscripts. This was the codex, ancestor to our modern-day book. The codex was composed of pages of parchment or papyrus placed in sequence one on top of another and then stitched together on one side. The earliest examples we have of all the scriptural documents being collected into one book come from the fourth century after Christ.

In the codex, texts that formerly were written on different scrolls were bound together into one entity. Individual books that had been kept quite distinct and separate from one another were now made parts of the same volume. Your Bible is the result of a long and complex process of collecting, selecting, and editing manuscripts. Understanding how these books are classified will help us to appreciate the uniqueness of each book and its relationship to all the others.

The Hebrew Bible

Ancient tradition in Judaism divided the books of the Hebrew Bible into three categories: the Law (Torah), the Prophets (Nebi'im), and the Writings (Ketubim) (see Table I). Evidence of such a tripartite division is found as early as 130 B.C., when the translator of Ben Sira wrote of his grandfather's devoted study of "the Law, the Prophets, and other books of the Fathers" (Sir: translator's preface, vv. 8–10).

In the Gospel of Matthew, Jesus includes the whole of Scripture under the first two terms when he declares that he has come, not to abolish "the Law or the Prophets", but to fulfill them (Mt 5:17). A third component is added in the Gospel of Luke, when the risen Lord interprets for his disciples "the Law of Moses, . . . the Prophets, and . . . the Psalms" (Lk 24:44).

The Law. Consisting of the first five books (Genesis to Deuteronomy), the Law is the foundation of the Old Testament. It took its present form at least by the middle of the fifth century B.C. (450 B.C.) and was the norm for Judaism from the time of Ezra onward (Neh 8:1–3, 7, 8).

The Prophets. This collection was subdivided into "former prophets" (from Joshua to 2 Kings, but excluding Ruth) and "latter prophets" (from Isaiah to Malachi, but excluding Lamentations and Daniel). The "latter prophets" include the three major prophets (Isaiah, Jeremiah, and Ezekiel) and twelve minor prophets (from Hosea to Malachi). This collection of books about kings and prophets was standardized in the years after the Exile and is mentioned in a text from the first century B.C. (see 2 Mc 2:13).

The Writings. These works consist of all the remaining books not found in the previous two categories, including Ruth, Lamentations, and Daniel. Its chief components are Job, Psalms, and Proverbs. Some of the remaining books came to be grouped together in a subsection of the five "Megilloth", or "Scrolls". Each was read on a great feast: Ruth (Pentecost), Song of Songs (Passover), Ecclesiastes (Tabernacles), Lamentations (ninth of Ab), and Esther (Purim). Jews from the Greek-speaking world were inclined to include more books in the category of the Writings than were the Jews of Palestine. This lack of consensus eventually produced the diverse Catholic and Protestant opinions regarding the contents of the Old Testament.

The Greek Bible

By the time of his death in 323 B.C., Alexander the Great extended his empire throughout the Middle East to the borders of India. Greek became the international language of the world. Because Greek was the first tongue of an increasing number of Jews living outside Palestine, a need arose for the Hebrew Scriptures to be translated into Greek.

Less than a century after the death of Alexander, Jewish scholars in Egypt undertook the Greek translation of the Hebrew Scriptures called the Septuagint (LXX). In fact, a whole tradition of scholars spanning a number of generations worked on the project in Alexandria, the great center of Hellenistic learning and culture at the mouth of the Nile. The Septuagint version, which began as a translation project in the middle of the third century B.C. (c. 250 B.C.), reached completion sometime after the composition of the book of Wisdom (c. 30 B.C.) (see Table II below). The Septuagint became very influential in the early Christian Church since Greek was the native tongue of most of its members and the language of every document in the New Testament.

The Septuagint is remarkable in both organization and content. The books were grouped in a manner different from the Hebrew Bible, conforming more to perceived historical sequence, with common literary types gathered together. They were arranged in four, rather than three, categories: the Pentateuch, the Historical books, the Wisdom (poetic) books, and the Prophets.

The Pentateuch. Pentateuch is a Greek word meaning "the five books". These books in the Greek Bible correspond exactly to the Law in the Hebrew Bible.

The Historical Books. The historical books include all that has been designated as the "former prophets" in Hebrew, plus some historical literature that was previously classified under the Writings (1 and 2 Chronicles, Ezra, Nehemiah, Ruth, and Esther).

The Septuagint went beyond the contents of the Hebrew Bible, however, and added other works to this section. Among these were three books (Tobit, Judith, 1 Maccabees) that were probably written originally in Hebrew but were soon translated into Greek, after which the original texts were lost. Another addition was 2 Maccabees, a text originally written in Greek.

The Wisdom Books. In the Greek Bible, the Wisdom books include five works from the Writings: three major ones (Job, Psalms, and Proverbs) and two shorter works (Ecclesiastes and the Song of Songs). In addition to these books, the Wisdom category includes the book of Sirach (a Greek translation of the Hebrew original) and the Wisdom of Solomon.

The Prophetic Books. In the Septuagint, the prophetic books include all the latter prophets from the Hebrew Bible, but with some rearranging and some additions. Lamentations was moved from the Writings to a place just after Jeremiah, since the destruction of Jerusalem evokes its theme (narrated in Jeremiah 52). The book of Baruch (named after Jeremiah's scribe) is a late Greek translation from a Hebrew original inserted after Lamentations. Daniel was transferred from the Writings to a position preceding the Hebrew Bible's twelve minor prophets that begin with Hosea.

The Old Testament Canon

What books should be included in the Bible? This became a concern for Christians in the first century A.D. as they turned to the sacred texts to receive a deeper understanding of Jesus as the fulfillment of God's word. It was perhaps an even more critical issue for Judaism, especially after the destruction of the Temple and the fall of Jerusalem in A.D. 70. With that catastrophic event, Judaism lost its center of gravity and turned to the word of Scripture as the unifying force of its people. Both Jews and Christians felt the need to define the "canon" of sacred books.

"Canon" refers to the body of writings that are recognized as authoritative Sacred Scripture. The Greek root of the word means "rule" or "standard". Before the codex became popular, the canon was simply a list given to believers to identify for them the texts that were sacred and therefore appropriate for use in worship or instruction. The canon distinguished these books from other religious texts. With the codification of the sacred books into one volume, the canon came to mean simply those books inspired by God that belong in the Bible.

Jews and Christians worked independently of each other to identify the canon of sacred writings for their people. Toward the end of the second century B.C., rabbis still living in Palestine drew up a list for their people that did not include the extra works found in the Septuagint. By contrast, Christians who saw references to books such as Wisdom, Sirach, and Maccabees among the writings of Paul and John maintained sympathy for the Septuagint collection with its additional material.

The case, however, was not rigidly defined. Many Jews held some of the noncanonical texts in high esteem, while some noted Christian theologians (for example, Origen, Athanasius, and Jerome) argued for the adoption of the Hebrew canon alone. In the centuries that followed, successive councils of the Church identified as part of the Old Testament books that had not been contained in the Hebrew Bible. These included Sirach, Tobit, Judith, 1 and

2 Maccabees, and the Wisdom of Solomon, as well as additions to the texts of Esther and Daniel. These came to be termed "Deuterocanonical", or canonical in a secondary sense.

In the sixteenth century, Martin Luther advocated a return to the Hebrew canon. Nonetheless, he preserved the Deuterocanonical works in his first edition of a complete Bible, placing them in a separate category called the "Apocrypha" (from a Greek word meaning "hidden"). While early Reformers such as Calvin and Zwingli adopted this convention, the Dutch Reformed and Puritan congregations farther north abandoned it, denying the Apocrypha any inspired quality and excluding it from their editions of the Old Testament. In 1546, the fourth session of the Council of Trent certified the Deuterocanonical books as part of the canon for Catholics. The Apocrypha contains more books than the Catholic Deuterocanonicals. The texts that are in the Apocrypha but not in the Catholic canon are: 1 and 2 Esdras, 3 and 4 Maccabees, the Prayer of Manasseh, and Psalm 151.

A renewed sharing of the word of God has been the basis for developing unity among Christians in our day. Respect for one another's viewpoints has produced a consensus that the Bible is the common heritage and source of life for all Christians. Catholics and Protestants are jointly producing common editions of the Bible. These include the Deuterocanonical works, usually placed between the Old and New Testaments or included in a special section entitled "Apocrypha". The fact that the life-giving dynamism of the Scripture is gathering together Christians of all traditions provides clear evidence of the Spirit's activity in our world today.

STUDY QUESTIONS

1. How many books are in the Jewish and Protestant traditions as compared to the Catholic tradition?
2. What are the three categories of books of the Hebrew Bible?
3. When did the Law take its present form?
4. What is the Septuagint, and why was it written?
5. What does "canon" mean?
6. What does "Deuterocanonical" mean?
7. Why is it important to read the Bible?
8. Discuss how your attitude toward the Bible has changed over your life. How did you feel about it as a child? in church? during happy moments of your life (weddings, baptisms) or at tragic times (sickness, funerals)?
9. Have you ever experienced a lightening of your heart when you heard someone expound from the Bible and say something about Scripture or about God that had never occurred to you before? Why do you think that experience was so memorable?
10. What is there about the word of God that makes the Bible different than any other book?

Table I
The Hebrew Bible

I. *The Law (Torah)*
Genesis
Exodus
Leviticus
Numbers
Deuteronomy
II. *The Prophets*
  A. *The Former Prophets*
  Joshua
  Judges
  1 & 2 Samuel
  1 & 2 Kings
  B. *The Latter Prophets*
    1. *The Major
    Prophets*
    Isaiah
    Jeremiah
    Ezekiel
    2. *The 12 Minor
    Prophets*
    Hosea
    Joel
    Amos

Obadiah
Jonah
Micah
Nahum
Habakkuk
Zephaniah
Haggai
Zechariah
Malachi
III. *The Writings*
Job
Psalms
Proverbs
The Megilloth
  Ruth
  Song of Songs
  Ecclesiastes
  Lamentations
  Esther
Daniel
Ezra
Nehemiah
1 & 2 Chronicles

Table II
The Greek Bible (Septuagint)

I. *The Pentateuch*
Genesis
Exodus
Leviticus
Numbers
Deuteronomy
II. *The Historical Books*
Joshua
Judges
Ruth
1 & 2 Samuel
1 & 2 Kings

1 & 2 Chronicles
Ezra
Nehemiah
Tobit*
Judith*
Esther**
1 & 2 Maccabees*
III. *The Wisdom Books*
Job
Psalms
Proverbs
Ecclesiastes

Song of Songs	Joel
Wisdom*	Amos
Sirach*	Obadiah
IV. *The Prophets*	Jonah
Isaiah	Micah
Jeremiah	Nahum
Lamentations	Habakkuk
Baruch*	Zephaniah
Ezekiel	Haggai
Daniel**	Zechariah
Hosea	Malachi

*Deuterocanonical books.
**Contain additional texts beyond the Hebrew versions.

2

AN OVERVIEW: PEOPLES, PLACES, AND EVENTS
HISTORY AND GEOGRAPHY

Have you ever opened the Old Testament hoping to be carried aloft on the
wings of wisdom only to become bogged down by the names of peoples and
places you can barely pronounce? Such is the experience of most people who
either seldom read the Old Testament or give up after their initial resolve
wanes. How can the Bible be the normative word of God for all people when
it is so wrapped up with the particular times and circumstances of an ancient
world?

This is a very big question, one that we can treat here only in a partial
manner. Certainly, a major portion of the response comes from allowing the
same Holy Spirit who inspired the original authors to inspire us with the
salvific truth contained in the text. But another aspect of the response demands
that we respect the way God speaks through Scripture and realize that it
points out how he desires to work in our own lives.

Each person's life is governed by the specifics of time and space. We can be
only in one place at one time—a condition of existence we often find
exasperating. Especially when we are having a rough time, we try to flee—in
mind, if not in body—from the confinement of our circumstances. Unfortunately, too often we carry this habit into our spiritual life, thinking that God
cannot encounter us in our particular situation. That is why the Bible has to
be so down to earth: to counter our instinctive escapism and to teach us how
to face the grit of the reality at hand in such a way as to experience here the
revelation of God's power and love.

The Bible is too realistic to be a book of religious philosophy that merely
offers us abstract concepts or ideas about God. Rather, it proclaims the events
of God, his saving deeds, which he accomplished for his people in specific
times and places. The Bible teaches us who God is by showing us how he
works. As communicated in the Scriptures, these events of God—especially
the Exodus in the Old Testament and Jesus' Resurrection in the New Testament—
are not past memories but the shape of his action in our world today. More

specifically, the Bible always aims to teach us how the Lord wants to engage our unique personal lives here and now. Anything we can do to understand better the historical and cultural setting of the biblical world will enable us to appreciate the remarkable way God wants to deal with each of us and all of his people.

The Ancient Near East

We are going to take a panoramic view of the peoples and lands of the ancient Near East from 3000 B.C. until the time of Christ. This was the stage for the great drama of God's electing as his own an obscure and oppressed people.

Consulting a globe of our planet, we find the heart of the biblical world to be a relatively small area at the juncture of the continents of Asia and Africa. Here is a simple way to picture the ancient Near East. Begin by focusing your eyes on the five great bodies of water that circumscribe the biblical lands. Starting from the northwest and following a clockwise sequence, we see they are: the *Black Sea,* the *Caspian Sea,* the *Persian Gulf,* the *Red Sea,* and the *Mediterranean Sea.* Now turn your attention to the land mass that rests in the midst of these waters and identify the major rivers in this part of the world. Essentially, there are only two: in the north and east, the *Tigris-Euphrates* system, which flows south from the heights of Asia minor and Armenia to empty into the Persian Gulf; and, in the south and west, the *Nile,* which runs northward from the highlands of Africa to empty into the Mediterranean Sea. These two great waterways spawned the magnificent civilizations of *Mesopotamia* in the north and east and *Egypt* in the south and west.

Now consider the masses of terrain stretching from east to west along the north coast of the Mediterranean. The extensive landscape of *Asia Minor* gave birth to the ancient Hittite culture, another important element in the biblical world. Moving farther west, we see that *Greece* and finally *Rome* produced empires that controlled the world toward the end of the Old Testament era.

The Land of Israel

Against this background, we can perceive the territory of ancient Israel to be a tiny region in a strategic location. It was a crossroads where the great civilizations encountered one another in the ancient world. In times of international peace, it was a great location for developing trade and commerce, but, when the prospect of war overshadowed the world, it was a frontier squeezed between the superpowers who exerted pressure on it from all sides. The great empires of the ancient world realized that their security would be enhanced to a large degree by controlling the eastern Mediterranean regions of Lebanon and Palestine.

Let us take a closer look at this precious territory. It is not difficult to form a mental outline of Israel in your own mind. Picture the Mediterranean coast on the west. About 25–30 miles inland from the northern coastal area is the *Sea of Chinnereth* (the Sea of Galilee in the New Testament). The *Jordan River* flows 65 miles due south in the *Jordan Valley* from the Sea of Chinnereth until it empties into the *Dead Sea.* At its northern tip, the Dead Sea is approximately 55 miles from the Mediterranean coast. *Jerusalem* is some 20 miles west from the northern shore of the Dead Sea. *Samaria,* which would become the capital of the northern kingdom, is about 40 miles north of Jerusalem.

For a small territory, Palestine's landscape exhibits remarkable diversity and variation. You can think of it as comprised of four topographical bands running side by side from north to south. On the western fringe is the *coastal plain* extending inland from the Mediterranean Sea. At their eastern flank, these lowlands give way to the *central highlands,* which extend southward from the mountains of Lebanon until they are broken by the Plain of Esdraelon, only to rise upward again through Samaria to Jerusalem, which is situated on a height of land some 2500 feet above sea level. This explains why the ancient pilgrims describe their journey as going "up" to Jerusalem (Ps 122:3–4). Along their eastern edge, the highlands drop off sharply into the deep *Jordan Valley,* a cavernous depression in the earth that begins north of the Sea of Chinnereth, runs the length of the Jordan River to the Dead Sea, and then continues farther south as the arid indentation called the *Arabah,* which extends down to the *Gulf of Aqaba.* The point at which the Jordan River flows into the Dead Sea (about 5 miles from *Jericho*) marks the lowest ground on the face of the earth—almost 1300 feet below sea level. To the east, this great rift rises up dramatically to the heights of the *Transjordan,* an elevated arid tableland of rolling hills and barren mountains about 20 miles wide that eventually gives way to the great Arabian Desert.

Travel was easiest going north and south along the roads in the Transjordan, the central highlands, or the coastal plain. The best routes east and west passed through the lush *Valley of Jezreel* in the north or the *Negeb* in the south, Israel's arid frontier stretching all the way from the Arabah across to the west coast. Of course, south and west of the Negeb is the formidable *Wilderness of Sinai,* which separates Palestine from Egypt.

The Ancient Near East before Abraham

Remarkable civilizations existed in Egypt and Mesopotamia for over a thousand years before the time of Abraham. A closer look at these lands and their peoples will enable us to locate the biblical story within the context of world history.

As a land where rain is almost unknown, Egypt's lifeline has always been the Nile, the longest river in the world (4,100 miles). This wonder of nature originates in the high lakes of Uganda (the White Nile), is joined by a tributary (the Blue Nile) at modern Khartoum, and continues its descent northward through the full length of Egypt. The only arable land in the country lies along the shores of the Nile, which overflows its banks each year as the run-off from the torrential rains of equatorial Africa fills its channels. In the arid regions of the ancient Near East, Egypt was renowned for its crops of barley and wheat, vegetables and fruit, including the "cucumbers, melons, leeks, onions and garlic" that tempted the Israelites of the Exodus back into slavery (Nm 11:4–6). Famous Egyptian linen was produced from flax crops; and papyrus for scrolls and manuscripts was manufactured from reeds in the Nile delta.

Egypt's history as a united nation began not long after 3000 B.C. and endured until Alexander the Great conquered it in 332 B.C. The great pyramids built before 2200 B.C. provide an impressive testimony to the artistic genius and technical skill of these masters of the ancient world. For the most part, the great flowering of Egyptian power and culture took place prior to 1000 B.C.

On the other side of the ancient Near East, Mesopotamia is practically synonymous with the Fertile Crescent, a vast arching expanse of fields and pasture lands that stands out amid the dusty terrain characteristic of the more general region. Its life source is the 1700-mile Euphrates River, which flows leisurely in an arc to the southeast, where it joins the shorter (700-mile), swifter Tigris before emptying into the Persian Gulf. The marshlands between these rivers were the birthplace of some of the world's earliest civilizations. Sumer (3500–2350 B.C.) and Akkad (2350–1950 B.C.) were two highly developed city-states that established a cultural tradition in the region before the days of Abraham.

Shortly after 3500 B.C., the Sumerians developed the first nonnomadic civilization consisting of individual city-states that either a king or a priest ruled. By 3200 B.C., they had developed a system of cuneiform writing and arithmetic. Their remarkable palaces and temples were academic centers where scribes put into writing great epics and stories of creation. Ur was the principal city of Sumer until the Akkadians under the leadership of King Sargon overran it.

The Akkadians were originally a nomadic people from northwest of Sumer, whose capital was located south of present-day Baghdad, between the Euphrates and Tigris Rivers. Akkadian commercial enterprises expanded west to the Mediterranean, south into Arabia, and east as far as the Indus River in India. The recent discovery of 16,000 clay tablets at Ebla (south of Aleppo in Syria) turned up evidence of conflict and commerce between the Eblaites and Akkadians of this era. With the decline of the Akkadians, control of Mesopotamia was divided between Babylon in the south and Asshur in the north.

The History of Israel

With this sketch of the third millennium B.C. in the background, we now stand on the threshold of biblical history. The Old Testament story spans a time frame of almost two thousand years from Abraham to Jesus. Its dramatic development unfolds against the horizon of all that was happening in the great empires of the world throughout this era. For the sake of tracing a clear outline, we can divide the history of ancient Israel into ten periods.

1. The Age of the Patriarchs (1850–1550 B.C.)

The story of the Patriarchs takes us across the whole sweep of the ancient Near East from Mesopotamia to Egypt. When Abraham set out on his journey sometime around 1850 B.C., he did not blaze a new trail but followed the principal overland route from northeast to southwest. Leaving his native city Ur, he traveled north along the Euphrates to Haran in the upper regions of the Fertile Crescent (Gn 11:31). There God called him to continue south and west into Canaan, where he traversed the central highlands until he established himself about 20 miles south of Jerusalem around Hebron (Gn 13:18). Isaac seems to have gravitated more toward the Negeb in the region of Beersheba (Gn 26:15-25), and Jacob subsequently moved north into the central highlands around Shechem and Bethel (Gn 33:18-20; 35:1-15). The story of Joseph's rise to power in Egypt corresponds best with the period of the Hyksos, Semitic invaders who seized power for a century and a half (c. 1720-1550 B.C.). The arrival of Jacob in Egypt completed the movement of the Patriarchs from the eastern to the western empires of the ancient world (Gn 46:1-27).

2. The Egyptian Era (1550–1280 B.C.) through the Exodus and Wilderness
Period (1280–1240 B.C.)

We know practically nothing of the Hebrews in Egypt for the 200 years from
the death of Joseph to the birth of Moses (c. 1550–1300). It is certain that
during this interval, Egypt expanded her borders, notably under Thutmoses
III (1490–1436), who marched his troops through Canaan and Syria right up
the banks of the Euphrates. Rameses II (1290–1224), the pharaoh at the time of
the Hebrew Exodus under Moses, ruled Syria and Palestine as a condition of a
treaty with the Hittites following the battle of Kadesh on the Orontes River in
1286. Around 1280, Moses led the Israelites out of Egypt to sojourn in the
Sinai wilderness for forty years. Actually, they spent about thirty-five of those
years in the region of Kadesh-Barnea, located in the eastern Sinai directly
south of Canaan. At the end of the wilderness period, they passed through the
territories of Edom and Moab (on the eastern side of the Dead Sea) to encamp
in the Transjordan opposite Jericho.

3. The Conquest and Settlement of the Promised Land (1240–1030 B.C.)

Around 1240 B.C., under Joshua's leadership, the Israelites invaded Canaan and
established themselves in the Promised Land (Jos 1–12). During the period of
the Judges (1200–1020 B.C.), the twelve tribes dispersed throughout the
land organized themselves into a sort of confederation and confirmed their
presence amid the Canaanite cities (Jgs 1–16). The mantle of moral and
spiritual leadership was laid upon the shoulders of Samuel (c. 1050–1030 B.C.)
as the Israelites felt the menace of the Philistines, a people from the Mediterranean who had invaded the land from the west around 1200 B.C. (1 Sm
1–7).

4. The United Kingdom (1030–931 B.C.)

Around 1030 B.C., to unite the people against the Philistine threat, Samuel
anointed Saul as the first king to lead all Israel (1 Sm 9–10). Following Saul's
death in battle against the Philistines at Mount Gilboa, David was proclaimed
king in 1010 B.C. and organized the land into a legitimate kingdom that
merited recognition and respect from the surrounding nations (2 Sm 1–24). In
970 B.C., Solomon succeeded his father to the throne and brought Israel to the
apex of prosperity by expanding her trade, strengthening her military, and
transforming Jerusalem into a cosmopolitan center of learning. In spite of
Solomon's administrative talents, his kingdom was split in two as soon as he
died.

5. The Divided Kingdom (931–721 B.C.)

The people of northern Israel resented the burden Solomon had imposed on them to realize his ambitious projects. When he died and they received an unsympathetic hearing in Jerusalem from his heir Rehoboam, the ten northern tribes gathered together under one of Solomon's officials, Jeroboam (931–910 B.C.) and separated themselves from Judah (1 Kgs 12). Rehoboam (931–913 B.C.) and his successors maintained intact the Davidic line of rulers over Judah. By contrast, in the northern kingdom, now known as "Israel", rivals from diverse families seized the throne in a series of bloody revolutions. Judah and Israel exhibited an ambivalent love-hate relationship toward each other throughout their history.

The storm cloud of Assyrian might was gathering force on the eastern horizon. In 853 B.C., at the battle of Kharkah, an alliance of Israel, Judah, and other nations along the Mediterranean coast had a major confrontation with the armies of Shalmaneser III (858–824 B.C.). However, in 841 B.C., the Assyrians regrouped, invaded Israel, and exerted control over the region. Over a century later, the death-blow fell when the Assyrians under Shalmaneser V (726–722 B.C.) and Sargon II (721–705 B.C.) conquered Israel, overran its capital Samaria, and took its leading citizens into captivity in the east (2 Kgs 17:1–41). The ten northern tribes underwent such a radical transformation that they would never regain their original form.

6. The Kingdom of Judah (721–587 B.C.)

The leadership of Hezekiah (716–687 B.C.), a king devoted to the spiritual reform of his people, brought the southern kingdom through a critical period. Remarkably, Jerusalem was spared when the Assyrian troops of Sennacherib (704–681 B.C.) were at the very gates after ravaging cities throughout Judah in 701 B.C. The apostate King Manasseh (687–642 B.C.) practically surrendered the spiritual heritage of Judah to the forces of the world. However, by an amazing turn of events, the Assyrian Empire, which seemed indomitable under Ashurbanipal (669–629 B.C.), was erased from the map in 609 B.C. with the Babylonian victory at Haran.

The great reforms of Josiah (640–609 B.C.), a true spiritual son of David, tragically ended when Necho, the Egyptian leader, killed him at Megiddo. A series of inept kings in Judah allowed the Babylonians to destroy Jerusalem in a series of three invasions: first, in 597 B.C., when they deported the leading citizens to Babylon; again, in 587 B.C., when the city and Temple were destroyed after a horrible siege; and once more, in 582 B.C., in a follow-up campaign (2 Kgs 24:10–25:26).

7. The Exile in Babylon (587–538 B.C.)

The Davidic line came to an end with the death of Jehoiachin in exile sometime after his release from prison in 562 B.C. (2 Kgs 25:27–30). How could Judah survive without a king, a land, or the Temple? The marvelous story of the Exile is that of the spiritual transformation of God's people by the power of his word. Prophets and priests of great stature rose to leadership among the exiles.

On the international scene, after the death of Nebuchadnezzar (605–562 B.C.), Babylon lacked a sound leader. Around the same time, in the east, Cyrus II of Persia (550–530 B.C.) defeated the Medes and campaigned westward into Asia Minor and eastward into Afghanistan, before finally taking Babylon in 539 B.C. In 538 B.C., Cyrus' official decree ended the Exile and granted the Jews permission to return to their native soil and rebuild their city and Temple (Ezr 1:2–4).

8. Reconstruction and the Persian Period (538–332 B.C.)

A relatively small group of hearty Jews possessing a pioneering spirit returned to restore their land under the leadership of Zerubbabel the governor and Joshua the priest. Through persistent encouragement from the prophets Haggai and Zechariah, the people rededicated the modestly restored Temple in 515 B.C. (Ezr 1:1–6:22). The Persian Empire was distinguished by its respect for local religious and cultural traditions. In Judah, this led to a separation between spiritual and temporal rule, as appointees of the Persian Empire governed the region, but the priests who instructed their people from the Temple led the people in faith.

The last half of the fifth century represented a unique exception to this separation of spiritual and temporal when Nehemiah, a Jewish governor (from 445 B.C.), and Ezra, the priest-scribe (from 458 B.C.), instituted reforms that would shape Judaism for centuries to come.

The Persian Empire, whose boundaries far surpassed the dimensions of any previous world power, finally had to give way to the Greek armies of Alexander the Great, who conquered the eastern Mediterranean in 332 B.C. and the whole ancient Near East as far as India by 326 B.C.

9. The Greek (Hellenistic) Period (332–63 B.C.)

During his lifetime, Alexander conquered the world with his armies and after his death with his language and culture. Greek became the international tongue and the first language of most Jews, since more of them lived outside

Palestine than within its boundaries. By 250 B.C., the city of Alexandria was a center of Judaism where the Hebrew Scriptures were translated into Greek in a version known as the Septuagint. At his death, Alexander's empire was divided between the Ptolemies and the Seleucids, two dynasties who ruled from Egypt and Syria respectively. Seleucid oppression of the Jews reached a climax under Antiochus IV Epiphanes (175–164 B.C.) and provoked the Maccabaean revolt. Within Judaism, groups of Hasidim distinguished themselves as nonconformists in the world because of their adherence to the Torah. Traditions were being formed that gave rise to the Pharisees, Sadducees, Zealots, and Essenes of New Testament times.

10. The Roman Era (63 B.C. and onward)

In 63 B.C., the Roman armies of Pompey captured Damascus and then wrested control of Jerusalem from the descendants of the Maccabees. Palestine was placed under the authority of the Roman governor of Syria. Just over a century later, in 70 A.D., the Roman armies of Titus destroyed Jerusalem and its Temple. Tenacious Jewish resistance in the Holy Land continued until the revolt of Simeon Bar Kocheba, which was crushed in A.D. 135.

The Mystery of Election

A principle underlying God's election of his chosen people is that he did not direct his favor toward the mighty of the world but toward those who were helpless and enslaved (Dt 7:7–8). When he provided them with a land, he did not isolate them from the perils of the world but settled them in a place where they were vulnerable to the forces of history. From a political viewpoint, the Israelites were really in control of their own destiny in Palestine only during the reigns of David and Solomon, a period of some eighty years. Palestine was a defenseless country at the mercy of the world's superpowers: the Assyrians, Babylonians, Greeks, and Romans overran it successively, and the Persians controlled it. Such was the geographical and political position of the Promised Land in the world of its own day.

Here, geographical issues become theological concerns. Why did the Lord give his people a land in which they were so vulnerable to all the threats of war and violence in their world? Perhaps the reason is that the Israelites' vulnerable position enables peoples of all nations in every age, whom foreign domination threatens, to identify themselves with God's chosen ones. But more directly, the biblical authors perceived that the geographical and political vulnerability of Israel was part of God's design to teach his people the surpassing value of living by practical faith in him every day. History demonstrates that God's people always survived, even as the greatest empires expired into historical oblivion. In face of the hard evidence, they learned to pray with confidence in God's faithfulness, "Some call on chariots, some on horses, but we on the name of Yahweh our God. They will crumple and fall, while we stand upright and firm" (Ps 20:7–8). Only faith shared among God's people as divine wisdom and love can bring into the world genuine life that will last forever.

STUDY QUESTIONS

1. What role does the Holy Spirit have in our reading Scripture?
2. What relevancy does the Bible have to our lives?
3. Name the five seas and the two major river systems of the ancient world.
4. Name the two major regions of political power in the ancient Near East.
5. Draw a map of ancient Israel, including major cities, deserts, and bodies of water.
6. Describe the geographic movements from the time of Abraham to that of Joseph.
7. What happened to the united kingdom after the reigns of David and Solomon?
8. What were the circumstances of the Jews' return from the Egyptian bondage? From the Babylonian Exile?
9. What factors made Israel a precarious geographic area? How did the location of Israel affect the faith of the people?
10. What can we learn from the perdurance of the Israelites?
11. How do you think your location and the time in which you live affect your faith in God?
12. Do you belong to a rural, suburban, or urban parish? How does the locale of your parish affect the way in which you gather as a congregation for catechesis and liturgy?

3

THE HISTORY OF WRITING THE OLD TESTAMENT

Being able to locate the biblical events in their original historical and geographical setting enables us to think of what it must have been like to live then. For example, we can distinguish the times of Abraham from those of David and appreciate more immediately the factors that shaped Abraham's journey and David's rise to power. Nevertheless, for all its advantages, a chronicle of dates and times might have the detrimental effect of emphasizing just how far removed we are from the biblical era. Some people overemphasize the importance of chronological information to the point that, in the name of intellectual honesty, they treat the Bible as little more than an important artifact of history.

Anyone who takes Scripture seriously, however, cannot accept such a characterization. When we open the Bible and read of the great events of salvation, such as God's call to Abraham, the Exodus from Egypt, or the anointing of David as king, the question that preoccupies us most consistently is not "When did this happen?" but "What does this mean for us today?" Indeed, the primary reason we turn to the sacred text is to receive insight and direction for our lives. We do this, not because we are unreasoning fanatics, but because something in the text itself tells us we will never know what it is really saying unless we approach it with the eyes of faith. Every book of the Bible claims to tell us something important about our lives. Each text refuses any attempts we may make to reduce it to an artifact of history.

The Author's Concern: What Past Events Mean Today

When we question the Bible's meaning for our lives, we touch the very issue that motivated the inspired authors to write the Scriptures in the first place. Each of these anointed prophets, pastors, and teachers was proclaiming God's word to the community of faith in his own day. Furthermore, he was conscious of belonging to a sacred tradition. He was communicating a word resounding from ages past, and he expected his message to echo forth throughout the future generations of God's people. It was a living word that owed its vitality to the Spirit of God and not to the genius of his own mind.

The historical books of the Old Testament are perhaps the most important case in point. The authors of these books, describing events from the call of Abraham to the revolts of the Maccabees, did not intend us to read them as historical chronicles. They proclaim the action of God in the midst of his people. By their manner of describing what God *has done* in the past, the anointed authors want to proclaim what God *is doing* in the present.

For the most part, the authors of the historical books lived centuries after the events they were describing. At first we might be surprised to learn that the Yahwistic author, who wrote the earliest discernable history of the Patriarchs, lived nine hundred years after Abraham. The Priestly editors, who brought the Pentateuch to completion, looked back on the event of the Exodus from a distance of some seven or eight centuries. The Chronicler, who considers all history in light of David's reign, composed his work six centuries after the great king's death and more than two centuries after the Davidic line had disappeared. This perspective indicates to us that, in their description of the great events of salvation, the biblical authors were responding to precisely the same question we have as we think of the centuries separating us from Abraham, Moses, and David: "What do these events that happened hundreds of years ago mean for us today?" In his manner of presentation, each biblical author responds to the challenge of communicating to his people not just historical information but also God's revelation as it applies to his contemporaries.

The biblical writers worked with the conviction that the events of salvation affected the lives of their people not just indirectly through the unfolding of the ages but also directly through the experience of revelation and faith. By divine grace, they labored to illustrate how God was at work in their own day to redeem and form his people just as he had been when he first made himself known in deed and word. The vital component of sacred tradition is God's action revealing himself to every generation. Because we are the community of faith today, God is at work in our lives in the same way. That is why we need the Bible. The Sacred Scriptures are designed to teach us how to discern and respond to God's event in the present time.

A History of the Text

With all this in mind, we realize that knowing when the biblical events occurred is not sufficient for interpreting the Scriptures. We must know when the authors wrote the texts. Along with a history of the biblical events, we need a history of the biblical text. To interpret Scripture correctly, we must ask not only "What happened in this event?" but also "What is the meaning of this event according to the inspired author?" Our first objective in studying a text must be to discover the sense the original author intended. As we become aware of what the text *meant* to the biblical author and his audience, we will be able to appreciate what it *means* to us in our own day. In summary, when studying the Scriptures, we must be conscious of what the text is saying in view of two historical settings: (a) the times in which the events occurred, and (b) the times in which the author wrote about the events. This exercise will make us more perceptive about how Scripture speaks to a third historical setting, namely, (c) the times in which we are living.

In surveying the development of the Scriptures, we will follow the chronological schema introduced in the last chapter. We will keep in mind the categories of the biblical writings mentioned in the first chapter: Pentateuch, Prophets, Writings, and Deuterocanonicals. "Historical" narratives are found in all four categories: the Pentateuch contains the stories of Moses and the Patriarchs; the "Former Prophets" is another title for the Deuteronomic History (Joshua, Judges, Samuel, and Kings); the Writings include the compendium of Chronicles, Ezra, and Nehemiah; and Deuterocanonicals contain the books of Maccabees.

We will try to point out examples of the relationships between various books of the Bible. It is helpful to consider each text as a member of a family. When you look at a book of the Bible, ask yourself the question, "Where are its relatives?" Each text has two kinds of relatives: a "vertical" category and a "horizontal" category. The "vertical" category refers to tradition: these are relatives belonging to other generations (like grandparents, parents, children, and grandchildren; and even aunts, uncles, nieces, and nephews). The "horizontal" category consists of the book's contemporaries (analogous to brothers, sisters, cousins, or friends), namely, the other texts written in the same era, whether or not they originate from the same place. With this background, we can read the books of the Bible in light of each other and thus begin to appreciate the marvelous variety of ways God uses to speak his word anew to each generation.

1. The Age of the Patriarchs (1850–1550 B.C.)

Scholarship has been unable to identify any part of the biblical text written during the time of the Patriarchs. However, oral traditions consisting of stories about these figures originate in this period. In addition, we note that extrabiblical texts, such as ancient Mesopotamian myths of creation and the flood (such as *Enuma Elish* and *The Gilgamesh Epic*) and legal codes (such as the Code of Hammurabi), derive from this period.

2. The Egyptian Era (1550–1280 B.C.) and the Exodus (1280–1240 B.C.)

Nomadic societies do not have libraries, but they do have revered teachers and storytellers. The oral traditions recounting the Exodus originated with the generation of people who left Egypt under Moses' leadership. In the wilderness, Moses and his people proclaimed the Lord's mighty deeds with the result that other desert nomads joined their ranks (Nm 11:4; cf. 10:29–32).

3. The Conquest and Settlement of the Promised Land (1240–1030 B.C.)

As the Israelites settled in the land and occupied cities, they spoke of the wilderness experience from a new perspective. Furthermore, writing became part of their culture. For the first time, we can speak of "literature" in Israel.

Pentateuch: Oral traditions that would give rise to the Pentateuch became more fixed as schools of priests and teachers explained the Exodus in story form and taught the people how to apply the laws of Sinai to a settled way of life. Examples of early elements of the Pentateuch in written form deriving from this era are the Canticle of the Red Sea (Ex 15:1–18, 21), the Song of the Well (Nm 21:17–18), first editions of the Balaam oracles (Nm 22–24), and Jacob's blessing (Gn 49:1–27).

The Former Prophets (or Deuteronomic History): The most ancient oral and written traditions at the foundation of the Deuteronomic History were taking shape. The stories contained in Joshua, Judges, and the early chapters of Samuel are rooted in these times. The Song of Deborah (Jgs 5:1–31) is the best example of a text coming from this period.

4. The Period of the United Kingdom (1030–931 B.C.)

Cultural activity flourished in Jerusalem during the reign of Solomon. Poets, writers, and inspired researchers composed various forms of literature that became part of the Pentateuch, the Deuteronomic History, and the Writings.

Pentateuch: Around 950 B.C., the Yahwist completed the earliest written source in the Pentateuch.

Former Prophets: At the same time, a member of the royal court published his eyewitness review of David's reign that we recognize as a literary masterpiece (2 Sm 9–20; 1 Kgs 1–2).

Writings: David was a patron of music who encouraged poets to compose songs for worship, some of which are contained in the book of Psalms. The Song of Songs contains some lyrics of romance from this period. Solomon was a patron of the sages and sponsored the earliest collection we have in the book of Proverbs (Prv 10:1–22:16). The first edition of the book of Ruth might date back to this era.

5. The Divided Kingdom (931–721 B.C.)

When the kingdom of Solomon was divided into Israel and Judah, the literary traditions became more diversified.

Pentateuch: If the Elohist composed a source distinct from that of the Yahwist, he carried out his work in the northern kingdom between 900 and 800 B.C. Somewhat later, perhaps around 750 B.C., the Deuteronomic tradition originated in the northern kingdom.

Former Prophets: The Elohist's concern for prophecy probably reflected the influence of Elijah (c. 875–850 B.C.) and Elisha (c. 850–800 B.C.), the servants of the word in the north throughout most of the century. The stories of their exploits come from this era (1 Kgs 17 to 2 Kgs 13). Of course, throughout the period in both Israel and Judah, scribes maintained records of the various kings that served as sources for the writers of Kings and Chronicles.

Latter Prophets: Amos and Hosea, the first of the classical prophets, proclaimed their messages in the northern sanctuaries around 750 B.C. Their contemporaries to the south in Judah were Micah (c. 740–710) and Isaiah (c. 740–690 B.C.).

6. The Kingdom of Judah (721–587 B.C.)

After the Assyrians destroyed the northern kingdom (721 B.C.), traditions converged in Jerusalem as members of prophetic circles escaped from the north and headed south. Less than a decade after the fall of Samaria and the ten northern tribes, Hezekiah came to power in the south. He inaugurated a religious reform that encouraged the development of sacred traditions and literature.

Pentateuch: The Yahwistic and Elohistic sources were combined, perhaps during the reign of Hezekiah (716–687 B.C.). An early edition of Deuteronomy found its way to Jerusalem and was sealed in a Temple storeroom in the dark days of Manasseh, the apostate king (687–642 B.C.). People charged with renovating the Temple discovered this text in 622 B.C. (2 Kgs 23:3–10), and Josiah made it the basis for his reform. The Deuteronomic school edited the book of Deuteronomy and a history from Joshua to Josiah. Concern for the Temple motivated the Priestly writers to publish early editions of legislation governing ritual purity.

Former Prophets: In Josiah's reign, the Deuteronomists wrote the history of Israel, extending all the way from Joshua to Josiah.

Latter Prophets: The school of Isaiah's disciples produced an edition of their master's speeches. After more than a half century of silence during Manasseh's reign, the prophetic word echoed through Jerusalem from the mouth of Zephaniah (c. 635–630 B.C.). Jeremiah undertook his long ministry during which he and the Deuteronomic school influenced each another (627–580 B.C.). Jeremiah's scribe Baruch diligently recorded his master's teaching. Nahum sang his dirge over Nineveh (612 B.C.). Habakkuk encouraged Jerusalem to remain faithful to the Lord in face of the advancing Babylonian armies (604–599 B.C.). The young priest Ezekiel was among the first wave of deportees uprooted from Jerusalem to Babylon in 597 B.C.

Writings: Around 700 B.C., sages in Jerusalem made another collection of proverbs during Hezekiah's reign (Prv 25:1–29:27).

7. The Babylonian Exile (587–538 B.C.)

"Judaism" really began when the people of Judah went into exile in Babylon after the armies of Nebuchadnezzar destroyed Jerusalem and its Temple. To a large extent, the Exile forged the Old Testament text.

Pentateuch: The Priestly writers edited and composed the legislation governing life and worship in anticipation of returning to Judah after the Exile. Furthermore, they began shaping the traditions of the prehistory, the Patriarchs, and the Exodus into a cohesive narrative. The Deuteronomic school made additions to the text that Josiah's reform had used and published the final edition of Deuteronomy around 550 B.C.

Former Prophets: At the same time, the Deuteronomic school also completed their history of Israel's existence in the Promised Land and interpreted everything that happened from Joshua to the Exile in light of the book of Deuteronomy (Joshua, Judges, Samuel, and Kings).

Latter Prophets: Jeremiah remained in Judah after the destruction of Jerusalem but then reluctantly went to Egypt where he finished his days. Editors, perhaps from the Deuteronomic school, compiled an edition of his teachings during or shortly after the Exile. Ezekiel carried out his ministry to the exiles in Babylon and had a distinct influence on the Priestly school (593–571 B.C.). Sometime after 550 B.C., Deutero-Isaiah (Is 40–55) announced the Lord's words of consolation and promise to the exiles. Circles of disciples edited a collection of the prophets who worked until the early days of the Exile.

Writings: The book of Lamentations expresses the grief of survivors gazing upon Jerusalem, which foreign armies had ravaged.

8. Reconstruction in Judah and the Persian Period (538–332 B.C.)

After the Exile, literary activity developed both within Judah and beyond its borders in the "Diaspora" (Greek for "dispersion" [from the Promised Land]).

Pentateuch: The Priestly editors completed their work on the Pentateuch by 400 B.C. by joining their distillation of Yahwist, Elohist, and Priestly streams with the book of Deuteronomy.

Latter Prophets: Between 520 and 518 B.C., Haggai and Zechariah offered prophetic impetus for the reconstruction of the Temple. Later, at the turn of the century, Trito- (or Third) Isaiah (Is 56–66) worked to revitalize the community in Judah. Perhaps around 475 B.C., Malachi highlighted the importance of the priesthood and family life and thus served as an unsuspecting forerunner of the reformers Ezra and Nehemiah. After Malachi's time, prophecy developed an apocalyptic orientation. Obadiah made a final denunciation of Edom. The Isaian Apocalypse (Is 24–27) provided the final element of the whole book, which was edited between 450 and 400 B.C. Joel's vision of the end time, which was prompted by a locust plague, dates from between 400 and 350 B.C. Deutero-Zechariah (Zec 9–14) comes from late in the Persian era. Finally, we note that Jonah, written between 350 and 250 B.C., is distinct among the prophetic books, being a parable rather than an account of a particular prophet's life and message.

Writings: Individual scribes completed the final edition of Ruth and composed Esther by 400 B.C., perhaps during the missions of Ezra and Nehemiah. Sages from a wisdom tradition wrote the long introduction to Proverbs (Prv 1:1–9:18) and brought the whole book to completion around 400 B.C. The book of Job dates from the same time. Composers and liturgists edited the book of Psalms toward the end of the Persian period. Another composer completed the Song of Songs, perhaps around 350 B.C. The Chronicler's history, which includes Chronicles, Ezra, and Nehemiah, received its final form around 350 B.C.

9. The Greek Period (332–63 B.C.)

Once Alexander the Great conquered the eastern Mediterranean, Greek thought became a dominant influence on Hebrew literature. We note that the collections of the Pentateuch and the Prophets had been completed before this time.

Writings: The existential musings of Qoheleth come from a time of prosperity, perhaps around 250 B.C. Jewish Hasidim (or "devout ones") with pacifist leanings wrote the book of Daniel around 164 B.C. to encourage their people to die as martyrs rather than surrender under the persecution unleashed by Antiochus IV Epiphanes against them.

Deuterocanonicals: The turn of the century (around 200 B.C.) witnessed the publication of the book of Tobit, which offers us an engaging story of God's providence guiding a devout family. Still early in the second century B.C. (about 180 B.C.), Jesus Ben Sira, a revered teacher in Jerusalem, collected his teachings in Hebrew. Sometime after 132 B.C., his grandson translated them into Greek in Alexandria, Egypt. Did Ben Sira ever teach those who wrote Daniel? Militants who wanted to drive the foreign rulers from Palestine wrote 1 Maccabees around 100 B.C. Some twenty years earlier, a scribe from Alexandria offered a different perspective on part of the same period when he published 2 Maccabees, a summary of an earlier five-volume work. The book of Judith came to light around 100 B.C. to describe, in story form, how Jewish ingenuity can overcome foreign occupation. At approximately the same time, editors completed the Deuterocanonical editions to the books of Daniel and Esther. The final edition of Baruch might have been produced around 100 B.C.

Sometime around 250 B.C. (during the reign of Ptolemy II Philadelphus [285–246 B.C.]), Jewish scholars in Alexandria, Egypt, began translating the Hebrew Scriptures into Greek. Their work represents the beginning of the translation we call the Septuagint (LXX). The final collection of the Septuagint was completed in Alexandria sometime after the book of Wisdom.

10. The Roman Period (63 B.C. and onward)

The one book written after the end of the Greek period belongs to the *Deuterocanonicals.* A scholar in Alexandria wrote the book of Wisdom shortly after 30 B.C. as a catechism for intellectuals in a cosmopolitan center.

This survey of the Old Testament literature enables us to appreciate the development of revelation. God's word urges his people to move forward from promise toward fulfillment. Everything is not immediately evident. The word God spoke at a particular point in the past is understood in a new way much later. Two factors provided for the formation of the Scriptures: the Holy Spirit and God's people. God's people existed prior to the Scriptures. Indeed, the Scriptures were written out of the people's experience of God from generation to generation.

This perspective can lead us to appreciate something about the charism of inspiration. Inspiration is the unique action of the Holy Spirit in producing the Sacred Scriptures, which determines the books of the Bible to be the normative and inerrant word of God for all time. The Holy Spirit did a special work in the minds of the biblical authors. However, the Spirit was able to move in their lives because they were members of a faith community that was born out of a sacred tradition. The Holy Spirit was active throughout the whole community in every generation. The Spirit's work in the lives of the sacred authors was a particular manifestation of his presence in the people of God. Our survey of the biblical texts indicates that the Spirit moved throughout the community of faith over a span of eighteen centuries to produce the Old Testament. The Bible belongs to the community of faith. Sacred Scripture itself is a primary and inimitable fruit of the Holy Spirit's activity within the community of God's people.

The Scriptures will come alive in our hearts if we approach them conscious of being members of God's people and desirous of the guidance of the Holy Spirit. Our reading will bear meager fruit if we turn to the Scriptures with an individualistic attitude that sets us apart from the community of faith. Our study will be dry if we just approach the word intellectually without seeking the Spirit's guidance. It is exciting to know that we are never alone when we open God's word. The Bible intends to bring us into communion with God in the Holy Spirit, so that we might have the most intimate union possible with our brothers and sisters in faith.

This background prepares us to begin studying the Pentateuch, the five books that provide the foundation for all the others. The Bible is designed to bring us into the heart of God's revelation right at the beginning.

STUDY QUESTIONS

1. What was the intent of the authors in writing Scripture?

2. When did the Yahwist live, and what did he write?

3. What contribution did the Priestly editors make to the Bible? When did they complete their work?

4. When did the Chronicler live, and what did he write?

5. How does Scripture link past events to us?

6. What is our first objective in studying a biblical text?

7. Why is it important to distinguish between the times in which the events occurred and the times in which the author(s) wrote about the events?

8. What do we mean by the vertical and horizontal relatives of a text?

9. Identify some examples of early written elements of the Pentateuch.

10. What two factors determined the formation of the Scriptures?

11. How can we appreciate the operation of those factors as we read the Bible?

12. Have you ever tried to write a spiritual story? What would be some of the elements you would try to put in it? Would you create a hero or heroine? Would you concentrate on the characteristics of God? Would you end with a moral or a message? Would you use literary techniques like metaphor, simile, foreshadowing, dramatic irony, personification? Would prayer have a role in your writing the story and in the story itself?

PENTATEUCH

4

THE PENTATEUCH: ITS STRUCTURE

You have probably heard the word "Pentateuch" before. *Penta* is Greek for "five". *Teuchos* in Greek means "book". Thus the first five books of the Bible—Genesis, Exodus, Leviticus, Numbers, and Deuteronomy—are the Pentateuch. Jewish tradition calls these same books the "Torah", which in Hebrew means "instruction" or the "law".

The titles of the five books come from the Septuagint translation, which classified in one Greek word the material according to the predominant theme of each book. For instance, "Genesis" refers to the "Beginning"; "Exodus" describes the "Departure" of the Israelites from Egyptian slavery; "Leviticus" contains legislation governing sacred matters of worship and religious observance pertaining to the "Levitical" priesthood; "Numbers" contains a variety of census lists and administrative records; and "Deuteronomy" is erroneously called a "Second Law" after a mistranslation from Hebrew into Greek of Deuteronomy 17:18, which actually admonishes the king to write a *copy* of the Law (not a "second" law).

The Pentateuch spans history from the creation of the universe (Gn 1) to the death of Moses (Dt 34). During that enormous recounting of history, the Pentateuch describes how God intervenes to lay the foundations of his plan for the human race. Beginning with a vision of mankind as a whole, the authors of the Pentateuch progressively focus our attention on God's acts through his promise to the Patriarchs and his covenant with their descendants, the Israelites, to form a people of his own.

This journey into understanding the plan of God is a very personal one because it applies, not just to the ancient Israelites, but to us. The authors of the Pentateuch invite us to face the mystery of our existence as creatures of God who are unique in the universe. More deeply, the authors call us to travel the long and sometimes arduous path that culminates in experiencing the grace of the living God, who is not only our creator but our savior who wants us to be his people. Let us take a moment to survey in detail this pathway that God's promise has opened to us.

Genesis: The Beginning

The first book of the Pentateuch, Genesis, has two parts:

1. the primeval history of the origin of the world and its development up to Abraham (Gn 1–11); and
2. the story of the Patriarchs, Abraham, Isaac, and Jacob, ending with the tale of Joseph (Gn 12–50).

Genesis 1–11 introduces the whole Pentateuch. By describing the event of creation, these chapters provide the setting for the drama of redemption. This drama unfolds God's purpose, which is to draw all mankind to himself by forming a people of his own in the world. The authors composed the stories of creation with a theological intent. From the beginning, they want to draw our attention to the foundational relationships between God, the world, and humanity. All that God does is good, and his creation of the human race is very good. Yet the world is always teetering between glory and chaos because man has marred the divine image by sin and rebellion. The fall from life toward death, from truth toward deception, from communion with God into bondage to self accounts for the pervasive suffering we see throughout our world. We would be adrift on our own in the universe if God did not guarantee his mercy in the covenant. Therein lies our hope and the beginning of our salvation.

Genesis 12–50 introduces the history of God's saving action by focusing on God's choice of Abraham as the forefather of a holy people for himself. The narrative of Abraham and his descendants, Isaac and Jacob, not only spans historical time but geographic breadth. It takes us across the landscape of the eastern Mediterranean world from Mesopotamia through Canaan to Egypt. First Isaac and then Jacob inherit the promise in Canaan before Jacob's sons receive it in Egypt. From beginning to end, the narratives of the Patriarchs illustrate God's providence toward his chosen people.

Exodus: The Departure

The book of Exodus focuses our attention on the major salvation event in the Hebrew Bible: God's deliverance of his people from slavery in Egypt. Moses, the great man of God, now takes center stage, dominating the remaining books of the Pentateuch from Exodus through Deuteronomy. The book of Exodus spans the period from Moses' birth in Egyptian slavery to God's renewal of the covenant after Israel's first apostasy at Mount Sinai.

As in the case of the Patriarchs, so here we undertake a spiritual-geographic journey. We may view the Exodus narrative according to the four locations of the Hebrews as they move from human bondage to divine freedom:

1. While the Hebrews are in Egypt (1:1–12:36), Moses flees to Sinai, where God reveals himself to him and calls Moses to make known his plan of salvation through signs and wonders in Egypt;
2. The actual departure from Egypt and crossing of the Red Sea (12:37–15:21) demonstrate that only by the power of God do his people find deliverance;
3. The three-month journey from the Red Sea into the heart of the wilderness at Mount Sinai (15:22–18:27) reinforces the lesson that the people find security in God alone;
4. Finally, the people settle at Mount Sinai (19:1–40:38), where they enter into covenant with the Lord, break it by idolatry, and then renew it in the revelation of God's mercy.

Leviticus: Laws and Regulations

The people's sojourn at Mount Sinai provides the setting for the book of Leviticus. We remain stationary in order to study the lessons of the covenant. Leviticus maintains the tone established in the later sections of Exodus with the description of the Lord's sanctuary and its fixtures (Ex 25–31; 35–40). The ceremonial rubrics, regulations governing worship, the difference between the sacred and the profane all come under the umbrella of the divine assertion that undergirds the book, "You have been sanctified and have become holy because I am holy" (Lv 11:44).

The book of Leviticus contains four major legal collections: (1) laws governing sacrifices (1:1–7:38); (2) laws pertaining to the priesthood (8:1–10:20); (3) laws discriminating between clean and unclean (11:1–15:33); and (4) the Holiness Code (17:1–26:46). In addition to these laws, the book contains the ritual for the Day of Atonement (16:1–34) and guidance on the fulfilling of vows to the Lord (27:1–34).

Numbers: Administrative Lists and Journey Narrative

After nearly ten chapters that conclude our Levitical lessons at Sinai, the book of Numbers picks up the narrative by describing the Hebrews' departure from Mount Sinai to their encampment in the region of Moab on the eastern side of the Jordan River across from the land of Canaan. We can understand the book

best by dividing it into three sections according to the geographical indications in the text:

1. The compilation of institutional records associated with the sojourn
   of the Hebrews at Mount Sinai (1:1–10:10);
2. The people's movement from Mount Sinai to settle in the desert
   region south of Canaan at Kadesh-Barnea (10:11–20:13); and
3. More than a generation afterward, the people's movement from Kadesh-
   Barnea through Edom to their encampment in the land of Moab
   (20:14–36:13).

At this point, we can consider how the Hebrews distributed their years in
the wilderness. The journey from the eastern shore of the Red Sea to Mount
Sinai took three months (Ex 19:1). Next, they stayed at Mount Sinai for eleven
months (Nm 10:10; cf. Ex 19:1). Finally, we hear that the Hebrews' wilderness
period ended "in the fortieth year", when Moses addressed them in the
territory of Moab (Dt 1:3). The evidence indicates that the Hebrews spent
more than thirty-five years (thirty-eight years, according to Dt 2:14) in the
wilderness around Kadesh-Barnea, a major oasis located about fifty miles
south of Canaan (Nm 32:8; 12:16–19:22; 20:1, 14, 16, 22).

Deuteronomy: The Exposition of the Law

With the book of Deuteronomy, we halt our journey once again and listen to
a series of sermons and instructions that Moses gives to the people on the
plains of Moab at the end of their wanderings in the wilderness of Sinai in
preparation for their entrance to the Promised Land:

1. Moses' introductory sermon (1:1–4:43) recalls the people's Exodus
   from Egypt and their subsequent journey, stressing the Lord's fidelity
   in the face of his people's faithlessness;
2. Moses expounds the Ten Commandments with a commentary on
   their application (4:44–11:32);
3. He then presents the extensive Deuteronomic Law Code (12:1–26:15);
4. In response to his instruction, the people renew their covenant with
   the Lord (27:1–30:20);
5. Finally, Deuteronomy brings the Pentateuch to a close with Moses' last
   words, expressed in a hymn of praise to God and a song of blessing
   over Israel followed by a description of his death (Dt 31:1–34:12).

In the final scene of the Pentateuch, we contemplate the fulfillment of
Moses' life. The Lord speaks to him on the summit of Mount Nebo located

across the Jordan from Jericho. From there, he shows Moses the land he had promised to Abraham's descendants. Finally, God alone provides for Moses at his death. These final lines are suggestive of God's providential concern for his people, which shines through all the words and events of the Pentateuch.

STUDY QUESTIONS

1. What does "Pentateuch" mean?
2. Where does the title of each book of the Pentateuch come from, and what does each title mean?
3. What events does the Pentateuch cover?
4. Why does God choose a people?
5. Why has God chosen you?
6. What are the two thematic parts of Genesis?
7. What is the major salvation event in the Hebrew Bible?
8. Why may we consider Leviticus to be the book of holiness?
9. Where were the Israelites encamped when Moses spoke to them in the book of Deuteronomy?
10. What is the unique feature of each of the books of the Pentateuch?
11. What are the events in your life and in the life of your parish that you can recall and evaluate in the light of how they have affected your relationship with God and with others in the community of faith?
12. What does the journey narrative in the Pentateuch teach us about our pilgrimage on earth?

THE PENTATEUCH

I.   Genesis
      A.   Introduction: Creation and the State of the World (1:1–11:32)
      B.   The Patriarchs (12:1–50:26)
            1.   Abraham (12:1–25:18)
            2.   Isaac and Jacob (25:19–37:1)
            3.   The Story of Joseph (37:2–50:26)

II.   Exodus
      A.   Moses and the Israelites in Egypt (1:1–12:36)
      B.   The Exodus out of Egypt (12:37–15:21)
      C.   The Wilderness Journey: The Red Sea to Mount Sinai (15:22–18:27)
      D.   Sojourn at Mount Sinai (19:1–40:38)
            1.   The Ten Commandments (19:1–20:21)
            2.   The Covenant Code (20:22–23:33)
            3.   The Covenant Ceremony (24:1–18)
            4.   Instructions on the Tabernacle (25:1–31:18)
            5.   Apostasy and Renewal of the Covenant (32:1–34:35)
            6.   Building and Furnishing the Tabernacle (35:1–40:38)

III. Leviticus
      A.   Laws Governing Sacrifices (1:1–7:38)
      B.   Laws concerning the Priesthood (8:1–10:20)
      C.   Laws Distinguishing the Clean from the Unclean (11:1–15:33)
      D.   The Day of Atonement (16:1–34)
      E.   Laws of Holiness (17:1–26:46)
      F.   Appendix: Payment of Votive Offerings (27:1–34)

IV.   Numbers
      A.   Administration at Mount Sinai (1:1–10:10)
      B.   From Mount Sinai to Settlement at Kadesh-Barnea (10:11–20:13)
            1.   Issues of Leadership (10:11–12:16)
            2.   Attempt to Enter the Land of Canaan (13:1–14:45)
            3.   Laws and Miracles in the Wilderness (15:1–20:13)
      C.   From Kadesh-Barnea to Moab (20:14–36:13)

5

THE PENTATEUCH:
ITS OUTLINE AND HISTORICAL SETTING

One of the questions people most often ask when they read the first five books of the Bible is "When did these things actually happen?" This is more difficult to answer than we might first imagine because of the complex nature of the literature itself. An initial look at the material leaves us with the impression that we are seeing an unbroken chain of events following one another in a linear sequence. Historically, things did not happen exactly this way.

Serious review of the Pentateuch reveals that the narrative sometimes focuses on certain events in detail while, at other times, spans extensive time periods in a few lines. For example, in the description of the Israelites' forty years in the wilderness, the text devotes some fifty-eight chapters to the Hebrews' one year at Mount Sinai (Ex 19:1–Nm 10:10) while taking only ten chapters to describe their thirty-five years or more at Kadesh-Barnea (Nm 12:16–20:22).

This lack of proportion between the amount of text and the passage of time is even more evident when we compare the three generic eras that the Pentateuch describes. The immense span of time between the creation of the universe and the call of Abraham covers merely the first eleven chapters (Gn 1:1–11:32). But the shorter period describing the generations of the Patriarchs from Abraham to the sons of Jacob (Gn 12:1–50:26) covers the next thirty-nine chapters. We then encounter the remaining 137 chapters, which describe solely the life span of Moses from his birth to his death, with maximum concentration on the less than half-century between his prophetic call and his death (Ex 1:1–Dt 34:12).

If we search for the historical setting of the Pentateuch, we find that the authors of the biblical text are more precise about the Exodus and the journey of the people under Moses than they are about earlier events. The material in the first eleven chapters of Genesis is practically impossible to identify histori-cally both because it is comparatively short but also because it is a different literary type from the rest of the Pentateuch. In other words, the authors did not intend us to read the first eleven chapters of Genesis as a chronicle of history. We will reserve our discussion of these introductory chapters of the Pentateuch until our later consideration of the whole book of Genesis. Our study of the Pentateuch's historical context will focus on the chronology of the Patriarchs and the events from the Exodus from Egypt to the entrance of the Israelites into the land of Canaan.

The History of the Patriarchs

To be confident that we are determining biblical history properly, we should base our analysis of the biblical text on supportive evidence from external sources. The tremendous advance of archaeological discoveries in the last hundred years has greatly enhanced our vision of the ancient Near Eastern world and, in many cases, has provided historical verification of the laws and customs that governed the lives of the Patriarchs.

1. Abraham and Isaac

The description of Abraham in the Pentateuch fits well into the setting of the Fertile Crescent as we know it early in the second millennium B.C., perhaps around 1850 B.C. He was born into a clan of semi-nomadic herdsmen of Mesopotamia, who grazed their livestock on the grassy land along the Euphrates River between Ur in the south and Haran in the north (Gn 11:28, 31; 15:7). They did not live in houses, as farmers or city-dwellers would have, but in tents that they could set up in a particular place for a substantial period of time and, then, when the pasture was used up, move somewhere else.

Abraham's ancestors were likely Amorites, a northwest Semitic people that seem to have spread across northern Mesopotamia and Syria at the end of the third millennium B.C. By Abraham's time, the ancient Mesopotamian cultures of Sumer and Akkad had passed away. Power was concentrated in city-states of the region. Most notable among them was Babylon in southern Mesopotamia along with Assyria and Mari farther north.

We should note that until approximately 1750 B.C., Egypt prospered with a two-hundred-year period of political stability. This untroubled era provided the basis for remarkable cultural advancement and commercial prosperity. During the third millennium, the region of Syria and Palestine saw the development of significant cities, such as Byblos, Tyre, and Ugarit, along the coast, and Ebla, Megiddo, Ai, and Jericho inland. The Canaanites were the dominant people in the region and influenced the surrounding area from within their fortified cities such as those listed above. Archaeological evidence indicates that a number of cities and towns in Palestine were destroyed and rebuilt around the beginning of the second millennium B.C., perhaps due to an invasion of Amorites (an Akkadian word meaning "Westerners") into the region.

One of the marvelous aspects of Abraham's story is that his pilgrimage took him across all these ancient cultures. Having moved north along the Euphrates with his father Terah, he settled at Haran, the major city of the region, located on the Balikh River (Gn 11:27–32). From there, he left his ancestral land in Mesopotamia and drove his extensive herds from Haran south and west along the main caravan route down past Ebla and Damascus into the central highlands of Canaan around Shechem and eventually Bethel (12:1–8). He moved even farther south through the Negeb, eventually entering Egypt, where he stayed before returning to Canaan (12:9–13:1). The narrative describes Abraham pasturing his herds in the central hills from Bethel to Hebron as well as in the Negeb, the arid southernmost region on the edge of Canaanite civilization.

Information in archival documents unearthed in recent archaeological excavations at Mari on the Euphrates and Nuzi in the territory east of the Tigris supports placing Abraham in the first half of the second millennium B.C. Administrative records at Mari indicate that there was regular trade and commerce between Mesopotamia and Palestine in the eighteenth century B.C. Nuzi legal texts from the fifteenth century B.C. provide the background that explains how a household slave could become the legitimate heir of a family he served (15:1–6) and describes the rights protecting a concubine from banishment after she had given birth to her master's son (as in the case of Hagar in 21:8–21). The renowned Law Code of Hammurabi, king of Babylon (1792–1750 B.C.), also provides us with a source of legislation seemingly addressed to families and societal structures typical of the Patriarchal era as the Pentateuch describes them.

Archaeological evidence indicates that Abraham was a man of his times. He did not blaze a new trail when he traveled, because the route he followed was the main caravan pathway for trade between Mesopotamia and Egypt. From a strictly historical viewpoint, we can assume that in the land of Canaan, Abraham did not have the prominence that the Pentateuch ascribes to him. While researchers have found forms (cognates) of the names "Abraham" and "Jacob" in ancient records of the region, they have not uncovered anything identifying these two individuals in particular even though the Pentateuch gives primacy to them. This lack of historical prominence should not disturb us, because it makes it easier for us to identify ourselves with Abraham and Jacob as people who lived and moved among their peers in their own day just as we do, without fanfare or public acclaim.

While Abraham did have many herds of sheep and cattle, he was not the only herdsman in the land of Canaan. There were certainly many other Mesopotamian traders who traveled the same path as he did to do business on their western coast and down into Egypt. Abraham's uniqueness does not stem from his geographic journey from Mesopotamia to Canaan but from his spiritual journey, which was the motive for his departure from Mesopotamia. Abraham would never return to his ancestral homeland. He uprooted himself because God called him to go to Canaan, and he went because he trusted in God's promise. But this takes us beyond the bare historical data, which is our present focus. Let us wait to consider the biblical account in order to understand how God changed the course of history forever through his intervention in the life of this one person.

The authors describe Isaac as inheriting the mantle of his father Abraham as the wealthy herdsman at the head of his clan. He seems to have moved farther south than his father, making Beersheba and the surrounding Negeb the center of his activities. We should note with interest the hint of a societal change identified with his generation in the mention of Isaac's sowing a crop at Gerar on the edge of Philistine territory to the west of Beersheba (26:1-6, 12). Having grown up as a semi-nomadic herdsman, Isaac experimented with the more settled manner of life characteristic of a farmer.

2. Jacob and the Joseph Story

Jacob's story begins by returning us more than 500 miles northward, to the roots of Abraham in Haran, where Jacob went in flight from Esau and in search of a bride from the family of his mother's kinsman Laban (27:46-31:18). On his way, Jacob passed through the central hill country of Canaan and experienced a revelation of God in a dream at Bethel (28:10-18). During his lengthy stay in Laban's household, Jacob tended livestock across the general territory of Paddan-Aram around Haran (30:29-31:18). Throughout this period, the narrative describes Jacob's sons being born to the women he married, his cousins Leah and Rachel, as well as to their servants Zilpah and Bilhah (29:31-30:24). Jacob's and Laban's strained relationship tainted Jacob's departure to Canaan. This was legally resolved shortly thereafter when they ratified a treaty along a route south in the highlands of Gilead east of the Jordan River (31:43-55). In that region, Jacob wrestled with the angel of God on the banks of the Jabbok River at Peniel (32:22-32). His twin brother Esau came north from his southern territory in Edom to meet him and to be reconciled with him there (33:1-17). Jacob sojourned in the territory of the Canaanite hill country around Shechem and Bethel before moving south to Hebron.

In Egypt, after 1750 B.C., the Twelfth Dynasty collapsed, and the country underwent a period of political and cultural transition. Foreign populations from Asia gradually infiltrated the land and eventually rose to power. The "Hyksos" (literally, "foreign rulers") took control of Egypt for just over one hundred years (1720–1552 B.C.), establishing their capital at Avaris in the northeastern region.

The story of Joseph's brothers selling him into slavery and Joseph's rise to power in Egypt corresponds best with the political situation under the Hyksos rulers. At that time, it was common for various Semitic populaces, such as Midianites or Ishmaelites, to travel to Egypt by way of Canaanite centers, such as Shechem or Dothan (37:1–36). A Semite like Joseph could have attained a high government office more readily during the time of the Hyksos than at any other period in the history of ancient Egypt. The political conditions welcoming foreigners during the time of the Hyksos would have eased the movement of Jacob and his sons from southern Canaan into Egypt (46:1–47:12).

The Population of the Patriarchs

We can best understand the stories of the Patriarchs against the background of the ancient Near East between 1850 B.C. and 1550 B.C. Abraham is associated with the earlier date and Jacob and his sons with the later. Laws and records of the time give support to the basic historical accuracy of the narratives about and the uniqueness of Abraham, Isaac, and Jacob as individuals.

At the same time, we should recognize that the authors of the text had more than historical description on their minds. Their intent in writing these narratives of the Patriarchs was to describe the formation of a people holy to God. The authors identify Jacob with the whole of Israel (35:10). His sons bear the names of the tribes of Israel. The authors imply the comparative stature and relationship of the sons of Jacob to each other according to the identity of their respective mothers (29:31–30:24; 35:23–26). They portray the historical tension between Israel and Edom by describing the conflict of the brothers Jacob and Esau (25:19–34; 27:1–45; 32:1–33:20; cf. 36:1–43). The authors also narrate the story of Simeon's and Levi's killing of Shechem to explain these two Israeli tribes' destruction of the Canaanite city of Shechem at some point in history (34:1–29). While, on a primary level, we must understand the Patriarchs as historical individuals, on a secondary level, we should recognize that they are "eponymous" figures who personify in themselves the identity of their descendants. ("Eponymous" means giving one's name to a people or a nation.)

The Patriarchal period spans approximately three and a half centuries of actual history. The biblical narrative tends to streamline and simplify what was in reality a complex process of people interacting with each other, from which the Israelites emerged. Abraham's origins in Haran and Jacob's return there to marry and raise sons from the population of Paddan-Aram indicate that the Israelites traced their beginning to close ties with the Aramaeans (28:1–7; cf. Dt 26:5). They also acknowledged kinship with the Moabites and Ammonites (typified as the offspring of Abraham's nephew Lot: Gn 19:36–37) as well as with the Edomites (the descendants of Esau: Gn 36:1–43) and with diverse Arabian populations (the descendants of Ishmael: Gn 25:12–18).

The journey of Abraham probably typifies a general migration of semi-nomadic people from upper Mesopotamia into the land of Canaan early in the second millennium B.C. The movements of Isaac and Jacob represent the interaction of this people with others in the region of Canaan and the Transjordan over the next few hundred years. This group formed the nucleus of Israelites who eventually found their way to Egypt during the Hyksos period (c. 1720–1552 B.C.) according to the implications of the Joseph story.

In summary, we must account for the historical evidence as it relates to the biblical text. The Age of the Patriarchs extended over a time span of 300 years. Yet the biblical texts refer to only four generations within this time frame. The only way to explain such a long chronological period to cover so few Patriarchs is to realize that, while Abraham, Isaac, and Jacob and his sons were in a direct lineage of family descent, they did not follow immediately after one another as father, son, grandson, and great-grandson. The biblical authors present their story by telescoping the complex historical data in order for us to see only the significant steps in the development of God's promise. These steps unite the Patriarchs in the closest personal association with one another. Clearly, they are immediate descendants and successive heirs of the promise according to the unfolding of God's plan for the sake of the whole human race.

The History of the Exodus and the Wilderness Journey

Although the book of Exodus begins with a transition that links it to the preceding final events of the book of Genesis, there is probably a chronological gap of some two hundred fifty years between the era of the Patriarchs and the birth of Moses. Let us continue our study of the Pentateuch's historical background by locating the events that Exodus through Deuteronomy narrate against the background of their times. We should pay attention to three phases that the narrative outlines:

    1. the situation in the land of Egypt from the time of Joseph until the call of Moses;

2. the Exodus across the Sea of Reeds to Mount Sinai; and
3. the subsequent journey through the wilderness to the frontiers of Canaan.

1. The Israelites in Egypt

Rulers from southern Egypt, who had first established themselves at Thebes before taking control of all Egypt, deposed the Hyksos from power. Their dynasty controlled Egypt and expanded its influence for the next two hundred fifty years (c. 1552–1304 B.C.), bridging most of the gap between the death of Joseph and the birth of Moses. During this time, Egyptian power expanded over Palestine and Syria by a series of conquests. Egypt established governmental outposts in a variety of Canaanite cities to maintain its influence over the region and to protect its main commercial and military access through the land that led to the Hittite kingdom in the north and the Assyrian kingdom in the east.

Official correspondence from the time indicates that the Canaanite cities benefited from the stability of the Egyptian presence. Nevertheless, roaming bands of wayfarers on the edges of Canaanite society caused some civil unrest in the land and seem to have taken control at Shechem and its environs in the central region. Beyond the borders of Canaan, Assyria was rising to prominence in the east after subduing Babylon, and the Hittite kingdom to the north was expanding its influence as well.

Moses grew up in an Egyptian world that was undergoing a period of political transition. A new dynasty that would take Egypt through the next century (1304–1184 B.C.) replaced the old one, which had become too weak to cope with mounting internal friction and foreign pressure on its empire's borders. The pharaoh of the biblical accounts was most likely Rameses II (1290–1224 B.C.), whose family came from Avaris, the former Hyksos capital. When the biblical text describes the Hebrews working as slaves on the store-city called Rameses (Ex 1:11), it is most likely referring to his reconstruction project of this center in northeastern Egypt where he established his capital.

The evidence available does not permit us to date precisely when the Exodus from Egypt occurred. The most ancient reference to the Israelites in Egyptian archives is in a hymn extolling the victories of Pharaoh Merneptah (1224–1211 B.C.) in the land of Canaan sometime during the first five years of his reign. "Israel" is listed among the peoples whom the pharaoh defeated there. This indicates that the Israelites were in the land of Canaan by 1220 B.C. The Pentateuch notes in various places that the Israelites spent 430 or 400 years in Egypt—figures that could correspond with their possible arrival during the time of the Hyksos and their departure during the time of Rameses II (cf. Ex 12:40 and Gn 15:13). The only text conflicting with a thirteenth century B.C. date for the Exodus is the notation in 1 Kings 6:1, which places the beginning of Solomon's construction of the Temple (around 960 B.C.) 480 years after the departure from Egypt, a calculation that would place the Exodus around 1440 B.C. We note that the most recent archaeological excavations at Jericho indicate that fire and earthquake severely damaged the city in 1400 B.C. But the evidence both within and outside the biblical text continues to sustain the scholarly consensus that Moses led the Israelites out of Egypt rather early during the reign of Rameses II. We can thus date the Exodus at around 1280 B.C.

We should recognize that the Israelites were not a homogeneous people at this time. They were made up of more than the descendants of Jacob, who had come down to Egypt during the Hyksos era. Over the subsequent few centuries, other Semitic transients and refugees from Canaan and elsewhere would have found their way into Egypt. Some of their descendants who belonged to the lower social strata and also provided the slave labor for Rameses' construction projects probably joined themselves to the Israelites. The biblical text describes "a mixed crowd" departing with the Israelites under Moses (Ex 12:38). We read that they numbered 600,000, but this number is derived from a standard Semitic literary practice of scribes who wrote centuries later but wanted to emphasize the significance of the event that formed the whole people of God (Ex 12:37; Nm 1:46; 26:51). The Exodus of the Israelites is not recorded in Egyptian annals. More than likely, the departure of this humble and motley band of slaves was one of a number of social transitions in Egyptian society at the time. These oppressed and impoverished serfs from the lowest classes offer a marked contrast to their wealthy patriarchal forebears from Abraham to Jacob.

2. The Path from the Sea of Reeds to Mount Sinai

We may ask two questions that seem to dominate a study of the Exodus: "Where did the Israelites cross the Red Sea?" and "Where is Mount Sinai located?" When the Israelites left Rameses, Moses led them south and west to Succoth (Ex 12:37). Probably because he feared reprisals from the Egyptian forces, Moses decided not to take the shortest route to Canaan called the "Way of the Land of the Philistines" along the Mediterranean coast but chose instead to head farther south to Etham (13:17–22). Historians have not pinpointed the exact locations of Migdol and Baal-Zephon, but they most likely were farther south along the edge of the Sinai wilderness (14:1–4).

1. Where did the Israelites cross the Red Sea? The body of water that the Israelites crossed was actually called the "Sea of Reeds" (Hebrew: *yam suf*). This term could have meant the Bitter Lakes and surrounding marshlands as well as the Gulf of Suez. Most likely, the Israelites crossed the lakes or marshlands extending the Gulf of Suez. Their safe passage was made possible because of a perfectly timed wind that provided proper conditions for getting them across before it changed direction and caused the waters to consume their Egyptian pursuers (14:1–15:21).

2. Where is Mount Sinai located? Scholars have debated its general location. They have dismissed theories suggesting Mount Sinai is either in the northern region of Sinai or in Arabia. The consensus today is that Mount Sinai is in the south-central region of the Sinai peninsula, where pilgrim tradition has identified it with Jebel Musa (Arabic: "Mount of Moses"). The Israelites reached the mountain by going south along the eastern shore of the Sea of Reeds, camping at the oasis of Elim, before heading inland to Mount Sinai (15:27).

3. The Journey in the Wilderness

After a sojourn lasting for almost a year at Mount Sinai, the Israelites moved to the region of Kadesh-Barnea and encamped there for more than thirty-five years (Nm 12:16–20:22; cf. Dt 2:14). During this time, most of the generation that had come out of Egypt died, but their descendants increased in number. The addition of others to the band, such as the Arabian in-laws of Moses and perhaps a variety of dispossessed people (making up the notorious "rabble" who settled among the Israelites in the desert), added to the population (Nm 11:4; cf. 10:29–32).

From Kadesh-Barnea, Moses sent spies to survey the land of Canaan in order to prepare for their attack on it from the south. After rejecting Moses' command to launch an invasion, the troops subsequently changed their minds and precipitously charged into the southern regions, where a coalition of Amalekites and Canaanites defeated them (13:1–14:45). Nevertheless, after leaving Kadesh-Barnea, they attacked the Canaanite king of Arad and destroyed his city (21:1–3).

Following their departure from Kadesh-Barnea, the Israelites turned south as far as the Gulf of Aqaba and then went north, steering clear of any confrontation in either Edom or Moab (21:4–20; 33:1–49). Finally, they engaged Sihon, ruler of Heshbon, in a battle north of the Moabite territory on the eastern side of the Dead Sea and won. Their victory in the region provided for the beginning of their settlement on the eastern side of the Jordan (21:21–35). There Moses gave his final instruction to the people. Their foothold in the territory north of Moab served as their base of operations for entering and eventually possessing the land of Canaan after the death of Moses.

STUDY QUESTIONS

1. Why is history more important to the authors in Exodus and Deuteronomy than to the authors of Genesis?

2. When did Abraham live?

3. What significance can we derive from the fact that Abraham and Jacob were not important in their own worlds?

4. Why did Abraham go to Canaan?

5. What was God's promise to him?

6. Why was it probably advantageous to the Israelites that the Hyksos were in power in Egypt during the time of Joseph?

7. What significance did Jacob and his sons have for all Israel?

8. How long did the Age of the Patriarchs last?

9. How do we date the Exodus?

10. Who made up the Israelites at the time of the Exodus?

11. When have you experienced God's call in your life? In the various episodes of your life, do you see a pattern of God's revelation of himself to you over time?

12. How much do you know about the history of your parish or diocese? In your lifetime, what do you think have been the most important events in the history of your parish, your diocese, and the universal Church?

6

THE PENTATEUCH: ITS SOURCES AND FORMATION

Our study of the historical background framing the events narrated by the Pentateuch indicates that the events span a period of more than six centuries, from the call of Abraham (c. 1850 B.C. [Gn 12:1–3]) to the death of Moses (c. 1240 B.C. [Dt 34:1–12]). We may well ask, in view of this vast period of history, "How did the Pentateuch take shape?" and "Who authored the work?"

Moses and the Writing of the Pentateuch

Ancient religious tradition attributed the authorship of the Pentateuch to Moses. Clearly, he is the central figure in the work, and the text mentions that he wrote certain articles, e.g., the Lord's judgment upon Amalek (Ex 17:14), the covenant laws (Ex 24:4), legislation governing worship (Ex 34:27–28), the logbook of the wilderness journey (Nm 33:2), the Deuteronomic Law Code (Dt 31:9, 24), and a song extolling God's faithfulness (Dt 31:22, 30).

In spite of this evidence, we know that Moses did not actually write the Pentateuch because of three overriding factors: (1) there are very few writings ascribed to him, (2) the ancient concept of authorship normally ascribed works to famous people in order to give the works prominence, and (3) evidence shows that the actual writers of the Pentateuch worked long after the Israelites had settled in Canaan.

First, we must admit that, at best, the writings attributed to Moses are only fragments of the final product. We can be comfortable with this fact. After all, the leader of a band of desert nomads was far more likely to be a prophetic figure who guided his people by the power of the spoken word rather than to be a scribe devoted to the intricacies of the written text. Nomadic leaders communicate almost exclusively by word of mouth, whereas a permanently settled population produces written documents, texts, and libraries. That Moses was not the author of the Pentateuch does not reduce his stature. Without Moses, we would not have a Pentateuch; however, his importance derives from his essential role in prophetically mediating the word of God to his people, not in his writing the text itself.

Secondly, the ancient world's concept of authorship differed markedly from our own. The sense of individualism that dominates us in our modern Western world did not dominate the people of the ancient Near East. They identified themselves within the context of families, clans, tribes, and traditions. Their scholars understood themselves as disciples and had no difficulty ascribing their work to the master who stood at the head of their tradition. Understanding this perspective, we can see that the ancient attribution of the Pentateuch to Moses does not mean that he authored the text himself but that he was its primary and central inspiration. We can understand that everything within the Torah is derived from the tradition that originated with Moses.

Even when the text describes Moses as "writing" something, we need not interpret that description as an assertion that the precise words came from his hand. What that description means is that the author solemnly attests that the writing belongs to the mainstream of the Mosaic tradition. We can apply this analogous understanding of transcription even more emphatically to the description of God himself "writing" the commandments on the tablets he gave to Moses (Ex 24:12; Dt 9:10). This anthropomorphic portrayal of God's activity in revealing his plans for his people is a magnificent method of insisting that these words do not originate with man but with God and that they will forever be at the heart of God's personal relationship with his people in the covenant.

Thirdly, if we look at the text attentively, we will see evidence that people who lived during the period after the Israelites had settled in the land of Canaan wrote the Pentateuch, which, of course, describes the period before their settlement. Fragmentary indications are scattered throughout the text. For instance, parenthetical remarks (noting that Canaanites and Perizzites inhabited the land at the time of Abraham) had to be addressed to the readers in order to clarify the historical situation of earlier years (Gn 12:6; 13:7). Apparently the Joseph story was written sometime after the territory had been designated the "land of the Hebrews" (Gn 40:15). The writer's geographical standpoint within the Promised Land looking eastward "across the Jordan" indicates that he viewed the world from the environs of Jerusalem (Gn 50:10–11). Both a scribal comment and explicit legislation focusing on kingship in Israel had to have come from the era after the establishment of the monarchy (Gn 36:31; Dt 17:14–20). The writer's mention of how situations described in the text have endured "to this day" betrays his own historical distance from the events he narrates (Dt 34:6; cf. 3:14; 34:10). In some cases, the writer even seems to have written with the perspective of living in exile from Palestine centuries after its settlement (Lv 26:40–45; Dt 4:25–31).

Tradition: Oral and Written

Let us consider the evidence we have accumulated up to this point. Even those who assert that Moses wrote the Pentateuch would have to admit that he received material concerning the Patriarchs that had been handed down from one generation to the next for more than three hundred years. If we admit that indications embedded in the text itself suggest that Moses was not the author but that his people in subsequent generations were, we can begin to appreciate the significance of sacred tradition in the formation of the inspired Scriptures.

Scripture and tradition are intimately related to one another. Sacred tradition is the divinely guided process whereby the people of God personally communicate their faith from generation to generation throughout history. Sacred Scripture is born through the unique action of the Holy Spirit shaping the centuries-long tradition of the people of God. Thus the Pentateuch is the fruit of divine tradition. In the postbiblical era in which we live, the definitive word of God inscribed in the Scriptures is the standard for the tradition of faith. Not only does sacred tradition give birth to Scripture, but also Scripture is the source of all subsequent sacred tradition.

We can differentiate between two kinds of tradition according to the mode of transmitting the message of faith: oral tradition and written tradition. Oral tradition is simply communication by word of mouth spanning successive generations. Written tradition is the process of passing on information across centuries by means of inscribed documents. Oral tradition is more ancient than written. All people learn to speak and listen before they can write. In the case of the Israelites, we have already mentioned that oral tradition would have been characteristic of the Patriarchs' semi-nomadic existence and of Moses and his people in their wilderness journey. Written tradition would have come into being among the Israelites after their settlement in Canaan, and it would have flourished around intellectual centers, such as the royal court and schools for training talented youth. In ancient Israel, oral tradition and written tradition would have existed side by side and influenced one another.

Where do we see oral tradition? Oral tradition is particularly evident in songs, stories, and catechesis. The ancient song proclaiming Sihon's conquest of Moabite territory (Nm 21:27–30), Miriam's acclamation of victory (Ex 15:21), the extended canticle of the Israelites (Ex 15:1–18), their subsequent refrain at the well (Nm 21:17–18), and Moses' psalm and blessing (Dt 32:1–43; 33:1–29) are all examples of oral tradition inscribed directly into the Pentateuch. They serve to illustrate the important role music and balladeers played in the transmission of faith among God's people. The great narratives about the Patriarchs rest on the secure foundation of the tradition that communicated them orally so that each generation could have personal contact with the sources of God's revelation.

The Pentateuch as a whole derived its shape from the revered profession of faith that formed the heart of ancient Israel's relationship to God:

> My father was a wandering Aramaean, who went down to Egypt with a small group of men, and stayed there, until he there became a great, powerful and numerous nation. The Egyptians ill-treated us, they oppressed us and inflicted harsh slavery on us. But we called on Yahweh, God of our ancestors. Yahweh heard our voice and saw our misery, our toil and our oppression; and Yahweh brought us out of Egypt with mighty hand and outstretched arm, with great terror, and with signs and wonders. He brought us here and has given us this country, a country flowing with milk and honey (Dt 26:5–9).

This sacred creed traces the history of God's dealings with his people beginning with the Patriarchs, particularly Jacob ("My father was a wandering Aramaean") and his descent into Egypt, then describing the affliction of slavery there as a prelude to the joyous event of God's deliverance of his people from bondage, and concluding with his provision of the land for his people. Each Israelite made this profession of faith annually when he presented the first fruits of his crops to the Lord. Its confession provided the overall blueprint for the Pentateuch and beyond, from Genesis to Joshua (Gn 12–Jos 24).

The family setting provided the primary context for oral tradition. The Passover ritual and the dedication of the first-born were occasions for parents to explain the redemptive work of God to their children (Ex 12:26–28; 13:14–16). The parents had the primary responsibility for instructing the next generation about the meaning of God's commandments (Dt 6:7, 20–25).

Evidence of Written Traditions

The most obvious examples of written tradition are elements of archival material that the authors inserted into the Pentateuch. They refer to a certain "Book of the Wars of Yahweh" (Nm 21:14–15); ancient poems and oracles that supplement the narrative at various points (Gn 4:23–24; 27:27–29, 39–40; Nm 23:7–10, 18–24; 24:3–9, 15–24); and genealogies that they copied from ancient records and that play an especially prominent role in Genesis (Gn 5:1–32; 6:9; 11:10–26, 27; 25:12–20; 36:1, 9; cf. 37:2). Beyond all these, the major collections of legal material must have been transmitted in written form (Ex 20:22–23:19; 34:10–27; Lv 17:1–26:46; Dt 12:1–26:19).

If we carefully study the text, we see that the Pentateuch is not the work
of a single author, nor is it the fruit of a single written tradition. We can
explain the evidence of repetitions, inconsistencies, and divergencies in literary style and vocabulary within the Pentateuch by recognizing that the final
edition developed from a variety of literary traditions whose theological
integrity the final editors respected and left intact within the text.

The existence of different traditions in the Pentateuch permits us to
explain the repetition of the same story pattern. For instance, there are three
narratives that follow the same basic story line describing a Patriarch identifying his attractive wife as his sister on account of his fear of the foreign ruler in
whose territory they are sojourning (Gn 12:10–20; 20:1–18; 26:1–11). Similarly,
the presence of different traditions explains the two renderings of the Decalogue with slightly altered supplementary notes (Ex 20:1–17; Dt 5:6–21).

Each of the clusters of legal material in Exodus (20:22–23:19; 34:10–27),
Leviticus (17:1–26:46), and Deuteronomy (12:1–26:19) shows a unique perspective because each came from a distinctive tradition. For example, the
Deuteronomic legislation on slavery, which gives equal protection to women
as to men, represents a development beyond the statutes in Exodus (Ex
21:1–11; Dt 15:12–18). This development stems from a different tradition.
Again, while the Levitical Code is occupied with all the details pertaining to
the priesthood, the Deuteronomic Code calls our attention to the overriding
importance of the Temple's location in Jerusalem as "the place chosen by
Yahweh your God as a home for his name" (e.g., Dt 12:11, 21; cf. Lv 21:6;
22:2). The difference in emphasis is due to the difference in traditional source.

Inconsistencies within the Pentateuch suggest that the authors brought
different traditions together to form the final version. For instance, if we
carefully read the opening chapters of Genesis, we see that two distinct
creation accounts occur one after another (1:1–2:3; 2:4–25). While they both
describe the creation of man and woman within the setting of the creation of
the world, each of the accounts has a unique perspective. The first account
offers a panoramic view of God's creation of the whole universe and then his
systematic introduction of life, beginning with plants, then animals, and
finally human beings (1:1–2:3). If we contrast the second account, we see that
it has a more personal approach, immediately focusing on the relationship
between the Lord God and the human being (Adam) before referring to the
plants and animals (2:4–25). In the first account, God creates man and woman
at the same time, while, in the second, God brings the woman into existence
after he creates man.

Our study becomes more interesting when we note that the distinguishing features of the two creation accounts are woven together in the subsequent
Flood story (Gn 6:5–8:22). The elements from the Flood story that derive

from the first creation narrative are: (a) the manner in which the waters inundate the land, thus reversing the creation process (7:11, 23; 8:2; cf. 1:6–10); (b) the list of creatures inhabiting the earth (7:21; cf. 1:28); and (c) the preference for the word "God" in whole narrative segments (6:9–22; 8:1–5, 14–19; 9:1–17; see also 1:1–2:3). Ingredients that harmonize with the second creation account are: (a) the reference to those "with the least breath of life in its nostrils" (7:22–23; see also 2:7, 20); (b) the Lord's personal solicitude for Noah (7:16b); and (c) mention of the divine name of "Yahweh" (6:5–8; 7:1–5; 8:20–22; cf. 2:4–25). In other minor inconsistencies in numerical details, we see additional remnants of the two originally independent traditions that were combined in the Flood story. According to one tradition, seven pairs of clean and one pair of unclean animals were brought into the ark for the flood that would last forty days and nights (7:1–5). In the other version, one pair of each species was brought onto the ark, which floated until the waters began to recede after 150 days, when it rested on a mountain after a little more than a year (7:6–11, 12–16a; 8:1–5).

Scholars distinguish four written traditions in the Pentateuch, which the authors combined to produce the final version. Scholars have classified these traditions on the basis of vocabulary, literary style, historical and geographical concern, and theological intention. Let us designate them as "traditions" rather than as "sources" to emphasize that an intricate historical process of handing on the faith orally and then in writing went into producing each of them. "Tradition" refers to the transmission of revelation over a span of time, while "source" refers to the written document formed out of that tradition and available to those who finally composed the Pentateuch. The authors of the Pentateuch would have set aside each of these written sources as they incorporated their contents into the Pentateuch, and, thus, they became part of the normative expression of ancient Israel's faith. We must admit, however, that archaeologists have not discovered such written sources of the Pentateuch. Thus we have only a hypothetical model constructed by scholars to explain the formation of the Pentateuch.

Turning our attention now to the four traditions underlying the Pentateuch, we should recognize that we are oversimplifying a very complex historical process. We can provide only the basic structure of a model with which to understand the whole text. To appreciate the vitality of the pentateuchal traditions, we should think of them as streams and tributaries—which smaller brooks have fed—whose waters converge at various points to make up a large river. When we read the Pentateuch, we are drinking from the river itself. Our investigation of its written traditions takes us upstream to trace our way to the headwaters of this life-giving current of divine revelation.

The Yahwistic Tradition (J)

Scholars designate the author of the earliest written pentateuchal source as the "Yahwist" because he uses the personal divine name—*Yahweh* or "the Lord" —from the very beginning, in narratives that come before God's revelation of his name to Moses on Mount Sinai (Ex 3:14–15). We call this source "Yahwistic".

The Yahwistic source covers the broad outline of the whole Pentateuch, beginning with a narrative of creation (Gn 2:4–25) and concluding with the account of Moses' death (Dt 34:1–12). The Yahwist devotes considerable attention to humanity's fall from union with God and the cataclysm of the flood as a consequence of the disorder that human sin introduced into creation (Gn 3:1–24; 6:5–8:22). This condition sets the stage for God's call of Abraham and his merciful dealing with the Patriarchs (Gn 15:7–18). The Joseph story bridges the gap between the era of the Patriarchs and that of Moses (Gn 37–50). The Yahwist highlights Moses, the great servant of God, in the description of his birth, his prophetic call, his union with the Lord at Mount Sinai, and his leading the people through the wilderness (Ex 1–Nm 32). The prophetic oracles of Balaam bring the Yahwistic narrative to a climax (Nm 22:1–24:25).

The Yahwistic tradition developed a rich and profound theology that we can summarize in three principal themes:

1. the nearness of God;
2. the alienation of humanity; and
3. the hope contained in God's abiding faithfulness to his promises.

1. *The Nearness of God.* The Yahwist describes God in anthropomorphic terms to emphasize divine personhood and God's desire to enter into an ever-deeper intimacy with the human race he created with great care and affection. In act after act, the Yahwist portrays God as merciful and loving. The Lord personally breathes his own life into the clay he forms to bring each human being into existence (Gn 2:7). God walks in the garden, seeking his creatures, voicing the plaintive question, "Where are you?" to a humanity that is hiding in its guilt and shame (3:9). In his mercy, God makes provision to cover the nakedness of Adam and Eve and even to defend Cain, a murderer (3:21; 4:15). The Lord, deeply grieved at the sin of humanity, reaches out to Noah in order to rescue the human race from oblivion (6:5–8; 7:16b; 8:20–22). He speaks person to person with Abraham and enters into a penetrating dialogue with Moses (Gn 12:1–4a; 18:22b–33; Ex 3:1–4:17). He reveals himself directly to Moses on Mount Sinai when he establishes and renews the covenant with his people (Ex 19:2–25; 33:18–34:28).

2. *The Alienation of Humanity.* The Yahwist exercised the spiritual gift of

penetrating discernment in his portrayal of human nature. The human race is alienated from God because its primal will is to become God's equal. This will manifests itself in the sin of rebellion against God's authority. Sin begins in the mind, and the Yahwist offers a graphic description of both the subtlety of sin's suggestiveness and the enormity of its consequences. His description of the Fall masterfully exposes the consent to inner deception that expresses itself in sin, which, in turn, produces the debilitating effects of shame, guilt, and fear (Gn 3:1–13). From then on, sin multiplies and breeds death in contradiction to the Lord's plan for life in the world. God warns Cain of the sin in his mind before Cain externalizes it by murdering his brother (Gn 4:6–7). The evil suffusing the thoughts and intentions of the human heart provokes God into releasing the flood waters (Gn 6:5–6; 8:21). Humanity lives in a state of alienation from the Lord because the power of sin has dominated people's hearts, leading people to withdraw farther and farther from the communion of life that the Lord desires.

3. *The Promises of God.* The tragic situation of a humanity dominated by sin puts in perspective the enormity of God's mercy as the only basis for hope. At every point where human sin progresses, the Lord intervenes to protect the sinner. First, he promises a separation between the offspring of the serpent and the offspring of the woman (Gn 3:15). Then he commits himself to be Cain's protector (4:15). Finally, by solemn oath, he swears never to destroy life from the earth in spite of the darkness subsisting in the human heart (8:21–22).

In light of this perspective, we can appreciate God's election of Abraham as his merciful intervention to restore life to the human race in view of its own trajectory toward death. Abraham will be the source of blessing for all peoples on the face of the earth (12:3). The Lord binds Abraham to himself in a covenant that sets before him the prospect of a land (15:17–18). This theme provides a focus for the promise that will now shape the history of God's people. Thus, the Yahwist describes God's revelation to Moses as a definitive step toward the fulfillment of the promise he made to the Patriarchs, identifying the land as one "flowing with milk and honey" (Ex 3:6–8).

We find the climax of these promises in the prophecies concerning the descendants of Jacob as a people who will rule over the surrounding nations and who will be a source of blessing for all their allies (Gn 27:29; Nm 24:3–9). The final prophecy of Balaam describes a star or scepter rising out of Israel to exercise authority over regions east of the Jordan (Nm 24:15–19). In Jacob's blessing, the Yahwist applies the image of a scepter even more specifically to the tribe of Judah from whom will come a leader to subdue foreign powers (Gn 49:10).

The Yahwist offers us a theology of history in which the Lord brings life to the human race through the fulfillment of his promises. His commitment to

Moses reinforces his earlier promise to Abraham. However, the trajectory of God's word applies not only to the mere occupation of the land under Joshua but also to its mature extension manifested by the kingship of David.

Evidence that scholars derive from the source material indicates that the Yahwist most likely composed his work in Jerusalem around 950 B.C., not long after the death of David. The Yahwist was probably a scholar who taught at the royal academy established by Solomon. If this is true, we have some interesting perspectives for reading the text. For instance, the firsthand chronicle of the dark side of David's reign (2 Sm 9–20; 1 Kgs 1–2), including his sin with Bathsheba, might have contributed to the Yahwist's penetrating understanding of the origins of sin in and after the Fall (2 Sm 11:1–12:25; cf. Gn 3:1–24; 4:6–7; 6:5–7). Also, the ethos of international wisdom literature was a likely influence on both the Yahwistic narrative of the Fall and the story of Joseph in Egypt (Gn 2:4–3:25; 37:2–50:26; cf. Prv 10:1–22:16; 22:17–24:22).

The Elohistic Tradition (E)

Scholars designate a source for the Pentateuch that seems to have contained material paralleling the Yahwistic tradition as "Elohistic" because that author exclusively employed the Hebrew term "Elohim" for God up to the time when God reveals the divine name (in Hebrew, *Yahweh*) to Moses (Ex 3:14–15). After that point, the author uses both "Yahweh" and "Elohim" when he speaks of God. Scholars find it difficult to configure the original Elohistic source because the authors of the Pentateuch incorporated that material into the Pentateuch only to supplement the overall writing that the Yahwistic source provided. Indeed, recent studies have questioned whether there ever was a distinct "Elohistic" source. The tradition might have simply provided editorial emendations to the work of the Yahwist.

The Elohistic narrative seems to bypass primeval history and begin with the call of Abraham (Gn 15). The Elohist covers basically the same ground that the Yahwist does, concluding with the death of Moses. In the patriarchal narrative, the Elohist tends to highlight the figure of Jacob by calling attention to details about his life. Among the important expansions the Elohist makes of the Yahwistic material are the following: the presentation of the Ten Commandments (Ex 20:1–17), the Covenant Code (Ex 20:22–23:33), the narrative of the Israelites worshipping the image of the calf (Ex 32:1–35), and the words of Moses' final blessing (Dt 33:1–29).

We might characterize the Elohistic tradition by its reinforcement of these themes:

1. the sovereignty of God,
2. the spiritual identity of God's people, and
3. the importance of prophecy for authentic worship of God.

1. *The Sovereignty of God.* In contrast with the Yahwist's portrayal of the intimate association of God with human beings, the Elohist maintains a separation between the heavenly realm of God and the earthly sphere of humanity. God mediates his revelation to people through heavenly messengers or dreams. The narratives describing God's challenge to Abraham (to sacrifice Isaac) and Jacob's dream are examples of Elohistic literature. In each of them, angels of God play an essential role (Gn 22:1–19; 28:10–12, 17). Human beings bow down in reverence before the overwhelming presence of the living God (Ex 3:6). The Elohist communicates God's divine majesty through the symbolic media of fire, lightning, thunder, trumpets, and clouds (Ex 19:16, 19).

2. *The Spiritual Identity of God's People.* The Elohist emphasizes that Israel's distinctiveness from others comes from her identity as a people belonging exclusively to the Lord as "a kingdom of priests, a holy nation" (Ex 19:5–6). The children of Jacob are therefore set apart to comprise a unique category in contrast to all other nations, for the Lord himself is Israel's true king (Nm 23:9b, 21–22).

Sin is the greatest threat to God's people because it separates them from him. Their destruction would rise up from within their midst as a consequence of apostasy. At Bethel, Jacob commands those in his group to set aside all foreign gods in order to worship the living and true God (Gn 35:2–3). One of the most important contributions of the Elohistic tradition to the Pentateuch is the elaboration of this theme in the description of Israel's worship of the golden calf (Ex 32:1–35). The incident is unmistakably similar to the apostasy Jeroboam perpetrated in the early days of the northern kingdom when he had images of golden calves erected at the principal sanctuaries of Dan and Bethel to discourage the people from going south to worship at the Temple in Jerusalem (1 Kgs 12:25–33). The Elohistic narrative of Israel's heresy concludes with the foreboding prospect of God's judgment on Israel's sin looming over them in the future (Ex 32:33–34).

3. *The Prophetic Voice in Israel.* The Elohistic tradition highlights the significance of prophecy for the people of God. This is the source that identifies Abraham as a prophet (Gn 20:7). God demands that the people cease their rebellion and respect Moses as a prophet unlike all others because God has granted him alone the grace to enter into personal conversation with him (Nm 12:6–8). On this foundation, the Elohistic theology develops a more

comprehensive vision expressed in Moses' desire that the whole of Israel would become a prophetic people (Nm 11:24–30).

The Elohist's respect for prophecy, his attention to Jacob and the places in the central highlands associated with him, and his conviction about God's impending judgment on Israel's sin are some indications that the Elohist likely wrote in the northern kingdom of Israel after its partition in 931 B.C. but before the destruction of Samaria in 721 B.C. A probable date for publication of the Elohistic material would be around 750 B.C. Therefore, the Elohistic source was the northern counterpart of the Yahwistic source, which was composed in the southern kingdom of Judah at an earlier date.

The great prophetic movement in the north identified with Elijah and his successors would have influenced the Elohistic tradition. The Elohist's focus on God's sovereign revelation to Moses at Mount Sinai would have fueled Elijah's zeal to overturn the massive apostasy that swept through Israel during the reign of Ahab and his wife Jezebel (1 Kgs 19:1–18). In turn, the words and witness of Elijah probably enhanced the Elohist's understanding of God's judgment on the sin of his people. The earliest classical prophets, Amos and Hosea, emerged in the northern kingdom around 750 B.C., just before Micah and Isaiah emerged in the south. Amos' and Hosea's condemnations of Israel's idolatry and their prophecies of her impending doom mesh with the Elohist's presentation of God's impending judgment on his people's sin (Ex 32:34; cf. Hos 8:5; Am 8:2). Their prophecy would find its tragic fulfillment in the destruction of the northern kingdom by the Assyrian forces in 721 B.C. (2 Kgs 17:1–41).

After the fall of the northern kingdom, the Elohistic document seems to have come south to Jerusalem, where it was edited and incorporated into the Yahwistic source possibly during the reign of Hezekiah, which was a time of religious reform and scholarly advancement (716–687 B.C.) (cf. Prv 25:1–29:27).

The Deuteronomic Tradition (D)

In 622 B.C., workers who were cleaning out a storeroom adjacent to the Temple in Jerusalem discovered a scroll of the Law (2 Kgs 22:8–10). This document was so important that it became the basis for the spiritual reformation undertaken by the great King Josiah (2 Kgs 22:11–23:30). The fact that Josiah's reforms targeted issues central to the Deuteronomic legislation indicates that the newly uncovered scroll was an early edition of the book of Deuteronomy. At practically every point, Josiah's initiatives corresponded with the Deuteronomic statutes. Josiah centralized all worship at the Temple in Jerusalem beginning with the Passover celebration in the year the workers discovered the scroll (2 Kgs 23:8–9, 19, 21–23; cf. Dt 12:1–31; 16:1–8). He expunged from the land every element pertaining to the worship of foreign gods: the worship of the stars and other cosmic entities (2 Kgs 23:5–6, 11–12, 14; Dt 16:21; 17:3); cultic prostitution (2 Kgs 23:7; Dt 23:18); and occult practices and child sacrifice (2 Kgs 23:10, 24; Dt 18:10–12).

We find that the Deuteronomic source in the Pentateuch is limited almost exclusively to the book of Deuteronomy except for a few supplementary notes that it contributed to the Elohistic version of the Decalogue (see Ex 20:1–17) and for the ordinances governing the celebrations of Passover, Unleavened Bread, and the dedication of the first-born (Ex 12:24–27a; 13:3–16).

We can see that the book of Deuteronomy has a distinctive form if we compare it to the rest of the Pentateuch. Its contents are presented as Moses' final addresses to his people in the land of Moab on the eastern side of the Jordan. Moses' bearing seems similar to the bearing of the classical prophets in that exhortation, warning, and encouragement characterize his manner of teaching. Consistently, Moses issues an urgent appeal for the people to submit in obedience to God's commandments (Dt 5:32; 11:26–32; 28:1). The word of God confronts his hearers with a decision that they must make now, "today" (Dt 5:1–3; 8:1, 11; 13:19).

Some central themes of the Deuteronomic tradition are the following:

1. the uniqueness of God;
2. the primacy of the Temple in Jerusalem; and
3. human responsibility before God.

1. *The Uniqueness of God.* The basic principle of Deuteronomic theology is that the Lord alone is God (Dt 6:4). The people must banish all foreign gods from the land so that they can set their hearts on the living God. The people must remove from their midst prophets and leaders advocating idolatry in the name of religious pluralism (Dt 13:1–19). The uniqueness of the Lord is manifest in the grace of his word and the power of his deeds. The gods of other nations have done nothing compared to the salvation the Lord provided for his people in redeeming them from slavery and teaching them his laws and statutes (Dt 4:32–40). The personal love the Lord has demonstrated in dealing with his people distinguishes him. This love is the foundation of his gracious election of them and his call for them to be a holy people (Dt 7:6–11).

2. *The Centralizing of Worship.* Because God is one and he wills that his people be united, they are to celebrate all forms of solemn worship in "the place chosen by Yahweh your God as a home for his name" (Dt 12:11 within 12:1–31 [see also 12:21]; 14:23; 16:11). The Deuteronomic source authorized the exclusive identification of one sanctuary where the people would gather for public liturgy in order to purge the land of various pagan cults that were

flourishing throughout the countryside. After they fled southward in 721 B.C., the Deuteronomists identified this sanctuary with the Temple in Jerusalem. This Deuteronomic legislation contrasts with the ancient practice in Israel of erecting an altar in places where the Lord had revealed himself (Gn 12:7; Jgs 6:24, 28; 1 Sm 10:8; 1 Kgs 3:4). It provided the basis first for Hezekiah (716–687 B.C.) and then for Josiah (640–609 B.C.) to destroy all the altars outside Jerusalem that had been erected during the periods of apostasy immediately preceding them under Ahaz (736–716 B.C.) and Manasseh (687–642 B.C.), respectively. The statute was so important to the tradition that it was foremost in the Deuteronomic Code of law (Dt 12:1–26:19). This was a reform that endured, for people recognized the Temple in Jerusalem as the only place for official worship from the time of Josiah throughout the following centuries.

3. *Personal Responsibility before God.* Because God revealed his love in his election of Israel and in his word addressed to them, each of his people faced the decision of responding to him. The Deuteronomist insists that absolute love demands absolute surrender. Love that emerges from the depths of one's being and includes the commitment of all of one's life is the only adequate response to God's initiative in forming the covenant. "You must love Yahweh your God with all your heart, with all your soul, with all your strength" (Dt 6:5). This form of love is not sentimental; it is intelligent. It demands a discipline of the mind through adherence to the word of God. One must "remember" the deeds of the Lord and his commandments, because "forgetting" them leaves one vulnerable to the onslaught of pride that turns the heart from God and therefore leads to destruction (8:2, 11; 9:7; 16:3). Ultimately, this love manifests itself in obedience to all that God demands (6:25; 13:4; 28:13).

Like its Yahwistic and Elohistic forebears, the Deuteronomic tradition developed over an extensive period of time. It seems to have originated in the northern kingdom before the destruction of Samaria in 721 B.C. During that time, the influence of the Elohistic tradition might have fueled the development leading to the vehement rejection of foreign gods and pagan practices that is so pervasive in the Deuteronomic literature. An early version of Deuteronomy was probably brought from the northern kingdom to Jerusalem in 721 B.C. This version might have been expanded and supplemented as the tradition developed, first in support of the reforms that Hezekiah attempted (716–687 B.C.), and then in secretive resistance to the apostate policies of Manasseh (687–642 B.C.). Therefore, the text that the workers discovered in the Temple storeroom during the reign of Josiah was probably a revised version of the original one that had come from Samaria a century earlier.

In any case, the text of Deuteronomy discovered in 622 B.C. had to undergo further emendation to reach the completed form that now concludes the Pentateuch. It is probable that a Deuteronomic school flourished under Josiah and continued in Jerusalem up to the time of its destruction in 587 B.C. During this period, the prophet Jeremiah would have drawn inspiration from its precepts, and he probably influenced the further development of its formation in the course of his ministry. However, the final editors composed the definitive version of Deuteronomy in light of the destruction of Jerusalem and the Temple, completing their work in Babylon during the Exile, perhaps around 550 B.C. (sometime after 562 B.C.: 2 Kgs 25:27–30).

The Priestly Tradition (P)

The Priestly tradition gave the Pentateuch its ultimate form. Scholars identify the final editors of the whole work as priests because of their evident preoccupation with matters of liturgical rubrics, ritual purity, and Temple piety.

We must clarify our nomenclature concerning the Priestly contribution to the Pentateuch. We speak of Priestly authors and editors in the plural because a variety of hands worked on the text over the course of generations. A "tradition" and "school" of priests were responsible for the Priestly notes and additions. Nevertheless, we can speak of the Priestly writer or editor in the singular when we refer to the person who was responsible for the final edition of the Pentateuch.

Although the Priestly writers did not develop their own comprehensive narrative of the events in the Pentateuch, we cannot overestimate their contribution to the final product. The Priestly writers reworked the Yahwistic and Elohistic materials into their present form. By contrast, there is scant indication of the Priestly influence on the book of Deuteronomy except in its concluding verses, which summarize the life of Moses and conclude the whole work (Dt 34:1, 7–9, 10–12).

The most obvious Priestly contribution to the Pentateuch is the legislation contained in the whole book of Leviticus (Lv 1:1–27:34), the preceding material pertaining to the Temple (Ex 25:1–31:17; 35:1–40:38), and the subsequent liturgical and census data on the Israelite tribes (Nm 1:1–10:28). The most renowned examples of their craft are the majestic account of creation that introduces the whole Pentateuch (Gn 1:1–2:3) and their portrait of God's covenant with Noah after the Flood narrative (Gn 6:9–8:22 [P and J]; 9:1–17 [P]). The narrative skill of the Priestly writers is apparent in two stories that are theirs alone: a unique description of God's covenant with Abraham (Gn 17:1–27) and the account of Abraham's purchase of a field for family burials (Gn 23:1–20).

The influence of the Priestly writers is not isolated to these examples of pure composition. It is present throughout the text, especially from Genesis to Numbers, in the form of brief notes that blend the material to describe cohesively God's action in redeeming and forming a people of his own. An important Priestly contribution to the book of Genesis is the series of genealogies that serve to link Adam through Noah to Abraham, Isaac, Jacob, and, by implication, his sons (Gn 2:4; 5:1–32; 6:9–10; 10:1–32; 11:10–26, 27–32; 25:12–17, 19–20; 36:1–2; 37:2). Periodic editorial insertions and explanatory comments maintain the narrative flow (Gn 16:1a; 21:2b–5), and longer summaries bridge historical gaps (Ex 1:1–5).

In all their endeavors, the Priestly writers were people who maintained a reverential concern for the integrity of the tradition they inherited. The conviction of their intentions stemmed from three themes:

1. the transcendence of God as Lord of creation;
2. the perfection of God's plan revealed in history; and
3. the call to holiness that God addresses to his people.

1. *The Transcendence of God.* In spite of their preoccupation with minute liturgical details in Leviticus, the Priestly writers' contribution to primeval history in Genesis demonstrates that they were not narrowminded in their understanding of God. To them, the Lord of Israel was not just a national god but the Sovereign One who created the world out of nothing by the power of his word and now rules over the whole of the universe (Gn 1:1–2:3). He sets the stamp of his image and likeness on every man and woman, not just on the Israelites (1:26–27). God's work of creation is not haphazard but orderly and perfect, corresponding to the symmetry of life that the laws ordaining the Sabbath rest revealed among the Israelites (2:1–3). The Priestly writers saw clearly that creation as the handiwork of God was profoundly "good" (1:10, 12, 18, 25, 31).

The Priestly editors were not naive concerning the nature of sin, for they placed the Yahwistic narrative of creation and the Fall (2:4–3:24) immediately after their own. In the face of human wickedness, God ratified a covenant with his creation through Noah, decreeing that he would not destroy it on account of sin (9:1–17). The Priestly editors set God's call to Abraham against the background of the Priestly Table of Nations (10:1–32) to illustrate the point that God's choosing a particular people was for the sake of realizing his purposes for all. God is always transcendent but not remote from all things. He definitively revealed himself at Mount Sinai, and he continues to encounter his people in the holiest sanctuary of the Temple (Ex 24:15b–18a; Lv 16:2). The God of creation is the Lord of history.

2. *The Plan of God.* The spiritual genius of the Priestly editors is evident in their presentation of the successive stages in the unfolding of God's revelation.

History always moves forward in a linear fashion with God as both its beginning and its end. The plan of God is revealed in the sequence of his covenants, first with Adam (implied), then with Noah, next with Abraham, and finally with Moses on Mount Sinai. To both Adam and Noah, he is revealed as God (Hebrew: *Elohim*) (Gn 1:1–2:3; 9:1–17), but to Abraham he makes himself known as God Almighty (Hebrew: *El Shaddai*) (Gn 17:1). Finally, to Moses, he fully manifests himself as the Lord (Hebrew: *Yahweh*) (Ex 3:14). Like the Elohist, the Priestly writer refrains from using the divine name "Yahweh" as a title until after God's revelation to Moses at Mount Sinai (Ex 6:2–7:7).

3. *The Call to Holiness.* A refrain echoing through the priestly legislation, "You have been sanctified and have become holy because I am holy", summarizes the vocation of God's people (Lv 11:44–45; 19:2; 20:7, 26). Because of the recurrence of this theme, we call the ancient collection of laws at the heart of Leviticus the "Holiness Code" (Lv 17:1–16 to 26:1–46). The Hebrew concept of holiness emphasized the glorious otherness of God, his distinctiveness and separation from that which belongs to the world. God calls Israel as his people to be "set apart" from all other nations to serve the Lord alone. God's presence fills the Temple sanctuary so that its name is "the holy place" (Lv 6:30; 10:17; 16:2).

So overwhelming is the holiness of God that his people are able to approach him in the sanctuary only through the mediation of priests. Practically everything pertaining to the priests' ministry is "holy" because of their association with the place of the Lord's presence (Ex 28:2, 4; 29:6; Lv 16:4). The precise attention to sacrifices and oblations is concerned with purging the people of their sin precisely so that they can come together as a "holy assembly" to celebrate their major feasts (Lv 16:1–34; 23:4, 7, 8). We should not accuse the Priestly tradition of arid ritualism, for we should remember that this is the source that commanded the Israelites to "love your neighbor as yourself. I am Yahweh" (Lv 19:17–18).

A preliminary examination of the plans for the Lord's sanctuary and its liturgy is sufficient to indicate that the authors intended to construct the Temple in Jerusalem, not the Tent of Meeting in the wilderness (Ex 25:1–40 to 31:1–18; 35:1–35 to 40:1–38). Although many of the components of the Priestly tradition originated in antiquity, the final writers produced their work as a program for the reconstruction of the people following their exile in Babylon. The Priestly tradition developed within the Temple precincts over centuries, but it assumed definitive form after the destruction of the Holy Place in 587 B.C. Ezekiel, the great prophet of the Exile, who was himself a priest, influenced the Priestly tradition during the Exile. Ezekiel absorbed the Priestly tradition that had developed up to his time. But his adamant concern for the holiness of God's name also must have had an impact on the final edition of the Priestly work (Ez 36:22; cf. Lv 22:31–33). His prophetic vision of the Temple restored in Jerusalem after the Exile must have inspired the hearts of those who worked on the details of the blueprints (Ez 40:1–47:12; cf. Ex 25:1–40 to 31:1–18).

The Priestly writers seem to have completed their work sometime in the fifth century, before 400 B.C. The "Book of the Law of Moses" that Ezra, the great priest and scribe, read in Jerusalem was a late, if not the final, edition of the Pentateuch (Neh 8:1–3). By our dating of Ezra's mission, he would have brought it to Jerusalem from Babylon in 458 B.C. (the alternate date of his mission being 398 B.C.). Ezra may possibly have played a vital role in bringing the Pentateuch to its present inspired fullness.

In summary, we can look back only in wonderment at the activity of God's Holy Spirit at work in the midst of his people to bring the Holy Scriptures to birth from the resources of sacred tradition. We have contemplated a process that extended across some 1,400 years from the call of Abraham to the mission of Ezra (1850–450 B.C.). In this perspective, we have seen the traditions of Moses nourish the people of God through some eight centuries (1280–450 B.C.) before taking definitive form in the Pentateuch. Surely, we must approach such documents with reverence and prayer that the same Holy Spirit who inspired their formation would enlighten the darkness of our minds so that we could surrender our lives to the divine revelation contained in them.

In our study of the individual books of the Pentateuch, we will put ourselves in the position of the Jews living in the exilic and postexilic periods (c. 550–400 B.C.). The Priestly tradition gave these works their present form in order to address both those who were living in Babylon and those who had returned to Jerusalem after the Exile. By now, we can appreciate that the inspired authors were concerned not simply with recounting the stories of past ages but also with indicating how the events of salvation from creation to Moses' death revealed the nature of God's action in their immediate situation. They perceived obvious parallels between the forty years of existence in the wilderness under Moses (1280–1240 B.C.) and the fifty years of captivity in Babylon (587–538 B.C.). Shortly after 550 B.C., Deutero-Isaiah ("Deutero" means "second") proclaimed that the return to Judah from exile would be nothing less than a second Exodus (Is 40:3–5; 43:16–21).

Like the Israelites under Moses, the Jews of the sixth century B.C. were undergoing their wilderness experience in exile. Now they needed to hear God speak directly to them through the mouth of his servant Moses. Obedience to his commands would guarantee their entrance into the Promised Land and their survival there as a witness to all people of the earth.

STUDY QUESTIONS

1. Contrast the two Genesis accounts of creation.
2. Contrast "source" with "tradition".
3. What are the four traditions of the Pentateuch?
4. How does the Yahwist describe sin and mercy?
5. What is the Yahwist's theory of history?
6. How does the Elohist expand the Yahwistic material?
7. Describe the central theme of love in Deuteronomy.
8. What was the contribution of the Priestly editors?
9. When and where did the Priestly tradition assume definitive form?
10. Who was the intended audience of the Priestly writers?
11. What were the needs of this audience?
12. Of the four Pentateuchal traditions, which one do you find most appealing? Why? How can the other three traditions bring you a more fully developed understanding of God and his people?

7

GENESIS 1–11: THE PREHISTORY

The Exile in Babylon (587–538 B.C.) changed the Israelites' world view and caused them to ask primary questions about their faith. Far from the provincialism of their homeland, they lived under the spell of a sophisticated metropolis that was undergoing splendid renovations throughout the reign of Nebuchadnezzar (605–562 B.C.). The Temple of Marduk was refurbished to unprecedented grandeur to complement the king's magnificent palace and spectacular hanging gardens. Mathematicians, astronomers, and engineers were busy studying the nature of things in order to improve their technology.

At the annual New Year's festival, the whole populace gathered to extol the god Marduk as the one who made heaven and earth. All of this could only deepen the spiritual turmoil of the Israelite refugees, who would recall how armies of this glorious empire had destroyed Jerusalem and ravaged its Temple. The contrast between the splendor of Babylon and the desolation of Jerusalem was enough to provoke a crisis of faith of the most profound order.

The end of the Exile did not resolve this crisis of faith among the Jews. When the Persians overthrew the Babylonians and decreed the restoration of the exiles to their homeland (Ezr 1:2–4), the people of Judah became all the more conscious of being a relatively insignificant and powerless people in a very large world that was beyond their control. The Exile had produced a Copernican revolution in the Jewish mind: the Exile and its aftermath had forced the Jews to realize that Jerusalem was not the fixed center around which the rest of the world moved.

By the grace of God, times of deepest questioning can be times of greatest revelation. In the decades following the Exile, the Priestly writers assumed the task of discerning God's action in Israel within the broader horizon of his activity in the whole cosmos. They communicated to their people a vision of the universe that could give them access to God's innermost designs at the center of all existence. Insofar as these Priestly writers were responsible for the final edition of the Pentateuch, they produced the Bible's first book in its present form. Genesis is a vast and majestic work that takes us all the way from the creation of the world to the settlement of the Israelites in Egypt. This is a complex symphony that blends into harmony a variety of literary forms, such as genealogies and poems, sagas and stories, narratives and doxologies.

The book of Genesis can be subdivided into four sections. The first eleven chapters are best designated as "the prehistory"—they provide an introduction not just to this book but to the whole of the Pentateuch (1:1–11:32). The actual historical narration begins with the stories of the Patriarchs: Abraham (12:1–25:18), Isaac (25:19–26:35), and Jacob (27:1–37:1). The Joseph story concludes the book (37:2–50:26).

The first eleven chapters of Genesis set the stage for the great biblical drama of God reaching out to embrace man with the fullness of his divine love. The authors of these texts did not intend them to be read as history in our contemporary sense of the term. They provide a sort of "prelude" to the biblical story by introducing the major themes they address in the remainder of Scripture. These were the questions most pressing on the minds of the postexilic Jews, and they probe the mystery of existence in every age: Why is there something rather than nothing? Where do we come from? What is the place of man within the cosmos? Why do we suffer and die? Why must we work so hard and yet gain so little? Why is there confusion and turmoil on the international scene of human relations? Why is marriage at once so essential and yet so problematical for spouses? Why is there conflict in family life?

Creation: Man and the Cosmos (1:1–2:3)

The opening chapters of the Bible show that creation itself is the first word God speaks to us. The text describes creation from two complementary perspectives. The first one is cosmic and sketches the panoramic design of God in the emergence of the universe (1:1–2:3). The second one is personal and concentrates on the mystery of the human person in relationship to God and to others (2:4–25).

The author of the cosmic perspective on creation composed it after the rest of the Pentateuch. The Priestly writer, who was the Pentateuch's final editor, composed it after the Exile and before 400 B.C. as an introduction to the whole collection. He wrote it in part as a response to the ancient Mesopotamian myths of creation (known to us from an Assyro-Babylonian document entitled *Enuma Elish* ["When above"]) that were performed at the annual New Year's festival. The narrative celebrating Marduk's deeds includes an epic depicting the world as the product of a divine combat in which, by craft and might, Marduk overcomes the goddess Ti'amat and brings forth the universe out of her remains. We should note that such stories were known throughout the ancient world. For example, ancient Canaanite myths offer similar portraits of creation as the result of wars and rivalries between the gods.

The Priestly authors needed to expose the error inherent in the Mesopotamian myths and instruct their people in the truth concerning the origins of the universe. In this work, they followed the lead of Deutero-Isaiah, their predecessor in the ranks of the prophets. He carried out his ministry to the exiles around 550 B.C., probably over a century before the Priestly writers completed their work on the Pentateuch. In the face of oriental doctrine about Marduk, Deutero-Isaiah proclaimed the Lord of the Israelites to be the true Creator of Heaven and earth (Is 40:12–31). He is the one who introduced the concept of God "creating" (Hebrew: *bara'*) the universe (Is 42:5; 45:7, 12, 18). The Priestly writer received this concept from the prophetic school and developed it into his portrait of the origin of the universe.

In Deutero-Isaiah, God's work of creation refers to both his bringing all things into existence at the beginning (Is 40:26; 45:7, 12, 18) and his forming his people by delivering them from sin and bondage (Is 43:1, 7). When the Priestly writer uses the term at the beginning of Genesis, he is demonstrating that the Lord who called his people and redeemed them from slavery is the One who created the universe.

In the mind of the inspired author and his audience, an awareness of the Lord as redeemer preceded the awareness of the Lord as creator. However, in the mind of one who reads the text, creation is the first manifestation of God to man. The biblical narrative maintains the unity between creation and redemption by demonstrating that the God who creates all that exists continues to act in history by bringing mankind to salvation through his election of a people and through his mighty works to free them and make them his own in the covenant.

We can more clearly appreciate the Bible's teaching on creation by understanding how the Priestly account differs from other ancient Near Eastern literature about the origin of all things. The universe is not a chance happening, a chaotic environment that still reflects the primitive rivalries of warring deities. Rather, the universe is orderly and makes sense, because there is only one God (see Dt 6:4), and he makes all that exists according to his divine will and providence. The universe is the event of God's personal word: he speaks and it comes into being. The Babylonian religion viewed the sun, moon, stars, and the sea as deities. By contrast, the Genesis account clearly asserts their creaturely status and thus illustrates the truth that God is without rival in the universe. Moreover, the astral elements serve a liturgical purpose precious to the mind of the Priestly author: they delineate the times and seasons of major festivals (Gn 1:14).

Another indication of the Priestly author's mentality is his portrait of creation in seven days, which reflects his perception that the climax of all life is the observance of the Sabbath rest (Gn 2:2–3; Ex 20:8–11). God's activity has a marvelous cadence, proportion, symmetry, and order. He brings all that exists into being step by step in accordance with his word. There is no confusion; light is distinguishable from darkness, the land from the sea. Vegetation is abundant and guarantees a rich array of food for humanity. The categorization of animals, fish, and birds again reflects a priestly appreciation for order (Lv 11:1–30). God blesses all living beings, thus guaranteeing their survival. Over and over, the author marvels at the propriety of everything: God sees that it is "good" (1:4, 10, 12, 18, 21, 25).

However, one aspect of creation surpasses all others: when God creates man and woman, he sees that it is "very good" (1:31). The only time during creation when the author portrays God as being in deep reflection is before God creates human beings. Surely this illustrates his special attention in bringing into existence man and woman as the apex of the universe (1:26). The human person is distinct in the order of all creation in that only human beings bear the image and likeness of God (1:27). To speak of a creature bearing "the likeness" of God is a radical statement about human dignity because it comes from priests who were so conscious of idols and images of God (Ex 20:3–5).

Beyond this, another remarkable feature of the text within the culture of its time is its application to both woman and man equally and in union with each other: each shares in the image and likeness of God. Furthermore, the text is unique in its universal application: not just members of the covenanted people but rather everyone without qualification bears the image of God.

Human beings are the ambassadors and servants whom God commissions to exercise proper stewardship over all creation. God speaks directly to them about his intentions and plans for all that he brings into existence. God guarantees human survival through the free bestowal of his blessing and the offer of all vegetation for the family table (1:28–30). That God enters into his Sabbath rest after empowering the man and the woman to take care of his creation suggests that God's creation is perfect. Insofar as God establishes a perfect order, creation is complete; yet it must reach fulfillment through human stewardship in obedience to the divine command (2:1–3).

Creation: The Centrality of Marriage (2:4–25)

The Priestly editors placed their cosmic description of creation in front of the older Yahwistic presentation, which considers creation from a personal view (2:4–25). The final arrangement of the text produces the effect of directing our attention from the vast panorama of the universe to the husband-wife relationship, which the editors introduce in a few masterful lines of poetry (1:27).

The Yahwist's perspective provides a movement toward intimacy. The sovereign and almighty "God" of the cosmos now draws near to man as his personal "Lord God" (or "Yahweh God") to care for him and share his friendship with him. God forms man (Hebrew: *adam*) from the earth (Hebrew: *adamah*) and gives him directly the breath of life. The Lord works like a master potter to shape meticulously his precious creation (2:7; cf. 3:19). Man is a combination of something godly and something earthly. Later theology would say man is the meeting point of spirit and matter.

The man lives in the garden where the Lord dwells. Insofar as the man is alone, he has tension in his life even in God's paradise. His freedom to name all the living creatures suggests his God-given dominion over creation (2:19–20). Still he is incomplete by himself. Human beings need one another. God constitutes human beings so that nothing else in creation can bring them fulfillment. Ever solicitous for the man's welfare, the Lord resolves to make one who is distinctive from, yet complementary to, the man (2:20: "suitable for", in Hebrew *'ezer kᵉnegdo*). Having induced a divine slumber upon the man, the Lord takes one of his ribs (suggesting equality of dignity) and fashions a woman. The man (*'ish*) names the woman (*'ishshah*) and declares her to be "his flesh and bone", his closest kin (2:21–24; cf. 29:14). Unless God graces them with a special calling (Jer 16:1), God designs an individual man and woman to find the fullness of life in a permanent union with each other. Marriage is at the heart of God's plan for the human race since it is in the communion of life and love shared by husband and wife that each one finds the completion of his or her personal character (Gn 2:18–25).

The Fall: Creation's Wound in the Human Heart (3:1–24)

As we have seen, the first pages of Scripture set before us the vision of how God intends us to live: securely in God's presence, gratefully sharing the intimacy of marriage, and submitting all of creation to the glory of God's divine plan. When faced with this idyllic portrait, anyone, including the inspired author, has to face the question, "What went wrong?" Elementary experience tells us that life is not like that vision. We live every instant against the dark horizon of death. Every relationship struggles against the tensions that threaten to fracture unity into division and chaos.

Genesis 2:4–4:16 was originally a unified work from the hand of the Yahwist. Having described God's attentive love in creating man and woman

(2:4–25), the Yahwist goes on to describe the roots of disorder in our lives due to the Fall (3:1–24) and the tragic power of sin to breed death as it passes from generation to generation (4:1–16).

The whole narrative is a highly nuanced work of art that illustrates that sin originates in the human heart and is the root cause of human suffering and death in the world. Aspects of a wisdom tradition run through the text. Disorder in the world begins with confusion of *the mind* about God's commandments. God forbids the man and woman to eat from *the tree of the knowledge of good and evil,* a symbol of the power to determine for themselves the moral standards of right and wrong. The forbidden fruit is desirable on account of its potential for offering *wisdom.* The promise of having their *eyes opened* lures the man and woman (3:1–7).

Evil is both intelligent and personal, symbolized in the serpent, who is a creature hostile to God and malicious toward humanity. He speaks the anti-word that distorts the divine precept (3:1; cf. 2:16–17) and depersonalizes God (referring to the Creator as "God" [3:1, 2] rather than employing the more familiar title "Yahweh God" [3:1, 8]). The serpent thereby sows suspicion in the human mind and fixes the man's and woman's attention on themselves rather than on companionship with the Creator (3:4–6). The man's and woman's consideration of the serpent's word generates antagonism toward God, distrust of his motives, and an absurd rivalry with him. The serpent insinuates, "You can become like God by disobeying God." The human will to carry on the mental battle evaporates. As their ears yield to the serpent's voice, their eyes desire what God has forbidden them. As craving replaces reflection and sensation overcomes reason, rebellion disrupts their relationship with God.

As a consequence of doing what the Lord forbade, the couple has their eyes opened in a way they never anticipated (3:7; cf. 3:5–6). Their minds turn inward on themselves. By a tragic introversion, they are overcome by self-absorption. Shame in each other's presence (realizing they are "naked"), fear in the Lord's presence (indicated by their "hiding"), and guilt over their behavior (blaming their actions on the other or the serpent) dominate their lives.

The scene that follows is a study in contrast between the Lord's reaching out to share the joys of the garden and the couple's withdrawal into guilty seclusion. The stage is set for the biblical drama that ensues. God's first question is like the anxious call of a parent in search of a child who has not come home at the customary hour and who might have fallen into bad company. "Where are you?" (3:9). This divine appeal echoes throughout the ages. The question introduces the dialogue between God and every person who reads the Scriptures from the beginning. The biblical narrative describes, not our search for God, but rather God's search for us, as we hide in fear and self-preoccupation over the very possibility of his finding us (3:8–13).

The Lord's response to sin is not rejection but promise. He asserts his intention to free mankind from the tyranny of the serpent in a statement that the early Church Fathers call the "proto-evangelium" (meaning, forerunner of the Gospel) (3:14–15). Human rejection of God's commandment is the root of suffering and struggle that characterize common life. Strain now accompanies all that God intended to be unalloyed joy. The pain of childbirth, tensions in marriage, the meager effectiveness of human labor, and the certitude of eventual death are all consequences of mankind's primeval rebellion against God (3:16–19). The greatest sorrow of all is banishment from the Lord's presence (3:23–24). Yet, even in this most tragic event, the Lord's compassion is symbolized in his humble service of making clothes for the couple before they leave him (3:21).

The Fall: Effects on Family Life (4:1–16)

A sign of the Lord's continued love for the couple even following their banishment from the garden is their experience of his blessing in the gift of children (4:1–2). The author expands the focus on marriage to encompass family life. Another generation is born, and brotherhood becomes the central issue.

After the Lord indicates his preference for Abel's offering, he still illustrates his concern for preserving Cain's integrity by exposing his interior state of turmoil. It is the Lord who mentions "sin" explicitly for the first time in the Bible and personifies it as a beast about to spring forth and devour its prey. God warns Cain that he is in mortal combat. Again, evil emerges from within the heart to manifest its chaos in external action. Envy, jealousy, and anger are the roots of murder (4:5–7).

The Lord's response to Cain's sin parallels his correction of Adam and Eve:

   a. The Lord beckons the sinner with a plaintive question. This time, the Lord extends his inquiry in scope: "Where are you?" now becomes "Where is your brother?" (3:9; 4:9);

   b. The sinner attempts to evade responsibility. Cain's cynical retort is ironic because it reflects the truth: of course, God intended him to be his brother's keeper. Compared to his father, who admitted his state when questioned, Cain seems more hardened in his sin (4:9; cf. 3:10–12);

   c. The earth suffers consequences: the soil, which human blood has contaminated, will yield even less than after Adam's sin (4:10–12a; cf. 3:17–19);

d. God must banish the sinner from his home. Just as God sent Adam and Eve from the garden, so now he uproots Cain from settlement to wander the earth as an estranged nomad;

e. The Lord still extends his love to the sinner. Divine compassion is evident in God's commitment to protect Cain as his nearest kin (4:15–16; cf. Nm 35:19).

As we review the wealth of insight into marriage and family life that Genesis 2:4–4:16 contains, we might ask, "What inspired the Yahwist to write this?" In view of this contemporary social problem, the Spirit of God enlightened the Yahwist to describe the theological dimensions of marriage with a previously unrivaled depth of understanding. Possibly the Yahwist's deep concern about these issues arose from the family crises in David's life. If the Yahwist wrote around 950 B.C., he was a contemporary of the literary genius who wrote the firsthand account of David's sin with Bathsheba and the subsequent turmoil in his family life (2 Sm 9–20). He writes the narrative in such a manner as to indicate that the sin of the father unleashed forces of darkness in his home that culminated in brother (Absalom) murdering brother (Amnon) (2 Sm 11:1–12:25; 13:1–37). The wisdom motifs in Genesis 2:4–4:16 are developed under the partial influence of the school of sages that produced the Proverbs of Solomon, some of which express deep concern with family life (see Prv 10:1–22:16; 25:1–29:27). How impressive is the Yahwist's courage in proclaiming a vision of marriage that neither David his hero nor Solomon his king was able to realize in his life. This illustrates the radical nature of the Yahwist's prophetic vision of marriage and family life.

Returning to Genesis, we see that the author mentions the descendants of Cain in quick succession so that the narrative can reach Lamech, the one who illustrates the development of inhumanity. Lamech's taunting song addressing his wives at once reflects both his cavalier attitude toward a murder he committed and his expectation of vengeance should someone attack him. Human life becomes less and less sacred for Adam's descendants as they become more and more ferocious with the passing of each generation (Gn 4:19–24).

The Flood: Creation Returned to Chaos (5:1–9:29)

The power of sin begins to dominate the world. Periodic genealogies illustrate its advance as life expectancy gradually declines from over 700 years (from

Adam to Noah: Gn 5:1-31) to under 600 years (from Noah to Abraham: Gn 11:10-26) and finally to less than 200 years for the Patriarchs (Abraham to Jacob: Gn 25:7; 35:28; 47:28). Man continues to go beyond his boundaries, searching for divine powers to rival God, and so must have a limited term for each generation (illustrated in 6:1-4; see also 11:1-9).

The darkness that sweeps across the earth stems from its source in the human mind. Although God originally brings human beings into existence as the apex of a universe that he divinely decrees to be "good", they descend to the point of preoccupying themselves only with what is "wicked" (6:5). As a result, creation returns to chaos.

The flood story is more than a description of a natural disaster. It depicts an event of cosmic proportions—the reversal of creation itself. The waters above and below the earth, which God separated from each other on the second day (1:7), now converge from above and below (7:11), and all are in danger of returning to their most primitive state when there had been only a watery abyss (1:2).

The story of Noah represents a Hebrew counterpart to Babylonian tales, such as the *Gilgamesh Epic* and the myth of *Atrahasis*. A comparison of the narratives reveals the uniqueness of the Genesis story. According to the Babylonian myths, the whim of the gods causes the flood, but one of them warns Utnapishtim to build a boat so that he is able to journey successfully toward immortality. The Genesis narrative insists that sin brought forth the watery chaos and God mercifully spares the human race by preserving one righteous man and his family so that they can provide a new beginning for the human race. Through their service, a remnant of all created things escapes obliteration in the flood. All takes place according to the Lord's plan to purge his creation from evil. He mercifully reveals his plan in commissioning Noah to exercise stewardship for the survival of all living things (6:13-7:5; 7:11-16; cf. 1:28-31) and then symbolizes his concern by personally shutting Noah into the safety of the ark (7:16).

The flood recedes as God remembers Noah and the living creatures in the ark (8:1). The waters wash away the old world of Adam. Noah and the creatures are a bridge to a new world order that will reign. This is the new era of God's covenant and promise. The universe will endure because of God's faithfulness. Mercifully, its survival is not contingent on human virtue. The rainbow is a natural sign of God's unconditional covenant with all living creatures (9:8-17).

The flood narrative is the first biblical illustration of redemption. In love and mercy, God reaches out to rescue mankind and to advance his plan for all creation. In spite of sin, God preserves man and woman as creatures who bear his image and likeness (5:1-2; 9:6; cf. 1:27). Even the profound disorder in the human heart does not provoke him to jeopardize his creation ever again (8:21–22). Having rescued mankind from the chaos that threatened to engulf all living beings, he commissions Noah and his descendants to exercise stewardship over creation according to his original intention for man and woman. Only this time, there are subtle traces that indicate a lack of perfection: all other living creatures will live in "terror and . . . dread" of man; animals as well as plants will become his food; and God must admonish men never to kill each other (9:1–7; cf. 1:28–31). God cannot trust any man fully. (Even the righteous Noah will soon fall into drunkenness: 9:20–22).

The covenant with Noah is practically unconditional. Its fulfillment does not depend on man but only on the graciousness of the Lord. Thus, the security of God's faithfulness and love embraces wounded humanity and creation. Here is the foreshadowing of God's ultimate universal purpose in calling Abraham and making a covenant with him in which "all clans on earth will bless themselves by you" (12:1–3).

Babel: Technology and International Tension (10:1–11:9)

The "Table of Nations", listing the descendants of Noah, illustrates the conviction that all peoples belong to one family (10:1–32). However, the Tower of Babel story (11:1–9) portrays the impossibility of all people in the world maintaining their unity with one another on their own best efforts. Human pride always frustrates good intentions. Everything collapses under the weight of human ambition.

Like the narratives of the Fall (3:1–24) and of intermarriage with quasi-divine beings (6:1–4), the story of Babel highlights the futility and destructiveness of human pride to usurp the place of God in the world. The tale has a surprisingly modern ring with its focus on technology and international relations. Captivated by the potential of his science and inventiveness, man attempts to reach God on the strength of his own efforts. The narrator indicates that this attempt is completely laughable. From the heights of his sovereignty, God stoops down to look at this puny little heap of bricks people think is the ultimate skyscraper (11:5).

The Lord develops his plan further as he scatters the people across the earth. By diversifying their languages, he maintains their well-being, because he prevents them from accomplishing what they had desired and preserves them to some degree from further disaster (11:6). Furthermore, their dispersal enables mankind to fill the earth according to God's original intention (9:1, 7).

With the last story of the prehistory, the Priestly writers bring us to the heart of the Exile in the city of Babylon. The Tower of Babel story represents the ultimate confrontation with the city populace's pretentious mind set. The Hebrew author seems to have in mind a *ziggurat* or temple-tower, such as the one at Marduk's sanctuary in Babylon. These structures were made out of bricks and reputed to house the gods in their summits. The term "Babel", which resembles the Hebrew word for "confusion", was a derisive term for the great city of Mesopotamia. In the mind of the inspired author, far from being a masterpiece of civilization, this cosmopolitan city was a testimony to human arrogance and defiance of God.

The primeval history concludes with a vision of the human race fragmented and scattered across the face of the earth. There seems no point of convergence, no epicenter, no source of unity. It is against this international background that the author directs our attention to the vast region of Mesopotamia extending in all directions beyond Babylon. There he brings us far outside the city and introduces us to the particular family of Terah. He directs our focus more precisely to one of Terah's sons, Abram, married to a barren wife, Sarai. Through this couple, who drive their herds north and westward along the Euphrates River from Ur to Haran, God's promise for the whole human race becomes manifest (11:10–26, 27–32).

Toward the New Testament: Christ in Creation and Redemption

Jesus highlights the overriding importance of Genesis with his radical instruction on the indissolubility of marriage, which overturns Moses' dispensation for divorce (Mt 19:3–12; Mk 10:2–12; cf. Lk 16:18). In Jesus' mind, the creation texts contain something more primary and essential than what the Mosaic legislation allows. These passages present God's design for how men and women are to live in light of how he constitutes them. Jesus emphasizes how God "made them male and female" "from the beginning" (Mt 19:4; Mk 10:6; cf. Gn 1:27), and he highlights the fact that "the two become one flesh" (Mt 19:5; Mk 10:8; cf. Gn 2:24). Thus he indicates that the new order his teaching and preaching inaugurate will be, in fact, the fulfillment of God's original intention for mankind, which is not yet realized. Of course, Jesus' references to Genesis on marriage are central to the Church's teaching in subsequent generations (see Eph 5:31; cf. 1 Cor 6:16).

From the first Easter, the earliest Christians knew through the intuition of faith that the Resurrection of Christ transformed the whole of creation. Christ raised life, humanity, and the cosmos itself to a new order, the one that corresponds to God's plan from the beginning. Furthermore, contemplating the mystery of Christ in light of Genesis 1–11 inspired the New Testament writers to replace any narrow earthbound conceptions of Jesus with the true revelation of him as the center and fullness of the Father's plan for the universe. We will consider four aspects of Christ highlighted against the background of the Bible's first chapters.

1. Christ, the New Adam, Lord of a New Creation

Reading the Genesis narratives of the creation and the Fall in light of the wisdom tradition (see Prv 8:22–31; Sir 24; and Wis 2:23–24; 7:22–26), Paul proclaims Christ as the New Adam and divine Lord who establishes his reign over the new creation that his Resurrection from the dead inaugurates. Even in the early 50s A.D., he presents Christ as the center of creation in his confession that "for us there is only one God, the Father from whom all things come and for whom we exist, and one Lord, Jesus Christ, through whom all things come and through whom we exist" (1 Cor 8:6). At our conversion, the Father brings us into Christ, and this makes us a new creation. Paul describes his own encounter with the risen Lord as a revelation coming from "God who said, 'Let light shine out of darkness'" (2 Cor 4:6; cf. Gn 1:3). The true light, which is the first event of the new creation, is the radiance of Christ shining in our hearts.

Christ is the New Adam whose obedient death conquered the sin and rebellion of the First Adam. He is the source of life-giving grace that over-powers death, the characteristic of sin's reign (Rom 5:12–21; cf. Gn 3:17–19). As God creates him, Adam before the Fall is only a foreshadowing of the reality now manifest in the risen Christ. The first Adam, when God creates him, becomes a living being. The second Adam, when the Father raises him from the dead, becomes a life-giving spirit (1 Cor 15:45–49; cf. Gn 2:7). Paul contrasts Adam after the Fall with Christ. In Adam, all have died, but, in the risen Christ, all are brought to life (1 Cor 15:20–28; cf. Gn 3:17–19).

The first ones to participate in Christ's transformation of the cosmos are those he makes the true children of God by their sharing in his risen life through faith and baptism (see Rom 8:18–25; cf. Gn 3:17). God does not just forgive them or restore them to a prior state of innocence; he transforms and exalts them to an unprecedented state of existence. In Christ, we experience a totally new mode of being. The cross demolishes the whole old order. It overcomes the alienation of sin and reconciles mankind to God (Gal 6:15; see also Rom 6:5–7). At its heart, this reconciliation is a holy communion, a dynamic participation in the glory of God that changes us ever more fully into the image of Christ (2 Cor 3:17–18).

2. Christ, the Image of God

Paul and the tradition shaped under his influence perceive that we can bear the image and likeness of God only insofar as Christ forms himself in us. Because of the Fall, sin darkened the divine image in humanity. As Son, Christ alone is the realized image of God, and, in him, God's original intention for humanity is fulfilled. When we consent in faith to his grace, God conforms us to the image of his Son so that we can share in God's life as children of the Father and as brothers and sisters of Christ (Rom 8:29). Only when we put off the false old self and put on Christ, who forms a new self in the divine image, do we truly become who God intended us to be (Col 3:10–11; Eph 4:24; cf. Gn 1:27).

Christ, "the image of the unseen God", as he exists for all time, is the center of the divine plan for all that comes into being (Col 1:15–20; cf. Heb 1:2–3). To know him fully, we must contemplate his existence with the Father prior to creation. In Christ, God has known each one of us personally from before he created the world (Eph 1:3–14).

3. Christ, the Eternal Word and Son of the Father

The Gospel of John starts by further echoing the creation account, the very first lines of Scripture, and this is because Christ is the beginning of all things. The words "In the beginning" no longer refer solely to when God created the world (Gn 1:1); they now refer to the ultimate reality of the eternal communion shared between the Divine Word and the Father (Jn 1:1). The Word is the eternal Son of the Father who took flesh in order to empower those who would receive him to become children of God through a divine new birth (Jn 1:13; 3:3–5). Christ has come to bring all people into the unity he shares with the Father (Jn 10:16, 30). He reverses Babel by gathering together the children of God whom God scattered across the world (Jn 11:52; cf. Gn 11:9). Jesus dies on the cross to bring all people to himself and make them one in the life he shares with the Father (Jn 10:16; 12:32; 17:20–23).

4. Christ, the Conqueror of Satan

A particular stream of the Johannine tradition portrays how God fulfills his promise of separating the offspring of Eve from the attack of the serpent. The book of Revelation symbolizes the people of God as the New Eve, the mother of Christ, who reigns over the universe and gives birth to the Messiah (Rv 12:1–6; cf. Gn 3:15–16). The victory of Christ's death and Resurrection crushes and defeats Satan. In our era, between the victory of Christ in his exaltation and the final event of his second coming, the continual protection and intervention of God on the Church's behalf preserve the Church from the attacks of the evil one (Rv 12:13–17; cf. Gn 3:15).

With our minds on how God forms and protects his people, we can return to Genesis and read of the first initiatives God takes to raise a community of faith, truth, and life.

STUDY QUESTIONS:

1. What was the conflict in the minds of the Israelites in exile in 587–538 B.C.?

2. What was the overriding concern of the Priestly writer in his account of creation?

3. What are the nature and consequences of sin as Genesis describes them?

4. What is the thematic significance of the flood story?

5. What is the thematic significance of the Tower of Babel story to the audience of the Priestly writers? To you?

6. How does Jesus use the Genesis texts on marriage in his instruction concerning divorce?

7. Compare Jesus to Adam. How are they similar? How different?

8. How does "In the beginning" relate to Jesus Christ?

9. How is Jesus the fulfillment of the promise in Genesis 3:15?

10. Reflect on the lies that the snake told Eve: the half-truths, the misinterpretations, the goading. What in your experience confirms the Yahwist's insight on the deceptive nature of sin: we are fooled and we believe what we want, even though it is not true and leads to our sorrow.

11. How does your belief in Jesus Christ as Son of God and sovereign Lord influence the way you understand the world and live your life?

12. What does it mean to you to be your brother's keeper?

GENESIS

I. The Primeval Story (1:1–11:32)
    A. Creation of the World (1:1–2:3 [P])
    B. Creation of Man and Woman; Their Fall (2:4–3:24 [J])
    C. Cain and Abel (4:1–26 [J])
    D. Genealogy from Adam to Noah (5:1–32 [P])
    E. The Flood (6:1–8:22 [J & P])
    F. God's Covenant with Noah (9:1–17 [P])
    G. Canaan Cursed by Noah (9:18–29 [J & P])
    H. The Table of Nations (10:1–32 [P & J])
    I. The Tower of Babel (11:1–9 [J])
    J. Genealogy from Noah's Sons to Abraham (11:10–32 [P & J])

II. The History of the Patriarchs (12:1–50:26)
    A. Abraham (12:1–25:18)
        1. Abram's Call (12:1–9 [J&P]) and Sojourn in Egypt (12:10–20[J])
        2. Abram and Lot (13:1–18 [J&P]); Abram and Four Kings (14:1–24[–])
        3. God's Promise to Abram (15:1–21 [J & E])
        4. Ishmael and Hagar (16:1–16 [J & P])
        5. Covenant and Circumcision (17:1–27 [P])
        6. Story of Sodom and Gomorrah (18:1–19:38 [J])
        7. Sojourn in Gerar (20:1–18 [E])
        8. Isaac and Ishmael (21:1–21 [J & P])
        9. Abraham and Abimelech (21:22–34 [E])
        10. Sacrifice of Isaac (22:1–24 [E])
        11. Burial Plot Purchased (23:1–20 [P])
        12. Isaac's Betrothed (24:1–67 [J])
        13. Abraham's Descendants (25:1–18 [P])
    B. Isaac (25:19–26:35)
        1. Jacob Gains Esau's Birthright (25:19–34 [P & J])
        2. Isaac in Gerar and Beersheba (26:1–35 [J, E, P])
    C. Jacob (27:1–37:1)

Pentateuchal sources of particular sections are noted in parentheses.

8

GENESIS 12–50: THE PATRIARCHS

The grief-stricken refugees whom the Babylonians deported from Jerusalem to Babylon in the tragic summer of 587 B.C. had to question the reality and meaning of the Lord's providence. How could exile in a foreign land be part of the divine plan? Indeed, how does the Lord of Israel work in history? After all, the ten northern tribes whom the Assyrians took captive in 721 B.C. faded into oblivion, never to be heard from again. They would have thought: What basis do we have for expecting anything but the same fate for Judah a century and a half later (2 Kgs 17:5–6; 18:9–11)? They questioned whether there was any genuine hope for their future. Such basic concerns demanded a new look at the origins of God's people. The scribes who reshaped the traditions during the Exile provided a magnificent response in their presentation of the stories of the Patriarchs (Gn 12:1–50:26).

The exiles had no difficulty relating to the themes of uprooting and migration, as we read in the narratives from creation to Babel, which were already characteristic of Genesis. The prehistory (Gn 1–11) depicts humanity's alienation from God in terms of banishment and dispersal: first, God must expel Adam and Eve from the garden, then Cain becomes a tormented and homeless fugitive, and finally God scatters from Babel all peoples across the face of the earth. Ultimately, everyone seems lost and disoriented; history becomes directionless. Thus, arrogance and sin render human existence practically meaningless.

The stories of the Genesis prehistory confirm what the prophets were declaring to the exiles, namely, that it was their own sin and not the Babylonian armies that caused Judah's deportation (for example, see Jer 13:22; Ez 16:35–63). The good news, however, is that the dispersion resulting from sin is not the end but the beginning of God's founding a people.

The inspired scribes in Babylon introduced the exiles to migration of a different sort, one founded on God's promise. Abraham's journey contrasts with all previous dislocations of people because God orients it in a specific direction by speaking his word to Abraham. Just as in the beginning, God speaks and all things are created (Gn 1:1–2:3), so in the course of time, he speaks again to form a people. This happens precisely where the Israelites are in exile, in the region of Mesopotamia, not far from Babylon (Gn 12:1–3). The journey Abraham makes is the dream of the exiles: a departure from Mesopotamia westward into the Promised Land. Furthermore, they could take comfort in the fact that God spoke to Abraham in Mesopotamia, the very place of their exile, and could speak to them as Abraham in their own day.

By contrast with the tragic fragmentation that the prehistory narrates, the stories of the Patriarchs unveil a dynamic movement toward convergence and unity. The underlying principle is one God, one people, one land. Abraham and his descendants teach us that hearing God's word provides for a whole new way of being and moving in the world.

Three major cycles of texts comprising the narratives of the Patriarchs illustrate this new way of life (Gn 12–50). The text devotes a complete cycle first to Abraham (12:1–25:18), then to Jacob (27:1–37:1), and finally to Joseph and the sons of Jacob (37:2–50:26). The stories of Isaac (25:19–26:35) are not really a major unit in themselves but rather serve as a bridge between the sagas of Abraham and Jacob. The largest portion of material is concerned with Jacob, the "wandering Aramaean" who gives birth to the people Israel (27:1–50:14; see Dt 26:5–9).

A central theme distinguishes each of the three major cycles: the stories of Abraham highlight God's promise; the Jacob narratives revolve around the issue of blessing; and the fine artistry of the Joseph story illustrates how God's providence achieves fraternal peace. We will note that the author expresses each of these themes within the dynamics of family relationships.

Abraham: Responding to the Promise (12:1–26:35)

God's word to Abraham consists of a command ("Leave your country ... ") and a promise ("and I shall make you a great nation") that bears implications for all peoples ("and all clans on earth will bless themselves by you") (12:1–3). The promise has two dimensions: the provision of a land and the genesis of a people or nation. It speaks of concrete realities, not abstractions. And human resources cannot possibly bring these realities into existence. (We have already noted the barrenness of Abraham's wife in the text [11:30].) Only God can accomplish the promise.

Faith on man's part is necessary as the sole adequate response to God's word (15:6). Faith has two dimensions: trust in God's promises and obedience to his commands. Promise and command belong together as complementary dimensions of God's word. Obedience is possible in view of the promise, and what God promises is realizable only through obedience. God's initial revelation of his plan to Abraham provides the agenda for the restoration of the exiles to the Promised Land. In the middle of the sixth century B.C., the Jewish people of Judah in Babylon were in the same position as Abraham in the middle of the nineteenth century B.C. Like Abraham, they had to receive God's word as promise and respond to it with a trusting and hopeful faith. The Scriptures were revealing that the Exile did not remove them from God's plan but, in fact, put them in the shoes of their father Abraham. The Jews in Babylon had to realize that God was calling them to a new beginning as the people of the promise.

God does not fulfill his promise immediately. Through years of testing and experience, Abraham has to learn what it means to live by faith. He himself is the first to jeopardize God's promise by not remaining in Canaan but going to Egypt, where he puts his wife at risk out of fear for his own life (12:10–20). He repeats the same folly years later, and only God can rescue him, amazingly, by speaking to the foreign king in a dream (20:1–18). Earlier, in the interim, God ratifies his promise in the form of an unconditional covenant (15:1–21). Eleven years after Abraham leaves his homeland, Ishmael is born to Abraham's slave Hagar (16:1–16). A full twenty-five years after his departure, when Abraham is almost a hundred years old, God establishes the covenant marked by circumcision. Furthermore, he promises Abraham a son to be born of Sarah (17:1–27). Sarah greets the promise with derision, even as God delivers it to Abraham in the guise of three sojourners (18:1–15). Finally, Isaac is born as the child of the promise (21:1–7). Even then, there remains one further test for Abraham. This one God himself designs to ascertain Abraham's fidelity even at the cost of sacrificing his son (22:1–19). Once Abraham meets this challenge, the Lord bestows upon him the fullness of the blessing he had announced in his original declaration (22:15–18).

All along, the Lord continually keeps before Abraham's mind the promise he made when he first called him (12:1–3; 15:1–6; 17:4–8, 15–22; 22:17–18). While Abraham witnesses the fulfillment of the promise in the birth of Isaac, this marks only the beginning of God's forming a people over a series of lifetimes. With each successive generation, first with Isaac (26:3–4, 24) and then with Jacob (28:13–14), the Lord repeats his commitment to Abraham. The promise of a mighty nation finds its culmination in the birth of Jacob's twelve sons, who are the forebears of the tribes of Israel (29:31–30:24; 35:16–20, 23–26). As the book draws to a close, the author gives them center stage in Jacob's characterization of each one while bestowing his final blessing (49:1–28).

By the end of Genesis, there is evident fulfillment of God's promise of a people. However, his promise of a land (12:7) stretches our vision beyond Genesis throughout the Pentateuch (Ex 3:7–8; 6:4; Dt 7:1) to the entrance of

Joshua into Canaan (Jos 1–12). Abraham establishes his people's claim to the Promised Land in his purchase of the cave at Machpelah where he and each of the Patriarchs are buried (23:1–20; 25:8–10; 35:27–29; 50:13).

Jacob: God's Blessing (27:1–36:43)

God's blessing is the power that generates life in fulfillment of his promises. A blessing is God's word unleashed in power and effectiveness to accomplish what it announces. Divine blessing is the driving force that brings about the formation of God's people throughout Genesis. In the opening chapters, God blesses people whenever he makes a new beginning in the realization of his plan. In creation, he blesses man and woman to guarantee that they will produce offspring in abundance (1:28). His blessing of Noah after the Flood announces the dawning of a new era (9:1).

Most especially, God enshrines his call to Abraham with a blessing that guarantees he will have the promised offspring (12:2). The fact that God extends this blessing to all peoples suggests that now there is a power active in history to overcome the curses deriving from sin in the prehistory (12:3; cf. 3:17–19; 4:11–12). Isaac owes his whole life to God's blessing, which brings him to birth (17:16), identifies Rebekah to be his wife (24:48), consoles him at his father's death (25:11), increases his crops and livestock (26:12–14), and guarantees his descendants (26:24).

With Jacob, the narrative reveals that blessing is the most essential ingredient in life. God's blessing is solemnly communicated once and for all from father to son. At his mother's initiative, Jacob defrauds Esau of his father's blessing and thereby receives the power of life that his father hands on (27:1–45; cf. 25:24–34). His kinsman Laban testifies to the efficacy of the blessing upon Jacob (30:27, 30). God's blessing gives Jacob his new name Israel, making him the head of a nation (35:9–10; cf. 32:23–33). Toward the end of his life, he acknowledges the blessing of God as the source of his progeny, and so he blesses the two sons of Joseph, Ephraim and Manasseh (48:1–20). His life reaches completion with the bestowal of his blessing upon all his sons, who stand at the head of the twelve tribes of Israel (49:1–28).

Thus, Genesis illustrates that the nation of Israel is the fruit of God's efficacious blessing, not of natural descendance. God carries forth his primeval blessing, which he declared over the human race at its creation, in the formation of his people. By his wise and merciful plan, God overcomes the curse of sin by the efficacy of his blessing all people through Abraham. For the exiles, this means that their endurance as a people ultimately does not depend upon their natural instincts for survival but rather on the anointing God provides through blessing them.

At various points, the text provides supplementary evidence of God's concern for peoples other than the Israelites. God's solicitude for the Arabian tribes is particularly evident in his revelation to Hagar and blessing upon Ishmael after Sarah banishes them to the wilderness (16:1–16; 17:20; 21:8–21; 25:12–18). The text makes special mention of the Moabites and Ammonites (19:30–38). It highlights the Edomites by their identification with their patriarch Esau, who, on one occasion, reflects the very disposition of God to Jacob (33:1–11; 32:22–33; see also 26:34–35; 28:6–9; 36:1–43). By way of extension, such texts in Genesis would encourage the exiles to look fraternally on all kinds of foreigners they would meet in Babylon.

Marriage and Family Life

If we glance back over the stories of the Patriarchs, we can see that they suggest it might be more accurate to identify the couples and their families as the true protagonists of Genesis. Abraham and Sarah, Isaac and Rebekah, Jacob and Rachel—husbands and wives are intimately involved in working together to respond to God's call in their lives. Genesis offers a series of family portraits that are remarkably honest and realistic.

The first effects of the Fall occur within marriage (Gn 3:7, 16), and the experience of Adam and Eve is reflected in diverse ways in the marriages of the Patriarchs and their wives. Out of fear and self-concern, Abraham twice endangers his wife (12:10–20; 20:1–18). Sarah's depression from having no children is evident in her cynicism toward God's declaration of his promises (16:1–6; 18:9–15). Isaac imitates his father's weakness in not protecting his wife amid foreigners (26:6–11). Rebekah sides with her son Jacob in opposition to her husband Isaac and their elder son Esau (27:1–45). Jacob and Rachel quarrel over her inability to have children early in their marriage (30:1–2). Consistent with our common experience, human frailty is primarily manifest in the most intimate relationships and wounds most deeply those whom we are to love most fully.

Where human weakness is most evident, God's grace is most abundant. His blessing to overcome barrenness comes first upon Sarah and then upon both Rebekah and Rachel (21:1–3; 25:21; 30:1–24; 35:16–19; cf. 16:1–6; 18:1–15; 21:1–7). God works his plan out through married life even when one of the spouses fails to uphold the marriage relationship. Two instances stand out. God rescues Sarah from the clutches of foreigners when Abraham is too fearful to care for her as his wife (12:10–20; 20:1–18). God even uses Rebekah's deception of Isaac for the good purpose of furthering his plan to bring the tribes of Israel into existence (27:1–29).

The love of husband and wife grows through trial and testing and reaches maturity in old age. In death, the rich quality of their commitment to each other is most evident. Overcome with grief at Sarah's death, Abraham purchases an estate in Canaan to secure his burial with her (Gn 23:1–20; 25:7–10). Likewise, Isaac is buried with Rebekah (49:31). Jacob's love for Rachel is evident in the manner in which he erects her tomb at Bethlehem and informs their beloved son Joseph of the event (35:19–20; 48:7).

The Joseph Story: Providence and Reconciliation (37:2–50:26)

Throughout the book of Genesis, the focus on marriage and family gives rise to a theme of brotherhood. This motif has its origins in the prehistory with the Lord's acceptance of Abel's offering and his rejection of Cain's, which foreshadows the surprising divine preference for the younger over the elder in the families of the Patriarchs. God will favor Isaac over Ishmael (Gn 21), Jacob over Esau (25:23, 27), and Joseph over his brothers (Gn 37–50).

In the biblical sense of the term, brotherhood does not develop by natural instinct. Rather, it is the fruit of reconciliation. Suspicion, jealousy, and rivalry characterize natural family relationships throughout Genesis. Cain murders Abel (4:1–8), Sarah has Ishmael driven out into the desert away from Isaac (21:8–21), Jacob deprives Esau of their father's blessing (27:1–45), and Joseph's brothers sell Joseph into slavery (37:2–36).

Reconciliation among brothers forms the climax of Genesis. We clearly see the embrace of forgiveness in two places: first, in Esau's reception of Jacob (33:1–11) and, ultimately, in the hospitality Joseph extends to his brothers (45:1–15).

The Jacob story indicates reconciliation between brothers is practically equivalent to the revelation of God himself. Esau's tearful embrace of his guilt-ridden brother to forgive him for all the injuries Jacob had committed in the past compels Jacob to exclaim, "In fact I have come into your presence as into the presence of God, since you have received me kindly" (33:10). His remark refers to the episode on the banks of the Jabbok the night before, when he encountered God "face to face" (32:23–33). The message is that we touch God by encountering our brother or sister in reconciliation.

The whole book of Genesis reaches its culmination when Joseph embraces his brothers at table and pronounces his forgiveness of the ways they had injured him (45:1–15). At various points throughout the narrative, he makes his brothers conscious of their guilt and hopelessness (42:21–22; 44:16). When he finally gathers them together and discloses to them who he really is, he exhibits the same gestures as Esau did with Jacob, embracing them, kissing them, weeping with them, and offering them his pardon (45:14–15; cf. 33:4, 11). Later, after the death of their father, his brothers explicitly ask Joseph's forgiveness for the evil they did to him. Here, again, he consoles them and assures them that he has forgiven all (50:15–21). The book of Genesis concludes on this note of fraternal reconciliation as a counterpoint to the division and hostility we first saw in the story of Cain and Abel (4:1–16).

The whole Joseph narrative (37:2–50:26) is a beautifully crafted short story illustrating how God's providence works to overcome all evil and division. Here we see how God uses everything, even human sin, to accomplish his designs.

In retrospect, Joseph realizes that, although he was sold into Egyptian slavery by his brothers' treachery, God uses the event to position him in Egypt, where he eventually provides for his father and for the next generation. He tells his brothers, "The evil you planned to do me has by God's design been turned to good" (50:20).

His discernment reaches its pinnacle with his insightful description of God's providence in using all events to form a people of his own. While a common human perspective would assert that Joseph goes to Egypt because his brothers sell him into slavery, Joseph discerns for his kinsmen what really happened: "God sent me before you to assure the survival of your race on earth and to save your lives by a great deliverance. So it was not you who sent me here but God . . . " (45:7–8). God's plan involves something more than the mere preservation of Joseph and his brothers. His providence is always directed toward the development of his people in the next generation and beyond.

The Joseph story answers the Babylonian exiles' question: "How could our deportation from Jerusalem to Babylon be part of God's providence?" Joseph is the best example of a person who is violently and unjustly removed from the Promised Land to a pagan empire. Just as with Jacob all the tribes went down into Egypt, so, too, in the Exile, the last remaining tribe, Judah, was taken to Babylon. But why? Joseph asserts what the exiles must believe, namely, that God will turn evil into good (Gn 50:20). Out of the people's very sins that brought about banishment from their land, God will bring life for his people. More specifically, through Joseph, the Lord reveals why he has brought his people into a foreign land: to preserve a remnant on the earth (45:7–8; see Jer 31:7). From these words, the people of Judah could realize that God brought them to Babylon, not to drive them into extinction, but to preserve them for a future as a holy people.

The whole manner in which the Priestly authors put the book of Genesis together exhibits their concern to reveal the perfection of God's plan to form his people. The Priestly editors inserted genealogies at strategic points in the text to link one generation to the next and to present the clear linear precision of God's design for those who would have the eyes to behold it. The second account of the creation begins with the formula: "Such was the story of heaven and earth as they were created" (Gn 2:4). This phrase is typical for introducing narratives (Gn 6:9; 11:27; 25:19; 37:2) and genealogies that trace the pathway from Adam to Noah to Abraham to Jacob (5:1; 10:1; 11:10; 25:12; 36:1). The editors were not hesitant to include the genealogies of the neighboring peoples who were offshoots of Abraham's descendants. The genealogies illustrate the order and continuity in God's plan as it unfolds stage by stage in history as in creation. God will never let a link fall from the chain of the generations of his people. All peoples of the world will find their identity within the framework of his divine plan for Israel.

Toward the New Testament: God's Children by Faith

In the New Testament, the figures of the Patriarchs become prominent in debates over the nature of salvation and the identity of God's people. In Judaism at the time of Jesus, the Patriarchs were not considered only in view of past history but also as identified with God's ultimate Kingdom in heaven. In his discussion with the Sadducees over the resurrection, Jesus refers to the God of Abraham, Isaac, and Jacob as the God of the living (Mk 12:18–27; Mt 22:23–33; Lk 20:27–40). They are the great figures presiding over the divine banquet (Mt 8:11; Lk 13:28). Abraham is the one to receive the poor into heaven (Lk 16:22–31). In these last two examples, Jesus insists that not only Jews but also Gentiles and the marginalized will be received into final glory.

"Who are the children of Abraham?" This was a recurring question in the New Testament churches at various points during the first century. The Matthaean tradition highlights at the beginning of the Gospel John the Baptist's insistence that physical descendance from Abraham means nothing by comparison with the necessity of repentance (Mt 3:8–9). So, too, in the Johannine tradition, Jesus challenges the religious leaders over their reliance on descendance from Abraham, which prevents them from placing faith in him as the divine Son who preexisted the Patriarch himself (Jn 8:31–59). Each of these traditions indicates that Abraham's importance rests, not in his status as the genealogical forefather of a nation, but rather in his status as the model of submission and obedience to God.

Paul becomes more focused and identifies faith as the distinguishing feature of both Abraham and his true children (Rom 4:1–25). Noting the priority of Abraham's faith in God's promise (Gn 15:5–6) over his act of circumcision (Gn 17:10–11), Paul uses the texts in Genesis to illustrate his assertion that justification comes through faith, not observance of the Law.

In his presentation of the theme in Romans, Paul builds on what he had previously written to the Galatians. There he insisted that Christ is the true offspring of Abraham as the ultimate child of God's promise (Gal 3:15–18). With Christ, the grace of sonship received through justifying faith in Christ overcomes and brings to an end the era of slavery under the Law (Gal 3:19–4:7). By a rabbinical form of argumentation, Paul uses images of Hagar and Ishmael in comparison with Sarah and Isaac to contrast the life of slavery under the old Sinai covenant (Hagar) with the life of freedom under the new covenant of the Jerusalem from above (Sarah) (Gal 4:21–5:1). All of this demonstrates the validity of Paul's basic assertion that "it is people of faith who are the children of Abraham" (Gal 3:7).

The Letter to the Hebrews indicates that Abraham's tithe to Melchizedek means that Christ's priesthood takes primacy over that of Abraham's descendant, Levi (Heb 7:1–28; cf. Gn 14:17–20). Later on, the author presents Abraham and Sarah as models of persevering faith and endurance through trial and testing as they look forward to the heavenly city God builds (Heb 11:8–19). The lives of Isaac, Jacob, and Joseph connote successively the same faith (Heb 11:20–22).

Preventing a misinterpretation of the Pauline emphasis that contrasts faith and works as in opposition, James insists that in Abraham's case, "his faith was working together with his deeds; his faith became perfect by what he did" (Jas 2:22). James takes this alternate perspective of Abraham because he is dealing with a different issue. Certainly, he finds basic agreement with the Apostle to the Gentiles, who asserts that faith has to work through love so as to fulfill the perfect law of Christ (Gal 5:6; 6:2; cf. Rom 8:2).

Clearly, Abraham stands at the beginning of God's plan that God brings to fulfillment in Jesus Christ. This is evident in Matthew's genealogy (Mt 1:1–17; cf. Lk 3:23–38) and in the great hymns of both Mary and Zechariah in Luke's infancy narrative (Lk 1:55, 73). Referring to Christ's Resurrection as the fulfillment of the Father's plan, the earliest evangelists proclaim the faithfulness of God to the religious authorities in Jerusalem: "It is the God of Abraham, Isaac and Jacob, the God of our ancestors, who has glorified his servant Jesus whom you handed over and then disowned in the presence of Pilate . . ." (Acts 3:13).

As the Resurrection is the central event of salvation in the New Testament, so the Exodus is in the Old Testament. Our reading of Genesis in light of Christ has prepared us to consider how God redeems a people and makes them his own. We turn now to the book of Exodus to pursue this issue in detail.

STUDY QUESTIONS

1. Why was the disappearance of the ten northern tribes important to the exiles in Babylon?
2. What themes were the Priestly writers trying to teach the Babylonian exiles concerning sin and personal identity?
3. What are the three major cycles of patriarchal stories, and what are the themes of each?
4. What are the two dimensions of faith?
5. What is the significance to us of God's blessing of Abraham?
6. How does the text reveal God's concern for people other than Israelites?
7. What is the significance of reconciliation in the patriarchal texts?
8. What is the purpose of the Priestly use of genealogies in Genesis?
9. How does the New Testament use the themes of the patriarchal texts?
10. How much do you know about your own genealogy? Which individuals of a preceding generation had the greatest influence on your growth in faith?
11. How can leadership of a family enlightened by prayer and faith change your own life and affect the life of your parish?
12. How does the theme of reconciliation in Genesis apply to you, your family, your parish, and the universal Church?

9

EXODUS: FREEDOM AND COVENANT

The Priestly writers who composed the early editions of the Pentateuch during the Exile knew that the Jews living in Babylon during the sixth century B.C. would easily identify with the Israelites living in bondage in Egypt prior to the thirteenth century B.C. Like the Israelites of Moses' day, the exiles lived in a mighty and prosperous nation but under the dominion of foreigners. Furthermore, a great, forbidding desert separated each group from the Promised Land: the Sinai wilderness between Egypt and Canaan; the Arabian desert between Babylon and Judah.

Around 550 B.C., Deutero-Isaiah heard the call to prepare a way for the Lord to lead his people through the wilderness back to Judah (Is 40:3–5). The return from exile would be a new Exodus. God would work wonders among the returning exiles modeled on his parting of the Sea (Is 43:16–21; 51:10), guiding and protecting them (Is 52:12) and bringing forth water from the rock (Is 48:21). In their recounting of the events in the book of Exodus, the Priestly writers wanted the exiles in Babylon to realize that they, in fact, were the people of Moses of their day. The Lord would bring them out of captivity, lead them across the wilderness, enter into covenant with them, and finally reveal his glory to them from his holy sanctuary.

The book of Exodus has two halves, the first narrating the event of liberation from slavery in Egypt (1:1–18:27) and the second focusing on the covenant at Mount Sinai (19:1–40:38). The first half primarily consists of God's deeds, while the second concentrates on his words. The first half is a dramatic and fast-paced portrait of the Israelites' struggle to gain freedom (1:1–13:16) and their eventual flight from Egyptian bondage across the Sea into the wilderness (13:17–18:27). By comparison, the second part slows down as if to offer us a desert experience with God's people, who now remain encamped at Mount Sinai. The writers present minute details for the construction of the Tabernacle (25:1–31:18; 35:1–40:38) amid God's awesome revelation in his establishment of the covenant (19:1–24:18) and subsequent reconciliation with his people after their failure to keep it (32:1–34:35).

We will consider the message of Exodus by focusing on four central themes: (1) revelation, (2) salvation, (3) covenant, and (4) glory. Exodus teaches us that these principles are the vital ingredients God uses to form a people of his own in the world.

The Way out of Slavery (1:1–13:16): Revelation

Revelation is God's making himself known to human beings directly through a personal encounter. The three times God reveals himself to Moses on Mount Sinai represent the critical turning points in God's dealings with his people. First, he speaks his name to Moses and tells him of his plans to redeem his people from slavery in Egypt (3:1–4:17). Later, he discourses with Moses on the mountain when he enters into covenant with Israel (19:1–20:21; 24:1–18). Finally, God makes his glory known to his servant when he renews the covenant (33:11, 18–23; 34:6–9, 29–35). Each case shows God revealing himself when his people are in their deepest need, first of all in Egyptian bondage (1:1–2:25), then in the insecurity of the wilderness (15:22–27; 16:1–17:7), and, finally, after they break the covenant by their sin (32:1–35). Let us look more closely at the issue by asking: "What is it like to experience revelation?" and "What does God reveal?"

1. Experiencing Revelation

The Exodus account would have encouraged the exiles in Babylon to realize that God reveals himself when times are difficult and makes himself known to those who suffer deeply even at the hands of their own people. The theme of God's providence carries over from the end of Genesis to the beginning of Exodus. Just as the treachery of his brothers drove Joseph away from his own people, so the threat of betrayal by a fellow Hebrew forces Moses to flee into the wilderness (2:11–15). As in the case of Joseph, so for Moses: banishment from the clan and life with strangers becomes the setting to prepare God's chosen one to rescue his people (2:16–25). A time of suffering can be a time of great revelation.

The description of Moses' prophetic call offers us a fascinating insight into what it is like to experience God's revelation for the first time (3:1–4:17; cf. Jer 1:4–10; Jgs 6:11–24). We listen to an extended dialogue that God initiates and which Moses intersperses with five objections (3:11; 3:13; 4:1; 4:10; 4:13). The conversation reflects the difference between the minds of God and man. The Lord speaks positively, offering an extensive outline of his plan to redeem his people and care for every eventuality in the process. By contrast, Moses exhibits an emerging pessimism in his abrupt, short questions and protests. At first, his questions appear to reflect humility and an honest search for comprehension (3:11, 13); however, they are increasingly charged with self-concern and manifest a desperate attempt to avoid the call, climaxing with his anxious plea, asking the Lord to send someone else (4:1, 10, 13).

Moses' reactions must have struck a chord with the exiles, who responded with cool suspicion upon first hearing the "good news" of their impending deliverance from Babylon (Is 49:1–7). Moses' objections are rooted in past experiences, while God's responses promise a qualitatively new future (3:12, 18, 21–22; 4:9, 15). The Lord is patient but resolute, repeatedly assuring Moses with the phrases, "I am well aware ... " (3:7), "I shall be with you ... " (3:12), "I shall help you ... " (4:15). His very name promises that he will be with the people always to rescue them from their oppressors and provide them with a "Promised Land" (3:17–18).

Moses' example indicates that while the experience of God's revelation can be disconcerting at first, such an encounter with God will become more important than anything else for the person who allows God to work in his or her life. As Moses becomes more acquainted with the grace of divine revelation, he eagerly seeks out the presence of God. The reluctant attitude he demonstrates in his first encounter stands in marked contrast with his desire to experience fully the glory of God during his last meeting with the Lord on the mountain (Ex 33:17–23).

2. The Content of Revelation

Basically, God's revelation consists of two elements: the announcement of his plans to redeem his people and the declaration of his name. When the Lord speaks his name to Moses, everything about the relationship between God and mankind is cast in a new light. No matter how much we may "know about" a person from observation or hearsay, we cannot claim to "know" that person really until we have introduced ourselves by speaking our names to one another. When God introduces himself as "Yahweh", he reveals himself to Moses in the most personal and definitive way. The expression "I am he who is" represents an interpretation of the word *YHWH* ("Yahweh"), which is derived from the verb "to be" (*hwh*) (Ex 3:14). This name is so holy that later Jewish tradition would consider it unutterable and, instead of "Yahweh", Jews would say "the Lord" (*Adonai*) whenever coming across *YHWH* in the sacred text. (The term *Jehovah* is a rendering in English of what would be impossible in Hebrew due to mixing the Hebrew consonants of *Yahweh* with the vowels of *Adonai*). When God forgives the sin of his people and renews the covenant, he reveals his name again but with a deeper accent on his compassion and mercy (33:19).

The Israelites become known as those who call upon the name of the Lord (Ex 15:1–3; see Pss 99:6; 116:4, 13). Deutero-Isaiah alerted the exiles in Babylon to the importance of the divine name (see Is 42:8; 43:10–12). The Priestly editors wanted to keep this message alive by focusing their audience's attention on the source of the prophet's teaching in Exodus.

The Israelite captives in thirteenth-century Egypt and in sixth-century Babylon received a revelation surpassing that of the Patriarchs. Abraham, Isaac, and Jacob encountered *El* (in Hebrew, "God": Jos 24:2) under a variety of aspects: *El Shaddai* ("the God of the mountain" or "God Almighty" [Gn 17:1; 35:11; 43:14; 49:25; cf. Ex 6:3]), *El-Elyon* ("God the Most High" [Gn 14:18–24]), and *El Bethel* ("God of Bethel" [Gn 31:13; cf. 28:10–22]).

Until Moses, faithful people thought of God in light of his associates. He was "the Kinsman of Isaac" (Gn 31:42), "the Mighty One of Jacob" (49:24), or simply "the God of Abraham" (Gn 31:42) or "the God of my father" (26:24; 28:13; 31:5, 42; 32:10). Beginning with Moses, every one of his people could know him directly as "Yahweh" (Ex 6:2–13). Knowledge of the divine name leads to salvation.

Across the Sea and through the Wilderness (13:17–18:27): Salvation

The Exodus event is the biblical paradigm of salvation that stands at the heart of the Old Testament. It teaches us the way God works to bring about our redemption. A close study of the text exposes some radical truths about salvation. God saves us, not in isolation from each other, but as members of his people. God's ways of bringing about our salvation meet opposition from the world and resistance from within ourselves. Because God desires our salvation far more deeply than we do, he overcomes all obstacles to liberate us so we can live in obedience to him.

God redeems a people whom he chooses to be his own (3:7–10). The people Moses leads out of Egypt are not a homogeneous or harmonious group but a "mixed crowd" who have one thing in common: they know God is calling them out of their slavery (12:38). No one can get out of slavery alone without joining the people of God.

Salvation begins when Moses proclaims to Pharaoh and to the Hebrews God's divine name and his intention to bring his people out of Egypt (5:1–6:1). A dynamic tension fills the air. In his series of audiences with Pharaoh, Moses resembles the later prophets of Israel who confront her kings by declaring, "This is what Yahweh says . . . " (5:1; 7:17; 7:26; 9:1; cf. 1 Kgs 21:19). Each time, Moses meets with more determined resistance.

Not only the Egyptians protest against God's plans. The Hebrews protest as well, immediately reinforcing Pharaoh's resistance. Moses' people initially receive the news of their redemption with joy (4:31) but quickly become bitter toward God's servant as Pharaoh's reactions cause their hardships to increase (5:21). Even Moses begins to fall back into his original pessimism (5:22–23). Everyone except the Lord wants to give up on the idea of redemption for the Hebrews.

The Lord demonstrates his love for Israel by confronting the pride of Egypt with his mighty works that chastise the land of slavery (7:8–11:10). The tension mounts until the tenth wonder. The death of the first-born of the Egyptians contrasts with the life of the first-born Hebrews and highlights the fact that Israel itself is God's "first-born son" (11:1–10; 12:29–34; 13:1–16; cf. 4:22–23). The Egyptians' surrender to the Israelites of everything they asked for upon their departure vindicates the Lord's word of promise (12:35–36; cf. 3:21–22; 11:2). Israel leaves the land of captivity as a victorious people.

At the narrative's climax, there is an insertion of a late form of the Passover ritual (12:1–28, 43–51), which alerts every generation of Israelites to realize that God is at work in their own day to set them free from bondage. Because God has set them free in this great work of deliverance, Israelites of every generation must renounce slavery to the world by responding to God's call (12:11–12, 14, 17, 24–27). The exiles who returned to Judah and celebrated the first Passover at the restored Temple in 515 B.C. would have had a special appreciation of this biblical "memorial" (Ezr 6:19–22).

Up to this point in the narrative, the authors demonstrate that God desires his people's salvation more than they do. The question that remains is: "Will the Israelites trust him?" They vacillate between elation and despair. The confidence they exhibited in plundering the Egyptians (12:35–36) vanishes into terrified disbelief when the Egyptian forces trap them on the shores of the Sea of Reeds (14:5–14). So that they will realize God saves them by his grace alone, Moses demands nothing except that they stand fast and look to what the Lord will do (14:13–14). Upon passing through the parted waters of the Sea, the same Israelites who had vehemently protested God's plan now profess their faith (14:31; cf. 14:12; 5:21; 6:9).

But this kind of shallow faith cannot stand the test of harsh circumstances. Whenever the Lord is at work to save them, the people fear his bringing about their destruction and prefer slavery to freedom (17:2–3; 16:3; 14:11–12; 6:9; 5:21). Biblical salvation involves a paradox that challenges our human preferences. Egypt, the land of prosperity and security, is the place of slavery, while the life-threatening desert is the place of freedom. When God redeems them, his people forfeit houses for tents, a settled urban life for a nomadic existence, and a productive land for an arid wilderness. At first glance in this light, the call of God seems harsh and demanding. However, we must always realize that in the desert, there was something available to the Israelites that they did not have in Egypt, namely, God's presence and his power to meet every one of their needs.

At every step of the people in the wilderness, God provides them with healing and life (15:26, in 15:22–27). He reveals his glory in the form of manna and quail for food (16:7, in 16:1–36), and he manifests his presence by drawing water from the rock (17:7, in 17:1–7). He defeats the Amalekites in response to Moses' prayer and thereby demonstrates his power to overcome all enemies of his people (17:8–16). Every hardship is an occasion for Israel to experience God's love and deliverance (18:8). But the people are unstable in their faith. They need to enter into covenant with God.

This perspective on salvation challenges us in the same way it confronted both the Jewish exiles who found comfortable positions in Babylon and the pioneers who returned to Judah shortly after 538 B.C. The story of the Exodus forced the vast majority of Jews who remained in Babylon after Cyrus' decree of liberation to examine their motives for staying. Were they like the reluctant Israelites whose attachment to security enslaved them in the land of captivity so that they would not venture out into the freedom of God's call? And did those who returned to Judah tend to complain like the Israelites when difficulties they encountered in Judah tempered their initial enthusiasm for liberation (see Ezr 1:1–6:22; Hg 1–2; Zec 1–8)? The fear and instability of our hearts expose our need to enter into a covenant relationship with God. God invites us into covenant with him so that his work of salvation will become the secure foundation on which we build our lives together as his people.

The Sinai Event (19:1–24:18; 32:1–34:35): Covenant

Covenant is an agreement that God initiates to protect, sustain, and bring to completion the salvation he has already brought about in the lives of his people. In the covenant at Sinai, God makes Israel his own people.

From where does the idea of covenant come? Biblical covenants took the form of treaties between an overlord and his vassals typical of the ancient world. Hittite pacts of the fourteenth century B.C. consisted of six parts: (1) a *preamble* mentioning the overlord's title (Ex 20:2); (2) a *historical prologue* summarizing the past relations between the two parties (Ex 20:2); (3) the *obligations of the vassal* (Ex 20:3–17); (4) the *stipulations for writing and proclaiming* the text at regular intervals (Ex 31:18; 24:12; 34:1–2, 27–28; 40:20; see Dt 27:1–10; 31:9–13); (5) the *list of heavenly witnesses* to the agreement (Dt 32:1–43); and (6) the *blessings and curses* for compliance or noncompliance respectively (Dt 27:11–28:46).

Acquaintance with this cultural background reinforces our understanding that a covenant was far from being a partnership agreement. The parties in the biblical covenant are the all-powerful God and a helpless, even rebellious, people. That God would even enter into a covenant indicates his love and mercy. As his people, Israel finds her identity in obedience that she expresses by proclaiming in solemn oath, "Whatever Yahweh has said, we will do" (Ex 19:8; 24:7). Through the covenant, God transforms the "mixed crowd" who depart Egypt (12:38) into "a kingdom of priests, a holy nation" (19:6).

The book of Exodus contains two accounts of God making covenant with his people, once when they first arrive at Sinai and again when they renew their commitment after breaking the first agreement. We shall note that the second event of covenant might have been more relevant to the exiles than the first.

1. The Original Covenant at Sinai (19:1–24:18)

The "theophany" or revelation of God dominates the biblical account of the covenant at Sinai (19:1–25). The elements of trumpet, cloud, fire, and smoke combine to reflect the transcendent splendor of God that would consume any flesh approaching the mountain (19:16–25). So great and powerful is the divine otherness that only Moses can stand in God's presence as mediator while the whole people must purify themselves (19:9–25). From the time the Israelites leave Egypt, they see God's presence reflected in the fire and cloud that lead them and in the miracles that provide for their needs. Now at Sinai, they meet God personally.

Within the context of the revelation of himself to the people, the Lord communicates his commandments. Law, if we correctly understand it, is an essential ingredient of the covenant relationship between God and his people. The Ten Commandments, or the "Ten Words" (34:28), which are the stipulations of the covenant, do not produce salvation but protect God's work of salvation and deepen our response to it. God gives his commandments to his people after he has set them free from bondage. Before he communicates his precepts, he introduces himself as their and our Liberator: "I am Yahweh your God who brought you out of Egypt, where you lived as slaves" (Ex 20:2). God's commandments guarantee freedom and preserve the new life that he has freely given his people by bringing them through the sea.

God's commandments provide the foundation for community life in both vertical (toward God) and horizontal (toward each other) dimensions. The first commandment, requiring exclusive commitment to the Lord who has redeemed his people, is the primary condition of the covenant. All the other commandments identify various implications of this first one in the course of practical living. Obedience to the Lord demands respect for all members of the covenant community so that their unity would reflect the oneness of God. Thus, the first three precepts reflect the believer's relationship to God, while the remaining ones describe the essentials of justice toward other human beings.

2. Breaking and Renewal of the Covenant (32:1–34:35)

Before the Babylonians ravaged the city, Jeremiah and Ezekiel told the people of Judah that Jerusalem would be destroyed because the people had broken the covenant with God (Jer 11:1–11; Ez 17:19–21). Nevertheless, once the people were in exile, both prophets proclaimed that God would establish a new covenant, one in which the Law will be written on their hearts (Jer 31:31–34; cf. Ez 36:26–28), an everlasting covenant of peace (Ez 37:26; cf. 16:60–62). For the exiles, the original covenant at Sinai has already been broken. The only one that gives hope to the exiles is the new covenant God will establish as he forgives his people their transgression. The influence of Jeremiah and Ezekiel probably made the Priestly editors aware that the account of renewing the covenant would speak more directly to the exiles than the story of the original covenant at Sinai. They took the Yahwistic narrative, which by this time was combined with Elohistic and Deuteronomic elements, and inserted it into the narrative at this point in order to encourage their audience in exile to repent and renew their covenant with the Lord.

We have noted how the people's failure to trust the Lord gave rise to great turmoil among the Israelites prior to their arrival at Sinai. Now we realize that even ratification of the covenant did not bring the Israelites' unbelief to an end. When the Israelites break the covenant, they do so by trespassing the first and foremost of the commandments. The narrative of their worshipping the golden calf is a finely tuned description of the primary temptation that threatens to destroy God's people throughout their history. The calf-idol calls to mind the images constructed at sanctuaries at Dan and Bethel to seal the religious separation of the northern kingdom under Jeroboam in 931 B.C. The very words of the first king of the northern tribes are on the lips of the people at Sinai as Aaron presents the idol to them (32:4; 1 Kgs 12:28).

The exiles in Babylon might have associated the calf-idol with the various images of Mesopotamian deities that their captors worshipped. Deutero-Isaiah had already exposed the futility of pagan idolatry (Is 44:9–20; 42:8; 48:11) and had declared the primacy of the Lord who made heaven and earth. While proclaiming the many attributes of God, Deutero-Isaiah placed special emphasis on the Lord's mercy and compassion. Indeed, God told him to proclaim before anything else that he now forgives the sin that had brought his people into exile (Is 40:1–2). The Exodus account of the covenant renewal reinforces the same message to the exiles. When God restores his relationship with his people, he reveals himself in a new and even more personal way than in the original Sinai covenant (Ex 33:18–23; cf. 19:16–25; 20:18–21). Without the overwhelming power of thunder, fire, clouds, darkness, and smoke, he reveals himself to Moses as " 'Yahweh, Yahweh, God of tenderness and compassion, slow to anger, rich in faithful love and constancy, maintaining his faithful love to thousands, forgiving fault, crime and sin . . . ' " (Ex 34:6–7). All of this indicates that when God's people repent of their sin, they receive a deeper grace of revelation than ever before (32:19–20, 25–35).

The radiance of Moses' face as he descends the mountain to hand over to the people the new tablets containing the terms of the covenant indicates the power of God's revelation to transform one's life (34:29–35). Ten precepts (originating in the Yahwistic source) emphasizing renunciation of idolatry and the call to holiness point back to the original Decalogue as the essence of the covenant (34:10–26; cf. 20:1–17). The whole narrative illustrates that reconciliation and renewal of the covenant bring about a new and fuller manifestation of God in his faithfulness than people experienced before God forgave their sin. God reveals his glory to the people who receive his mercy in the covenant renewal.

The Tabernacle (25:1–31:18; 35:1–40:38): Glory

Deutero-Isaiah prophesies that through the return of the exiles to their Promised Land, the Lord will manifest his glory to all humanity (Is 40:3–5). This theme of the Lord's revealing his glory develops throughout Exodus to form the climax of the book. Once they depart the land of captivity and cross the Sea, the Israelites first behold the glory of the Lord in the miracle of manna and in the luminous cloud guiding them (Ex 16:4–12). The cloud that goes before them later hovers above them and covers the mountain when the people enter into covenant with the Lord (Ex 24:16–18). The Lord draws even closer when he allows Moses to experience something of his glory during their dialogue on the mountain, which reconciles God with the people after they had broken the covenant by their sin (Ex 33:18, 22). Finally, the book reaches its climax when Yahweh establishes his abode among his people by filling the sanctuary with his glory (Ex 40:34).

The Priestly writers describe the desert tabernacle in terms identifying it with Solomon's Temple, which the exiles needed to restore upon their return to Jerusalem after 538 B.C. (Ex 25:1–31:18; 35:1–40:38; cf. 1 Kgs 6:1–7:51; see Ezr 1:1–6:22). Exodus provides a promise to the exiles: the Lord will reveal his glory to the people through the ministry of the priests at the Temple (Ex 28:2, 40; 29:43–44). To find a source of inspiration for the Priestly writers' highlighting the theme of the divine glory dwelling in the Temple, we should turn to Ezekiel, the great prophet and priest who ministered exclusively to the exiles in Babylon. As a priest who carried out his mission (593–571 B.C.) well before the completion of the Pentateuch, he must have exerted a formative influence on the Priestly tradition. Ezekiel's vision of the Lord's glory departing the sanctuary at the Temple's destruction (Ez 10:18–19; 11:22–23) and returning there at its restoration (Ez 43:1–12) had a significant impact on the shape of the Exodus literature.

The Priestly editors elaborate the extensive plans for construction of the sanctuary (25:1–31:18; 35:1–40:38) to indicate the importance of providing a dwelling place for the Lord's glory (29:43; 28:2, 40). They gave this text to the Jews to open their minds to the greatness of God's call for them either to return to Judah and rebuild the Temple or to support its reconstruction with all of their means. As the people God called to renew the covenant at the end of the Exile, the Jews needed to make the reconstruction of the Temple their greatest priority. Covenant reaches a fullness when the Lord pitches his tent among his people.

The narrative of apostasy and reconciliation (32:1–34:35) separates the planning of the sanctuary (25:1–31:18) from its actual construction (35:1–40:38). The latter texts repeat the former to emphasize how the Israelites obey the commands of the Lord to their smallest details. Undoubtedly, the plan of Solomon's Temple is suggested in the description of this desert tabernacle, for example, in its distinction between the "Holy Place" and the "Holy of Holies" separated by a curtain (26:33; cf. 1 Kgs 6:15–30). Foremost among the furnishings is the ark, a wooden box containing the two stone law tablets (25:10–16). It is covered by a "mercy-seat" of pure gold, overshadowed by cherubim on each side (25:17–21). The Lord will speak to his people from above the mercy-seat (25:22). The plans climax with the description of the Sabbath (31:12–17), the seventh time the text mentions "Yahweh spoke to Moses . . ." (25:1; 30:11, 17, 22, 34; 31:1, 12). As the rainbow was the sign of the covenant for Noah and circumcision for Abraham, so the Sabbath is the sign of the covenant at Sinai (cf. Gn 9:12–13; 17:11).

The Lord's supervision of the construction is evident in his anointing craftsmen with his Spirit to accomplish the work (35:30–35; cf. 1 Kgs 7:13–14). Moses inspects the final product to insure its conformity to the word of the Lord (39:33–43). Finally, the glory of the Lord comes upon the sanctuary to complete the experience of the covenant people in whose midst the Lord is present in the same way as he was with Moses on top of the mountain (which they saw from a distance) (40:34–38; cf. 19:16–25).

Toward the New Testament: The New Covenant and the New Law

In surveying the New Testament, we will limit ourselves to considering the influence of the Exodus literature on our understanding of the Eucharist, Jesus, and the commandments in the early Church.

Jesus' death and Resurrection fulfill God's work of salvation foreshadowed by the Exodus. At the Last Supper, Jesus celebrates a Passover meal with his disciples (Mk 14:22–25; Mt 26:26–29; Lk 22:14–20; 1 Cor 11:23–26; cf. Jn 6:51–59). In the course of the meal, both when breaking the bread and blessing the third cup of wine, he redirects the symbols from the Exodus to point to his death on the cross. By doing this, he indicates that his death will be God's final work to redeem mankind from slavery and make them his own. In particular, mention of his "blood of the covenant" recalls the ceremony of ratification at Sinai (Ex 24:8). His injunction for the disciples to celebrate the Eucharist as a "memorial" is faithful to the demands of the Exodus ritual and promises that Christ, in the saving power of his cross and Resurrection, will be present to them in an unprecedented manner (cf. Ex 12:14).

Jesus uses the same eucharistic gestures to multiply the bread in the wilderness. Thus he indicates that Moses' provision of manna is but a foreshadowing of his gift of himself (Mk 8:1–10; Mt 15:32–39; Lk 9:12–17; Jn 6:1–15; cf. Ex 16:1–36). As the Word of God, Jesus is the living bread that the Father sends from heaven to fulfill what the miracle in the wilderness only promised (Jn 6:22–51).

Christ is the Passover Lamb who is sacrificed, and the new life he brings demands that we sweep away old sinful ways like the old yeast of Egypt (1 Cor 5:7–8; cf. Ex 13:6–7). In the Johannine tradition, as the "Lamb of God", Christ overcomes the sin of the world by his exaltation on the cross (Jn 1:29). He is condemned at the precise hour when the Passover lambs are being sacrificed (Jn 19:14). After his death, the fact that "not one bone of his [was] broken" indicates that he fulfilled his mission as the Passover Lamb who brings deliverance to the human race (Jn 19:36; cf. Ex 12:46). This meditation is developed in the book of Revelation, which primarily focuses on the victorious "Lamb that was sacrificed", now enthroned in glory, whom the heavenly court worships (Rv 5:6–14).

In the Gospel of John, as the divine Son, Jesus reveals himself in light of God's name pronounced to Moses from the burning bush. Three times in the same dialogue, he challenges his opponents to acknowledge his divine identity implied in the phrase "I am" (Jn 8:24, 28, 58; see also 13:19; cf. Ex 3:14). Among the prophets, Deutero-Isaiah emphasizes that the name God reveals to Moses at Sinai is his divine title (Is 45:18). At the time of Jesus, people may have associated the phrase "I am" with the Messiah (Mk 13:6). Its occurrences in the Fourth Gospel suggest a very high Christology that emphasizes Jesus' divinity.

Throughout the New Testament, the risen Jesus is acclaimed as *Kyrios* ("Lord"), the Greek term used to translate *Yahweh* or *Adonai*. In his Resurrection, Jesus offers the most complete revelation of God, and, therefore, it is only proper that he should bear the name above all others. In the essential Christian confession of "Jesus Christ as Lord", we reverence the glory of God the Father (Phil 2:9–11).

By way of comparison, the Gospel of Matthew refers to Exodus in order to identify Jesus as the new Moses. The wicked king's slaying of the children at the time of Jesus' birth recalls the circumstances of Moses' earliest days (Mt 2:1–12, 16–18; cf. Ex 2:1–10). Jesus goes up the mountain to teach his disciples the new Torah (Mt 5:1–7:29). He has come to fulfill the whole of the Law by revealing the interior aspect of God's commandments, which demand more than mere external compliance (Mt 5:17–48). Later, at the end of his ministry in Galilee, Moses and Elijah appear with him on the mountain in the midst of a cloud as he is transfigured in a manner recalling the experience of Moses on Mount Sinai (Mt 17:1–8; Mk 9:2–8; Lk 9:28–36; cf. Ex 34:29–35). The parallel text in the Gospel of Luke mentions that the three figures were discussing Jesus' "passing" (Greek: *exodus*) from earth to heaven by way of the cross (Lk 9:31). Finally, in Matthew's Gospel, Jesus reveals himself as the risen Lord on the mountain and sends his disciples forth to proclaim the Gospel with the assurance that he will be with them (Mt 28:16–20). Behind the "Immanuel" theology of this text (Is 7:14; Mt 1:23; 18:20; 28:20) may be an allusion to the divine presence of the Lord dwelling with his people. Certainly, the Prologue of John's Gospel alludes to the image of the Lord "pitching his tent" among his people, which forms the climax to Exodus (Jn 1:14; Ex 25:8; 40:34–38).

The Letter to the Hebrews illustrates the superiority of Jesus to Moses as the mediator of a new covenant. The greatness of Christ is manifest in part by his entering into the heavenly sanctuary of which the earthly one is but a shadowy prefiguration (Heb 9:1–12; cf. Ex 25:1–26:37). The covenant that Christ inaugurates surpasses the one Moses instituted because Christ's blood, not the blood of animals, has ratified it (Heb 9:13–28; cf. Ex 24:6–8). This blood accounts for the difference in character between the two covenants. It purifies the conscience of dead works and effectively intercedes for mercy. Those who come to God through the blood of Christ do not encounter the fear of Sinai reflected in storm, fire, and thunder but rather enter into the communion of saints in the heavenly Jerusalem, where God's graciousness and love receive them (Heb 12:18–29; cf. Ex 19:16–19).

Ultimately, Paul declares that Moses' experience of the luminescence of God foreshadows that of every Christian who now contemplates the glory of the Lord on the face of Christ. "And all of us, with our unveiled faces like mirrors reflecting the glory of the Lord, are being transformed into the image that we reflect in brighter and brighter glory: this is the working of the Lord who is the Spirit" (2 Cor 3:18; cf. Ex 34:29–35).

We will reflect such radiance as we grow in holiness. If we are asking the question, "How can I be changed by the glory of the Lord?", we are ready to turn to the book of Leviticus.

STUDY QUESTIONS

1. List the parallels between the Jewish exiles living in Babylon and the Israelites living in bondage in Egypt.
2. Distinguish between the two halves of the book of Exodus.
3. What are four central themes of Exodus?
4. What are the three instances of revelation in Exodus?
5. What are the various names of God in Exodus?
6. What are the six ingredients of covenant?
7. Describe the vertical and horizontal dimensions of God's commandments.
8. How does Exodus foreshadow the new covenant in the blood, the bread, and the lamb? How does Exodus deepen your appreciation of the Eucharist?
9. How is Jesus the new Moses?
10. Have you ever experienced a need to escape from something: a job, a harmful relationship, a location? How did you deal with that urge? What role did God play in your handling of the situation?
11. The Dogmatic Constitution on the Church (*Lumen Gentium*, chap. II, pars. 9–17) calls the Church, "the People of God". What does the book of Exodus teach you about the Church as a pilgrim people in the world today?
12. How does God's redemption of the enslaved Israelites indicate his preferential love for the poor and the oppressed? What does the book of Exodus teach you about the relationship between faith and justice?

EXODUS

LEVITICUS: THE CALL TO HOLINESS

We must bow down in worship when we encounter the revelation of God's glory. This explains why the prescriptions of Leviticus follow immediately after the Exodus narrative. As the last verses of Exodus describe the presence of the Lord coming upon the Tabernacle (Ex 40:34–38), so it is most fitting here that the author give instruction about the proper response God demands of his people.

Leviticus is the worship guide of the Hebrew Scriptures. Like any good manual, its style is less than exciting, but its contents are clearly arranged—here, in four sections: (1) laws governing sacrifices (1:1–7:38); (2) notes on the consecration of priests (8:1–10:20); (3) standards for distinguishing clean from unclean (11:1–16:34); and (4) the Holiness Code with an appendix on dispensation from vows (17:1–27:34).

Let us admit that a basic question in our minds is, "Why was all this material collected in the first place?" The contents of Leviticus were particularly meaningful in two different periods following the Exile. During the early years of restoration, the priests used an early edition of Leviticus in order to resolve debates about issues of sacrifice, ritual, and worship at the reconstructed Temple, which was dedicated at Passover in 515 B.C. (see Ezr 6:13-22). The final edition of Leviticus exercised an important role during the reformation under Ezra (beginning in 458 B.C.) (see Ezr 9:11, in 9:1–10:44; cf. Lv 18:24–30; Neh 8:14, in 8:1–9:5; cf. Lv 23:33–44). The priests in Exile had composed this edition from earlier traditions that they wove into a unified body of legislation.

Since the Davidic line of kings was extinguished during the Exile, the priests became the leaders of the people who returned to Judah. Jewish society revolved around the Temple. Order in the Temple precincts set the standard for order in the society. As the manual for the Temple, Leviticus exercised a determinative role on the society of Judah.

The Sacrifices (1:1–7:38)

Through the covenant, God's people can share in a communion of life with one another and with the Lord. Divisions can be healed, sin can be forgiven, and, by the grace of God, union among people and between people and God is possible. This remarkably optimistic view is the conviction of Priestly theologians that underlies their extensive concern for sacrifices throughout the first quarter of Leviticus (1:1–7:38). God ordains sacrifice to dispel evil and strengthen bonds of unity.

Ratification of the covenant did not render the people incapable of sinning. In fact, it made possible their turning from the Lord in a radical fashion that was unknown to them before coming to Sinai. While Moses was seeing the Lord's glory on the mountain, the people broke the covenant and were in need of reconciliation (Ex 24:12–18; 32:1–35). When the glory of the Lord ultimately came upon the Tabernacle in their midst (Ex 40:34–38), the people had to understand how to become free of the sin that the light of God's presence would expose even more.

God speaks to Moses solely in the Tent of Meeting at the camp and no longer on the mountain (Ex 33:7–11). The manner of his address remains the same: the Lord directs his servant to communicate these precepts as his personal word to the Israelites (1:1–2). Thus, the Priestly writers present all the legislation in Leviticus as constitutive of the Sinai covenant. By prefacing the texts with the words, "Yahweh spoke to Moses . . .", the postexilic Priestly writers asserted a divine origin for their collection of laws, which had developed over the seven hundred years between the generation of Moses and their own time.

Sacrifice is the offering of a gift to God for the sake of healing or strengthening a relationship with him or another member of the community. The book of Leviticus identifies five principal categories of sacrifices, first, in a general fashion (1:1–5:26) and, then, with details specifically pertinent to the priests (6:1–7:38).

1. The burnt offering was a complete holocaust of an animal to make atonement or to offer thanksgiving (1:3–17; 6:18–23).

2. The cereal offering was the same type of sacrifice only using grain as the oblation (2:1–16; 6:7–16).

3. Like the burnt offering, the peace offering involved the sacrifice of an animal, but with the difference that only the entrails and kidney fat ("suet") were burned up. The priests (representing God) and the one presenting the sacrifice ate the rest. Hence, this offering is known as a "communion sacrifice" to emphasize the fellowship between the Israelites and God symbolized by the meal (3:1–17; 7:11–36).

4. The sin offering did not deal with offenses against one's neighbor but rather with offenses against God and the sanctuary (4:1–5:13; 6:17–23).

5. The guilt offering was sacrificed for sins of desecration and for offenses against one's neighbor (5:14–6:6; 7:1–10).

Ritualism is the great enemy of worship and the inherent temptation when implementing liturgical precepts. Safeguards against such arid formalism are embedded within the text. For example, the guilt offering alone is not enough to produce reconciliation with the offended party. The offending party must admit his guilt and provide personal restitution along with the sacrifice (5:1–6, 5:14–6:6). The ritual by itself does not cause forgiveness but rather is the occasion in which God sovereignly communicates his mercy (4:20, 26, 31). We should keep in mind that the editors established the final form of the legislation after the great prophetic declarations condemning arid formalism (Am 5:21–22; Is 1:11–17; cf. Ps 50:7–15). The common ground that Leviticus and Ezekiel share indicates that the Priestly traditions influenced the prophets and, in turn, the prophets' announcement of God's word shaped them (for example, Ez 44:10–31; Lv 6:3–4; 21:1–24).

The Priesthood (8:1–10:20)

It is likely that an earlier version of Leviticus began immediately with the material on the function of priests (8:1–10:20). This section of the book has close affinity to the Exodus literature pertaining to the planning and erection of the sanctuary (Ex 25:1–31:18; 35:1–40:38). The consecration of priests and the sanctuary that Exodus prescribes (29:1–46; 30:22–37; 40:1–15) is actually carried out in Leviticus (8:1–36). The authors emphasize obedience to the Lord in the details of observance with the repetition of the phrase ("which Yahweh prescribed to Moses" or "had ordered Moses") that recurs throughout the description of building the sanctuary (8:9, 13, 17, 21, 29, 35; 9:7, 10, 21; cf. Ex 35–40).

The glory of the Lord that came upon the sanctuary (Ex 40:34) is present to the people as the Lord sends fire to consume the first sacrifices of the priests, thereby signifying his approval (Lv 9:23–24).

The rite of priestly ordination is an extensive ceremony taking seven days, presumably the time needed to pass from a common state to a holy state (8:1–35; cf. 13:29–37; 14:8). On the eighth day, Aaron and his sons begin carrying out their priestly functions of offering sacrifice on behalf of the community (9:1–24). The dramatic story of fire from the Lord consuming Aaron's two sons illustrates the power of the divine glory and the importance of exact compliance with his precepts (10:1–3). Their names, Nadab and

Abihu, and the reason for their deaths relate this event to the fates of Nadab and Abijah, the sons of Jeroboam I, who died because of either personal sins (Nadab) or those of his father (Abijah) (1 Kgs 14:1–18; 15:25–30). We can recall that the author related worship of the golden calf permitted by Aaron to Jeroboam's placement of golden bulls in the northern sanctuaries after his separation of the northern tribes from the south (1 Kgs 12:28–33). Within its context, the narrative of the death of Aaron's sons (Lv 10:1–3) serves the same purpose as the story of the golden calf (Ex 32:1–35). Both episodes occur after the Lord has given precise instructions about how to serve him, and they illustrate the Lord's power in judgment for not obeying his commands in detail.

In view of their office, the priests have a higher standard of conduct than the general public. They are not to mourn like others (10:6; cf. Ez 24:15–27). Under no circumstances can they withdraw from the sanctuary once they have begun their service (10:7). And they must renounce intoxicating drink, which would affect their judgment (10:8–9). As well as offering sacrifice, their primary duty is to teach the Law of the Lord to the people (10:10–11). In the final edition of Leviticus, the author intended the whole section on Aaron and his sons (8:1–10:20) to prevent the abuse of clerical privilege during the period of restoration after the Exile when the priesthood exercised increasing authority over the people.

The Call to Holiness (11:1–27:34)

Leviticus 11–16 presents the standards of ritual purity. Leviticus 17–27 (the Holiness Code) provides the legislation governing ethical conduct. Binding these two units together is the overall theme of Leviticus summarized by the Lord's admonition, "[B]e holy because I am holy" (11:45; 19:2; 20:26).

The Hebrew root for the word holiness (*qdsh: qadosh* or *qodesh*) implies a sense of otherness, distinctiveness, and separation from the ordinary that is characteristic of the transcendent God. Association and communion with God in the covenant make God's people holy. They are the people whom he chose and set apart from the world, and he calls them to live in a manner that reflects the glory of the Lord who is in their midst.

Nevertheless, holiness is not other-worldliness. In fact, it is a whole manner of being within the setting of God's creation. The Priestly theologians who present the vision of God's creative work (Gn 1:1–2:3) were inspired to perceive a divine order in all living beings. Each creature belongs to a proper category, and all things are in harmony insofar as they correspond to God's design.

In the Priestly theology, we evaluate everything about life in light of the Lord's presence in the Temple. The Priestly vocabulary provides important distinctions. "Clean" or "pure" creatures correspond to the Lord's order, while some defect distinguishes "unclean" or "impure" beings. Not only people but also creatures and inanimate objects can be clean or unclean. The people are to use and associate with all that is "clean". Contact with whatever is impure will render an individual "unclean" and therefore unable to enter the Temple (11:1–15:33). On the other hand, a person who is unclean is "cleansed" in order to return to a condition of purity (14:1–15:33). Clean things are "consecrated" or "sanctified" in order to become holy (16:18–19), while holy things that are "defiled" or "profaned" return to a state of being common (11:44).

Holiness implies wholeness, a condition of being genuine and complete. In a primary sense, God alone is holy, and so is his name as the revelation of his person (20:3; 22:2, 32). He alone can sanctify or make his people holy, and he has done this by redeeming them from Egypt and associating himself with them in the covenant. In response to God's initiative, the people must sanctify themselves by observing his commandments (22:31–33; cf. 20:8; 21:8). In other words, the people cannot make themselves holy but receive holiness as a grace and incorporate it into their character through obedience to the commandments.

As the source of life, God wills that his people be whole. The text is saturated by a concern for the well-being of people. For example, as one whom God particularly calls to holiness, the priest is required to be the most complete person (21:17–21). For the common person, means exist to obtain holiness once uncleanliness has happened. For example, people with contagious skin diseases were unclean and had to be set apart from the camp (13:1–59). After they were healed, they were readmitted to the community, and sacrifice was offered to mark their purification and restoration to God and his people (14:1–57). Matters of sexuality and childbirth receive particular attention because they are totally concerned with one's relationship to God as the author of life (12:1–8; 15:1–33).

Once a year, the people were to celebrate the Day of Atonement (*Yom Kippur*) to cleanse the sanctuary of all defilement and to free the people from their sins (16:1–34). Since there is no mention of this feast in preexilic literature, it is likely that only after the Exile was the Day of Atonement actually celebrated each year. First, a bull was sacrificed for the sins of the priest and then a goat for the sins of the people. At the beginning of the liturgy, the priest entered the Holy of Holies, took incense, put it on coals in front of the ark, and caused a cloud to overshadow the mercy-seat protecting him from the immediacy of the Lord's presence. Then he performed the identical ritual, first with the blood of the bull and then with the blood of the goat. He took the blood (symbolizing life sacrificed for sin) and sprinkled it seven times on the mercy-seat to purge the sanctuary of defilement due to the state of the people. Next, in a similar fashion, he went out to the Holy Place and purified the altar (16:3–19). Furthermore, the sins of the people were confessed over a second goat, which was led away from the camp into the wilderness region, considered the habitation of the demonic powers of Azazel (16:8–10, 20–22).

Our relationship to God is only one dimension of holiness. We must also manifest holiness in righteous action toward the whole community. The book of Leviticus insists on the obligation to love one's neighbor as oneself (19:18). The motive for the extensive legislation governing family life and sexuality is the need to act with justice toward every person (18:1–30). In addition, the author strongly emphasizes care for the poor. At harvest time, the landowners are obligated to leave something in the fields that the underprivileged can glean (19:9–10; 23:22). The Israelites must love the resident alien as themselves since they shared the same status through their history in Egypt (19:33–34).

Most of the legislation pertains to the social situation after settlement in the land. The Israelites are admonished to reject the practices of the Canaanites who previously occupied the territory and of the peoples in the surrounding countries (18:21, 24–30; 20:2–5; cf. 2 Kgs 16:3; 21:6). Because the land of the Israelites belongs to the Lord, the people must treat it as a gift. Even the soil must observe the Lord's Sabbath rest (25:1–7). Since the land was distributed among the people as an inheritance from God, the people cannot sell it absolutely even among the Israelites. The jubilee year is established to guarantee the continual just distribution of property in Israel. In every fiftieth year, real estate that had been transferred as debt payment has to be returned to its ancestral proprietor (25:8–34).

Leviticus contemplates the gift of settled life in the land surrounding the Temple from the perspective of the wilderness journey. Even when they are in the land belonging to the Lord, God admonishes the Israelites to understand themselves as "strangers and guests", the recipients of God's gracious hospitality (25:23). They are able to stay as long as they observe the Lord's commandments (26:3–5).

The authors address the book's conclusion (26:1–46) particularly to the people who resettled in Jerusalem after 538 B.C. It reflects on the experience of the Exile and interprets it in light of the wilderness journey that Moses led. The authors interpret the destruction of Jerusalem and the dispersion of God's people into exile in Babylon and elsewhere as an action, not of Nebuchadnezzar's armies, but of the Lord himself (26:1–33). They single out for special mention the Israelites' neglect of the laws governing the Sabbath year for the land. The inspired authors perceived that the fifty years of exile (587–538 B.C.) were the Lord's provision to allow the Promised Land a period for observing the

Sabbath rest (26:34–35, 43). The time of exile represents another wilderness journey and is a period of gracious discipline, when the hearts of the people will be humble and they will confess their sin (26:40–43). Another Exodus will accomplish their return to the land in that the Lord will bring his people out from the land of their oppressors in remembrance of his covenant (26:44–45).

Ultimately, God wants to give his people dignity and union with himself. He promises that they will be free to "walk erect" and "walk with" him in his land. At every point in the people's history, God's promise is sealed in the covenant and governs all his interaction with his people. "I shall fix my home among you and never reject you. I shall live among you; I shall be your God and you will be my people, I, Yahweh your God, who brought you out of Egypt so that you should be their slaves no longer, and who broke the bonds of your yoke and made you walk with head held high" (26:11–13).

Toward the New Testament: Christ's Atoning Sacrifice

The legislation in Leviticus is reflected in the background of Jesus' life and ministry. In his earliest days, his parents offer the sacrifice of the poor to accomplish the rites of his mother's purification (Lk 2:22, 24; cf. Lv 12:8). At the beginning of his ministry, Jesus astonishes people by his association with the marginalized, notably lepers. Accepting the charge of becoming "unclean" himself, Jesus reaches out to touch the diseased man who had asked Jesus to cleanse him. Then he admonishes the man to fulfill the requirements of Leviticus by showing himself to the priests (Mk 1:40–45; Mt 8:1–4; Lk 5:12–16; cf. Lv 13–14). The new Law that Jesus proclaims is distinguished by his relating the proclamation of the great *Shema'* (to love God) directly to the admonition to love one's neighbor that we find in Leviticus. In the Gospel of Matthew, after proclaiming the command to love God, he declares that the second "resembles it", namely, to love your neighbor as yourself (Mt 22:34–40; cf. Dt 6:4–5; Lv 19:18).

The Letter to the Hebrews uses the role of a sacrificial victim's blood in Leviticus to interpret the significance of Christ's death (Heb 9:11–14). Leviticus demonstrates that blood is necessary for purification from sin (Lv 8:15, 23–24, 30; 9:18; 16:14–16, 18–19). The image of the high priest entering the Holy of Holies each year on the Day of Atonement provides the background for the Letter to the Hebrews' explanation of the supremacy of Christ's sacrifice on two accounts. First, by his sacrifice, Jesus enters once and for all into the perfect tent, the presence of God in heaven, which the earthly sanctuary only foreshadowed (Heb 9:6–12). Secondly, the blood of Jesus, the spotless victim, is eternally effective in cleansing our conscience from dead works and freeing us from sin (Heb 9:13–14, 25–28; cf. Lv 16:2–29).

In the Letter to the Romans, Paul says that God presents Christ as a sacrifice for reconciliation through his blood (Rom 3:25). The language comes from the rites the priests performed in the Holy of Holies on the Day of Atonement (Lv 16:2–29). It seems that here he identifies Christ in his sacrificial death with the mercy-seat covering the ark in the Holy of Holies. God manifests his glory immediately above it. The mercy-seat itself was the object that the High Priest anointed with blood in the rite of purification (Lv 16:15). In this interpretation, not only does the blood of Christ cleanse us from all sin, but he himself in the power of the cross is the full revelation of God's mercy and glory, which the Holy of Holies had only foreshadowed.

Reflecting the theme of Leviticus, Jesus teaches his disciples, "You must therefore set no bounds to your love, just as your heavenly Father sets none to his" (Mt 5:48; cf. Lv 11:44–45; 19:2). However, to attain this goal, he commands his disciples to go beyond the limitations of the former law by loving not just their neighbors but also their enemies (Mt 5:43–48; cf. Lv 19:18). The Christian churches took up the call to holiness. The First Letter of Peter quotes the same text in Leviticus and indicates that the source of holiness is the blood Christ shed. In response to this ransom of Christians from the world, they must put off their former ways of life (1 Pt 1:13–21). Moreover, the Letter describes our walk of faith in time and space as a period of exile in which we must have the identity of an exile who does not expect comfort in the present age (1 Pt 1:17; 1:1; cf. Lv 25:23).

Remaining in our place offers us the stability of learning about holiness. However, the trials of life in the world must test us. We have been encamped with the Israelites at Sinai for almost three months. The book of Numbers will give us marching orders so that we can experience the tests to determine whether our holiness can withstand the rigors of a hostile environment.

STUDY QUESTIONS

1. What is the purpose of the book of Leviticus?
2. What are its four sections?
3. What was the purpose of offering sacrifices?
4. What were the five categories of sacrifice?
5. What is the meaning of holiness in Leviticus?
6. How is Christ's sacrifice supreme?
7. What is the liturgical meaning of sacrifice? What sacrifices to God have you offered in your life other than giving charitable contributions?
8. Why is the shedding of blood significant as part of the offering of sacrifice? How do we see this most importantly in the Eucharist?
9. How does the book of Leviticus deepen your understanding of holiness?
10. In what manner have you experienced the grace of holiness in each of the sacraments you have received?
11. Do you have a daily pattern of prayer, reading Scripture, and worship? What effect do your devotional exercises have on your manner of living each day?
12. Holiness is one of the four marks (one, holy, catholic, and apostolic) of the Church. From your perspective, which people and ministries reflect the holiness of the Church most clearly to the world?

LEVITICUS

II

NUMBERS: JOURNEY THROUGH THE WILDERNESS

The authors of the book of Numbers designed it to give young people a vision for their lives. The book calls them to risk, to step beyond the confines of the ways their elders had gone about living. Numbers tells young people they can and must forge a future about which people of former times had only dreamed. It challenges them to be a generation that will bring about a whole new way of life and set the standard for God's people in future centuries.

The scribes who edited the text in the exilic and postexilic period were devout scholars in their mature years. Those who wrote during the Exile either had been born in Babylon or had been deported from Jerusalem at a young age. In either case, during their time in Babylon, they witnessed the death of a complete generation of their elders. Now, the parallels between the fifty years of exile (587–538 B.C.) and the forty years of Exodus wandering (1280–1240 B.C.) started to strike home. For the faithful, exile in Babylon was their wilderness experience. We recall that Moses and the generation who had left Egypt did not enter the Promised Land. Joshua and his peers who succeeded them did. So, too, the next generation of exiles in Babylon would be those who entered the Promised Land. They were to be the new Joshua and his brothers and sisters for their own time.

As they shaped the book of Numbers, the exilic scribes knew they had to reach the young Jews who were coming to maturity in Babylon. They were concerned to highlight the passing of the former generation, which had been weak in faith (Nm 1–25), and the emergence of a new generation, which would be stronger insofar as it refused to imitate the unbelief of its parents (26–36). Two census lists, one at the beginning (1:5–47) and one beyond the halfway point in the book (26:1–65), offer a key to appreciating the book's message. The first list identifies the older generation, who left Egypt but did not sustain their faith in the wilderness. The second list marks a new beginning with the next generation, who are stationed in Moab, poised to enter the Promised Land.

If the Israelites spent just under a year at Sinai (10:11), then Numbers covers practically the whole span of the forty-year wilderness period. At

Mount Sinai, the Lord instructs his people in the ways of holiness. Through-out the book of Leviticus, the Israelites stay in the same place and attend the school of the covenant to be formed in godliness. The book of Numbers presents the final lessons in their education at Sinai before narrating their journey through the wilderness as a venture of integrating into real life the wisdom they had received. The distinction between the holy and the profane now works itself out in life or death for the Israelites. Theirs is a journey through the harsh realities of the world, and only union with God in holiness of life guarantees safe passage.

In order to adapt ourselves to the sense of movement that contrasts Numbers with Leviticus, we can best survey the text according to the geo-graphical setting of the Israelites:

1. the final days of the Israelite encampment at Sinai (1:1–10:10);
2. long years of journeying throughout the wilderness around Kadesh-Barnea (10:11–20:13); and
3. the journey east of the Dead Sea and north around Edom to Moab (20:14–36:13).

Encampment at Sinai: Organizing the People (1:1–10:10)

As the period of training at Sinai draws to a close, God marshals his people into formation and gives them their marching orders. The opening census list demonstrates that the Lord has been faithful to his ancient promises by redeeming them and entering into covenant with them. Although the Israelites went into Egypt as a mere seventy people, God brings them out as a great multitude and preserves their numbers during their time in the wilderness (Nm 1:1–47; cf. Ex 1:1–6; Gn 46:8–27). While the figure approximating 600,000 seems to come from a later period after the settlement, theologically it serves as testimony to the Lord's fidelity in keeping his promise to give Abraham innumerable descendants (Nm 1:46; 26:51; Ex 12:37; cf. Gn 15:5; 17:4–8).

The people are carefully organized for their journey as a holy regiment in successive rows around the Tent of Meeting, with the Levites stationed nearest the Tent and the twelve tribes posted farther away in strict compliance with the Lord's instructions (2:1–34). The overriding motive for so structuring the community is to allow the Lord to dwell in their midst while at the same time protecting them from the overwhelming power of his holiness (1:53).

The assembly will depart Sinai as a holy people, for the Lord's blessing communicated to them by Aaron and the priests empowers and sets them apart (6:22–27). The pillar of cloud overshadowing the Tent signals the Lord's presence among them to guide and protect them (9:15–23). Far from becoming a memory left behind at the place of the covenant, the people's experience of the Lord at Sinai is only the beginning of communion with him, which now has to be the governing principle of their lives at every step in the journey. Just as the pillar of cloud provided for their deliverance from the Egyptians through the Sea (Ex 13:21–22; 14:19–20; 40:34–38), so it now signals the beginning of a new era as the Israelites move from Sinai to the Promised Land. Zeal, anticipation, and obedience to the word of the Lord characterize the people on the point of breaking camp (9:17–23). Under the authority of the priests, the trumpets sound and the people move out in triumphant procession (10:1–12).

This portrait of community would have made a strong impression on the people who settled around Jerusalem after the postexilic rededication of the Temple in 515 B.C. From that time onward, the priests took the role of leadership and the Levites assumed a prominent position. After the Exile, Jewish society was structured in a hierarchical fashion of priests—Levites—people. The Lord's presence and word, which all the priestly classes mediated, emanated from the Temple. It is the ideal community that heads for the Promised Land (cf. Neh 11:1–12:26).

The Wilderness Years: Breaking Faith (10:11–20:13)

The community that leaves Sinai gives every indication of being a loyal, well-trained, disciplined troop ready to make a straight path to its destination. Yet how quickly they change! The narrative of their movement (10:11–20:13) describes how the direct march degenerates into a listless wandering as the trained squadron becomes an unruly rabble (11:4). The people challenge the whole authority structure that God established. A volatile mixture of insecurity, personal ambition, and nostalgia for the old days fuels rebellion at all levels of the community (see 11:1–6, 18–22; 12:1–2; 14:1–4, 10; 16:1–3; 17:6; 20:2–5).

Precisely when the Lord has the people on the quick route to the Promised Land, they protest and voice their desire to return to Egypt. Indeed, the closer they get to the Promised Land, the more vehement becomes their demand to return to Egypt (11:5; 14:3). Seemingly, their experience of glory at Sinai, the covenant with the Lord, and his abiding presence in their midst have not made any significant difference. They complain now just as they had before they ever came to know the Lord and receive his love. As on the journey from the Sea to Sinai, they demand the food they had had in slavery (11:4–6; cf. Ex 16:1–3). In reaction, Moses regresses almost to the state he was

in when the Lord first called him, and he complains about the burden of
leadership that God has laid upon him (11:10–15; cf. Ex 3:11; 4:1; 5:22).

The Lord responds to both parties with the abundant provision of his
spirit or wind (both are implied in the one Hebrew word *ruah*). He pours out
a prophetic spirit on seventy elders at the Tent and two in the camp, a work of
such profusion as to suggest to Moses the possibility of all the people becoming prophets (11:24–30). Next, God blows his wind to send quails in an
abundance surpassing anything the people had ever witnessed. The way he
answers their prayer is a lesson in irony. They want an experience of Egypt,
and that is what he gives them: an oversupply of food, which a plague
accompanies to remind them of another aspect of their life in the land of
slavery that they seem to have forgotten (11:31–35).

Rebellion spreads to the higher ranks as prophetess and priest, Miriam
and Aaron respectively, attempt to usurp the primacy of Moses in proclaiming
God's word. God vindicates Moses' authority when it is evident that only his
prayer can heal Miriam of the leprosy (due to her ambition) that excludes her
from the community (12:1–16).

Numbers indicates that the Lord's intention was to have the people enter
the Promised Land from the south almost immediately after the covenant at
Sinai. Unbelief in the hearts of his people, however, frustrates this plan and
necessitates the long, difficult years of the wilderness sojourn. The rebellion of
Israel against the Lord reaches its climax in the narrative of the spies surveying
the land and the people's reaction to their report (13:1–14:45).

The leaders of the twelve tribes who carry out the spy mission confirm
the promise of the Lord that it is indeed a land "flow[ing] with milk and
honey" (13:27). However, they become preoccupied with the strength of the
present inhabitants of the land—as if the Lord had not also made note of them
in his original promise to Moses (13:28–29, 31–33; 14:1–4; cf. Ex 3:7–9;
23:20–33; 33:1–2). Fear causes their imagination to misrepresent reality. When
they think of Egypt, the Israelites contemplate only the rich produce without
recalling their slavery. Now, as they picture the Promised Land, they consider
only the imagined strength of their foes and neglect the actual evidence of the
land's fruitfulness provided by the enormous clusters of grapes (13:21–14:4). In
other words, when recalling their old life of slavery, they highlight the
benefits and deny the agony, but when considering the new life of God's
promise, they highlight the struggle and deny the benefits. The Israelites'
demand to return to Egypt reaches a crescendo precisely as they are standing
on the frontiers of the Promised Land.

The whole scene repeats in a new way their breaking of the covenant at
Sinai (Ex 32:1–6). They demand a leader who will take them back to Egypt
(14:4; cf. Ex 14:11–12; 16:3; 32:1). Moses must plead with the Lord not to

destroy them but to reveal himself once again as one who is full of mercy and ready to forgive (14:10–19; cf. Ex 33:14–34:9). In the end, the Lord does forgive the sin of his people but determines that the present generation must pass away in the wilderness and the new generation will be the ones to experience the fulfillment of his promise (14:20–35).

At this point, we must ask, "What does it mean to be a community of faith?" Just as God had told Abraham to go into the foreign land of Canaan (Gn 12:1–5), so now he was asking the whole people to do the same in fulfillment of his promise to the Patriarch. Although Abraham believed, his descendants refuse to trust the Lord. Their sin is magnified because their refusal occurs after they have already entered into covenant with God and witnessed his wonders ever since leaving Egypt (14:11). Nevertheless, just when the apostasy of the older generation is most evident, signs of faith and leadership become prominent among their children. Joshua and Caleb take the role of Moses and Aaron and present the Lord's promises to his people, encouraging them to overcome all fear through the commitment of faith (14:6–9). Already the Lord is training the new generation by raising those who will lead them into the Promised Land through faith in his promises (13:30; 14:38).

The defeat of the guilt-ridden Israelites who attempt an invasion on their own shows the old generation beginning to pass away because of disobedience to God's word (14:39–45). Nevertheless, rebellion continues to move up the ranks as the Levites attempt to usurp the authority proper to Aaron and the priests, and the Reubenites rise up against Moses (16:1–35). Their mental perversity is evident in their acclamation of Egypt as the "country flowing with milk and honey" and their cynicism toward the land of Israel's inheritance (16:13–14). Because they refuse to acknowledge the difference between the land of slavery and the land of promise, it is only fitting that the earth itself should devour them in death (16:31–34). But the people become angry again. Moses and Aaron act to forestall Yahweh's anger. Aaron's rite of expiation halts a plague (17:11–15). The sprouting of his staff in the Tent of Meeting vindicates Aaron's authority over the priests and Levites (17:16–26).

The Israelites express their pessimism in the constant chorus of complaint that more and more sounds like a communal death wish (17:27–28; 20:2–5; cf. 17:6). The people repeat a complaint from their early precovenant days in their demand for water (20:1–11; cf. Ex 17:1–7). This is the setting in which rebellion reaches even to the pinnacle of the Israelite community. Now Moses proves to be lacking in faith and therefore unfit to enter the Promised Land (20:12–13). His rebellion is subtle but substantial since it consists in not adhering to God's word. To bring forth water, the Lord orders Moses to speak to the rock while holding Aaron's staff in his hand (20:8). Instead, Moses does something that seems more practical—he strikes the rock with the staff two times (20:11). It is a subtle indication of his lack of trust that the word of God could produce its effects by its own power. With this gesture, unbelief penetrates the whole community, and it is time to leave Kadesh-Barnea and find the way for the next generation actually to enter the Promised Land.

The postexilic scribes probably had a strong conviction about how the message in this section of Numbers applied to their audience. Jerusalem and Judah around 500 B.C. were spartan environs compared to the luxury of Babylon where the people had been in exile. The cry of Moses' people to return to Egypt almost certainly echoed the longing for Babylon of some exiles who had returned to their native soil. It is also likely that the rebellion of the people against the leadership of the priests was as strong a temptation after the Exile as it had been during the Exodus.

From Kadesh-Barnea to Moab: The New Generation (20:14–36:13)

The journey from Kadesh-Barnea to Moab represents the transitional phase in which the old order gives way to the new, triumph replaces tragedy, and prophecy replaces pessimism. The theme is introduced when Aaron dies and his son Eleazar succeeds him to the priesthood (20:22–29).

Immediately, victory overshadows defeat as Israel reverses its fortunes in the Negeb by conquering the Canaanite city of Hormah (21:1–3; cf. 14:39–45). Two more great triumphs quickly ensue as the Israelites move up the eastern side of the Dead Sea and defeat, in succession, Sihon, king of the Amorites, and Og, king of Bashan (21:21–35). Because they involve seizing territory, these events in the Transjordan offer the people a prophetic foretaste of what taking possession of the Promised Land will be like.

As they camp on the plains of Moab, the Israelites experience a great renewal. All the world knows it and begins to fear. Balak, the king of Moab, resembles Pharaoh of the former generation in the way the prospect of new life for the Israelites in his territory threatens him. He sends a delegation to Mesopotamia to commission Balaam, the visionary of international repute, to curse the Israelites. However, Balaam knows the Lord and therefore is a man of truth unable to suppress God's prophetic word (22:1–21). The fact that he, rather than Moses, releases the power of God's word to shape the future indicates that all people on the earth must acknowledge the significance of what is happening to the Israelites.

Balaam does not understand everything at once. His experience with his donkey on the way to Moab is God's lesson to prepare him for his encounter with Balak. Three times the donkey sees the angel of the Lord on the road and stops in spite of Balaam's beating him. Only after the third episode does the Lord open Balaam's eyes to appreciate that the donkey was saving his life by obeying God rather than his human master (22:22–35). This foreshadows the three times Balaam must proclaim the Lord's word in spite of the abuse Balak heaps on him.

Just as in the experience with the donkey, so there is heightening of intensity from one prophecy to the next. The first contrasts Balak's desire to curse with God's ancient determination to bless Israel, reflecting back on his promise to Abraham (23:7–10; cf. Gn 12:1–3; 13:16; 15:5). The second emphasizes the decisiveness of God's will and asserts the emerging strength of Israel in spite of its present appearance (23:18–24). Finally, the prophet's eyes are fully open for the third oracle, in which he speaks of a messianic leader to arise out of God's people and establish a great kingdom (24:3–9, 14–19). Balaam's oracle looks to the kingship of David, but his words open the future to the hope of a messiah who will fully establish God's reign on the earth.

Up to this point, we must admit that Israel has not clearly realized its renewal. Some negative carryovers from the past spot the picture. Shortly after leaving Kadesh-Barnea, we hear the familiar voice of complaint about wanting to return to Egypt, which then results in the plague of serpents (21:4–9). Only one final rebellion remains: the apostasy of the Israelites in Moab (25:1–18). Their worship of foreign gods and defilement with pagans give this event a tone similar to that of the episode with the golden calf (Ex 32:1–35). However, this time, the younger generation of priests typified by Phinehas, the grandson of Aaron, disciplines the Israelites. The worship of the Baal of Peor is the final action that brings about the end of the older generation.

The new census marks the beginning of a new age and describes a young, vibrant, and purified community ready to enter into the new life promised by the Lord (26:1–65). Moses, through the laying on of hands, appoints Joshua as its leader (27:12–23). The assembly is given a short course in covenant life that summarizes the instruction at Sinai (28:1–30:17). The renewed people of God manifest their authority in the world through their conquest of Midian to wipe out the sacrilege of the last rebellion (31:1–54).

Now Israel can look forward to settlement in the Promised Land. The occupation already begins with the settlement of the tribes of Reuben, Gad, and half of Manasseh in the Transjordan (32:1–42). The journey in the wilderness is now a memory for the people to recount (33:1–49). The Israelites must look westward to their future across the Jordan in the land of Canaan, whose boundaries God clearly defines for them (34:1–35:34). It is God's will that everyone have a proper inheritance in the land. Concern for the exceptional case of daughters' inheritances, which frames the whole section on the new era for the Israelites, highlights this fact (36:1–13; cf. 27:1–11).

Toward the New Testament: Signs of New Life

Remarkable symbols, which the New Testament uses to describe the event of Christ and the Spirit, have emerged from the book of Numbers. The trumpets the priests blow to begin the sacred procession from Sinai to the Promised Land are heard in the New Testament announcing the victorious passage from death to life in the Resurrection (1 Cor 15:52–53; 1 Thes 4:16–17; cf. Nm 10:1–8). Jesus himself fulfills Balaam's prophecy of the Messiah symbolized in the rising star. He is the ruler who arises out of Israel to establish his kingdom throughout the world (Mt 2:2; Rv 2:28; 22:16; cf. Nm 24:7, 17).

Both the Pauline and Johannine traditions identify Christ as the rock that pours forth abundant waters in the wilderness (Nm 20:7–11). Paul is convinced that Christ is the rock already present to the people in the wilderness. He locates the event, however, within the broader context of its original setting because he wants his people to take seriously the more general lesson in the book of Numbers: that God is always giving the new life of freedom to his people, while they long for the old life of slavery. Although God's people "drink" from Christ as their spiritual source, they still turn from him in complaint and debauchery. Every Christian must learn from his or her folly and not slip into a complacency that excuses moral laxity (1 Cor 10:1–13; cf. Nm 20:1–11; 11:4–23, 31–35; 17:6–15; 21:5–6; 25:1–9). The Gospel of John employs the image of the rock pouring forth water to present the life-giving character of Jesus' cross. This symbol forms the background for Jesus' words about his communication of the Holy Spirit in his prophecy that "From his heart shall flow streams of living water" (Jn 7:38–39). This outpouring is actually fulfilled in the event of his death (Jn 19:35).

The event in Numbers of Moses' healing the people by holding a bronze serpent above them (Nm 21:6–9) is the reference the Gospel of John introduces to emphasize the cross as the source of life. The serpent is not a symbol of Jesus, but the manner of its being "lifted up" prefigures the death of Jesus as being an event of exaltation to the Father. The effectiveness of Jesus' death is also foreshadowed in the Old Testament text: just as the people "looked at" the object and "lived", so those who "believe" in Jesus will have "eternal life" (Jn 3:14–15). In the Gospel of John, believing is a new form of seeing (Jn 20:28; cf. 20:29).

The Lord's plan for his people in the Exodus can be fulfilled in the Church through the outpouring of the Holy Spirit. Moses' desire for the whole people to receive the gift of prophecy turns out to be a prophetic vision that is realized in the Christian community at Pentecost (Acts 2:1–36; cf. Nm 11:24–30 and Jl 3:1–2). Paul is convinced that the Church will be fully edified when each of the people prays for prophecy above the other gifts (1 Cor 14:1–5). The Church is the new people of God, whom he calls to live in obedience to his word and to proclaim it to the world.

If we desire to hear deeply God's word, we are ready to turn to the book of Deuteronomy, the Old Testament's great homiletic book.

STUDY QUESTIONS

1. How is the idea of community important in Numbers?
2. What misperceptions did the people have about Israel and the Promised Land?
3. Of what does Moses' rebellion consist?
4. What was Balaam's role, and how did he fulfill it?
5. What is the significance of the new census in Numbers?
6. What are the symbols from Numbers that the New Testament uses?
7. How does Jesus compare to the rock pouring forth water? To the bronze serpent?
8. What is the significance of prophecy in Numbers and the New Testament?
9. How is God calling you to build community within your family? at your job? in your church? What practical steps will you take this week to heal and strengthen relationships?
10. From your own experience or in light of the witness of others, how have you seen faith in God overcoming fear?
11. Do you pray every day for your pastor and other leaders of the Church? Among family, friends, and associates at work? Whom is God calling you to support in faith?
12. What can the book of Numbers teach us about how to give young people a sense of God's vision for their lives?

NUMBERS

12

DEUTERONOMY:
COVENANT AND THE LOVE OF GOD

Imagine you are in Jerusalem during the early months of 622 B.C. The city is astir with new religious vigor and the people exhibit a new-found confidence. Remarkable young people have risen to leadership and are opening up new horizons. King Josiah, although only thirty years of age, has reigned officially for the last eighteen. In the past decade, he has shown himself to be a veritable new David in all he has undertaken (2 Chr 34:2–3). Just as Josiah was reaching his early twenties, the Assyrian overlords turned on one another and, because of their internal disputes, they withdrew the pressure they had exerted over Judah for the previous hundred years.

At that time Zephaniah, the first great prophet to be heard in Jerusalem for over fifty years, called for an end to all the idolatry left over from Manasseh's reign (687–642 B.C.) (Zep 1:1–2:3; 3:1–5). Josiah heeded his admonition and initiated a program of spiritual renewal around 629 B.C. He received support from Jeremiah, the remarkable young prophet (then only in his early twenties) who showed promise to be Zephaniah's successor as the Lord's spokesman in Jerusalem. Foremost among Josiah's priorities has been the renovation of the Temple that Manasseh's sponsorship of paganism had abused.

Something remarkable has just happened. King Josiah, at the urging of the prophetess Huldah, has decreed that all the people must renew their covenant with the Lord, and he demands that everyone celebrate the Passover only in Jerusalem this year (2 Kgs 22:11–23:3; 23:21–23). It seems that in 622 B.C., in the course of cleaning out a storeroom in the Temple, the high priest Hilkiah found a text of the Law that has induced King Josiah to call everyone to a deeper form of repentance. From this point forward, this text will serve as the basis for his reform of the land. What kind of document could provoke the king to speak with such urgency, indicating that everyone must now go far beyond the kind of reform he had had in mind earlier? (2 Kgs 22:1–23:30; 2 Chr 34:1–35:27.)

Josiah's reaction indicates the powerful impact for renewal that the book of Deuteronomy communicated. Josiah correctly understood the nature of the document. Deuteronomy is a program for the renewal of the covenant, complete with all the necessary rites, including the reading of the ordinances, the call for the people's response, the inscribing of the Law, the declaration of blessings and curses, and the solemn depositing of the Law alongside the ark of the covenant (4:44–26:19; 27:1–28:46; 31:9–13, 24–27).

Certainly, as it stands within the Pentateuch, Deuteronomy is concerned with the people's renewal of the covenant under Moses' leadership on the plains of Moab before they enter the Promised Land. They glance backward in order to cut themselves off from their previous faithlessness (11:1–7), and they look forward to renewing again the covenant at Gerizim and Ebal following their entrance into the land under Joshua (11:26–32; 27:4–8, 11–13; cf. Jos 8:30–35).

Nevertheless, Deuteronomy defies any attempt to pin it down to one historical setting. By the text's very design, Moses speaks to the present moment. In the course of his addresses, he uses the word "today" over fifty times (compared to some six occurrences elsewhere in the Pentateuch) and often reinforces it with an emphasis on the "now" that defines the moment of decision in everyone's life. He speaks directly to the current generation when he says, "Yahweh made this covenant not with our ancestors, but with us, with all of us alive here today" (5:3). Anyone reading this text stands among the Israelites as they renew their commitment and hear Moses say, "Today you have become a people for Yahweh your God" (27:9).

Now we begin to appreciate why Deuteronomy provoked Josiah to reform the people with such urgency. Unlike the first four books of the Pentateuch, Deuteronomy takes the form of direct speeches by Moses, who addresses the people in the "I–You" language of person-to-person discourse. It is existential; it puts us on the spot by challenging us to enter into covenant with the Lord now.

Deuteronomy is the last will and testament of Moses. His speeches in the first four sections follow the outline of a covenant renewal program, beginning with (1) a historical prologue recounting God's faithfulness to the Israelites throughout their wilderness journey (1:1–4:43), followed by (2) a presentation of the general laws of the covenant (4:44–11:32) and (3) the specific precepts deriving from the laws (12:1–26:19), concluding the speeches with (4) the rites of covenant renewal at Moab (27:1–30:20). The final section of the book (5) brings to a conclusion the Pentateuch as a whole by communicating Moses' last words and account of his death (31:1–34:12).

The Formation of Deuteronomy

Deuteronomy is able to speak to all ages because it grew out of a tradition of preaching whose mission was to renew God's people at various critical junctures during the course of over two hundred years in Israel's history. The "Deuteronomists" were anointed prophets, priests, and spiritual leaders who developed a distinctive theology that was sensitive to both legal and prophetic traditions in ancient Israel. We can identify five stages in the development of the Deuteronomic tradition:

1. In the northern kingdom of Israel sometime prior to 750 B.C., perhaps during the reign of Jeroboam II (783–743 B.C.), a circle of prophets (who interacted with Hosea) created a distinctive collection of the traditions deriving from Moses and Joshua;

2. After Assyria took over the northern kingdom and seized its capital Samaria in 721 B.C., the Deuteronomists of the time fled southward for refuge to Jerusalem and brought their text with them. They edited their text during the reign of Hezekiah (716–687 B.C.) and made it the basis for the history they wrote to explain the destruction of the northern kingdom. In Jerusalem during those days, the Deuteronomists would have encountered Isaiah and Micah, and together they concentrated their efforts on supporting the king's religious reforms (2 Kgs 18:1–20:21);

3. During the long reign of the apostate King Manasseh (687–642 B.C.) (2 Kgs 21:1–18), the Deuteronomists who escaped martyrdom would have gone underground, but a copy of their text found its way into the Temple storeroom;

4. As we saw, the Levites and workmen discovered this text during the Temple renovations in 622 B.C. From the time of its discovery until the death of Josiah (622–609 B.C.), Deuteronomy became the basis for the renewal of Judah. The Deuteronomic school experienced a revival in Jerusalem and made a new edition of the book of Deuteronomy the theological basis of the revised Deuteronomic History (consisting of Joshua, Judges, Samuel, and Kings). Throughout the period from the discovery of the scroll until the destruction of Jerusalem (622–587 B.C.), while Deuteronomy served as the basis for Josiah's reform, the Deuteronomic school would have interacted with Jeremiah to a significant degree. Was Baruch, the prophet's scribe, a member of the Deuteronomic school (see Jer 32:11–16; 36:1–32; 43:3, 6; 45:1–5)?

5. Finally, after Nebuchadnezzar's armies destroyed Jerusalem, the Deuteronomists took their work into exile in Babylon, where the final editor completed the work around 550 B.C. (after Ezekiel had completed his mission and while Deutero-Isaiah was exercising his ministry). Sometime later, before 400 B.C., the Priestly editor who completed the Pentateuch joined Deuteronomy

to the first four books, leaving the text untouched except for some additions and adjustments to the material pertaining to Moses' last days. Deuteronomy serves a dual role as the culminating volume of the Pentateuch and the foundational volume of the Deuteronomic History, providing a magnificent bridge extending across the whole panorama of Israel's history, all the way from the creation of the world (Gn 1:1) to the release of Jehoiachin from prison in exile in 561 B.C. (2 Kgs 25:27–30).

Themes in Deuteronomy

Deuteronomy offers us a formation in the language of the covenant. It mediates to our hearts God's design for the renewal of his people in our day as in the days of first Hezekiah, then Josiah, and finally the Jews in Babylonian exile. For Christians, the text functions in a manner analogous to the Gospel of John insofar as its vocabulary (outside of the Deuteronomic Code) is simple but mediates truth at a profound level by reinforcing itself through repetition. We will absorb the thrust of the text by considering the covenant relationship from the alternate perspectives of both parties to the covenant: God and his people. First, we will contemplate the God of the covenant before reflecting on the response his initiative invites from the people of the covenant.

The Lord Revealed in the Covenant

In Deuteronomy, Moses invites us to acknowledge how God draws near to us and wants to form a people who know him from their hearts on the basis of his self-revelation. There is one truth underlying all others, namely, the uniqueness of the Lord: "Listen, Israel: Yahweh our God is the one, the only Yahweh" (6:4). During the Exile, the Deuteronomists highlight this perennial truth in a poem reflecting the influence of the whole prophetic tradition culminating with Deutero-Isaiah, the prophet of their times (32:1–43). While the Lord is sovereign, he is not distant. Indeed, his nearness to his people surpasses the claims of any nation concerning its relationship to its gods (4:7). When the Lord draws near, he does so reflecting his holiness: "Yahweh your God is a consuming fire" (4:24). We cannot contain the Lord with our minds. He has no form so that we might behold him with our eyes (4:15). However, he has spoken to us from the midst of the fire (4:15, 33, 36; 5:22, 24).

The Lord mediates his presence by the personal utterance of his word. However, the word itself is not primarily a concept or an idea but a sound mediating the divine presence. From the midst of the fire, the Lord speaks so that his people hear the sound of his voice (4:32–33; 5:23–25; cf. 5:26–27). The Law embodies God's voice. This Law that he gives to his people is not some remote or ethereal wisdom but rather an accessible personal word (30:11–14).

The Lord who speaks from the fire is, above all else, the God of love. God's love alone accounts for his election of Israel to be his people. His love is infinitely more than a warm sentiment; he has expressed it in the concrete acts of delivering his people from bondage in Egypt, blessing them in the words of the foreigner Balaam, and promising to remain faithful to them in the future (4:32–40; 7:7–15; 10:15; 23:6).

The divine fire also conveys an impression of the undivided or "jealous" nature of the Lord's love. The Lord will not tolerate his people's turning to other gods (4:23–24). In the covenant, he demands that his people make a decision and take personal responsibility for remaining faithful to him (11:26–32; 30:15–20). If they remain faithful, he will bless them with prosperity in the land he has given them as an unmerited gift (28:1–14; 8:7–20; 9:5–6). If they turn from him, he will send them into exile, but then he will express his love to them as mercy when he brings them back from exile to their own land (4:27; 28:20–28; 36–37; 47–68; 30:1–14). The clearest evidence that the Lord wants to remain close to his people in the land consists in his choice of a place where he will cause his name to dwell (12:4–5; 14:23; 16:2,6).

The People of the Covenant

Deuteronomy's preoccupation with the unity and extension of God's people is evident from its insistence from the very first to the very last lines of the book that Moses deal with "all Israel" (1:1; 34:12; 5:1; 11:6; 13:12; 27:9; 29:1; 31:1, 7, 11, 30). Because God is one, his people must be one. Such unity is possible only by sharing in the love God communicates in the covenant.

Because the Lord has first loved them, he calls his people to respond in kind. One bedrock admonition summarizes the whole Law, "You must love Yahweh your God with all your heart, with all your soul, with all your strength" (6:5). The people can love God because they remember how he revealed himself as a father who cared for them as his children by offering them actual protection and support in their journey through life's wilderness (1:31; 7:6; 14:1; 32:6).

Loving God means obeying his commandments (10:12–13; 11:1, 13, 22). This obedience must never degenerate into servile legalism. The people "obey the voice" more than the precept; in other words, their obedience is a response to love rather than to law (30:2, 10). As Jeremiah and Ezekiel point out, at its roots, this is an issue of the heart. External observance is not enough. While

Jeremiah speaks of the Lord making a new covenant by inscribing it on the heart (Jer 31:31–34) and Ezekiel promises that the Lord will take from his people their hearts of stone and give them hearts of flesh (Ez 36:26; 11:19; cf. 18:31), Deuteronomy demands that the people "circumcise" their hearts lest they remain proud and easily lured to idolatry (10:16; cf. 30:6; 8:14; 11:16; 29:17–20). Jeremiah certainly influenced Ezekiel's thinking on the matter, and both prophets seem to have been in touch with the Deuteronomic tradition that emphasized the centrality of the heart in relating to God personally.

In concrete terms, obedience to the Lord's commands focuses primarily on renouncing all forms of idolatry. All other commandments and precepts of the Law depend upon observance of this first commandment of the Decalogue. Israel must renounce the three primary forms of idolatry: the casting of images, the participation in worship of foreign gods, and the announcement of false prophecy. Israel must refuse any attempt at making an image of Yahweh, just as Moses had refused at Sinai (4:15–16; 5:8–10; cf. Ex 32:1–24). By contrast, Jeroboam's rebellion was founded on the idolatry he instituted at Dan and Bethel (1 Kgs 12:28–30). Furthermore, people must not attend the pagan cults even if their own families invite and encourage them to attend (12:29–13:1; 13:7–19). The people will be alert to the false prophet if they listen carefully to hear whether he or she purportedly prophesies a word coming from another god (13:2–6). The Deuteronomic Code obligates the people to reject all shrines in the countryside in order to present their offering at the one sanctuary where the Lord causes his name to dwell (12:4–7, 11, 13–14, 18; 14:23; 16:2, 6).

In conclusion, we must note that Deuteronomy requires everyone to satisfy the obligations of the Law. Indeed, a special regulation applies to the king, who must write for himself a copy of the Law (in Greek, *deuteronomion*), to which he will submit himself throughout the duration of his reign (17:14–20). The Lord promises to send his people a prophet like Moses who will teach them his ways by faithfully communicating all that the Lord tells him (18:9–22). We must note that the covenant obliges everyone, from king to common folk, to care for the poor and needy (10:18–19; 14:28–29; 15:1–18; 24:14–15).

In his love, the Lord has chosen his people. However they, in their turn, must decide to respond to his invitation to renew the covenant. Furthermore, we can take encouragement from the one characteristic every generation that enters into the Deuteronomic covenant shares in common: they all knew sin and failure in the past. The covenant in Deuteronomy is a special expression of God's forgiveness and the beginning of new life for his people.

The Hebrews whom Moses addressed on the plains of Moab in 1240 B.C. were the children of parents who turned from the Lord first at Sinai and then again at Kadesh-Barnea (9:7–29; Ex 32; Nm 13–14). The people of Judah who

received the first edition of Deuteronomy during the reforms of Hezekiah
(716–687 B.C./2 Kgs 18:1–8) experienced the call to purge themselves of the
previous generation's idolatry during the reign of Ahaz (736–716 B.C./2 Kgs
16:1–20). Josiah's Deuteronomic reform aimed at expelling the elements of
apostasy stemming from Manasseh's reign (640–609 B.C./2 Kgs 22:1–20;
687–642 B.C./2 Kgs 21:1–18). Ultimately, the final Deuteronomic editor
addressed the whole book especially to the second generation of Jewish exiles,
whose parents witnessed the fall of Jerusalem because of their sins (29:21–28).

Considered in this light, we can appreciate why the book of Deuteronomy
is a charter for the spiritual renewal of God's people in every generation. In
Deuteronomy, we see how God endows his people with dignity and respects
their freedom to choose. By their own strength, they cannot free themselves
from the bondage of their dark deeds of the past. However, they can decide to
respond to his love and invitation to enter into the covenant. Thus, they stand
at a crossroads and must choose between the two ways, one leading to life and
the other to death (30:15–20). Depending on their choice, they will experience either blessing or curse (27:11–28:46). There is no middle ground, no
gray area of compromise. The people choose for themselves either freedom or
bondage. Now God sets before them the joyous possibility of putting an end
to the past, of redeeming the times by turning from death and entering into a
communion of life and love with the God of the covenant. Moses begs every
generation down to our own, "Choose life, then, so that you and your
descendants may live, in the love of Yahweh your God, obeying his voice,
holding fast to him; for in this your life consists . . . " (30:19–20). No wonder
Josiah responded with such zeal and urgency when he heard the words of this
book.

The Last Days of Moses: Song, Blessing, and Death

The Priestly editor who set the Pentateuch in its present form reserved most of
his emendations to Deuteronomy for the concluding section, which recounts
the final acts of Moses (31:1–34:12). Moses appoints Joshua to be his successor
and proclaims the hymn of praise that echoes the teaching of the great
prophets extending down to Deutero-Isaiah (31:1–8; 32:1–43). Finally, in the
tradition of the Patriarch Jacob, he pronounces God's blessing upon each of
the tribes (33:1–29; cf. Gn 49:1–28).

The depiction of Moses' death is a subtle portrait of God's mercy and
faithfulness. The great servant's return to the mountaintop recalls the times of
his personal encounters with the Lord on the peak of Sinai (Ex 3–4; 19–20;
32–34). This time, he sees, not the face of God, but the land that reveals the

Lord's faithfulness to Moses and to his people (34:1–4). In death, Moses is taken into the mystery of God. No one is able to find his grave as only the Lord could have buried him and thus taken him into his care in death (34:5–6). The Pentateuch thus concludes with a mountaintop scene of a death that suggests life is just beginning. The Lord has been faithful to Moses, the most faithful of his servants (34:1–12).

Toward the New Testament: Jesus, the Prophet like Moses

As the sermon collection *par excellence* in the Old Testament, Deuteronomy inspired the ministers of the word who were evangelists, pastors, and teachers in the early Christian communities. They discerned that Jesus redeemed the history of his people, and they knew him to be "the prophet like Moses" (see Dt 18:15). Furthermore, resonances of Deuteronomy echo through Jesus' vocabulary as he implants God's word on the hearts of all who believe in him.

The Gospel narratives of Jesus' temptations portray him at the beginning of his public life reliving the experience of Israel. Just as the Israelites pass through the Red Sea and then journey in the wilderness for forty years, so Jesus goes through the waters of the Jordan in his baptism and remains in the desert forty days and nights (Mk 1:9–13; Mt 3:13–17; 4:1–11; Lk 3:21–22; 4:1–13). To each of Satan's temptations, Jesus responds with a quotation from Moses' reflection on the Israelites' wilderness experience in Deuteronomy (Mt 4:1–11; Lk 4:1–13). According to their sequence in Luke, Jesus' replies refer to the three times when the Israelites doubted the Lord, first in demanding bread (Dt 8:3; Ex 16:1–36), then in crying out for water (Dt 6:16; Nm 20:2–13), and finally in facing the idolatry in the land of Canaan (Dt 6:13). Whereas Israel succumbed to temptation, Jesus is victorious. Thus, in his temptations, Jesus redeems the history of Israel by reliving their experience and overcoming the power of Satan precisely where they had weakened.

Jesus is the prophet like Moses, "the one who is to come" (Mt 11:3; Dt 18:15–19). At the transfiguration, the Father speaks and, in an allusion to Jesus as the fulfillment of Moses' promise, admonishes the audience: "Listen to him" (Mk 9:7; Mt 17:5; Lk 9:35; cf. Dt 18:15). We have already noted how the Gospel of Matthew portrays Jesus as the New Moses who positions himself on the mountain to give the people the new Law (Mt 5:1–7:29). In Deuteronomy, Moses commissions Joshua and then is last seen on a mountain. The Gospel of Matthew portrays Jesus the risen Lord in a similar fashion: in the last scene, he commissions his disciples on a mountain (Mt 28:16–20; cf. Dt 34:1–12).

Deuteronomy's concern for the state of the believer's heart prepares us for Jesus' correction of the Pharisees' preoccupation with externals (Mk 7:1–9,

20–23; cf. Dt 6:4–6; 10:12–22). The Deuteronomic presentation of love as obedience provides a foretaste of Jesus' teaching in the Gospel of John, "If you love me you will keep my commandments" (Jn 14:15; 15:10; cf. Dt 6:4–9; 7:9–11; 10:12–13; 11:1). As in Deuteronomy, so in John: the disciples of Jesus are not rigid legalists, for they heed the voice, not just the words, of their shepherd (Jn 10:1–5; cf. Dt 26:17).

Paul rejoices in the nearness of God's word that Deuteronomy announces. However, for Paul, there is a difference: the word is no longer the Law but rather the Gospel, namely, "the word of faith" that the apostles preach to bring salvation to everyone in the world. The word God places on our lips is the confession that "Jesus is Lord." We can utter this truth because God has revealed Christ in the power of his Resurrection within the inner depths of our hearts (Rom 10:5–13; cf. Dt 30:11–14).

God's release of his word through the mouth of his prophets guides the course of history. The Deuteronomists were so convinced of this that they wrote a complete history of Israel's existence in the Promised Land to illustrate how the prophetic word shapes the community of faith. For an extensive meditation on this theme, we must turn to the Deuteronomic History.

STUDY QUESTIONS

1. Describe the reforms of Josiah.
2. What are the elements making up the book of Deuteronomy?
3. What is the significance of the word "today" in Deuteronomy?
4. How does the form of Deuteronomy differ from that of the first four books of the Pentateuch?
5. What are the five stages in the development of the Deuteronomic tradition?
6. What books comprise the Deuteronomic History?
7. What is the significance of love and unity in Deuteronomy?
8. What are three primary forms of idolatry?
9. How does Jesus relive and redeem the experience of the Israelites? How does Jesus reveal himself as the new Moses?
10. Why is love essential to a life of faith? Describe your personal awareness of God's love. How can you teach young people about God's covenant love?
11. What role do the commandments play in teaching you how to love God and your neighbor?
12. How does the book of Deuteronomy provide an outline of genuine renewal for the Church today?

DEUTERONOMY

HISTORICAL BOOKS

THE DEUTERONOMIC HISTORY: JOSHUA TO 2 KINGS

"Why did this happen to us?" The question haunted the mind of everyone who survived the great catastrophe when the Babylonians destroyed Jerusalem in 587 B.C. The best way for grief-stricken survivors to collect the shattered fragments of their lives is to tell their story and go over their history until they can picture the tragedy within the whole context of their lives. They require a special ministry of God's word. Anointed teachers from the Deuteronomic tradition provided this ministry when God's people were in the depths of desolation.

The Deuteronomists communicated God's word in the form of the biblical compendium comprising the books of Joshua, Judges, Samuel, and Kings. We call this collection the Deuteronomic History. Together, these volumes tell the story of God's people from their entrance into the Promised Land until their deportation from it into exile. They offer a prophetic interpretation of history spanning almost seven centuries, from Joshua's conquest of the land (1240 B.C./Jos 1:1–4) through the destruction of the northern kingdom (721 B.C./2 Kgs 17) up to Jehoiachin's release from prison in Babylon about twenty-five years after the desolation of Jerusalem and the beginning of the Exile (562 B.C./2 Kgs 25:27–30).

Joshua, Judges, Samuel, and Kings developed in light of Deuteronomy. However, the tradition undergirding the book of Deuteronomy developed somewhat distinctly from that underlying the Deuteronomic History. To reflect this difference in tradition, we have adopted a simple nomenclature:

1. The adjective "Deuteronomic" describes the unique theological perspective deriving from the book of Deuteronomy;
2. The "Deuteronomists" are teachers in the Deuteronomic tradition and members of the Deuteronomic school who contributed to the tradition history of the book of Deuteronomy and to Joshua–2 Kings; and
3. The "Deuteronomist" edited the final edition of Deuteronomy while the "Deuteronomic Historian" edited the final edition of Joshua to 2 Kings.

Our biblical text is the second of two discernible editions produced by different generations of Deuteronomic writers. In the last chapter, we traced

the outline of the two-hundred-year history of the Deuteronomic tradition, from its origins in the northern kingdom prior to the middle of the
eighth century B.C., through its development in Judah during the seventh
century B.C. and in Babylon after 587 B.C., up to the middle of the sixth
century B.C.

When the Deuteronomic school rose to prominence under Josiah's patronage (622–609 B.C.), its scholars produced the first edition of Israel's history
suggesting that its development was reaching a climax in their day with the
reforms that their venerable king mandated (2 Kgs 22:1–23:30; 1 Kgs 13:2; 2
Kgs 23:16–18, 25). Decades later, the Deuteronomists had established themselves among the exiles in Babylon after the destruction of Jerusalem in 587
B.C. They revised the work, producing a definitive edition of the history to
explain why the Lord had allowed the destruction of the holy city and the
pillaging of the Temple.

The Deuteronomists completed the final edition of the work after the
event that concludes their narrative: Jehoiachin's release from prison, which
took place in 562 B.C. (2 Kgs 25:27–30). They finished the present edition of
their compendium around 550 B.C. At the same time, they finished their
editorial work on the book of Deuteronomy itself and placed this text of the
Law at the head of the whole collection. A few editorial additions (notably in
Kings) were later inserted into the text of the Deuteronomic History during
the Persian era (e.g., 1 Kgs 5:4–5; 8:41–51).

Deuteronomy and the Deuteronomic History

Scholars use the title "Deuteronomic History" to designate Joshua, Judges,
Samuel, and Kings because these texts interpret Israel's history in the Promised
Land in light of Deuteronomy. We must hasten to note that the Deuteronomists'
work involved both editing sources and authoring their own commentaries
on the materials to comprise this collection. They brought together various
types of documents, such as census lists, land surveys, annals of the royal court,
prayers, and previously written histories. Their task consisted in shaping these
texts and literary units into a cohesive narrative that conveyed the message
that God was anointing them to communicate to their people.

The manner in which the Deuteronomic scribes edited the texts they
received reflects their respect for God's work in the tradition. For example,
they made very few adjustments to the magnificent biography that runs
throughout Samuel. By contrast, in Kings, they did not hesitate to offer their
editorial evaluations of whether or not a monarch lived up to the standards of
God's commission of him (e.g., 1 Kgs 14:22; 15:11, 26, and so forth). We can

discern strong evidence of Deuteronomic influence in the common perspective and vocabulary that characterize the speeches of Yahweh and the great figures: Joshua (Jos 1:2–9; 22:1–8; 23:1–24:28), Samuel (1 Sm 12:1–24), Nathan (2 Sm 7:5–16), David (2 Sm 7:18–29), and Solomon (1 Kgs 8:22–61). The hands of the Deuteronomists account for the inner consistency of the editorial comments explaining, first, Israel's inability to dispel foreign nations from the land (Jgs 2:6–3:6), secondly, the fall of the northern kingdom (2 Kgs 17:7–23), and, finally, the destruction of Judah (2 Kgs 23:26–27; 24:3–4).

The Former Prophets

Jewish tradition reserves a special place among the prophetic collection for Joshua, Judges, Samuel, and Kings by calling them the "Former Prophets". If this title seems odd to us at first, it is only because we are unfamiliar with the real message of these books. In fact, "Former Prophets" is the best designation for understanding these texts from the perspective of faith. While, on the surface, they appear to concentrate on the heroics and crimes of powerful leaders and kings, at a deeper level, they draw our attention to the prophetic word. These books teach us that it is God's word that really governs history.

From reading these books, we learn to turn our attention away from the figures who dominate the center stage of life and direct our attention to the humble prophets who bear the burden of God's word in the world. It is worth noting some of the lesser-known servants of God's word, whom we often bypass in our preoccupation with the proud and the mighty kings: Ahijah of Shiloh (1 Kgs 11:27–39; 14:1–18), Shemaiah, the man of God (1 Kgs 12:22–24), Jehu ben Hanani (in Hebrew, *ben* means "son of") (1 Kgs 16:1–4, 7), and Micaiah ben Imlah (1 Kgs 22:5–28). Faithful messengers such as these were true brothers of those from among their ranks who suffered martyrdom in times of persecution (1 Kgs 18:4; cf. 2 Kgs 21:16). They merit a place alongside the great prophetic figures, such as: Joshua (Jos 1:6–9; 24:1–24), Deborah (Jgs 4:1–5:31), Samuel (1 Sm 1:1–19:24; 25:1), Nathan (2 Sm 7:1–17; 12:1–15; 1 Kgs 1:1–53), Elijah (1 Kgs 17:1–2 Kgs 2:13), and Elisha (1 Kgs 19:16–21; 2 Kgs 2:1–9:10; 13:14–21).

Over the course of the whole collection, we should make note of five different kinds of people who mediated God's word to Israel. The Deuteronomists applied the term "prophet" to the last four but not to God's first servant in the land, who was Joshua. Nevertheless, he was the "one-like-Moses" of the earliest days who united in himself the two offices of administrative leader and messenger of God's word (Jos 1:5–9; see Dt 18:15). In their collection, the Deuteronomists reserved the term "prophet" for individuals who were distinct from the judges and kings (see Jgs 6:7–10). Nevertheless, they had a broad understanding of the term, since they employed it to designate at least four different types of people who exercised a ministry of the word to Israel.

First, there is Samuel, the priest at the sanctuary of Shiloh, who is also called a "seer" (1 Sm 3:20; 9:9). Secondly, we note the bands of ecstatics who wander the countryside spontaneously announcing their message (1 Sm 10:10; 19:20). Thirdly, Elijah and Elisha belong to a category of their own because of their powers to heal, which support the authority of their proclamation (1 Kgs 17:1–24; 2 Kgs 4:1–5:27; cf. 1 Kgs 19:16; 2 Kgs 3:11). Fourthly, Nathan is an example of the king's adviser on religious and moral issues who is an official member of the royal court (2 Sm 7:2; 12:25; cf. 24:11).

Everyone who held the title "prophet" was anointed to declare God's word to the king and to the people. Much of the Deuteronomic History reveals the tension between king and prophet. The Deuteronomic legislation carefully sets forth guidelines to govern both the office of prophet, on the one hand (Dt 13:2–6; 18:9–22), and king, on the other (Dt 17:14–20). It obliged the king to be the first one to submit his life to the Law of God. The prophets throughout the Deuteronomic History call the kings to obey God's instruction in the manner in which they live their lives and exercise their office.

The whole Deuteronomic History reveals the effectiveness of the word God consistently speaks through the servants of his word. In fact, God allows the destruction first of the northern kingdom and then of Jerusalem because the people and their kings refuse to heed the prophets' message (2 Kgs 17:7–23; 21:10–15). God's people go into exile in fulfillment of the word he spoke to them throughout history from their first days until their last days in the land before the Exile (Jos 24:19–20; 2 Kgs 20:16–19).

The majority of the people and their kings sin against the first commandment by compromising their allegiance to the Lord with elements of idolatry. This sin is the source of all others, and it accounts for the great desolation, first of Samaria and then of Jerusalem (see Jgs 2:11–19; 1 Kgs 11:1–13; 12:26–33; 16:26; 2 Kgs 17:7–23; 21:1–18; cf. 1 Sm 13:8–15).

The message the Deuteronomists communicate to the exiles is: we must learn from our pain. We cannot indulge in self-pity; we must allow our sufferings to bring us to repentance. The Deuteronomists show us that God disciplines those whom he loves (see Heb 12:5–13; cf. Dt 8:5). Their message encourages us to acknowledge our responsibility for the weakened state of God's people today. They call us to become a source of new life for the community of faith by giving our lives in total response to the first of all God's precepts, "Listen, Israel: Yahweh our God is the one, the only Yahweh.

You must love Yahweh your God with all your heart, with all your soul, with all your strength" (Dt 6:4-5).

A closer look at Joshua and Judges will give us a better understanding of the Deuteronomic work.

STUDY QUESTIONS

1. Why did the Deuteronomists produce their history?
2. Why is "Former Prophets" an appropriate title for this collection of books?
3. What was the role of the prophet?
4. Why did God permit the destruction of Samaria and of Jerusalem?
5. Discuss how history is more than a scattering of events but a pattern in God's revelation of himself to us.
6. Do you see how in your own life the events making up your life are God's revelation of himself to you? How does that knowledge affect the choices you will make from now on?
7. How attentive are you to hearing the word of God proclaimed at the celebration of the Eucharist? Are you developing the habit of reading the texts and incorporating them into your prayer before you attend the Liturgy?
8. How does your faith in God affect the way you reflect on tragedy and suffering in your life?

14

JOSHUA AND JUDGES: SETTLEMENT IN THE LAND

Everyone living in today's rapidly changing world experiences the stress that a period of cultural transformation generates. All of us know the struggle of adapting to the climate that computers, mass communication, and high technology produce. Christians today are becoming increasingly aware that cultural transition produces a spiritual crisis. How can you preserve your faith when your whole world is changing? How can God's people maintain their spiritual and moral values when confronted with the glamor of modern civilization? Is it possible for faith to shape contemporary culture rather than for contemporary culture to reinterpret faith so as to conform it to society's trends? Can parents bridge the generation gap and communicate to their children a sense of the dignity faith offers as a sign of contradiction to the present world? The Bible's literature of conquest and settlement in the Promised Land offers us a perspective for considering issues such as these.

The books of Joshua and Judges span a time frame of almost two centuries between the Israelites' entrance into the land of Canaan and their final decades as a tribal confederation (1240–1050 B.C.). This was an era of great social transition when the Israelites were bound to experience "culture shock". These desert nomads had to become farmers and even city-dwellers, exchanging tents for houses, learning the science of agriculture, and understanding how to govern themselves in towns and tribal regions.

The Land of Canaan

In order to gain a historical perspective on what the Israelite occupation of the land entailed, let us consider the Canaanite civilization and culture that predated the Israelites in the territory. The excavations at Ras Shamra (otherwise known as Ugarit), which were undertaken in 1928, have made a wealth of information available to us. This Canaanite city, located on the coast of what is now Lebanon, flourished between 1400 and 1200 B.C., a time frame that overlapped with the Israelite occupation of the Promised Land.

The greatest treasures unearthed at Ras Shamra were a vast array of texts inscribed on clay tablets in cuneiform script. It is worth mentioning that the discovery of the Ugaritic language cast light on ancient Hebrew owing to their similarities in vocabulary and syntax. Evidence from the tablets and excavations of the city indicates that the Canaanites had a highly developed civilization. Ugarit itself was a commercial center. It was located on the overland route connecting Mesopotamia with Egypt, and its ports offered access to the Mediterranean islands of Cyprus and Crete as well as to the region circumscribing the Aegean Sea. Ugarit was a cosmopolitan marketplace with its own merchant navy on the water and agricultural economy on the surrounding land. Its scribes could write in the languages of both Mesopotamia and Egypt as well as their own. Its religion was embodied in myths and legends celebrating the deeds of gods such as El and Baal and the goddesses Asherah and Anat. Worship in its temple exhibited a pronounced sexual aspect in fertility rites aimed at guaranteeing abundant herds and crops. In the world of its day, this was an advanced culture that would not easily yield to a comparatively primitive nomadic population infiltrating its territory after forty years of wilderness existence.

Canaan was not a unified political state like Egypt; rather, it was comprised of a number of independent city-states that shared a common culture and formed alliances with each other for purposes of defense and mutual economic gain. Thus, the Israelites could enter the land and approach one city at a time without fearing that a national Canaanite army would meet them. Furthermore, they could settle in particular districts without drawing unwarranted attention from more distant regions.

The History of Israel's Occupation of the Promised Land

An Egyptian stela dating from 1220 B.C. provides the earliest extra-biblical evidence of the Israelites living in the land of Canaan. This basalt tablet lists "Israel" among the peoples and places (including Ashkelon and Gezer) that the Egyptian forces defeated in "the fifth year" of Pharaoh Merneptah, who succeeded his father Rameses II.

This historical artifact offers suggestive clues pertaining to the Israelites' occupation of Canaan. Most important of all, it provides extra-biblical evidence that indeed the Israelites had entered the land and were living in the hill country at least by 1220 B.C. However, the fact that they are not associated with specific settlements on the stela seems to indicate that, at first, the Israelites continued living as semi-nomads in the open land outside the city walls. Evidently, the Israelites did not conquer the land in one successful campaign. On a more general plane, it is certain that the Egyptians asserted political control over Canaan at the time. The fact that the Egyptians disciplined the Israelites as early as 1220 B.C. indicates that the latter must have experienced their share of setbacks from the beginning. All of this suggests that the Israelite occupation of the Promised Land was a more complex historical process than we might imagine upon a preliminary reading of the biblical account.

Indications within the biblical text and archaeological evidence combine to suggest that Israelite settlement in Canaan took place through a gradual process of social transformation. Scholarly opinion offers three portraits of how the Israelites actually occupied the land. The oldest image is that of a military invasion whereby Joshua's forces took control of Canaan by conquering its principal cities in a relentless display of force. A second picture describes a peaceful settlement of the land by the semi-nomadic tribes who first infiltrated the countryside and then occupied the cities. The most recent proposal suggests that a peasant revolt took place throughout Canaan and the victorious lower classes came to identify themselves with the Israelites and their faith.

What actually happened? Obviously, the issue will continue to be a subject of debate. However, it seems most likely that Israel's occupation of Canaan was not a homogeneous event but rather the result of developments represented in all three hypotheses. The biblical text notes that military conquests were limited to specific regions. Archaeological evidence indicates that they took place over a period of time.

The Israelites who invaded *from the east* under Joshua advanced across the · Jordan into the territory north and west of the Dead Sea identified by the sites of Gilgal, Jericho, Bethel, and Ai (Jos 3:1–8:29). Later, Joshua led his army from Gilgal to defend the Gibeonites against an attack that a league of five Canaanite cities had launched (10:1–15). They probably took the *southern hill country* (called the "Shephelah") and its major cities of Libnah, Lachish, and Eglon at a later date, perhaps at the death of Pharaoh Merneptah (d. 1204), when a politically unstable Egypt would not have been able to intervene (10:29–39). Israelite victories *in the north* are limited to only two major battles, both of which they carried on against Jabin, king of Hazor: one at the waters of Merom, and the other in the region of Mount Tabor under instructions from Deborah (Jos 11:1–14; 12:19–23; Jgs 4:1–5:31). *From the south,* the victory at Hormah (Nm 21:1–3) seems to have provided a base of operations for an invasion by Calebites, Kenites, and other elements that became absorbed into the tribe of Judah (Jos 10:36–39; 14:6–15; 15:13–20; Jgs 1:1–21).

Significantly, the Israelites took over much of *the central highlands* almost without a skirmish. Shechem became their principal sanctuary and meeting place (Jos 8:30–35). The Israelites seem to have occupied this territory in a peaceable fashion, perhaps because of their influence on those who had previously settled there. It is likely that elements of the local population, especially from the poorer classes, entered into covenant with the Lord and joined themselves to Israel (see Jos 24:1–28). The small number of battles Israel fought in the north suggests the possibility that local inhabitants found an affinity to the faith of Israel and were incorporated into their numbers as the tribes spread out to occupy the territory. Some scholars have suggested that local peoples who converted to Yahwism made up the majority of the northern tribes of Israel.

The book of Joshua describes the Israelite conquest, while the book of Judges portrays their settlement in the land of Canaan. From a historical perspective, each of these texts offers a distinctive impression of what the Israelite occupation was like. The book of Joshua conveys the impression of Israel's being a unified army led by one commander that swept through the region in a triumphant crusade. By contrast, the book of Judges offers a multifaceted portrait of various tribes settled in diverse regions facing ongoing conflict with other local peoples and even with one another.

JOSHUA: CONQUEST OF THE LAND

The book of Joshua consists of three major parts: (1) the Israelite conquest of the Promised Land (1:1–12:24); (2) the distribution of the land to the tribes (13:1–22:34); and (3) the renewal of the covenant in the land (23:1–24:33). The book covers the full span of Joshua's career as leader over Israel, opening with his appointment by the Lord to take the place of Moses (1:1–9) and closing with his death (24:29–31) (c. 1240–1200 B.C.).

It is difficult to overestimate the significance of this book since it provides the climax of what the Pentateuch anticipated. The Israelites' entrance into the Promised Land represents the fulfillment of the promise God made to the Patriarchs and to Moses (Gn 15:18–21; Ex 3:8). The narrative illustrates how God's grace and his people's obedience work in harmony with each other to accomplish the divine plan. The description of every episode brings to mind the dynamic tension that defines the relationship between God and human beings. The Lord "gives" the land to his people (1:2); yet, at the same time, the Israelites must "take possession" of it through the rigorous efforts conquest demands (1:11).

The Israelites' entrance into the Promised Land is not a human work but an event of God's grace that provides a mirror image of the Exodus from Egypt. The parting of the Jordan's waters reflects the previous generation's passage through the Sea of Reeds (3:14–17; Ex 14:15–31). The Israelites' celebration of the Passover upon their arrival in Canaan recalls the inauguration of the feast in Egypt on the night God delivered them from bondage (5:10–12; Ex 12:1–28).

Joshua is the new Moses whom God raised up to lead his people (Dt 18:15). His personality and actions are almost indistinguishable from those of his great forebear. Identification with Moses is evident in: (a) his commissioning spies to survey the land (2:1–24; Nm 13:1–33); (b) his encounter with God on "holy ground" (5:13–15; Ex 3:5); (c) his admonition that the people sanctify themselves prior to the Lord's revelation (3:5; Ex 19:10–11, 14–15); (d) his intercession for the Lord to forgive the sin of his people (7:6–9; Ex 32:11–14); and (e) his mediation of the covenant between God and his people (24:1–28; Ex 24:1–18; see also Ex 19:1–23:33; 34:1–35). As the successor to Moses, Joshua is presented as the ideal leader of Israel and a model for the great kings of the future, such as David, Solomon, and Josiah.

On a superficial level, the book of Joshua seems to be a piece of military history recounting the victories that enabled the Israelites to establish themselves in Canaan. However, for the Deuteronomic editors and their audience, the military concepts served as metaphors describing the continual battle of God's people in every age, especially in the Exile, where the paganism of Babylon surrounded them. Canaan represents the world (including Babylon) that man creates without knowledge of God. The story of Israel's conquest of this land provides an instruction about how God's people must take control of this environment that is hostile to faith. No compromise is possible. The world will turn the people away from true fidelity to the Lord unless the community of believers subdues it and takes it captive. The real battle is about preserving faith in a glamorous world of distraction and temptation—a theme most relevant to the exiles living under the spell of Babylon's enchantments in the middle of the sixth century B.C.

The book of Joshua teaches us that three elements are essential in order for faith to be victorious. First, the people must listen to the word of God and allow it to form their minds and hearts. Secondly, they must banish all worldly idols from the land. And thirdly, they must renew the covenant to confirm their commitment to the Lord so they can secure their future in the land.

While the Lord takes the initiative in bringing his people into the Promised Land, they must respond to his word at every juncture. The Israelites conquer the land insofar as they obey God's word. In fact, the Deuteronomists initially describe the Israelites' manner in taking possession of the territory as an act of worship. The Deuteronomists were teaching their people that true worship of the Lord rather than military conquest causes God's people to take authority over their world. The prime example is the conquest of Jericho. Not an advancing military squadron but the acclamations of the people whom the priests lead in a liturgical procession, carrying the ark of the covenant and sounding the ram's-horn trumpets, bring the walls of the city down (6:1–21). The Deuteronomists were suggesting to the exiles in Babylon that their first priority in reestablishing themselves in the land must be the restoration of the Temple under the administration of the priests (see Ezr 1:1–6:22; Hg 1–2). Genuine liturgy in praise of God will conquer the world. By contrast, disobedience to the Lord's word produces defeat and humiliation—such is the harsh lesson deriving from the first unsuccessful attempt to overrun Ai (7:1–26).

Even the primitive practice of devoting all that is plundered to the Lord highlights the fact that the war belongs to the Lord. The practice of "the curse of destruction" (*herem*) obliged the Israelites to commit all the spoils of war to the Lord either by sacrifice or dedication. They placed precious metals and stones in the treasury to adorn the place of worship at a later time (6:17–19). Israel had to destroy her enemies and their possessions so as not to provide a source of temptation for the people to turn from a life of pure devotion to the Lord (7:16–26).

How are we to read the violent texts describing the complete extermination of Israel's enemies? Clearly, the Deuteronomists' original audience of exiles in Babylon did not draw the conclusion that they were to kill their pagan captors or attack their enemies in the land upon their return from exile (cf. 4:1–6:21; Neh 3:33–4:17; 6:1–7:3). They appreciated the actions of Joshua's army as graphic illustrations highlighting the importance of keeping the first commandment. The threat of judgment did not hang over the foreigners as much as over Israel herself. She had to banish from her environment every temptation to worship the idols of the world. For the exiles in Babylon, this imposed an obligation on the Jews to construct an environment free from the allurements of the pagan culture.

Deuteronomy's version of the Law of Moses is the norm for Israel's entrance into the land. Meditation on this Law must have shaped Joshua's mind so that Israel's campaigns and activities would be successful (1:6–9). Once the Israelites gain a foothold in the central highlands, Joshua carries out Moses' demands by stationing the people facing one another on the slopes of Mount Ebal and Mount Gerizim to renew the covenant by reading to them the blessings and curses written in the "Book of the Law" (8:30–35; Dt 27:4–26). Joshua's final discourse in old age testifies to his constancy as he insists that future generations remain steadfast in their observance of what is written in the "Book of the Law of Moses" (23:6–10).

According to Joshua, the Israelite conquest of Canaan bears witness to the power of God's word to accomplish what it promises. Such is the lesson we gain from surveying the distribution of the land among the twelve tribes

(21:43–45). In his final testament, Joshua speaks to each successive generation of God's people and to everyone reading the text when he insists, "Acknowledge with all your heart and soul that of all the promises made to you by Yahweh your God, not one has failed: all have been fulfilled—not one has failed" (23:14).

In view of the Lord's fidelity to his promises, the people are invited to renew their covenant with the Lord at Shechem in the event that brings the whole book to its climax (24:1–28). The covenant seals the work the Lord has accomplished in providing his people with the Promised Land. A Deuteronomic emphasis directs attention exclusively to the first commandment (24:14–18; Dt 5:6–10; 5:32–6:25). The covenant provides the foundation upon which the people will construct their future. The Deuteronomists make sure the exiles understand their banishment from the land to be a consequence of Israel's infidelity. This makes it all the more urgent for the Jews in Babylonian exile and every member of God's people down to our own generation to alter the course of history and to respond to the Lord with the wholehearted declaration, "Yahweh our God is the one whom we shall serve; his voice we shall obey!" (24:24).

JUDGES: SETTLEMENT IN THE LAND

When they settled in the land after the death of Joshua, the Israelites organized themselves into a confederation of tribes without one primary head or central authority. They were country people of a lower economic status who provided for themselves through farming and agriculture. In times of crisis, a leader or "judge" emerged from a particular tribe to guide Israel through the emergency. This leader did not hold a permanent office and was in the forefront only for the duration of the crisis.

Times of emergency were bound to arise since Israel was never able to banish completely other peoples from the land (Jos 13:1–5; Jgs 3:1–3). In fact, around 1200 B.C., just when the Israelites were spreading across the land from the south and east, the Philistines invaded Canaan from the north and west. Apparently, they were a subgroup of so-called "Sea Peoples", who came from the region of the Aegean Sea and had conquered the Hittite Empire in Asia Minor before heading south along the Mediterranean coast to enter Phoenicia and even destroy Ugarit. Some Philistines then advanced farther south until they entered the land to which they would give their name ("Palestine"), and they established their own league of five cities, consisting of Gaza, Ashdod, Ashkelon, Gath, and Ekron. The Philistine threat would be a source of preoccupation for the Israelites for two centuries, from the time of Samson until David's victory over them (c. 1150–965 B.C./Jgs 13:1–16:31; 2 Sm 5:17–25; 21:15–22).

The book of Judges describes the era of the Israelites' settlement in Canaan from the death of Joshua (Jos 24:29–31) until the birth of Samuel (1 Sm 1–2). The duration of their existence as a tribal confederacy distinguished by the periodic leadership of judges extends beyond the book of Judges into the first part of 1 Samuel (c. 1200–c. 1020 B.C./Jgs 1 to 1 Sm 7).

We may divide the text of Judges into three sections: (a) an introduction summarizing Israel's incomplete conquest of the land (1:1–3:6); (b) the stories of twelve individual judges representing each of the tribes (3:7–16:31); and (c) two appendices mainly concerning the tribes of Dan (17:1–18:31) and of Benjamin (19:1–21:25).

While the book of Joshua highlights Israel's successes, Judges assesses her failures. As the first volume of the Deuteronomic History, Joshua describes what Israel should be like as God's people who experience victory because of their obedience to his word. As the second volume in the collection, Judges offers a more sobering portrait that explains how God's people's weakness and submission to the very world they should have overcome frustrates God's designs.

The introduction to Judges (1:1–2:5) interrupts the natural flow of the narrative from the end of Joshua to Judges 2:6ff. It inserts material designed to nuance the almost exclusive emphasis on Israelite conquests described in Joshua. Judges offers a more subdued and complex summary of Israel's campaign in Canaan. The tribe of Judah and its associates primarily vanquished the Canaanites and alien peoples in the south (1:1–21). By contrast, with the exception of the tribe of Joseph's victory at Bethel (1:22–26), Israel's northern tribes were unable to dislodge the Canaanites and other peoples from their cities (1:27–36). Throughout the northern territory, the Israelites settled into coexistence with those who preceded them in the land. Thus, they failed to fulfill the demands of the covenant outlined in Deuteronomy and so made themselves vulnerable to domination by the world in which they had made their home (Jgs 2:1–5; cf. Dt 7:1–6).

As God's people who first took possession of the Promised Land, Joshua's generation is held up as the model for Israel throughout the centuries of her settlement. All generations after Joshua's fell short of the standard set by their earliest forebears in the land (2:6–10). Their inadequacy concerns primary issues, specifically, transgression of the first commandment. We find the roots of their apostasy and idolatry in their failure to extricate the other peoples from the land as the Lord had commanded them. The Lord had to accommodate himself to Israel's reluctance to take decisive action. Thus, contrary to his original perfect design, the Lord relents from his determination to drive out the Canaanites, Hittites, Perizzites, Hivites, and Jebusites. Instead, he allows them to remain in Canaan and makes use of their presence as a continual means of testing Israel's fidelity (2:20–3:6; cf. Dt 7:1–6).

Israel's disobedience to the Lord, who had graciously redeemed her from slavery and brought her into the Promised Land, sets her history on a tumultuous downward spiral. The spiral follows a pattern consisting of seven movements: (1) the people turn from the Lord to worship the gods of other peoples; (2) the Lord allows them to suffer the consequence of their sin in the form of their enemies' domination over them; (3) their anguish provokes the people to turn back and cry out to the Lord; (4) he sends a judge to rescue them from their oppressors; but (5) only with hesitation do the people abandon their idolatry; (6) the judge saves the people, securing peace for them throughout his or her lifetime; but (7) the people return to their apostasy after the judge's death, and so the spiral repeats itself from the beginning (Jgs 2:11–19). The biblical authors depict this pattern being reinforced in the career of each judge God raises up to rescue his people (see 3:7–11 for the prototype of the Deuteronomic description of the judges).

Within the framework of this historical pattern, administering justice did not necessarily define the role of "judges". The greatest of them were "saviors" who, by their heroic deeds, rescued their people from destruction. Twelve judges emerge to rescue Israel at various points in the history of the tribal confederation. Six were "minor" judges, most of whom were concerned with the administration of justice (10:1–5; 12:8–15; cf. 3:31). They are the subjects of brief notices interspersed between the adventure stories of the six "major" judges, who were more renown for their military leadership and prowess than for their administrative skills.

The stories of Deborah, Gideon, and Samson testify to the literary skills of the inspired authors. The events surrounding Deborah likely occurred around 1125 B.C. She provided the wisdom and encouragement for the Israelite army under Barak to defeat the forces commanded by Sisera, a general who served Jabin, the Canaanite king of Hazor, the foremost city in the north. The narrative (4:1–24), of later origin than the ancient Song of Deborah (5:1–31), makes the point that the obedient servant of God's word wields more authority than commanders of armies to change the course of history. As a prophetess, Deborah admonishes the general Barak to trust in the Lord's commands. In accordance with her prophetic word, the humble bring down the mighty as the Kenite woman Jael disposes of General Sisera and thus humbles King Jabin (4:9, 17–24).

Sometime afterward, God raises up Gideon to deal with the Midianites and other marauding bands from the east, who were more likely to pillage the northern countryside after its main center, Hazor, had been weakened. In the manner of his call, Gideon resembles both Moses and Jacob. When God tells him that he will deliver his people from oppression, he protests his own unworthiness. In response, God gives him a sign that will overcome his self-doubt (Jos 6:16–18; cf. Ex 4:1–9). Then he is overcome with reverence at beholding the Lord's angel face to face (6:19–24; cf. Gn 32:31; cf. Ex 33:20). Gideon's willingness to reduce his troops to the barest minimum serves to glorify the Lord as the one who delivers his people (6:33–8:21). His refusal to become an established ruler over Israel serves as a warning to future monarchs that the Lord alone will always be the true king over Israel. "I will not rule you, neither will my son. Yahweh shall rule you" (8:23). Such sentiments cautioned Israel against excessive enthusiasm for kingship in future generations (cf. 1 Sm 8:7–8).

Samson, from the tribe of Dan in the south, differs in character from the other judges. He is a tragic hero whose personal story conveys a moral lesson. A magnificent narrative filled with divine revelation reminiscent of Moses' encounters with the Lord on Mount Sinai is devoted solely to his conception and birth (13:1–25; cf. Ex 3:13–14; 33:20). God endows this anointed deliverer with great physical strength and even courage, yet he lacks emotional stability and spiritual wisdom. Like Solomon of later years, involvement with foreign women proves to be his downfall (14:1–15:20; 16:1–3, 4–31; cf. 1 Kgs 11:1–8). Nevertheless, even after Delilah dupes him and his enemies capture him, the blind Samson brings down the temple of the foreign god Dagon and so illustrates the Lord's power to deliver Israel from the Philistines (16:21–31).

The concluding appendix to the book of Judges (17:1–21:25) indicates that the greatest threat to Israel's survival in the land would not arise from the other people who exerted pressure on her but from within the hearts of God's people themselves. The stories focusing on the tribes of Dan (17:1–18:31) and Benjamin (19:1–21:25) point out Israel's tendencies to become wayward when lacking a strong leader. Kingship seems to be the only remedy for Israel's lack of inward discipline. Hence, one theme echoes throughout this section, "In those days there was no king in Israel" (17:6; 18:1; 19:1; 21:25). Without one central authority, "everyone did as he saw fit" (17:6; 21:25), giving rise to the atrocities, division, and moral chaos that the Benjaminites typified (19:1–21:25). The book's conclusion offers evidence for Israel's need of one king who would be a savior such as the judges in Israel had only foreshadowed.

Toward the New Testament: Heralds of the Messiah

Neither Joshua nor Judges is quoted in the New Testament. Nevertheless, their heroes provide early images of John the Baptist, Mary, the mother of Jesus, and even of the Messiah.

Joshua is the namesake of Jesus (in Hebrew, *Jehoshua* means "Yahweh saves": Mt 1:21). The manner in which Joshua leads Israel into the Promised Land and mediates the renewal of the covenant between God and his people foreshadows how Jesus forms the new people of God through the ministry of his word and then establishes the new covenant in his blood on the night before he dies (Lk 19:47–48; 21:37–38; 22:14–23; Mk 14:22–24; Mt 26:26–28; 1 Cor 11:23–25).

The story of Samson's conception and birth (Jgs 13:1–25) contributes to the background for the infancy narrative of John the Baptist (Lk 1:5–25, 80; cf. 2:40, 52). Like Samson, John the Baptist is born to a woman unable to have children. Announcing his birth is an angel of the Lord, who appears to tell his parent that he must pledge a nazarite vow from his earliest days. As in the case of Samson, so for John the Baptist and Jesus: the infancy account concludes with mention of the child growing in the spirit of the Lord.

Mary, the mother of Jesus, is related to the great figures who were instrumental in bringing God's salvation to his people. The angel of the Lord greets her as he did Gideon (Jgs 6:12) with the declaration, "The Lord is with you!" (Lk 1:28). Elizabeth's acclamation to Mary echoes Deborah's reference to Jael as the "most blessed of women" (Jgs 5:24; Lk 1:42).

In the pages of Joshua and Judges, the Christian community found examples of the faith that brings salvation to God's people. Rahab, one of the four women mentioned in Matthew's genealogy, is a model of one who exercises her faith at the risk of her life (Jos 2:1–24; Mt 1:5; Heb 11:31; Jas 2:25). After his conversion, Paul was lowered down by rope from a window in the Damascus wall, much like the spies who had surveyed Jericho (Jos 2:15; Acts 9:25; 2 Cor 11:33). Gideon's obedience to the Lord in reducing his army to a ridiculously small number before defeating the Midianites (Jgs 7:1–25) taught Paul the paradoxical wisdom of the cross, that "God chose those who by human standards are fools to shame the wise; he chose those who by human standards are weak to shame the strong, those who by human standards are common and contemptible—indeed those who count for nothing—to reduce to nothing all those that do count for something so that no human being might feel boastful before God" (1 Cor 1:27–29).

STUDY QUESTIONS

1. Describe Canaanite life at the time the Israelites lived among the Canaanites.
2. How does the book of Joshua convey the Israelite conquest?
3. How does the book of Judges convey the Israelite settlement?
4. What are the three parts of the book of Joshua?
5. What is the importance theologically of the Israelites' entrance into the Promised Land?
6. How is Joshua the new Moses?
7. How are the military concepts in Joshua metaphors for the Babylonian exiles?
8. What are the three elements necessary for the victory of faith?
9. What was a "judge" in ancient Israel?
10. What are the three parts of the book of Judges?
11. How is the story of Samson's conception and birth related to the background for the infancy narrative of John the Baptist?
12. Modern technology has a tendency to distance people from one another. How do the books of Joshua and Judges guide us to develop a community of faith that is attractive to young people?

JOSHUA

JUDGES

15

1 AND 2 SAMUEL:
THE BEGINNINGS OF KINGSHIP:
SAMUEL, SAUL, AND DAVID

Without knowing it, perhaps you have experienced the drama of the books of Samuel (1 and 2 Sm) even if you were not particularly interested in the Old Testament. Just ask yourself, "What were the Bible stories that spoke to me as a child?" and "What stories cause me to reflect as an adult?" It is quite likely that in answer to the first question, David and Goliath will be close to the top of your list; and, in answer to the second question, David's sin with Bathsheba and his consequent desolation will soon come to mind. The stories in the books of Samuel get into our hearts and demand that we take them personally.

The books of Samuel are the greatest biographical work in the Hebrew Bible. They offer an intimate, sometimes firsthand, portrait of three chosen leaders: Samuel, Saul, and David. They describe events of their lives in such a way as to bare their souls. The events are almost always interpersonal encounters that unmask hidden dimensions of the personalities involved. The books of Samuel teach us that we shape our innermost character by the way we relate to one another. However, the greatest burden of our lives is not other people but ourselves. Our most painful experience is having to confront the darkness within us, which our contacts with others bring to light. Ultimately, the great figures in the books of Samuel do not deal with one another as much as with God.

The text heightens our sensitivity to the fact that every period of solitude, every meeting with another person, and every moment of decision are points when God encounters us personally and challenges us to grow in faith and in knowledge of him. Furthermore, the books of Samuel demonstrate that our knowledge of God is solely personal, that is, we do not know him from our head (where we seek control) but from the inner depths of our heart and spirit (where we pray and listen to God's word).

The Days of Samuel, David, and Saul

The books of Samuel span the critical juncture in Israel's existence, from the birth of Samuel to the last days of David (1080[?]–970 B.C.). They describe the great turning point that transformed Israel from a tribal association into a legitimate nation ruling its own territory. Here, within the same period, we come across both the beginning and the pinnacle of kingship in Israel. The kings of this period succeeded in uniting the twelve tribes as at no other time in the course of their history.

The Israelites' pathway toward nationhood advanced in three successive stages corresponding to the careers of its three great leaders. Under Samuel's leadership (1040–1020 B.C.), the system of a confederation of twelve tribes under the judges gave way to the model of one governor leading all the people. Samuel was remarkable for the fact that he exercised both spiritual and temporal offices at the same time. He was prophet and judge for all Israel (1 Sm 3:1–4:1; 7:2–17). He alone could anoint Israel's first kings, Saul and David (1 Sm 9:26–10:8; 16:1–13).

Saul (1030–1010 B.C.) seemingly came into prominence in the same manner as the judges of earlier days: by gaining a reputation as a military commander. In part, the force of circumstances propelled his career beyond that of any previous leader. A variety of hostile neighbors, including Philistines, Moabites, Ammonites, and Edomites, threatened Israel's tribes individually as they were scattered in isolation from each other across Canaan (1 Sm 14:47–52). The Israelites who advocated kingship were convinced that they needed one permanent leader to unite them in a common defense against their enemies who were pressing in on all fronts. Saul gained a reputation beyond the tribal borders of Benjamin when he led his army across the Jordan to defeat the Ammonites at Jabesh in Gilead (1 Sm 11:1–11). This feat won him the attention of other tribes and identified him as the popular choice for king. In fact, Saul was more a military commander than a monarch and relied on subsequent victories against Israel's foes to consolidate his position (1 Sm 14:47–52).

David (1010–970 B.C.) was Israel's first king in the strict sense of the term in that he was a ruler as well as a military commander. His rule extended over a whole territory that other peoples recognized as the kingdom of Israel, whereas Saul's influence had been limited to the tribes in the central highlands around Gibeah and across the Jordan in Gilead. David was the first to bring all Israel under one domain and establish a central administration to govern a national territory. He demonstrated cleverness in making Jerusalem, the former Jebusite stronghold, his capital since it was located between the northern and southern tribes without previous attachment to either side (2 Sm 5:6–12). David secured his borders with military victories against all the surrounding nations: Zobah, Damascus, and Hamath in the north; Moab, Ammon, and Edom across the Jordan in the east; and the Amalekites and Philistines on the fringes of Israel in the Canaanite territory (2 Sm 8:1–14). Internal discord in Egypt and Assyria throughout David's reign permitted him to lay the foundations upon which his son Solomon could build a genuine empire.

The Structure of 1 and 2 Samuel

We should read the two volumes of Samuel as one continuous book. The Septuagint (Greek) translation (after 250 B.C.) first separated the text into two parts. The Hebrew edition first appeared in a two-volume format much later, in A.D. 1517.

We can subdivide the complete text of Samuel according to the three figures who successively occupy center stage: (1) Samuel (1 Sm 1:1–12:24); (2) Saul (1 Sm 13:1–31:13); and (3) David (2 Sm 1:1–24:25).

We can see each of them in the context of the others. Samuel introduces us to the two rivals, Saul and David. He is the bridge between them and assures the transfer of kingship from Saul to David. We come to know Saul in the context of his negotiations with Samuel and his tortuous relationship with David. We come to know David in the context of his overshadowing the other two as the main character of the whole work. According to our present arrangement, we could call the whole of 2 Samuel the "Book of David" since it is entirely devoted to his reign, from his rise to power through to his later years.

This masterpiece went through a series of editions that knitted various stories together. We can detect at least six sources underlying the narrative: (1) the Samuel stories (1 Sm 1–12); (2) the Saul stories (1 Sm 8–31); (3) the stories of the ark (1 Sm 4–6; 2 Sm 6); (4) the stories of David's rise to power (1 Sm 16 to 2 Sm 5); (5) the story of David's family at the royal court (sometimes called the "Court History" or the "Succession Narrative": 2 Sm 9–20; 1 Kgs 1–2); and (6) the diverse stories in the appendix (2 Sm 21–24).

Scholars propose various complex theories about how the text passed through a series of editions to reach its present form. We will concentrate on the following contributions: (a) the original writers who composed the sources during the reign of Solomon (970–931 B.C.); and (b) the two generations of Deuteronomists, the first being those who directed this work to the spiritual needs of Judah during the time of renewal under Josiah (622–609 B.C.) and the second being the people who produced the final edition of this book as part of the Deuteronomic History in the middle of the Babylonian exile (550 B.C.). We should keep in mind that the prophetic circles in the northern kingdom beginning with Elijah and Elisha significantly affected the work's transmission.

Particularly important is the contribution of the literary master who wrote the Court History that extends into the first two chapters of Kings (2 Sm 9–20; I Kgs I–2).

Themes in Samuel

The text of Samuel reveals the complexities and inconsistencies in human nature that the most powerful of us experience in vacillating between dignity and degradation, courage and cowardice, righteousness and remorse. We will focus on three themes in the narrative: (a) family life; (b) personal integrity and repentance; and (c) kingship and prophecy.

Family Life

The books of Samuel and Genesis share an emphasis on marriage and family life more than any other texts of biblical narrative. Their common concern derives in part from the likelihood that the Yahwist and the author of the Court History (2 Sm 9–20; I Kgs I–2) were contemporaries in Jerusalem during Solomon's rule (970–931 B.C.). They saw the tragic condition of family life even within the royal household, and they devoted themselves to discerning God's intentions for home life (2 Sm 9–20; cf. I Kgs II:I–I3). In addition, we should note a third circle of scholars, namely, the sages in the academies, who worked under Solomon's patronage and also expressed a concern for the quality of relationships within families (Prv 10:1–22:16: cf. 13:1; 15:5; 17:25).

Because the Samuel literature is so complex, we will consider all three categories of relationships within family life, namely, those between (a) parents and their children; (b) husbands and wives; and (c) brothers and sisters.

A. Parents and Children: Samuel offers a number of dramatic family portraits that invite comparison with each other. The very first lines of the book draw us into the marriage relationship between Elkanah and Hannah prior to the birth of Samuel. The atmosphere is charged with deep emotional tension because Hannah is barren and Elkanah's other wife Peninnah taunts her. The whole scene recalls the home life of Abraham and Sarah, suggesting that Samuel's birth will be a new beginning in the history of God's people just as Isaac's birth had been (I Sm 1:1–8; cf. Gn 16:1–5).

New life for Israel begins with humble prayer. In this story, Hannah, the barren woman, is closer to the Lord than the priest Eli is at the sanctuary. Eli's dullness is a symptom of the spiritual fog hanging over the whole people (1 Sm 1:9–18). Once Hannah gives birth to Samuel, she fully dedicates him to the Lord's service (1 Sm 1:19–2:11). Her success stands in marked contrast to Eli's failure as a parent to teach his sons proper devotion. Both of Eli's sons are a scandal to the priesthood from the beginning, in spite of their father's futile appeals for them to reform (1 Sm 2:12–17, 22–25, 27–36).

Unfortunately, as parents, both Samuel and David share Eli's faults instead of Hannah's virtues. The corruption of Samuel's sons is so deep that the people demand a king to succeed him (1 Sm 8:1–5).

David is astonishingly inept at correcting the faults of his children once he establishes them as the royal family in Jerusalem. He is reluctant to admonish Amnon, his eldest son and heir-apparent, after he rapes his half-sister Tamar (2 Sm 13:1–22). The passivity of David contributes to his son Absalom's rage, which provokes him to have Amnon murdered (2 Sm 13:23–37). Finally, when Absalom leads a revolution deposing his father from the throne in Jerusalem and then chases him into the Transjordan, the cycle of family violence and turmoil reaches a crescendo (2 Sm 15:1–17:29). With rape-incest, fratricide, and insurrection seething through its corridors, the royal household becomes a chaotic network of intrigue and conspiracy. The lowest point in David's life occurs when he receives news that his troops have killed Absalom (2 Sm 18:19–32). David could not be king and father at the same time. At the news of Absalom's death, David the king did not celebrate reclaiming his kingship: David the father had to mourn. Instead of the shout of victory, the anguished lament for a lost son issues from the heart of David for all the world to hear (2 Sm 19:1–9).

Paradoxically, the most unstable of the three principal figures has the most noble son. Saul's son Jonathan stands out from all the other offspring mentioned in 1 and 2 Samuel. Jonathan's integrity does not come from his father's influence. This young man cultivated a nobility of soul in spite of his father, who looked upon him as a threat and a rival (1 Sm 14:40–45; 20:30–34). Saul attempted to use his children to control David and thereby forfeited the loyalty of both Jonathan and Michal, his daughter, to his archrival David (1 Sm 18:20–27; 19:1–17; 20:1–21:1).

B. *Husbands and Wives:* The text of Samuel highlights the relationship between parents and their children more than between husbands and wives. It does not tell us about the marriages of Eli, Samuel, or Saul. However, we do hear of David's marriages to Abigail (1 Sm 25:1–42) and Michal (1 Sm 18:20–27; 19:11–27; 2 Sm 6:16–23), but more especially to Bathsheba (2 Sm 11:1–27; 12:16–25; 1 Kgs 1:11–37), since the latter plays a pivotal role in the narrative.

At the conception of Samuel, the narrative presents the relationship between Elkanah and Hannah as the model for genuine family life, which originates in the union of husband, wife, and the Lord (1 Sm 1:19). Hannah's prayer not only opens the way for her to conceive Samuel but also heals her relationship with her husband.

David's wives lack Hannah's character. Michal's father Saul intrudes upon the genuine love she has for David in the early days of their marriage (1 Sm 18:20–30; 19:11–17). Saul takes her from David and passes her to another (1 Sm 25:44). After David regains Michal, strangely enough, she begins reflecting her father's contempt for David's popularity (2 Sm 3:13–16; 6:16–23).

We learn that violation of the marriage covenant destroys family life by seeing the history of the royal family after David defiles the union of Bathsheba and Uriah, a marriage suffused with genuine love according to Nathan's parable (2 Sm 12:1–4). Once David attempts to cover up his affair by having the noble Uriah killed in battle, the forces of passion leading to death begin to sweep through his family. We see no sign of corruption in David's children until after his affair with Bathsheba. By his manner of arranging the story, the author of the Court History wants to show us that a disordered relationship in a marriage pollutes even the most important of families (2 Sm 12:11–12; cf. 13:1–20:26).

C. Brothers and Sisters: Throughout the books of Samuel, we see families ravaged by jealousy and ambition. The descriptions of the sons of Eli and of Samuel suggest that cooperation between these brothers occurs more often in a conspiracy to commit evil than in an alliance intent on righteousness (1 Sm 2:12–17, 32–34; 4:4, 11; 8:1–3). In David's family, brother violates sister and brother kills brother (2 Sm 13:1–37). Throughout the narrative, tensions between blood relatives generate an atmosphere of suspicion and violence that fills the world.

The evidence forces us to ask, "Is brotherhood possible?" and "Where is there hope for unity between people?" Both questions find their response in the bond between David and Jonathan. They enter into a covenant of friendship based on their personal determination to act righteously in the face of Saul's treachery (1 Sm 18:1–4). This brotherhood is deeper than blood because it is rooted in God's purposes for their individual lives and for the world. Such brotherhood matures when Jonathan demonstrates covenant loyalty at the risk of his life and reputation (1 Sm 19:1–7; 20:1–42; 23:15–18). David's later life bears out the truth he expresses in grieving over Jonathan's death: covenanted brotherhood with Jonathan proves to be more genuine to him than his marriage relationships (2 Sm 1:26).

Personal Integrity and Repentance

The text of Samuel encourages us to contemplate the figures of Saul and David in light of one another so we can understand how to respond to God. The careers of Saul and David exhibit many parallels: (a) just before being designated leader of the people, each is tending his father's livestock (1 Sm 9:1–10; 16:1–13); (b) Samuel anoints each of them after receiving interior guidance from the Lord (1 Sm 9:11–10:8; 16:1–13); (c) in the earliest days of their reign, each of them conducts successful military campaigns beyond Israel's borders (1 Sm 11:1–11; 2 Sm 5:6–12, 17–25; 8:1–14; 10:6–19); (d) at the height of their success, each of them sins against the Lord (1 Sm 13:8–15; 15:1–9; cf. 14:31–35; 2 Sm 11:1–27); (e) a prophet confronts each of them with God's word in response to their sin (1 Sm 15:10–23; 2 Sm 12:1–12); and (f) after their sin, their lives are marked by personal turmoil and alienation from their children (1 Sm 18:6–31:13; 2 Sm 13:1–20:26).

By no means do these parallels suggest that Saul and David are equals. To the contrary, they serve to pinpoint exactly what makes David far superior to Saul. It is not a matter of human talent; both were gifted men. It is not a matter of personal virtue; both men sinned. It has everything to do with their relationship to God. David took confidence in the Lord's anointing, and he accepted the Lord's mercy, while Saul never really put his trust in God.

Look at the way each of them reacts to his sin, and you will find a key to the underlying difference in their make-up. Saul sins by allowing his people to take plunder from the Amalekites instead of consigning it all to the Lord (1 Sm 15:7–9). When Samuel confronts him, Saul acknowledges that he acted to curry human respect and trespassed the Lord's commands because he feared the people (1 Sm 15:24). However, Saul's deepest personal failure does not consist in his act of sinning but rather in his refusal to uproot sin from his life. He admits his sin but does not repent (1 Sm 15:30). Self-preoccupation prevents him from grounding his life in God through repentance. His primary concern is that Samuel not cause him to lose face in the sight of Israel's important people. His religion remains a pretense that Samuel unmasks. He even says to Samuel in reference to the Lord "your God" as if to imply that he himself has no personal relationship to the One whom Samuel worships (1 Sm 15:10–31).

In the early days, Samuel was suspicious that Saul's character was flawed by a weak self-image that made him easily swayed by the opinion of others (1 Sm 9:21; 15:17–18). God offers Saul a moment of grace when Samuel confronts his weakness (1 Sm 15:16–31). When Saul neglects the invitation to repent deeply, his sin releases a power within him ("an evil spirit") that eventually destroys his sense of God, wounds his family, and brings about his death (1 Sm 16:14-15). He exhibits dramatic mood swings indicative of a personality increasingly dominated by depression and paranoia, the fruit of brooding over rather than repenting of past sin and failure (1 Sm 16:23; 18:8-16, 28-30; 19:8-17; 28:3-25; cf. 31:4).

By contrast, when the prophet Nathan confronts David with his sin with Bathsheba, the king confesses his sin and yields himself to the Lord in prayer and fasting. When the child conceived by the unholy union dies, David draws closer to the Lord, worshipping him in the sanctuary, and then serves the Lord as best he can (2 Sm 12:1-25). The Lord brings good out of human evil: Bathsheba's next child will be David's heir, Solomon. Although David's sin unleashes the forces of violence within his home, David himself remains humble, accepting his dismissal from Jerusalem as a chastisement and persevering in prayer to the end of his life (2 Sm 16:5-14; 22:1-51 = Ps 18). Thus, he is able to designate Solomon to succeed him (1 Kgs 1:11-40; cf. 2 Sm 12:24-25).

In his early days, David learns integrity by dealing with Saul's psychoses. The saga of the two men begins with them together in the same room, the young musician ministering to the king, trying to lift him out of his morose introspection (1 Sm 16:14-23). However, the "evil spirit" (16:14; 18:10; 19:9) cultivated by Saul's brooding quickly drives them apart, one heading toward unbelief and death and the other aiming toward faith and life. Whenever their paths cross, they are alone in each other's presence and one of them is faced with the temptation to kill the other. Invariably, Saul succumbs and makes an attempt on David's life (19:8-10; 18:11-12), while David renounces the opportunity and instead extends protection to the king (24:1-8; 26:1-12).

From the beginning, David joins himself to the Lord from the heart (1 Sm 16:7, 13; 17:37). He trusts God enough to lay down his life for his people, and so he wins the victory over Goliath (1 Sm 17:45-51). When Saul makes him an outcast and counts him an enemy of the people, David upholds the dignity of Saul, to the point of risking his life in reverential deference to him as "Yahweh's anointed" and "father" (24:7-23; 26:8-23). In his days as a fugitive, David is the model of one who is falsely accused and must suffer for his fidelity to the Lord.

Saul's desperate rampage in pursuit of David sets him on the road to personal destruction. First, he loses sight of Israel's welfare by resenting David's success instead of rejoicing over the Philistines' defeat (18:6-16; 19:8-10). Then, his jealousy of his children's affections for David alienates him from his son Jonathan and then his daughter Michal, each of whom preserves David's life by securing his escape from their father's designs (18:1-5; 19:1-7, 11-17; 20:1-43). Finally, he alienates himself from the Lord by losing a sense of all that is sacred. So atrocious is his massacre of the priests of Nob that even his most loyal soldiers refuse to obey his orders, leaving only a mercenary from the ranks of Israel's enemies, Doeg the Edomite, to carry them out (22:6–23). Now he hears only deathly silence from the Lord. In desperation for guidance, Saul trespasses the very laws he had imposed on the land and consults a necromancer, the witch at En-Dor (28:3–25; cf. Dt 18:9–12). From the other side of death, Saul hears the word of God spoken by his faithful prophet Samuel, telling him once again of the Lord's election of David and foretelling Saul's defeat at the hands of the Philistines (28:16–19). In the end, it is tragically fitting that Saul delivers his own death blow, impaling himself on his sword (31:4). Yet we may detect providential mercy toward him in the reverence with which the people of Jabesh in Gilead bury him (31:11–13).

The stories of Saul and David were particularly applicable to the Jews who were suffering the humiliation of exile in Babylon. Twice in Deutero-Isaiah, we note the prophet referring to the identity crisis of the exiles in terms of their lack of self-worth (Is 40:27; 49:13–16). In presenting the stories of David and Saul to the exiles, the Deuteronomists were addressing the issue of the peoples' self-understanding. They proposed David as the model for the exiles as one who seeks the Lord, appreciates the grace of election, remains steadfast under persecution, and repents of sin. For all of its trials and afflictions, life in Babylon offered Judah the opportunity to grow into the stature of David. If they remained burdened by insecurity and introspection, the exiles would be vulnerable to the deeper forces of self-destruction that Saul exhibited.

Kingship and Prophecy

In every era of Israel's history, the people asked how they could maintain some form of stability from one generation to the next. The strongest voices among Samuel's contemporaries were convinced that kingship was the only remedy for the turbulence characterizing Israel's history in the Promised Land (1 Sm 8:1–5). Samuel was not totally convinced and neither were the Deuteronomists in Israel's later history that kingship was the only remedy (cf. 1 Sm 8:7–9, 10–18).

Did Israel really need a king in order to survive? The issue generated heated debate not only in Samuel's day (1050 B.C.) but also throughout the duration of the northern kingdom (930–721 B.C.) and in Judah's exile in Babylon (587–538 B.C.). In the northern kingdom, the monarchy was a source of instability as one dynasty overthrew another to take the throne. In the Exile, the future of the Davidic line seemed doubtful because it depended on the weak Jehoiachin, who was released from prison in 561 B.C. (2 Kgs 25:27–30). We have already noted that the Deuteronomic tradition originated in the northern kingdom. The Deuteronomists who produced the final edition of Samuel around 550 B.C. intended their reflections on kingship to offer the people a perspective for interpreting God's designs in their own situation.

The books of Samuel offer an ambiguous evaluation of kingship. The Deuteronomists preserved alongside one another texts from contrasting sources that alternately favor the monarchy (1 Sm 9:1–10:16; 11:1–15) and oppose it (1 Sm 7:2–8:22; 10:17–27; 12:17–24). Samuel is the spokesman for the Deuteronomists who oppose it (1 Sm 8:1–22; 12:17–24). In order for Israel to gain control of her destiny, she does not need kingship but rather obedience to the first commandment, which she demonstrates by renouncing all vestiges of idolatry (1 Sm 7:2–4; cf. Dt 6:13–15). Insofar as Israel desires kingship in order to be "like the other nations", she is sinning against the Lord by renouncing her election as a nation set apart and refusing to allow the Lord to be her true king (1 Sm 8:1–9; 12:12). Israel will survive on the condition that both the people and the king submit themselves to God's word (1 Sm 12:14–15; cf. Dt 17:14–20). In summary, the Deuteronomists admitted the monarchy might have been a historical necessity but, at the same time, suggested that it threatened the integrity of Israel's faith.

God guarantees the survival of his people through prophets who direct the king in the path of the Lord. He governs history by means of his anointed word rather than through human authority. We see this truth demonstrated throughout the lives of the great figures. Samuel is distinguished by the fact that when Israel is in a deep spiritual vacuum, he receives the Lord's word and proclaims it to his people (1 Sm 3:20–4:1; 7:2–12; 8:1–22; 12:1–24).

The king might exercise some dominion over the people, but the prophet must exercise the authority of God's word over the king. The cases of both Saul and David show the prophet anointing the king (1 Sm 10:1; 16:13). The prophet discerns the heart of the king and must confront him when he sins. Whether the king accepts or rejects the message, God's word that the prophet speaks determines the course of history (1 Sm 13:14; 15:28; 28:15–19; 2 Sm 12:11–12). The prophet works also to protect the people against the excesses and abuses of the king (1 Sm 8:1–22; 12:1–24).

While the Deuteronomists soberly evaluate kingship in general, they enthusiastically support David and his line in particular. Through his prophet Nathan, God enters into an eternal covenant with David and his descendants (2 Sm 7:1–17; 23:5). David's kingship provides not just a replacement for Saul's but rather a whole new order of service in the Lord's plan. David's vocation consists, not in accomplishing a human work, but in responding to a divine calling. The prophecy develops out of a play on words. Instead of David's building the Lord a wooden "house" (the Temple), the Lord will make of David an "everlasting house" (a royal descendance). The Lord's adoption of

David's son as his own will resound through the Temple at the enthronement ceremony of each successive king (2 Sm 7:14; cf. Ps 2:7).

Nathan's prophecy is a pinnacle of revelation as a fulfillment of the past and a promise for the future. The Lord's covenant with David brings to a climax the series of covenants he made in the Pentateuch, first with Noah (Gn 9:1–17), then with Abraham (Gn 17:1–27), and finally with all Israel at Mount Sinai (Ex 19:1–24:11; cf. 34:1–28). We recall that the Israelites renewed the Sinai covenant at Shechem after they entered the Promised Land under Joshua (Jos 24:1–28). Up to this point, the Deuteronomic presentation has shown how Israel broke the Sinai covenant throughout her history in the land (Jgs 2:6–3:6). Now, in the covenant with David, Israel receives new hope from the fact that this covenant resembles the Lord's pact with Abraham more than the one with the people at Sinai. At Sinai, the Lord stipulated conditions; with Abraham and with David, his covenant is unconditional. The Davidic covenant is one of promise that guarantees fulfillment solely because God is faithful. As for Abraham so for David, the Lord's promise focuses on a descendance that will become a source of life for all his people.

In her worship, Israel expresses her hopes based on the Lord's covenant promise to David (Pss 89:20–37; 132:11–12). Even in the Exile, with the Temple destroyed and the Davidic line fading from view, she receives direction by questioning the Lord's ways in light of his promise to David (Ps 89:38–52). In 550 B.C., the Deuteronomists wanted their people to hear that they were the generation whom the Lord was going to establish in the Promised Land (2 Sm 7:9–11). One question remained. The physical line of Davidic kings was dying out in the Exile. How would God fulfill his promise concerning David's son? God uses this most disturbing question to lift his people's minds from an earthbound horizon in search of the true Messiah who would come from heaven. As David had returned in triumph to Jerusalem, so would the exiles and ultimately the Messiah.

Toward the New Testament: The Son of David

The infancy narrative of Samuel (1 Sm 1:1–2:11) is a partial backdrop for Luke's account of the annunciation to Mary. Hannah's song of praise in the sanctuary at Shiloh is the forerunner of Mary's Magnificat (Lk 1:46–55; cf. 1 Sm 2:1–10). Hannah's psalm is an introductory acclamation directing our attention to David, the "Anointed" (Hebrew: *Messiah*) of the Lord (1 Sm 2:10). The manner in which the Lord lifts Hannah from her low estate of barrenness to give birth to Samuel is a prophetic indication of how he would raise David from his humble origins to lead all Israel. By echoing Hannah's song, Mary's hymn reveals God working again among the humble to bring forth the true son of David who would fulfill all his promises to Abraham and those who followed after him (see Lk 1:32–33; cf. 2 Sm 7:12–16).

The Deuteronomists perceived that God fulfilled Nathan's prophecy to David in every successive king who ascended to the throne in Jerusalem from Solomon on. However, in our next chapter (on the books of Kings), we will see that few of those kings approached and none surpassed the standard of kingship that David set. The Lord was faithful in treating each of them as his "son" in the sense that he protected them and preserved them in spite of their folly and imprudence. The Deuteronomists never thought that anyone could surpass David in terms of his union with God. This indicates the unique quality of Jesus as Son of David, which the New Testament authors reveal. He is David's "son", not as an inferior descendant but as the superior fulfillment. David's identity is fulfilled in Christ. In Jesus, God fulfills his promise to David in an all-surpassing manner. David is not the standard but only the foreshadowing for Christ. Jesus insists on this point when he astonishes the scribes by saying that David points beyond himself to one who is even greater (Mk 12:35–37; cf. Ps 110:1; cf. 2 Sm 7:9–11). The early apostles proclaim the superiority of Jesus to David in light of his Resurrection from the dead (Acts 2:30; cf. Rom 1:3–4).

Jesus fulfills Nathan's prophecy by bursting the limits that our minds place around sonship. The people acclaimed the kings of Judah as God's adopted sons (Ps 2:6–7; cf. 2 Sm 7:14). However, when God applies this title to Jesus, he reveals him to possess a status and an identity superior even to that of the angels (Heb 1:1–14). The various and fragmentary ways God spoke to us in the past serve only to highlight the supremacy of his speaking to us now in his Son. Jesus, the risen Christ, is God's Son, not by adoption, but by essence from the very core of his being. The central theme of the Gospel of John is the revelation of Jesus as the divine Son in this sense (Jn 20:30–31; 10:30).

Returning to the books of Samuel, we discern a foreshadowing of Christ in David's sufferings as we consider David's afflictions at the hands of Absalom. David and Jesus follow the same path, have similar types of friends, and bear the same title. When David flees Jerusalem, he passes eastward down through the Kidron valley and up the slope of the Mount of Olives, weeping in grief-filled prayer (2 Sm 15:23, 30–31). Jesus takes the same route until he finds his destination on the Mount of Olives, where he expresses his suffering in prayer (Jn 18:1; Lk 22:39–46). As Ittai of Gath insists that he will remain loyal to David in face of all trials, so does Peter assert to Jesus (2 Sm 15:19–22; cf. Mk 14:27–31; Mt 26:30–35; Lk 22:31–34; Jn 13:36–38). David's adviser Ahithophel conspires against his master and then later hangs himself, presaging the later course of Judas (2 Sm 15:12, 31; 16:15, 20–23; 17:23; cf. Mt 27:3–10).

Besides all this, we must contemplate the resemblance between David and Jesus in the context of what "King of the Jews" means, a concept that dominates the scenes of both Jesus' trial and crucifixion (see Jn 18:28–19:22; Mk 15:16–20, 25, 32; Mt 27:11–14, 27–44). Similarly, we can depict David's triumphant return to Jerusalem as a foretaste of Jesus' victorious post-Resurrection appearances in the holy city (2 Sm 19:10–44; Lk 24:1–49; Acts 1:1–11).

The exiles in Babylon drew inspiration from David's return to Jerusalem because it encouraged them in their hope of returning as well. David's journey is the first biblical portrait suggesting that the fulfillment of our life consists in a return to Jerusalem. As David's triumphant return presented an ideal to inspire the exiles in Babylon, so it presents a vision for all who look toward the heavenly Jerusalem as the goal of their lives (see Rv 21:1–22:5).

Paul applies to Christians Nathan's prophecy of eternal covenant with David in order to illustrate what makes them distinct from pagans. By his own free decision fulfilled in the outpouring of the Holy Spirit, God has adopted us as his sons and daughters and has made himself known to us as "Father" (2 Cor 6:18; Gal 4:4–6; cf. 2 Sm 7:14). By applying Nathan's prophecy to Christians, Paul indicates that God has bestowed on us a royal dignity. The prophecy emphasizes the responsibility that accompanies regal status in the eyes of God. Because they constitute a kingly people, those who have received the Spirit of Christ must exercise spiritual authority over their lives and over their environment by freeing themselves from wrongful attachment to a world that is insensitive to the holiness of God (2 Cor 6:11–7:1).

The portraits of Saul and David respectively in 1 Samuel provide us with the substance for a meditation on the difference between the "old self" and the "new self" in the Pauline tradition of the Gospel. God's divine action in baptism consists in destroying ("crucifying") the false egocentric self so as to bring forth our new self, which is transformed by participating in the risen life of Christ (Rom 6:6; Col 3:9–10). In Saul, we find a compelling illustration of our old self-life, which is "corrupted by following illusory desires" (Eph 4:22). We can all identify with the tendencies of Saul as he fell into deeper bondage to insecurity, rationalization, fear, anger, and jealousy, leading him down the path to self-destruction. The Good News consists in the fact that God has set us free from this nature through the power of Christ's cross applied to our lives. Now, we can clothe ourselves in the nature illustrated by the young David. He is the one whose desires conform to the Lord's own heart as he refuses to harm his adversary and, instead, consistently chooses to revere him (1 Sm 13:14; 24:1–23; 26:1–25; cf. Mt 5:43–48; Lk 6:27–36).

In Christ, we have put on the new self in union with our brothers and sisters in the Church so that, by responding to the indwelling Spirit, we can be renewed in the spirit of our minds "in the uprightness and holiness of the truth" (Eph 4:23–24). Consider how God, in Christ, works this marvelous exchange in us, replacing the character of the old Saul with that of the young David. Paul describes this as the reality of God's activity in the life of every Christian when he says, "I have been crucified with Christ and yet I am alive; yet it is no longer I, but Christ living in me. The life that I am now living, subject to the limitation of human nature, I am living in faith, faith in the Son of God who loved me and gave himself for me" (Gal 2:19–20).

The books of Samuel teach us that human beings relate to others with justice insofar as they heed the prophetic word. People exercise authority properly to the degree that they first submit to God in trust and obedience. We will see that the books of Kings illustrate the devastating consequences of a lack of submission to God on the part of the leaders and their people.

STUDY QUESTIONS

1. Contrast Hannah and Eli as models of parenthood.
2. How does David's affair with Bathsheba affect his family life?
3. What are the parallels in Saul's and David's careers?
4. What is Saul's "evil spirit"?
5. Describe the ambivalence toward kingship in the books of Samuel.
6. How is Nathan's prophecy a pinnacle of revelation?
7. How does the Davidic covenant more closely resemble the covenant with Abraham than the one at Sinai?
8. How is David's identity fulfilled in Christ?
9. Compare Saul and David with the old life and the new life in Christ.
10. Discuss the role of leadership in government, in the church, in schools, in the family. Do you see how the quality of the leader in each institution affects everyone who follows him or her? How would you rate your leadership in your: (a) family, (b) work, (c) community, (d) church? What are your strengths and weaknesses? How has the quality of your leadership affected those whom you lead and with whom you interact? Do you see areas for improvement? What relationship does your prayer life have to making you a better leader?
11. Why do you think God had such a special relationship with David considering the enormity of his sin with Bathsheba and his role in Uriah's death? Read Psalm 51, which was composed after the Exile (51:18–19; cf. Is 60–62) but which the editor applied to David by inserting the subheading "Of David". According to the editor of the psalm, how did David view his own sin? How do you see your relationship to God when you sin?
12. What do the books of Samuel tell you about how God is going to renew the Church in this generation and in the next generations? How does the Lord raise people who are capable of hearing his word?

1 AND 2 SAMUEL

1 AND 2 KINGS: FROM SOLOMON TO THE EXILE

Nothing is constant in world politics. Every month we hear news of developments on the international scene that affect large portions of the world's population. Daily fluctuations in the stock markets reflect the rapidity of change in our world. People try to predict trends, but almost no one with any credibility suggests he or she can foresee even the major changes that lie ahead in the next five years. In a rapidly changing world, we are forced to search for the ultimate ground of history by trying to uncover the constants at the root of all developments.

Are there any absolute principles that undergird our history? With wisdom and prayer, the Deuteronomists labored for generations to answer this question for God's people. By personal conviction, they were certain that the Deuteronomic legislation contained the key to unlock the meaning of Israel's history. They probably formulated their hypothesis on the basis of spiritual conviction, but they had to look into the hard evidence of Israel's past in order to demonstrate their case.

The Deuteronomists researched a wide range of sources in their endeavor to show the unity and meaningfulness of Israel's history. They consulted the palace archives, the Temple archives, and the prophetic traditions extending over centuries. The materials from the royal archives covered over four hundred years of the monarchy after David and included the "Annals of Solomon" (1 Kgs 11:41), the "Annals of the Kings of Judah" (1 Kgs 15:7), and the "Annals of the Kings of Israel" (1 Kgs 15:32). They sorted through the Temple archives, looking at building designs (1 Kgs 6–7), noting when money was withdrawn from the treasury (1 Kgs 15:18), identifying whenever someone removed the precious materials used for decoration or liturgy (2 Kgs 18:15–16), and pinpointing major alterations affecting worship (2 Kgs 16:10–18). Furthermore, the Deuteronomists collected the traditions of the prophets, notably Elijah and Elisha (1 Kgs 17 to 2 Kgs 13), but also including others, from Ahijah of Shiloh to Micaiah ben Imlah, down to the great Isaiah in Jerusalem (1 Kgs 11:27–39; 22:1–28; 2 Kgs 19–20).

The books of Kings represent the result of the massive research project that the Deuteronomists undertook. Kings offers us not so much a chronicle of the succession of monarchies as an illustration of the specific principles by which God relates to his people throughout the course of history. These principles can speak to our situation in a manner similar to that of the original audiences whom the Deuteronomists were addressing.

We should read the books of Kings as a unit as we suggested for reading the books of Samuel. In fact, the books of Samuel and of Kings blend into each other and overlap in sequence, one after another. (The Septuagint tradition recognizes their cohesiveness by designating them as 1–4 Kingdoms.)

We can discern two editions of the text that point to the two audiences — separated by over half a century — to whom the Deuteronomists were addressing their work. It seems that the Deuteronomists completed the first edition in Jerusalem during the reign of Josiah after the scroll of Deuteronomy was discovered in the Temple storeroom in 622 B.C. (2 Kgs 22:3–10). This text included the vast majority of material now in our present edition up to the end of Josiah's reign (1 Kgs 1:1 to 2 Kgs 23:30). The Deuteronomists of Josiah's time highlighted the important role their king played in God's plan for his people (1 Kgs 13:2; 2 Kgs 23:25). However, it remained for another generation of Deuteronomists to complete the work. The anointed scribes who brought the whole Deuteronomic compendium (the foundational Deuteronomy and Joshua to 2 Kings) to completion in Babylon around 550 B.C. gave the work its ultimate shape and added the final chapters covering the period between the death of Josiah and the release of Jehoiachin (2 Kgs 23:31–25:30). After the Exile, during the Persian era, a scribe inserted a few additions into the text (e.g., 1 Kgs 5:4–5; 8:41–51).

The Deuteronomists were confident that they had discovered the principles of God's action that were valid for all the excesses of history, from the heights of success to the depths of failure. We gain this impression from the fact that the two audiences who received the successive editions were in extremely different circumstances compared to each another. The Deuteronomists of Josiah's time were encouraging the people of Judah to celebrate their days of freedom from Assyrian tyranny and religious renewal throughout the land. By contrast, the Deuteronomists of the Exile were addressing a broken and humiliated people who had been uprooted to a foreign land. The Deuteronomic tradition spoke the same message to both generations of God's people, inviting them to learn from their history so they would not have to repeat the errors of their ancestors.

The Historical Background (970–561 B.C.)

The books of Kings cover more than four centuries of history, from Solomon's rise to power (970 B.C./1 Kgs 1:1–2:46) until Jehoiachin's release from prison in Babylon (561 B.C./2 Kgs 25:27–30). The text divides this era into three periods: (1) the reign of Solomon (970–931 B.C./1 Kgs 1:1–11:43); (2) the era of the divided kingdom from the death of Solomon to the destruction of Samaria, the capital of the north (931–721 B.C./1 Kgs 12:1 to 2 Kgs 17:41); and (3) the kingdom of Judah from the fall of Samaria through the destruction of Jerusalem to Jehoiachin's pardon by the king of Babylon (721–561 B.C./2 Kgs 18:1–25:30).

David, Solomon's father, appointed him to the throne, but he had to take ruthless action against his half-brother Adonijah and his supporters in order to secure his position (1 Kgs 1:1–2:46). While he lacked the military prowess of his father, Solomon was a skilled administrator and diplomat. He opened up international trade with Arabia for spices, with Cilicia for horses, and with the coast of east Africa for ivory. Solomon transformed Jerusalem into a cosmopolitan center of culture. He established an academy where sages could teach young diplomats (Prv 10:1–22:16). Liturgists composed psalms, poets wrote masterpieces for the royal weddings (Ps 45; Sg 3:6–11), a court scribe penned the story of David's royal family in Jerusalem (2 Sm 9–20), and the Yahwist wrote the first history of the people from creation to the death of Moses. The construction of the Temple and royal palace occupied center stage and reflected the growing stature of Israel as a nation to be reckoned with on the international scene.

Solomon did not die beloved by all the people. His concern for status abroad alienated him from the common folk, who also served in forced labor crews to complete his ambitious building projects (1 Kgs 5:27). Even before Solomon's death, Jeroboam, a crew foreman, was marshaling the support of his laborers from the northern tribes for a revolt (1 Kgs 11:26–40). When Solomon's son and heir, Rehoboam, offered no promise of lifting the burden of oppression that his father had imposed, the northern ten tribes united under Jeroboam's leadership and declared their independence from Judah and Benjamin (1 Kgs 12:1–25). The ten northern tribes called themselves "Israel", while the two southern tribes were known as "Judah". Jeroboam established his capital first at Shechem and later at Tirzah. Around 880 B.C., Omri made Samaria the royal city (1 Kgs 16:23–28), and it remained the capital of Israel until the Assyrians seized it as they overran the whole territory in 721 B.C. One of Jeroboam's first initiatives was the construction of sanctuaries at Dan to the north and Bethel to the south to eliminate the need for his people to go to the Temple in Jerusalem for worship (1 Kgs 12:26–33).

Because Jeroboam was not from the royal household, there never was a Davidic lineage of kings ruling Israel (the ten northern tribes) during the two centuries of the divided kingdom. In fact, there was really no lineage of any kind that lasted more than four generations. Kingship was a very unstable institution in the north as only in the cases of five rulers did succession go to their sons or grandsons (Jeroboam I, Baasha, Omri, Jehu, and Menahem), and only two families could be called dynasties (the House of Omri [876–842 B.C.] and the House of Jehu [842–745 B.C.]). Insurrection and revolution were the order of the day as rulers from nine different families seized the throne at one time or another over the course of two centuries. By comparison, the history of kingship in Judah was miraculous if for no other reason than that the Davidic line remained intact throughout the duration of the southern kingdom and into the Exile (587–561 B.C.).

Throughout the existence of the divided kingdom, Israel and Judah exhibited a love-hate relationship typical of unreconciled siblings. They attacked one another at the beginning of the period (c. 900 B.C./1 Kgs 15:7, 16–22) and again toward the end (c. 785 B.C./2 Kgs 14:12; and c. 735 B.C./2 Kgs 16:5 [the Syro-Ephraimite war]). By contrast, in the intervening period, they formed alliances to protect their mutual interests in the Transjordan (c. 853 B.C./1 Kgs 22:8–23) and to maintain their control over Moab (c. 845 B.C./2 Kgs 3:6–8).

On the international scene throughout the period, Israel and Judah were mostly preoccupied with developments in Mesopotamia. It is true that around 918 B.C., Pharaoh Shishak invaded Palestine and Syria with great ferocity and plundered from the Temple treasury (1 Kgs 14:25–28). Nevertheless, after that time, the main threat came from the east. In 853 B.C. in the battle of Kharkah on the Orontes River in Syria, a coalition of kingdoms from the Mediterranean coast, including Judah and Israel, formed an alliance and engaged the Assyrian forces of Shalmaneser III (859–825 B.C.) in an important but inconclusive battle. However, in 841 B.C., the Assyrians again invaded, defeated Damascus, and exacted tribute from Israel. These were only faint premonitions of the cataclysm to come a century later. In the autumn of 721 B.C., after a three-year occupation of the land, the Assyrian troops, first under Shalmaneser V (726–722 B.C.) and then under Sargon II (721–705 B.C.), conquered Israel, seized its capital Samaria, and deported its leading figures into captivity in the east. The ten northern tribes would never again be recognizable as a distinctive entity (2 Kgs 17:1–41; 18:9–12). Only the southern kingdom of Judah remained.

Twenty years later, in 701 B.C., the Assyrian armies of Sennacherib (704–681 B.C.) invaded Judah and came up to the walls of Jerusalem before turning back just when they were about to deliver the death blow to the city

(2 Kgs 18:17–37; 19:32–37; Is 36:1–22; 37:36–38). After exacting heavy tribute from Hezekiah for the duration of his reign, the Assyrians exerted complete control over his son Manasseh throughout his reign (687–642 B.C./2 Kgs 21:1–18).

Assyria fell from the status of a major world power to a nonentity in a span of only twenty years. The Assyrian empire began to disintegrate from within toward the end of Ashurbanipal's reign (669–629 B.C.). The Babylonians broke the Assyrians with their capture of Nineveh in 612 B.C. Tragically in 609 B.C., King Josiah was cut down by Pharaoh Necho of Egypt as he tried to prevent the Egyptians from passing through his territory to support the Assyrians' final futile attempt to dislodge the Babylonians from Haran.

The Babylonians took control of the eastern Mediterranean. In 604 B.C., Nebuchadnezzar made Judah a vassal state. He invaded Jerusalem for the first time on March 16, 597 B.C., and deported King Jehoiachin and many of the leading citizens to Babylon (2 Kgs 24:10–17). The Babylonians placed Zedekiah on the throne in Jerusalem. However, when he threatened rebellion, the armies of Nebuchadnezzar surrounded the city in January of 588 B.C. After hemming in the populace for eighteen months and depriving them of food and supplies, the Babylonians broke through the walls and destroyed the city and Temple on either the seventh (2 Kgs 25:8) or the tenth (Jer 52:12) of Ab (July/August) 587 B.C. At that time, they deported the second wave of exiles to Babylon (2 Kgs 25:1–21). Finally, in 582 B.C., the Babylonians again overran Judah in a clean-up operation to rid the territory of vestiges of potential insurrection (Jer 52:28–30; cf. 2 Kgs 25:22–26). The last news we hear in the books of Kings mentions Jehoiachin's release from prison by Nebuchadnezzar's successor Evil-Merodach (2 Kgs 25:27–30).

Themes in Kings

The books of Kings depict the rueful story of Israel's decline from the height of magnificence under Solomon to the depths of ruin in the Exile. Everything that Solomon constructs in the beginning the Babylonians destroy in the end. We have noted that the Deuteronomists follow a simple three-stage chronological outline describing in sequence: (1) the reign of Solomon (1 Kgs 1–11); (2) the kingdom divided into Judah and Israel (1 Kgs 12 to 2 Kgs 17); and (3) the kingdom of Judah (2 Kgs 18–25). Nevertheless, their text is not a monotonous chronicle. Within this general framework, the Deuteronomists were very selective in deciding what to emphasize. For example, they devoted the fourteen chapters in the middle of their text to the dynasty of Omri in Israel (1 Kgs 16:23 to 2 Kgs 8:24: from Omri to Jehoram [885–841 B.C.]) while dedicating only a few lines to each of the forty-year reigns of Jehoash (835–796 B.C.) and Manasseh (687–642 B.C.) in Judah (2 Kgs 12:1–22; 21:1–18). A closer look at the text indicates that the sacred writers were not as interested in the Omrides as in the prophets of their day. They arranged the text so as to make the missions of Elijah and Elisha the centerpiece of the whole work (1 Kgs 17 to 2 Kgs 13:21). Prophecy is the key for unlocking the treasure-house of God's purposes in history.

Kings brings us to a climax in our search for an answer to the question dominating the whole Deuteronomic History: "Why did God allow the Assyrians to destroy Israel and then the Babylonians to destroy Jerusalem and the Temple?" We can grasp the response of the sacred authors by focusing on three themes that form the primary undercurrents of Kings:

1. the mission of kingship;
2. the importance of the Temple; and
3. the role of prophecy.

The King's Mission

As we read the sections in Kings that offer brief analyses of the reigns of individual kings, we might become frustrated with the manner in which the Deuteronomists take us back and forth as they alternate between northern and southern kings (1 Kgs 14:21 to 16:22; 2 Kgs 9:1–17:4). Their arrangement serves a theological purpose of causing us to consider Israel and Judah as one people, "all Israel" whom Moses addressed in Deuteronomy (Dt 1:1; 34:12). The division between north and south is a consequence of sin and is not in accord with God's purposes.

The Deuteronomists evaluated each of the kings in light of the two divine decrees that made Israel's monarchy distinct from that of other nations. First, the Lord's word revealed in Nathan's prophecy led the sacred authors to compare each king with the standard of David (2 Sm 7:5–17). Secondly, Deuteronomic legislation on kingship decreed that the monarch's first obligation was personal submission to the Law of the Lord. By implication, the king had to conceive of his mission as obedient service to the Lord in which he would lead his people to conform their lives to the requirements of the Deuteronomic Code (Dt 17:14–20). Foremost among the dictates of the Law was the primary commandment to worship the Lord alone and to banish every form of idolatry from the land (Dt 5:7–10; 6:4–5; 7:1–6; 12:29–13:1).

The kings of the north failed under both standards. Although prophetic sanctions at first supported Jeroboam's revolt as a discipline against Solomon's excesses, the breakaway tribes of the north were seen as a constant rebellion against the House of David (1 Kgs 11:28–39; 12:19–20). By installing as king a person outside the line of David, the northern tribes cut themselves off from God's covenant that Nathan decreed.

Furthermore, when Jeroboam erected the sanctuaries at Dan and Bethel in opposition to the Temple in Jerusalem, he acted like Aaron in the Sinai by casting images of the Lord in the form of two golden bulls and thus trespassed the primary prescription of the Law (1 Kgs 12:26–33; Ex 32:1–6). In the north, religious practice continued to mix elements of Canaanite religion with Yahwism as the Israelites worshiped on the "high places" and "under the trees" where the pagans practiced their fertility rites in the name of Baal (1 Kgs 13:32; 14:22–23). The prophet chastised Jeroboam for his idolatry (1 Kgs 14:8–9), and every king in the north after him was tainted insofar as he refused to correct the tradition of apostasy and followed Jeroboam's example (e.g., 1 Kgs 15:26; 16:2, 19, 25–26; 2 Kgs 15:28).

The Deuteronomists evaluated as well each successive king of Judah according to the standard of David. We should note that they presented David as the model of one who fulfills the demands of the Deuteronomic Law by serving the Lord with his whole heart and not permitting idolatry in the land (1 Kgs 15:5). Over one-third of Judah's kings after Solomon received acclaim for following the example of David to some degree (Asa, Jehoshaphat, Jehoash, Amaziah, Uzziah, Jotham, Hezekiah, and Josiah) (1 Kgs 15:9–15; 22:41–45; 2 Kgs 12:1–3; 14:1–3; 15:1–3, 32–34; 18:1–8; 22:1–2, 11–20; 23:25). Of these, the Deuteronomists single out three in particular (Asa, Hezekiah, and Josiah) for special mention in view of their energetic reforms to rid the land of all forms of idolatry and worship of foreign gods (1 Kgs 15:9–15; 2 Kgs 18:1–8; 22:2; 23:25). While over half of Judah's kings fell short of the mark, Ahaz and Manasseh merit greater contempt than the others for their tolerance of the degrading pagan practices (including child sacrifice) that marked their two reigns (2 Kgs 16:1–4; 21:1–18).

Solomon was the original "son of David" who fulfilled the promise contained in Nathan's prophecy and received his father's instructions to observe the Deuteronomic ordinances (1 Kgs 2:1–4; 2 Sm 7:5–17; Dt 17:14–20). Solomon stands above all the kings who followed both in Judah and in Israel. However, he is not an unalloyed figure. He offers both an impression of the Davidic line's greatness but also a premonition of its human imperfections. Solomon builds the Temple in fulfillment of the Lord's word to his father, but, at the same time, he intermarries with foreigners and becomes influenced by their idolatry (1 Kgs 3:1–3; 11:1–13).

Divine revelation frames Solomon's career, as the Lord appears directly to the king first at the beginning of his reign and then after the dedication of the Temple (1 Kgs 3:4–15; 9:1–9). Even his father David did not receive the gift of such intimacy with God. Nevertheless, we detect a divine urgency in the Lord's dealings with Solomon. While the first encounter takes the form of a dialogue, the second takes the form of a prophetic warning to the king. No sooner has the Temple been constructed than the Lord warns Solomon (and every king after him) that the Lord will destroy the sacred precincts and ravage the land if the king and people turn away from him to idolatry. The Lord pronounces the judgments consequent upon breaking the covenant to explain prophetically the Exile to come four centuries later (1 Kgs 9:6–9; cf. Dt 28:15, 36–37, 41, 43–44, 47–57, 63–68; 29:23–27). Looking at the more immediate future, the Lord declares to Solomon that the Lord himself will split the kingdom between north and south because Solomon has given in to the lure of idolatry (1 Kgs 11:9–13). The Deuteronomists emphasize that from the first son of David onward, the determining factor in Israel's history has not been political but spiritual. The people suffer division because of idolatry in their highest ranks. Only allegiance to the Lord expressed in a living faith will produce unity.

Already at this point, we realize why the Lord allowed the Babylonians to destroy the Temple and to take the people into exile. Indeed, the Babylonians were merely the Lord's instruments for accomplishing his word in accordance with the sacred terms of the covenant. The Deuteronomists insist that the king's primary responsibility consists in maintaining an environment of genuine Yahwistic faith untainted by idolatry. The editors who labored on the history during the days of Josiah rejoiced that they had a king who fulfilled the ancient prophecy of a son of David who would inaugurate a renewal of faith by ridding the land of every vestige of paganism (1 Kgs 13:2; 2 Kgs 23:15–16). Nevertheless, even the virtues of the great Josiah could not overcome the damage caused by Manasseh, whose forty-five year sponsorship of apostasy was the determining cause of Jerusalem's ruin, the Temple's destruction, and the people's exile (2 Kgs 23:12; 24:3–4).

At this point, we must pause and ask, "What is the use of talking to the exiles about apostasy in Israel? Isn't it rather like closing the barn door after the horse has escaped?" Once again, we must highlight the fact that the polemic against idolatry was very relevant to the Jews who lived in the shadow of Marduk's temple and breathed the air of Babylonian myths. Around 550 B.C., Deutero-Isaiah admonished his people on the same issue as the Deuteronomists were emphasizing in their narrative. Practicing idolatry is utter foolishness (Is 44:9–20; 42:8; 40:19–20). The Lord alone is God, and he will redeem those who renounce other gods and turn to him alone (Is 45:20–25).

The people experience salvation when their worship is genuine. In order to pursue this topic further, we must direct our attention to the Temple, which is a focus of concern throughout the books of Kings.

The Temple

The theme of the Temple links the reign of Solomon back to David and forward to the destruction of Jerusalem. The Deuteronomists perceived that whatever took place at the Temple determined the course of Israel's history. God's promise to David reached fulfillment through Solomon not only when he succeeded his father to the throne but especially when he dedicated the Temple to the Lord's service (1 Kgs 8:14-21; 2 Sm 7:4-16). The Temple theme then defines the boundaries of the text of Kings, which opens with its construction and closes with its destruction (1 Kgs 6-7; 2 Kgs 25:8-17). From Solomon onward, the history of kingship is relative to the mystery of the Temple. The king always stands in the shadow of the Temple as its custodian.

The Temple is the place where the Lord makes himself known to his people. The book of Exodus describes the successive stages by which the Lord draws near to his people in the form of a cloud, first ahead and then behind them as they cross the Sea, then on top of the mountain when they enter into covenant, and, finally, overshadowing the wilderness sanctuary on the edge of their camp (Ex 13:21-22; 24:16-18; 40:34-35). When the Lord fills the Temple with his glory in the form of a cloud after the priests set the ark in the Holy of Holies, he brings to fulfillment what he foreshadowed in Moses' day. Now the Lord has a permanent dwelling in the midst of his people (1 Kgs 8:10-13; see Ez 43:4-5).

Nevertheless, the Deuteronomists emphasize that the Lord cannot be confined to a physical space (1 Kgs 8:27). They prefer to describe the Temple as the dwelling place of the Lord's "name" (1 Kgs 8:16, 29; cf. 2 Kgs 21:7; Ez 48:35; Dt 12:5, 11-12). The name communicates the divine presence in the most genuine and powerful manner but without limiting the mystery of God to a particular setting.

Throughout Kings, the Deuteronomists accentuate the Temple's holy character by directing our attention to various changes in its details. They offer a careful description of the design, structural materials, furnishings, and utensils that went into Solomon's edifice (1 Kgs 6-7). They make special note of any adjustment to this original order, such as Jehoash's repairs, Ahaz's redesign of the altar and rearrangement of the fixtures, Manasseh's introduction of idols, and—on a more positive note—Josiah's renovations to restore everything to its proper place (2 Kgs 12:5-17; 16:10-18; 21:1-9; 22:3-9). They identify the enemies who looted the Temple treasury, such as Shishak of

Egypt (I Kgs 14:25–26) and Jehoash of Israel(!) (2 Kgs 14:13–14), and they specify which of the kings had to delve into the Temple's resources to pay tribute exacted by foreign powers (I Kgs 15:18–19; 2 Kgs 12:19; 16:8–9; 18:14–16).

Finally, we experience the poignancy of the Temple's destruction by going over the meticulous list of materials, furnishings, and instruments of worship that the Babylonians carried off (2 Kgs 25:13–17). The pillars, basins, and spoons take on the character of sacred relics for the author. We recall the immense care for detail that went into the original construction (I Kgs 7:15–39), and we realize that the account describes not so much the demolition of a building as the withdrawal of a Person (cf. Ez 10:18–22; 11:22–25). Without the Lord's presence in the Temple, the people have no reason for being in the land. Divine logic correlates destruction of the Temple with exile of the people.

We should also note that the Deuteronomists instruct us that concern for the Temple is the basis for social responsibility. Their history proves that insofar as the king reverences the Lord at the Temple, to that extent he governs the people with justice. The reigns of Ahaz and Manasseh are the best witnesses to the principle that when the king fails to revere the Lord's presence in the Temple, he also allows injustice and immorality to ravage the people (2 Kgs 16:1–20; 21:1–18). By contrast, the examples of Hezekiah and Josiah demonstrate that reverence for the Lord's holiness expresses itself in concern for justice and truth among the people (2 Kgs 18:1–20:21; 22:1–23:30).

Prophets

When the Lord is present, he speaks his word to his people (cf. Dt 4:32–33). The books of Kings bear out the truth of an editorial comment in Amos, "No indeed, Lord Yahweh does nothing without revealing his secret to his servants the prophets" (Am 3:7). Throughout their work, the Deuteronomists assert that the vital principle governing history is the prophetic word. As a messenger of the divine word, the prophet does not predict the future as much as shape it. The word the prophet announces from the Lord releases an effective power that brings about its own fulfillment in history.

The Deuteronomic Code identifies two distinguishing characteristics of genuine prophets: (a) they insist that the Lord alone is God (which motivates them to oppose every form of idolatry), and (b) what they declare actually reaches fulfillment (Dt 18:9–22; 13:2–7). The books of Kings indicate that God always provided his people with such servants of his word who shaped the course of their history.

Furthermore, the exiles who read Kings made the astonishing discovery that the downward spiral of Israel's history from Solomon's reign to the Exile actually demonstrated the power of God's word. Everything happened in fulfillment of what the prophets announced. Jeroboam's movement to separate north from south was not a political action of some malcontents but rather the accomplishment of God's word spoken through Ahijah of Shiloh, who announced the event as a punishment for Solomon's idolatry (1 Kgs 11:29–39). The extension of Josiah's reform to the northern territory was not a minor effort to turn back the tide of apostasy but rather the fulfillment of what the anonymous man of God from Judah had announced three centuries prior to the great renewal in Jerusalem (1 Kgs 13:1–10, 31–32; 2 Kgs 23:15–20).

The exiles saw prophetic fulfillment in many other instances. Jehu ben Hanani promised the overthrow of Baasha because of his tolerance of paganism, and Zimri's revolt accomplished the prophet's word (1 Kgs 16:1–7, 8–20). An anonymous prophet advised Ahab that Israel would defeat the great army of Damascus so that the people would know that Yahweh is God (1 Kgs 20:13–30). Shortly after the victory, a member of the prophetic brotherhood promised Ahab that he would pay with his life for his indecision about really breaking the power of the conquered enemy (1 Kgs 20:31–43). Micaiah ben Imlah followed up this word by contradicting the king's false seers who promised another triumph; he announced instead the death that awaited Ahab for precipitously engaging the Syrian forces at Jabesh (1 Kgs 22:5–28). Isaiah admonished Hezekiah not to capitulate to the Assyrians who surrounded Jerusalem since the Lord would rescue the people. The city witnessed the fulfillment of the prophet's words when the Assyrian troops withdrew at the point of making an absolute conquest (2 Kgs 19:1–37). The prophet announced the king's imminent death, and, after Hezekiah's prayer, the Lord willed that he recover (2 Kgs 20:1–11). Finally, the prophetess Huldah told Josiah of the Lord's plans to render Jerusalem and her populace desolate, but not during the lifetime of the noble king (2 Kgs 22:14–20).

Far from discrediting the sovereignty of God, the destruction first of Samaria and then of Jerusalem really served to highlight the authority of the word he spoke through the prophets. The Assyrians were able to seize Samaria, not because of their superior strength, but because of Israel's idolatry and refusal to respond to the prophets' words (2 Kgs 17:7–18; 18:12). Similarly, the Babylonians ravaged Jerusalem and destroyed the Temple almost a century and a half later in fulfillment of the Lord's word that the prophets declared throughout the period (2 Kgs 21:10–15; 24:2–4).

Now we must ask, "What did this message imply for the exiles in Babylon?" They could accept that the conquests of Samaria and Jerusalem were in keeping with the Lord's plan, but where was the hope for their future?

Although it might not be obvious to us at first glance, in fact the Deuteronomists were directing the exiles to sure ground for their hope. The prophetic word is an absolutely reliable and sure guide to the future. Since history vindicated every genuine prophet throughout the history of Israel and Judah, then the exiles had every reason to trust the word of the prophets who spoke to them in exile. The three who merited their attention were Jeremiah, Ezekiel, and Deutero-Isaiah. When the final Deuteronomic editors were completing their work around 550 B.C., scribes were producing written editions of the teachings of Jeremiah and Ezekiel; about the same time, Deutero-Isaiah was proclaiming his word of consolation to the exiles (Is 40–55). The three prophets shared two qualities: (a) after the destruction of Jerusalem, they promised a triumphant return to the land following a time of purification (Jer 30:1–31:40; Ez 36:1–37:28; 40:1–48:35; Is 40:1–11); and (b) each of them knew a deep experience of suffering in union with the people (Jer 20:7–18; Ez 24:16–27; cf. Is 52:13–53:12). Since the prophets were correct when they promised disaster, the people could certainly believe them when they announced a time of return and restoration. In addition, the Deuteronomists adopted from the Isaian tradition the vision of the Lord preserving a remnant that would return to the land and provide the seeds of a new beginning (2 Kgs 19:4; Is 10:20–22; cf. 1 Kgs 19:18; 2 Kgs 19:31; Is 4:3).

The Deuteronomists insist that while the prophets must chastise the people for idolatry, their mission always brings life to God's people in the long term. They present the ministries of Elijah and Elisha at the center of Kings to illustrate how God works through his prophets to open up the future by healing and caring for his people when they suffer oppression in an idolatrous land. Faithful Jewish exiles in Babylon could identify with the Deuteronomists' portrait of the reign of the Omrides in Israel (885–841 B.C.): God's people were in spiritual disarray, the pagans had triumphed, the cult of the foreign gods dominated the land where God's people were living, and the prophets of Yahweh had either been killed or were suffering (1 Kgs 16:23 to 2 Kgs 8:29). In a word, the people in exile, like those in Israel during the forty-year rule of the Omrides, suffered a crisis of faith and questioned, "Is Yahweh truly God?" (see Is 40:12–31; 43:8–13; 44:6–8, 24–28; 45:20–25). The ministries of Elijah and Elisha offered the exiles assurance that through his prophets, God can heal and deliver his people even in their darkest days.

Because we usually associate them together, we must begin by distinguishing Elijah and Elisha from one another. Elijah was a radical reformer who roamed the margins of society, living in caves and camping on mountains throughout Ahab's reign over the northern kingdom (874–853 B.C./1 Kgs 17:1 to 2 Kgs 2:13). By contrast, Elisha was a farmer who moved into a house in the city of Samaria and walked among the common folk in the northern kingdom for the half century from Ahaziah to Jehoash (853–c. 783 B.C./1 Kgs 19:19–21; 2 Kgs 2:1–11:20; 13:1–21).

Elijah devoted his life to combating the militant paganism and persecution of Yahwism by Jezebel, the daughter of the king of Sidon, who controlled her husband, the indecisive King Ahab (2 Kgs 16:29–34). It is likely that underground groups of prophets authored the Elijah cycle of stories, which encouraged fidelity to Yahweh during the oppressive reign of Manasseh, who martyred some of the Lord's servants (687–642 B.C./2 Kgs 21:16; cf. 1 Kgs 18:4). Everything about Elijah's ministry reveals the sovereignty of Yahweh over the pagan gods. Baal, whom the Omrides reverenced, had the reputation of being the god of fertility and the god of the storm. When Elijah proclaims a three-year drought in the name of the Lord, he demonstrates that Yahweh, not Baal, rules the land and its crops (1 Kgs 17:1; 18:41–46). He goes right into Sidonia, the native territory of Jezebel and her god, to show the extent of the Lord's dominion over all people by providing food for the widow of Zarephath and then raising her son from death to life, again in the name of Yahweh (1 Kgs 17:7–24). His great confrontation on Mount Carmel with the priests of Baal illustrates the folly of pagan-cult antics and shows that the Lord, not the reputed storm god Baal, sends lightning from heaven to bring his fire to the earth (1 Kgs 18:20–40). All who cry "Yahweh is God" are professing the core of Deuteronomic faith (Dt 6:4), which the remnant of Manasseh's day and the exiles in Babylon must echo in their respective situations.

In fear and despair, Elijah flees to Mount Horeb (Sinai), where Yahweh reveals himself to this prophet whom he is making into a new Moses (1 Kgs 19:9–18; cf. Ex 33:18–34:9). Here again, we see the distinction between Yahweh and Baal: the true Lord is not in the storm but in the murmuring sound of a voice speaking to the prophet who will form a remnant of those who will survive because of their faithfulness.

The last days of Elijah indicate how much God has conformed him to Moses. The prophet parts the Jordan as Moses had the Sea (2 Kgs 2:8; Ex 14:16, 21–22), relates to Elisha as his successor in a manner analogous to Moses' relation to Joshua (2 Kgs 2:1–13; 1 Kgs 19:19–21; cf. Nm 27:18–23; Dt 31:7–8; 34:9), and cannot be found by a human being when he departs this earth (2 Kgs 2:11–12, 17–18; Dt 34:6).

Elisha was a healer who cared for ordinary people and, at the same time, advised the king on military strategy. His counsel enabled the Israelites first to defeat Moab and then to survive a prolonged siege of Samaria by the Aramaeans (2 Kgs 3:1–27; 6:24–7:20). His disciple anointed Jehu, the king who carried out a bloody purge of the Omrides, killing Jezebel in the process (2 Kgs 9:1–37).

Elisha's example reassures us that the Lord's concern extends beyond international developments to focus on the needs of individuals and families who struggle with life's difficulties. At his word, the Shunammite woman conceives and gives birth to a son whom the prophet later brings back from death (2 Kgs 4:8–37). He reflects the Lord's compassion on the poor and the needy by multiplying oil for the prophet's widow, purifying the poisoned soup of the prophets during a famine, and multiplying bread for a hundred men (2 Kgs 4:1–7, 38–41, 42–44). When Elisha's instructions bring about Naaman's healing, the pagan professes faith in Yahweh as the sovereign God above all others worshipped by the nations, and so he calls our attention back to the main theme of the whole book (2 Kgs 5:1–27).

Toward the New Testament: Jesus, Prophet and Healer

Elijah and Elisha are the only Old Testament figures who perform healings. Insofar as their ministries combine preaching with miracles, they foreshadow Jesus as the Messiah who brings the Kingdom of God in word and deed. Elijah's and Elisha's work of raising the widows' sons from death to life prefigures Jesus' work of the same type at Nain (Lk 7:11–17; 1 Kgs 17:17–24; 2 Kgs 4:18–37). Paul repeats the gestures of both Elijah and Elisha when he restores the young man who fell from the window sill during Paul's farewell address to the church in Troas (Acts 20:7–12; 2 Kgs 4:33–36). Elisha's dialogue with his servant prior to multiplying the bread for the man from Baal-Shalishah echoes through Jesus' conversation with his disciples prior to his feeding the five thousand (2 Kgs 4:42–44; Mk 6:31–44; Mt 14:13–21; Lk 9:10–17; Jn 6:1–13). In the Gospel of Luke, at the very beginning of his ministry, Jesus indicates he came to bring salvation to Gentiles as well as to Jews by alluding to Elijah's concern for the woman of Zarephath and Elisha's healing of Naaman the Syrian (Lk 4:25–27; 1 Kgs 17:7–24; 2 Kgs 5:1–14).

The ascension of Elijah is reflected in the accounts of Jesus' transfiguration in the three Synoptic Gospels and in Luke's account of his exaltation in the Acts of the Apostles. Jesus' transfiguration on the mountain with Moses and Elijah indicates that he is the fullness of revelation that the Lord's manifestation of himself on Mount Sinai to Moses and to Elijah only foreshadowed (Mk 9:2–8/Mt 17:1–8/Lk 9:28–36; Ex 3:1–4:17; 33:18–34:9; 1 Kgs 19:9–18). By their presence, both Moses and Elijah point toward the promise of Jesus' Resurrection, since these are the two servants whom God took directly to himself, leaving no trace of a tomb that a human being could find (Dt 34:6; 2 Kgs 2:11–12, 17–18). The description of Jesus' Ascension reflects the last event in Elijah's ministry (Acts 1:9–11; cf. 2 Kgs 2:1–13).

During Jesus' ministry, many people thought of Jesus as a new Elijah (Mk

6:15; 8:28). Like Elijah, he experienced persecution at the hands of the king of the northern territories, and he worked signs and wonders (see Lk 13:31–34). However, especially Matthew and Mark are careful to identify John the Baptist as the new Elijah, since they interpret him to be the forerunner of the end time in light of later tradition (Mt 17:10–13; Mk 9:11–13; cf. Mal 3:23–24).

We must note that Jesus' prophecy of the destruction of the Temple and of the desolation of Jerusalem places him squarely in the line of practically all the prophets we have met in the books of Kings (Mk 13:1–2, 14; Mt 24:1–3, 15–16; Lk 21:5–6, 20–21; 19:41–44). When the Sanhedrin condemns Jesus to death for this teaching, they set the stage for him to reveal himself as the "son" who fulfills the missions of the previous messengers whom the Father sent but whom their people persecuted (Mk 14:61–62; cf. Mk 12:1–12; Mt 21:33–46; Lk 20:9–19).

In the Letter to the Romans, Paul insists that God is forming a faithful remnant of the Jews who believe in Christ. To appreciate the Lord's plan, Paul appeals to the Lord's promise to Elijah on Mount Horeb. This faithful remnant, born of grace, constitutes the sign of God's fulfilling his promises to the Jewish people (Rom 11:2, in 11:1–36; cf. 1 Kgs 19:10, 14).

Having completed our survey of the Deuteronomic History, we now have the opportunity to review the story of kingship from another perspective, that which the Chronicler offers.

STUDY QUESTIONS

1. Compare the two audiences for the successive editions of the Deuteronomic collection.

2. What are the three periods that the books of Kings cover?

3. Why did the kingdom split? Describe the difference in kingship in the north and the south.

4. Describe the fall of the northern and southern kingdoms.

5. What are the three themes of the books of Kings that underlie the answer to the question, "Why did God permit the destruction of the kingdoms?"

6. How was the polemic against idolatry in the books of Kings relevant to the Babylonian exiles?

7. What is the significance of the Temple in the books of Kings?

8. What are the two salient characteristics of prophets?

9. Distinguish Elijah from Elisha. How does Elijah compare to Moses? How do Elijah and Elisha foreshadow Jesus?

10. Have you seen in the crises of your life that there is always someone who speaks the truth of God to others? Is it you?

11. In your estimation, who are the prophetic figures (after the fashion of Elijah and Elisha) in the Church today, both on the universal and local levels?

1 AND 2 KINGS

THE KINGS AND PROPHETS OF ISRAEL

Saul (c. 1030–1010)   *Samuel (c. 1040–1020)*
David (c. 1010–970)   *Nathan (c. 1010–960)*
Solomon (c. 970–931)

Israel (Northern Kingdom)		*Judah (Southern Kingdom)*	
Jeroboam I (931–910)	*Ahijah of Shiloh*	Rehoboam (931–913)	
Nadab (910–909)		Abijah (913–911)	
Baasha (909–886)	*Jehu ben Hanani*	Asa (911–870)	
Elah (886–885)			
Zimri (885)			
Omri (885–874)	*Elijah (874–853)*		
Ahab (874–853)		Jehoshaphat (870–848)	
Ahaziah (853–852)	*Micaiah ben Imlah*		
Jehoram (852–841)		Jehoram (848–841)	
Jehu (841–814)	*Elisha (c. 853–783)*	Ahaziah (841)	
		Athaliah (841–835)	
Jehoahaz (814–798)		Jehoash (Joash) (835–796)	
Jehoash (Joash) (798–783)			
Jeroboam II (783–743)	*Amos (c. 760–740)*	Amaziah (796–781)	
Zechariah (743)		Uzziah (781–740)	
Shallum (743)	*Hosea (c. 745–736)*		
Menahem (743–738)		Jotham (740–736)	*Isaiah (c. 740–690)*
Pekahiah (738–737)			
Pekah (737–732)		Ahaz (736–716)	*Micah (c. 740–710)*
Hoshea (732–724)			
[Fall of Samaria (721)]			
		Hezekiah (716–687)	
		Manasseh (687–642)	
		Amon (642–640)	
		Josiah (640–609)	*Huldah*
			Zephaniah (c. 635–630)
			Jeremiah (c. 627–580)
			Nahum (c. 612)
			Habakkuk (c. 604–599)

Jehoahaz (609)
Jehoiakim (609–598)
Jehoiachin (598–597)

Ezekiel (593–
c. 571)

Zedekiah (597–587)
[Fall of Jerusalem
   (587)]

17

1 AND 2 CHRONICLES:
DAVID, THE TEMPLE, AND THE LITURGY

Why does the Bible contain two enormous works that cover the same material? This question is bound to cross our minds as we read the books of Chronicles and find them going over much the same subject matter that we already considered in Samuel and Kings. Our first impulse might be to excuse ourselves from a serious reading of the texts on the ground that we have heard it all before.

At the outset of this chapter, we might as well admit that Chronicles has suffered from some negative publicity. For instance, the Septuagint (Greek) translation calls these books literally "Leftovers" (*Paraleipomenon*). But, before you pass them over, take a moment to see if your curiosity is not already aroused. The inspired authors and the people who defined the canon of Sacred Scripture surely knew that we might find the material in Chronicles redundant after the Deuteronomic History. Let us take a closer look in order to find out why they were convinced that these books would increase our appreciation of God's manner of forming his people.

The books of Chronicles are not simply a repetition but a rereading and reinterpretation of Samuel and Kings. Some scholars have designated them as "midrash" (from the Hebrew verb *darash,* meaning "to seek"), which was a technique of retelling the biblical story with apparently minor alterations in order to draw out the hidden meanings and practical applications of the text. Strictly speaking, it was the rabbis of the postbiblical era who fully developed the literary form of midrash as a means of seeking out the deeper implications of the biblical text for their contemporaries. Those rabbis claimed as their mentor and model the great Ezra, who was renowned for his "studying the Law of Yahweh" so as to teach the people how to put it into practice in their daily lives (Ezr 7:10). According to Chronicles, the great kings insisted that seeking the Lord and his instruction would heal God's people of sin and guarantee them a long life in their land (1 Chr 28:8; 2 Chr 30:18–19: cf. Ps 119:45, 94, 155).

The writer of Chronicles was searching the Scriptures to discern the ways of the Lord for his people. We can consider Chronicles as a sort of commentary on Samuel and Kings. It represents a new reading of those texts in view of a later and radically different pastoral situation compared with that which the Deuteronomists addressed. The copy of Samuel and Kings that the author of Chronicles possessed was different in some details from the canonical Hebrew ("Masoretic") text of our Bible today. He refers to these volumes as the "Book of the Kings of Israel and Judah" or variations of this title (2 Chr 27:7; cf. 28:26). We should note that, in addition to these texts, the author of Chronicles mentions over a dozen other sources, including diverse works containing the sayings of various prophets such as Nathan, Ahijah of Shiloh, Jehu ben Hanani, and Isaiah ben Amoz (e.g., 2 Chr 9:29; 20:34; 26:22).

We call the author of our text the Chronicler. Although we do not know him by name, his writing gives evidence that he possessed a colorful personality, loved the Temple liturgy, and appreciated good preaching. More precisely, the Chronicler was a Levite cantor who offers us a theology centered on the Temple not only as a religious institution but also as the place where the community gathers to worship in song and praise. He views the Temple from the inside, actually from the perspective of the choir, not of the priest. The Chronicler might have included his own genealogy in the introductory prologue (1 Chr 3:17–24). In any case, the fact that he mentions the Levites ninety-nine times while Samuel and Kings together contain only three references to them offers us significant evidence about the Chronicler's background (see 1 Chr 23:1–26:32).

The Chronicler's History

What was the extent of the Chronicler's writing? The books of Ezra and Nehemiah together contain some sixty references to the Levites. Furthermore, they share other characteristics in common with Chronicles, such as: (a) an appreciation for genealogies (Ezr 2:1–70 = Neh 7:6–72) and census lists of the diverse orders of Levites (1 Chr 9:1–34; Neh 10:1–30; 11:3–36; 12:1–26); (b) a particular concern for Judah and Benjamin as distinct from the northern tribes (2 Chr 15:9; Ezr 1:5; Neh 4:10); and (c) a highlighting of the completed text of the Law of the Lord that priests and Levites interpreted to the people (2 Chr 17:8–9; Ezr 7:25; Neh 8:1–12).

However, in spite of their similarities, Ezra and Nehemiah differ from Chronicles in style and perspective. For example, Nehemiah brings up Solomon's weakness for foreign women, a failing that the Chronicler is loathe to mention (Neh 13:26). While Chronicles is practically an extended tribute to David,

Ezra and Nehemiah scarcely refer to the great king. Furthermore, Chronicles maintains a hope that the remnants of the northern kingdom will rejoin Jerusalem through an act of repentance, while Ezra-Nehemiah consider the people of that region to be the enemies of Judah's attempts at renewal (2 Chr 30:18–20; cf. Ezr 4:1–3).

What can we conclude from this evidence? Chronicles, along with Ezra and Nehemiah, form a compendium of texts traditionally called the Chronicler's History. However, the Chronicler's style and inspiration are not consistent throughout all these works. His hand is most evident in both books of Chronicles and in the biographical material about Ezra (Ezr 7–10; Neh 8–9). His influence is greatly reduced in the Nehemiah documentation (Neh 1–7; 10–13). The complexity of the evidence suggests it is prudent for us to separate our study of Chronicles from our examination of Ezra and Nehemiah while recognizing that these texts are related to each other.

We will take the following position. After 400 but before 350 B.C., the person whom we call the Chronicler wrote the book of Chronicles (1 Chr 1 to 2 Chr 36) along with the history of the reconstruction (Ezr 1–6); he also edited Ezra's Memoirs (Ezr 7:1–8:36; Neh 8:1–9:2; Ezr 9:1–10:17). A later editor who shared the Chronicler's pastoral concerns but not his exegetical preoccupations rearranged Ezra's Memoirs in order to incorporate Nehemiah's Memoirs (Neh 1:1–2:20; 3:33–7:5; 12:27–43; 13:4–31) and the remaining material into the work. This second editor completed the final edition of Ezra-Nehemiah shortly after 350 B.C.

The Historical Situation from the Exile to the Chronicler

The Chronicler lived in Jerusalem after both Ezra and Nehemiah had completed their missions but before Alexander the Great brought the Greek culture to the eastern Mediterranean. We date his work during the later part of the Persian era (538–332 B.C.), between 400 and 350 B.C.

We have scant information about the situation in Judah throughout the Persian era. However, we must make a quick survey of religious developments in Judah from the end of the Exile until the time of the Chronicler. Generally speaking, a pervasive spiritual lethargy seemed to hang in the atmosphere of Jerusalem from the Exile to the time of Ezra.

Even in the early years immediately following Cyrus' decree of 538 B.C. permitting the Jews to return to Jerusalem from the Exile in Babylon, initial enthusiasm gave way to a concern for security and survival, which delayed even the rudimentary completion of the second Temple until 515 B.C. (2 Chr 36:22–23; Ezr 1:1–6:22; cf. Hg 1:4). Actually, credit for completing the project was due in large measure to the strong leadership of Zerubbabel the governor and Joshua the priest, who were supported by the preaching of Haggai and Zechariah after 520 B.C. (Hg 1:1–2:23; Zec 1:1–8:23). Zerubbabel was the last person from the Davidic line actually to govern Judah, even as a delegate of the Persian authorities. Once his term of office ended and he died, the prophets' hopes of maintaining the rule of the Davidic dynasty in Judah were frustrated by Persian administrative pragmatism (cf. Hg 2:20–23; Zec 4:6b–10; 6:12–14). Because the Persians could appoint as governor whomever they fancied, the priests at the Temple had to assume the role of leadership among the Jews from this point onward.

By the turn of the century (500 B.C.), the prophet we call Trito-Isaiah had to address a populace composed of the arrogant and the disconsolate. He admonished the wealthy for their superficial piety and encouraged the down-trodden not to be ashamed of their humble city but to appreciate its stature in the eyes of the Lord, who promised to bestow on it unsurpassed glory (Is 56–66; 60:1–22; 62:1–12). Perhaps a quarter century later, the prophet Malachi again confronted the spiritual inertia, this time as it manifested itself in the priests' negligence to uphold the standards of dignified worship at the Temple and in the widespread breakdown of family life due to divorce (Mal 1:6–2:16).

We will accept the accuracy of the biblical text in dating the beginning of Ezra's mission to Jerusalem in 458 B.C. (Ezr 7:7). The great priest set about transforming the life of Judah according to the prescriptions of the complete text of the Pentateuch (Neh 8:1–18). Nehemiah's arrival as governor just over a decade later secured the work of reformation by annulling marriages with foreigners, rebuffing the threats of officials in Samaria, rebuilding the walls of Jerusalem, adding to its populace, and increasing revenue for the Temple (Ezr 9:1–10:17; Neh 1–13). The combined efforts of Ezra and Nehemiah generated the greatest renewal Judaism experienced at any time in the Persian era.

The Chronicler carried on his work perhaps a half century after Ezra and Nehemiah completed their missions. Actually, the labors of these two great reformers gave birth to the pastoral situation of the Chronicler and his contemporaries. In his time, Jerusalem was spiritually stable, and the people did not question the importance of the Temple. Orthodoxy had triumphed, and everything was in relatively good order. However, the Chronicler was sensitive enough to notice that the one ingredient missing from the faith was vitality. Religious practice was sound but lifeless. The people did not need more reform but new vigor in their worship and zeal in their personal appropriation of faith. The Chronicler aimed at bringing life to his people while not jeopardizing the religious stability they had attained.

Themes in Chronicles

The books of Chronicles trace the history of God's people from Adam to the end of the Exile (1 Chr 1:1 to 2 Chr 36:23). The narrative portion actually begins only with David's reign, which is highlighted throughout the work. The first and second books of Chronicles should be read as a single unit. We can divide them into four major sections: (1) the genealogies, which provide a prologue to the whole work (1 Chr 1:1–9:44); (2) the reign of David (1 Chr 10:1–29:30); (3) the reign of Solomon (2 Chr 1:1–9:31); and (4) the kings of Judah from Rehoboam to the time of the Exile (2 Chr 10:1–36:23).

A preliminary survey of the books indicates two striking factors that differentiate the Chronicler's work from that of the Deuteronomists. First, the Chronicler offers no history of the kings of the northern territory after the division between Israel and Judah following Solomon's death. He is consumed with an exclusive devotion to David and his line in Judah. Secondly, the Temple stands in the foreground as the focus of attention from the beginning to the end of his narrative.

We will consider the Chronicler's message under the headings of three themes that pervade his work: (1) the relationship between the Davidic line and the Temple; (2) the Lord's guidance of the history of his people through retribution and repentance; and (3) the Temple perceived from the standpoint of the Levites as the place of congregational worship and liturgy.

David, His Descendants, and the Temple

History according to the Chronicler really begins with David (1 Chr 10:1–29:30). A series of genealogies summarizes the whole span of time from Adam to Saul (1 Chr 1:1–9:44), and then mention of Saul's death serves only as an introduction to David's reign (1 Chr 10:1–14). The tribe of Judah and the line of David receive prime attention amid the genealogies (1 Chr 2:1–3:24). The Chronicler edits the material in the books of Samuel and Kings so as to offer a portrait of David reflecting the brilliant light of unsullied virtue. In Chronicles, we read nothing of David's struggle with Saul (1 Sm 18:6–26:25), his association with the Philistines (1 Sm 27:1–29:11), his affair with Bathsheba, or his plot on Uriah's life (2 Sm 11:1–12:25). Also missing are mention of David's subsequent family problems, including Absalom's murder of Amnon (2 Sm 13:1–37), his insurrection against his father, and his death at the hands of David's troops (2 Sm 15:1–19:9). The Chronicler's concern for the reputation of the Davidic line extends to Solomon, as we hear no whisper of his bloody struggle to gain the throne (1 Kgs 2:12–46), his marriages to foreigners, or his idolatrous practices (1 Kgs 3:1–3; 11:1–13).

Throughout his work, the Chronicler scarcely refers to the Exodus and the Sinai covenant, although he cherishes the Law of Moses (2 Chr 23:18; 30:16; 35:12). According to the Chronicler, salvation flows to the people from God's covenant with David (1 Chr 17:1–27). This explains why the Chronicler refuses to consider the rulers of the northern kingdom after Solomon and instead concentrates exclusively on the successors to David's line in Judah up to the Exile (2 Chr 10:1–36:13). "But", we must ask, "if God's covenant with David is of primary importance, how does the Chronicler account for the fact that the Davidic line disappeared more than a century before his own day?"

This question allows us to touch the nucleus of the Chronicler's wisdom. David's line might have faded, but the Temple that stands in the heart of Jerusalem embodies the essence of God's promise to David and his descendants. The Chronicler interprets David's career primarily in terms of his labors on behalf of the Temple. David prepares the holy site for construction first by capturing Jerusalem (thus making it the City of David/1 Chr 11:4–9), then by bringing the ark into its precincts (1 Chr 13:1–16:43), and finally by purchasing the land and erecting the altar in the proper location for the Temple (1 Chr 21:18–22:1). David makes all the arrangements for the building (1 Chr 28:1–21), provides the precious materials for its decor (1 Chr 29:2–5; 18:7–11), and appoints some Levites to head the music ministry (1 Chr 15:16–16:38; 25:1–31), others to serve as doormen and keepers of the treasury (1 Chr 26:1–32), and still others to assist the priests in their responsibilities (1 Chr 23:1–24:31).

According to the Chronicler's description, although Solomon actually constructs the Temple, David remains its true founder and inspiration. Because he follows his father's orders, Solomon is able to bring the project to completion (2 Chr 3:1–7:22; 1 Chr 22:2–19; 28:1–29:30).

The Chronicler casts the spotlight on two other kings who best illustrate the Davidic line's vocation of service to the Temple: Hezekiah and Josiah, who were also favorites of the Deuteronomists. However, by comparison with the Deuteronomists, the Chronicler makes Hezekiah the greater hero by expanding the presentation of his reforms from one verse (2 Kgs 18:4) to eighty-four (2 Chr 29:1–31:21). Hezekiah's program inspires Josiah's initiatives (2 Chr 34:1–35:18). Thus, the Chronicler presents Hezekiah as the first great reformer. The manner in which the king addresses his sermons to the Levites and to the people provides an overture for the great discourses of Ezra (2 Chr 29:5–11; Ezr 9:6–15; Neh 8:1–18). The people's celebration of the Passover in the restored Temple calls to mind the atmosphere in Jerusalem at the time of its dedication under Solomon (2 Chr 30:25–26; 7:9).

An indication of the Chronicler's overriding concern for the Temple is evident in the closing lines of his books. Although the Davidic line has practically receded from view during the Exile, the Chronicler raises a voice of confident optimism focused, not on the monarchy, but on the Temple. Cyrus' decree of 538 B.C. makes the joyous announcement that the people of Judah can return to rebuild the Temple in Jerusalem. Even more astonishing is the manner in which Cyrus, a Gentile, speaks as a new Solomon who has received a divine commission from the Lord to construct the Holy Place in accordance with the Lord's covenant to David (2 Chr 36:22–23). Is this portrait of Cyrus influenced by Deutero-Isaiah's conviction that the Persian king was the Lord's instrument to bring new life to his people (45:1–7)?

Retribution, Repentance, and God's Action in History

The Chronicler insists that the Lord guides history by rewarding virtue and punishing vice. David's words to Solomon serve as an admonition to all who read the books and recognize their validity borne out in the experiences of subsequent kings: "And you, Solomon my son, know the God of your father and serve him with an undivided heart and willing mind; for Yahweh scrutinizes all hearts and understands whatever plans they may devise. If you seek him, he will let you find him; but forsake him and he will cast you off forever" (1 Chr 28:9).

Thus, Asa's reign was marked by peace and success because he sought the Lord by destroying idolatrous objects, and he heeded the word the Lord spoke through the prophet Azariah; but the king hastened his own death by not turning to the Lord in his illness (2 Chr 14:1–16:10; cf. 16:11–14). Uzziah prospered as long as he was attentive to the Lord, but he suffered a skin disease when he defiled the Temple and tried to exercise the ministry of the priesthood (2 Chr 26:1–15; 26:16–23; cf. Nm 12:1–10). Even Josiah, who experienced consolation when he sought the Lord in his reforms, died because he neglected to heed the Lord's word before engaging the Egyptians in battle (2 Chr 34:3–35:18; cf. 35:22).

When the people worship in the Temple and obey the prophetic word, the Lord makes them victorious in battle (2 Chr 13:4–18; 14:8–14; 20:13–30). However, when they practice idolatry and refuse to listen to his word, they experience the humiliation of defeat (2 Chr 12:1–11; 21:2–20; 24:19–24; 25:14–24; 28:1–8, 16–25). Ultimately, it is the people's neglect of and resistance to the message of the prophets that cause the Lord to use the Babylonians to break down the walls of Jerusalem and to destroy the Temple (2 Chr 36:14–20). Nevertheless, even in exile, he continues to offer them hope through his servants, the prophets. The Chronicler interprets the Exile to be God's fulfillment of the word he spoke through Jeremiah about allowing the land to lie fallow for seventy years (2 Chr 36:21; cf. Jer 25:8–13; 29:10).

Retribution for sin is never the Lord's last word. He consistently offers his people mercy and healing through the gift of repentance. The Lord promises Solomon that he will forgive and restore his people whenever they humble themselves in prayer at the Temple (2 Chr 7:13–14). The Lord acts on this word by preserving Rehoboam from total devastation at the hands of Shishak and by sparing Hezekiah from an illness occasioned by his own arrogance (2 Chr 12:6–12; 32:24–26). Most amazing of all is the Chronicler's assertion that the apostate King Manasseh experiences the Lord's mercy and gains release from the Assyrians because of his deep repentance (which provides the background for the apocryphal psalm called "The Prayer of Manasseh"/2 Chr 33:11–13, 18).

Chronicles sustains the hope that even the remnants of the northern tribes can be reunited with the mainstream of Judah and Benjamin by means of repentance. Hezekiah's attempts to extend his reform into the northern territory occupied by the Assyrians after 721 B.C. reflect an ideal of the Chronicler that the northern tribes of his own day would return to Jerusalem in humility and renewed faithfulness (2 Chr 30:6–12; cf. 2 Chr 13:5–11).

A pervasive concern for the unity of "all Israel" imbues the Chronicler's writing. Part of the glory of both David and Solomon consists in the fact that, of the various kings, they alone keep all of God's people together. In fact, the Chronicler emphasizes the close relationship between the people and the monarchy at its foundation by indicating that the whole populace anoints David as king (1 Chr 11:1–3; 12:1–41; cf. 29:22–25). This represents a very different picture from the Deuteronomists' version of Samuel anointing David in the private setting of his family (1 Sm 16:1–13). While David and Solomon serve all Israel throughout their reigns, the Chronicler gives special priority to Judah and Benjamin, since these are the tribes that remain faithful to the Lord's covenant with David while the northern ten tribes cut themselves off from this source of divine promise (2 Chr 10:1–11:12; 13:4–12). In his own day, the Chronicler encourages the majority representing Judah and Benjamin to welcome into their midst the descendants of the northern tribes, such as Ephraim, Manasseh, Zebulon, and Asher (1 Chr 9:2–3; 2 Chr 30:11). His vision should inspire Christians of our own times to cultivate an ecumenical concern for the healing of centuries-long divisions within the body of Christ.

Levites, Worship, and Prayer

The Chronicler sometimes describes the glory and prosperity of Judah in terms of stupendous armies numbering in the hundreds of thousands and, at least on one occasion, more than a million (2 Chr 13:3; 14:8; 17:14–19; 26:13)! Nevertheless, Judah is victorious in battle, not by force of arms, but by the strength of praise that ascends to the Lord (2 Chr 13:13–18; 20:13–30). It is not the military commanders but the Levites who stand at the forefront to lead the people to triumph by song.

The Chronicler knows all the Levites by name, rank, and responsibility. He mentions every one of them, not to bore us with details, but to impress on us the importance of each one from the least to the greatest. Far from being mere functionaries, the Levites are the ones who bring life to God's people. As the Chronicler describes them, you can never just think about the Levites; you always hear them. Wherever they are, there is music, song, joy, worship, and prayer. None of them is alone; they form a community that will gather together the whole congregation in lively, creative, but traditional worship.

Who were the Levites? They underwent a long development to attain the stature accorded them in Chronicles. These Levites were different from the original tribe of Levi, which was a violent group that associated with the tribe of Simeon and disappeared at a rather early date (Gn 34:25–31; 49:5–7; cf. 1 Chr 5:27–6:38). The Levites were a priestly group set apart by God (instead of the first-born) to assist Aaron and his descendants in the priesthood (Nm 1:48–53; 3:5–13; cf. Ex 32:25–29). Since Yahweh was their inheritance, the Levites had no territorial allotment in Israel (Jos 13:14, 33; 14:3–4). They settled in "levitical towns" scattered throughout the various tribal regions, and they survived on tithes from the rest of the people (Nm 18:21–24; 35:1–8; Jos 21:1–42). They functioned as priests in the rural areas, and, according to Deuteronomy, their responsibilities included teaching and interpreting the Law (Dt 17:18; 33:10). However, when Josiah centralized all worship in Jerusalem, the Levites who came from the outlying regions were accorded a lower status than the priests at the Temple (2 Kgs 23:8–9; cf. Dt 18:6–8). Because of their association with the sanctuaries outside Jerusalem, Ezekiel accused the Levites of idolatry and clearly subordinated them to the sons of Zadok, whom he considered to comprise the legitimate priesthood (Ez 44:10–15).

Following the Exile, the Levites attained a prominence in their own right, distinct from the priests (2 Chr 29:34). In Chronicles, they exercise a variety of ministries at the Temple, including carrying the ark of the covenant, supervising the entrances to the Temple, overseeing the treasury, leading the music in the assembly's worship, assisting the priests in Temple ritual, interpreting the Law, and preaching sermons (1 Chr 9:19–34; 15:11–16:38; 23:3–32; 2 Chr 17:7–9; 19:8–11; 35:3).

The Levites are models for all congregational ministers of music and song. They are renowned for their joy and capacity to uplift the assembly in its worship. They employ a wonderful variety of instruments to accompany their songs, including lyres, harps, cymbals, and trumpets (1 Chr 15:16–24). In fact, some of their singers are so anointed that their service to the assembly is called prophecy (1 Chr 25:1–3). Two of their great choral leaders, Asaph (a "seer"/2 Chr 29:30) and Korah, become patrons of two collections of psalms (Pss 50, 73–83; 42–49, 84, 85, 87, 88; cf. 1 Chr 6:16–32).

The Chronicler teaches us that the ingredients of genuine renewal are good preaching, genuine personal prayer, and vibrant liturgical celebrations. At various points in his work, we hear the echoes of fine levitical preaching coming from David, as well as Abijah and other prophets, and Hezekiah (1 Chr 28:2–10; 2 Chr 13:4–12; 15:1–7; 28:9–11; 29:6–11). We find further resonances in the Lord's address to Solomon and in Hezekiah's letter to the northerners (2 Chr 7:11–22; 30:6–9). The Chronicler indicates that prayer is the foundation of character for both David and Solomon (1 Chr 14:8–17; 17:16–27; 21:7–17; 29:10–20; 2 Chr 6:12–39). When the assembly gathers and acknowledges the Lord's presence, they invariably lift their voices in psalmody (1 Chr 12:19; 16:8–36; 2 Chr 7:3; 20:21). Their prayer, their song, and their joy are not superficial but emerge from the depths of hearts that acknowledge the Lord's faithfulness to his covenant with David (2 Chr 7:10; cf. 15:15; 30:21–27).

Toward the New Testament: The Son of David and the Temple of God

The New Testament writers never quote the books of Chronicles. However, the Chronicler's focus on David and the Temple prepares our minds to appreciate the stature of Jesus, of the Christian, and of the community in the preaching of the early Church.

The Chronicler's version of Nathan's prophecy is even more open to an interpretation pointing to the Messiah than the original text of the Deuteronomists (1 Chr 17:11–14; cf. 2 Sm 7:12–16). The Chronicler omits the prophetic reference to the failings of David's son (2 Sm 7:14: regarding Solomon). Furthermore, we note the difference made by the Chronicler's "midrash" (exposition) on 2 Samuel 7:16. According to the original text, God promises that *David's* house and kingdom will be secure and *David's* throne will be established forever (2 Sm 7:16). By contrast, according to the Chronicler's commentary, God promises to set *David's son* over *God's* house and kingdom, and the throne of *David's son* will be secure forever (1 Chr 17:14). It seems most likely that the Chronicler interpreted Nathan's words in light of Ezekiel's prophecy of the new David who would come and be the one shepherd for God's people (Ez 34:23–24; cf. Jer 23:5–6).

We know that when the Chronicler wrote his commentary on Samuel and Kings, the Davidic line had receded from power for over a century. We cannot be sure if he expected it ever to be rejuvenated in its traditional form. We do know that his words inspired future generations to look for the coming of the true son of David who would fulfill God's promise to David. We noted that 1 Chronicles 17, in comparison with 2 Samuel 7, speaks more about David's son than about David. The focus on David's son prepares for the description of Jesus in the New Testament. In Jesus, we meet the Son of David who surpasses his forefather according to the flesh by proclaiming the Good News of God's Kingdom and by taking authority over God's house (see Mk 12:35–37; Rom 1:3–4; cf. Heb 1:5; Mk 1:14–15).

Jesus' identity and destiny were intimately related to the Temple. In the Gospel of Luke, it is clear that he cleanses the Temple in order to take possession of it by filling its precincts with his teaching (Lk 19:45–21:38; cf. 2:41–49). At his trial and crucifixion, his accusers charge him with conspiracy to destroy the Temple (Mk 14:57–58; 15:29). In view of the Resurrection, the Holy Spirit enlightened the Johannine community to understand that the true Temple of God is the body of Jesus, crucified and transformed in risen glory (Jn 2:19–22).

Understanding the body in light of the Temple is also an important theme in Paul's letters to the Corinthians. He employs the Temple symbol in reference to both the corporate body of the whole Christian community (1 Cor 3:16–17; 2 Cor 6:16) and the corporeal body of the individual Christian (1 Cor 6:18–20). In the first instance, the community itself is God's Temple because this is where the Holy Spirit dwells (1 Cor 3:16; cf. 1 Chr 22:7). The character of holiness deriving from God's gift of the Spirit distinguishes the Christian community from all human institutions. Each person must reverence the community in the same way the people of Judah reverenced the Temple. Paul describes the community as God's Temple within the context of his admonition to the Corinthians for their factions and rivalries, which break down the unity of the body (1 Cor 1:11–13). Every form of behavior that causes division in the community constitutes a sacrilegious action.

In another context in the same letter, Paul uses the Temple symbol to develop a theology of the body. Surrounded by the decadence of Corinth, many of his newly baptized people lacked a sense of their own dignity and so remained in their pagan bondage to illicit sexual behavior. Paul teaches them to have an esteem for themselves based on the indwelling of the Holy Spirit. As the Temple of God, the Christian's body merits the same respect the Jews accorded the sanctuary in Jerusalem. Again, sexual immorality constitutes a sacrilege, since, like the Temple, the Christian's body must reveal the glory of the Lord through acts of virtue and service (1 Cor 6:18–20).

In Chronicles, we considered the Temple as it was built in Jerusalem through the efforts of David and Solomon. We will find that their initiative served as the model for the renewal of the city and the sanctuary accomplished through the reforms of Ezra and Nehemiah.

STUDY QUESTIONS

 1. How are the books of Chronicles "midrash"?
 2. What elements do the books of Ezra and Nehemiah share with Chronicles?
 3. Describe the spiritual atmosphere at the time of the Chronicler.
 4. What are three themes in the books of Chronicles?
 5. What does the Chronicler omit and why?
 6. Why is the Temple important in the books of Chronicles?
 7. What is the significance of repentance in Chronicles?
 8. Who were the Levites?
 9. How does the interpretation of the Davidic covenant differ for the Chronicler and for the Deuteronomists?
10. How is the symbol of the Temple appropriate to Jesus? To the Christian community? To the individual Christian?
11. What does your Church symbolize to the people of your village, town, or city? In your congregation, how do various people express their love and concern for the Church?
12. Try taking a Scripture story and rewrite it for your family or friends for a holiday, making it applicable to them.

I AND 2 CHRONICLES

18

EZRA AND NEHEMIAH: BUILDING COMMUNITY

How do you build a community of faith among an apathetic people? What does it take to overcome the spiritual inertia of nominal believers and form them into a body of people who are alive to God and to one another? The books of Ezra and Nehemiah tackle these concerns, which are so vexing to any pastor who sees his people suffering from spiritual desolation. They describe one of the most significant renewals in the Old Testament era, in fact, the one that gave Judaism a definitive shape that endured throughout the New Testament period and even to our own day.

In Ezra and Nehemiah, we find a model of clergy and laity complementing one another's offices and personal talents. Ezra, the priest, scholar, and pastor, communicates to his people a love for God's word while he teaches them the Law of Moses and offers them a sense of the dignity that will be theirs as they conform their lives to its precepts. Nehemiah, the governor, manager, and politician, is a pragmatist whose gifts of leadership marshal the people to complete his plan for the urban renewal of Jerusalem.

The texts of Ezra and Nehemiah form a single book. The Hebrew editions published them as one volume up to the fifteenth century A.D. Their separation into two books seems to derive from their transmission through Christian circles under the influence of the Septuagint.

Their contents span a time frame of more than a century, from Cyrus' edict permitting the Jews to return to their homeland from the Exile up to the end of the careers of Ezra and Nehemiah in Jerusalem (Ezr 1:1–Neh 13:31). Within this general framework, only two particular periods receive attention. The first part deals with the era of reconstruction in Jerusalem, from Cyrus' decree of 538 B.C. until the rededication of the Temple at the Passover of 515 B.C. (Ezr 1:1–6:22). After silently leaping over a gap of a half century, the editor uses the remainder of the text to describe the missions of Ezra and Nehemiah in Jerusalem, probably from 458 B.C. until sometime before 400 B.C. (perhaps a decade) (Ezr 7:1–Neh 13:31).

The dating of Ezra's mission and the relationship between the careers of Ezra and Nehemiah have been a central preoccupation of research on these books. We can be certain that Nehemiah served as governor of Judah under the Persian King Artaxerxes I (464–423 B.C.) for the twelve years from 445–433 B.C. (Neh 1:1; 2:1; 5:14). Later, following an interval of perhaps five years during which he returned to the Persian court, Nehemiah received a second appointment as governor for another twelve-year term (Neh 13:6).

The scholarly debate focuses on the date of Ezra's mission in Jerusalem. The most obvious reading of the text presumes the king to be Artaxerxes I (464–423 B.C.) and pinpoints Ezra's arrival in Judah in 458 B.C., "the seventh year of Artaxerxes", a dozen years before Nehemiah's arrival (Ezr 7:7). However, a significant pool of scholars defends a second proposal: that Nehemiah must have preceded Ezra to Jerusalem. They point out that Nehemiah does not mention Ezra or his reforms explicitly, and, indeed, many of Ezra's accomplishments seem to presuppose a situation that Nehemiah's activities created. These scholars prefer to date Ezra's arrival in 398 B.C., interpreting the "seventh year of Artaxerxes" (Ezr 7:7–8) in reference to the reign of Artaxerxes II (404–358 B.C.). A third proposal tries to do justice to the manner in which the text intermingles the missions of Ezra (Ezr 7–10; Neh 8–9) and of Nehemiah (Neh 1–7; 10–13) and a few times mentions them together (Neh 8:9; 12:31–43). This school of thought would emend the text of Ezra 7:7–8 to read "the thirty-seventh year of Artaxerxes" and date Ezra's arrival as 428 B.C.

The most recent scholarship tends to support the earliest date (458 B.C.). We will follow the most obvious reading and date Ezra's arrival in Jerusalem at 458 B.C., although there remains a number of indications that favor the alternative of 398 B.C. We will presume that Ezra arrived in Jerusalem over a decade before Nehemiah and leave open the possibility that there might have been some overlapping of their missions in Judah.

In its present arrangement, the text does not accurately represent the historical development of events in all details. For instance, the correspondence between Rehum, governor of Samaria, and Artaxerxes, the Persian king, could not have preceded the completion of the second Temple (when Cyrus, Cambyses, and Darius I succeeded each other as kings) but must be dated a half century later, probably around 456 B.C., when the Persians were concerned about turmoil in the west and took action against a revolt in Egypt (Ezr 4:6–23). The census list of the returning exiles in Nehemiah is a duplicate of the one in Ezra (Ezr 2:1–70 = Neh 7:6–72). Furthermore, the respective autobiographies of the heroes were originally self-contained units independent from one other: Ezra's Memoirs (Ezr 7:1–10:17; Neh 8:1–9:2) and Nehemiah's Memoirs (Neh 1:1–2:20; 3:33–7:5; 12:27–43; 13:4–31). The sections that present the exchange of correspondence between Persia and Jerusalem about the Temple are written in Aramaic, the international language of the empire (Ezr 4:8–6:12; 7:12–26).

The present arrangement of the text derives from the final editor's concern for pastoral ministry rather than history. First of all, the editor organized his material to demonstrate the continuity between preexilic and postexilic Judah. The restored Temple is the true spiritual descendant of Solomon's original structure. Even after the Davidic line of kings receded from prominence and the era of the classical prophets drew to a close, God continued to raise up gifted leaders to renew his people. And in a practical vein, the editor suggests that teamwork in ministry is an important part of God's design. By intertwining the memoirs of Ezra and Nehemiah, he shows how their ministry parallels that of Joshua and Zerubbabel. In both cases, new life comes to God's people from the combined talents of the priest and the governor, the cleric and the layman. By concentrating only on the era of reconstruction (538–515 B.C./Ezr 1:1–6:22) and on the era of reform (458–c. 410 B.C./Ezr 7:1–Neh 13:31), the books of Ezra and Nehemiah emphasize how to form a community of faith among people gripped by stress and suffering from spiritual lethargy.

The design of the text charts the process of building community according to successive stages that we will identify by five "Rs": roots, repentance, renaissance, reeducation, and reinforcement:

1. The *roots* of renewal under Ezra and Nehemiah reach back to the reconstruction of the Temple supervised by Zerubbabel and Joshua (538–515 B.C./Ezr 1:1–6:22);
2. *Repentance* is the stage when Ezra begins to mold the people into a community by calling the leaders to repentance (Ezr 7:1–10:44);
3. The *renaissance* of Jerusalem is symbolized in the reconstruction of its walls when Nehemiah's leadership skills motivate the people to express their interior change by working together (Neh 1:1–7:72);
4. Next, the *reeducation* of the people begins when Ezra steps forward again to strengthen the interior life by taking the people through a study of the Law of Moses (Neh 8:1–9:37); and
5. Finally, the *reinforcement* of Ezra's teaching occurs when the people, using the practical skills of Nehemiah, apply the Law to daily life in Jerusalem (Neh 10:1–13:31).

The five stages of this outline represent five principles that harmonize with one another in the development of community. We will be able to appreciate the interrelationship of the five "Rs" by focusing on the three points of reference that guide the course of renewal in Ezra and Nehemiah: (1) the Temple, (2) the remnant, and (3) the Law.

The Temple

Roots: The Temple identifies the members of the restored community in Jerusalem as the legitimate spiritual descendants of God's people who had lived under the prophets and kings prior to the Exile. Just as a foreign king destroyed the original Temple, so now a foreign king rebuilds the holy sanctuary: Cyrus the Persian reverses the damage caused by Nebuchadnezzar the Babylonian. Is not divine providence marvelous! The continuity between the first Temple (built by Solomon) and the second Temple (built under Zerubbabel the governor and Joshua the priest) is guaranteed when Cyrus puts into the hands of Judah's prince (Sheshbazzar) the very articles that Nebuchadnezzar had plundered. The precious relics of the original are the prime ingredients of the reconstructed Temple (Ezr 1:1–11; cf. 2 Chr 36:17–23).

The celebrations attending the preliminary initiatives at reconstruction in September of 538 B.C. echo the original establishment of the Temple. The leaders imitate David by first building the altar and offering sacrifices on it even before erecting the Temple walls. Mention of the tradesmen, the Levites, the trumpets, the singing, and the people's acclamation of praise recall the scenes of David placing the ark in Jerusalem and of Solomon building and dedicating the Temple. The mixture of weeping and praise makes it clear that the first Temple is foremost in the minds of the people working on the reconstruction (Ezr 3:1–13; cf. 1 Chr 21:18–30; 22:2, 15; 2 Chr 5:1–7:22). Reference to the Passover a few weeks after the dedication of the Temple in March or April of 515 B.C. links this event in spirit with the reforms of Hezekiah and Josiah (Ezr 6:13–22; cf. 2 Chr 30:1–27; 35:1–18).

Repentance and Reeducation: Concern for the Temple connects Ezra's mission of 458 B.C. with the events that took place in Jerusalem up to 515 B.C. Ezra received a written commission from King Artaxerxes to make the journey to Jerusalem with gifts of silver and gold to refurbish the Temple. Thus, Ezra's ministry begins with the same pattern that brought about the end of the Exile and the completion of the rebuilding project: in each case, the Persian king (first Cyrus, then Darius, then Artaxerxes) expresses his regard for the Temple in an official document accompanied by a financial commitment to its restoration (Ezr 7:1–26; cf. 1:1–11; 6:1–12).

Ezra's strategy suggests to us that concern for the building and the furnishings of worship is important to the renewal of a faith community. The physical enhancement of the Temple and its liturgy made possible with the king's silver and gold provides a symbol of the spiritual transformation promised to the people through repentance (Ezr 8:24–34; 9:1–10:17). At the Temple, the people gain a sense of their own dignity and receive motivation to live a new life according to God's word. Ezra brings the people to the newly enhanced environs of the Temple first to call them to repentance and later to celebrate the feast of Shelters (Tabernacles) as the climax of instructing them in the study of the Law (Ezr 10:1–17; Neh 8:13–17).

Reinforcement. "We will no longer neglect the Temple of our God" (Neh 10:40). This is the banner slogan of Nehemiah's administration as he applies Ezra's teaching to Judah's daily life. Foremost among the priorities he presents to the whole populace during his first term of office are the payment of proper tithes, the dedication of the first-born, and the provisions for the priests (Neh 10:33–40). Again in his second term as governor, some thirty years after the beginning of Ezra's mission, we find Nehemiah purging the sacred precincts of unsavory characters and rekindling the morale of the Levites at the Temple (Neh 13:1–14). In summary, we recognize that the Temple provides the theme that binds the whole work together since it is the focus of concern from beginning to end (Ezr 1:1–11; Neh 13:1–14, 30–31).

The Remnant

Roots: God forms the community of faith out of a remnant that has experienced the test of hard times. About five years before the fall of Jerusalem, Jeremiah had prophesied that those returning to the land from exile in Babylon would make up the remnant (Jer 24:4–10). The 42,360 indicated on the census list of returning exiles (not counting slaves and singers) represent the first wave of people to fulfill the prophet's word (Ezr 2:64; Neh 7:66).

By its very nature, the remnant does not simply blend into the preexisting populace but generates something of a spiritual counterculture. Some of the deepest resistance can arise from those who claim nominal allegiance to the faith. The strongest opposition to the renewal of Judah came from Samaritans who had descended from the intermarriage between Assyrians and Israelites after the destruction of the northern kingdom in 721 B.C. (Ezr 4:1–16; 5:8–16; Neh 3:33–4:17; 6:1–19; cf. 2 Kgs 17:24–41).

Repentance: Ezra shows us how to build community on the foundation of a faithful remnant. Even before leaving Babylon, he trains a nucleus who, by the witness of their lives, will bring Jerusalem out of its lethargy and apathy (Ezr 8:1–23). This is very personal work; each family and leader is so important that he tells us their names. Their basic training for protection is not the government but fasting, humble prayer, and reliance on God even during their journey from Babylon to Judah.

Repentance has the power to form a genuine community out of people who had been indifferent to the life of faith. Repentance of this quality is the fruit of anointed preaching and prayer, not just of moral exhortation. Ezra gives the people a sense of their history, identity, and vocation in the world as God's "remnant" (Ezr 9:6–15). New life comes to them when he leads the assembly in prayer, fasting, and confession, culminating in his invitation for them to leave behind their old life by renewing the covenant (Ezr 10:1–17). He reserves his most radical correction for a limited number of the ruling class and religious leaders whose marriages he dissolves on account of the scandal they caused to the whole community (Ezr 10:18–44; 9:1–2).

Renaissance and Reinforcement: The liturgical celebration of repentance and healing within the community must carry through to the practical situations of the work place. Nehemiah's example highlights two ingredients essential to building community: a concern for social justice and a commitment to hospitality. On the construction work site, he boosts the corporate morale by persuading the wealthy Jews to cancel the debts their poorer brothers had incurred in trying to keep up with their tax payments (Neh 5:1–13). In order to influence the magistrates in the land, he leads the way by example, canceling his governor's tax and opening his home (Neh 5:14–18). Like Ezra, Nehemiah knows his people; the various lists of names might seem tedious to us, but they indicate how Nehemiah counted each family as important to the whole community (Neh 11:4–12:26).

The Law of God

Roots and Repentance: Good teaching of God's word forms community. Ezra is the model interpreter of the sacred text. Indeed, we may see in him indications of a new Moses. Jewish tradition reveres him as the "Father of Judaism" because he is the first one to teach the whole Torah, that is, all five books of the Pentateuch in its final form. He was learned in the Scriptures but not bookish, having "devoted himself to studying the Law of Yahweh so as to put into practice and teach its statutes and rulings" (Ezr 7:10; cf. 7:6).

Although Ezra devotes himself to making the Scriptures accessible to God's people, he does not open the sacred text to them until his people are ready to appreciate its value. He refrains from explicitly teaching the Scriptures to them until they experience repentance or what we might call conversion. Prior to the people's exhibiting a basic change of heart and renunciation of sin, Ezra limits himself to preaching, basing his proclamation on the Law and the

Prophets (Ezr 9:1–10:17). Preaching brings the unbeliever to conversion. Teaching enables the converted believer to grow in the life of faith.

Reeducation: Ezra brings the "Book of the Law of Moses" into public view for the community that has already committed itself to enter into covenant with the Lord (Neh 8:1–18; cf. Ezr 10:3). A sign of a healthy community of faith is its apparently paradoxical reaction to God's word: the community's initial joy at the prospect of hearing the Sacred Scriptures becomes muted as God's word cuts to the heart and lays bare the community's failure to live according to the divine precepts. However, unlike the sullenness of the hardhearted in their preconversion days (Ezr 10:1–17), this sorrow is godly and opens up the prospect of deeper conversion and new life. Such a hearing of God's word is a cause for joy and celebration because the Lord will heal and forgive a people who cling to his word (Neh 8:1–12).

The community reaches maturity as its members personally study the words of the Law. Ezra, ever the concerned strategist, trains his Levites to answer the people's practical questions about issues of interpretation and application of the Law to their lives (Neh 8:7). Ezra's methodology of first instructing the clergy and heads of families so that they in turn can teach others to reflect on the Scriptures is an effective means of building the community (Neh 8:13).

Reinforcement: Teaching and study bear fruit through application. Nehemiah's organizational talents provide the perfect complement to Ezra's teaching skills. Under Nehemiah's administration, the Torah governs daily life in Jerusalem (Neh 10:29–40; 12:44; 13:3). The community that hears and studies the word now constructs an environment of faith as its members help one another to apply its life-giving truths to their situation. By animating the lives of his people, God's word can transform a culture.

By way of conclusion, the dedication of the city walls offers us a charming portrait of the success achieved by the efforts of Ezra and Nehemiah. A thread of sorrow runs through the people's reactions, from their mixture of weeping and praise at the Temple site in the earliest days, to their sitting in the rain listening to Ezra's call to repentance, and finally to their shedding tears of regret upon hearing the teaching of the Law (Ezr 3:12; 10:9; Neh 8:9). However, all this sorrow is transformed into undiluted joy as the choirs march in two processions—one led by Ezra and the other led by Nehemiah—going in opposite directions around the walls of Jerusalem (Neh 12:31–43). Part of the experience of building genuine community is to express the joy of God, who gathers his people to share life with each other.

Toward the New Testament: The Ministry of Teacher

Although the New Testament documents contain no direct references to the texts we have been considering, the ministries of Ezra and Nehemiah undoubtedly inspired the leaders of the first-century Christian communities. We will focus our attention on how the figure of Ezra in particular foreshadows the importance of the office of teacher in the body of Christ.

We preface our comments with two preliminary remarks, one about ministry and the other about community. We have seen that the editor of Ezra-Nehemiah structured the text in such a manner as to interweave the missions of the two main figures. His efforts had the effect of presenting Ezra and Nehemiah practically as partners of one another. The New Testament verifies the importance of his insight for the exercise of ministry. Jesus sent out his disciples in pairs (Mk 6:7). In his ministry to the churches, Paul almost always works with a companion, such as Barnabas, Silas, Timothy, or even a couple such as Priscilla and Aquila (Acts 13:1–3; 15:40; 16:1; 18:1–4). Ezra and Nehemiah introduce a concept verified throughout the New Testament: building community requires teamwork in ministry.

Such cooperation is important partly because of the stress involved in establishing a community of faith in the midst of a world that often resists the Gospel. Nehemiah, like the apostle Paul, suffered false accusation and risked his life to build the community (Neh 6:1–19; cf. Acts 21:27–40; Gal 2:1–10). The opposition of the Samaritans to the efforts of Ezra and Nehemiah offers a foreshadowing of the tensions experienced by some of the early communities Paul founded. The examples of the Thessalonians and the Philippians are sufficient to reinforce the point that forming community sometimes involves taking a stance that the world might not find acceptable (see 1 Thes 1:1–2:16; Phil 1:29–30).

Ezra can provide us with the model of the teacher in the Christian community. To highlight the importance of this office within its Christian context, we need only recall that the crowds called Jesus a teacher and prophet (Jn 3:2; Mk 6:15). Barnabas and Paul were among the teachers and prophets of the Church in Antioch (Acts 13:1–2). In Paul's list of offices in the Church, he mentions "apostle", "prophet", and "teacher", in order of priority (1 Cor 12:28). In later Pauline tradition, teachers are further qualified as "pastors and teachers" (Eph 4:11).

Ezra's example foreshadows the manner in which the teachers exercised their ministry in the Christian community. The "preachers" announced the word to unbelievers in order to bring them to conversion (see 1 Tm 2:7; 2 Tm 1:11; cf. Ezr 9:1–10:17). The "teachers" communicated the word of God to those who had been baptized so that the people could become ever more deeply rooted in the life of Christ (Heb 5:12; cf. Neh 8:1-12). The gifts of discernment and discretion we saw exemplified in Ezra remain the primary requirements of the teacher in the Christian community (Jas 3:1-18). Just as Ezra applied the word to his own life before teaching others, so Timothy must adhere to the standard of apostolic instruction by submitting his whole life to the Scriptures in order to preserve the community from floundering in a sea of popular opinion (2 Tm 2:14-3:17; cf. Ezr 7:10).

Because God's word alone has the power to distinguish between soul and spirit (Heb 4:12), when obedient hearts receive it, God's word forms community (1 Pt 1:22-2:3). As we reflect on Ezra's witness, we can pray for the grace to respond to Paul's admonition that, in our concern for others, we would correctly handle the word of truth so that our work of service would contribute to a solid foundation for life in the Christian community (2 Tm 2:15).

In Ezra and Nehemiah, we have studied the formation of the remnant. We now will turn to the roots of this concept in the prophets, especially in the prophet Isaiah.

STUDY QUESTIONS

1. Compare the individuals Ezra and Nehemiah.
2. What are the five "Rs" in building community?
3. What are the three points of reference guiding the renewal in Ezra and Nehemiah?
4. Why is it fitting that a foreign king permit the restoration of the Temple in Jerusalem?
5. How is Ezra the "Father of Judaism" and the model for the New Testament teacher?
6. Have you ever had to rebuild something—a marriage, a career, a place to live? If you were to rebuild your life of faith now, how would you go about doing it?
7. What do the books of Ezra and Nehemiah teach you about the process of renewal that brings the community of faith into greater harmony with the plan of God?
8. What qualities in Ezra and Nehemiah make them models for leadership for the Church today?

EZRA

NEHEMIAH

PROPHETS

INTRODUCTION TO THE PROPHETS

Prophecy is the discernment of God's action and the communication of his will at a specific point in history. A prophet is a man or woman anointed by God and ultimately recognized by the people to announce God's word to his or her generation. The prophet is a servant of the word who receives revelation and personally experiences its power for judgment and salvation even as he or she proclaims it to others. Therefore, prophecy is an intensely personal event that begins in God and shapes the prophet's life to foreshadow the manner in which the prophetic word will form the community of God's people.

Prophecy is both a grace (because it originates in God) and a ministry (because it directs people toward God). Over the course of its long history in ancient Israel, extending at least from the time of Samuel (c. 1040 B.C.) until the advent of Alexander the Great (c. 332 B.C.), prophecy exhibited a magnificent diversity in form and content. We will trace the history of prophecy in Israel and then reflect on some of its qualities that are consistent throughout the Old Testament literature of the three major and twelve minor prophets.

The History of Prophecy in Israel

Prelude to Prophecy—The Pentateuch and Judges (Prior to 1100 B.C.): The phenomenon of prophecy was common throughout the ancient Near East. The Mari texts, which date from the eighteenth century B.C. in Mesopotamia, refer to men and women who proclaimed oracles on behalf of a variety of deities. In Babylon of later times, priests at the temples communicated messages to devotees who approached them. Diviners and ecstatics also played a role in the religious life of both ancient Egypt (cf. Ex 7:8–13, 22) and Canaan (cf. 1 Kgs 18:20–40). Consideration of the religious background of the ancient world allows us to appreciate the uniqueness of prophecy in Israel. In Israel, prophecy takes authority over both king and people in a manner unparalleled elsewhere. Moreover, in contrast to the phenomena in other cultures, the prophetic word in Israel is not a momentary fragment but a dynamic power that exhibits a consistency strong enough to generate a tradition extending for almost a millennium.

The Elohist and Priestly authors traced the roots of prophecy back to the Pentateuch. According to the Elohist, Abraham (Gn 20:7 [E]), Aaron, and Miriam (Nm 12:2–8 [E]) were prophets along with Moses (Dt 34:10–11 [E]; cf. Dt 18:13–18 [D]). The Priestly writer lends his support to this assessment of Aaron (Ex 7:1 [P]) and Miriam (Ex 15:20 [P]). The Elohist is so bold as to highlight Balaam the foreigner from Mesopotamia as Yahweh's prophet (Nm 22:2–24:25). The Deuteronomists similarly designate Deborah as a prophetess during the early days after the settlement in Canaan (Jgs 4:4). Designation of these people as prophets is an important theological insight by the sacred writers who labored in the ninth (Elohist source) and sixth (Priestly source) centuries B.C. However, we will begin our examination of prophecy from the time of Samuel because the accepted office of prophet is tied historically to the advent of the kings of Israel.

The history of prophecy in Israel really begins with the time of Samuel (c. 1040 B.C.) and extends into the period when the culture of Greece held sway over the world (c. 250 B.C.). We will survey the development of Old Testament prophecy in four stages: (a) the formative era prior to the first written collection of oracles (1100–750 B.C. [Amos]), (b) the preexilic era (750–587 B.C.), (c) the exilic era (587–538 B.C.), and (d) the postexilic era (538–250 B.C.).

The Formative Period (1100–750 B.C.): The first prophets we meet in Israel are the groups of ecstatics who roamed the countryside at the time of Saul's anointing (1030 B.C.), announcing their oracles to the accompaniment of music and dance (1 Sm 10:5–13; cf. 19:18–24). The fact that Samuel was priest, prophet, and leader of Israel at the same time indicates that prophecy was not limited to the fringes of society represented in the radical ecstatic brotherhoods (1 Sm 3:20). When Samuel the prophet designates first Saul (1 Sm 9:11–10:16) and then David (1 Sm 16:1–13) as king over Israel, we receive an indication of the official role that prophecy would play in relationship to the monarchy throughout Israel's history.

The prophet Nathan became a member of David's royal court in Jerusalem with the authority to advise (2 Sm 7:1–17) and to admonish (2 Sm 12:1–15) the king in a manner unheard of in other cultures. Distinct from the court prophets, we find the sanctuary prophets who carried on their activities where the Israelites gathered for worship in the early days at Shiloh (1 Kgs 14:1–2), Bethel (2 Kgs 2:3), Gilgal (2 Kgs 4:38), and later at the Temple in Jerusalem (cf. Jer 23:11; 35:4). In summary, we note that as the court prophets dealt with kings, so the Temple prophets worked with priests.

However, the distinction between court and sanctuary was never absolute among the prophets who operated with individual freedom. Thus, Ahijah of the sanctuary at Shiloh prophesies first the success of Jeroboam's rebellion (1 Kgs 11:27–39) and then the Lord's removal of Jeroboam (1 Kgs 14:1–11). In similar fashion, Shemaiah (1 Kgs 12:22–24), Jehu ben Hanani (1 Kgs 16:1–3, 7), and Micaiah ben Imlah (1 Kgs 22:5–8) were prophets who reprimanded, admonished, and judged their kings.

Micaiah ben Imlah represents an important witness to the priority of reason over ecstasy in exercising the prophetic gift. Micaiah lacks the spiritual manifestations of the ecstatics, contradicts their advice to King Jehoshaphat (870–848 B.C.), and is vindicated by the outcome of events in the battle in the Transjordan (1 Kgs 22:5–38). Around the same time in the northern kingdom, Elijah's coolness contrasts with the antics of the prophets of Baal when Elijah successfully calls down fire from Yahweh (1 Kgs 18:20–40). We must note, however, the intimate association of Elijah and Elisha with the prophetic brotherhoods (2 Kgs 2:7; 3:15; 4:1).

The Preexilic Period (750–587 B.C.): Amos, the first servant of the word to have his oracles preserved in written form, is reluctant to call himself a prophet, apparently because he wants to dissociate himself from the ecstatic brotherhoods (Am 7:14). It is not by chance that the first literary prophets emerged from the northern kingdom of Israel, since this had been the territory of Elijah and Elisha in the previous century. Nevertheless, Hosea is the only literary prophet who was native to the northern kingdom; all the others, including Amos (who served in the north), came from the southern territory of Judah.

Chronologically, the preexilic prophets are clustered in two groups, the first arising from the middle through last half of the eighth century B.C. (760–700 B.C.: Amos and Hosea in Israel; Isaiah and Micah in Judah) and the second coming from the last part of the seventh century and the first decade of the sixth century B.C. (635–587 B.C.: Zephaniah, Jeremiah, Nahum, Habakkuk, and Ezekiel). No literary prophets emerged during the repressive days of Manasseh (687–642 B.C.), which even witnessed the martyrdom of some prophets (cf. 2 Kgs 21:16).

The literary prophets whose words are preserved in the sacred text represent only an elite few of those who exercised the prophetic ministry. The names of Huldah, the Temple prophetess who strongly supported Josiah's reforms (2 Kgs 22:14–20), and Uriah, the prophet-martyr under Jehoiakim (Jer 26:20–23), probably reflect many others who will remain forever anonymous as faithful servants of the Lord. On the other hand, the preexilic prophets had to confront a majority of others bearing the same title who proclaimed a false word because of their own vanity, fear, or ignorance. Their chastisement of the false prophets both at the Temple and in the royal court became so constant that it represents a theme common to most of the preexilic prophets (Mi 3:5–6; Zep 3:4; Jer 5:13; 23:9–40; Ez 13:1–23; cf. Am 2:11–12; Is 9:14–15).

The preexilic prophets shared in common a focus on certain themes. They were concerned with calling Israel and Judah to repentance in light of the people's neglect to live up to the covenant demands of serving the Lord and caring for one another. In general, the prophets of this era saw God's judgment coming upon both Israel and Judah in the form of invasion by the major foreign powers Assyria, Egypt, and Babylon. They prophesied the preservation of a remnant of faithful ones whom the Lord would preserve as a nucleus for rebuilding his people (Am 9:8; Is 4:3; 8:16–20; 10:20–23; 37:32; Mi 2:12; 4:7; Zep 2:7; 3:12–13; Jer 23:3). In a related theme, they foresaw the coming of a Davidic Messiah who would surpass the kings of their own day in faithfulness to the Lord (Is 9:1–6; 11:1–9; Mi 5:1–3; Jer 23:5–6; Ez 34:23–31; 37:24–28).

The Exilic Period (587–538 B.C.): Ezekiel marks an astounding development in prophecy by the fact that he received his call outside the Promised Land in Babylon (Ez 1:1–3:21). Some twenty years after Ezekiel receded from view, Deutero-Isaiah received his vocation as a prophet (Is 40:1–11). Just as Ezekiel proclaimed the Exile's beginning, so Deutero-Isaiah proclaimed its ending (Ez 12:1–20; Is 40:1–11). By contrast with their preexilic forebears, the exilic prophets looked forward to the advent of salvation, not to judgment for Judah. God was going to do a new work (Is 48:6–7), promising his people a new covenant (Jer 31:31–34) by giving them a new heart and spirit (Ez 36:24–32) under the prospect of raising them from the death of the Exile to a new life (Ez 37:1–14) and leading them back to Jerusalem by way of a new Exodus (Is 40:3–5).

However, the exilic prophecies offered diverse portraits of Jerusalem's restoration. The early promises of Jeremiah and Ezekiel, which contemplated the restoration of the Davidic line (Jer 23:5–6; Ez 37:24–28), echo only once in Deutero-Isaiah (Is 55:3), who boldly called attention to the foreign King Cyrus as Yahweh's servant in the liberation of the Jews from exile (Is 45:1–7). Ezekiel presented a vision of a holy and purified society gathered around the Temple (Ez 40:1–48:35), while Deutero-Isaiah was less concerned with specific institutions, such as kingship, priesthood, and the holy sanctuary (cf. Is 44:28), and more preoccupied with the restoration of Zion in general as a manifestation of divine grace (Is 52:1–12; 54:1–17). During the Exile, especially through the work of Deutero-Isaiah, prophecy took on a more cosmopolitan perspective that contemplated God's action among the foreign nations as well as among his chosen people.

The Postexilic Period (538–250 B.C.): Numerous prophets, both men and women, carried on the prophetic ministry after the Exile in the environs of the Temple (see Zec 7:3; Neh 6:14). With the demise of hope for the restoration of kingship and the Davidic line in Judah after the Exile (cf. Hg 2:20–23; Zec 4:1–14), prophetic activity focused on the priesthood, the Temple, its laws, and its liturgy (Hg 1:1–2:9; Zec 3:1–10; Mal 1:6–2:9). The postexilic prophets appealed to observance of the precepts of the Law as the means of preserving Judah's distinctive identity in the world. By comparison with their preexilic forebears, the postexilic prophets tended to be more protective of Judah by offering her the promise of salvation in contrast with the judgment Yahweh pronounced against the nations (Obadiah, Joel, Zechariah 9–14).

Among Judah's prophets in the postexilic era, we detect two tendencies that are in tension with one another. On the one hand, we note a defensive trend toward sectarianism, which portrays Judah as an enclave of the elite whom God will protect as he overthrows the nations (Jl 3:1–4:21; Zec 12:1–14:21; Ob vv. 1–21). On the other hand, we note the growth of a vision for God's design to extend redemption beyond the frontiers of his chosen people to embrace the Gentiles (Is 56:1–7; 66:18–23; Zec 14:16–19). Issued as the last text in the prophetic collection, the book of Jonah offers assurance of God's desire to show mercy to the Gentiles as well as to the Jews in its portrait of his compassion on the people of Nineveh (Jon 3:1–10).

The postexilic prophets extend our vision to the limits of world history by interpreting history in view of God's universal judgment at the end time, when he will overthrow the present world order and bestow his everlasting peace upon his elect (Ob vv. 1–21; Jl 3:1–4:21; Zec 12:1–14:21). This perspective provides the bridge by which late prophecy passes into apocalyptic literature (Dn 7–12).

The Qualities of Prophecy

By way of review, we can reflect on the uniqueness of the prophetic word by comparing it to the other two categories of biblical literature, namely, the Law and the wisdom books. We highlight three characteristics that distinguish prophetic literature in the biblical canon: its personal quality, its focus on Israel, and its orientation toward the future.

In contrast with both the legislation in the Pentateuch and the wisdom literature, prophecy is intensely personal and emerges from the life experience of the individual prophet. This principle holds true especially for the major preexilic and exilic prophets. Amos' experience as a herdsman sensitizes him to injustice in the marketplace (cf. Am 5:10–13), just as Hosea's broken marriage is a metaphor of God's covenantal love, which Israel rejected (Hos 1:1–3:5). We detect other examples of how deeply the word unites with the individual prophet, for instance, in the names of Isaiah's children (Is 7:3; 8:3, 18), Jeremiah's Confessions (e.g., Jer 11:18–12:6; 20:7–18) and celibacy (Jer 16:1–4), Ezekiel's lack of mourning over his wife's death (Ez 24:15–27), and Deutero-Isaiah's Servant Songs (e.g., Is 50:4–11; 52:13–53:12). In all the literary prophets, the personality of the servant shines forth. We need only consider the vehemence toward the mighty nations that Nahum and Obadiah expressed, the conviction of divine judgment in Joel and Zechariah 9–14, the passion for the Temple in Haggai, Zechariah 1–8, and Malachi, and the constancy of faith under trial in Habakkuk.

The prophets looked at the world from the standpoint of life in Israel and Judah at a certain point in history. The historical setting of each prophet greatly affected the shape and content of his message. By contrast, the legislative texts in the Pentateuch aim at universal application for each member of God's people in every time and place. Furthermore, the sages who authored the wisdom literature exhibit a cosmopolitan perspective by describing principles of life that are true for all people, for Gentiles as well as Jews. Each of the prophets is committed to the renewal of covenant faith in Israel in his own generation. Even when the prophets describe the extending of salvation to the nations beyond Judah's frontiers, they conceive of redemption in terms of the nations joining God's people in the renewed Israel and new Jerusalem (Is 56:1–7; 66:18–22; Zec 8:20–23; 14:16–19).

Although each of the prophets speaks to his own generation, the word he announces releases a power to shape history far beyond his own vision. Because it originates in God, the prophetic word always bears fruit (Is 55:10–11). The word is the divine agent that makes history. History conforms to God's word rather than vice versa. Prophecy is not the prediction of a predetermined future. Rather, prophecy is the release of God's power to affect history and bring salvation to the world. Once he proclaims the word through his prophet, God attentively guards the word in order to fulfill it (Jer 1:12; 28:6; Nm 23:19).

God's word always reaches fulfillment, but seldom in exactly the way the prophet originally imagined. For instance, in 701 B.C., Isaiah correctly prophesied God's intervention to cause Sennacherib's Assyrian army to retreat from Jerusalem, but the affliction the Assyrians suffered differed from Isaiah's expectation (Is 37:29–33; cf. 37:36–38). More important for our consideration is the evidence that, by God's design, the prophetic word always reaches a greater fulfillment in Christ than the Old Testament prophet could have imagined. For example, while Isaiah thought of a young married woman giving birth to a child named "Immanuel" in 734 B.C., his prophecy reached fulfillment in the virginal conception of Jesus in the womb of Mary (Is 7:14; cf. Mt 1:23).

The Books of the Prophets

Prophets exercise their ministry through oral proclamation of the word. When the oral word is written, it becomes fixed as a permanent record. The fact that disciples of the prophets wrote down the words of their masters indicates their conviction that the prophetic word that God addressed to their historical moment would be vital to every future generation of his people. Once the prophetic word becomes part of a text, it takes on a new vocation. Now it becomes a divine resource expressing God's promises that form the memory and shape the mind of Israel so that the people in successive generations know how to orient their lives toward God with confident hope.

Isaiah (Is 8:16–20), Jeremiah (Jer 36:1–32), and Ezekiel (Ez 2:8–3:3) were prophets who seem to have taken an active role in the writing of their words. The book of Jonah is exceptional in the collection of the prophets as a text originating in a written rather than an oral form. For the most part, disciples of the prophets produced the books bearing the names of their masters. In some cases (e.g., Ezekiel, Habakkuk), disciples produced the complete text within a generation of the master prophet. In other cases, the final text was issued centuries after the original prophet: for example, the final edition of Isaiah (Is 1–66) seems to come from late in the fifth century (450–400 B.C.), some three hundred years after the ministry of the original prophet (740–700 B.C.).

Sirach's reference to the twelve (minor) prophets indicates that the whole collection of the prophetic books was completed by 180 B.C. (Sir 49:10). Thus, the prophetic tradition in the Bible spanned a millennium. As we read through the prophets, we can marvel at the constancy of God, who inspired his people with divine gifts in order to produce this source of revelation pointing to Christ.

STUDY QUESTIONS

1. What is prophecy?
2. What are the four stages of the development of Old Testament prophecy?
3. What are the themes of the preexilic prophets?
4. How did prophecy change during the Exile?
5. What was the focus of postexilic prophecy?
6. What was the perspective of postexilic prophecy that led to apocalyptic literature?
7. How does prophecy compare with the two other categories of biblical literature, i.e., the Law and the wisdom books, in terms of personal interaction and outlook on the world?
8. Do we see prophets today? Who are they? How do you recognize them?
9. If the family is a minichurch, then we should be able to be prophets to build up the church that is our family. How do you exercise prophecy at home to enhance the spiritual life of your family?

THE PROPHETS

I. Prelude to Prophecy: The Pentateuch and Judges (Prior to 1100 B.C.)
    "Prophets" before Samuel: Abraham (Gn 20:7); Aaron (Ex 7:1); Miriam (Ex 15:20); Moses (Dt 18:18; 34:10); Balaam (Nm 22:2–24:25); Deborah (Jgs 4:4).

II. The Formative Period (1100–750 B.C.)
    Ecstatic bands of prophets by the time of Samuel (c. 1040–1020 B.C.): 1 Sm 10:10–12 (10:5–6); 1 Sm 19:18–24. Samuel as prophet (1 Sm 3:20; 9:9).

    Nathan the prophet at David's court (c. 1010–960 B.C.): 2 Sm 7:1–17; 12:1–15 (cf. 12:25)

    Northern Kingdom (Israel)
    Elijah (874–853) (1 Kgs 17 to 2 Kgs 2)
    Elisha (c. 853–795) (2 Kgs 2–13)

III. The Preexilic Period (750–587 B.C.)

Northern Kingdom (Israel)	*Southern Kingdom (Judah)*
Amos (c. 750–740)	
Hosea (c. 745–736)	Isaiah (c. 740–690)
	(Is 1–39)
	Micah (c. 740–710)
Fall of Samaria and end of northern kingdom (721 B.C.)	
	Kingdom of Judah (721–587 B.C.)
	Zephaniah (c. 635–630)
	Jeremiah (c. 627–580)
	Nahum (c. 612)
	Habakkuk (c. 604–599)
	Fall of Jerusalem and beginning of the Exile (587 B.C.)

IV. The Exilic Period (587–538 B.C.)
    Ezekiel (593–c. 571)
    Deutero-Isaiah (c. 550–525) (Is 40–55)

V.   The Postexilic Period (538–250 B.C.)
      Haggai (520)
      Zechariah 1–8 (520–518)
      Trito-Isaiah (c. 525–500) (Is 56–66)
      Malachi (c. 475)
      Obadiah (c. 450[?])
      Joel (c. 375[?])
      Deutero-Zechariah (c. 350[?]) (Zec 9–14)
      The book of Jonah (c. 275[?])

AMOS AND HOSEA:
JUSTICE FOR THE NORTHERN KINGDOM

How can a society experience restoration when its primary values are being washed away in a flood of materialism? There comes a point at which material progress becomes an enemy of cultural and spiritual development. When the profit motive rules a society, concern for possessions overtakes care for people, and religious ritual replaces personal faith. Those of us who live in Western society today might find it noteworthy that the earliest of the classical prophets, Amos and Hosea, experienced God's call in a period of Israel's history distinguished by remarkable economic prosperity, individual self-assertion and consequent spiritual complacency.

Amos and Hosea were distinctive individuals who undertook their missions as prophets in the northern kingdom during the reign of Jeroboam II (783–743 B.C.). They each came from a different background and had a distinct personality. Amos, the older of the two, came from Judah and brought the practical mind of a herdsman to his ministry. By contrast, Hosea was a native of Israel who exhibited the sensitivities of a family man throughout his service. These two individuals had the same reaction to the times in which they lived: both were overwhelmed by the loss of traditional values in their society. Amos, the livestock man, was dumbfounded at the corruption in the marketplace. Hosea, the family man, experienced turmoil and breakdown in his marriage. By teaching them how to respond to the shocks of life characteristic of their times, the Lord formed both of them into singular prophets who could speak from their day to ours.

AMOS

The Northern Kingdom under Jeroboam II

Jeroboam II (783–743 B.C.), a most capable monarch, expanded Israel's territory at a time when Assyria was preoccupied with internal tensions. He issued a stinging defeat to Damascus and took control of the whole Transjordan all the way down to the southern end of the Dead Sea (2 Kgs 14:25–27). He capitalized on Israel's control of the main trade route linking Egypt to the nations in the north and east so that his kingdom flourished as a crossroads of commerce. Signs of prosperity multiplied. The wealthy class built mansions, purchased two houses (one for summer and one for winter), bedecked them with fine stone, appointed them with ivory and furnished them with elegant couches (Am 3:12, 15; 5:11; 6:4). Peace was at hand, business was good, and opportunities for expansion were abounding. Into this world of urban extravagance came Amos, the herdsman and fig-dresser from the village of Tekoa, located in the vast rolling hills of Judah.

The Book of Amos

The introductory verse (1:1) suggests the contents of the book of Amos fall into two categories: the first part communicates the prophet's words (1:1–6:14), while the second part describes his visions (7:1–9:10). An elaboration of the Lord's promise to restore the house of David and to bring greater prosperity to his people concludes the whole work (9:11–15).

Most of the contents originate with the prophet himself. However, the book went through a series of editions before achieving its present form. Either the prophet himself during his lifetime or a circle of scribes who fled to Jerusalem after the destruction of Samaria in 721 B.C. brought a text of Amos' words south to Judah.

The three doxologies distributed throughout the book (4:13; 5:8–9; 9:5–6) come from one author at a later date, perhaps just after 621 B.C., when Josiah ordered the destruction of the sanctuary at Bethel as part of his reforms (2 Kgs 23:15–20). The concluding promise of reestablishing the line of David comes from the postexilic era either during or following Zerubbabel's terms as governor (Am 9:11–15; cf. Ezr 4:1–6:22; Hg 2:20–23). It seems that a circle of scribes produced the final edition of the book around 500 B.C.

The Vocation and Message of Amos

Amos exercised his ministry when the northern kingdom was at the height of prosperity before the Assyrian resurgence under Tiglath-Pileser III in 745 B.C. A suitable estimate would date his career in the decades of c. 760–740 B.C.

The one biographical passage in the text indicates the degree to which officials of the kingdom considered Amos to be a thorn in their side (7:10–17). Perhaps around 750 B.C., Amaziah, the high priest of the sanctuary at Bethel (where Amos issued most of his pronouncements), expels Amos from the hallowed precincts, accuses him of sedition against Israel, and demands that the "visionary" return to his native Judah (7:10–13).

In response, Amos offers the story of his vocation. First, he dissociates himself from the guild of professional prophets officially trained to work at the sanctuary or court (7:14; cf. 1 Kgs 20:13–34, 35–43; 2 Kgs 2:1, 3; 4:1; Mi 3:5–8). By trade, he was a cattleman and a sheepherder who also knew the science of cutting figs at the proper time to sweeten the fruit. Amos asserts that the only basis for his ministry is God's intervention and command that he leave his home in Judah to issue a warning about the impending doom about to descend on unsuspecting Israel (7:10–17).

This biographical glimpse of Amos offers us some indication of the issues central to his teaching. We will survey his message by focusing on three recurrent themes: (a) social justice in relation to worship; (b) the shape and sound of God's word; and (c) the Day of Yahweh.

Social Justice: From beginning to end, Amos issues a withering attack on religious ceremony that camouflages social corruption. His vehemence is all the more striking for the fact that he voices his accusations precisely within the setting of the sanctuary at Bethel (7:10–13; cf. 3:14; 4:4; 5:5–6) and extends his references to the other shrines of the northern kingdom at Dan (8:14) and Gilgal (4:4; 5:5) and even to Beersheba, Abraham's place of residence, which was a pilgrimage site in the south (5:5; 8:14; cf. Gn 22:19).

Amos exposes the hypocrisy of elaborate rites devoid of social consciousness. Fascination with ritual divorced from concern for neighbor amounts to an offense against God (5:21–24). Everywhere he turns, Amos sees injustice that breeds an increasing disparity between rich and poor. Extortion and cheating in the marketplace deprive the farmer of a just price for his grain (5:11; 8:4–6). Incidences of oppression by the upper class include sexual abuse of servants (2:7) and debt slavery of the poor (8:6). Amos' scathing criticism cuts across the spectrum of the aristocracy touching the king (7:10–11), the high priest (7:16–17), and the wealthy of Samaria (4:1–3; 6:1–7).

The force of the prophet's words derive from his consciousness that by such deeds Israel has betrayed the Lord who knew them so intimately in the covenant (3:1–2). Because of their injustice, the people's worship constitutes an act of rebellion against the Lord (4:4–5; 5:21). The sinister quality of such false religion lies in its capacity to perpetuate the delusion that ritual without deeds guarantees redemption. In fact, restoration of the society will come through the practice of justice, the primary quality of relationship to God in the covenant (5:15, 24).

This does not mean that Amos would cast aside liturgy as irrelevant and delusive. To the contrary, he insists that authentic worship is the source of power for the redemption of society. The Lord responds to the prayers of those who intercede for mercy on behalf of the people (7:1–6). New life comes to the land through a humble seeking of the Lord in repentance (5:4). The future, whether it be restoration or deterioration, begins with what takes place in the sanctuary of worship (see 7:7–9; 8:1–3; 9:1–4).

The Word of God: Because Amos knew that spiritual lethargy derives from ritual without God's word, he established himself at Bethel in order to preach where the community assembled for worship. From Amos, we hear not only God's words but also the sound of his voice. Yahweh roars like a lion (1:2; cf. 3:4, 8). His utterances reverberate with a tenor that would have kept a herdsman like Amos on guard throughout the night.

Imagine the impact Amos would have had on his audience at Bethel (1:3–2:16). Speaking to the urbane and finely dressed audience at Bethel, Amos would have won nods of approval as he depicted God's judgment hanging over each of the countries surrounding Israel (beginning with Damascus and ending with Judah: 1:3–2:5). But the audience's reaction would have changed when the prophet refused to stop at the borders but instead reserved the harshest of divine reprimands for Israel, indicating that her crimes far exceeded those of the other nations (2:6–16)! Amos communicates his blunt message through a refined oratorical style. He makes artistic use of repetition to unfold the crimes of the nations ("for three ... for four": 1:3–2:6) and to reinforce God's call for repentance ("and still you would not come back to me": 4:6–11).

By rejecting the words of Amos (7:10–13) and by silencing other prophets (2:12), Israel demonstrates an unwillingness to hear the Lord. Amos perceives that the Lord will correct Israel precisely by giving in to her demand for silence: he will not speak to her for some time. In the near future, this materially prosperous land will experience a deep, pervasive famine, not for physical bread, but for hearing God's word (8:11–12; cf. Dt 8:3). By her refusal to listen to the voice of God, Israel is cultivating for herself unparalleled affliction.

The Day of Yahweh: The sequence of Amos' visions indicates that he became increasingly conscious of impending doom hanging over Israel because of the injustice in the land. In his early visions of locusts and drought, the prophet is able to avert disaster by means of intercessory prayer (7:1–6). However in the last three visions of the plumb-line, the ripe fruit, and the sanctuary (7:7–9; 8:1–3; 9:1–4), the prophet shows that calamity has become irrevocable. The Lord seems to be indicating that by rejecting the prophet's word, Israel had crossed the line of no return.

We might note that Amos' visions offer precedent for the images of God's holiness and judgment, which characterize the vocations of the great prophets (Is 6:1–7; Jer 1:11–19; Ez 1:1–3:3). Symbolic visions for interpreting the times will recur in subsequent prophets and will lead to the development of apocalyptic literature (see Ez 8:1–18; 11:1–13; Zec 1:7–6:8; 14:1–21; Dn 7:1–12:13). Amos introduces a foundational concept into this vast tradition when he speaks of the "Day of Yahweh" (Am 5:18–20; cf. Zep 1:14–18; Jl 1:15–20; 2:1–11).

Whereas Amos' audience had previously looked upon this day as a time of reward, the prophet declares it will be a time of divine judgment and terror for the unrighteous (5:18–20). Instead of joy, it will provoke lamentation; instead of rejuvenation, it will cause fainting (8:9–10, 13–14). Within the setting of his times, long before anyone else, Amos foresaw the threat to Israel coming from Assyria (3:11; 5:27; 6:14). His promise of Samaria's destruction and exile would find its fulfillment in the events of 721 B.C. (4:2–3; 5:2; 6:7, 8–14; cf. 2 Kgs 17:1–6). Most importantly, Amos instructed the people about how to interpret the Assyrian invasion. It would represent the fulfillment of God's word, and it would have an aspect of the divine visitation on the injustice rampant among his people (3:13–15; 9:1–4, 7–10).

In spite of all the destruction to follow, Amos knew that the Lord would preserve "a remnant of Joseph" who would persevere in practicing justice (5:14–15). This remnant on the side of the oppressed provides the seeds of hope for Israel's future. The postexilic addition to the end of Amos is much more than a happy ending to a gloomy message. It reveals the ultimate goal of all God's actions by describing beyond "that Day" when the Lord brings the remnant to the fullness of life in fidelity to his promises to David and to all Israel (9:11–15).

Toward the New Testament: Genuine Worship and Restoration

We have noted how the book of Amos prescribes an end to the old order of life and worship in Israel as a precondition for the restoration of the people.

The manner in which the Acts of the Apostles quotes the text of Amos on two occasions corresponds to this two-stage sequence by which God forms his people.

In Stephen's speech, which summarizes the history of God's relationship to Israel, Stephen applies Amos' critique of arid ritualism to the idolatry of the ancients in the wilderness (Acts 7:42–43; cf. Am 5:25–27). We should note that in the Hebrew text, Amos upholds the virtue of the Hebrews in the wilderness by dissociating them from the idolatry of his own time in Israel (see Am 5:25–27). By contrast, the Septuagint version that Acts quotes makes no distinction between the Israelites of the wilderness period and those whom the Assyrians exiled from the land in 721 B.C. Furthermore, the text in Acts passes over reference to Assyria in order to focus on the more famous exile of the people of Judah to Babylon in 587 B.C. (Acts 7:43; cf. Am 5:27). These rereadings of the Amos text by the Septuagint translators and by Luke, the author of Acts, serve only to highlight the fact that Stephen, "a man full of faith and of the Holy Spirit" (Acts 6:5), spoke as a new prophet, the Amos of his day insofar as he was exposing the falsity of ritualized Temple worship (cf. Acts 6:13; 7:35–50). The high priest and elders in his audience interpreted his words and reacted in a manner consistent with Amaziah's expulsion of Amos (Acts 6:15–7:1, 51–53, 54, 57–59; cf. Am 7:10–17). Just as Amos' words declared an end to the empty cult in Bethel so that God could restore a humble remnant by obedience to his word, so Stephen's speech announced the bankruptcy of empty Temple ritual to be replaced by personal submission to the Lordship of Jesus revealed in the power of his Resurrection (Acts 7:51–60).

At the Council of Jerusalem in A.D. 49, the apostles decreed that Jew and Gentile together make up the new people of God (Acts 15:1–35; cf. Gal 2:1–10). In his speech advocating the admission of the Gentiles into the fold of God's people on equal terms with the Jews, James, the kinsman of the Lord and elder of the Jerusalem community, quotes the vision of restoration that concludes the book of Amos (Acts 15:16–17; cf. Am 9:11–12). James seems to use a version of Amos adapted from the Septuagint. In so doing, he emphasizes that God's intentions of restoring David's house extend far beyond the boundaries of Judaism to encompass "the rest of humanity" (Acts 15:17; cf. 1:8; Lk 3:6). We note that Amos would have agreed with his words, since Amos asserted in his own time that the Lord cared for the Cushites, the Philistines, and Aramaeans as well as for the children of Israel (Am 9:7).

HOSEA

Although both Amos and Hosea began their ministry during the reign of Jeroboam II (783–743 B.C.) (Am 1:1; Hos 1:1), evidence in the text suggests that Hosea arrived on the scene shortly before the death of Jeroboam and therefore a few years later than Amos' departure just after 750 B.C. Hosea's mission extended well into the turbulent years leading up to the Assyrian takeover of the northern kingdom. He certainly witnessed the war between Israel and Judah in 735–734 B.C. and the Assyrian occupation of Galilee in 732 B.C. (2 Kgs 15:27–31; 16:5–9; cf. Hos 5:8–12). We lack solid evidence indicating that Hosea witnessed the fall of Samaria in 721 B.C. Thus, we date his ministry between 745 and 730 B.C. in the kingdom of Israel.

When Jeroboam II died in 743 B.C., the northern kingdom became destabilized by insurrection and anarchy as five different aspirants ascended to the throne within the following decade. Amos' prophecy that Jeroboam would be assassinated did not prove true for the king himself but for his son Zechariah, whom Shallum ben Jabesh murdered (2 Kgs 14:28–29; 15:10; cf. Am 7:11). A month later, Menahem ben Gadi murdered Shallum and went on a bloody rampage through the city of Tappuah (2 Kgs 15:13–16). During Menahem's reign (743–738 B.C.), the Assyrians under Tiglath-Pileser III (Pul) (745–727 B.C.) made their presence felt by exacting substantial sums from Israel (2 Kgs 15:17–22; cf. Hos 5:13; 7:11). Within a year of succeeding his father to the throne, Pekahiah (738–737 B.C.) was assassinated by Pekah ben Remaliah (737–732 B.C./2 Kgs 15:23–31). This king foolishly entered into an anti-Assyrian coalition with Damascus, went to war against Judah in reprisal for not joining their alliance, and (by 732 B.C.) ended up losing the verdant northern part of his kingdom (including Galilee [733–732 B.C.] and Naphtali [743 B.C.]) when the Assyrians took possession of the area to quell the uprising (2 Kgs 15:27–31; 16:5–9; cf. Is 7:1–9:6; Hos 5:8–12). The vanquished Pekah was assassinated by Hoshea ben Elah, whose subsequent ill-advised attempt at an alliance with Egypt sealed Samaria's fate by provoking the ultimate Assyrian invasion that extinguished the northern kingdom in 721 B.C. (2 Kgs 15:30; 17:1–6). This sorry history vindicated Amos in everything he had said. God spared Amos the ordeal of living through the doom he had foreseen for Israel. The task of preaching the word amid the treachery, intrigue, and revolution (Hos 7:3–7) fell to Hosea, the prophet whose marital difficulties symbolically resonated with his society's chaos.

The Book of Hosea

The book of Hosea consists of three parts: (1) a description of Hosea's marriage to Gomer, which provides an analogy for the Lord's relationship to Israel (1:1–3:5); (2) a large collection of the prophet's teachings that illustrate the Lord's love, judgment, and promise for rebellious Israel (4:1–14:1); and (3) a concluding invitation for Israel's return to Yahweh in repentance and reconciliation (14:2–10).

While most of the contents come from the prophet's ministry in the kingdom of Israel, the final edition of Hosea is the product of editorial work undertaken in the scribal academies of Judah, first in Jerusalem and then in Babylon. After the fall of Samaria in 721 B.C., disciples of Hosea brought the text south to Jerusalem. There, perhaps during the reforms of Hezekiah (2 Kgs 18:1–8), a prophetic school edited the original so that the words Hosea had originally spoken to the northern kingdom were now applied to Judah (1:7; 2:2; 4:15; 5:5; 6:4, 11; 8:14; 12:1, 3; cf. 3:5). During the Exile in Babylon, later editors indicated how the prophet's words opened up a vision of restoration to the land for their own generation (11:10–11; 14:2–9). The wisdom tradition exerted some influence on the final editor, who completed the book during the Exile in Babylon (587–538 B.C.) (14:10).

The Message of Hosea

Hosea teaches us that God knows his people with the love of a husband for his wife and a father for his children. In spite of this, the family is in great crisis because the wife has proven unfaithful and the children rebellious. The book of Hosea indicates the process by which God plans to heal his people and restore them to himself. This process has three components: (1) a portrait of the foundations offering God's view of the relationship under the symbol of marriage; (2) an analysis of the problem focusing on Israel's infidelity in worship and life; and (3) an outline of the steps toward a solution pictured in terms of a new Exodus.

The Marriage Relationship: Although the text leaves us unclear about the details, we know that Hosea married Gomer and that she was unfaithful to him either before or after the wedding. At some point, she took part in the orgiastic rites at the Canaanite sanctuary, and she might even have been a temple prostitute (1:2; 3:1–3). So dissolute had life become in Samaria that she was not alone in her behavior among the young women of Israel (4:13–14). The Lord made an astounding claim on the prophet's life when he demanded that Hosea enter, maintain, and renew his marriage in spite of Gomer's infidelity. Hosea's marriage to Gomer would become the prophetic symbol of the Lord's relationship to Israel (2:4–25).

Hosea understood that in the covenant, God bound himself to Israel after the manner of a husband to his wife in marriage (2:18; cf. 6:7; 8:1). The requirements of such a union are loyalty of affection and an ever-deepening personal knowledge of one another. Covenant loyalty (Hebrew: *hesed*) goes beyond the minimal requirements of fidelity to include compassionate, trusting, self-giving love expressed in action. Primarily, it refers to God's disposition toward his people manifested in his redeeming work (Ps 136). In response to God's loyalty, his people are called to exhibit the same quality in gratitude to the Lord and in service of one another (6:6; 10:12; 12:7). A dynamic and serene interpersonal knowledge (Hebrew: *da'at*) accompanies the development of covenant loyalty (6:6). The Lord who knows his people in love desires them to share in a communion of life with him (2:21–22).

Hosea reinforces the same principles by alternately describing God's relationship to his people in terms of a father's affection for his children. Here, we find evidence suggesting that Hosea belonged to an early Deuteronomic circle. It was purely out of love that the Lord redeemed his people in the Exodus event and has cared for them like a father raising his beloved son (11:1–4; cf. Dt 7:7–11; 1:31; Hos 1:3–9).

Israel's Infidelity: Hosea discerns that the root of the problem is the manner in which Canaanite practices have invaded Israel's worship. The Israelites have blended into their worship of the Lord elements of the fertility cults that extol Baal as the god of abundant crops and herds (4:7–14; 10:1–2; 13:1–3). By the incorporation of fertility rites, Israel's liturgy has become a source of adultery in both personal and spiritual senses of the term (2:4–15; 5:5–7; 9:1–5). All the chaos that now overwhelms Israel comes from her infidelity. She has forsaken the Lord's self-giving love for Baal's eroticism. Israel's love has proven no more substantial than the morning mist, and she lives as if she had never known God (6:4; cf. 13:3; 4:1; 5:4).

The corruption of worship coincides with the intrigue and treachery in the royal palace and on the streets (7:1–7; 8:4; 10:3–4). There is no witness to moral standards (4:1–3). The foreign policies of arbitrary alliances represent yet another instance of betraying the Lord (8:8–10; 10:5–8; 12:2).

The whole society is perishing for lack of knowing the Lord (5:3–5). The priests at the sanctuary no longer teach their people God's ways (4:6). The people want to claim a relationship to Yahweh while they reject his Law (8:1, 12). We must note here that the people's lack of knowledge is not due to intellectual ignorance but to willful rejection of Yahweh's presence. Their only hope for restoration lies with the Lord, who refuses to give up his love in spite of the grief and affliction he has suffered because of his people's scorn (11:8–9).

The New Exodus: Hosea's restoration of Gomer to the family home foreshadows the Lord's plan to win his people back to his love (3:1–3). The movement toward new life in the relationship will involve two stages: (1) a period of destruction to eliminate the vestiges of the past leading into (2) a time of new beginnings.

Yahweh will destroy Samaria and deport her people into captivity amid great affliction (9:11–17; 13:9–14:1). However, by the Lord's design, the circumstances of exile will provide the setting of a new Exodus. Not Egypt as in the days of Moses, but Assyria this time will be the land of captivity (11:5; 8:13; cf. 9:3, 6, 17).

In the land of exile, the Lord will be able to win Israel back to his love (2:16–25). In the wilderness of the foreign territory, Israel will experience a new betrothal. God will seal his love in a new covenant that will extend to all creatures (2:20; cf. Gn 9:8–17; Ez 34:25; cf. Jer 31:31–34). Israel's promised new existence will consist of all the genuine qualities of covenant life, including fidelity, knowledge of God, and justice (2:21–25; cf. 2:1–3). The exilic editors of the text appreciated that such healing is available to God's people whenever they accept the prophetic invitation to turn from the gods of this world to the Lord who is ever faithful (14:2–9).

Toward the New Testament: The Union between Christ and His Church

Hosea's introduction of the marriage symbol to describe the relationship between the Lord and his people continued to develop through the tradition of other prophets (Jer 2:1–7; 3:1–13; Is 54:1–10; 62:4–5) and flourished in the New Testament writings. Jesus drew upon this tradition when he referred to himself as the bridegroom (Mk 2:19–20; cf. Jn 3:29), performed his first sign at a wedding feast (Jn 2:1–11), and selected the customs of marriage to illustrate the nature of God's kingdom (Mt 22:1–14; 25:1–13). By his death and Resurrection, Jesus establishes the new covenant in which God weds himself to his people (see 1 Cor 11:25; cf. Rv 19:7–9; 21:2, 9).

When addressing the Gentiles in Corinth, Paul reflects Hosea's previous concern for the Israelites. For the New Testament apostle as for the Old Testament prophet in a different context, sexual immorality represents a betrayal of the community and infidelity to the Lord (1 Cor 6:15–20). Furthermore, Paul develops Hosea's images of marriage to symbolize the union between the community and Christ achieved by the apostolic preaching and baptism (2 Cor 11:2; cf. Hos 2:18–25). By bringing them to conversion and new life through word (cf. 1 Pt 1:23) and sacrament (cf. Ti 3:5), Paul betrothed the community to Christ. His concern that the Corinthians not be seduced into infidelity by following the gnosticism of the "super-apostles" echoes Hosea's correction of the Israelites who mixed elements of Baalism with their worship of the Lord (2 Cor 11:1–21; cf. Hos 8:1–14).

Later Pauline tradition describes Christian marriage as a symbol of Christ's love for the Church (Eph 5:21–33). Heightening the tradition begun with Hosea, primary emphasis in Ephesians falls on the self-emptying love that Christ has revealed in his cross to manifest most completely the covenant affection (*hesed*) God has always had for his people. By sharing in the love of Christ, husband and wife manifest the divine *hesed* to one another in their mutual self-giving. In the book of Revelation, marriage symbolizes the union between the Lord and his people in the heavenly Jerusalem (cf. Rv 21:2, 9; 19:7–9).

The New Testament writers quote the text of Hosea in order to uncover God's vision for the life of his Church. By referring to Hosea 11:1, the infancy narrative of Matthew's Gospel reveals Jesus' solidarity with God's people throughout their history. In Hosea, God called Israel out of Egypt in the Exodus (Hos 11:1). Matthew identifies that from the very beginning of Jesus' life as the Son of God in the fullest sense of the term, he identifies with God's people by reliving their journey from Egypt to the Promised Land (Mt 2:13–23).

Twice in the body of the same Gospel, Jesus refutes the protests of the Pharisees against his actions by referring to Hosea's thematic concern that the Lord desires love not sacrifice (Mt 9:13; 12:7; cf. Hos 6:6). Of the many connotations associated with covenant loyalty (Hebrew: *hesed*), the Greek translations emphasize mercy (Greek: *eleos*). Hosea made his statement as an appeal for the people of Israel to act with integrity toward God and neighbor and to avoid participation in any worship tinged with Baalism (Hos 6:6). When the Pharisees criticize Jesus' fellowship with sinners and actions on the Sabbath, Jesus responds by referring to Hosea's statement as a basic principle of God's mind. Because *hesed* is a primary characteristic of God, compassion toward others must override self-concerned legalism in the way his people work out their lives together (Mt 9:10–13; 12:7).

In conclusion, Paul applies Hosea's texts about God's restoration of his covenant with Israel to support the incorporation of the Gentiles into the full people of God (Rom 9:25–26; cf. Hos 2:25; 2:1). Within the context of Hosea's time, the Lord referred to Israel as "not-my-people", because her infidelity had shattered the covenant, and later called her "my people" when he promised to establish a new covenant with her (Hos 1:9; 2:1–3, 18, 25). When Paul read Hosea in light of his own mission, he received revelation that when the Lord called Israel "not-my-people", the term actually applied to the Gentiles in Paul's day. Now that they have received the preaching of the Gospel and have been justified by faith in Christ, the Gentiles along with Jews in the Christian community are "children of the living God" (Hos 2:1) and can rejoice in the Lord calling them "my people" through the new covenant (Rom 9:25–10:13).

Having considered the missions of Hosea and Amos, the two great prophets in the northern kingdom up to its destruction in 721 B.C., we can now direct our attention to Isaiah and Micah, their contemporaries in the southern kingdom of Judah.

STUDY QUESTIONS

1. Compare Amos and Hosea as to background and personality.
2. What are the three themes in Amos?
3. Describe the "Day of Yahweh".
4. How was Stephen in the New Testament the Amos of his day?
5. What is the message of Hosea?
6. How is Hosea's marriage prophetic for the people of Israel?
7. What is the "new Exodus"?
8. How is the marriage symbol appropriate to the New Testament understanding of Jesus and the Church?
9. How does Paul expand Hosea's concept of God's people?
10. Discuss how, in your experience of the single life or marriage, you have seen the importance of repentance, forgiveness, and mercy.
11. How does the image of the Bride of Christ contribute to your appreciation of the Church as the "sacrament of salvation" in the world (*Lumen Gentium,* par. 1)?

AMOS

HOSEA

ISAIAH AND MICAH:
THE REIGN OF JUSTICE IN JUDAH

Where are people able to find genuine life in an era characterized by upheaval internationally and oppression at home? The prophetic word possesses the unique authority to anchor our lives in God and preserve us from drifting into disaster on the superficial tide of the world's trends. We must renounce worldliness, but we cannot flee the world for which we are responsible as God's people today. Authenticity distinguishes the community of faith in a world that has become destabilized. A study of the missions of Isaiah and Micah within the setting of their times will assist us in learning the art of our vocation.

Isaiah and Micah were contemporaries of one another in Jerusalem for perhaps three decades. Isaiah's career extended at least forty years, from the death of King Uzziah (740 B.C.) until sometime after the Assyrian siege of Jerusalem in 701 B.C. (Is 1:1; 6:1; 36:1–37:38). Micah arrived on the scene some years after Isaiah—once Jotham had become king—and his mission might have extended up to the turn of the century as well (Mi 1:1; cf. Jer 26:18). In their early days, Isaiah and Micah were the counterparts in Judah to Amos and Hosea, who labored in the northern kingdom of Israel. Reading Isaiah and Micah together affords us the opportunity of seeing Jerusalem from the two perspectives that the city and the country represent. Isaiah, the refined man of letters and a native of the capital, loves the city and discerns the subtleties of its citizens' minds. Micah, by contrast, comes from the rural southwestern regions (near the Philistine frontier) and betrays his suspicions of the city in the frankness of his speech (Mi 1:1, 14).

Judah in the Times of Isaiah and Micah

The succession of four able kings in Assyria changed the course of history in the eastern Mediterranean in the last half of the eighth century B.C. Each of them invaded Judah at least once. In 734 B.C., the armies of Tiglath-Pileser III (745–727 B.C.) swept down the Mediterranean shore, took possession of Philistia, and controlled the whole territory up to the Egyptian frontier. As soon as the Assyrian king turned his attention away to the eastern front of his empire, Razon of Damascus and Pekah of Israel tried to form a coalition of states to drive out the Assyrian presence. When Ahaz of Judah refused their invitation to join the anti-Assyrian alliance, Damascus and Israel launched an attack on Jerusalem. Ahaz appealed to Assyria for help, and the armies of Tiglath-Pileser returned to defeat the rebellious coalition, overrunning the northern part of Israel and exiling segments of its population to Assyria in the process (2 Kgs 15:29; 16:5–9). Assyria exacted a large sum of tribute from Judah but at least allowed it to remain intact while the imperial armies captured Damascus and all of its territory in 732 B.C.

In 724 B.C., Shalmaneser V (726–722 B.C.) laid siege to Samaria until Hoshea the king of Israel paid him tribute. A short time later, Hoshea foolishly joined himself with Egypt in an attempted rebellion. This move brought about Samaria's ultimate destruction in 721 B.C. as the Assyrians under Sargon II (721–705 B.C.) invaded the land, took control of the capital, deported a large segment of the Israelites, and settled an assortment of people from various parts of the empire in the territory (2 Kgs 17:1–6, 24–41). The northern kingdom practically disappeared. Now the Assyrians were literally just a few hills beyond Jerusalem! Judah survived by complying with Assyria's dictates.

The situation remained unsettled over the next two decades. In 711 B.C., Sargon's armies moved against the coastal region of Ashdod, which had formed an ill-advised alliance with Egypt. Judah became even more confined, lacking any access to the Mediterranean as the Assyrians controlled all the territory on its northern and western frontiers.

Yet the Assyrian military machine was unable to silence the voices of revolt that echoed again in 705 B.C. with the death of Sargon. This time, Judah was a leading player in forming an anti-Assyria coalition with Egypt and some cities of Philistia. The project received encouragement from Babylon, Assyria's primary adversary in the east (cf. Is 39:1–8). In 701 B.C., the Assyrian King Sennacherib reacted with a characteristic show of force by sending his armies to attack Philistia and Judah. Just when the city was about to fall, something amazing took place: the Assyrians withdrew from Jerusalem for no apparent reason (2 Kgs 19:35–37; Is 37:36–37).

ISAIAH

The Book of Isaiah

Before describing the career of Isaiah within the setting of his times, we will survey the contents of the book that bears his name. The complete book of Isaiah as we have it in our Bible is actually a collection of writings representing a tradition that extended over a span of some three hundred years. The whole text can be subdivided into three major sections: (1) Isaiah 1–39, for the most part, presenting the teaching of the prophet himself, who labored in Jerusalem from 740 until sometime after 701 B.C.; (2) Isaiah 40–55 (generally called "Deutero-Isaiah" ["Second Isaiah"]), containing the oracles of another prophet in the tradition of Isaiah, who announced God's word to the exiles in Babylon sometime between 550 and 539 B.C.; and (3) Isaiah 56–66 (designated "Trito-Isaiah" ["Third Isaiah"]), reflecting the same tradition at a later stage in Jerusalem after the Exile but before the arrival of Ezra and Nehemiah, perhaps around 500 B.C.

It is difficult to estimate when the whole book of Isaiah reached completion. The latest texts within the compendium make up the "Isaian Apocalypse" (24:1–27:13), a collection whose unique style and special concern for the end time suggest that it must have been written after 450 B.C. While admitting that the question remains open, we propose that the complete book of Isaiah came from the hands of scribes working in Jerusalem around 400 B.C. in light of the city's reformation inaugurated by Ezra and Nehemiah. Certainly, this is the last in a long series of editions, the first of which Isaiah's disciples issued shortly after the prophet's death early in the seventh century B.C. In view of the rich, centuries-long heritage from which the text comes, we do well to think of it as the product of the School of Isaiah, a 250-year-old tradition of disciples stretching from the time of Isaiah to the era of Ezra.

In this chapter, we will limit our attention to Isaiah 1–39, postponing our reflections on Deutero-Isaiah (40–55) and Trito-Isaiah (56–66) until we deal with the exilic and postexilic prophets respectively. In outline form, the first part of Isaiah consists of six sections: (1) announcements concerning Jerusalem's situation internally and internationally (1–12); (2) oracles against foreign nations (13–23); (3) the Isaian Apocalypse (24–27); (4) oracles about Judah's alliances and survival (28–33); (5) promise of healing and victory for Zion (34–35); and (6) the Assyrian attack on Jerusalem in 701 B.C. (36–39).

In order to focus on the original Isaiah's teaching, we will bypass the later material that editors incorporated into this part of the book. The later added material is not limited to the sections of Deutero- and Trito-Isaiah. Within the first section of the book, we find some of the last pieces incorporated into it. Among these texts are: the oracles against Babylon (written during the Exile: 13:1–14:23; 21:1–10); the prophecy against Edom (composed during or shortly after the Exile: 34); the history of the Assyrian invasion (adapted from 2 Kgs 18:13–20:19/36–39); the promise of healing for Jerusalem (closely related to Deutero-Isaiah: 35); the promise of return to Jerusalem (composed toward the end of the Exile: 11:10–16); the psalm of deliverance (a non-Isaian composition: 33); and the Isaian Apocalypse (24–27). Although we pass over these texts, we should appreciate that all of them are vital to the message of the inspired book. Studying them in light of the original prophet's words will enable the reader to appreciate the dynamic manner in which God's word addresses each period in history through sacred tradition. We must limit our attention to the magnificent figure of Isaiah, the patriarch of the tradition.

The Life and Message of Isaiah

Isaiah was born in Jerusalem around 765 B.C. and grew up in the atmosphere of prosperity and optimism that characterized the reign of Uzziah (781–740 B.C./2 Kgs 15:1–7). He may have trained in a school for scribes (Is 30:8). He married a prophetess who gave birth to at least two sons (8:1–4). While venerable tradition suggests that he was martyred under Manasseh, the apostate king, we know for certain only that he died sometime after 701 B.C., when he uttered the last oracles contained in his book (cf. 2 Kgs 21:16).

We divide Isaiah's career into four periods corresponding to the activities of the Assyrians as they bore down upon Judah: (1) from his prophetic call until the war with Damascus and Israel (740–734 B.C.); (2) from the beginning of the war with Damascus and Israel until the Assyrian takeover of the northern kingdom (734–721 B.C.); (3) from the accession of King Hezekiah until Assyria's advance on Ashdod (716–711 B.C.); and (4) from the death of Sargon II until the Assyrian invasion of Judah (705–701 B.C.). In the process of studying the development of the prophet's mission, we will note three of his chief concerns: (a) the holiness of God; (b) the vocation of David's son, of Zion (Jerusalem), and of the remnant; and (c) the experience of faith.

1. Isaiah's Call and Early Ministry (740–734 B.C.)

Isaiah's vocation-event indicates to us what can happen to a person while taking part in the regular worship services of the congregation. In 740 B.C., Isaiah experienced the revelation of God's holiness in the Temple, perhaps during a liturgical celebration that included the offering of a sacrifice on the altar (6:1–13). We can imagine that as he observed the smoke rising up and listened to the choir acclaim the Lord to be thrice-holy, he received the divine grace "to see" beyond all appearances into the very life and presence of God. The smoke was no longer that of the sacrifice but rather of the Lord's awesome presence over Sinai when he first made himself known to the whole people (Ex 19:18). The voices he heard were no longer those of the choir but of the heavenly seraphim represented in the figures that hovered over the ark (Ex 25:18–20). In his heart, the prophet entered into the Holiest of Holies as he encountered the Lord's glory, which formerly had entered the Tent during the wilderness journey and then had filled the sanctuary at the dedication of Solomon's Temple (Ex 24:16–17; 40:34; I Kgs 8:10–11).

His experience was like that of Moses on the mountain after the people turned to idolatry. In a manner of speaking, he "saw" the Lord while confessing his and his people's sin and receiving a divine purging from guilt (Is 6:1–7; Ex 33:18–34:9). Actually, a close reading of the text indicates that perceiving just the outer fringe of the Lord's "garment" was sufficient to overwhelm the prophet with an awareness of God's glorious otherness (6:1). Like his predecessors, Moses and Micaiah ben Imlah, Isaiah experienced the revelation of the Lord's glory as the constitutive element of his call to be a prophet (Is 6:8–10; see I Kgs 22:19; Ex 3:1–4:12). This encounter with God provided the foundation for his preaching beginning with the oracles of his earliest days, which comprise almost all of the first five chapters of the book.

The majesty, glory, and holiness of God permeate the prophet's message. First and foremost, Yahweh is the "Holy One of Israel" (Is 1:4; 5:19, 24; 10:17, 20; 29:19, 23; 30:11, 12, 15). While he transcends history, Yahweh is never distant or remote. Isaiah's own experience taught him how close the Lord remains to his people. The Holy One has plans to rule in the midst of his own and to guide history toward the fulfillment of his intentions (28:21).

However, under the pretense of knowledge, human beings tend to be cynical about a divine plan (5:19, 21; 29:15). The monstrous pride and self-determination of meager human flesh pose the major obstacle to trusting the Lord and receiving divine wisdom. This is why the Lord sends the prophet to tell the people first of all that, contrary to what they presume, in fact, they do not see, hear, or understand the Lord's ways (6:9–10). Isaiah could speak this message from his personal experience at the Temple liturgy, when God opened his eyes to "see" truly the Lord's glory, his ears to "hear" truly the heavenly chorus acclaim God's great holiness, and his heart to confess his sin and thus "understand" and be healed (6:1–7; cf. 6:9–10).

Social injustice offers primary evidence of resistance to divine revelation. In the earliest days of his mission, Isaiah echoed in Jerusalem the concerns

Amos and Hosea expressed in Bethel and Samaria. In spite of the prosperity characteristic of Uzziah's reign, the wealthy oppressed the poor for maximum profit and neglected the needs of widows and orphans (1:23; 3:14–15). Preoccupation with extravagant houses and high fashion had made the city rife with greed and bribery (1:23; 3:16–24; 32:9–14; 5:8–10).

Jerusalem, the Lord's cherished vineyard, had produced bitter fruit contrary to his intentions (5:1–4). Isaiah perceived that divine pruning would have to cut back the wild growth so that the remaining stock could produce genuine fruit (5:5–7; cf. 6:13). Thus, within the same general section, we find the prophet speaking alternately of Jerusalem's desolation and glory. The Lord will purge his beloved city with a devastation that will humble the proud and punish the unjust who offend God's holiness by their attitude and actions (1:21–31; 2:6–4:1). Nevertheless, the destruction will not be total, since the Lord will leave the fragile shoots of new and fresh life to spring forth from the desolation. He will preserve a remnant who will experience the Lord's glory just like the people of the Exodus and Isaiah himself at the Temple liturgy (4:2–6; cf. 6:1–7; Ex 13:21–22). The life of this remnant will generate a magnetism within Jerusalem that will attract all nations to learn the ways of the Lord so as to produce a new international order of peace and justice (Is 2:1–5 = Mi 4:1–3).

2. Immanuel: The Years of War (734–721 B.C.)

When war loomed on the horizon shortly after Ahaz's accession to the throne, Isaiah's career took a dramatic turn as he devoted his energies to two projects. He began confronting the king directly, and he started to form a school of disciples to become the nucleus of the remnant he had been describing. Most of the material in Isaiah 7–12 originated in this era.

Isaiah's concern for the quality of faith in Judah united both dimensions of his ministry. Over the course of Ahaz's reign (736–716 B.C.), the king would develop a reputation for apostasy and religious compromise (2 Kgs 16:1–4). Isaiah discerned the king's flaws early, when Pekah of Israel and Razon of Damascus were planning to launch their attack on Judah for not joining in their anti-Assyrian coalition. The prophet demanded that the king trust in the Lord's protection and not fear these states, which Isaiah foresaw to be passing away soon (Is 7:3–9). In the prophet's mind, faith is not simply an interior assent to a credal formula but a posture of confidence in facing the world based on the premise that the Lord is more present to his people than are enemy armies.

Sometime in 734 B.C., Isaiah announced the Immanuel prophecy to Ahaz. In his attempt to dissuade the king from entering into an alliance with Assyria in order to protect Judah from attack, Isaiah pleaded with the king to ask God for a sign. When the king refused under the pretense of not wanting to test the Lord, Isaiah declared that a woman has conceived a child and, at his forthcoming birth, she would give him the name that summarized the prophet's message to Ahaz: "Immanuel", "God is with us" (7:14; 8:8, 10). Furthermore, Isaiah wanted the king to realize that in another decade—before this child would reach the age of reason—the kingdoms of both Israel and Damascus would lie in ruins (7:15–17). Within the historical setting, we are unsure whether Isaiah was referring to a son to be born to his own wife or a son to be born in the royal court (cf. 9:5).

We know that Ahaz did not follow Isaiah's advice but appealed for Assyrian protection instead. In 732 B.C. the Assyrians quashed the rebellion by taking over Damascus, invading the northern territories of Israel (including the tribal lands of Zebulun and Naphtali: Is 8:23) and deporting a significant portion of its people to the east (2 Kgs 15:29). These events provide the historical setting for Isaiah's prophecy of a light of revelation to break forth on these people who have suffered oppression, banishment, and death at the hands of the Assyrians. The light will be revealed in the person of the true son of David, who will extend his dominion outward from Jerusalem in a reign of everlasting peace (Is 9:1–6; cf. 2 Sm 7:12–16; Mi 5:1–3). Another prophecy expresses Isaiah's belief that God will trim away the barren branches of the Davidic line and bring forth a king from David's roots in the house of Jesse who will establish the reign of peace (11:1–9; cf. 32:1). This king will exercise the same type of role for the monarchy as Isaiah's disciples will for the people of Judah: each will constitute the genuine "remnant" to bring forth new life corresponding to God's primary intentions (Is 10:20–23).

When Isaiah realized that his counsel against an alliance with Assyria was falling on deaf ears, he turned his attention to forming a body of disciples who would learn the Lord's ways (8:11–20). The king and the general populace were shortsighted and easily swayed because they had no awareness of the holiness of the Lord. In fact, Yahweh himself had become so alien to the people as to be the stumbling block that would bring about their downfall. After the events of 732 B.C., it seems that Isaiah went into relative seclusion for over a decade in order to form his disciples into a remnant (8:13–16; 10:20–23). The contrast between the mentality of his school and that of the general public in Jerusalem was extreme. Withdrawing from the public eye, the prophet asserts, "My trust is in Yahweh who hides his face from the House of Jacob; I put my hope in him" (8:17).

3. Hezekiah's Reign up to Ashdod's Rebellion (716–711 B.C.)

The fall of the northern kingdom in 721 B.C. seemed to correspond to Isaiah's prediction over a decade earlier (Is 7:16; 2 Kgs 17:5–6). No longer could king or people ignore the prophet and his disciples. The arrival of religious refugees from the north, such as the members of the Deuteronomic circles, would have brought a new seriousness to some quarters of the city. When Hezekiah succeeded his father to the throne, Judah had a king who admitted that his people were in need of reformation (2 Kgs 18:1–8). Isaiah emerged back into the public light as an adviser to Hezekiah. While the king reversed his father's programs in religious matters, he continued his father's obstinacy to Isaiah's counsel against alliances in matters of foreign policy.

For three years (714–711 B.C.), while Ashdod was gathering support from other cities in Philistia as well as from Egypt and Ethiopia (Cush) for a rebellion against Assyrian hegemony in the region, Isaiah walked naked through the streets of Jerusalem to communicate his conviction of the wrongheadedness of Hezekiah even to consider entering into such an alliance (20:1–6). Isaiah was convinced that Israel's supposed allies would either turn toward Jerusalem in search of wisdom or they would perish. In either case, peace and security would come when Judah turned to the Lord rather than to the nations for defense and liberation (18:1–7; 19:1–15; cf. 19:16–25 as a comment written after 587 B.C.). History demonstrated the correctness of the prophet's counsel when the Assyrians invaded and took control of Philistia in 711 B.C.

4. Hezekiah's Reign during the Assyrian Invasion (705–701 B.C.)

Restlessness prevailed in the states under Assyrian domination. With the death of Sargon II in 705 B.C., the simmering rebellion seethed to a boiling point, this time with Judah playing a major role in spite of Isaiah's protests. In 703 B.C., King Hezekiah welcomed to Jerusalem a delegation of Babylonians, the foes of Assyria in the east (2 Kgs 20:12–19; Is 39:1–8). Then he cast his lot with Tyre, Philistia, and Egypt, Assyria's most powerful enemy in the south and west.

While the ambassadors were traveling back and forth between Judah and Egypt, Isaiah steadfastly denounced them with a message that must inform our own consciences today when we consider the role of military force on the international front. The prophet declared that Judah was renouncing her faith in Yahweh by putting her trust in Egypt's military strength. Because Judah was looking to someone other than the "Holy One of Israel" for her security, both the protector (Egypt) and the protected (Judah) were destined to fall (Is

31:1–3). The king's prophets and advisers in the matter were renouncing the truth in favor of shoring up the king's vain hopes by telling him what he wanted to hear (30:1–17).

By contrast, Isaiah was proposing a strategy of faith such as he might have learned from the witness of Moses commanding the Israelites of the Exodus to remain calm and steadfast as they stood on the shore of the Sea while their enemies descended on them (see Ex 14:14). The prophet insisted that faith, not force, would lead to freedom from Assyrian oppression: " 'Your salvation lay in conversion and tranquility, your strength in serenity and trust' " (Is 30:15).

However, he knew that, far from being dynamically attentive to the word of God that shapes all history, the faith of Judah amounted to little else than a religious system. All knew the right words and could recite them on their lips but refused to allow them to penetrate their hearts and form their minds (29:13–14). The people would suffer because of their spiritual lethargy. However, from the resulting desolation, the Lord would raise up a humble and therefore a wise people who truly knew him as the Holy One of Israel (29:1–24).

While Sennacherib's armies were marching toward Judah in 701 B.C., Hezekiah took the opportunity to make some provision for defense by fortifying the city wall and by digging the trench through rock to bring water from the Gihon spring inside the city to the pool of Siloam (2 Kgs 20:20; Is 22:8–11; cf. Jn 9:7). The Assyrian military machine swept through Judah with speed and ferocity. An Assyrian list details some forty-six cities that Sennacherib captured before he surrounded Jerusalem (see Is 10:28–32; Mi 1:10–16).

Although Isaiah had protested Hezekiah's folly in drawing the Assyrian wrath down upon Jerusalem, he supported the king and encouraged the people when the enemy surrounded the city. The prophet declared that Yahweh would still preserve his city by terrifying the Assyrians with the authority of his presence (30:27–33). Although the narrative section describing the events is a copy from the Deuteronomic source, it clearly illustrates the prophet's insistence that the king not concede the city to the Assyrians (36:1–37:38). The city's deliverance was miraculous. For some unknown reason, just when they were about to break through the walls, the Assyrians silently broke camp and moved off elsewhere. Isaiah's prophecy was fulfilled: the people experienced deliverance, not by military strength, but by the mysterious movement of Yahweh on their behalf (37:36–38; cf. 30:15, 27–33). Now it remained for the prophet to teach his king how to experience personal healing through prayer and repentance (38:1–20) and to call his people to give up their empty-headed ways (22:1–14).

Toward the New Testament: The Messiah King and the Life of Faith

Isaiah the prophet-poet spoke of God revealing his holiness through his actions of judgment and promise in history. The Lord disciplined his people in order to concentrate their lives on the revelation of his glory. He needed to prune both the Davidic line and the whole people so that they would produce a new and pure life from the original stump of Jesse and from the remnant of the faithful. Isaiah's focus on the Davidic heritage and on the purified remnant made a significant contribution to the understanding of Christ and the life of the Church in the New Testament.

The Gospel of Matthew employs the acclamation of Jesus as "Immanuel", "God-is-with-us", to provide the overall basis for its portrait of Christ in the beginning, middle, and end of the Gospel. First, the angel quotes Isaiah telling Joseph that Mary's child will be "Immanuel" (Mt 1:23); then Jesus promises the Church that when two or three gather (especially to be reconciled) in his name, "I am there among them" (Mt 18:20); finally, as the risen Lord, he assures his apostles whom he sends out to the world with his last words, "I am with you always ... " (Mt 28:20).

We note that, when quoting Isaiah 7:14, the evangelist prefers the narrowness of the Septuagint (Greek) translation to the breadth of the Hebrew original. The unknown scribe who translated the text into Greek sometime after 250 B.C. in Alexandria rendered the Hebrew term for "young woman" (*'almah*) by the term "virgin" (*parthenos*). The Jewish tradition in Egypt of the third century B.C. was inspired to contemplate an unprecedented divine intervention in the birth of the Messiah. The insistence on a virginal conception that the Greek text asserts allows Matthew to demonstrate that not only Jesus' title as Immanuel but also the manner of his birth fulfills the Scripture. We have seen that the original prophet was thinking of a young married woman who conceived a child around 734 B.C. at the beginning of Judah's war with Israel and Damascus. By deciding to quote the Septuagint, Matthew associated himself with a tradition that proclaimed the promise of the Messiah in a manner far more marvelous than Isaiah had imagined.

Galilee became known as the "land of the Gentiles" as a consequence of the Assyrian invasion and conquest of 732 and 721 B.C. Matthew discerns that Jesus' growing up in Galilee is the fulfillment of Isaiah's prophecy that God's light would come upon this territory (Mt 4:13–16; Is 8:23–9:1). In addition, this same Isaian text contributes to the background of Jesus' declaration of himself as the final revelation of God in his word, "I am the light of the world" (Jn 8:12; cf. Is 9:1). Finally, we note that Jesus, upon whom the Spirit rests, is the promised shoot to spring from the root of Jesse (Rom 15:12; 1 Pt 4:14; Rv 22:16; cf. Is 11:1–9).

The Lord commissions Isaiah to tell the people that, contrary to appearances, they are not receiving God's revelation (Is 6:9–10). This is one of the few Old Testament texts that Jesus quotes in all four Gospels (Mk 4:12; Mt 13:14–15; Lk 8:10; Jn 12:40; cf. Acts 28:26–27). Jesus uses this text to indicate to his disciples that even the misunderstanding and incomprehension of the crowds concerning his message are foretold in Scripture. The populace does not understand his parables. Most of the Jewish elders refuse to believe. All these events, far from discrediting his ministry, reveal it to fulfill his mission as prophet. When grappling with the tension between acceptance and rejection of the Gospel, Paul and Peter refer to two other Isaian texts, both of which focus on the image of a stone. Around 735 B.C., Isaiah declared that the Lord would be "a stumbling-stone" causing the downfall of those elders in Judah who would demonstrate their unbelief by making a treaty with Assyria to defend Jerusalem against the coalition of Israel and Damascus (Is 8:14–15). Over twenty years later, to the leaders who wanted to make a pact with Egypt against Assyria, Isaiah declared that the Lord was establishing his presence in Zion as a foundation-stone that merits their trust (Is 28:16–17). In Romans, Paul makes the "stone" a symbol of the Gospel. Those who seek justification by faith appreciate the Gospel as a reliable foundation-stone, but those who try to save themselves by works of the Law find the Gospel to be a stumbling-stone (Rom 9:33; 10:11). In 1 Peter, the "stone" is Christ, who is the precious cornerstone for those who believe but a scandal to unbelievers (1 Pt 2:6, 8).

Now we can appreciate how Isaiah's prophecy concerning a remnant reaches fulfillment in the Christian community. In Paul's mind, the true remnant of Israel are those members of the chosen people who confess their faith in Jesus as the Messiah and are joined to his universal people in the Church where Jews and Gentiles together make up one Body (Rom 9:25–29; cf. Is 1:9; 10:22–23).

Isaiah foreshadowed Jesus' ministry insofar as he confronted the arrogance of those who presumed to be the wise ones of the community. Jesus' indictment of the Pharisees' focus on externals, such as rituals and rites without considering the heart, echoes Isaiah's chastisement of religious practice devoid of interior faith (Mk 7:6–7; Mt 15:8–9; cf. Is 29:13–14). The Pauline tradition uses the same text to admonish the Christian community against legalism and scrupulosity in observance of rituals (Col 2:20–22). Paul reiterates Isaiah's words to explain why the Gospel confounds the "wise" as it manifests its authority in power (1 Cor 1:19, quoting Is 29:14). Finally, he indicates that unbelief comes from a spirit of lethargy in the people (Rom 11:8, quoting Is 29:10).

We will gain another perspective on the roots of messianism and the call to faith issuing from Judah in the eighth century B.C. as we turn to Isaiah's contemporary Micah of Moresheth.

MICAH

The Prophet and His Times

Micah was a younger contemporary of Isaiah whose ministry in Judah seems to have covered some thirty-five years, from the reign of Jotham (740–736 B.C.) until the Assyrian attack on Jerusalem (701 B.C.). Micah's roots in Moresheth account for two aspects of his teaching. First, being from the country, Micah lacked Isaiah's sympathy for the city life of Jerusalem. Secondly, the Assyrian invasions of Philistia in 711 B.C. and of all Judah in 701 B.C. had a pronounced impact on him because his native region felt their effects before Jerusalem did (Mi 1:1, 14). Micah's instruction echoes the themes of Amos and Hosea, the prophets of the northern sanctuaries. In Micah's earthy style and straightforward manner, we might detect a reflection of Amos, the herdsman from Tekoa (less than twenty miles west of Moresheth), who was his elder by a generation from the Judaean countryside. So effective were Micah's warnings to Jerusalem that the leaders in the capital a century later would recall how he provoked Hezekiah to reform his people and thus provided a precedent for Jeremiah's ministry (Jer 26:16–19).

The Book of Micah

We can divide the book of Micah into three parts, each of which consists of an announcement of God's judgment followed by a declaration of his promise for the people. In the first part (1:1–2:13), the description of Judah's impending desolation owing to her crimes (1:1–2:11) is followed by the vision of God gathering the scattered sheep back into one flock (2:12–13). The second section (3:1–5:14) focuses on the corruption of Judah's leaders (3:1–12) before revealing God's promise of Zion's future restoration (4:1–5:14). The third part (6:1–7:20) brings to a climax the Lord's confrontation with his people by revealing the charges making up the divine lawsuit against Israel (6:1–7:7) and then expressing Israel's prayer of repentance, which allows God to bring healing and deliverance (7:8–20).

    This structure offers a vision of history consistent with the prophet's conviction that, by God's design, a period of injustice will lead to a time of desolation to be followed by the Lord's intervention to restore his people to new life. Our final edition of the book, while true to the prophet's teachings, is not the work of the prophet but of an editor who completed the text after the Exile in Babylon, perhaps around 500 B.C.

The book is a testament to the richness of the inspired prophetic tradition to which Micah's teaching made a primary contribution. Later scribes reworked his message of Jerusalem's doom before the fall of the city to the Babylonians in 587 B.C. (4:6–8). In the early days of the Exile, the inheritors of the prophetic tradition reshaped his promise that the Lord would restore his people after their desolation so that it offered hope to the people of Judah who had been deported to Babylon (7:8–10/after 587 B.C.). This hope became more certain as the end of the Exile came into view (2:12–13). The announcement of the Lord's will to restore Jerusalem, while consistent with Micah's original teaching, derives its present shape from the prophetic vision of the community after the Exile (7:11–13, 14–17). The final editor incorporated the concluding psalm to teach us that a confession of faith accompanied by a prayer of repentance expresses the proper response for us upon hearing the prophet's message (7:18–20).

The school of Isaiah seems to have taken responsibility for transmitting Micah's teaching immediately after the prophet's death. An early Isaian editor copied the text from his master's work into the book of Micah to provide the foundation for the vision of Jerusalem's future status (Mi 4:1–4 = Is 2:2–4). When we read the text, we must not allow ourselves to consider such elements as later editorial intrusions into the original. Instead, they represent the dynamic of tradition by which God's prophetic word remains always active so as to guide his people in each new historical setting.

The Message of Micah

We will reflect on the complete text by focusing on three central themes: social injustice, the Lord's case against his people, and the promise of a future Davidic king who will restore Zion. These topics represent three stages in the movement of salvation history: because he can no longer tolerate the injustice toward the poor from the past to the present, the Lord is about to bring desolation upon his people to put an end to the old order and to prepare for his new reign of justice and peace.

In the tradition of Amos, Micah was appalled by the corruption that was rampant in the city. His words have a contemporary ring for us today because we find the forms of injustice he confronted everywhere in our world. The wealthy class amassed vast real-estate holdings by taking possession of the inherited properties of the poor in lieu of debt payments (2:1–5). The numbers of homeless people, especially single women with children, increased as the rich seized land, houses, and the pledges of the poor (2:8–10). Farmers could not get fair prices for their goods because of the crooked dealings in the city markets (6:10–12). The civil authorities oppressed the poor (3:1–4); magistrates accepted bribes (7:3); even the court prophets and Temple priests were so tied into the system of fiscal and social favors that they seemed to languish in a stupor and spoke no truth (2:6–7, 11; 3:11). Without the support of society, family life broke down as suspicion alienated spouses from one another and rebellion propelled children away from their parents (7:5–6).

The false prophets' concern to speak words that soothed the corrupt brought a deathly silence and darkness upon the people. Now there was no word, no vision from God (3:5–7). More out of dismay than pride, Micah asserts that he alone is filled with the Lord's Spirit to possess a sense of what is right (3:8).

Through Micah, the Lord takes his people to court. Yahweh does not take the role of judge but of the offended party who initiates a lawsuit against Israel for breach of covenant. Micah acts as the spokesman who presents the Lord's case (1:2; 6:1–16). The Lord begs his people to tell him what offense of his might have provoked them to betray the covenant so completely. While he formed them by his justice in redeeming them from slavery in the Exodus, they have reduced the covenant relationship to an empty ritual to mask lives that are devoid of integrity (6:1–7). Micah practically capsulizes the teachings of all the biblical prophets that follow him when he declares what the Lord asks of his people, "Only this, to do what is right, to love loyalty and to walk humbly with your God" (6:8).

In face of the present reign of injustice, the Lord presents a two-stage vision of the future in which desolation will precede restoration. Micah saw the Lord's judgment coming upon Judah in the movement of the Assyrian armies across Judah in 701 B.C. (1:8–16). He speaks of "that day" when the unjust will experience the divine sanctions for their behavior (2:4). "That day" will not be without hope, for it will be a time of discipline, when the Lord will rid the land of the sources of temptation (5:8–14). Once the old order has been demolished, the time will come for the people to rebuild a new social order (7:11–13).

God will bring forth the true son of David to drive out the Assyrians and to establish peace in the land (5:4–5). Consistent with his mistrust of the city and confidence in the country, Micah points out that the anointed king will come from the almost-forgotten territory of Bethlehem-Ephrathah, David's ancestral home (5:1; 1 Sm 17:12). This king will be the Immanuel of whom Isaiah had spoken (Is 7:14). Future prophets will richly develop Micah's image of Immanuel shepherding his people (Mi 5:2–3; Mi 7:14; Ez 34:1–31; Is 40:11). This shepherd will gather the scattered flock of God's people and authorize the remnant to bring Zion to the fullness of glory God intends for it (Mi 4:6–8; cf. 2:12–13).

Toward the New Testament: The Messiah from Bethlehem

According to Matthew's infancy narrative, it is the text of Micah that leads the Magi to find Jesus as the Messiah. These wise people can follow the signs of the cosmos (represented in the star) to the vicinity of truth, but they must consult Scripture in order to meet Christ personally (Mt 2:1–12). The passage in Micah demonstrates that Jesus' birth in Bethlehem identifies him as the promised Messiah who will shepherd his people (Mt 2:5–6; cf. Mi 5:1–3; 2 Sm 5:2).

The infancy narrative in Luke makes another allusion to Micah to illustrate that in Jesus, the son of David, God fully restores his people in accordance with his promise to Abraham (Lk 1:73; cf. Mi 7:20; Gn 22:16–18). The Pauline tradition appeals to the messianic focus in Micah and Isaiah by proclaiming Christ to be "our peace" (Eph 2:14; cf. Mi 5:4; Is 9:5–6). Within the Church, there is a development of God's plan. Whereas, in Micah, the son of David would establish peace by conquering the gentile enemy (Assyria), within the Christian community, Jesus establishes new relationships in reconciling Jew and Gentile by breaking down the walls of division between them (Eph 2:14–22).

Jesus does not bring the peace of deceptive and soothing compromise that Micah condemned (Mi 3:5–8). To the contrary, the sword of his word can divide family members from one another (Lk 12:49–53). Considered within the setting of the general New Testament teaching, this type of family tension is very different from the destructive mistrust and rebellion of which Micah spoke. The Gospel speaks of family tension arising from allegiance to the word of God, whereas Micah spoke of family breakdown resulting from ignorance of God's word (Mi 7:5–6). By demanding that each of his disciples give his life to him first of all, Jesus introduces a creative tension through which truth and integrity can enter the home to bring healing, salvation, and reconciliation over the long term (see 1 Cor 7:14, 16; 1 Pt 3:1–2; Eph 5:22–6:4).

We will realize more fully how the prophetic word brings life to the community as we consider the ministry of Zephaniah, who was the first prophetic voice heard in Jerusalem following more than a half century of desolate silence after the deaths of Isaiah and Micah.

STUDY QUESTIONS

1. Compare Isaiah and Micah as individuals.
2. What are the three major sections of the book of Isaiah?
3. Describe Isaiah's vocation-event.
4. What was the Immanuel prophecy?
5. How is Jesus "Immanuel"?
6. What is Micah's vision of history?
7. What are the three central themes of Micah?
8. How does Jesus fulfill the messianic focus in Micah?
9. Compare Isaiah's experience of the Lord at his call with that of the people at Sinai.
10. How does Isaiah represent a model for teachers and catechists in the Church today?
11. How do you think God wants to restore us to himself?
12. In your personal life, have you experienced a time of desolation? Was it followed by a period of restoration? What role did your life of faith have in leading you from desolation to restoration?

ISAIAH 1–39

I.   Jerusalem's State Internally and Internationally (1:1–12:6)
       A.   Introductory Judgment Oracle (1:1–31)
       B.   The Glory and Shame of Jerusalem and Judah (2:1–5:30)
       C.   Isaiah's Personal Recollections (6:1–8:23)
       D.   Judah under Threat from Foreigners (9:1–12:6)

II.   Oracles against the Nations (13:1–23:18)
       A.   Against Babylon and Its King (13:1–14:23)
       B.   Against Assyria, Philistia, and Moab (14:24–16:14)
       C.   Against Damascus and Israel (17:1–14)
       D.   Concerning Ethiopia and Egypt (18:1–19:25)
       E.   Isaiah's Symbol for Ethiopia and Egypt (20:1–6)
       F.   The Fall of Babylon; Words to Edom and Arabia (21:1–17)
       G.   A Vision concerning Jerusalem (22:1–25)
       H.   Against Tyre (23:1–18)

III.   The Apocalypse of Isaiah (24:1–27:13)
       A.   The Collapse of Earth and the Reign of God (24:1–23)
       B.   The Heavenly Banquet of God in Zion (25:1–12)
       C.   Psalms of Deliverance (26:1–27:1)
       D.   The Vineyard, the City, and the Israelites' Return (27:1–13)

IV.   Concerning Judah's Alliances and Survival (28:1–33:24)
       A.   Words against Samaria and Jerusalem's Rulers (28:1–29:24)
       B.   God Will Protect Jerusalem against Assyria (30:1–31:9)
       C.   Judgment and Promise on Jerusalem (32:1–20)
       D.   Deliverance and the Glorious Future of Jerusalem (33:1–24)

V.   Judgment on Edom and Healing for Jerusalem (34:1–35:10)

VI.   Isaiah, Hezekiah, and Assyrian Gloom (36:1–39:8 = 2 Kgs 18–20)
       A.   The Assyrian Invasion of 701 B.C. (36:1–37:38)
       B.   Hezekiah's Illness, Healing, and Prayer (38:1–20)
       C.   The Letter from Babylon and the Prophecy of Exile (39:1–8)

MICAH

ZEPHANIAH, NAHUM, HABAKKUK:
JUDAH BEFORE THE EXILE

The life of faith cannot be limited to the private sphere of existence. Faith has implications for national identity and international relations. When a society loses its sense of God, pride overtakes the hearts of its citizens, and violence spills out into its streets. Such a civilization can have prosperity but not integrity. It is doomed to a limited life span unless it can find the grace of humility born out of a living knowledge of God.

Zephaniah, Nahum, and Habakkuk were three prophets convinced of the fundamental importance of faith to their society and to the whole world. They announced God's word to Jerusalem in the times of elation and grief that marked the last third of the seventh century B.C. Zephaniah was a forerunner while Nahum and Habakkuk were contemporaries of the great Jeremiah. All these prophets shared in common the conviction that Judah's very survival depended upon her will to renounce her pride and to live by a humble trust in the Lord. Furthermore, in the disposition of faith, they found a key to understanding how God reveals himself on the stage of international politics. Their message teaches us that authentic faith is the only foundation that can promise the survival of civilization.

After the Assyrian forces overran Samaria in 721 B.C. and decimated the ten northern tribes of Israel, they dominated the political arena of the ancient Near East for the next one hundred years. Although Sennacherib's army returned from Jerusalem without invading the city in 701 B.C., Assyria's influence in Judah went beyond the political and economic to the religious spheres of life. Upon Hezekiah's death, his reforms did not continue, because his son Manasseh succeeded him to the throne and resumed idolatrous practices in the tradition of his grandfather King Ahaz (736–716 B.C.).

Manasseh's reign of almost a half century (687–642 B.C.) represented a period of unrelenting spiritual disintegration. Pure Yahwism evaporated with the introduction of Assyrian and native Canaanite elements into Judah's worship. Shrines in the countryside propagated astral worship, ritual prostitution, and divination. In the Temple, the Assyrians set up altars and sacred images of gods and goddesses, relegating the altar of Yahweh to a subsidiary position in the process. Judah's leaders even tolerated the anathema of child sacrifice on the southern outskirts of Jerusalem in the Valley of Ben-Hinnom (2 Kgs 21:1-16; cf. 2 Chr 33:1-10). Manasseh's reign was a time of martyrdom for the faithful when he silenced the voices of authentic prophecy (2 Kgs 21:16). We can imagine that genuine Yahwism survived in underground associations of the faithful, such as the circles of Isaian disciples and the Deuteronomic guilds.

Amon (642-640 B.C.) succeeded Manasseh to the throne of Judah but was assassinated within two years (2 Kgs 21:19-26). A group of elders arranged for the transmission of the kingship to Amon's eight-year-old son, Josiah, who would reign for the next thirty years (640-609 B.C./2 Kgs 22:1-2). Indications in Chronicles suggest that, while still in his teens, he set his heart on a return to the traditions of David, and, in 629 B.C., he initiated a reform movement in Judah (2 Chr 34:3-7). The timing of his initiative coincided with a period of turmoil in the high ranks of Assyria as the sons of Ashurbanipal (669-630 B.C.) provoked five years of civil unrest in their quarrel for succession to their father's throne.

The providential discovery of the early edition of Deuteronomy in the Temple storeroom in 622 B.C. provided Josiah's reformation with direction and authority deriving from Mosaic tradition (2 Kgs 22:3-20). In accordance with the Deuteronomic legislation, Josiah purged the land of the practices that had characterized the reign of Manasseh (2 Kgs 23:4-14, 21-25; 2 Chr 34:1-35:19). He even extended his reform to encompass some of the northern kingdom, which the Assyrians had overtaken a century earlier (2 Kgs 23:15-20; 2 Chr 34:6-7).

Throughout this period, the ponderous Assyrian empire was· rapidly disintegrating. In 626 B.C., Nebupolassar (626-605 B.C.) dislodged the Assyrians from Babylon in a victory that would eventually identify him as the patriarch of the neo-Babylonian empire. In 614 B.C., the Medes from the north and west of Persia captured Asshur. Finally, in 612 B.C., a coalition of the Babylonians and the Medes overran the Assyrian capital of Nineveh. In 609 B.C., the Babylonians repelled a final desperate attempt by the Assyrians to retake Haran. Preparations for this battle brought tragedy to Judah as the Egyptian army of Necho killed Josiah at Megiddo when the king of Judah tried to prevent him from supporting the Assyrian assault on Haran (2 Kgs 23:29-30).

Although Egypt had backed the losing side at Haran, Necho was able to take control of Judah until the Babylonians further developed their power. Necho deposed Josiah's heir, Jehoahaz, and replaced him with another son, Jehoiakim (609-598 B.C.), who offered the promise of greater fealty to Egypt (2 Kgs 23:31-35). The Egyptians relinquished control of the region four years later, when the Babylonian forces under Nebuchadnezzar defeated them in 605 B.C. at Carchemish on the northwestern estuary of the Euphrates. Judah then came under Babylonian control. However, around 600 B.C., when Necho's forces turned back the Babylonians from the Egyptian borders, Jehoiakim rebelled against his overlords. Nebuchadnezzar responded by sending troops of mixed nationalities against Jerusalem. Jehoiakim died (perhaps violently) at the end of 598 B.C. (2 Kgs 24:1–7). His eighteen-year-old son, Jehoiachin, succeeded him to the throne but reigned only three months before Nebuchadnezzar's forces invaded Jerusalem for the first time on March 16, 597 B.C., and deported the king along with thousands of the leading citizens to exile in Babylon (2 Kgs 24:8–17).

ZEPHANIAH

Zephaniah was the first classical prophet to surface in Judah after more than a half century following Isaiah's career. The introduction to the collection of Zephaniah's teachings informs us that he exercised his ministry under the favorable conditions provided by King Josiah in Judah (1:1). Furthermore, the text indicates that he was a fourth-generation descendant of King Hezekiah (716–687 B.C.) and, therefore, a distant relative of Josiah. When we add to this evidence his apparent familiarity with Jerusalem and its officials (1:4–11), we can surmise that he was a native of the capital and perhaps even a member of the royal court. If this represents an accurate portrait, his indictment of the priests (1:4–6), prophets (3:4), and princes (1:8–9) is all the more personal and stunning. Because nothing in Zephaniah indicates that the prophet knew of the king's reforms, we date his ministry to the years 635–630 B.C., prior to Josiah's reforms. Did Josiah begin to seek the Lord in response to Zephaniah's preaching (2 Chr 34:3)?

We can divide the book of Zephaniah into four sections: (1) the impending visitation of divine judgment upon Judah and Jerusalem reserved for the Day of Yahweh (1:1–18; 2:1–3); (2) God's judgment on the nations (2:4–15); (3) God's judgment on Jerusalem (3:1–8); and (4) God's promise of salvation and joy for a remnant in Judah (3:9–20).

Most of the book's contents come from the mouth of the prophet. However, the clarity of vision about other nations being converted to the Lord (3:10; cf. Mal 1:11), the final invitations to joy (3:14–18; cf. Is 40:2; Zec 2:14), and the description of restoration (3:19–20) all derive from exilic and postexilic editors. These scribes found in Zechariah's words God's vision for the restoration of his people in their own generation. We can date the final edition of Zephaniah after the Exile, perhaps around 500 B.C.

The Message of Zephaniah

Zephaniah considered himself to be living in the breach between the closing of an era awaiting its final overthrow and the beginning of a period of restoration. He surveyed history with a broad vision by which he could locate the destiny of Judah and Jerusalem within the framework of what was happening in the surrounding nations of the world. We will examine his message in light of two themes he derived from his predecessors Amos and Isaiah, respectively: (a) the coming Day of Yahweh, and (b) the remnant who will survive in Judah.

The Day of Yahweh: Zephaniah called for elimination of all vestiges of corruption and idolatry deriving from the reigns of Manasseh and Amon. Jerusalem had provoked the Lord's anger by the hospitality it had extended to Assyria's astral deities and to the pagan gods Baal and Milcom (1:4–5). The elders of Judah along with her priests and court prophets had neglected the Lord and his commandments (3:1–4). The lavish dress of the princes, the extravagant new houses of the city, and the feverish activity of the marketplace — all indications of a prosperous society — served only to provoke the Lord because they were the fruit of ill-gotten wealth (1:8–13). The root of Judah's corruption was its pride, its arrogant suggestion that the Lord was irrelevant, and its refusal to approach him in faith (1:12–13; 3:1). Its attitude toward the Lord made Judah indistinct from other nations (3:7).

In face of all that the Lord was showing him about the state of his people, Zephaniah announced to Judah the message Amos had preached to Israel in the middle of the previous century. The Day of Yahweh was coming, this time upon Jerusalem and Judah (1:2–2:3; cf. Am 5:18–20). Zephaniah's description develops the theme beyond the scope Amos had had in mind. In Zephaniah, the Day of Yahweh extends outward from the borders of his people's land to take on cosmic proportions affecting all creatures (1:2–3; cf. Hos 4:3). It will be the "Day of Yahweh's anger", when all that sin has corrupted will be consumed in a fiery holocaust (1:14–2:2). The Lord's visitation will come upon each of the nations surrounding Judah: Philistia to the west (2:4–7), Moab and Ammon on the east (2:8–11), Egypt-Ethiopia in the south (2:12), and Assyria in the north (2:13–15). Zephaniah's dark picture would be taken up again in Joel (1:14–18; cf. Jl 2:1–11).

The Remnant: Up to this point, we have seen only one side of the Day of Yahweh: destruction. The other side represents the reverse. The Day of Yahweh will destroy the pride of Judah and bring forth a purified remnant who will survive because of their humility and submission to the Lord's ways

(2:3). In Judah, the remnant of the Lord will replace "Baal's remnant" (3:11–13; cf. 1:4). Just as arrogance, pride, and faithlessness had marked the leaders of the old era, so lowliness, docility, and trust in the Lord will define the remnant. With this inspired vision, Zephaniah advances a vision of community focused on "the poor of the Lord" (Hebrew: *'anawim*), which will be developed in later Isaian tradition and in the Psalms (2:3; 3:12; Is 57:14–21; Pss 22; 34; 37; 69; 74; 149).

A great promise lies in store for this remnant who will inherit the surrounding lands (2:7, 9). For them, in the future lies "that Day" when the Lord will gather them into Jerusalem and make of them a community of grace, peace, and joy (3:11–18). Zephaniah and the tradition under his influence advance beyond Amos by insisting more strongly on the point that God's last word is not the Day of Yahweh's wrath but "that Day" of joy and redemption (1:14–18; cf. 3:11–18). In fact, the "Day of Yahweh's anger" (1:18) only initiates the final time of salvation that bursts into light as on a day of festival (3:18). Zephaniah makes another important advance by introducing the suggestion that the grace of conversion will extend beyond Judah to embrace all peoples (2:11; 3:9–10; cf. Is 42:4; 51:5; 56:1–7).

Toward the New Testament: Judgment and the Remnant of the Meek

The words of Zephaniah contribute to the tradition that Jesus draws upon when he speaks of judgment and promise in the Gospel of Matthew. When explaining the meaning of the parable about the weeds growing among the wheat, he uses Zephaniah's introductory words of divine judgment to describe the actions of the angels whom the Son of Man sends to expel all who do evil from his kingdom (Mt 13:41; cf. Zep 1:3). Thus, Jesus indicates to us that Zephaniah's words should awaken us from spiritual complacency by causing us to examine whether we are the wheat or the weeds in the Church (Mt 13:24–30, 36–43).

Zephaniah exhorted his people to examine themselves in a similar manner according to his distinction between the proud and the humble (1:12–13; 3:1–4; cf. 2:3; 3:11–13). In Zephaniah, we discern a clear foreshadowing of Jesus' description of God's people in the Sermon on the Mount. It is not the mighty but the meek who will inherit the earth (Mt 5:4; cf. Ps 37:11). Zephaniah offers a graphic illustration of this principle in his promise that the humble remnant of Judah will take over the lands of surrounding nations (2:7, 9).

The action of God to overthrow the most powerful of nations while caring for Judah is a theme we encounter once more in the book of Nahum.

NAHUM

We know almost nothing about Nahum except that he was a prophet from Elkosh, a village outside of Jerusalem whose location is still subject to debate (1:1). His writing style indicates that he was a gifted poet. He composed his text in 612 B.C., just as Nineveh, the capital of the Assyrian Empire, was falling to the alliance of the Medes and Babylonians.

The book of Nahum consists of two parts: (1) (1:1–2:1): a psalm (1:2–8) and meditation (1:9–2:1) concerning the Lord's revelation of himself to Assyria and Judah; and (2) (2:2–3:19): a poetic depiction of the attack on Nineveh (2:2–11) followed by a series of meditative reflections on the event (2:12–3:19). In general, Nahum belongs to the category of prophetic literature concerned with the Lord's judgments on the nations (see Am 1–2; Is 13–23; Jer 46–51; Ez 25–32).

We will contemplate Nahum's message by reflecting on two of his primary concerns: (a) the revelation of Yahweh to Assyria and to Judah; and (b) the implications of Nineveh's fall for God's people and mighty nations in every period of history.

The Lord's Self-Revelation: Every reader must pause and offer his or her own response to the central question in Nahum, "What are your thoughts about Yahweh?" (1:9). Deeper than Nahum's fascination with the astounding collapse of a presumably invincible empire is his preoccupation with how the Lord makes himself known in history. The opening psalm provides a meditation on the Lord's sovereignty over all creation (1:3–5) and, in the process, indicates his personal qualities. The Lord reveals a different aspect of himself to people according to their position in the world. To those who put their faith in him, he is more than a fortress and a protection from all threatening catastrophes (1:7–8), but, to those who resist him, he becomes a predator who will devour them (1:8).

In the commentary following the psalm (1:9–2:1), Nahum makes it clear that the Assyrians now have a different experience of Yahweh than do the people of Judah. The fact that Assyria had existed for centuries is a testament to the truth that "Yahweh is slow to anger" (1:3), but the rapid demise of the empire within a few short years reveals also that Yahweh is "great in power" (1:3; cf. Ex 34:6–7). Because Assyria constantly worked against the Lord and his people, even its king will have no surviving offspring, and the images of its gods will be thrown away (1:11, 14). By contrast, the very events by which Yahweh reveals his fury against his enemies provide freedom for his faithful. In the fall of Nineveh, Judah experiences new freedom and receives the good news of "peace" with an assurance that she will no longer suffer the oppressions of the past (1:12–13; 2:1; cf. Is 52:7–10).

God's People and the Mighty Nations: The whole work of Nahum serves to relativize every form of human power to the sovereignty of God. No matter how dominant an empire might become, God will judge it on the basis of the justice it demonstrates in international affairs (3:1, 4). A capital replete with ambassadors and financial negotiators can become a hollow ghost town with shocking suddenness if the Lord wills it (3:16–17). At her collapse in 612 B.C., Nineveh was no better off than the city of Thebes in Egypt when the Assyrians overran it in 663 B.C. (3:8–11). The nation whose cruelty had made it the mightiest upon the earth now hears the Lord of hosts declare, "I am against you" (2:14; 3:5; cf. 3:19). Nahum wanted his people to realize that the Medes and the Babylonians were acting as agents of the Lord's judgment when they attacked Nineveh. By contrast to the extinction of Assyria, at one time the most imposing of all nations, Judah continues to survive successive waves of invasion and plunder (2:1). The Lord reveals himself to be the surest of all defenses for those who trust in him (1:7).

Toward the New Testament: Faithful Resistance to the Great City

The book of Nahum demonstrates that there is an application to international affairs for Jesus' maxim about the exalted being humbled (Lk 14:11; 18:14) and for James' admonitions concerning the futility of pride in accumulated wealth, power, and status (Jas 4:13–5:6). Nahum's assertion of the Lord's being the sure defense of those who trust in him contributes to the background of Jesus' encouragement to his disciples that they persevere in their faith amid wars and rumors of wars, confident that their endurance will bring them salvation (Mk 13:5–13). Nahum's conviction about the conditional nature of political power is consistent with Jesus' word to Pilate that all earthly authority is relative to God, who permits its exercise (Jn 19:11).

Nahum's portrait of Nineveh foreshadows the picture of Rome offered in the book of Revelation under the symbol of Babylon the Great (Rv 17–18). Nineveh, Babylon, and Rome were all cities that, at the height of their power, oppressed God's people. Like Nahum's Nineveh, Rome in the book of Revelation is a corrupt and abused harlot about to fall into decay (Rv 17:1–18:24; cf. Na 3:4). With an awareness that the Roman Empire would follow Assyria and Babylon into extinction, the Christians were strengthened in their resolve not to worship the Emperor in spite of the persecutions of Domitian around A.D. 95 (cf. Rv 1:9; 2:13; 13:1–17).

The prophet Habakkuk will instruct us further on the importance of exercising faith when God's people face affliction at the hands of the most powerful nation in the world.

HABAKKUK

Habakkuk was both a visionary (1:1) and a psalmist (3:1–19). The sparse references in captions above texts that have a pronounced liturgical aspect suggest that, by his office, he was intimately associated with the Temple in Jerusalem. He had a high perch in Jerusalem from which he performed his service as Israel's watchman (2:1–3). He wrote his composition after 605 B.C., when the Babylonians defeated the Egyptians at Carchemish. The best date for his work seems to be around 598 B.C., when the forces of Nebuchadnezzar were approaching Judah in response to Jehoiakim's ill-fated rebellion (1:6–11). Habakkuk composed his text before the Babylonian invasion of Jerusalem in March of 597 B.C.

The book of Habakkuk consists of three sections: (1) a two-part dialogue in which the prophet voices his complaint about injustice and receives God's response (1:1–2:4); (2) the pronouncement of five woes on the Babylonian invaders (2:5–20); and (3) a concluding psalm announcing the revelation and victory of God (3:1–19).

The structure of the text exhibits an inner logic and progression as it takes us from complaint (1:1–2:4) to a vision of God's judgment (2:5–20) and finally to the revelation of God (3:1–15). The methodology of the book brings us from doubt and confusion over what is happening all around us (1:2–4, 12–17), to reception of God's vision of the present (2:1–20), and finally to fundamental trust in God irrespective of our circumstances (3:16–19). We will examine the three parts of the book as stages of growth in order to consider how our faith can develop in response to divine revelation.

Questioning and Dialogue with God (1:1–2:4): We must take our complaints about life to God. Habakkuk's complaint concerns the "violence" (1:3, 9; 2:8, 17) he sees in the world around him (1:2–4). His complaint echoes that of Jeremiah first against King Jehoiakim and, then, against King Jehoiachin for neglecting the needs of the poor in Judah (cf. Jer 22:13–17, 24–30). In response to the inequity of Habakkuk's time, the Lord speaks of sending the Babylonians as instruments of his judgment on Judah (1:5–11). This response provokes Habakkuk to issue a second complaint, this time on the side of Judah precisely against the advent of the powerful Babylonians. How could the Lord allow this powerful oppressor to descend upon his people (1:12–17)? The Lord's response is now different: he instructs Habakkuk to wait for the vision. This is the act of faith that will cause the righteous to survive (2:2–4). It is a basic trust and reliance on God that is distinguished by fidelity in times of difficulty (cf. Is 7:9). So far, we can appreciate that dialogue with God deepens our trust in him.

The Vision of Faith (2:5–20): Now, with the perspective of faith, Habakkuk sees into Nebuchadnezzar's behavior. He perceives that the Babylonian leader stands under God's judgment. He announces the five woes of divine condemnation on the Babylonians' international plunder (2:7–8), ill-gotten wealth (2:9–11), barbarism (2:12–13), mercilessness (2:15–17), and idolatry (2:18–20). In fact, seen through the eyes of faith, the Babylonian oppressor is not the most powerful but the most doomed of God's creatures (2:5–6). In the midst of the woes, Habakkuk calls his mind back to the sovereignty of God over the earth and in the Temple (2:14, 20).

The Revelation of God: Habakkuk's final psalm turns the mind from preoccupation with human adversaries to the authority of God manifest first in creation (3:3–7) and then in his conquest of the hostile forces in the world represented in the waters of chaos (3:8–15). He will perform a new act of deliverance to subdue the sea and its monsters (3:15; cf. Is 43:16–17). As in the days of the wilderness journey and the conquest, now the Lord comes to save his people and make them secure (see 3:8; cf. Dt 33:26–29).

Once the prophet is set at ease, he appreciates the greatness of the Lord's majesty and the strength of his will to save his people (3:16–19). The barren circumstances of the present struggle no longer affect the person who knows the greatness of God and his care for his people. Habakkuk teaches us that when our situation seems desolate, we can have greater cause for rejoicing and renew our strength because of the revelation the Lord will offer to those who seek him. Patient trust in God bears the fruit of joy and vigor (3:17–19).

Toward the New Testament: Justification by Faith

Paul develops our understanding of faith when he quotes Habakkuk to support his assertion that human beings are justified by faith (Gal 3:11; Rom 1:17; cf. Heb 10:38; Hb 2:4). Habakkuk's intention was to contrast the faith of Judah with the arrogance of Babylon. Faith to Habakkuk is a trusting reliance on the Lord in the face of great adversity. This basic trust will cause the righteous ("upright") people of Judah to survive beyond the term of the unrighteous Babylonians (Hb 2:4). Paul quotes the prophet's statement in a manner that corresponds neither to the Hebrew nor to the Septuagint (Greek) text. However, he is inspired to see more deeply into the revealed meaning of the text than Habakkuk did. In Paul, faith alone makes us righteous and therefore able to live. Because all of us have sinned and fallen short of God's glory, we cannot be made right with God through works. Justification comes only through faith, which is an active consent to the redeeming work of Christ applied to our life (see Rom 3:20–28).

When quoting the same text in Habakkuk, the author of Hebrews returns to another emphasis found there by stressing faith's need to persevere through times of trial (Heb 10:38, in 10:32–39; cf. Hb 2:3–4).

Finally, we note how Habakkuk contributes to Luke's theology of the poor of the Lord (Hebrew: *'anawim*). The arrogance of the rich, exemplified in the Babylonians, is a cause for woe because it cuts them off from God's Kingdom (Lk 6:24–26; cf. Hb 2:5–6). By contrast, in her song of praise, Mary, the mother of Jesus, exemplifies the fullness of faith foreshadowed in Habakkuk when she declares, "my spirit rejoices in God my Savior" (Lk 1:47; cf. Hb 3:18).

Together, Zephaniah, Nahum, and Habakkuk provide a kind of background chorus for the great prophetic figure of their time, Jeremiah of Anathoth.

STUDY QUESTIONS

1. What are two themes of Zephaniah?
2. What are the characteristics of the remnant?
3. How does Zephaniah's message relate to Jesus' parable of the weeds and the wheat?
4. What are Nahum's two concerns?
5. What are the characteristics of the Lord that Nahum reveals?
6. How is Nahum's vision international?
7. What are the similarities among Nineveh, Babylon, and Rome?
8. How does Paul interpret Habakkuk's understanding of faith?
9. How does Habakkuk contribute to Luke's theology of the *'anawim?*
10. Discuss how what appears on television and in the movies today resembles Nineveh, Babylon, and Rome. How do you counter the effects of these media in your life of faith?
11. How would you persuade a young person susceptible to temptation (drugs, sex, and alcohol) to prefer a life of holiness and worship? What insights in the matter do you receive from Zephaniah, Nahum, and Habakkuk?
12. What might these prophets suggest to us about the Church's role in calling for peace and justice among the nations of the world?

ZEPHANIAH

I.   The Day of Yahweh for Jerusalem and Judah (1:1–18)

II. God's Judgment on the Nations (2:1–15)

III. God's Judgment on Judah (3:1–8)

IV. The Promise of Conversion and Restoration (3:9–20)

NAHUM

I.   The Lord, Assyria, and Judah (1:1–2:1)
     A.   Introductory Psalm: Revelation of the Lord's Wrath (1:1–8)
     B.   Judgments for Assyria and Promises for Judah (1:9–2:1)

II. Nineveh's Desolation (2:2–3:19)
     A.   The Final Assault on Nineveh (2:2–11)
     B.   Meditation on Nineveh's Ruin and Futility (2:12–3:19)

HABAKKUK

23

JEREMIAH: THE PROPHETIC LIFE

God speaks his word through the prophet's life more than simply through his mouth. We should not think of biblical prophecy as a mere message that suddenly enters the mind as if from another world, momentarily alters the speaker's state of consciousness, and then passes through his lips. The book of Jeremiah teaches us that such an experience is typical of counterfeit prophecy (see 23:25–40). Genuine prophecy is a word from God intended to take flesh permanently in the life of his people. By God's action, the word is first embodied in the prophet's life and, over time, shapes his whole existence. The prophet stands in the midst of God's people as a sign illustrating the effectiveness of God's judgment and promise contained in the word he speaks. We find the interaction between the divine word and human life illustrated most fully in Jeremiah, whose life is described in detail unparalleled among all the prophets.

Jeremiah's service to the Lord and his people spanned more than forty years (627–c. 582 B.C.), long enough for Judah to pass under the rule of five kings and a governor who were subservient to the dominion of three successive foreign empires. His life as a prophet is a revelation of the dynamic of God's word constantly in action across a half-century, from a time of optimism and renewal (under Josiah) to days of despair and desolation (in the fall of Jerusalem and its aftermath). Ultimately, in Jeremiah, we experience the movement of God's word not just through time but through space as we follow the prophet, in his final years, on his reluctant journey beyond the frontiers of the Promised Land down into Egypt.

We will devote ourselves to a meditation on Jeremiah's words according to the historical development of his ministry. But first, we must consider how the biblical authors arranged his teachings in the inspired text.

The Book of Jeremiah

Because the text is more than a biography, it does not follow a chronological sequence. Rather, it presents the life and message of Jeremiah in five parts

organized around one predominant theme, namely, God's dealings with Judah
in relation to his judgments on the nations of the world. Judah is unique
among all nations because of God's word. This theme recurs in each major
section of the book: (1) God's judgments on Judah and Jerusalem (1:1–24:10);
(2) the prophet's words and deeds concerning the matter of Judah's interaction
with other nations (25:1–35:19); (3) the sufferings of the prophet, who ends up
in one foreign nation (Egypt) after another foreign nation (Babylon) destroys
Jerusalem (36:1–45:5); (4) the prophecies of divine judgment on the foreign
nations (46:1–51:64); and (5) the fall of Jerusalem, the deportation of the
people from Judah to Babylon, and the eventual release of Judah's king from
imprisonment in exile (52:1–34 = 2 Kgs 24:18–25:30).

The text is composed of four different types of material:

a. The actual words of the prophet expressed in poetic oracles, comprising the most obvious category (e.g., 2:1–6:30; 8:4–10:25; 21:11–14; 22:6–30;
30:1–31:22). We should reserve a special subsection of this category for the
autobiographical pieces, which include his "Confessions" (11:18–12:6; 15:10–21;
17:14–18; 18:18–23; 20:7–18) and other personal statements (4:19–21; 5:3–5;
8:18–23; 16:19–21);

b. The biographical passages describing events in the prophet's life, written in prose narrative (e.g., 26:1–28:17; 29:1–32; 32:1–44; 36:1–32; 37:1–45:5);

c. Sections that reflect the tensions between Jeremiah and his adversaries,
offering direct speech in the style of ordinary nonpoetic discourse (e.g.,
7:1–8:3; 11:1–14, 15–17; 16:1–13, 14–18; 18:1–12; 19:1–20:6; 21:1–10; 22:1–5;
25:1–13; 34:1–35:19). Particularly in this type of material, we can detect a
strong Deuteronomic influence; and

d. Prophecies against the nations belonging to another distinct category
of expression (46:1–51:64).

The richness of the book's contents manifests the grace of inspiration
God gave to a tradition of disciples who devoted themselves to probing
the depths of the revelation given to the prophet by God. We can detect
three major stages of composition culminating in the present edition of the
text:

1. Jeremiah provided the first edition of his message in 605/604 B.C.,
when he dictated his words to Baruch, who wrote them on the scroll that
court officials received and then passed on to King Jehoiakim (36:1–32). After
the king destroyed the original scroll in disgust, Jeremiah composed another
version, again through the hand of Baruch. This second text he kept safely out
of the reach of his adversaries (see 36:32).

2. The prophet's scribe, Baruch, composed a biography of Jeremiah covering some twenty-five years of his life and ministry, from the beginning of
Jehoiakim's reign (in 609 B.C./26:1–24) through the destruction of Jerusalem

(in 587 B.C./39:1–41:18) to the subsequent time when the prophet reluctantly took up residence in Egypt (42:1–44:30; cf. 45:1–5).

3. During the Exile, Deuteronomists collected the documentation containing the prophet's words and deeds and reshaped the material into the final edition of the text. The version we have in the Bible comes from the hand of a Deuteronomic editor, who completed the work either in the last days of the Exile (c. 538 B.C.) or in the early years of Jerusalem's reconstruction (c. 500 B.C.). By our estimation, the Deuteronomists produced the final edition of Jeremiah within decades of putting the finishing touches on the book of Deuteronomy and the Deuteronomic History.

The Words and Deeds of Jeremiah

Our survey of the book's contents now affords us the opportunity to consider the unfolding of God's word in the prophet's life. We will contemplate the development of Jeremiah's message in relation to the episodes that affected him most deeply. We can distinguish four successive periods in the life of Jeremiah: (1) under the reign of Josiah, from the prophet's call to the king's death (627–609 B.C.); (2) under the reign of Jehoiakim (609–598 B.C.); (3) under the reign of Zedekiah (597–587 B.C.); and (4) in the aftermath of the fall of Jerusalem, concluding with Jeremiah's final residence in Egypt (587–c. 582 B.C.). Those who are interested in considering spiritual development according to the stages of a person's life can calculate the prophet's age in each of these periods based on the estimation that Jeremiah was born around 645 B.C., in the last years of Manasseh's reign (687–642 B.C.).

1. Years of Renewal under Josiah (627–609 B.C.) (1:1–6:30; cf. 11:1–17, 18–23; 30:1–31:40)

Jeremiah grew up in Anathoth, a township only a little more than an hour's walk north and east of Jerusalem. The fact that he came from a priestly line that might have traced itself back to Abiathar of King David's court (see 1 Kgs 2:26–27) makes Jeremiah's later confrontations with the priests all the more remarkable (2:8, 26; 4:9; 5:31). Jeremiah experienced his prophetic call in 627 B.C., the thirteenth year of Josiah's reign (1:1–2). We acknowledge that a minority of scholars equate the prophet's call with his birth (1:4–5) and date the beginning of his ministry under Jehoiakim as 609 or 605 B.C. However, evidence throughout the book supports the conclusion that he received God's life-changing word as a "young man" (na'ar: 1:7) in his mid- to late teens (1:2–3). In light of information we discussed in the last chapter, we note that

Jeremiah began his prophetic career within five years of Zephaniah's ministry and two years after Josiah had initiated his movement toward reform.

Unlike Isaiah of the previous century and Ezekiel, his contemporary at a distance in later days, Jeremiah does not mention a vision of the Lord's glory in his call (1:4–10; cf. Is 6:1–13; Ez 1:1–3:21). God's word stands at the center of Jeremiah's experience. The dialogue between the prophet, overwhelmed at his own inadequacy, and the Lord, who indicates his resolute decision, recalls the primary event in Moses' life at Sinai (Ex 3:1–4:17). Like Isaiah and Ezekiel, Jeremiah's vocation primarily entails announcing God's word to people who are obstinate and unreceptive (1:9–10, 17–19; cf. Is 6:9–13; Ez 3:4–11; 12:2). Jeremiah's mission is distinguished by an international aspect that will bring about a change in the world order. Through him, the word of God will overthrow nations, destroying what existed and planting the seeds of new life (1:10; cf. 18:7; 31:28; 45:4).

The two visionary components of Jeremiah's call indicate that the word is going to be fulfilled through the advancing armies of the destructive foe from the north. In his early years, Jeremiah might have identified this foe with the Assyrians, but he refocused his gaze once the neo-Babylonians under Nebupolassar (626–605 B.C.) came into prominence. His certitude about what would take place came from inspired insights he received while looking at such ordinary objects as an almond tree (common in the region of Anathoth) and a cooking pot tilting on the fire (1:11–14).

In his formative years, Jeremiah studied Hosea. In his early preaching, he employs Hosea's symbol of marriage to image God's covenant relationship with his people (2:2; Hos 2:16–17). Using terms Hosea had addressed to Israel prior to its destruction over a century before, Jeremiah describes Judah as a spouse who has become unfaithful because of idolatry (2:1–3:5; 3:19–20; 6:29–30) and injustice (5:1, 26–29; 6:13–14). Unless Judah repents, her only prospect is the deathly silence of what we might now term the "nuclear winter" (4:23–26). A further indication of Jeremiah's stance in line with his eighth-century forebears is his withering attack on the prophets of false consolation (4:10; 5:12–13, 30–31; 6:13–14; cf. Hos 4:5; Mi 3:5, 6, 11; Is 9:14; 28:7). In his first days, Jeremiah devoted himself to purging the land of the elements of paganism coming from the reign of Manasseh.

We lack precise indications about Jeremiah's role in the Deuteronomic reformation Josiah undertook after the discovery of the scroll in 622 B.C. (2 Kgs 22:8–10; 23:1–27). He certainly welcomed the king's devotion to the Law as a salutary correction of priests who neglected to teach its precepts to their people (cf. Jer 2:8). Jeremiah offered his support for adherence to the terms of the Deuteronomic covenant as the source of hope for survival in the land (cf. 11:1–14).

The pace of the reforms and the prominence given to the Deuteronomists might have made Jeremiah optimistic, inspiring him to contemplate even the possibility of the restoration of the northern kingdom as Judah became renewed (see 30:1–31:40). We can surmise that as the reforms continued, Jeremiah would have been concerned that they were not deep enough to change the people's hearts. The reform movement lost its momentum when the Egyptian troops of Necho killed Josiah at Megiddo in 609 B.C. (2 Kgs 23:29–30).

2. A Decade of Confrontation with Jehoiakim (609–598 B.C.) (7:1–15/11:15–17/26:1–24; 7:16–20:18; 22:13–19; 25:1–13/36:1–32)

Upon Josiah's death, Jehoahaz succeeded his father to the throne. However, after just three months, Necho deposed him, took him into captivity in Egypt, and installed his brother Jehoiakim as a vassal king of Judah (2 Kgs 23:31–37; cf. Jer 22:10–12). Almost immediately after the king's enthronement in 609 B.C., Jeremiah took center stage in Jerusalem by preaching his famous Temple Sermon (7:1–15; 26:1–19). His theme was in the tradition of his classical forebears: because ritual sacrifice without obedience to God and justice to neighbor provokes God's wrath, he will destroy even the Temple in Jerusalem as he had obliterated the sanctuary at Shiloh (cf. Am 2:6–4:12; Hos 4:1–19; Mi 7:1–7). Because of idolatrous pagan rituals and moral dissolution, the Temple had become "a den of bandits" (7:11). Reacting swiftly, the priests and prophets officially assigned to the Temple summarily brought Jeremiah to trial and demanded his execution. Jeremiah escaped with his life only through the intervention of some prominent civic leaders, who perceived in his speech resonances of the now-venerable Micah. The leader of Jeremiah's defenders was the scribe Ahikam, whose father had been a prime advocate of Josiah's reforms (26:24; cf. 2 Kgs 22:8).

This was only the beginning of Jeremiah's protest against Jehoiakim and his regime. By the prophet's estimation, the king betrayed every principle his father had upheld. Jehoiakim's self-indulgent building projects combined with the heavy taxation that Egypt demanded put an insupportable burden on the populace. The king deserved a donkey's funeral (22:13–19; see 2 Kgs 23:33, 35)! Because Jehoiakim's policies contradicted his father's, idolatry and injustice were returning and the whole society was going to disintegrate like a rotten waist cloth or be smashed like wine jugs (13:1–11, 12–14; cf. 9:1–21; 10:1–25; 18:13–17). King, Temple priests, and prophets alike would have to learn that true wealth comes from knowing the Lord and living in justice (9:22–23). These were not pleasant days for prophets: sometime in the early part of his reign, Jehoiakim executed Uriah of Kiriath-Jearim for saying what Jeremiah was now saying (26:20–23).

The simmering tensions between Jeremiah and Jehoiakim reached a boiling point once again in 605 B.C., when the Babylonians defeated the Egyptians at Carchemish. With the armies of Nebuchadnezzar advancing southward, Judah was in the midst of a national crisis. To illustrate what he perceived, Jeremiah rounded up important officials of state and Temple, took them to the Gate of Potsherds, showed them the heaps of potsherds that the craftsmen had thrown away, and declared that the Lord was about to visit a similar desolation on Jerusalem. The prophet's words were provocative enough for Pashhur, the chief of the Temple police, to put him in stocks even as Jeremiah berated him with the nickname "Terror-on-every-Side" (19:1–20:6).

The Temple officials forbade Jeremiah to enter the sacred precincts (36:5). We gain an impression of Baruch's courage because he enters the picture precisely at this juncture when all the public forces are turning against Jeremiah (36:1–31). ("Baruch" literally means "blessed" in Hebrew.) The prophet dictates his message, which Baruch inscribes on a scroll and then, on behalf of the prophet, reads to the populace who are gathered in the Temple square on a day of national fasting in December of 604 B.C. The Temple and state officials might have called the day of fasting in response to the crisis that Nebuchadnezzar's invasion of Philistia at this time generated (47:5–7). Credible leaders, such as Gemariah and Micaiah, the son and grandson of Josiah's scribe Shaphan, took the message seriously and requested Baruch to read it to them and other officials in a private sitting. They, in turn, arranged for the scroll to reach the hands of someone who would read it to the king (36:10–20). Because the Deuteronomists in the Exile edited both the Deuteronomic History and the book of Jeremiah, we should compare Jehoiakim's reaction to Jeremiah's scroll with his father Josiah's response to the text of Deuteronomy (36:21–26; cf. 2 Kgs 22:11–20). While his father repented when he heard the words of the scroll, Jehoiakim heard the scroll read and then simply sliced it up and cast it into the winter fire piece by piece. Jeremiah and Baruch then set about inscribing a replacement document to be stored for safe keeping (36:32). It seems the prophet went into relative seclusion for a few years after this.

The "Confessions of Jeremiah" (11:18–12:6; 15:10–21; 17:14–18; 18:18–23; 20:7–18) express the prophet's experience of God's word deriving from his years under the reign of Jehoiakim. These texts take us to the heart of the prophet and bring to light the interior conflict and suffering of the Lord's servant. Jeremiah's honesty is impressive as he refuses to cover up his resentment (11:20), despair (15:10–11; 20:14–18), and desire for retaliation (18:19–23). To our minds, these are understandable reactions for someone who has undergone his ordeal: assassination plots in his hometown (11:19–23), a courtroom trial with the threat of execution in the city (26:7–24), and confinement in stocks in the city square (20:1–6). In spite of all this, Jeremiah's struggle is not with other people but with Yahweh, whose word, which originally brought him such joy, now brings deep affliction (15:10–11, 16). His alienation from others comes from his obedience to the word. He feels as if the Lord has seduced him (20:7). Nevertheless, the confessions are more than complaints because they lead the prophet to repentance.

Jeremiah's honesty extends well beyond the communication of his own feelings to his reception of God's word. After his protests, he accedes to the Lord's admonition that he learn perseverance because the struggle is only beginning (12:4–5), that he become stronger in keeping with his original calling (15:20–21), and that he allow the Lord to test him so as to prove the quality of his devotion (20:11–13).

Returning to the world of politics, we recall that Jehoiakim's alliance with Egypt provoked Nebuchadnezzar to send his troops toward Judah shortly after 600 B.C. (2 Kgs 24:1–2). The advent of the Babylonian troops provides the setting for Habakkuk's prophecies (Hb 1:1–3:19). Before the Babylonians actually moved on Jerusalem in 598 B.C., Jeremiah received his insight at the potter's shop. Just as the potter has to destroy misshapen earthenware, so the Lord would have to shatter Judah in order to form a new people (18:1–12). Jeremiah's words about the advent of the foe from the north came to fulfillment on March 16, 597 B.C., when Nebuchadnezzar's army invaded Jerusalem and exiled a large number of its leading citizens (2 Kgs 24:10–16). Death came to Jehoiakim in December 598 B.C. Nebuchadnezzar deposed Jehoiakim's eighteen-year-old son, Jehoiachin, from the throne and imprisoned him in Babylon (2 Kgs 24:15–16; cf. Jer 52:31–34). Jeremiah saw this as divine justice against the unjust King Jehoiachin (22:20–30; cf. 13:18–19). The Babylonians sanctioned the passing of the crown to Jehoiachin's uncle, Zedekiah, a third son of Josiah, who reigned until the destruction of Jerusalem (2 Kgs 24:17).

3. Counselor and Prisoner under Zedekiah (597–587 B.C.) (21:1–22:9; 23:1–24:10; 27:1–29:32; 30:1–34:22; 37:1–39:18)

Being only twenty-one years old when he took the throne, Zedekiah lacked the experience and sober judgment required to stabilize life in Judah (52:1). Public opinion too readily swayed him so that he could not formulate a policy that was manifestly his own. The king's ambivalence and indecisiveness caused the battle lines in the debate to fall between Jeremiah on one side and the state prophets, Temple priests, and most public officials on the other. The dominant issue of the decade was, "What is the nature of a genuine prophetic word?"

The policy-makers of the day sounded like partisan propagandists who run political conventions in our own day. They portrayed the Babylonian invasion in the most optimistic light. The court prophet Hananiah serenely promised that the exiles would return within merely two years as the Babylonians would soon be overthrown (28:1–4). For some reason, perhaps because of the Temple's presence, the endurance of the Davidic monarchy through four centuries, or the memory of Jerusalem's survival even when Sennacherib had surrounded Jerusalem (701 B.C./Is 37:1–38), the officials could not face the fact that Judah was in danger of annihilation. Not many held the opinion of the sobering realism of a prophet like Habakkuk. Numerous prophets, both in Jerusalem and among the exiles in Babylon, were offering cheerful assurances of a quick return from exile and a resumption of normalcy in Jerusalem (28:3, 4; 29:8, 9, 15). Zedekiah was taken in by their false optimism.

In 594 B.C., with Nebuchadnezzar waging campaigns on his eastern fronts, Zedekiah invited delegates from Edom, Moab, Ammon, Tyre, and Sidon to a conference in Jerusalem to consider the possibility of forming an anti-Babylonian alliance. Jeremiah sent letters to the delegates and then confronted the king, not only declaring to him the folly of his ways but also insisting that the Lord was working on the side of the Babylonians. He asserted that, at this time, to oppose the empire was to oppose Yahweh and, conversely, to serve Babylon was to submit to the Lord (27:1–22).

Next, Jeremiah took the debate to the public square, put a yoke on his shoulders, and exhorted officials and populace alike to put on the Babylonian harness. When Hananiah broke the yoke from his shoulders and advocated rebellion against Babylon, Jeremiah foresaw the eventual destruction of city and land because of its leaders' pride, naiveté, and folly (28:1–17).

Jeremiah continued his efforts to make the people face reality by writing to the exiles in Babylon, counseling them to make the best of their situation because their sojourn was to last some seventy years by his estimation (29:4–23). This would be a time of new beginnings, when the Lord would bring his people peace and hope. In the end, Yahweh will restore his people to their land.

Jeremiah never spoke a pessimistic message to the exiles. In fact, his whole tone changed from judgment to promise when he thought of the exiles. He considered the Exile to be a grace. The Lord had taken his people into exile precisely so that he could transform them and provide a future that would include restoring them to their land. God's people were now separated into two parts, like two baskets of figs. The good ones were in Babylonian exile, and the rotten ones remained in Jerusalem. The Lord was even now bestowing his blessing on those in Babylon as the source of hope and promise for the future (24:1–10).

It was likely sometime in this period that the Lord inspired Jeremiah to understand the depth of renewal he wanted to accomplish. The Lord is going to make a new covenant with his people, distinguished from the old one by its radical interiority. The commandments will remain the same as ever. But in the new covenant, the Lord will write his Law on the heart of each person so each one will have a personal, living knowledge of God. In other words, the Lord will transform the minds of his people so they will be able to live in joyous harmony with his will (31:31–34; cf. Dt 10:16; 30:6).

In line with the vision of restoration to a new level of existence previously unknown in Israel was Jeremiah's perception of the future for the Davidic line. Zedekiah was unreliable, and the other leaders just fragmented the people with their shallow pronouncements. However, in the future, the Lord will restore a remnant of his people to be ruled by a Branch from David's house who would bear the title "Yahweh-Is-Our-Saving-Justice". A new Exodus will follow the period of exile (23:1–8). As things worsened for Jerusalem and Judah, Jeremiah's teaching became more oriented away from God's judgment and toward God's promise for the future of his people.

The constant debate with the public officials forced Jeremiah to examine the difference between authentic and counterfeit prophecy (23:9–40). He knew that the false promises of peace without repentance or correction left the people vulnerable to increasing dissolution and ultimate despair (23:9–17). In fact, the false prophets' greatest deception was claiming a divine authority for their own narrow hopes (23:25–28, 30–40). Counterfeit prophecy compares to a genuine word from the Lord as straw compares to wheat (23:29). What, then, are the distinguishing characteristics of the Lord's word? For his answer, Jeremiah returns to two images deriving from his personal experience of the word in his life. God's word is a fire that purifies by refining and testing the prophet. The prophet speaks such a word while recognizing his own resistance to it (23:28–29; cf. 5:14; 20:9). We should note how this image of fire relates the divine word to the Deuteronomic metaphor of God in his revelation at Sinai (cf. Dt 4:24). The second image, that of the hammer shattering rock, seems related to Jeremiah's meditations on the potsherds (cf. 18:1–12; 19:1–15; 13:12–14).

Nebuchadnezzar sent his army into Judah in 589 B.C. because he wanted to break up Zedekiah's alliance with Egypt and to quell Judah's surge toward independence. In January 588 B.C., the army set up siege works around Jerusalem to hedge in the population. In the early days of the siege, Jeremiah counseled capitulation to the Babylonians as the only way to survive (21:1–10). Within a few months, when the king finally approached him for a word, Jeremiah foretold the fate in store for the city and for the monarch himself (34:1–7). There was a brief respite in the siege when Egyptian forces diverted the Babylonians' attention for a few weeks or months (37:5, 11). During this time, Zedekiah announced the liberation of all Jews enslaved to pay off outstanding debts, but the measure did not last (34:8–22). Jeremiah again declared that the Babylonians would return to take the city (37:6–10). Nevertheless, the most hopeful of symbolic gestures was Jeremiah's purchase of property outside Jerusalem as an indication of his certainty that the people of Judah would eventually resettle the land (32:1–44). When the Babylonians surrounded the city, he tried to leave Jerusalem in order to survey his property. For his efforts, he was charged with attempted desertion and thrown into a prison (37:11–21).

After Zedekiah consulted Jeremiah again, a committee of officials demanded that the prophet be put to death for discouraging the people with his promise that the city would fall. They cast Jeremiah in the storage pit, but Ebed-Melech the Ethiopian rescued him so he could have a final audience with the king (38:1–28).

The Babylonians broke through the walls of Jerusalem in June or July 587 B.C. (2 Kgs 25:3–4). One month later, the Babylonians burned down the Temple (2 Kgs 25:8–9). After their invasion of the city, they captured Zedekiah at Jericho and dispatched him to Nebuchadnezzar, while they released Jeremiah from prison and allowed him to remain in the land (39:1–18). While many considered Jeremiah to be a Babylonian sympathizer, his prophecies reveal his conviction that Nebuchadnezzar was but a momentary instrument of the Lord's judgment. Once Jerusalem had fallen, the Lord would destroy Babylon for its arrogance and redeem his people from captivity (50:1–51:64).

4. The Aftermath: From Judah to Egypt (587–582 B.C.) (40:1–44:30)

Jeremiah stayed on in Judah among the common folk who were allowed to remain after the destruction of Jerusalem (52:16). Nebuchadnezzar appointed a governor over Judah, Gedaliah, whose father Ahikam had been an old ally of Jeremiah (40:1–10; cf. 26:24). Many of the Judaeans who had fled to the surrounding countries settled around Mizpah, the new capital. However, Ishmael ben Nethaniah, a member of the royal household, gained the backing of a party of Ammonites and murdered Gedaliah and his company (40:7–41:3). After hearing of Ishmael's cruelty and fearing Babylonian reprisal, Johanan ben Kareah, the leading survivor in Judah, decided to move to Egypt against the protestations of Jeremiah (41:11–43:7). Jeremiah and Baruch went down to Egypt with the other refugees (43:1–7).

In 582 B.C., the Babylonians swept through Judah for a third time and deported the remaining people into exile (52:30). Our last glimpse of Jeremiah provides us with an appreciation of his faithfulness. At the end of forty-five years of service, he could have applied to himself the lament he had composed in 609 B.C. for King Jehoahaz when he had been taken captive to Egypt

(22:10–12). The people of Judah who accompanied Jeremiah were returning to the goddess worship he had denounced at the time of his Temple Sermon (44:15–23; cf. 7:18). They rejected his word now as generations had done in the past (44:1–13, 24–27). He knew the Lord would maintain only a few from Egypt sensitive to his word (44:14, 28). Thus, we leave the prophet in the land of Israel's ancient bondage. Jeremiah was in a perfect situation to contemplate his words concerning the Lord's promise of a new Exodus, a new covenant, and even a new David (23:1–8; cf. 31:31–34).

Toward the New Testament: The Life of Jesus

Some people who heard Jesus preach identified him with Jeremiah (Mt 16:14). Their perception has value for us as we reflect on Jeremiah as a foreshadowing of Christ. Jeremiah prefigures Jesus at least in these dimensions of his life: (a) his call to prophetic celibacy (Jer 16:1–4; cf. Mt 19:10–12); (b) his rejection in his native village (Jer 11:18–23; cf. Mk 6:1–6); (c) his prophecy of the destruction of the Temple (Jer 7:1–15; 26:1–6; cf. Mk 13:1–4); (d) his prophecy about the fall of Jerusalem (Jer 28:5–17; cf. Lk 19:41–44; 21:20–23); and (e) his trial because of his preaching about the Temple (Jer 26:10–15; Mk 14:57–58). In his sufferings at the hands of his own people, Jeremiah is the "lamb being led to the slaughterhouse" foreshadowing the figure of the Servant of the Lord who is fulfilled in Jesus (Jer 11:18–19; cf. Is 53:7; Mk 15:5).

Jeremiah's teaching on the Temple, the heart, and the new covenant introduces themes that Jesus most fully develops and then the New Testament authors describe. When Jesus expels the merchants, he quotes Jeremiah's great sermon by accusing them of turning the Temple into "a bandits' den" (Mk 11:17; cf. Jer 7:11). By insisting that the distortions and impurity in mankind reach to the depths of the heart, Jesus develops another of Jeremiah's themes (Mk 7:21–23; cf. Jer 17:9–10). In the death and Resurrection of Jesus, God communicates the grace of the radical transformation Jeremiah promised. When Jesus declares in the Eucharist that the chalice is the cup of the "new covenant", he directs our attention to Jeremiah's prophecy (Lk 22:20; 1 Cor 11:25; cf. Jer 31:31–34). In the blood of Christ, we receive the forgiveness of our sins and the living knowledge of God in the heart that Jeremiah promised. Jesus is the "Branch of David" who forms a righteous remnant by his death and Resurrection (Jer 23:1–6; 33:15–16; cf. Zec 3:8; 6:12).

The Letter to the Hebrews twice quotes Jeremiah's prophecy of the new covenant, once in its entirety and then again in part with particular emphasis on the effectiveness of Christ's redemptive work (Heb 8:8–12; cf. 10:16–17; Jer 31:31–33). By his obedient sacrifice on the cross, Jesus has inaugurated a covenant that is "new" in the sense that it is divine. He has pierced through the veil to the very presence of God where he intercedes for us. His priesthood, sacrifice, Temple, and covenant are all "new" because they are of a totally divine order that infinitely surpasses their earthly foreshadowings (Heb 8:1–9:28). The one, efficacious sacrifice of Christ absolutely reconciles us to God in a manner far surpassing the repetitive sacrifices, which were only a "reflection of the good things which were still to come" (Heb 10:1).

In conclusion, we note how Paul makes one of Jeremiah's admonitions a thematic principle of his own spirituality when he insists, "If anyone wants to boast, let him boast of the Lord" (1 Cor 1:31; 2 Cor 10:17; cf. Jer 9:22–23). Jeremiah made the original statement after 609 B.C. to reprimand Jehoiakim and his cohorts for their arrogant manner of pursuing wealth, power, and status without reverence for the Lord's commandments or concern for justice to the oppressed. When Paul uses the statement, he applies it more specifically and deeply to warn about the danger of spiritual arrogance. For Paul, the person who boasts in the Lord does not just respect the commandments but also relies on Christ for all spiritual wisdom. "To boast in the Lord" means to live according to the Spirit (*pneuma*), not merely according to one's subjective powers (*psyche*) (1 Cor 2:6–16). By contrast, the "super-apostles" who claim special revelations and interior divine knowledge that set them above other Christians are people who boast in themselves (2 Cor 11:1–21; cf. 10:17). When confronting those who flaunt their spiritual progress, Paul, like Jeremiah, demonstrates that the true messenger of God learns humility by what he suffers as the servant of God's word (2 Cor 11:21–33). In the end, Jeremiah would probably agree with Paul's assertion that "it is when I am weak that I am strong" (2 Cor 12:10).

The drama of God's word transforming his people through its impact on his prophetic servant continues in the next biblical text concerning Ezekiel, Jeremiah's disciple-at-a-distance.

STUDY QUESTIONS

1. Distinguish between genuine prophecy and counterfeit prophecy.

2. What is the predominant theme of Jeremiah?

3. Describe Jeremiah's vocation.

4. Compare Jehoiakim's reaction to Jeremiah's scroll with Josiah's response to the rediscovered text of Deuteronomy.

5. What are some of the symbolic actions Jeremiah took to dramatize his messages?

6. Why did Jeremiah consider the Exile to be a grace?

7. How is the new covenant different to Jeremiah than the old?

8. How does Jeremiah prefigure Jesus?

9. How does Jesus inaugurate the new covenant?

10. Read the "Confessions of Jeremiah" (11:18–12:6; 15:10–21; 17:14–18; 18:18–23; 20:7–18). Have you ever faced a time of crisis where you had to bear bad news to others in distress? How did you exercise your faith in God and seek his will in prayer in order to communicate a difficult message? How does God's grace enable the proclamation of truth to bring healing and peace?

11. On the other hand, have you been receptive to others who, in bringing God's word to you, have called up within you thoughts or memories that you suppressed because they were too painful to deal with? How have you experienced God's grace in order to resolve the difficulty?

12. From your viewpoint, what does Jeremiah say to the Church today?

JEREMIAH

EZEKIEL: PROPHET IN A FOREIGN LAND

We experience the need for spiritual renewal most acutely in an age when the public is suspicious of religious institutions in view of their apparent failures and shortcomings. How does God bring about a spiritual renaissance in a time of uncertainty for his people, who live under the criticism of public opinion? We find a most fruitful source of meditation on such issues in the book of Ezekiel, the prophet who received God's call when his people were reeling in the depths of spiritual desolation and confusion.

Ezekiel, the son of Buzi, was a priest born in Judah during the reign of Josiah (640–609 B.C.). He was among the ten thousand people exiled to Babylon along with King Jehoiachin after the Babylonians invaded Jerusalem for the first time on March 16, 597 B.C. (2 Kgs 24:12–16; cf. Jer 38:28). He settled with the exiles in the village of Tel Abib just south of Babylon, across the River Chebar from Nippur (Ez 3:15). He was married, but his wife died in Tel Abib in the early summer of 587 B.C., just before the fall of Jerusalem (24:15–27).

The vast quantity of his teachings preserved in book form testifies to the magnitude of Ezekiel's stature among the people. The book of Ezekiel follows a well-defined order of four sections, each of which contains a specific category of pronouncements: (1) the prophet's call, followed by the oracles of judgment against Judah and Jerusalem (1:1–24:27); (2) the oracles against the foreign nations (25:1–32:31); (3) the promise of future restoration for Judah (33:1–39:29); and (4) the vision for the restored Temple and land (40:1–48:35).

The book actually falls into perfect halves: the first twenty-four chapters proclaim God's judgment, and the second twenty-four announce his promise to Israel. Overall, the text follows a trajectory from glory to glory by way of judgment. The revelation of the Lord's glory in the prophet's call at the beginning (1:4–28) balances with the ultimate manifestation of divine glory in the new Temple (43:1–3; 44:4; 47:1–12; 48:35; in 40:1–48:35). The intervening chapters describe how the glory revealed to the prophet will become present to the people, namely, through acts of divine judgment on Judah (3:22–24:27), followed by fulfillment of the divine promises to God's people (33:1–39:29).

The prophecies of judgment on the nations (25:1–32:31) provide the transition from the oracles of judgment to the oracles of promise addressed by Yahweh to Israel.

For the most part, the contents of Ezekiel follow a chronological sequence according to the fifteen dates pinpointed in the text (see the table at the end of this chapter). The prophet experienced his call in July 593 B.C. (1:1-3; 3:16), four years after his deportation from Jerusalem into exile. He exercised his ministry at least until the spring of 571 B.C. (29:17), the latest date indicated in the book. Most of his oracles come from a period of approximately eight years, between the summer of 593 B.C. (1:2-3) and the early spring of 585 B.C. (32:1). Most noteworthy is the way he announces his prophecies in successive stages. He confines his prophecies of judgment against Judah and Jerusalem to the period between his call (1:2-3; 3:16) and January of 588 B.C., when the Babylonians lay siege to Jerusalem (24:1). Once Jerusalem comes under attack, Ezekiel announces God's judgments on the nations, concentrating most of his attention against Egypt, with whom Zedekiah had attempted an alliance in order to stave off the Babylonians (29:1-2; 30:20-21; 31:1-2; 32:1-2, 17-18). He declares his pronouncements against foreign nations (25:1–32:31) through the years immediately after the fall of Jerusalem (587–585 B.C.). According to the notation in the text (40:1), it was approximately fourteen years after the destruction of Jerusalem that Ezekiel completed his vision for the restoration of the Temple, the people, and the land (40:1–48:35).

All this information indicates that the fall of Jerusalem was the turning point for Ezekiel's personal transformation: his preaching changed from oracles of judgment (3:22–24:27) to God's judgment on the nations and promise of salvation to Judah (25:1–48:35). This change is not absolute, since we find some salvation promises in the first part of the book (6:8-10; 11:14-21; 14:21-23; 16:60-63; 20:40-44) and admonitions in the second part (33:17-20, 23-29; 36:20). Nevertheless, it is true that both historically in his life as well as thematically in his book, once the fall of Jerusalem became inevitable, the prophet devoted himself to preaching a message of restoration. The death of Ezekiel's wife, which foreshadowed the destruction of Jerusalem, was the decisive event in the prophet's ministry (24:15-27).

The Book of Ezekiel

The autobiographical form of the book suggests that Ezekiel wrote a large portion of the text himself. Writing would have afforded the prophet the opportunity to address an audience in Judah and even in Egypt as well as in Babylon. Parts of the text would have made poor preaching but very intriguing reading (e.g., 1:4–28; 38:1–39:29; 40:1–48:35). The description of the prophet devouring a scroll suggests his association with the written as well as the spoken word (2:1–10; cf. Jer 15:16).

Ezekiel had a large following among the exiles, and he seems to have formed a school of disciples in Babylon. He certainly taught people in his home (8:1; 14:1; 20:1). His concern for matters of ritual purity and issues related to the Temple suggests that priests comprised the nucleus of his students. Ezekiel and his disciples interacted with the tradition underlying the Holiness Code (Lv 17:1–26:46). Because Ezekiel's school used early editions of the material in the Code for classroom texts, Ezekiel and his tradition played a formative role in the final biblical version of the Code (e.g., Lv 26:1–13; Ez 20:12–13; 34:26–27; 48:35). We should note that Ezekiel's circles represented one tradition of priestly schools that became strong during the Exile. We can only speculate about the indirect relationship his school had to the Priestly tradition that shaped the Pentateuch during the Exile and completed it perhaps a century and a half after Ezekiel's death.

Ezekiel's ministry ended in 571 B.C. In his last years, he might have worked with his disciples to edit a personal version of his teaching. In subsequent years, before 550 B.C., his disciples working in Babylon produced our final biblical edition of the text.

The book of Ezekiel is a unique piece of literature among the collection of the prophets and, indeed, within the whole biblical canon. The text is completely in the form of an autobiography. The author writes the whole text in the first person, never in the third person. Furthermore, this is a highly unusual autobiography because seldom do we read of Ezekiel's interacting directly with anyone except God. The only dialogue he has with others is when his compatriots ask him why he is not carrying out the traditional rites of mourning over his wife's death (24:19–24). Beyond that, the purpose of the mere mention of elders consulting him is to provide a setting for his reception of the Lord's word (14:1; 20:1). Throughout the rest of the text, we gain an impression of Ezekiel's relationship to others only through Yahweh: the questions, comments, and protests in their minds that Yahweh notes (11:14–15; 12:8–9; 18:25; 33:10, 17); Yahweh's observation of their behavior (33:10–33); Yahweh's references to their criticisms of Ezekiel (12:26–28; cf. 21:5); and Yahweh's questions to Ezekiel about what the people are saying (12:21–22; 14:2–4; 18:1–2; cf. 37:3). We do not read about Ezekiel interacting and debating with people in the public square as Jeremiah did. If we were to enact this book on stage, the only character in the performance would be Ezekiel listening to the voice of God, describing for us by word, gesture, and symbol what he was privileged to apprehend.

The Prophetic Character and Style of Ezekiel

Ezekiel is a poet and an artist who always remains an enigma to us in spite of the fact that his whole book takes the form of an autobiography. The fact that he is a question mark for us is part of his genius: the prophet always points beyond himself to the revelation of Yahweh. Ezekiel's life is an art form that directs our attention outward toward God and his sovereign glory. Because the land of exile alienated Israel from her religious institutions, such as the Temple, the sabbath, and the major feasts, Ezekiel himself takes up their role insofar as he becomes the beacon that points away from the world to the majestic transcendence of God over his people.

This prophet communicates by means of symbolic gestures intended to jar our conventional sensitivities. To announce the impending siege of Jerusalem and its aftermath, he does the following: sets up a battle in miniature around a brick (4:1–3); lies on his side for months at a time (4:4–8); eats rations of bread and water (4:9–17); shaves his head and beard and disposes of his hair by chopping it with a sword, burning it, and casting it to the wind (5:1–4); packs his baggage, digs a hole in the wall, and walks through it (12:1–20); traces a map pointing the king of Babylon's way to Jerusalem (21:23–32); and boils fine meat and bones in a rusty cooking pot (24:4–8). Consistent with his intuition of the power contained in symbols, he employs metaphors to describe Judah, her kings, and her adversaries. Israel is a wanton woman (16:1–52), a useless burnt vinestock (15:1–6), a lioness (19:1–9); her youthful kings are cubs (19:1–9); and the people in Jerusalem are meat in a cauldron (11:4). Nebuchadnezzar is an eagle (17:3–10), the Egyptian pharaoh is a crocodile (29:3; 32:2), and the island fortress of Tyre is a seafaring boat (27:4–9). To these, we must add the metaphors of Israel's salvation, which include the shepherd and the sheep (34:1–31), the dry bones coming to life (37:1–14), and the new Temple (40:1–48:35).

Ezekiel's words and gestures express the perceptions of a person deeply moved by God. He speaks of Yahweh's hand coming upon him to occasion deep perceptions of reality (3:22; 33:22). He describes his experiences of translocation by the power of God's spirit (3:12, 24; 8:3; 37:1; cf. 40:1). Among the physical effects of receiving God's revelation, he lists: stupor (3:15), muteness (3:25–27; 24:27), paralysis (4:8), trembling (12:17–18), and heart-breaking groans (21:11). The obvious sensitivity of the man makes his lack of grief over his wife's death the most shocking and climactic of his personal demonstrations (24:15–27). His wife's death is the ultimate sign-event revealing God's decision to permit the destruction of Jerusalem. By his refusal to mourn, Ezekiel becomes the sign to the people of God's sovereignty over all things (24:24, 27; cf. 12:6, 11).

When we first survey Ezekiel's behavior, we might attempt to psychoana-
lyze the prophet and judge him unbalanced. But such a reaction would be a
gross misreading of his character. In fact, his bizarre behavior recalls the roots
of prophecy in the ecstatic brotherhoods and in the ministry of Elijah (1 Kgs
19:1–21; 2 Kgs 2:1–18). Indeed, Israel's first two kings, Saul and David,
experienced God's spirit in the manner of Ezekiel (1 Sm 10:9–12; 16:13). By his
behavior, Ezekiel intends to break down the boundaries of convention in
order to demonstrate that the culture has become so self-contained that it has
no place for God's revelation. Ezekiel's life is a demonstration that the culture
is out of touch with the reality of God.

This man is radical because God's grace has given him perception into the
divine depths of existence. However, by no means can we consider Ezekiel a
fanatic. He was a well-known and gifted teacher (cf. 33:30–33) with good
contacts that informed him about what was taking place in Jerusalem and
elsewhere (cf. 8:1–11:13; 33:21–22; 29:1–32:31). Above all, he was an expert in
the Law, which he studied and taught. He based his reprimands of Jerusalem
on his expertise in the legislation governing worship and life in Israel (e.g.,
18:5–13; cf. Ex 20:22, 24; Lv 19:1–37; 25:35–37; Dt 24:14; cf. Ez 22:6–12).
Clearly, the admonitions of the prophets against the priests who refused to
teach the Law did not apply to Ezekiel and his school (cf. Jer 2:8, 26; 5:31;
6:13; Is 28:7; Hos 4:4, 9; cf. Ez 7:26).

Ezekiel was a revolutionary thinker both in how he wrote and what he
said. His symbolic literature with its concern for the ultimate future God
would reveal to his people is the earliest example of Hebrew apocalyptic and
prepares the way for the tradition of Zechariah (Ez 38:1–39:29; cf. Zec 1–8;
9–14) and the visions in Daniel (Dn 7–12), advancing Hebrew thought in the
way it considers God's judgments and promises. We now direct our attention
to his message under these titles.

God's Judgments (1:1–24:27)

Ezekiel develops his theology of divine judgment out of his appreciation
of God's holiness, on the one hand, and of individual responsibility, on the
other. We can summarize his teaching under the headings of revelation and
responsibility.

Revelation: The manifestation of the Lord's glory is the essence of Ezekiel's
prophetic call (1:1–28). His apprehension of divine majesty represents a
heightening of Isaiah's experience in the Temple (Is 6:1–8). The astounding
aspect in the case of Ezekiel is that God reveals his glory in an alien unclean

land. The winged creatures and coals of fire recall Isaiah's encounter (Is 6:1–8), and the fire, storm, and clouds reflect the revelation at Sinai (Ex 19:1–25; 24:1–18). But unique to Ezekiel are the images of chariot, wheels, and wings swirling together and offering a sense of the dynamic freedom and agility of Yahweh's splendor (cf. 2 Kgs 2:11).

This movement of the divine glory has two implications. First, it is a sign of hope and promise that the Lord can and does reveal himself to his people in exile (cf. 3:22). Secondly, it is a sign of judgment, because the glory of the Lord is about to depart from the Temple in Jerusalem (10:18–22; 11:22–25). The movement of the Lord's glory away from the Temple in Jerusalem (10:18–22; cf. 1:3–28) and the promise of its returning to the restored Temple (43:1–3; cf. 48:35) provide the theme framing the text. By means of the Exile, the Lord will transform his people so that he will be able to dwell in their midst (48:35; cf. 3:12).

The prophet consumes the decrees of God and receives his commission to be the watchman for his people (2:1–3:15; 3:16–21). As for Isaiah and Jeremiah, so also for Ezekiel: the prophet's audience will be defiant and resistant to his word (2:4–8; 3:7–11; cf. Is 6:9–11; Jer 1:8, 17). Ezekiel cannot determine the people's response, but he must be faithful in proclaiming the divine word whether or not his audience is receptive (3:11; 3:16–21).

In all that he does, God acts in order to bring his people to the knowledge that he is the Lord. His acts of judgment are like his works of salvation insofar as they reveal the Lord to his people. The destruction of Jerusalem (7:9), the death of the impious (7:15–27), the end of the false prophets and diviners (13:14, 23), and the dispersal into exile (12:15; 22:16) communicate a knowledge of the Lord just as will his raising of the lowly (17:24) and his restoration of his people in the covenant (16:63; 20:44). Because Jerusalem is the center of the nations (5:5), his judgments will issue forth from there to affect all peoples, so that the foreigners also will come to know that Yahweh is God (25:5, 7, 11, 17; 26:6; 28:24, 26; 29:6, 16; 30:19, 26; 32:16).

Responsibility: Ezekiel describes sin as sacrilege, an offense against the holiness of God's name. Although Hosea, Isaiah, and Jeremiah all considered the Exodus as a period of fidelity (Hos 2:17; Is 4:5–6; 11:15–16; Jer 2:2), Ezekiel offers a more severe analysis in his historical allegories, which indicate Israel was unfaithful to the Lord from the beginning (Ez 16:1–52; 23:1–49). Nevertheless, Ezekiel asserts that his people are not victims of their history. God offers each generation the opportunity to make a break with the past and forge a new future of life and grace. His teaching on individual responsibility opens the way to hope.

Three times, the prophet reinforces his insistence on the freedom of each person to make his or her own response to God (14:12–23; 18:1–32; 33:1–33). He confronts the error of a popular saying that suggests that the faults of the parents will always hold their children in bondage (Ez 18:2; Jer 31:29). In spite of all his decrees of judgment, Ezekiel insists that the Lord delights, not in the death, but in the life of his people (18:23; 33:11). The way to life consists in receiving God's revelation and responding to his commandments (18:5–9). Repentance brings freedom because it puts an end to the influence of the past and opens one's life to the future that God will form. In repentance, one takes on a new heart and a new spirit (18:30–32).

God's promises of salvation begin with this teaching on personal responsibility (18:1–32; 33:1–33). The prophet's vocation as watchman is intimately related to the people's call to freedom through personal responsibility (3:16–21; 33:1–9). To the exiles who are burdened with guilt and hopelessness because of their sins, Ezekiel offers the absolute promise of life contained in the grace of repentance (33:10–11). As the prophet begins his elaboration of God's promises of salvation, he seems to experience a renewal of his vocation as watchman (33:1–9; cf. 3:16–21). However, from this juncture on, he will direct his people's gaze, not to the guilt of the past (as in 3:22–24:27), but to a vision of the new community of faith (33:1–48:35).

God's Promises (33:1–48:35)

The promises of salvation in Ezekiel center around four images: (a) the shepherd and the sheep (34:1–31); (b) the new heart and mind (36:16–38); (c) the raising of the dead to life (37:1–28); and (d) the new Temple and the new Land (40:1–48:35). A theology of covenant links the first three images together. The references to both the flock and the new heart climax with the covenant promise, "You will be my people and I shall be your God" (36:29; cf. 34:30–31). The passage from death to life culminates in the unity of God's people in an "eternal covenant" with him (37:26). These three sections on covenant climax in the vision of the fourth image, the new Temple in which the Lord who had promised to be with his people now is "there" in the midst of them (34:30; cf. 48:35).

The Shepherd and the Sheep: We recall that Jeremiah noted the bankruptcy of Zedekiah's reign and perceived that the Lord's plan consisted in providing his people with a king who had the genuine qualities of a descendant of the Branch for David (Jer 23:1–6). Ezekiel elaborates this prophecy into a more extensive judgment on Judah's recent kings and leaders (34:1–10), a reflection on God's personal care for his people (34:11–22), and a promise of a renewed covenant of peace through David (34:23–31).

His criticisms of the leaders' self-indulgence recalls Jeremiah's reprimand of Jehoiakim (34:1–6; cf. Jer 22:13–19) but probably extends beyond Jehoiakim to Zedekiah and those in Jerusalem who prophesied peace and prosperity in the last days (cf. 19:1–14; cf. Jer 28:1–4, 10–11). The self-preoccupation of the kings has brought about the dispersal of God's people across the world to Egypt and to Babylon (Jer 42:1–44:30; 52:1–30).

During the Exile, when the people have no king, the Lord will draw near to them as their personal shepherd (cf. Ps 23). He will restore them to their own land and heal them (Ez 34:11–22). Ezekiel's images at this point will inspire Deutero-Isaiah's vision of the Lord's action in restoring his people to their land following the Exile (Is 40:10–11).

Ezekiel brings his vision to a climax by rooting Isaiah's vision of a final age of peace under David (Is 11:1–9) in a "covenant of peace" (Ez 34:25; 37:26). Most central to this covenant will be the presence of Yahweh in the midst of his people.

A New Heart and New Mind: Ezekiel now shows us the type of interior transformation that must underlie the regathering of the scattered sheep (36:24; cf. 34:13). He takes Jeremiah's prophecy about the new covenant (Jer 31:31–34) and develops it in light of his own sensitivity to God's spirit (cf. 1:20; 2:2; 3:14; 11:1, 5). But he speaks of a more perduring presence of God's spirit than he had known in his own fragmented experiences. God now promises that his spirit will dwell within his people permanently (36:27–28). The covenant of peace (34:25) will constitute the inauguration of a new order of existence based on God's action to transform the minds and hearts of his people (36:27–28). The source of God's covenant is a "new spirit" that he will put within the people (11:19; cf. Ps 51:12–14). The divine activity originates with God (36:26–28) but demands the response of each individual consenting to God's action of transforming his or her heart by the grace of the spirit (18:31). This communication of God's spirit provides the source of life for the civilization God had always intended (36:33–38).

From Death to Life: Ezekiel's action in the valley of the dry bones illustrates the power of the prophetic word to bring God's people from death to life by the work of his spirit (breath) (37:3–10). The bones take on flesh when, in obedience to God's command, Ezekiel prophesies to the breath (37:4–5, 9–10). The image of human forms coming to life by the breath of God recalls the Yahwist's story of creation (37:8; cf. Gn 2:7). God's work of restoring his people after the Exile will be of the same magnitude as his creation of human beings.

Next, the image of the dead rising from their graves (37:11–14) focuses the meaning of the dry bones (37:3–10) on the restoration of the exiles to their land. In the depths of their despair, they feel as if they were dead. However, God promises to bring them from the grave of the Exile to new life in the resettlement of his people in Judah. Four centuries after Ezekiel, the Hasidim writing the book of Daniel will perceive in Ezekiel's image God's revelation of an actual risen life beyond death (resurrection) for his saints in the Kingdom of heaven (Dn 12:2–3; cf. 2 Mc 7:9).

The image of the sticks joined together is another metaphor that further emphasizes the unprecedented quality of Israel's restored life (37:15–28). Under the "one shepherd" David, Judah and Israel will be reunited in the "covenant of peace" that is "eternal" (37:24–28; cf. 34:23–31).

The New Temple: The vision of the new Temple and order of service provide an outline of the new community the Lord will establish when he restores the people to their land following the Exile (40:1–48:35).

The prophet's vision for the reconstruction of the Temple recalls Moses' blueprints for the construction of the wilderness sanctuary (Ex 25:1–31:18; 35:1–40:38) and Solomon's provisions for the holy structure in Jerusalem (1 Kgs 6:1–8:66). All three narratives climax in the same event: the Lord comes to dwell in the Temple by overshadowing it with his glory (Ex 40:38; 1 Kgs 8:10–13; Ez 43:1–3; 44:4; cf. 48:35). Ezekiel emphasizes the point by quoting the Lord's promise to establish his presence among the people within the sacred precincts of the Temple (43:7; cf. Ex 25:8). A life of holiness reflecting the presence of the Lord will distinguish the restored people (43:4–12).

The stream flowing from the Temple communicates the life-giving quality of the Lord's presence to the whole of creation (47:1–12). Just as the dry bones will come to life through the divine breath (37:3–10), so even the arid wilderness of the Arabah rift (south of the Dead Sea) will become verdant with the waters of the Temple (47:1–12). Creation seems to be returning to its original state in Eden (cf. Gn 2:10–14). The whole cosmos experiences the transforming effects of Yahweh's returning to make his residence among his people in the new Jerusalem (48:35).

Toward the New Testament: The Shepherd and New Life for His Flock

Ezekiel's images of restoration open our minds to the vision of salvation realized in the coming of Christ. We will consider how the New Testament brings into full light the promise contained in the prophet's instruction concerning the Shepherd, the Spirit, the risen life, and the heavenly Jerusalem.

The Shepherd: Whenever Jesus employs the image of the shepherd to describe his ministry or that of the Church, he draws upon the words of Ezekiel (Ez 34:1–31). By his preaching to tax collectors and sinners, Jesus reveals himself as the shepherd who brings back to the fold all who have strayed from God (Lk 15:4–7; Ez 34:16). He demands that his Church exercise the same ministry toward those who fall away from their membership (Mt 18:12–14; cf. 1 Pt 5:2–4; Jn 21:15–17). When he shows compassion for the crowds who seem "like sheep without a shepherd", he manifests the affection of God for his people (Mk 6:34; Mt 9:36; cf. Ez 34:5, 8; Nm 27:17; Zec 10:2). Furthermore, he applies Ezekiel's criticism of the self-concerned leaders of Judah who brought about the downfall of the people (Ez 34:1–10) to the religious authorities of his own day (Jn 10:8).

As the Good Shepherd, Jesus fulfills God's promise to come and care for his sheep (Jn 10:7–15; cf. Ez 34:11–22). He far surpasses Ezekiel's vision because not only does he heal the sheep but he lays down his life for their sake in order to do so (Jn 10:10–11; cf. Ez 34:11–16, 22).

Jesus is the true David who establishes the eternal covenant of peace between God and his people (Ez 34:23–31; 37:24–28). Whereas Ezekiel had foreseen the restoration under David in terms of the reunification of Judah and Israel (Ez 37:24–28), Jesus has come to unite all humanity, both Jew and Gentile, into one flock under himself as the one Shepherd (Jn 10:16–18; cf. 11:52; 12:32; 17:20–23).

What Ezekiel said about the people of Judah scattered from Jerusalem into the Exile, the New Testament applies to the whole human race. At the end of time, Jesus will gather all peoples from the ends of the earth (Mt 25:32; cf. Ez 34:13). At that time, he will pass judgment, separating the just from the unjust in view of their service of him in the poor and the oppressed (Mt 25:32–46; cf. Ez 34:17–22).

The Spirit: The Gospel of John formulates its theology of baptism by intimately uniting Ezekiel's reference to water (Ez 36:25) with his mention of God's spirit (Ez 36:26). In Ezekiel, the water symbolizes the exiles' purification from idolatry, which was a precondition of their receiving God's spirit (Ez 36:26–27). In the Gospel of John, the water has a sacramental quality that signifies and mediates the communication of the Spirit in baptism (Jn 3:5). The Spirit testifies to the truth of God's indwelling presence in the life of the Christian, communicating a living knowledge of Christ that expresses itself in love of the brethren (Jn 4:23–24).

Furthermore, the Gospel of John relates Ezekiel's waters of cleansing from idolatry (Ez 36:25) with the waters flowing from the Temple (Ez 47:1–12) to develop an image of life that flows from Christ in his death on the cross. Jesus describes the waters of new life to the Samaritan woman (Jn 4:13–14) to introduce the theme of the living waters that will flow from his side as the manifestation of divine life he communicates from the cross (Jn 19:34; cf. 7:37–39).

The Risen Life: In his vision of the bones receiving life through the breath (spirit), Ezekiel saw an image of his people's restoration beyond the Exile (Ez 37:3–10). This work, by which God makes his people a new creation (cf. Gn 2:7), reaches fulfillment in the way Jesus, the risen Lord, "breathes" on his disciples to bring them to new life in the Spirit (Jn 20:22–23).

Furthermore, the new life of the dry bones (Ez 37:3–10) and the raising of the people from their graves (Ez 37:11–14) foreshadow the promise of the resurrection first fulfilled in the risen Christ (1 Cor 15:1–58). Those who have received the Spirit of Christ now rejoice in this sure basis of their hope for eternal life (Rom 8:11; cf. Ez 37:10).

The Heavenly Jerusalem: Both Ezekiel and the book of Revelation describe a new Jerusalem, but they are of different orders, the first within history, the second beyond history. Ezekiel's sketch of the restored community of faith in the new Temple provides an earthly foreshadowing of the heavenly Jerusalem, which is the ultimate promise God extends to all people in Christ (Ez 40:1–48:35; cf. Rv 21:1–22:5). When the heavenly messenger showed Ezekiel a vision of the new Temple, the prophet believed that he and his disciples received the commission to undertake its construction. (In fact, they never started the project.) By contrast, the heavenly Jerusalem cannot be made by human hands because it is a pure gift that descends from God (Rv 21:1–2). The mountain, the walls, the gates, and the river are all images derived from Ezekiel (Rv 21:9–22:2; cf. Ez 40:1–4; 48:31–35; 47:1–12). But there is a marked difference. The whole structure that was the Temple in Ezekiel (Ez 40:1–42:20) is the heavenly city Jerusalem in Revelation (Rv 21:9–21). In the Jerusalem from above, there is no Temple, because God and the Lamb are immediately present to the people (Rv 21:22–23).

Having considered the vision of promise Ezekiel offered at the beginning of the Exile, we can now direct our attention to the promise of return that Deutero-Isaiah voices at the turning point of the Exile.

STUDY QUESTIONS

1. What are the themes of the two halves of the book of Ezekiel?
2. How is the book of Ezekiel unique?
3. What symbolic gestures does Ezekiel use to communicate his messages?
4. How does the movement of the Lord's glory provide a major theme for the text?
5. Explain Ezekiel's theme of individual responsibility.
6. What are the four images of the promises of salvation?
7. How does the action in the valley of dry bones foreshadow the working of God's spirit in his people?
8. How does Jesus embody and surpass the image of shepherd in Ezekiel?
9. Distinguish between Ezekiel's and Revelation's descriptions of the new Jerusalem.
10. Every Christian is a witness to the Gospel. What aspects of your life are the most important signs to others?
11. In what ways do you see the Holy Spirit at work to renew the Church today (see Ez 37)?
12. What does it mean for you to receive a new heart and spirit from God through the grace of baptism (Ez 36:26–28)?

EZEKIEL

Dates (B.C.) for Ezekiel's Prophecies and Visions

1:1	?	Visions from God
1:2	July 593	The Celestial Chariot
3:16	July 593	Commission of the Watchman
8:1	Sept–Oct 592	Jerusalem's idolatry
20:1	July–Aug 591	Exile and return
24:1	Dec 589–Jan 588	Babylon surrounds Jerusalem
26:1	Mar–Apr 586	Babylon attacks Tyre
29:1	Dec 588–Jan 587	Judgment against Egypt
29:17	Mar–Apr 571	Babylon attacks Egypt after Tyre
30:20	Mar–Apr 587	The breaking of Egypt
31:1	May–June 587	Egypt, the fallen tree
32:1	Feb–Mar 585	Dirge for the crocodile pharaoh
32:17	Mar–Apr 586	Pharaoh in the netherworld
33:21	Dec 586–Jan 585	Messenger from fallen Jerusalem
40:1	Sept–Oct 573	The future Temple

In the text of Ezekiel, the author calculated years from the exile of King Jehoiachin (March 597 B.C.; 2 Kgs 24:8–17; Jer 52:28; 2 Chr 36:9–10). The new year began in springtime on the first of Nisan (March–April). Therefore, the "first year" dates from the Spring (Nisan) of 597 B.C. until the Spring of 596 B.C., and the "fifth year" begins in the Spring (Nisan) of 593 B.C. and ends in the Spring of 592 B.C.

(Adapted from Lawrence Boadt's *Reading the Old Testament. An Introduction* © 1984, p. 389, by permission of Paulist Press, New York, NY, and Mahwah, NJ.)

25

DEUTERO-ISAIAH: REDEMPTIVE SUFFERING

What is God's response to the profound suffering of his people? Does he truly have a word for human beings who grow up in an environment of pain born out of shattered dreams, frustrated hopes, and wounded memories? God can seem very distant to people raised in families and communities affected by generations of suffering. To them, his words of promise can seem like a fantasy from a bygone age or another world. They need a word spoken by God not from outside but from within the circumstances of their affliction. Only a word of divine compassion (literally "suffering with") can bring them healing. The text of Deutero-Isaiah (literally "Second Isaiah") (Is 40:1–55:13) communicates such a word brought forth by God from the heart of his troubled people. In this sacred text, the Lord announces a message of unparalleled hope to every person who is seeking him amid pain and despondency.

Deutero-Isaiah is the name we give to a prophet whom we know only by way of the message he proclaimed. Scholarly convention gave him his name, maintaining that he came from the Isaian tradition but carried out his ministry during the Exile in Babylon a century and a half after Isaiah completed his mission in Judah. In order to locate his mission with greater precision and to appreciate his message within its historical setting, we will survey the development of events in world history from the fall of Jerusalem until the end of the Exile (587–538 B.C.).

Israel's Years in Babylonian Exile (587–538 B.C.)

After destroying Jerusalem, the army of Nebuchadnezzar (605–562 B.C.) undertook a thirteen-year (587–574 B.C.) siege of the island fortress of Tyre, which they did not succeed in capturing (cf. Ez 26:1–28:26; 29:17–20). We have noted that Nebuchadnezzar's forces passed through Judah in 582 B.C. to sweep into Babylonian exile a final group who had survived the destruction of the city and the overthrow of Gedaliah the governor (Jer 52:30; cf. Jer 40:7–41:18).

In 568 B.C., Nebuchadnezzar ended decades of tension with Egypt by invading the land and securing its allegiance with Babylon.

The neo-Babylonian Empire reached its zenith under Nebuchadnezzar and began to crumble as soon as he died in 562 B.C. His son Evil-Merodach (Avilmarduk) was able to maintain power for only two years (562–560 B.C.), long enough to release Jehoiachin, king of Judah, from prison (2 Kgs 25:27–30). Neriglissar (560–556 B.C.) deposed his brother-in-law, Evil-Merodach, and ruled for four years. When Neriglissar died, Nabonidus (556–539 B.C.), an Aramaean from Haran, seized the throne. The Babylonians so disliked this man and his preference for the god Sin over their god Marduk that they forced him to move from Babylon and take up residence in Teima, a desert oasis located east of Edom. Belshazzar, the crown prince of Babylon, carried on the affairs of government in the capital.

As dissension grew in Babylon, a revolution was unfolding beyond its eastern frontier. In 555 B.C., Cyrus, the leader of the southern kingdom of Persia, initiated a successful rebellion against the northern kingdom of the Medes and their King Astyages. By 550 B.C., Cyrus had taken over the empire of the Medes and began directing his attention to Babylon. He marched his armies west and took control of most of Asia Minor by 547 B.C. before turning back east to take possession of the region comprising what is now Afghanistan. Finally, in 539 B.C., his army defeated the forces of Nabonidus at Opis on the Tigris River, and Cyrus took possession of Babylon, where the local citizenry applauded him for freeing them from the regime of Nabonidus.

Cyrus foresaw the advantage of having loyal support on his southern and western fronts. For this reason, in 538 B.C., he issued the official decree putting an end to the Exile and allowing the people of Judah to return to their land to rebuild their city and Temple (Ezr 1:2–4). Sheshbazzar, the prince of Judah, led the first wave of returning exiles. Sometime after the death of Cyrus (530 B.C.), Zerubbabel and Joshua the priest arrived in Judah. Under the inspiration of Haggai and Zechariah, they undertook the restoration of the Temple in 520 B.C. (Ezr 3:1–6:22). The reconstructed Temple was dedicated prior to Passover in March or April of 515 B.C.

The Text of Deutero-Isaiah

Isaiah 40:1–55:13 represents a section of text distinct from the first part of the book (1:1–39:8). Whereas, in the first part, the prophet lives within Jerusalem and speaks to Judah's king about how to protect the city (6:1–8:23), in the second part, the prophet presupposes Jerusalem has been destroyed and looks to its reconstruction (44:26; 51:11). Furthermore, in the second part, the prophet refers to only one king, David, just once by a messianic reference in keeping with the "everlasting covenant" that Jeremiah and Ezekiel mention (Is 55:3; cf. Jer 32:40; Ez 37:26; cf. Is 54:10). In the first section, Judah's principal foe is Assyria (10:5–19), and one of her potential, although suspect, allies is Babylon (39:1–8). By contrast, in the second part, her oppressor is Babylon (cf. 46:1–13; 47:1–15), and her ally is Persia under Cyrus (45:1–7). The message of consolation that introduces the second part (40:1–2; cf. 49:13; 51:12; 52:7–12) contrasts with the judgment on sin at the beginning of the whole book (1:2–31).

The references to Cyrus (44:28; 45:1–7) provide the primary indications for dating Deutero-Isaiah. The prophet speaks of the Persian king as if he is appearing on the horizon, coming to liberate Israel from her captivity (41:1–7). On the basis of such evidence, we can date the ministry of Deutero-Isaiah in the period after 550 B.C., when Cyrus had overthrown the Medes and was advancing against Babylon.

The text of Deutero-Isaiah consists of four sections: two main parts encompassed by a choral introduction and a concluding appeal for a response to its message. The introduction (40:1–31) announces Zion's deliverance from captivity; the first main part (41:1–48:22) speaks of Judah's impending deliverance from exile by the hand of Cyrus; the second main part (49:1–54:17) describes the promise of restoring the land amid joy and sorrow; the conclusion invites God's people to turn to the Lord in this time of grace (55:1–13).

The introduction (40:1–11) and conclusion (55:1–13) resonate with the themes of God's forgiveness (40:2; 55:6–8) and the reliability of his word over all human capability (40:8; 55:11). We note a difference in theme, tone, and emphasis between the two interior parts of the text. In the first main section (41:1–48:22), the prophet speaks to "Israel" or "Jacob" (44:1, 21), describes the coming of Cyrus (44:28; 45:1–7), satirizes the making of idols (44:9–20; 46:5–7), and describes the Lord as "the first" and "the last" in his manner of governing the course of events (44:6; 48:12). None of these elements occurs in the second main section. Instead, there we find the prophet addressing "Zion" or "Jerusalem" (49:14; 51:11; 52:8–9) while making no mention of idols or Cyrus. In the first main section, the prophet is more prone to refer to Israel's past sinfulness, ingratitude, and stubbornness, which led to the Exile (42:19–20, 24; 43:22–28; 48:4; cf. 50:1–3). In the second main section, he concentrates on encouraging the people to awaken and become strong in order to undertake the task at hand (51:9, 17; 52:1).

The prophet's teaching developed in two different stages of history. The first main section (41:1–48:22) presents the announcement of liberation that he proclaimed to the exiles from the time Cyrus arose on the eastern front (550 B.C.) until he captured Babylon (539 B.C.). The second main section (49:1–54:17)

summarizes his preaching in the years following Cyrus' decree ending the
Exile (after 538 B.C.), when the prophet exhorted his people to return to
Jerusalem and undertake the restoration of the land. The fact that he makes no
reference to the restored Temple or to Zerubbabel or Joshua the priest suggests
that Deutero-Isaiah completed his mission prior to 525 B.C. but long enough
after the end of the Exile to appreciate the suffering and struggle involved in
the work of restoration (see Ezr 3:1–6:22).

Our summary of Deutero-Isaiah remains incomplete until we make reference to the most salient texts in the collection, namely, the four Songs of the
Lord's Servant (42:1–9; 49:1–7; 50:4–11; 52:13–53:12). The theme and tone
that these texts share distinguish them from the rest of Deutero-Isaiah. The
fact that each of them can be removed from its present context without
interrupting the general flow of the text suggests that they were composed in
light of each other and that together they comprise an independent collection.
However, we must note a development of theme in them along the lines we
have mentioned for the major portions of Deutero-Isaiah. The first Servant
Song (42:1–9) speaks of the servant's call to ministry in a manner consistent
with the international perspective characteristic of the first stage of the prophet's
ministry under the shadow of Cyrus' advance (cf. 41:1–48:22). By comparison,
the remaining three Servant Songs (49:1–7; 50:4–11; 52:13–53:12) reflect a
personal aspect of suffering and affliction that corresponds with the tenor of
the stressful days of restoration (49:1–54:17).

Disciples of the prophet produced their final version of the text prior to
515 B.C. The last editors of the complete Isaian collection located it in its
present setting in the book when they completed the whole work between
450 and 400 B.C.

The Message of Deutero-Isaiah

Deutero-Isaiah communicates the good news of salvation to Jerusalem in a
resonant manner to all nations of the earth (52:7). We can contemplate the
substance of his proclamation by focusing on three of his primary concerns:
(a) Yahweh revealed as Creator of the universe and Lord of all history; (b)
Yahweh revealed as the Redeemer of his people and the source of righteousness;
and (c) Yahweh's universal plan for all nations in light of his revelation to
Israel. We will reserve a special section for our reflections on the Servant of the
Lord.

1. Yahweh, the Creator and Lord of History

Deutero-Isaiah perceives that at the root of the exiles' despondency is a narrow, earthbound understanding of God. His mission consists in making known the presence of God to his people (40:9). To do this, he engages the minds of the exiles by challenging their melancholy suppositions about Yahweh. They are disconsolate in Babylon because they think the Lord has forgotten them (49:14), ignored their plight (40:27), and abandoned and forsaken them (cf. 49:21). An audience whose minds are dulled by resignation and spiritual passivity will not respond to ideas about God. The prophet must break through their inertia and get them to think about God. Thus, Deutero-Isaiah employs a technique of posing a series of rhetorical questions, demanding that his people simply consider the vastness of the universe and the short duration of national empires in order to appreciate the incomparability of God's everlasting nature (40:12-31; cf. 44:7, 8, 25; 50:1-2; 49:15). His manner of illustrating God's majesty as reflected through creation foreshadows God's approach to Job in a later book (cf. Jb 28:21-28; 38:1-41:26).

Deutero-Isaiah's elaboration of Yahweh as the Creator of the cosmos represents an advancement in Hebrew theology (40:21-28; 44:24; 45:12, 18; 51:13, 16). Yahweh is beyond comparison with other gods (40:25; 41:21; 42:7, 18; 45:16, 20; 46:5-7). In fact, only Yahweh is God (43:8-13; 44:6-8; 45:5, 14, 21). This assertion would have struck a responsive chord in the exiles living under the shadow of the Babylonian Marduk, hearing the debate over Nabonidus' devotion to Sin, a god of Haran. In the first part of his ministry, Deutero-Isaiah derided the making of idols (41:6-7; 41:21-29; 42:8-9, 17; 44:9-20; 45:16-20; 46:5-7). In contrast to these nothings, Yahweh's name itself announces his existence. He alone can say "I am" (42:8; 43:10-11; 45:3-7, 14-22; 46:9), thus revealing himself through his prophet to the people in the Exile as he did to Moses at Sinai (cf. Ex 3:13-14).

The prophet proclaims the sovereignty of Yahweh by means of two titles for which he has a particular preference. Taking up the tradition of Isaiah, he identifies Yahweh as the "Holy One of Israel" (41:14, 16, 20; 43:3, 14, 15; 49:7; 54:5; cf. 1:4; 5:19, 24; cf. 6:3; 44:6). Furthermore, Yahweh's second title is "the first" and "the last" in his governance of all history (41:4; 44:6; 48:12). By his word in the past, he has already made known what is taking place now (42:8-9; 44:8; 45:21; cf. 41:22). Now, he reveals the new event he is bringing about in the midst of his people (42:9; 48:6). This event is the Lord's making himself known as Israel's Redeemer.

2. Yahweh, the Redeemer of Israel

Deutero-Isaiah illustrates the basic coherence of the Lord's activity in creation and redemption. Yahweh who created the universe (40:26, 28; 45:12, 18) is also the "Creator of Israel" (43:15; cf. 43:1). Significantly, the prophet employs the same verb (*bara'*: to create) to describe God's works of both bringing the cosmos into existence and forming Israel as his own people. In this way, Deutero-Isaiah depicts redemption as a divine creative event that continues God's action in the universe throughout history (see 45:7, 8). By his election of Israel and the work of salvation that he accomplishes for the sake of his people, the Lord transforms the world and continues to bring about a new creation (41:20; 43:7; 44:24; 45:11).

When the prophet calls Yahweh the "redeemer" of Israel (41:14; 43:14; 44:6, 24; 47:4; 48:17; 49:7, 26; 54:5, 8), he implies an intimate kinship exists between the Lord and his people. In Hebrew thought, the "redeemer" (*go'el*) is the nearest relative, whose responsibilities included punishing the oppressors of his kin (Nm 35:16–19; Dt 19:12) and guaranteeing payment to maintain family possession of the ancestral land belonging to his indebted relatives (Lv 25:23–25; Ru 2:20). When he calls Yahweh the "redeemer", Deutero-Isaiah indicates both that the Lord claims a closer relationship to his people than anyone else and that he has come to bring them justice.

In his work of redeeming his people from captivity, Yahweh is pouring forth saving justice (*zedek/zedekah*) upon the earth (45:8). More is taking place than a liberation from exile: the Lord is communicating to the world an aspect of his own divine quality, something unique to his sovereign realm. In Deutero-Isaiah, justice refers both to the mercy (41:10) of God and to his saving action (45:22–25; 41:2; 42:6, 21; 45:13, 19). Justice is the unmerited gift God communicates to his people simply on the basis of their election. " 'In Yahweh alone are saving justice and strength' " (45:24). Deutero-Isaiah describes salvation in terms of the Lord's work of bringing his people to a state of righteousness or justification, a theme that reaches its climax in his presentation of the Suffering Servant (51:1–8; 53:11).

Yahweh redeems his people by accomplishing a new Exodus when he brings them back from the Exile to their land (43:16–21; 51:9–11; 55:12–13). The prophet uses images from the original Exodus to describe the passage to the Promised Land: the people will move through the desert (40:3–4; Ex 15:22); Yahweh will conquer the monstrous evil symbolized in the sea (51:9–10; cf. Ex 14:5–31); his protective presence will surround them (52:12; cf. Ex 13:21; 14:19); water will flow in the wilderness (41:18–19; cf. Ex 17:1–7), and the Lord will reveal his glory (40:5; cf. Ex 24:7). In this Exodus from Exile, the Lord is not merely repeating the past; he is doing something that is radically "new" (42:9, 10; 43:19; 48:6). One aspect of the newness in this event is the Lord's use of a foreigner as his agent to accomplish the liberation of his people from Babylon.

3. Israel and the Nations

Cyrus the Persian works as Yahweh's deputy in bringing the Exile to an end (44:28; 45:1–7; 41:1–5). The fact that Yahweh works through someone who does not know him (45:4) is a further indication of the Lord's sovereignty over all nations. Just as Jeremiah and Ezekiel had perceived that the Lord used a foreign king (Nebuchadnezzar) to execute his judgment on Jerusalem (Jer 28:14; Ez 24:1–14), so also Deutero-Isaiah discerns the Lord's using another foreigner (Cyrus) to overthrow the remnants of Nebuchadnezzar's regime in order to deliver his people and initiate the restoration of Jerusalem.

Although Cyrus is Yahweh's agent, Israel remains his servant, his chosen one (41:8–9; 43:10; 44:1–2; 45:4). The Lord has corrected Israel as his servant for her past transgressions that resulted in her exile to Babylon (42:18–25; 43:22–28). Through Deutero-Isaiah's proclamation, Yahweh bestows his consolation and declares his forgiveness to Israel (40:1–2; 49:13; 51:12; 52:7–12). Israel, who had been blind and deaf according to the word of Isaiah, now becomes the servant of the Lord's plans for the world (42:18–25; cf. 6:9–10). Yahweh will provide Israel with the strength and resources to serve him arising from a personal union with him (41:8–9; 44:21, 26; 45:4; 48:20). Israel redeemed from captivity will be his witness to the nations (43:10).

Because of his awareness of God's greatness and the power of his justice, Deutero-Isaiah perceives that Yahweh extends his salvation to all peoples. When beholding the Lord's redeeming work taking effect in his servant Israel, all people will see the glory of the Lord (40:5), and they will have the opportunity to turn to him for redemption (45:22–23). God accomplishes his work among his own people in order to reveal himself to all nations (52:10). Eventually, all people will seek the Lord among the people he has chosen and redeemed (45:14–19, 20–25; 55:3–5). God's revelation will extend to the whole world through one Servant in particular, who will be the source of astonishment and righteousness because of his suffering (52:15; cf. 52:10).

The Servant of the Lord

Who is the Lord's servant acclaimed in the Songs of Deutero-Isaiah (42:1–9; 49:1–7; 50:4–11; 52:13–53:12)? The matter remains a subject of debate. Scholarly proposals cluster around three primary candidates: Israel (called a servant elsewhere in Deutero-Isaiah: 41:8–9; 43:10; 44:1, 2, 21; 48:20); Cyrus (called a servant in 44:26); or the prophet himself (in light of the first-person style: 49:1; 50:4). Closer analysis indicates that neither Israel nor Cyrus is the servant: Israel's sinful past runs contrary to the character of the servant in the Songs (cf. 42:18–25; 43:22–28); Cyrus does not exhibit the self-effacing qualities described in the poems. Therefore, the evidence in the text leads us to conclude that, in their original setting, the Songs refer to Deutero-Isaiah himself, but they also point beyond him to the perfect Servant whom God will send in the future (42:1–12; cf. 9:1–6; 11:1–9).

Before examining the Songs' contents, we note that the literary form of the Servant Songs derives from the "Confessions" of Jeremiah (Jer 11:18–12:6; 15:10–21; 17:14–18; 18:18–23; 20:7–18). Indeed, the witness of Jeremiah's prophetic career and suffering introduces the theme of the last three Songs (Is 49:1; cf. Jer 1:5; Is 50:4–11; cf. Jer 20:7–13; Is 53:7; cf. Jer 11:19). We will consider each of the Songs individually in order to see how they indicate a development in the prophet's vocation.

1. The First Song (42:1–9): The Prophet's Call

The servant exhibits the bearing of the promised David by virtue of his endowment with God's spirit (42:1; cf. 11:1–10; Ez 34:23–24) and his vocation to bring justice to the earth (2 Sm 8:15). The servant is primarily a prophet who brings discernment by his teaching (Is 42:4). Because Yahweh's saving justice (*zedek*) is the source of the servant's instruction (42:4, 6), the servant's word will be a light of revelation to heal the blind and free the captives (42:6–7).

2. The Second Song (49:1–7): Renewal of the Prophet's Call

In the new historical situation created by Cyrus' decree ending the Exile (49:1–54:17), the prophet receives the commission to restore Israel to Yahweh (49:5), recalling the vocation and life of Jeremiah (Jer 1:4–10). His resemblance to Jeremiah consists of the following: he protests his inability to succeed (49:3–4; cf. Jer 1:6–8; cf. Moses' protest in Ex 3:1–4:17); his call originates in his mother's womb (49:1, 5; Jer 1:5); and his labors appear futile (49:4; Jer 42:1–44:30).

3. The Third Song (50:4–11): The Disciple's Submission

The servant who proclaims the good news announcing peace (52:7) experiences affliction on account of the word he preaches (50:5–6; cf. Jer 20:7–13). His capacity to accept suffering stems from his training as a prophet in the school of Isaiah. By his obedience, he contradicts the rebellious who refuse to listen to the Law (50:4–11; cf. 30:8–14). In him, we contemplate an intimate connection between suffering and God's word both in listening and in speaking. For one whose heart is set on God, affliction can be a means of purification leading to a deeper hearing of the divine word. The Lord does not neglect but speaks most deeply to the afflicted. This truth is in opposition to the traditionally held view that suffering is God's punishment for sin (Gn 3:14–19; 12:17; 42:21; Jos 7:6–13; Jb 33:19–30). In this Song, however, the servant provides the axiom for apostolic preaching when he testifies that God's word releases a life-giving power for "the weary" as his prophet speaks from his tribulation (50:4; cf. 40:29–30; cf. 2 Cor 4:7–5:10; 11:21–12:10). Even as he suffers, the Lord's servant has a boldness to confront his adversaries in court to prove righteousness (50:8–10). This righteousness comes from trust in the Lord (50:10; cf. 30:15).

4. The Fourth Song (52:13–53:12): The Suffering Servant

In his final Song at the end of his life, the prophet looks both backward at his mission and forward to the perfect Servant whom God will send. The Song's structure consists of a three-part dialogue between Yahweh and his people about the Suffering Servant. Yahweh's words at the beginning (52:13–15) and at the end (53:11b–12) envelop the confessions of the congregation about their misapprehension of the servant (53:1–11a). The structure has the effect of showing us the difference between God's perspective and man's perspective on the suffering of the righteous and the innocent (cf. 55:8). The Song is similar in content to a psalm of personal lament (cf. Ps 22).

Yahweh Introduces His Servant (52:13–15): In the Song's opening line, Yahweh promises the ultimate victory of his servant (52:13). He reveals the servant as a sign of contradiction to the world, which looks at appearances but not at the heart (52:14; cf. 1 Sm 16:7). The servant instructs kings and nations not so much by the power of his words as by the depth of his suffering (52:14–15; cf. 42:4; 50:4–7). God reveals himself precisely where human beings declare his absence, namely, in the most abject human misery.

Mankind Confesses Its Guilt and Ignorance (53:1–11a): God's people express their astonishment through two rhetorical questions of the type in Deutero-Isaiah that leads to revelation (50:1; cf. 40:12, 13, 28). The congregation is astonished at the servant's passage from humiliation (53:2–9) to exaltation (53:10–11a). In the process of describing the servant's suffering, they confess their lack of compassion for him (53:3–5). Insofar as they lack empathy for him, they lack unity with each other. Hence, they are lost in their isolation like scattered and straying sheep (53:6; cf. Ez 34:1–31). In contrast to this fractious flock stands the silent lamb who is a persecuted prophet (53:7) like Jeremiah at the hands of his kinsmen (Jer 11:19). The people express their rejection of the Servant by dragging him to court (53:8; cf. 50:8–10; cf. Jer 26:1–24). They expel him from their midst (53:8). For Deutero-Isaiah, mention of being "cut off" and of having a "tomb" probably refers not so much to physical death as to descending into a spiritual abyss (Is 53:9–10; cf. psalms of lament: Pss 28:1; 30:3; 40:2; 143:7). The servant's silence, nonviolence, and lack of deception contrast his innocence with the congregation's guilt (53:7–9; cf. 53:2–6).

The voice of the congregation concludes its confession by proclaiming Yahweh's vindication of his servant (53:10–11a). This victory means deliverance for his persecutors as well. The servant provides a new revelation of the way God works. The servant's suffering is redemptive. His affliction is not an annihilation but an oblation. In tribulation, the servant's life does not go down toward Sheol but up toward God, and not just for his own sake but for the sake of his people and all humanity. The outpouring of the servant's life is a sin-offering (*'asham*), a sacrifice of reparation according to the Priestly Code (53:10; cf. Lv 5:14–26; Nm 5:5–8). Here, the text speaks of salvific reality beyond the mission of Deutero-Isaiah. It describes the Servant to come, who will offer his life as an atoning sacrifice, the righteous one who dies for the unrighteous (53:5–7, 10–11a; cf. 1 Pt 3:18). Light has overcome darkness, an image that we find in all the Servant Songs (53:11a; cf. 50:10; 49:6; 42:6; cf. Jn 8:12).

Yahweh Promises Justification (53:11b–13): The servant brings about the justification (*zedek/zedekah*) promised by the Lord (45:8) and desired by the humble (51:1–7; cf. 53:11b–13). The servant's knowledge that mediates this saving justice arises from his suffering at the hands of others in obedience to God (cf. 50:4–11). God's final word describes the servant's new life beyond torment. He promises forgiveness of sin, which is a central preoccupation of Deutero-Isaiah (53:12; cf. 40:2; 55:7).

Toward the New Testament: The Suffering Servant of the Lord

Jesus revealed himself as the Suffering Servant (e.g., Mk 8:31; 10:45). After Jesus' death and Resurrection, the early Church turned to the words of Deutero-Isaiah in search of an ever more profound understanding of Christ as the fulfillment of the Servant Songs. Owing to the vast number of references to Deutero-Isaiah in the New Testament, we will limit our study to how the

New Testament authors treat the message of the introductory voice (Is 40:3–5) and the Servant Songs (42:1–9; 49:1–7; 50:4–11; 52:13–53:12).

The voice that cries out at the beginning of Deutero-Isaiah announces the end of the Exile by demanding the construction of a level road across the wilderness from Babylon to Jerusalem (40:3–5). All four Gospels insightfully quote this text in reference to the mission of John the Baptist (Mk 1:3; Mt 3:3; Lk 3:4–6; Jn 1:23). In the original, the wilderness provides the setting for the road project (Is 40:3), but, in the Gospels, the wilderness is the theological environment in which the voice cries out (in reference to John the Baptist; e.g., Mk 1:3–4). This minor alteration opens new depths of revelation because, in the Synoptic Gospels, "the way" connotes more than a physical road (cf. Is 40:3); it refers to the spiritual path of discipleship. By his preaching of repentance, John the Baptist prepares people to follow "the way" of Jesus in the sense of sharing in his manner of life. In the Gospels, the way still leads toward the experience of salvation in Jerusalem (as in Deutero-Isaiah), but this time through the event of Jesus' cross (see Mk 10:52). In the early Church, "the Way" becomes a designation of the Christian life (see Acts 9:2).

We should note that the Gospel of Luke extends the quote to the full length of the text (Lk 3:4–6; Is 40:3–5) in order to emphasize the universality of salvation: "All humanity will see the salvation of God" (Lk 3:6; see Is 40:5) when the apostles preach the Gospel to the ends of the earth (Acts 1:8; cf. Paul's arrival in Rome: Acts 28:17–31).

1. The First Servant Song (Is 42:1–9)

The commission of the Lord's Servant provides the basis for the Gospel accounts of Jesus' baptism (Mk 1:9–11; Mt 3:13–17; Lk 3:21–22; cf. Jn 1:32–34; cf. Is 42:1). In Deutero-Isaiah, God identifies his servant as the one upon whom he bestows his spirit (Is 42:1). The Gospel scene echoes this text insofar as it describes the coming of the Spirit upon Jesus and God's uttering the message of revelation (e.g., Mk 1:9–11). However, the baptismal accounts exceed Deutero-Isaiah's comprehension by introducing vocabulary indicative of the Trinity. God calls Jesus "my Son" rather than "my servant" and thereby implies that God is Father. Furthermore, the Spirit (or "the Holy Spirit:" Lk 3:22) exhibits a more distinctive bearing than was implied by "my spirit" in the text of the prophet (Is 42:1). When we recognize that the Servant Song provides the background for the baptism scene, we can appreciate that submission to the Father distinguishes the Sonship of Jesus. As the Son of God, Jesus obeys the Father in all things (cf. Heb 5:8).

The Gospel of Matthew quotes the first Servant Song at length in order to emphasize that, by the unique combination of his humility ("does not cry out or raise his voice") and love of the poor ("he does not break the crushed reed"), Jesus fulfills the prescriptions of the Servant (Mt 12:15–21; cf. Is 42:1–4). Again, Jesus surpasses what Deutero-Isaiah had foreseen in that his healing of the blind is actual, not merely metaphoric. In Deutero-Isaiah, the promise of opening the eyes of the blind is a symbol for the release of the Jews from captivity in Exile, whereas, in Jesus, the symbol becomes reality in the physical cures (Is 42:7; cf., e.g., Mt 12:9–14; 20:29–34).

2. The Second Servant Song (Is 49:1–7)

Paul and Luke applied the renewed commission of Deutero-Isaiah (Is 49:1–7) to Paul's apostolic ministry. By insisting that his vocation originated when he was in his mother's womb, Paul defines his conversion on the road to Damascus as a prophetic call in line with that of Jeremiah and the Servant of the Lord (Gal 1:15; cf. Jer 1:5; Is 49:1). Furthermore, when he turns his attention from a strictly Jewish audience to the Gentiles of Antioch in Pisidia, Paul again reflects the mission of the Servant who came to address not only the people of Israel but all the nations (Acts 13:47; cf. Is 49:6).

The simile of the "sharp" sword to describe the mouth of the prophet (Is 49:2) provides the background for the New Testament description of God's word as a "two-edged" sword (Heb 4:12). The same image describes the prophetic aspect of Jesus, the glorious Son of Man, who speaks his word in the midst of his Church and in the final judgment of the nations (Rv 1:16; 19:15).

3. The Third Servant Song (Is 50:4–11)

The Song that describes the Servant as the disciple who confronts the world applies to Jesus in its first half (Is 50:4–7) and to every Christian in its second half (50:8–10). When the members of the Sanhedrin spit on Jesus and strike him in the face after finding him guilty of blasphemy, ironically, they are revealing him to be the Servant of the Lord for whom such treatment was prophesied (Mk 14:65; Mt 26:67). Again, the gentile soldiers demonstrate the same point in the Praetorium when they mock Jesus as a deluded king just before taking him outside to be crucified (Mk 15:19; Mt 27:30).

Paul alludes to the second part of the Song when he encourages all Christians to take up the attitude of the Lord's Servant by challenging every accusation of guilt (Rom 8:31–33; cf. Is 50:8–11). Because the Christian has received justification through faith in Jesus Christ, he or she has been freed from all condemnation before God (cf. Rom 3:26; 5:1–11). Therefore, following the model of the Servant, the Christian must confront interior accusation confident of the vindication that comes through faith.

4. The Fourth Song of the Suffering Servant (Is 52:13–53:12)

This poem is God's revelation that points unmistakably to Jesus as the Messiah and Savior by virtue of his suffering and death. Only Jesus totally fulfills its precepts. The Song tells us what is unique about Jesus compared to other figures in the Bible and in other religions. Both in structure and content, the Song of the Suffering Servant reveals Jesus as the source of our salvation (cf. Acts 8:32–33, within 8:26–40).

When preachers in the early Church read the Song of the Suffering Servant, they must have noted how the second (Is 53:1–11a) and third (53:11b–12) parts of the Song foreshadow the stages of Jesus' passage from death to life. By its structure, the Song prefigures the sequence of events that Jesus noted in his Passion predictions (Mk 8:31; 9:31; 10:32–34; cf. I Cor 15:3–5): he suffered (53:7), died (53:8), was buried (53:9), and was raised from the dead (53:10–12). Furthermore, Christians discern allusions to the days of Jesus' ministry in the description of the Servant's beginnings when his compatriots disrespected him (53:1–6). The anger of Jesus' opponents spills over in their desire to destroy him: the Pharisees and Herodians plot his assassination (Mk 3:6; cf. Is 53:5; cf. Lk 13:31–33), his neighbors and kinsmen at Nazareth mistrust him (Lk 4:16–30; Mk 6:1–6; Jn 7:5), and his opponents disdain his teaching (Jn 7:1–8:58; Lk 10:13–16).

We see Jesus revealed as the Suffering Servant especially in his Passion and death. When his disciples misinterpret his instructions by taking up arms, Jesus mentions that their action fulfills the Scriptures about his being counted among the rebellious (Lk 22:37, where the "rebellious" are the violent [cf. Lk 6:27–35]; cf. Is 53:12, where the "rebellious" are those who suffer for their sins). This association with the rebellious climaxes in Jesus' crucifixion between two criminals (Mk 15:27; Lk 23:32–33, 39–43). Leading up to his death, he maintains the silence of the Servant before the High Priest (Mt 26:63; Is 53:7) and before Pilate, who is amazed (Mk 15:5; Mt 27:14; cf. Is 52:15). Jesus becomes disfigured through the ordeal of the trial and subsequent abuse (Mk 15:16–20; Jn 19:1–5; cf. Is 52:15; 53:4–5). He receives the Servant's burial when the wealthy man, Joseph of Arimathaea, places him in his tomb (Mk 15:42–47; Mt 27:57–61; Lk 23:50–56; cf. Is 53:9).

The Song of the Suffering Servant is at the heart of the Gospel message because it shows us that Christ has atoned for our sin. This is the Good News of our salvation. The early Christian profession that "Christ died for our sins, in accordance with the Scriptures" primarily alludes to the Servant text (I Cor 15:3; cf. Is 53:4–5, 10). When Jesus declares his death will be "a ransom for many", he is revealing himself as the promised Servant (Mk 10:45; cf. Is 53:10–12). He makes the same point again at the Last Supper when he states that his blood will be poured out "for many" (Mk 14:24; Mt 26:28; see Is 53:11–12). His death is the sacrifice that makes atonement for sin and reconciles mankind to God in the new covenant. The term "for many" is not exclusive but inclusive in that the saving work of Christ reveals God's desire that all people be saved (1 Tm 2:4).

True liberation is ours when we base our life on the truth that "our Lord Jesus was handed over to death for our sins and raised to life for our justification" (Rom 4:25; cf. Is 53:4–6, 12). Christ's death is the sacrifice that delivers mankind from sin (see Rom 3:21–31). Jesus became the victim for sin in order to deliver us from its power and so as to assure our justification, which was the central concern of Deutero-Isaiah (2 Cor 5:21; cf. Lv 4:1–5:13; Is 53:11; cf. 45:8). Jesus' obedience makes his death the effective sacrifice that communicates God's righteousness to overcome the unrighteousness of Adam (Rom 5:19). When we put our faith in Jesus Christ, we receive this righteousness as an unmerited gift (Rom 3:24–26).

The First Letter of Peter teaches us that we can live a radically new way of life when we appreciate the deliverance Jesus offers us in his sacrificial death. Out of gratitude for what he has done for us, we can be free of resentment by allowing the Suffering Servant to show us how to respond to persecution (1 Pt 2:21–25; cf. Is 53:6–12).

When a Christian confesses that Jesus is Lord (Phil 2:11; Jn 20:28), he or she expresses the fullness of truth foreshadowed in Deutero-Isaiah's profession of faith. When Paul announces that every person in the world must confess that Jesus is Lord (Phil 2:10–11), he draws upon the words of the prophet who foresaw the Gentiles confessing their faith in Yahweh (Is 45:23–24). The terms that Deutero-Isaiah had used of Yahweh, Paul now applies to Jesus the risen Lord who reveals the glory of God the Father (Phil 2:11).

Having considered Deutero-Isaiah's ministry to encourage the exiles to return to Judah and undertake the restoration of the land, we can direct our attention to the missions of Haggai and Zechariah, the two prophets who were instrumental in bringing about the reconstruction of the Temple.

STUDY QUESTIONS

1. How does the text of Deutero-Isaiah differ from the first part of the book of Isaiah (1–39)?
2. Distinguish between the first and second parts of Deutero-Isaiah.
3. What technique does Deutero-Isaiah use to get his audience to think about God?
4. What are Deutero-Isaiah's two titles for Yahweh?
5. How will Israel be Yahweh's witness to the nations?
6. Who is the Servant of the Lord in the original setting of the Four Songs?
7. How does the prophet resemble Jeremiah?
8. How is Jesus the fulfillment of the Suffering Servant?
9. Discuss how in your own life and in the life of the Church, you have seen periods of suffering challenge your fidelity to God. How have those periods of suffering been times of grace?
10. What consolation does God desire to give his people? How can you be receptive to it through daily prayer, Scripture reading, and reception of the sacraments?
11. What are the elements of the new Exodus? How does the promise of a new Exodus in Deutero-Isaiah apply to the Church today?
12. Read the Servant Songs (Is 42:1–9; 49:1–7; 50:4–11; 52:13–53:12). How does Jesus' fulfillment of the Servant Songs by his Passion and crucifixion reveal to you the nature of God's love for you? How does Jesus' death on the cross heal you from sin and death?

DEUTERO-ISAIAH

26

HAGGAI AND ZECHARIAH:
THE REBUILDING OF THE TEMPLE

Constructing a building for worship represents a turning point in the history of every congregation. The project expresses the community's conviction of being called to grow in unity as God's people for generations to come. The enterprise symbolizes faith but entails stress. To reach completion, the undertaking demands a generous investment of time, talents, and finances on the part of all the faithful. The community requires strong leadership to prevent it from being splintered under the pressure.

The prophets Haggai and Zechariah reflect the combination of talents necessary for a building project to become an occasion for renewal. They were unique individuals. Haggai was a pragmatist, and Zechariah was a visionary. Together, they were responsible for motivating the people of Judah to restore the Temple after the Exile. In order to gain perspective on their ministries, we must examine the situation in Judah from the end of the Exile (538 B.C.) until the dedication of the restored Temple (515 B.C.).

The first group of exiles who returned to Jerusalem from Babylon immediately after Cyrus' decree in 538 B.C. consisted of the more rugged individuals of the community. Intellectuals, civic leaders, those who had enjoyed success in business and other members of Judah's upper class remained in Babylon because they preferred the benefits and opportunities afforded by a cosmopolitan center to the harsh challenge of starting over amid the ruins of Jerusalem. Those who accompanied Sheshbazzar to Jerusalem were a less numerous and elegant group than we imagine from the Chronicler's optimistic description of them (Ezr 1:1–2:70).

Perhaps as early as the autumn of 538 B.C., Sheshbazzar erected the altar at the Temple site, and the priests began offering the required sacrifices (Ezr 3:1–13). Then he undertook the task of rebuilding the Temple (Ezr 5:14–16). The people discontinued the Temple project after a brief initial effort. The interruption was due to pressure from outside interference and the basic hardship of the situation in Judah at the time. The governor and Samaritan leaders lodged official protests against the project (Ezr 4:1–23). The Persian armies disrupted it when they passed through Judah on their way to conquer Egypt in 525 B.C. In addition to the political difficulties, the returning exiles had to devote their attention to building houses for their families (Hg 1:4) while contending with drought and crop failure (Hg 2:15–19).

Cyrus II died in 530 B.C. and bequeathed the Persian throne to his son Cambyses II (529–522 B.C.). Cambyses' conquest of Egypt in 525 B.C. seems to have opened the way for a surge of exiles to return to Judah. When Cambyses died unexpectedly, a Persian army general, Darius Hystaspes (Darius I "the Great"), took the throne (522–486 B.C.). Darius reflected the broadminded vision of Cyrus so that his reign produced conditions more favorable to the reconstruction of the Temple. By the time Darius rose to power, Sheshbazzar faded from view and Zerubbabel took over the leadership of Judah.

It is difficult to ascertain Zerubbabel's official status with precision. The prophet Haggai calls him "governor" (Hg 1:1; 2:2, 21), but neither Ezra nor Zechariah accord him that title (cf. Ezr 3:8; 4:2, 3; 5:2; Zec 4:6b–10b). We are certain that Zerubbabel was a descendant of David (1 Chr 3:19; cf. 3:17). Since he was a member of Judah's royal line, the Persian authorities conferred on Zerubbabel the authority to direct the internal affairs of Judah and Jerusalem. Clearly, the people considered him to have filled the vacancy that Sheshbazzar left (Ezr 1:1–11; 3:1–13). The Jews but not the Persians might have called Zerubbabel "governor". He did not have the official status the Persians later accorded to Nehemiah by naming him "governor" (Neh 5:14–15). Zerubbabel was the last person in the line of David to fill the office of leader over Judah and Jerusalem. The biblical texts usually mention Zerubbabel in union with Joshua, a Zadokite priest, who was his clerical counterpart in leadership (Ezr 2:2; 3:8; 5:2; Neh 12:1; Hg 1:1, 12; 2:2; Zec 3:1–10).

In 520 B.C., Haggai and Zechariah inspired these two leaders to make a fresh start on the reconstruction of the Temple. Official work had ceased on the site for the previous fifteen years since the time of Sheshbazzar's brief initiative. The people of Judah were hardly responding to the wonderful visions of the restored Temple that Ezekiel had recounted (Ez 40:1–48:35)!

The ministries of Haggai and Zechariah overlap each other. Haggai proclaimed his messages between August and December of 520 B.C. Zechariah began in October of 520 B.C. (Zec 1:1–6) and continued to preach in February of 519 B.C. (Zec 1:7–6:15) and again in December of 518 B.C. (7:1–14). At the behest of Haggai and Zechariah, construction of the Temple began in autumn of 520 B.C. (Ezr 4:24–5:2; 6:14; Hg 1:1–15). The work reached completion before the dedication of the Temple in March or April of 515 B.C., prior to the celebration of Passover that year (Ezr 6:13–22).

HAGGAI

We know very little about Haggai other than that he was a persuasive speaker. Does his concern for the distinctions between clean and unclean indicate a formal association with the priests (2:10–14)? We can be certain that Haggai was a prophet imbued with a zeal for the Temple. He was one of the most successful of all the prophets in terms of getting immediate results. Almost as soon as he exhorted the people to restore the Temple, they took up the task (Hg 1:1–11, 12–15).

The book of Haggai consists of four messages the prophet delivered in the autumn of 520 B.C.:

1. There is no fruitfulness in the land because the Temple is still in ruins (1:1–15a);
2. Although the Temple seems a paltry replica at the moment, it will be restored to an unprecedented splendor (1:15b–2:9);
3.. The people will be freed from misery, and the Lord will bless the land as the Temple is restored (2:10–19); and
4. The Lord has a special place in his plan for Zerubbabel (2:20–23).

When an editor compiled the text, he inserted notations of dates to provide a framework for the quotations of the prophet (e.g., 1:1, 15; 2:1, 20). The editor seems to have been a disciple of Haggai who completed the book shortly after the prophet's ministry and perhaps even before the dedication of the Temple in 515 B.C.

The Message of Haggai

Haggai speaks as an organizer who possesses a practical mind and remarkable leadership skills. The fact that he was primarily responsible for initiating the successful reconstruction of the Temple indicates a great deal about the man's character and ability. Some people read the text and suggest that, while he was a remarkable manager, Haggai lacked spiritual depth. But they fail to appreciate his remarkable sense of the Temple's significance. Haggai was not a theologian but a gifted pastoral leader who possessed a unique combination of spiritual insight and practical judgment. His success in motivating his audience to undertake the Temple project arose from his inspired vision of the work as a cooperative effort between God and his people that would change the course of history.

From Haggai, we learn that constructing a sacred building can afford a congregation the opportunity of experiencing a renewal of faith. Haggai insisted that working on the Temple project offered Judah the possibility of leaving behind an old life and entering into a new life as God's people. Haggai associated the Temple project with a three-fold grace of repentance, glory, and promise. We will summarize his message under these headings.

Repentance: In Haggai's mind, the ruins at the Temple site reflected the spiritual desolation of Judah. He insists that self-concern has been the primary obstacle to reconstruction. The people have devoted themselves to building their houses while neglecting the Lord's House (1:2–4). Haggai admonishes them by alluding to the example of David in the earliest days when the people of Judah occupied Jerusalem (2 Sm 5:6). At that time, David was embarrassed by the fact that he lived in a house while there was no Temple to house the ark (Hg 1:4; 2 Sm 7:2). Haggai implies that his people can seize the opportunity to become faithful to Judah's traditions by thinking like David. For them, the Temple project will be an expression of repentance (cf. 2:17) in which they set aside their self-concern in order to reverence God in Jerusalem.

Both the people and the land will experience the benefits of this act of repentance. Haggai attributes the droughts and crop failures of recent memory to the people's lack of correct priorities (1:5–6, 10–11; 2:16–19). The land has been as barren as the unclean lives of the people who neglected to worship the Lord properly (2:1–14). As the people put the Lord first in their lives by reconstructing the Temple, the land will become productive. The recent harvest seems to have borne out the truth of his prophecy: the autumn crop yield increased once they set the Temple's cornerstone in place (2:15–19).

Glory: For Haggai, the Temple is the place where the Lord will reveal his glory (1:8; 2:9). Thus, the Temple project is really a work of God. Human effort represents only one side of the event. Indeed, it is because the spirit of Yahweh is among them that the people can work on the project (2:4; cf. 1:14). And, owing to their material poverty, the people will have to rely on the Lord even to provide the precious utensils for the Temple (2:7–8; cf. Ezr 1:7–11). The people of Judah must build the edifice, but Yahweh alone can make the Temple his House (1:8) by revealing his glory there (2:9; cf. 1 Kgs 8:11).

In response to the people's discouragement that the structure under reconstruction represents only a shadow of the grandeur of Solomon's Temple, Haggai promises that the glory of the new will exceed that of the old (2:9). Haggai foresees that "peace" or "healing" (Hebrew: *shalom*) will be the primary effect of the Lord's glory present in the Temple (2:9).

Promise: Haggai contemplates the Temple project against the horizon of God's total plan for the future of his people. He perceives that the order of creation and of international history will feel the repercussions of God's action of endowing the Temple with his glory (2:6–7). The other earth-shattering event in God's plan consists in his enhancement of Zerubbabel as the Davidic figure who will lead Judah to prominence among the nations (2:20–23). God's election of Zerubbabel (2:23; cf. 2 Sm 7:8) and his designation as a "signet ring" (cf. Jer 22:24) confirm his calling to be a figure endowed with a messianic role in Judah's history.

Toward the New Testament: The Unshakable Kingdom

Haggai's conviction about God's future intervention to jar the present world order contributed to the contemplation of the final days, which became an increasing preoccupation of later biblical tradition. In the only New Testament text to quote Haggai, the Letter to the Hebrews applies to the end time the prophet's image of the Lord shaking the heavens and the earth (Heb 12:26; cf. Hg 2:6). We have noted that in Haggai, the Lord's earth-shaking work was a promised event within history related to the rebuilding of the Temple (Hg 2:1–9). The author of Hebrews invokes the image to describe God's final judgment of the world. In the end, everything that does not belong to the unshakable Kingdom of Christ will be shaken into oblivion (Heb 12:25–29). The Christian and the community will remain because of their roots in the heavenly Jerusalem (Heb 12:22–24).

ZECHARIAH 1–8

Zechariah, the son of Iddo, was a priest whose father had returned from exile with Zerubbabel and Joshua (Neh 12:4, 16; cf. Zec 1:1). We know little about Zechariah other than that he united his efforts with Haggai's to encourage the restoration of the Temple (Ezr 5:1; 6:14). The fact that he was a priest with roots in Babylon who communicated his message by way of visions indicates his spiritual affinity with Ezekiel's tradition.

The book of Zechariah consists of two parts that are so distinct from one another in tone and perspective that they appear to come from different eras in Israel's history. The specific dates (1:1; 1:7; 7:1) and personalities (3:1–10; 6:9–14) mentioned in Zechariah 1–8 anchor this section in the period between 520 and 518 B.C. By contrast, Zechariah 9–14 has few historical indications and is preoccupied with the conflict at the end time, which places it in the category of early apocalyptic literature, possibly at the end of the prophetic tradition. While acknowledging that the matter remains a subject of debate, we will date "Deutero-Zechariah" ("Second Zechariah"/Zec 9–14) around the same time as Joel, another book that focuses on the end time. By this estimation, a prophetic editor completed the final version of Zechariah around 300 B.C.

We will devote our attention to the portion of the text that comes from the ministry of Zechariah (Zec 1:1–8:23). Three notations in the text indicate that his mission covered a period of just over two years, starting in the first months of the Temple project. He delivered his first message in October 520 B.C. (1:1) to add his voice to Haggai's appeal for Jerusalem to restore the holy site (cf. Hg 2:1–9). The text clusters all his visions in the night of February 16, 519 B.C. (1:7; cf. 1:7–6:15). Finally, his discourses date from November/December 518 B.C. While he and Haggai were instrumental in initiating the Temple project, there is no evidence in the texts indicating that either of them was in attendance at its dedication in 515 B.C.

The three dates in the book delineate the message of Zechariah into three parts: (1) an introductory summons to repentance (October 520 B.C./1:1–6); (2) eight visions of God's dealings with Israel and the nations (February 16, 519 B.C./1:7–6:15); and (3) Zechariah's instructions (November/December 518 B.C./7:1–8:23) concerning Israel's past ritualism (7:1–14) and future promise of the Lord's return to Zion (8:1–23).

An editor, possibly under the supervision of the prophet, has distinguished the visions (1:7–6:15) from the oracles (7:1–8:23). Apparently, a disciple of Zechariah completed the text (Zec 1–8) shortly after the prophet completed his ministry.

The Message of Zechariah

Both Zechariah and Haggai were convinced the days of earth-shattering change were at hand. The seventieth anniversary of the Temple's destruction was fast approaching (587–517 B.C.). The date had become a source of popular anticipation owing to Jeremiah's prophecy about restoration taking place after an exile of seventy years' duration (Jer 25:11; 29:10; cf. Zec 1:12; 7:5).

Like Ezekiel, Zechariah had the grace to break through the horizontal plane of history to perceive the events of his time from the perspective of revelation. He mediates his word by way of visionary symbols from the divine sphere to assure Jerusalem that God is now realizing his plan of restoration. The people might think that the Temple represents an arduous and frustrating effort (cf. Hg 2:3–4). However, with his visions of angels, horses, horns, smiths, olive trees, lamp-stands, scrolls, and chariots, Zechariah locates the project within the divine sphere of activity. God is the one who is really at work in the times, and he promises a reversal of fortunes. His people will rise in stature while the nations will recede into a position of subservience. We will summarize his message by considering his vision of what God was doing with Jerusalem, the nations, and the priesthood.

God's Promise to Jerusalem: Yahweh is returning to dwell in Jerusalem (1:16; 2:14; 8:3). The time of hardship and discipline is giving way to the time of peace and divine compassion (1:12–17). As the Lord returns to establish his glory in the Temple (2:9; cf. Hg 2:7), he will extend his presence as a wall of fire, protecting the whole city. In his vision, Zechariah sees a man who attempts to measure the city in the same way that the surveyor in Ezekiel's vision took the dimensions of his visionary Temple (2:5–9; cf. Ez 40:3–42:20). The servant in Zechariah's vision, however, is unable to calculate the city's dimensions because its population has become so abundant. This is because God's glory has extended beyond Ezekiel's imagined Temple to the city itself in Zechariah's vision, and this divine glory is boundless.

As the Lord returns to Jerusalem, so will his people. He has sent out his powers (chariots, horses, winds) to gain the release of his people from all the lands of their dispersion (6:1–8). By his saving action, he will bring them home to join the remnant in Judah (8:6–8). All he requires of his people is that they return to him in repentance (1:3) and practice covenant love toward the oppressed rather than merely express their devotion in ritual fasting alone (7:1–14). God's edict of judgment (the scroll) is going forth to banish the unjust (5:1–4). The work of redemption will endure because he is banishing to Babylon ("Shinar") the root of sin, which is "Wickedness" (5:5–11).

God's Work among the Nations: God is bringing about a reversal of fortunes. The nations that used to torment Judah will experience God's judgment, and then they will look to Jerusalem for life (1:14–15; 2:15). The angelic smiths have broken the power (symbolized by the horns) of the nations (Egypt, Assyria, Babylon, and Persia?) who caused Jerusalem's exile (2:1–4). Now it is Babylon who will suffer under the tyranny of Wickedness (5:5–11).

However, God's plan of salvation works itself out from Jerusalem to include the rest of the world. As the remnant in Jerusalem turns to him, the crops in Judah will flourish abundantly (8:11–13; cf. Hg 2:15–19; cf. 1:10–11). By exercising the covenant virtues of truth and peace, God's people will build a social order that will attract people from all nations (8:16–17). Because of the witness of life in Jerusalem, people from all nations will stream toward Zion in order to seek the Lord's mercy and favor (8:20–23).

God's Plan for the Priesthood: Whereas Haggai focused exclusively on the promised role of Zerubbabel in accomplishing God's plan (Hg 2:20–23), Zechariah envisions the important place of Joshua the priest along with Zerubbabel (Zec 3:1–10; 4:1–14; 6:9–14). Zerubbabel and Joshua (the two olive trees) represent the cooperation of temporal and spiritual authority as they attend to the presence of God (the lamp-stand) in the Temple (4:1–5, 10b–14).

Zechariah highlights Zerubbabel's mission to build the Temple (4:6b–10a; 6:12). For his generation, Zerubbabel is the "Branch" who fulfills the role of the descendant of David who acts wisely in governing his people (3:8; 6:12; cf. Jer 23:5). Nevertheless, the priest sits on his right, and the perfect healing peace (Hebrew: *shalom*) comes to the people through the cooperative reign of David's son and the Zadokite priest (6:13; cf. 8:16, 19; cf. Hg 2:9).

By an act of ritual purification, God invests Joshua as his high priest (3:1–10). God rebukes the accuser (Hebrew: *satan*) in the heavenly court and comes to Joshua's defense. When he takes off his dirty (impure) clothes and dresses in splendid robes, Joshua symbolizes the transformation God will bring about for the whole people (3:1–5). However, the Lord speaks exclusively to Joshua and his successors in the priesthood when he designates them as the ones who will watch over the Temple (3:7, 9a).

These texts of Zechariah prepare for a historical transition of leadership in Judah. Some scholars think Zechariah indicates that Joshua succeeded Zerubbabel as leader in Judah. Whether he did or not, either in their generation or shortly afterward, the high priesthood became the office of greatest authority in Judah and more or less maintained its position for almost six centuries until the destruction of the Temple in A.D. 70 by the Roman armies. The Zadokite priests administered the Temple from its founding (1 Kgs 1:38–40) until the Exile (Ez 40:46; 44:15–31) and then from the time of restoration (Ezr 7:1–5) until the second century B.C.

Toward the New Testament: Witnesses to the Heavenly Kingdom

The visions of Zechariah provided a prophetic introduction to the technique of apocalyptic literature, which interprets events in the present world by reference to what is taking place in heaven. We find an indication of the durability of Zechariah's symbols in the fact that John the elder of Ephesus uses some of them to express his inspired vision of God's work during the persecution under the Roman Emperor Domitian around A.D. 95. We will devote our attention to his description of the two witnesses in the book of Revelation and conclude with a brief reference to the importance of the Temple lamp-stand (Rv 11:1–13).

In Revelation, the prophet is the surveyor who will measure the Temple (Rv 11:1–2; cf. Zec 2:5–9; Ez 40:3–42:20). The Temple in Revelation, like the city in Zechariah, stands for the restored people of God. At this juncture in Revelation, the Temple symbolizes the Church (cf. 2 Cor 6:16; Eph 2:19–22; 1 Pt 2:5). The surveyor excludes those who inhabit the court of the Gentiles because they belong to the unbelieving world that profanes the Church by a persecution of a limited duration (Rv 11:1–2).

The forty-two months or 1,260 days (only half the perfect number of seven years) is the symbolic duration of persecution (Rv 11:2; Dn 7:25; cf. 4:13). During this time, God raises up the two witnesses symbolized by the two olive trees. This recalls the two olive trees that the book of Zechariah uses as images of Joshua the priest and Zerubbabel the descendant of King David (Rv 11:4; cf. Zec 4:1–14). The two Christian witnesses' association with the figures of Zerubbabel and Joshua indicates that God has given them a kingly (Davidic) and a priestly office. By surrendering their lives in the face of persecution, these two witnesses represent the Church martyred at the hands of the Roman Empire (Rv 11:7–10). They share in the resurrection of God's people and in an ascension like that of his prophet Elijah (Rv 11:11–13; cf. Ez 37:5, 10; 2 Kgs 2:11).

We cannot ascertain the precise identity of the two witnesses in Revelation (Rv 11:1–13). However, we do know that they represent the Church, which gives her life in faithful witness to Christ in a hostile world. The association of the witnesses with Zerubbabel and Joshua by way of the olive-tree image gives the witnesses a kingly and a priestly bearing. The combination of these qualities allows the two witnesses to represent the persecuted but faithful Church as a "kingdom of priests", a term of great importance in the biblical tradition (e.g., 1 Pt 2:9; Ex 19:5–6; cf. Zec 4:1–14).

Zechariah gives a greater priority to the lamp-stand in the Temple than we find in earlier books of the Bible (Zec 4:2; cf. Ex 25:31–40). He indicates that the lamp-stand is the most important element in the postexilic Temple, since the ark of the covenant had disappeared when the Babylonians destroyed Solomon's Temple (2 Kgs 25:13–17). In the absence of the ark, the lamp-stand becomes the primary locus of God's presence in the Temple (Zec 4:2). The book of Revelation uses this lamp-stand as its chief symbol of the Church (Rv 1:20) and thereby indicates that those who believe in Jesus reflect God's light to the world (cf. Mt 5:14–16; Phil 2:15).

In considering the messages of Haggai and Zechariah, we have encountered the people of Judah restoring the Temple. The teaching of Trito-Isaiah will enable us to see how ministry developed in the decades immediately following the dedication of the restored Temple.

STUDY QUESTIONS

1. What was the situation in Jerusalem immediately after the Exile was over?

2. What are four messages of Haggai?

3. What is the primary effect of the Lord's glory present in the Temple?

4. How does Zechariah use visionary symbols to show that God was restoring his people?

5. What is the significance of the two olive trees and the lamp-stand in Zechariah? in the book of Revelation?

6. What role does Zerubbabel fulfill?

7. Have you experienced a personal exile (job, marriage, school, friendships)? What did you do to restore your life, particularly your life of faith, when the exile was over?

8. Discuss how we never have to be in exile from God if we maintain a daily prayer life regardless of our external circumstances or the contingencies of life.

9. What is the Promised Land that you seek? What are the deepest desires of your heart? What would it take for you to feel you are at home, at peace, satisfied? Discuss how you must go beyond the particulars of your desires to see that the Promised Land is the Kingdom of God.

10. How can Haggai and Zechariah help us become aware that God must be first in our lives? How can they awaken us to our responsibility to take an active role in supporting our local church?

HAGGAI

ZECHARIAH 1–8

TRITO–ISAIAH AND MALACHI:
PROPHETS OF GOD'S NEW ORDER

The momentum of renewal among God's people is difficult to sustain after the early times of exciting changes. Initial enthusiasm becomes tempered by disappointment that the new order does not live up to our idealistic expectations. Prophets are necessary not just to initiate a new beginning but also to support God's people later when they struggle and sometimes give in to their own tendencies to fall back into self-serving patterns of life. We discover two such prophets in Trito-Isaiah and Malachi, who came to revivify their people when they were in danger of losing God's vision of restoration. Let us meet them by considering the times in which they served.

The repatriated exiles were dogged by drought, crop failures, and harassment from Syria. Completion of the second Temple took them twenty-three years. Not long after completing the restored Temple and dedicating it in March or April 515 B.C., the people realized that they were not going to attain their dream of a renaissance of the golden era under David and Solomon when the first Temple was built in the tenth century B.C. First, scarcity of materials, lack of manpower, and economic depression necessitated the erection of a bare and simple copy that could not hope to compare with the grandeur of the original. Secondly, because the Davidic line had practically faded into oblivion, there would no longer be an association between the king and the Temple. Hopes for the resurgence of the Davidic monarchy evaporated once Zerubbabel withdrew from public life sometime before 515 B.C. This last descendant of David had been an appointee of the Persians, and they certainly had no intention of allowing a ruling dynasty to reemerge in Judah.

The king's magnificent palace (1 Kgs 7:1–12), which Solomon built along with the Temple (1 Kgs 6:1–38; 7:15–51), was also gone forever, but there was no one to live in it anyway. The end of the monarchy heightened the importance of the Temple and of the priesthood in Judah. In the preexilic days, the people were joined together by their identification with the king.

Now, after the Exile, their sole locus of unity was the Temple, which became the exclusive domain of the priests.

The people of Judah would never again be the sovereign rulers of their own land. Throughout the next six centuries, they would be a vassal state under the successive hegemonies of the Persians, the Greeks, and finally the Romans. Because they lacked political independence, their distinctiveness as a people had to arise from religious grounds.

Since their governing regents were appointees of foreign powers, the Jews looked to the ranks of the priests to lead them as the people of God (see Zec 3:1–10). Everyone acknowledged that life in Jerusalem would be very different after the Exile from what it had been before. Disillusionment had so overtaken their dreams of idealism that most of the returnees were lowering their expectations and devoting their energies to the basic struggle to survive and attain some form of individual security in the land.

The missions of Trito-Isaiah and Malachi marked the high points of Jerusalem's history in the half-century between the dedication of the second Temple (515 B.C.) and the arrival of Ezra (458 B.C.). Although these two prophets labored in different decades from one another, they both exhibited a zeal for the Temple and a capacity to raise the people's sights by proclaiming God's exalted vision for life in postexilic Jerusalem. Each in his unique way called the people to repentance in view of God's promise for Judah.

TRITO-ISAIAH (ISAIAH 56–66)

Tradition was perhaps the most precious ingredient for Judah's reconstruction after the Exile. The bearers of tradition were primarily priests and prophets. The descendants of the Zadokite priests and of the Levites were among the first to return to the land (Ezr 2:36–54; 3:2). Foremost among their contemporaries from the prophetic circles were the disciples of the venerable Isaian tradition. The followers of Deutero-Isaiah must have responded quickly to their leader's call to return to Judah and build the new Zion (Is 49:8–26; 51:1–52:12; 54:1–17).

Scholarly convention gives the name "Trito-Isaiah" to their leader, an anonymous prophet who was a disciple of Deutero-Isaiah. In accordance with his mentor's instructions, Trito-Isaiah labored in Jerusalem during the time of resettlement and rebuilding of the Temple, perhaps for the quarter century between 525 and 500 B.C. By this estimation, in the early days of his mission, Trito-Isaiah was a contemporary of Haggai and Zechariah, but his career had a longer duration than theirs. We note that he shared with them a zeal for the reconstruction of the Temple (56:5; 60:13; 61:4; 62:9).

Concern for specific institutions, such as the Temple and the Sabbath

(56:2–6; 58:13–14), and for devotional practices, such as prayer (56:7) and fasting (cf. 58:1–12), distinguishes Isaiah 56–66 from Isaiah 40–55, which describes the renewal of Jerusalem in more general terms. Although there is a certain continuity of spirit linking the two collections, the vocabulary, style, and message of Isaiah 56–66 are distinctive from Isaiah 40–55. Each of these sections addresses a different situation. Isaiah 40–55 speaks to the refugees in the land of Babylon just before the end of the Exile (40:1–48:22) and in the early years after the liberation by Cyrus (49:1–55:13). Isaiah 56–66 speaks to the people who have returned to Judah in the early decades of resettlement. The two collections exhibit a variation in concern that indicates that they are dealing with at least two distinct situations. For example, Isaiah 40–55 emphasizes the consolation God extends to his people (40:1–11), while Isaiah 56–66 includes God's reprimands of his people's idolatry (57:3–13) and infidelity (63:7–65:25). Again, Deutero-Isaiah's focus on the foreign monarch Cyrus as God's agent (45:1–7; 48:12–15) differs in tone from the attention Trito-Isaiah devotes to God's judgment on the nations that have opposed his people (63:1–6).

Isaiah 56–66 represents a collection of diverse material that editors arranged according to three major themes: (1) the renewal of Jerusalem, which will take place through heartfelt repentance (56:1–59:21); (2) the glory of the Lord, which is about to overshadow the people and is the source of their new life (60:1–62:12); and (3) God's re-creation of his people through judgment and promise (63:1–66:24).

Mention of righteous foreigners entering the Temple provides the overarching theme at the beginning (56:1–7) and at the end (66:19–23) of the collection. The final arrangement of the material highlights the central section, which describes the divine glory rising over Jerusalem (60:1–62:12). Precisely at the midpoint of this section and of the whole collection, we find the description of the prophet's mission (61:1–11).

A number of indications within the text suggest that disciples of Trito-Isaiah edited the collection (56:1–66:24) not long after 500 B.C. For instance, the criticism of Judah's leaders (56:10–12) addresses a situation after the missions of Zerubbabel and Joshua, perhaps in the period between 515 and 505 B.C. The mention of the "holy Spirit" (63:10–11) is unique among the prophetic books (it occurs elsewhere in the Old Testament but only in Psalm 51:11 [translated as "spirit of holiness"] and in Wisdom 1:5; 9:17). God's overturning the present world order in favor of a new creation represents an early form of apocalyptic writing (65:1–66:24). Finally, as we stated in our reflection on the original Isaiah, the final edition of the book of Isaiah (1:1–66:24) comes from the hand of a redactor who completed his work in Jerusalem after Ezra's mission, sometime between 450 and 400 B.C.

The Message of Trito-Isaiah

We will survey the proclamation of Trito-Isaiah by concentrating on three primary ingredients that he insists will constitute the renewed Jerusalem: (a) humility distinguishing the renewed people of God; (b) the glory of salvation and justice dawning upon Jerusalem; and (c) the prospect of a new heaven and a new earth shaping the future. Let us examine more closely these essential elements of renewal: humility, glory, and a new creation.

Humility: Trito-Isaiah was not apologetic for the rudimentary quality of Jerusalem's restorations. Instead, he perceived through the sparse environs of David's once-splendid city that humility is the primary quality the Lord desires in the people he is reviving (57:14–21). Why was this humility necessary? The arrogance of leaders who succeeded Zerubbabel and Joshua provoked God's judgment (56:10–57:2). Such counterfeit leadership opened the door to recurring idolatry (57:3–13), arid ritualism (66:3–4), and simple disobedience of the divine precepts (66:17). God alone is the "Exalted One", and he looks with mercy on a people who are lowly, contrite, and obedient to his word (57:15; 66:2). To such "servants" of his, the Lord promises an abundant life in the end, while the arrogant will suffer privation (65:13).

The Lord announces his preferential love for the righteous who are oppressed (57:1–2). He insists that fasting will be effective only if it is accompanied by a commitment to works of justice on behalf of the downtrodden (58:6–7). The real gloom that hangs over Jerusalem does not arise from its paltry renovations but from the villainy of the powerful (59:1–20; 64:5). Yahweh will form his renewed people out of the righteous who maintain their integrity in spite of affliction (60:20–21).

The people's experience of Yahweh's justice will consist in something more than improved social conditions. Trito-Isaiah asserts that a new and intimate relationship with God constitutes the essence of salvation. He employs three metaphors from family life to express the personal union God promises his people: (a) a father to his child (63:16–17; 64:7), (b) a mother to her nursing infant (66:12–13), and (c) a bridegroom to his bride (62:4–5). As a variation on the same theme, he speaks of Jerusalem's becoming a mother to her children (66:10–11).

Glory: Renewal originates in God and consists in the revelation of his glory. By making the divine glory the centerpiece of his theology, Trito-Isaiah expands the richness of Temple spirituality and the whole Isaian tradition. The Temple was always considered the place where the Lord manifested the glory he had first revealed in the Exodus and covenant at Sinai (1 Kgs 8:11; Ex

16:10; 24:16–17; 40:34–35). Isaiah's encounter with Yahweh's glory in the sanctuary was the essential ingredient of his call to be a prophet (Is 6:3). Deutero-Isaiah developed the theme further two hundred years later when he spoke of the Lord's glory being revealed in the deliverance of his people from their Babylonian captivity (40:5; 48:11). Now, after the return to Judah, Trito-Isaiah brings the tradition to a climax by announcing the revelation of the Lord's glory over all of Jerusalem (60:1–2).

For Trito-Isaiah, the divine glory manifests the light of God's saving justice, which overcomes and dispels the darkness arising from man's unrighteousness (58:8, 10; 59:9, 19; 62:1–2). The Lord reveals his glory specifically in the work of salvation by which he restores his people. Again, the image of light overcoming darkness in Trito-Isaiah represents the climax of a central theme that had developed in the Isaian tradition over the course of two and a half centuries (see 2:5; 9:1; 42:6; 49:6; 60:1, 3, 20).

The prophet experiences his call as a commission in line with the Servant Songs (61:1–3; cf. 42:1–9; 46:1–7; 50:4–11; 52:13–53:12). The Lord bids him proclaim the saving work he is about to accomplish in Jerusalem. Trito-Isaiah is the new servant anointed with the spirit of Yahweh (61:1; cf. 42:1) to release the downtrodden of Judah from their despondency and to herald the jubilee year when all debts will be cancelled and the land restored to its rightful owners (61:2–3; cf. Lv 25:8–17). The people will express boundless joy in response to the announcement of salvation and to the revelation of the Lord's glory (61:7, 10–11). Out of such joy, they will restore their cities and towns that have lain in ruins for decades past (61:4).

As Jerusalem begins to reflect the Lord's glory, she will gain the attention of nations who will make their way to her in search of salvation (60:2–3; 62:2). Trito-Isaiah's inspired vision of peoples from all over the world streaming to Jerusalem to worship in the Lord's presence provides the conclusion to the whole book (66:18–23; 60:1–7; cf. Zec 8:20–23). Here we find a perception of God's universal offer of salvation. Furthermore, according to Trito-Isaiah, not only will converted foreigners enter the Temple but also they will even serve there in the ranks of the priests and Levites (66:21; cf. 56:3–7). This vision corresponds with the prophet's conviction that all who participate in the work of renewal will make up a priestly people (61:5–6; cf. Ex 19:3–6).

The New Creation: Trito-Isaiah foresees that what God is doing is nothing less than the foreshadowing of a new creation in which the new life of joy and gladness overtakes the old life of suffering and sorrow. Deutero-Isaiah's apprehension of the Lord as both Creator and Redeemer provides the background for his disciple's announcement that God is bringing forth "new heavens and a new earth" (65:17; 66:22; cf. 40:26; 43:1, 7; 45:8). The renewal in Jerusalem that began with redemption from the Exile now becomes a sign pointing to the future new creation of the cosmos (65:17; 66:22; cf. 43:18–19).

To his audience who are undergoing the stress of life in postexilic Jerusalem, Trito-Isaiah offers the prospect of pure joy as the identifying characteristic of life in the new creation. The manner in which God will bring about this new creation is so remarkable that the prophet likens it to giving birth without labor pains (66:7–14). So great will be the transformation of Jerusalem and her offspring that when the Lord reveals his glory, the city shall be "Joy" and the people "Gladness" (65:18).

Trito-Isaiah's conviction of God's breaking into history to create a radically new order that will replace an old one contributed to the emergence of apocalyptic literature over the course of the following centuries. The Isaian tradition continued to develop in the prophetic circles that followed in the generations after Trito-Isaiah. This prophetic tradition produced apocalyptic texts of a distinctly Isaian character that are the latest compositions in the whole book (Is 24:1–27:13). The final editors of Isaiah placed these texts in the first section of the book immediately after the judgments on the nations (13:1–23:18) and before the Lord's instructions to Jerusalem (28:1–35:10) because they show that in the end time, God will invert the order of the present world. The Isaian apocalyptic texts declare that God will replace the old order, which was dominated by human power (represented by the nations), with a new order of divine life (represented by the holy mountain of Jerusalem).

The "Isaian Apocalypse" (Is 24:1–27:13) stretches our sights beyond the time frame of Trito-Isaiah's vision to contemplate the final end of all existence. Drawing upon prophets such as Jeremiah and Ezekiel, its author uses the images of Yahweh destroying the city to announce the ultimate collapse of the world order under the judgment of God (24:1–23). Then, carrying on the spirit of Trito-Isaiah, he describes the new order in terms of the Lord's reconstruction of the city in which the lowly will be victorious (25:1–5; 26:1–6). Again, he carries a theme from Trito-Isaiah to its ultimate extent when he describes all nations coming to feast at the heavenly banquet on the Lord's holy mountain (25:6–12). Having considered how Trito-Isaiah influenced the prophetic tradition after him, we can reflect on the role his instruction played in forming a vision for life in the Christian communities.

Toward the New Testament: The Good News for the Poor

In the New Testament, the texts of Trito-Isaiah provide the agenda for Jesus' ministry and support the understanding of the Church as a body comprised of lowly people from both Jewish and gentile backgrounds.

In the Gospel of Luke, Jesus' first words in his public ministry consist of his reading the text of Trito-Isaiah describing the prophet's mission (Lk 4:18–19; cf. Is 61:1–2). Jesus came to fulfill this mission in a manner that was impossible for Trito-Isaiah. The holy Spirit (Is 63:10–11; cf. 61:1) as mentioned by Trito-Isaiah is an aspect of Yahweh's character but only a foreshadowing of the personal Holy Spirit the Father communicated to the Son at his baptism (Lk 3:21–22).

Jesus' ministry supersedes and opens up the prophecy of Trito-Isaiah not only through his anointing by the Holy Spirit but also by his healing the blind, an activity Trito-Isaiah does not mention (Lk 18:35–43; cf. Is 61:1–2). Yet, in the other works of healing, Jesus fulfills all that Trito-Isaiah foresaw so as to constitute proof to John the Baptist that indeed he is "the one who is to come" (Lk 7:18–23; Mt 11:2–6; cf. Is 61:1; 29:18–21; 35:5–7).

Jesus appeals to another prophecy of Trito-Isaiah to support his action of cleansing the Temple. His insistence that the people appreciate the Temple as God's house and a place of prayer reflects Trito-Isaiah's vision that the restored Temple was more than a place of sacrifice. Trito-Isaiah knew that God desired it to be a place where people from all nations would worship him. As he drives the merchants out of the sacred precincts, Jesus quotes Trito-Isaiah to indicate that he is bringing the Temple to its prophetic destiny (Mk 11:15–17; Mt 21:12–13; Lk 19:45–46; cf. Is 56:7).

In the Gospel of John, when Jesus declares that he has other sheep who are not of the Jewish flock, he echoes the words Yahweh spoke through Trito-Isaiah (Jn 10:16; cf. Is 56:8). In the Old Testament passage, Yahweh declares his intention to welcome people from the nations of the world to join the citizens of Judah in worship at the Temple. Jesus fulfills this divine plan by laying down his life to bring Gentiles into union with the Jews as members of his one flock, which is the Church (Jn 11:52; 17:20–21; cf. Is 56:7–8; 49:6).

In the Letter to the Romans, Paul quotes another passage of Trito-Isaiah to support his conviction that the manner in which the Gospel is spreading shows that God is offering salvation to all peoples, Gentiles as well as Jews (Rom 10:20–21; cf. Is 65:1–2). Trito-Isaiah was referring to the stubborn populace in postexilic Judah when he described God allowing himself to be found by people who did not seek him (65:1) and reaching out to a rebellious people (65:2). However, when Paul quotes the texts, he applies the first verse to the gentile Christians as those who found the Lord Jesus without seeking him (Rom 10:20; cf. Is 65:1) and the second verse to his Jewish brethren who have so far refused to accept the Gospel of Christ and thus are proving themselves to be a "rebellious people" (Rom 10:21; cf. Is 65:2).

In spite of their present resistance to the Gospel, the Jews maintain a primary role as God's people according to the apostle. Paul concludes his exposition of God's plan of salvation for all people (Rom 9:1–11:36) by quoting Trito-Isaiah once again to demonstrate the abiding importance of the Jews (Rom 11:26; cf. Is 59:20–21). To the repentant citizens of postexilic Judah, Trito-Isaiah announced the coming of a Redeemer to deliver Zion, who will always remain God's covenant partner (Is 59:20–21). Paul offers an inspired rereading of the text in order to highlight the role of Jewish people in God's plan. According to the apostle's teaching, the Redeemer will come from (not "for") Zion, and he will deliver the Jews from all godlessness by opening their hearts to receive the Gospel (Rom 11:26–27; see 11:25–32). These few lines summarize Paul's conviction that the Jews always remain central to God's plan. They have given the world the Messiah, Jesus the Lord, and God will bring them into the life of the Gospel in fulfillment of all his promises to them.

In addition, we note that Trito-Isaiah provides the background not only for the vision of the Church but also for the interior life of each Christian. The beatitudes Jesus announces in the Gospel of Luke echo the promises of Yahweh to his lowly people who suffer injustice and trial stemming from the difficulties of life in Jerusalem during its postexilic restoration (Lk 6:20–23; cf. Is 65:13–14). Jesus builds on the prophetic vision of God's preferential love for the lowly (Is 57:14–21) when he announces that those who are destitute in the present world will possess the Kingdom of heaven (Lk 6:20–23; cf. 16:19–31). Along the same line of thought, Trito-Isaiah's admonition concerning the priority of caring for the poor foreshadows Matthew's portrait of the final judgment when the Son of Man will separate the sheep from the goats according to how each person served the destitute and marginalized in human society (Mt 25:31–46; cf. Is 58:6–8).

Mary, the mother of Jesus, is the model disciple who assumed the qualities of humility and reliance on God characteristic of the poor (Hebrew: 'anawim), in the biblical sense of the term. Her song of praise echoes the joy of the Lord's servant clothed with the garments of salvation (Lk 1:46–55; cf. Is 61:10). By the grace of Christ, every Christian can dress in the clothes of righteousness that Yahweh dons symbolically when he comes to renew his people (1 Thes 5:8; Eph 6:14–17; cf. Is 59:17).

MALACHI

Malachi offers us an indication of Jerusalem's conditions perhaps a quarter-century after the mission of Trito-Isaiah. "Malachi" in Hebrew simply means "my messenger". Is it the actual name of a prophet (1:1) or a title describing the office of an anonymous figure (3:1) whom God sends to instruct his people? Although the Septuagint (Greek) translator interpreted the word as a title, we will take it as the personal name of the prophet. "Malachi" makes a play on his own name when announcing Yahweh's promise to send "my messenger" to herald his coming to the Temple (3:1).

We know nothing about Malachi other than what we can garner from his teaching. His preoccupation with the Temple and concern for the standards of ritual and sacrifice (1:6–2:9) relate him directly to Haggai (Hg 1:1–11; 2:10–14) and Zechariah (Zec 3:1–4:14). However, the manner in which Malachi refers to the Temple provides clear evidence that he undertook his ministry after the Temple's dedication in 515 B.C. and therefore well after Haggai and Zechariah had completed their missions. Malachi's preoccupation with divorce in Judah and marriage with foreigners (2:10–16) provides another clue to dating his ministry. The family issues he dealt with were similar to those of Ezra and Nehemiah (Ezr 9:1–10:44; Neh 13:23–27). Therefore, Malachi must have exercised his ministry in Jerusalem prior to the reforms of Ezra and Nehemiah. While it is impossible to be absolutely certain, a reasonable conjecture would date Malachi's mission around 475 B.C., well after the reconstruction of the Temple but before the arrival of Ezra and Nehemiah.

The structure of the book consists of six pronouncements: (1) the Lord loves Israel (1:1–5); (2) the priests have been unfaithful to their office by relaxing the standards relating to sacrificial offerings and teaching (1:6–2:9); (3) the Lord opposes divorce and marriage with foreigners (2:10–16); (4) the Lord will come to purify his Temple and the Levites (2:17–3:5); (5) a return to honest tithing at the Temple will bring prosperity (3:6–12); and (6) those who fear the Lord will receive salvation on the day of judgment (3:13–21). A later editor added the two appendices, one referring to Moses (3:22) and the other to Elijah (3:23–24).

It is difficult to estimate when the book of Malachi received its present form. It seems that either the prophet or a scribe who listened to him wrote the text of his pronouncements (1:1–3:21). We note that Malachi (1:1) begins with the same heading in Hebrew (*massa'*: "a message" or "a proclamation") as the two sections of Deutero-Zechariah (Zec 9:1; 12:1). This arrangement seems to be the work of the final editor of the collection of the prophets, who completed his labor well over a century after Malachi's mission.

The Message of Malachi

Malachi was a perceptive teacher who exposed and then challenged the mentality of the people. Each of his discourses takes the form of a debate that begins with an illustration of the darkened human heart attempting to justify its spiritual complacency and lack of zeal for God and his commands. He quotes the people directly ("You ask . . . " or "You say . . . ": 1:7, 13; 2:17; 3:7, 13) and then corrects them with a prophetic response. Spiritual aridity has dessicated Malachi's audience. For them, God is distant and indifferent. They lack awareness of his fatherly love (1:6–7) and respect for his authority to judge between right and wrong (2:17). Thus, they reduce their religious practice to monotonous ritual (1:13) that reflects lives almost devoid of personal reverence (3:14).

Malachi strives to develop the spiritual sensitivities of his people. He cultivates in them a sense of three ingredients essential to the life of faith: reverence, fidelity, and divine judgment.

Reverence: Contemplating the prosperity of the arrogant has led the people to surrender their appreciation for the distinctions between vice and virtue, right and wrong, good and evil (2:17; 3:13–15). To those who have become cynical about God, Malachi proclaims Yahweh's abiding love for Israel, thus reflecting the theology of Hosea and Deuteronomy (1:2; cf. Hos 11:1; Dt 7:7–11). Again, drawing upon a Deuteronomic background, he insists that God is a Father to his people (1:6; 2:10; cf. Dt 1:31; 32:6).

People who relate to God as their Father will respond to his love by honoring him. Malachi invites his people to realize that their dignity and salvation consist in living in reverence of the Lord. Indeed, only those who stand in reverent awe (or "fear") of him will survive the test of Yahweh's visitation (3:16–21). They will experience, not destruction, but healing when he comes in judgment (3:20–21).

The faithful would express their reverence for the Lord in concrete acts of offering the best of their flocks in sacrifice at the Temple (cf. 1:6–14) and in paying their full tithes (3:6–12). But the quality of his people's worship has sunk so low as to provoke Malachi to assert that pagans throughout the world are exhibiting greater reverence for the Lord than the people of Judah (1:11, 14). He comes to issue a call to repentance (3:7).

Fidelity: Judah's foremost sin is infidelity to God in covenants of two kinds, one pertaining to the exercise of the Levitical priesthood and the other to the state of marriage. Malachi reprimands the Levites for their laxity in overseeing the sacrificial offerings at the Temple (1:6–14) and for their negligence in providing the people with instruction in the Law (2:1–9). By accepting as Temple offerings what was blemished and useless to those who brought them (1:6–14), the priests have contributed to the people's lack of reverence for God. Furthermore, because of their lack of dedication to the word of God, the Levites have deprived the people of sound teaching that would call them to holiness of life (2:1–9). The Levites will be the first to experience the fires of purification from Yahweh's visitation to the Temple so that renewal can come to the people through them (3:1–5).

As the Levites had lost touch with the resources of God's covenant with them (2:4–6), so spouses were not living in fidelity to their marriage covenant (2:14–15). Young people were entering into marriage with pagans, taking no thought of the impact this would have on the integrity of their faith (2:10–12). Men were leaving their wives to whom they had been married for years (2:14). To provide proper perspective on marriage, Malachi appeals, not to the Deuteronomic legislation (Dt 24:1–4), but to God's original plan in creation (2:15; cf. Gn 2:24). Because a weakening of commitment to marriage mars God's creative intention, the prophetic word is abrupt and to the point, "I hate divorce, says Yahweh, God of Israel" (2:16).

Divine Judgment: Malachi takes up the theology of the "Day of Yahweh" that originated with Amos and applies it to the Lord's entering his Temple in order to purify his people (2:17–3:21). The fire of his holiness will mediate judgment that will consume the arrogant (3:19), refine the Levites (3:3), and heal those who fear his name (3:16–18, 20–21).

The later editor makes use of the prospect of the Lord's judgment to highlight the importance of observing the Law of Moses (3:22). Furthermore, he adds a new element to the vision of the end time by describing Elijah as the messenger who will come to heal family relationships and so preserve the people (3:23–24; cf. 3:1).

Toward the New Testament: Preparing a Way for the Lord

The evangelists saw in Malachi the foreshadowing of John the Baptist. The book's teaching on marriage provides an introduction to Jesus' instruction on the subject.

The Synoptic Gospels and Acts understand John the Baptist to be the messenger who comes to prepare the way for the Lord (Mt 11:10; Mk 1:2; Acts 13:24–25; cf. Mal 3:1). The background in Malachi allows us to appreciate that the Baptist's mission originates in heaven with God. He comes to purify the people by calling them to repent of their arrogance (Mt 3:8; cf. Mal 3:7) so that they will not be consumed when Jesus ushers in the final age by baptizing with fire and the Holy Spirit (Mt 3:12; Lk 3:17; cf. Mal 3:19). Jesus teaches his disciples that John the Baptist has fulfilled the mission of Elijah (Mt 17:10–13; Mk 9:11–13; cf. Mal 3:23–24; cf. Lk 1:17). The reason that he gives this instruction is to assure his disciples that his death and Resurrection herald the end time (cf. Mt 17:9; Mk 9:9–10).

Finally, we note that Malachi's inspiration to base his understanding of marriage on Genesis rather than on the Mosaic Code's permission of divorce (Dt 24:1–4) establishes the precedent for Jesus' teaching to the Church against divorce (Mt 19:3–9; cf. Mal 2:15–16).

We have observed how Malachi focused on the impending visitation of Yahweh in order to impress upon his people the urgency of responding to the prophetic call to repentance and renewal of life. We will detect an increasing fascination with the end time as we see Obadiah, Joel, and Deutero-Zechariah adopt a similar viewpoint.

STUDY QUESTIONS

1. How long did it take to complete the second Temple?
2. How does the text of Trito-Isaiah differ from that of Deutero-Isaiah?
3. What are three major themes of Trito-Isaiah?
4. What are the metaphors Trito-Isaiah uses to depict personal union with God?
5. What is the "Isaian Apocalypse"?
6. How does Jesus fulfill all that Trito-Isaiah foresaw?
7. How do the Jews maintain an important role as God's people according to Paul? What does he teach us about the importance of dialogue between Jews and Christians?
8. How do the beatitudes echo Trito-Isaiah?
9. What does Trito-Isaiah teach us about God's love for the lowly, the humble, and those who are struggling amid difficult circumstances?
10. What are three ingredients essential to a life of faith?
11. How is Malachi's understanding of marriage a precedent for Jesus' teaching?
12. Discuss the importance of integrating your "life decisions" (getting married, building a home, choosing an occupation) into your life of faith and worship.

ISAIAH 56–66

I. Renewal through Repentance (56:1–59:21)
    A. The New Temple: Open to Obedient Foreigners (56:1–8)
    B. Against Corrupt Leaders and Idolatry (56:9–57:13)
    C. The Exalted One Dwells with a Humble People (57:14–21)
    D. Genuine Fasting: Justice for the Oppressed (58:1–14)
    E. Psalm of Repentance: Yahweh's Justice (59:1–21)

II. The Glory of the New Jerusalem (60:1–62:12)
    A. Yahweh's Glory over Jerusalem (60:1–22)
    B. The Lord's New Servant (61:1–11)
    C. The New Jerusalem, Yahweh's Spouse (62:1–12)

III. Judgment and Promise (63:1–66:24)
    A. Yahweh Disciplines the Nations (63:1–6)
    B. Israel's History: The Father's Faithful Love (63:7–64:11)
    C. New Heavens and a New Earth (65:1–25)
    D. Judgment on and Promise to Jerusalem (66:1–17)
    E. Foreigners Come to Jerusalem (66:18–24)

MALACHI

28

OBADIAH AND JOEL: JUDGMENT AND SALVATION

If we are seriously concerned about the meaning of life, we try to make sense out of the history of our time. Often when we contemplate the global balance of power, the people who try to follow God faithfully seem very insignificant when compared to the great nations that appear to control the world's destiny. Indeed, the communities of those who trust in the Lord appear to struggle and suffer, while powerful international forces succeed in shaping history. Yet, if we are people of faith, then inside our hearts we know that God's designs for his people are more important than anything else. However, we are confused because we do not know how to read "the signs of the times" (cf. Mt 16:3 in 16:1–4). This is a prophetic skill that enables a person to discern which events are really important because they reveal how God is working in history. Obadiah and Joel are two prophets who can show us what it means to read the signs of the times. In order to appreciate their wisdom, we must first survey the history of Judah and the Persian Empire during their times in the fifth century B.C.

We can divide Judah's history in the fifth century B.C. (500–400 B.C.) into two contrasting parts, with Ezra's arrival (458 B.C./Ezr 7:1–8:36) providing the point of demarcation between them. Prior to Ezra, Jerusalem went through an extended period of spiritual stagnation, but Ezra, the great priest and scribe, set Judah on a whole new course of reform that transformed its life during the second half of the century.

The scarcity of data about what went on in Jerusalem from the dedication of the second Temple (515 B.C.) until the arrival of Ezra (458 B.C.) and Nehemiah (445 B.C.) suggests that this was a period marked by uncertainty. In spite of Zechariah's highlighting the primacy of the priesthood, Ezra was the first great leader since Joshua (Zec 3:1–10) to emerge from the ranks of the priests (Ezr 7:1–10:44; Neh 8:1–18). Again, until Ezra brought the materials from Persia (Ezr 7:13–20; 8:24–35), the reconstructed Temple remained a rather bare form lacking the finishing touches of artistic design and precious liturgical utensils and bowls. According to the census list in Ezra-Nehemiah, Judah's population numbered about 50,000 (Ezr 2:64–65 = Neh 7:66–67).

While they were growing in numbers, these people required the imagination, spiritual vigor, and stamina that Ezra and Nehemiah provided in order to undertake a prophetic rebuilding of Zion that would reflect the prophetic vision expressed by Zechariah, Trito-Isaiah, and Malachi.

The Persian Empire

During the fifth century B.C., the Persian Empire reached its zenith and dominated the world. The administrative and legislative genius of Darius I (522–486 B.C.) expanded the imperial frontiers eastward to the Indus River (in modern day Pakistan), northward to the Aral, Caspian, and Black Seas (in southern U.S.S.R.), and westward across Asia Minor up to the Aegean Sea and across northern Egypt as far as Banghazi (in what is now Libya). Persian architecture and engineering was immortalized in the construction of the magnificent capital at Persepolis.

Darius' only failure in a military campaign occurred in his renowned conflict with the Greek city-states. In 490 B.C., the vastly outnumbered Athenian forces turned back the Persian invaders on the Plains of Marathon. This marked the first episode of tensions between Persia and Greece that would escalate under the rule of Darius' son Xerxes I (486–465 B.C.), then lessen under his successor Artaxerxes I (465–423 B.C.) only to develop again over another century until Alexander the Great (336–323 B.C.) emerged from Macedonia to overtake the Persian Empire.

Darius manifested the Persian aptitude for government by organizing the empire into twenty satrapies. Each area came under the rule of a satrap who had his own court but who, in turn, also remained under the surveillance of his administrative secretary, finance minister, and military commander, each of whom was directly answerable to the king. As a further precaution against unbridled ambition and disloyalty in his appointees, the monarch commissioned an inspector (called "the king's eye") to make an annual tour through the provinces watching out for any signs of insurrection.

Yehud (Judah) was one of the territories of the fifth satrapy, called *Abar Nahara* ("Beyond the River": referring to its position on the western side of the Euphrates but east of Egypt, which was the sixth satrapy). The Persian system of government opened a free network of trade and communication across the Near Eastern world. This brought advantages and disadvantages to the spiritual life of God's people. The streamlined system made it easier for the descendants of the exiles to return with Ezra to their ancestral home in Judah. At the same time, the pervasive Persian rule threatened to infiltrate and vitiate the uniqueness of the Jewish culture.

Two aspects of their situation threatened to undermine the distinctiveness of the Jews. First, the Jews were not the only ones to settle in Judah. On returning from exile, they encountered elements of an indigenous population that had grown up in the land after the destruction of Jerusalem along with neighboring people from Samaria, Edom, and more distant regions of the Empire (Ezr 9:1–10:44; Neh 2:19; 6:1–14). Secondly, only a portion of the Jews expressed interest in returning to Jerusalem. Jewish settlements were now cropping up in far-flung areas of the world such as Babylon, Asia Minor, and Egypt. The most salient example of decentralization and, thus, dilution of orthodoxy was the building of a Jewish temple some distance up the Nile River at Elephantine. The establishment of this temple in contrast to the one in Jerusalem indicates a transition was taking place in Judaism that confirmed the suspicions of the prophets in Jerusalem concerning the influence of other nations on Jewish faith and worship.

Those other nations were indeed exerting both political and cultural influence over Judah and her people, who were scattered throughout the Persian Empire in the Diaspora. This situation brought to the surface a question nagging the hearts of God's people, who were conscious of belonging to a cosmopolitan empire. Does God really have a plan for Judah? How does the destiny of his people compare with that of other nations, especially Israel's ancient foes? How is it possible that God could favor the tiny territory of Yehud in the midst of the vast world empire that embraced a variety of nations far more imposing in stature?

Obadiah and Joel were two prophets inspired to discern the Lord's plan for his people in relationship to his dealings with other nations. Both of these prophets took as their theological focus the impending Day of Yahweh (see Am 5:18–20) and formulated a vision of history by interpreting their situation in view of the end time, when God would act with definitive judgment and salvation. They share in common the conviction that those who live on Mount Zion will experience salvation at the time of judgment (Ob v. 17 in Jl 3:5). Both of these prophets exercised their ministries in the fifth century. Joel came on the scene at the end of the century after the reforms of Ezra and Nehemiah. It is almost impossible to date Obadiah with precision, but, since Joel quotes him, we know that Obadiah predates him. This allows us to suggest that Obadiah issued his oracle in the earlier part of the century.

OBADIAH

The book of Obadiah is the only source of evidence we have for the prophet's ministry. Therefore, we must first survey the contents of this short text in the collection of the minor prophets in order to glean the barest evidence about Obadiah and his times.

The book of Obadiah is a prophetic "vision" of history that interprets God's plan for Israel in view of his dealings with Edom (v. 1). The prophecy consists of two parts, the first announcing Yahweh's judgment on Edom (vv. 1–15) and the second proclaiming the salvation of Zion (vv. 16–18). An appendix, perhaps from a later hand, describes the full extension of Israel's frontiers in the end time after God completes his final work (vv. 19–21).

The character of Obadiah's message as a pronouncement against Edom relates the text to a whole series of oracles voiced by prophets of various times against Israel's neighbor to the south on the far side of the Dead Sea (Am 1:11–12; Jer 49:7–22; Ez 25:12–14; 35:1–15; Is 34:5–17; 63:1–3; Mal 1:2–4). The parallels between Obadiah and Jeremiah have led some scholars to propose that the prophecy originated in the years prior to Jerusalem's destruction (Ob vv. 1–4/Jer 49:14–16; Ob v. 5/Jer 49:9; Ob v. 6/Jer 49:10). However, evidence within Obadiah demands that we date the oracle sometime after the fall of Jerusalem in 587 B.C. (Ob v. 11).

Our problem in dating Obadiah stems from the fact that we cannot determine with precision the historical event of Edom's desolation that provoked the prophet to announce his oracle. We recall that Malachi's first prophecy spoke of Edom's recent desolation in comparison with Israel's grace of endurance (Mal 1:2–4). Both Malachi and Obadiah reflect on a tragic experience for Edom. Are both prophets thinking about the identical event? If so, was it an attack by the Babylonians in the late seventh or early sixth century (Jer 49:7–22; Ez 32:29)? If they are not thinking of the same event, could Obadiah be thinking of the Nabataeans driving the Edomites from their ancestral territory in the Greek era prior to 300 B.C.? We are convinced that we must date Obadiah after the fall of Jerusalem and most probably after the end of the Exile (538 B.C.). While we admit the possibility of other options, we will date his prophecy sometime in the middle of the fifth century (475–425 B.C.). Either the prophet or a later editor probably added the final lines (Ob vv. 19–21) during the reforms of Ezra and Nehemiah.

While a particular event of destruction has turned Obadiah's gaze toward the pathos of Edom, his oracle reviews a much broader historical scope encompassing the long history of Edom's relations with Israel. The people of Edom were the descendants of Esau, the twin brother of Jacob, who was the father of Israel (Gn 25:19–28; 36:1–8). The stormy rivalry between Jacob and

Esau serves as a prelude to the tensions that perennially characterized the relationship between the two nations (Gn 27:1–45; cf. 33:1–17). Friction became manifest early in the days of the Exodus, when the king of Edom refused Moses and his people the right to pass through his territory on their way northward to the plains of Moab (Nm 20:14–21). After the Israelites settled in Canaan, they invaded Edom during some of their intermittent military excursions in the Transjordan. Saul conquered the Edomites among others in his early military expeditions across Israel's eastern frontier (1 Sm 14:47). During the century and a half between 875 and 725 B.C., Judah alternately ruled (2 Kgs 14:7, 22; cf. 1 Kgs 22:48) and surrendered control of Edom (2 Kgs 8:20–21; 2 Chr 28:17).

After 587 B.C., Edom became a source of deep resentment for the exiles, who recalled the Edomites supporting the Babylonians when they destroyed Jerusalem (Ps 137:7; Lam 4:21–22). It seems to be over a century later, when Edom came upon hard times, that Obadiah recalled this instance of Edom's betrayal of brotherhood with Jacob (Ob vv. 10–14; cf. Jer 27:2–3, 6).

The Message of Obadiah

Obadiah directs his attention to Edom in view of a specific historical event (vv. 1–15), but he does so in such a manner as to extend his concern both geographically to include all nations and historically to describe the end time (vv. 16–18). Edom represents all the foreign powers of the world. The destruction of Edom prefigures God's judgment of the nations in the Day of Yahweh. Israel's survival in the face of his kinsman's desolation foreshadows Yahweh's ultimate vindication of Zion in the time of salvation.

The oracle belongs in the category of the prophetic words against the nations (see Is 13–23; Jer 46–51; Ez 25–32). Obadiah's creativity shines through in his employment of the Day of Yahweh theme to distinguish between the Lord's promise of salvation to Israel and of judgment to the nations (cf. Zep 1:14–18; Jl 2:1–11).

Obadiah communicates a number of truths vital to the life of faith. First, Obadiah reinterprets the earlier prophetic tradition in which he asserts that the Day of Yahweh will bring about an inversion of the present world order. The earlier prophets Amos and Zephaniah foresaw divine retribution coming against Israel and Judah as other nations would conquer them (see Am 5:18–20; Zep 1:14–18). By contrast, Obadiah prophesies that, "on that Day", Yahweh will overthrow Israel's oppressors (v. 16) and will reveal his salvation to his own people (vv. 17–18). At a deeper level, the message concerns not so much the different destinies of nations but rather God's judgment of human arrogance and his vindication of the downtrodden. Edom's reputation for wisdom was a source of pride that only makes the nation more vulnerable to destruction (v. 8; cf. Jer 49:7). Ultimately, tyrants will suffer the effects of their own tyranny (Ob v. 15).

From beginning to end, Obadiah's vision announces that because Yahweh is the Lord of all history, he will bring his people salvation, while the nations will experience judgment (v. 21). The fact that Edom, the ancient brother of Israel, has become desolate while Judah continues to survive indicates that Yahweh has not withdrawn the grace of election from his people. To the people who inhabit the limited confines of Judah, Obadiah promises that the Lord will restore all the territories foreigners have occupied, and he will again unite ancient Israel (the "House of Joseph") and Judah (the "House of Jacob") (vv. 18–21). Obadiah portrays salvation in the end time in terms of the Lord restoring the Promised Land to his people.

Toward the New Testament: The Kingdom of the Poor

Although the New Testament writers do not cite Obadiah, as we read his book, we can detect a foreshadowing of two lessons central to the life of the Christian Church. First, his manner of describing the reversal of fortunes characteristic of the day of judgment allows Obadiah to foreshadow the Kingdom that Jesus announces in which the poor will reign while the haughty will experience desolation (see Lk 16:19–31; Mt 19:28). Obadiah's announcement of the futility of Edom's sages offers a prelude to Paul's castigation of the wise in the world in contradistinction to the wisdom of the cross (Ob v. 8; cf. 1 Cor 1:18–21).

Secondly, Obadiah provides a meditation on brotherhood, which is essential to relationships in the Christian community. The real tragedy at the root of Edom's destruction is the betrayal of brother by brother. Edom betrayed Israel by being an accomplice to Jerusalem's destruction (Ob vv. 10–14). The wounds of past rivalry never actually healed. Reading Obadiah should convince us that entire nations of the world need to receive the grace of reconciliation that Jesus Christ communicates most fully in the power of his cross (2 Cor 5:16–21). By describing the destructive effects of broken relationships, Obadiah can impress on us the urgency of responding to Jesus' demand that we be reconciled with one another, heal relationships, and live in community as brothers and sisters of one another (see Mt 5:21–26; 18:15–35). The prophet Joel will highlight for us another ingredient required for a new world order, namely, reception of the Lord's Spirit.

JOEL

All that we know for certain about Joel is that he was the son of Pethuel (1:1). He conveys an obvious love for the Temple and its spirituality in his concern for its priests and ministers (1:9, 13; 2:17) and in his conviction about the effectiveness of sacrificial offerings (1:9, 13) and fasts (1:14; 2:12, 15). The absence of any reference to either a king in Judah or to the Babylonians indicates that Joel carried out his ministry after the Exile and the dedication of the second Temple. Moreover, the fact that he does not have to correct disorder among the clergy or in family life suggests that he made his pronouncements after the reforms of Ezra and Nehemiah had taken effect. We date his mission around 400 B.C.

Like Obadiah, Joel announces his prophecies to interpret the meaning of a specific event. While Obadiah contemplates the destruction of Edom, Joel issues his oracles in response to a terrible plague of locusts that was ravaging the land of Judah (1:4–12; 2:3–9). Again, as in the case of Edom for Obadiah, we do not know precisely when the plague described in Joel took place. Once more, the exact date is unimportant because, after the fashion of Obadiah, Joel uses the particular event to elaborate a whole interpretation of history that focuses on the way God will overthrow the present state of the world when he comes to bring judgment and salvation on the Day of Yahweh (Jl 2:10–11; 3:4–5; 4:15–21; cf. Ob vv. 16–21).

The structure of the book of Joel is balanced between halves: the first (1:1–2:27) concerns the locust plague; and the second (3:1–4:21) focuses on the Day of Yahweh. The text artfully combines the halves by setting some of their components in parallel with each other: Joel parallels the invading army of locusts (2:1–11) with the nations of the world who enter into combat with the Lord (4:1–3, 9–17); the call to repentance (2:12–17) prepares Judah for the outpouring of Yahweh's spirit (3:1–5); and the Lord's restoration of the land (2:21–27) prefigures the final glory of Jerusalem (4:18–21).

The artistic symmetry of the book indicates that it comes from the hand of someone who shaped the prophet's words into a fine composition. The section mentioning specific peoples is a late addition (4:4–8). We can date the final edition of the book to the first half of the fourth century (400–350 B.C.).

The Message of Joel

Joel teaches us that liturgy provides the setting for revelation. In response to the plague of locusts, Joel assembles the people and leads them in worship and intercession. Within this experience of prayer, the people open their minds to apprehend the nature of the final Day of Yahweh. We will survey Joel's teaching by considering what a rite of reconciliation with God communicates about the Day of Yahweh.

A Rite of Reconciliation: As one who leads his people in prayer, Joel has a refined liturgical sense. He knows that a people suffering from natural calamity can best gain perspective on their lives by coming together in the presence of the Lord at the Temple. Once assembled, he leads them in lament, articulating the desolation experienced by the young and the old, the farmer and the priest (1:2–12). He summons them to fasting and prayer to enable them to express their grief and desire to repent from sin in the most genuine manner possible (1:13–20).

However, Joel does not allow the people to dwell on their temporal affliction. He wants them to realize what the Lord is teaching them through the scourge of the land. Yahweh instructs his people as he heals them. The plague of locusts is only a foreshadowing of the Day of Yahweh when the whole world will be consumed by divine judgment (2:1–11). If the locusts that sweep across the land in clouds so black as to obscure the sun are devastating, they are only a foreshadowing of the more awesome day when Yahweh will overshadow the world in judgment (2:2, 10–11).

This vision of the dark advent of God sets the stage for the prophet's call to a deep rending of the heart to replace a superficial regret of personal loss (2:12–17). To those who repent, the Lord comes, not as a foreboding judge, but as a merciful Redeemer. "Come back to Yahweh your God, for he is gracious and compassionate, slow to anger, rich in faithful love" (2:13). The prophet's words echo the Lord's revelation to Moses when he intercedes for mercy on behalf of his people at Sinai (cf. Ex 34:6–7).

The Lord responds to the prayer of his people in a wonderful manner: he dispels the plague of locusts (2:18; cf. 2:14). Again, the prophet insists that the people not only rejoice in the present act of deliverance but also realize its implications concerning Yahweh's fidelity to his people. By overcoming the locusts, the Lord reveals his promise for the future. He will restore the plague-ravaged land so that it will produce abundant crops (2:19–26). Most glorious of all is the news that he will dwell in the midst of his people in faithfulness to his covenant. "You will know that I am among you in Israel, I, Yahweh your God, and no one else" (2:27).

The events of the locust plague, the liturgy of repentance, and the restoration in answer to prayer (1:4–2:27) reveal a lesson about how the Lord will bring history to a climax in the end time. The Lord overcomes and destroys the powerful army (here, of locusts) that ravages his people, and he provides for Judah the promise of an abundant life she never before imagined

(2:18–27). The turning point that changes the course of history and allows the Lord to intervene with such power is the people's act of repentance expressed in prayer and fasting (1:11–20; 2:12–17).

The prophet tells us in the very beginning that we, the audience, are receiving this text precisely so that we can learn about the action of God in these events in order to tell our children how the Lord brings salvation to his people (1:2–3). In the second half of the book (3:1–4:21), Joel teaches us what he has learned about the Day of Yahweh from the events surrounding the plague of locusts (1:4–2:27).

The Day of Yahweh: The second half of Joel (3:1–4:21) describes the Day of Yahweh in images of cosmic proportions. His description of the sun losing its light and the stars growing dim derives from the prophetic tradition about the Day. However, Joel uses these images in such a manner as to heighten the impression that this Day is not a mere event within history but rather the absolute end of all history (4:15–16; 3:4; 2:1–2, 10–11; cf. Am 5:18–20; Zep 1:15–18).

Joel teaches us that the Day of Yahweh has two contrasting faces. The nations will experience the Day as a time of cosmic destruction, while Judah will experience it as the time of salvation and deliverance (3:4). On that Day, Yahweh will overturn the present system of world power. The mighty and oppressive nations of the world will enter into a final combat with the Lord, who will vanquish their armies just as he destroyed the plague of locusts (4:1–14; cf. 2:3–9). On that same Day, Yahweh will vindicate his people, establish his everlasting reign on Zion, and shelter his people with his protection (4:17; cf. 2:18–20, 27).

On the Day of Yahweh, God will pour forth his spirit on all his people as the first event that ushers in the end time (3:1–5). Here, Joel envisions the fulfillment of Moses' longing that all of God's people receive the prophetic spirit (Nm 11:29). In addition, Joel reflects the prophetic heritage of Ezekiel and the disciples of the postexilic Isaian tradition who spoke about God's pouring forth his spirit to transform the life of Israel (Ez 39:29; cf. 37:14; 11:19; Is 32:15). Yahweh's day of judgment on the world will be the day when he brings his people to new life by pouring out his spirit upon all of them without distinction of age, gender, or social class (3:2).

In Jerusalem, the Lord will establish his remnant composed of all who put their trust in his name (3:5). The contrast between Judah and the nations will be absolute. From his Temple, the Lord will cause a fountain to spring forth and water the land of Judah (cf. Ez 47:1), while he will make the territories of Israel's oppressors barren and desolate (4:18–21). In order to appreciate the impact of Joel's vision of the Day of Yahweh, we will direct our attention to the fundamental contribution his teaching made to the understanding of the New Testament event of Pentecost.

Toward the New Testament: The Holy Spirit of Pentecost

In the Acts of the Apostles, Peter quotes Joel in order to interpret the meaning of what happened to the disciples at Pentecost (Acts 2:17–21; cf. Jl 3:1–5). The way in which he applies the text of the prophet to the outpouring of the Holy Spirit has at least six implications for our understanding of the Church's birth to new life in the event of Pentecost.

First, the text in Acts introduces the prophecy by adding the phrase "In the last days" in order to recall Joel's future-oriented perspective (Acts 2:17; cf. Jl 3:1). By indicating this particular time frame in connection with the descent of the Holy Spirit, Peter asserts that the event of Pentecost is the first event of the end time. Because the Spirit now dwells in the hearts of human beings within the Church, the final, new age of salvation no longer remains in the distant future—it has already begun.

Secondly, "the Lord" who pours forth his Spirit is Jesus, who has ascended to the Father (Acts 2:17; cf. Jl 3:1; Acts 1:9–11). In union with the Father, he communicates the gift of divine life that the crowds witness in Jesus' disciples (Acts 2:33, 36).

Thirdly, it is the Holy Spirit whom Jesus the Lord pours out at Pentecost (Acts 2:17; cf. 2:4, 33). The trinitarian aspect of the Pentecost event bursts beyond the boundaries of Joel's limited understanding of Yahweh's spirit as a prophetic power (Jl 3:1–2; cf. Nm 11:25–30). The one whom the disciples receive is the Spirit of Jesus the Lord and also of the Father (Acts 2:33).

Fourthly, Luke capitalizes on Joel's reference to "all humanity" in the first line of his prophecy (Acts 2:17; cf. Jl 3:1). Once more, the prophetic word explodes beyond the confines of the prophet's original vision. When we recall Joel's adamant distinction between Judah and the nations (Jl 3:5; 4:17), we must acknowledge that by "all humanity", he was thinking of the various social classes but only within the confines of Judah (see Jl 3:1–2). Nevertheless, when quoted within the setting of Luke-Acts, the prophetic word refers literally to the whole human race. We have noted that when quoting Deutero-Isaiah at the beginning of the Gospel, Luke extends the reference to the line that announces that "all humanity will see the salvation of God" (Lk 3:4–6; cf. Is 40:3–5). In similar fashion here at the beginning of Acts, Peter insists that the Lord is pouring out the Spirit, not upon a select few, but upon all people. Although only Jews comprised Peter's audience at Pentecost, they came from all over the Roman Empire and therefore represented the universality of the human race upon whom God wants to bestow his Spirit (Acts 2:7–10). The "gentile Pentecost" occurs when Cornelius and his house receive the Spirit (Acts 10:44–48). From that point on, the Spirit will unite Jew and Gentile in the one community of the Church (1 Cor 12:13).

Fifthly, the events of Pentecost give definition to the gift of prophecy mentioned in Joel (Acts 2:17–18; cf. Jl 3:1–2). Prophecy at Pentecost consists in the capacity to proclaim the Gospel of the death and Resurrection of Jesus Christ (Acts 2:14–36). At the same time, it is "prophecy" that enables the people from the various countries of the world to hear the Gospel in their own tongue (Acts 2:5–13).

Sixthly, both Luke in Acts and Paul in Romans highlight Joel's insistence that everyone who calls on the Lord's name will experience salvation (Acts 2:21; Rom 10:9–13; cf. Jl 3:5). Again, we have an example of the prophetic word revealing more in its fulfillment than the prophet imagined when he first announced it. Joel intended the statement as an assurance to the people of Judah that Yahweh would preserve them from the judgment he will inflict on the nations on the Day of Yahweh. For Joel, the feature that distinguished the Jews from the other nations was their privilege to call on the name of the Lord, which meant worshipping at the Temple (Jl 3:5; 1 Kgs 8:29, 33, 35). The context of both Acts and Romans breaks open the prophetic word from its original constraint. Now all people in the world proclaim "the name of the Lord", not by worshipping in the Temple in Jerusalem, but by professing their faith in Jesus the risen one in whom they find salvation (see Acts 4:10, 12; Phil 2:11). Furthermore, as we have mentioned, all people, Gentile as well as Jew, will find salvation and new life as they reverence Jesus as Lord of all (Rom 10:11–13).

The New Testament writers expanded the original horizons of Joel by quoting his prophecy of salvation in reference not just to Judah but also to all peoples of the world. This is one indication that the inspired biblical tradition enlarges our perspective from a rather narrow exclusivism toward a universal vision of redemption. With this thought in mind, we direct our attention to Deutero-Zechariah and Jonah, two texts of differing styles that offer an early corrective of the narrowness in Joel and Obadiah by expressing the conviction that God's plan of redemption embraces all peoples.

STUDY QUESTIONS

1. What are the two parts of Obadiah?

2. How was the rivalry between Jacob and Esau reflected in the relationship of Israel and Edom?

3. What does Edom represent and what does its destruction prefigure?

4. How is Obadiah's meditation on brotherhood relevant to the New Testament?

5. What is the significance to Joel of the plague of locusts?

6. How does Joel describe the Day of Yahweh?

7. How does the Acts of the Apostles apply the book of Joel to Pentecost?

8. How does the meaning of "all humanity" change from Joel to Acts (Acts 2:17; cf. Jl 3:1)?

9. How does calling on the name of the Lord in Joel differ from that in the New Testament?

10. Discuss how the Day of Yahweh can be every day if you turn your undivided attention to the Lord.

11. According to the Acts of the Apostles, the era of the Holy Spirit is the final age. How does the concept of the end time in Acts differ from that in Joel?

12. At the beginning of the Second Vatican Council, Pope John XXIII prayed for a "new Pentecost". What developments indicate the revelation of this grace in the Church today?

OBADIAH

I.   The Destruction of Edom (1–15)

II. The Day of Yahweh (16–18)

III. Appendix: The Promised Land of the End Time (19–21)

JOEL

I.   The Plague of Locusts (1:1–2:27)
   A.   The Summons to Prayer in View of the Locust Plague (1:1–20)
      1.   The Locusts Ravage the Land (1:1–12)
      2.   Call to Prayer and Fasting (1:13–20)
   B.   The Day of Yahweh Foreshadowed in the Locusts (2:1–17)
      1.   The Enemy Army Ravages the City (2:1–11)
      2.   Call to Repentance (2:12–17)
   C.   The Lord's Response (2:18–27)
      1.   The Lord Removes the Enemy Army (2:18–20)
      2.   The Lord Makes the Land Abundant (2:21–27)

II. The Day of Yahweh (3:1–4:21)
   A.   The Lord Pours Forth His Spirit (3:1–5)
   B.   The Lord Judges the Nations and Vindicates Judah (4:1–21)
      1.   The Divine Judgment on the Nations (4:1–14)
      2.   The Day of Yahweh: Judgment and Salvation (4:15–17)
   C.   The Life of Everlasting Salvation in Judah (4:18–21)

DEUTERO–ZECHARIAH AND JONAH:
UNIVERSAL SALVATION

The citizens of Judah during the fourth and third centuries B.C. were tempted to fall back into a narrow sectarianism by identifying themselves in opposition to the surrounding nations. But people who live by faith in God's word must develop a global consciousness in order to be a prophetic presence in the world. The texts of Deutero-Zechariah (Zec 9–14) and of Jonah, each in its own way, communicate a conviction that God's mercy extends beyond the borders of Judaism to all peoples in the world. The collection of prophecies we call Deutero-Zechariah continues the tradition of Joel and Obadiah by juxtaposing Judah and the nations but succeeds in broadening the scope of salvation to include the Gentiles. By contrast to Deutero-Zechariah's rather somber specter of apocalyptic judgment, the book of Jonah is a humorous tale with a serious message asserting the priority of God's mercy over his judgment for all who turn to him in repentance. In order to appreciate these works within their historical setting, we will describe the turning point in history when Greek culture began to dominate the Mediterranean world.

From the Persian Empire to the Greek Empire

We have little information about the happenings in Judah from the period following Nehemiah's reforms (400 B.C.) until Alexander the Great's conquest of the region (332 B.C.). However, we can be certain of two trends that affected the shape of Judaism at the time: the balance of power was shifting from east to west as the Persian Empire was giving way to the Greeks; and increasing numbers of Jews were living in the various parts of the gentile world far beyond the shadow of the Temple in Jerusalem.

The Persians continued to dominate the stage of world history, but first Egypt, then a coalition of regional satraps around the Mediterranean, and finally Greece eventually challenged them. On the shores of the Aegean Sea,

Philip of Macedon (359–336 B.C.) brought all the Greek city-states under his control. From this foundation, his son Alexander the Great (336–323 B.C.) advanced against the Persian Empire conquering region upon region in spectacular succession. All of Asia Minor fell at the battle of Issus in 333 B.C. Alexander then brought the region of Syria and Palestine under his control on his way to seizing Egypt in 332 B.C. There, he established the city of Alexandria on the Nile delta. In 330 B.C., his troops headed east, overrunning first Babylon and then the Persian capital of Persepolis. In 327 B.C., he moved across the rugged terrain of what is now Afghanistan and then along the Indus River in what is now Pakistan. By 326 B.C., Alexander had conquered the whole Persian Empire. In 323 B.C., when he died in Babylon at the age of thirty-three, this student of Aristotle, the great philosopher, had a god-like stature in the minds of many of his contemporaries.

Anyone living in Alexander's lifetime had to develop a global vision as the world's political landscape underwent such a great transformation. We gain an impression of the perspective of the world from Judah at this time as we read Deutero-Zechariah and Jonah. By our estimation, Deutero-Zechariah was produced when Alexander the Great was a youth, while Jonah originated a number of decades following his death.

DEUTERO-ZECHARIAH

An attentive reading of the text causes us to realize that Zechariah 9–14 is so unlike Zechariah 1–8 that the two sections must come from different authors. First of all, we note that a title intrudes on the flow of the book to indicate a break in the text ("A proclamation": Zec 9:1; cf. 12:1). A closer examination of the contents turns up further indications that demarcate the book into two major sections. While chapters 1–8 contain precise historical references to people (e.g., Zerubbabel [4:6b–10a], Joshua [3:1–10], individual exiles [6:10, 14]) and dates (1:1, 7; 7:1), chapters 9–14 give no indication of a specific setting in history. For the most part in the first section (1–8), the prophet communicates his visions and words in the first person (e.g., 2:1–4, 5–9; 5:1–4, 5–11; 6:1–8; 7:4; cf. 1:1, 7), while in the second section (9–14), we receive no indication of the identity of the human being who speaks the Lord's word (e.g., 11:4; 12:2). The first section (1–8) describes the prophet's firsthand experience of God's revelation, while the second section (9–14) is an anonymous literary composition that collates material from earlier prophets (such as Ezekiel and Jeremiah).

In spite of their differences in origin, the two sections (1–8 and 9–14) do share common themes that provide for the unity of the book. Some of the themes that pervade the whole book are: (a) a preoccupation with the remnant of God's people (8:6; 9:7); (b) an appreciation of the value of prayer for new life (7:2; 8:21–22; 12:10); (c) a vision of restoration portrayed in terms of a new Jerusalem (2:5–9; 9:8; 14:8–11, 20–21); (d) God's judgment on the nations (2:1–4; 9:1–7; 14:12–14); and (e) the ultimate conversion of people from the nations (2:15; 8:23; 14:16–19). The journey of foreigners from distant places to Jerusalem serves as the culmination for each of the two sections (8:1–8, 23; cf. 14:16–21).

Previously, we indicated that the specific dates in the text (1:1, 7; 7:1) locate Zechariah's prophecies (1–8) in Jerusalem during the two-year period between October 520 and November 518 B.C., when he joined his voice to Haggai's in order to encourage the reconstruction of the Temple. Such precision is simply impossible for dating Zechariah 9–14. The literary evidence leads us to conclude that this second section (9–14) expresses a synthesis of tradition that drew its inspiration from the words and vision of Zechariah. One popular thesis dates the text in the Greek era sometime after 325 B.C. on the basis of perceived allusions to the conquests of Alexander the Great in the description of Judah's vanquished neighbors (9:1–17). However, in our opinion, such allusions are too weak to provide the primary evidence for dating the text. A preferable alternate thesis argues that the portions of the second section (e.g., 9:1–17; 10:1–2; 10:3–12; 11:1–3), which mention Judah's ancient neighbors, originated in the half century following Zechariah's ministry. Oracles such as these and others in Deutero-Zechariah originally referred to specific events, but, once the biblical author picked them up from the prophetic tradition and inserted them into the present book, the original event lost its importance and the names of Israel's ancient foes became symbolic of the nations of the world.

The present version of the whole work seems to come from the fourth century (400–300 B.C.), when the era of prophecy was coming to an end in Judah (see 13:2–6). The apocalyptic tone of the last chapter (14:1–21) and its reference to Yahweh gathering the nations for a final judgment relates the book to the final edition of Joel (Zec 14:2; cf. Jl 4:2, 12). The final editors might have inserted the titles to link the text with Malachi, which follows in the collection of the minor prophets (Zec 9:1; 12:1; Mal 1:1). In light of these indications, we propose that Deutero-Zechariah (9–14) comes from the hand of an editor who completed the arrangement of the whole book in Jerusalem not long after 350 B.C. Considered in this light, the book of Zechariah is a witness to God's grace inspiring sacred tradition to communicate his prophetic word, which becomes normative for all time in the Scriptures.

We use the term "Deutero-Zechariah" in a manner different from what we intended by using "Deutero-Isaiah". We can be certain that "Deutero-Isaiah" was a prophet who ministered to the exiles in Babylon and proclaimed to them the pronouncements collected in a specific part of the book of Isaiah (Is 40–55). By contrast, we speak of "Deutero-Zechariah" primarily to indicate that the texts at the end of Zechariah (9–14) postdate the original prophet, not that a later individual prophet wrote them. Our discussion of the geographical references indicates that it is most unlikely that all these oracles come from the same individual prophet. Therefore, when speaking of "Deutero-Zechariah", we have in mind an editor who collected elements of tradition and compiled the text in its present form.

In fact, internal evidence indicates that Zechariah 9–14 is composed of two distinct units, each of which bears the same title ("a proclamation": 9:1; 12:1). The basic material in the first unit (9:1–11:17) comes from an earlier date than the contents of the second (12:1–14:21) and is independent of it. Both halves of Zechariah 9–14 speak of God's final intervention on behalf of his people in the Day of Yahweh. While 9:1–11:17 speaks of an event within history in which the Lord defeats the enemies of his people, 12:1–14:21 describes God's ultimate intervention at the end of history. The phrase "when that day comes" occurs sixteen times in the second collection (12:1–14:21).

The first collection has more the aspect of a compilation of disparate oracles linked rather loosely by catch words (e.g., "sheep" in 9:16, 10:2, 11:4; "shepherds" in 10:2, 11:3, 5). The second collection has a more constant focus on one theme (judgment and salvation in Jerusalem) and advances more consistently from the final trials of the present age (12:1–13:9) toward the establishment of God's new order in the age to come (14:1–21). The description of the final battle (14:1–21), which mentions earthquake, war, plagues on nations, the transformation of Jerusalem, and the conversion of Gentiles, represents an important stage in the transition from prophecy to apocalyptic literature. The two are united by sharing a common theme of the Lord's judgment on Judah and on the nations preceding his final restoration of his people (9:1–8, 16; cf. 14:1–21).

The Message of Deutero-Zechariah

We will summarize the message of Deutero-Zechariah as a whole by considering three primary elements that pervade his composition: the final battle for salvation, the images of shepherd and sheep, and the promise of ultimate victory envisioned in the restoration of Jerusalem.

The Final Battle: Deutero-Zechariah is concerned with warfare that Yahweh initiates by entering into conflict with all the powers of the present age in order to establish his final rule over the world (14:9). Anyone reading the text carefully experiences mounting tension relieved only briefly in the beginning by reassurances of God's promise that he will restore his people (9:7–8; 10:6–10) and, in the end, by the certain declaration that the Lord will become king of all the world (14:9).

The book teaches us that we do not enter the final glorious age of God without enduring an intense struggle characterizing the end of the present age. The battle is between Yahweh and the gentile nations (Damascus, Philistia, Assyria, Egypt, Lebanon [9:1–6; 10:11–12; 11:1–3]; cf. 14:2), which, because they are the ones who have oppressed his people, symbolize the evil in the present age. We are not dealing with a worldly conflict but the battle between the Lord and the wickedness he overcomes by his judgment (9:7; 14:12). Yahweh initiates the warfare by advancing against the combined worldly forces of evil (14:2–3). Thus, his judgment on the world represents at the same time the final act of deliverance for his people (14:9–11, 20–21).

However, the people of God are not passive bystanders. They must take up their position as warriors armed by the Lord to rise up against their worldly foes (10:3–5). Yahweh must pass judgment on Jerusalem and Judah because only a purified remnant (9:7) can survive into the age of final restoration. There will be a battle in Jerusalem between those on the side of the Lord and their neighbors who have opposed him (see 11:6; 14:13).

The Shepherds and the Sheep: The first collection (9:1–11:17) most commonly images God's people as sheep (9:16; 10:2; 11:4, 7, 11, 17) and their leaders as shepherds (10:2, 3; 11:3, 5, 8, 15, 16, 17; cf. 13:7). A close study of its usage indicates that "shepherd" refers to two opposing types of overseer, namely, gentile rulers who abuse God's people (10:3; 11:3, 16) and the prophet who comes to replace them by caring for the flock in the name of Yahweh (11:4, 7). Deutero-Zechariah develops his meditation on the shepherds by reflecting on Ezekiel's exposition of the theme (Ez 34:1–31; cf. Zec 11:15–16).

The gentile shepherds ruled the flock through the cooperation of the Jewish wealthy class, who complied with the oppression of their own people (11:4–6). Yahweh sends the prophet as the shepherd to replace the oppressive gentile rulers (11:4–7).

The point of crisis at the center of Deutero-Zechariah occurs when the people reject this prophet-shepherd who serves them on behalf of Yahweh. They insult the Lord by dismissing his delegated shepherd with the paltry wages of thirty shekels, equivalent to the price of a slave (11:12–14). When he snaps the two staffs ("Goodwill" and "Couplers"), the prophet-shepherd reveals that breaking the covenant with Yahweh (symbolized in the staff called "Goodwill"—11:7, 10) has destroyed the unity of God's people (symbolized in the staff called "Couplers"—11:7, 14). By rejecting the prophet-shepherd, the people have declared that they have rejected Yahweh's rule over them. In response to the people's betrayal of the covenant, the prophet then equips himself with the gear of an evil gentile shepherd like the ones of former days in order to prophesy that such a ruler will take control of the land once again and harm the flock by his lack of concern for them (11:15–17).

The second collection (12:1–14:21) introduces the renewal of God's people at the end time with the conversion of their leaders, who confess their faith in the strength of "Yahweh Sabaoth their God" (12:5). At this time, the Lord will restore the House of David (12:7–8) through a mysterious intervention that will bring all the people to repentance. The people will turn to Yahweh as they gaze upon the "one whom they have pierced", a figure recalling the Suffering Servant of the Lord (Is 52:13–53:12), who, in this case, manifests Yahweh insofar as the people have rejected him (12:10).

Is the shepherd who is smitten by the sword (13:7) an evil shepherd (cf. 11:17) or the one who has been pierced (cf. 12:10)? The context suggests that he is the latter, a servant of Yahweh whose death provokes a period of suffering for the people prior to the Lord's restoring them to himself (13:7–9). The struggle over leadership in Israel comes to a resolution when the Lord establishes his rule as king over the whole world (14:9). In his victory, Yahweh reveals himself to be the only God (14:9; cf. 10:1–2).

The Final Restoration of Jerusalem: After the final battle between Yahweh and the powers of the world, Jerusalem rises to such heights that all the surrounding land seems like a plain (14:10). The city that had witnessed the death of evil wrought by God's judgment now becomes the place of light where there is only day and the source of life that pours forth water on the barren surroundings (14:7–11).

But the wonder of the new era of salvation is not the restored environs as much as the amazing variety of people who pass into salvation by entering the new Jerusalem. The remnant of Israel's faithful ones forms the nucleus of the population, but they are mentioned almost by allusion (14:14; cf. 10:6–12; 12:2–8). Deutero-Zechariah focuses our attention on the Gentiles, who had been God's ferocious enemies and who now experience conversion (14:16–19; cf. 14:2, 12; 9:1–6). God's desire to bring salvation to all peoples shines through the pilgrimage of the nations bringing their precious goods to adorn Jerusalem (14:14–19). Yahweh's reign is so pervasive that everything from animals to cooking utensils reflects the identity of Jerusalem as the holy city (14:20).

Toward the New Testament: The King and Shepherd

The New Testament writers found in Deutero-Zechariah (9–14) a wealth of prophetic texts that cast light on Jesus as the Messiah-Shepherd who, through his Passion and death, establishes God's reign over the world. We will concentrate our attention on the contribution of Deutero-Zechariah to the portrait of Jesus in the Synoptic Gospels and in the Gospel of John.

In their description of Jesus' triumphal entrance into Jerusalem, both Matthew and John quote Zechariah's reference to the king who will come to proclaim peace to all the nations of the earth (Mt 21:5; Jn 12:15; cf. Zec 9:9–10). In Deutero-Zechariah, the king receives salvation from Yahweh and comes riding on a donkey, because this animal was a symbol of peace while a horse suggested war (Zec 9:9; cf. 2 Sm 15:1). Matthew emphasizes the humility of Jesus manifest in his riding on a lowly donkey colt. Matthew places the text at the beginning of Jesus' ministry in Jerusalem to declare that Jesus is truly the Messiah-King whom Jerusalem has long awaited as the one who brings salvation. The title of king applied to Jesus links this scene with his final discourse at the end of his ministry in Jerusalem (Mt 25:34, 40), with his interrogation by Pilate (Mt 27:11), and with his death on the cross (Mt 27:29, 37, 42). As in Matthew, so in John, the title of king applied to Jesus at his procession into the city relates this event to his dialogue with Pilate (Jn 18:33) and to his exaltation on the cross (Jn 19:19–22).

Deutero-Zechariah contains a number of texts concerning the shepherd whom the people reject and kill that foreshadow Jesus as the Messiah-King in his Passion and death. Such texts belong in the same category as the Song of the Suffering Servant (Is 52:13–53:12) and Psalms 22 and 69, since they reveal Jesus as the Christ through his suffering. In the first century, the opponents of Christianity argued that Jesus could not be the Messiah because even his disciples did not display steadfast faith in him. All his disciples abandoned him in his Passion (Mk 14:50), and one of his own betrayed him to the chief priests (Mk 14:10–11; Mt 26:14–16; Lk 22:3–6; Jn 13:2, 27). The early evangelists and teachers found in Deutero-Zechariah prophecies revealing that Scripture foretells the disciples' apparently scandalous behavior and thereby revealing Jesus as the promised Messiah.

After the Last Supper, as he prophesies that his disciples will abandon him, Jesus quotes the passage mentioning the scattering of the sheep when the shepherd is struck (Mk 14:27; Mt 26:31; cf. Zec 13:7). In Deutero-Zechariah, the text refers to the murder of Yahweh's servant as the prelude to the struggle of the end time before God makes Israel his own people forever (Zec 13:7–9). By citing this text just before his arrest, Jesus indicates that the fact that his disciples flee from him does not contradict but, in fact, proves him to be the

Messiah foretold in the Scriptures. Just as Deutero-Zechariah implies that the Lord will restore his people to a new relationship with him after the time of trial (Zec 13:9), so Jesus indicates that he will regather his disciples in a new relationship to himself after his Resurrection, when he precedes them into Galilee (Mk 14:28; Mt 26:32).

According to Matthew, Judas received thirty silver pieces from the chief priests for betraying Jesus (Mt 26:14–16). The fate of these thirty silver pieces reveals that Jesus has the identity of God's rejected prophet-shepherd described by Deutero-Zechariah (Mt 27:3–10; cf. Zec 11:7–14). Judas' remorseful gesture of throwing the coins into the Temple corresponds to the action by which the prophet-shepherd casts away the money to express his disgust for the people's rejection of the Lord's authority (Mt 27:5; cf. Zec 11:13). In Deutero-Zechariah, the prophet casts the silver pieces into the Temple for "the smelter". Matthew prefers another meaning of the same term, namely, "the potter" (Hebrew: yotzar/ Zec 11:13). Matthew takes this meaning and combines the text with references to Jeremiah's purchase of a field (Jer 32:6–9). In this way, he perceives the significance of the "Potter's Field" that the Temple authorities bought with the funds Judas gave back to them (Mt 27:7; cf. Acts 1:17–20). By his inspired insight into the prophetic texts of the Old Testament, Matthew teaches us that even Judas' betrayal of Jesus was a fulfillment of the Scriptures (Mt 27:10).

All the messianic texts in Deutero-Zechariah point to the cross of Jesus for their fulfillment. This is most evident in the description of Christ crucified as "the one whom they have pierced" in the Gospel of John (Jn 19:37; cf. Rv 1:7; cf. Zec 12:10). Deutero-Zechariah first describes "the spirit of grace and prayer" bestowed by Yahweh on his people that causes them to look to him (Zec 12:10; cf. Ez 36:24–27). When he speaks about the people lamenting over "the one whom they have pierced", he refers to a figure who resembles the Suffering Servant of the Lord (Zec 12:10; cf. Is 52:13–53:12). The Gospel of John draws the fullest meaning out of the text by equating the one to whom the people look with the one whom they have pierced (Jn 19:37; cf. Zec 12:10). Jewish tradition provided a messianic interpretation for Zechariah 12:10, promising that people will look to Yahweh when they see the Messiah pierced. John draws upon this tradition in order to confirm the identity of Jesus as the Messiah. Who are "they" who gaze upon Jesus crucified? The Gospel has two groups in mind: first, the religious authorities who put Jesus to death (Jn 11:49–50; 12:19) and, secondly, his mother and the beloved disciple, who will draw life from Jesus' death (19:25–27).

The Gospel of John describes the death of Jesus as a life-giving event. When he died, he "gave up his spirit" (19:30; cf. 1:33; 20:22). The water that flows from his side (19:34) is the living water of the Spirit he promised would

flow forth from him (7:38), recalling Deutero-Zechariah's prophecy of the
fountain bursting forth for the House of David to cleanse Jerusalem (Zec 13:1)
and water the whole surrounding territory (Zec 14:8) in the end time. By his
death on the cross, Jesus pours forth the Holy Spirit upon his Church
(symbolized by his mother) and upon every beloved disciple (Jn 19:25–27;
20:22) and thereby inaugurates the end time that Deutero-Zechariah had
anticipated (cf. Zec 12:1–14:21).

Having considered how Jesus' death on the cross fulfills the promise of
God to initiate the final age of salvation, we can turn to the book of Jonah to
contemplate God's desire to reveal his mercy to all people.

JONAH

Jonah, son of Amittai, was a prophet who served in the northern kingdom
during the reign of Jeroboam II (783–743 B.C./2 Kgs 14:25; cf. Jon 1:1), but the
book of Jonah is not about him. The literary character who takes the name of
this ancient prophet in the book of Jonah is not a historical figure but typifies
a whole category of prophets and individuals belonging to the people of God
and ministering his word.

Jonah is not history but literary parable conveying a message applicable
to God's people in all places and times. The editors who compiled the
collection of the twelve minor prophets included the book of Jonah because
its story form somewhat resembles the legendary accounts of early prophets
such as Elijah and Elisha (1 Kgs 17 to 2 Kgs 13).

It is impossible to date the book of Jonah with precision. Its preoccupation with God's determination to extend salvation to all people
relates the text to the universalism evident in the exilic proclamation of
Deutero-Isaiah (Is 40:5; 45:1–7) and in the postexilic works of Zechariah
(Zec 8:20–23), Trito-Isaiah (Is 56:1–8; 66:18–23), and Deutero-Zechariah (Zec
14:16–19). Jonah tempers a strong form of judgmentalism against the nations
that surfaced even in the later prophetic texts (e.g., Jl 4:1–14; Zec 14:1–5,
12–15).

Joel proclaimed that Yahweh would extend his mercy to Jerusalem. In the
book of Jonah, however, the gentile king of Nineveh, who temporarily takes
the role of the prophet, encourages his people to put their faith in God's
compassion toward their gentile city (Jon 3:9, cf. 4:2; cf. Jl 2:13–14). Jonah
extends Joel's concept of God's mercy to include more than Israel. This
suggests that Jonah comes after Joel in time (c. 350 B.C.), at the end of the
Persian era or in the Greek period following Alexander the Great's conquest
of Judah (332 B.C.). We suggest that an author who was schooled in both the

prophetic and wisdom traditions produced the book of Jonah in the century between 350 and 250 B.C.

The Message of Jonah

A study of its outline indicates that the book of Jonah conveys its message through an artful balance of themes that recur in each of its halves (1:1–2:10; 3:1–4:11). Yahweh commissions Jonah as his prophet to Nineveh on two successive occasions (1:1–2; 3:1–2). Jonah's responses on each occasion contrast with each other. In the first instance, he tries to flee by heading in the opposite direction toward Tarshish at the westward edge of the world (1:3), while, in the second instance, he obediently goes eastward to the great city of Nineveh, where he preaches (3:3–4).

On both occasions, Jonah encounters gentile leaders and their people who are more open to the reign of Yahweh than he is. In the first instance, the gentile captain and the sailors call on Yahweh for deliverance from the storm (1:4–16), which foreshadows the second instance where the king of Nineveh and his people seek the mercy of God in response to Jonah's call to repentance (3:5–10). In each instance, Yahweh has to make extraordinary use of his creatures in attempting to bring his prophet to deliverance and new life. In the first instance, he uses the great fish to rescue Jonah from the depths of the sea (2:1–11), and, in the second instance, he causes a bush to spring up miraculously and save Jonah from dying under the hot sun (4:1–11). Yahweh offers the primary lesson of the story in his final words, which tell the prophet that salvation is a gracious work of divine mercy that no human being can merit but which God desires to bestow on all peoples (4:10–11).

The book of Jonah is a literary delight that entertains while it teaches. It shows us that humor can be wise and provides a most effective vehicle for breaking down the barriers of narrow sectarianism so that we can appreciate how deeply God desires the salvation of all people. The story is an astute tale designed to captivate young and old. It is thus a model of excellent catechesis or teaching. To gain an appreciation of its power to communicate divine revelation, we can think of the story as if a grandfather were telling it to his grandchildren after a family meal on a religious feast day. We will consider a few enchanting elements of the story along with its teaching on God's desire to have mercy on all people and its meditation on the prophet's spiritual struggle.

Elements of Enchantment: Typical of good storytelling that stimulates the imagination is the repetition of "great" in the book of Jonah. In the Hebrew text, all these elements are "great": the city (1:2; 3:2; 4:11), the wind (1:4), the storm (1:4, 12), the fish (2:1), the sailors' fear (1:10, 16) as well as Jonah's anger (4:1) and joy (4:6). Prayer is more important than human effort in bringing deliverance, first to the sailors (1:14), then to Jonah (2:2), and, finally, to the Ninevites (3:8). All creatures, including the wind, the sea, the fish, the bush, and the worm, serve Yahweh's purposes; even the animals in Nineveh repent, put on sackcloth, and receive the Lord's favor (3:7; 4:11). Only Jonah, the Lord's servant, seems out of step with Yahweh and his mercy.

The story communicates teachings on two planes: one concerning God's desire to redeem all people, and the other concerning the spiritual struggle of a prophet to respond to the word he preaches. By simultaneously drawing attention to these two issues, the book of Jonah offers a latter-day correction of the imbalance latent in the prophets who overemphasized the doom of God's judgment coming upon the nations in contrast to the salvation reserved to the chosen people of Judah (e.g., Nahum, Obadiah, and Joel).

Universalism: The ferocious tyranny of the Assyrian Empire, from its rise to world domination under Tiglath-Pileser III (745 B.C.) to its overthrow by the neo-Babylonians (609 B.C.), caused its capital Nineveh to become a legendary symbol of gentile society that was absolutely opposed to Yahweh. Nineveh's destruction in 612 B.C. is the cause of exultation throughout the book of Nahum (Na 1:1–3:19). By describing the king and citizens of this most deplorable of cities repenting and receiving God's mercy, the book of Jonah indicates that God wishes to extend his mercy to all people, in keeping with the principle of repentance that Jeremiah and Ezekiel announced (Jer 18:7–8; Ez 18:21–24; cf. 33:11).

The Prophet's Struggle: The abundance of God's mercy scandalizes his prophet. The Ninevites "repented" of their evil ways, and God "repented" of the disaster he threatened to bring upon them, but Jonah has difficulty "repenting" of his attachment to God's wrath so that he can rejoice in God's mercy (Jon 3:1–10; cf. 4:1–9). Jonah is downcast precisely because God is revealing himself to all peoples in the same way he had to Moses and his rebellious people in the wilderness: as a God of compassion and mercy who is slow to anger (Jon 4:2; cf. Ex 34:6–7). Jonah is angry because God is not angry!

Like Moses and Jeremiah, Jonah reacts against God's call to him (Jon 1:1–3; cf. Ex 3:11; 4:10; Jer 1:6). However, while Jeremiah later laments having to proclaim God's judgment (Jer 20:8–10), Jonah is depressed by the expression of God's mercy (Jon 4:1–2). While Elijah had wished death because of persecution (1 Kgs 19:4), Jonah wishes death because of God's generosity to others (Jon 4:3–4). What is Jonah's problem? It seems that in his lack of trust in Yahweh, Jonah has become consumed with self-righteousness and condemnation toward those beyond the circle of the chosen people.

Jonah's position is all the more untenable because, of all people in the story, he is the one who has experienced the greatest mercy. He has forgotten how Yahweh delivered him in answer to his prayer (2:1–11), just as God now delivers the Ninevites in response to their acts of repentance (3:7–10).

The first half of the book describes Jonah's flight from Yahweh as a spiritual descent into Sheol. When Jonah runs to the west (the sunset) instead of to the east (the sunrise), he really falls downward by stages, first to the bottom of the ship (1:5), then into sleep (1:5), and finally into the depths of the sea, where the monster of the deep swallows him (1:15, 2:1). The sea represents Sheol, the place of the dead (2:3–4; cf. Pss 49:15; 89:48) and, in later literature, of the wicked who die alienated from God (Pss 9:17; 55:15; cf. Nm 16:30, 33; Prv 1:12). Yahweh preserves Jonah by means of the great fish who serves as a refuge, the "belly" of Sheol. From this environment most alien to God, Jonah prays and Yahweh delivers him (Jon 2:1–11; cf. Pss 86:13; 116:3).

By an act of pure mercy, Yahweh rescues Jonah from the underworld, yet the prophet refuses to rejoice when God extends that same mercy to strangers, foreigners, and sinners of the world. Furthermore, God causes the plant to spring up to protect Jonah from the heat and shows him that everything good is an undeserved grace from God (4:5–9).

Since it comes at the end of the prophetic tradition, the book of Jonah teaches us that God's last word is one of mercy and compassion on the whole world (4:10–11). When we accept the evident truth that God has redeemed us out of pure, unmerited mercy, we give up our indignant self-righteousness, judgmentalism, and self-destructive anger represented in the figure of Jonah. At the end of the text, the question remains for us as for Jonah: will we repent and allow our anger to change into joy as we behold God's mercy extending to all people (Mt 5:43–48)?

Toward the New Testament: The Sign of Jonah

Jesus' association with tax collectors and sinners challenges the same type of self-righteous indignation that the book of Jonah reprimands (Lk 5:29–32). Jesus' declaration that, on account of their repentance, tax collectors and prostitutes will enter the Kingdom of God before the self-righteous (Mt 21:31–32) represents the same challenge to the sectarianism of Jonah who is angry when the Ninevites turn to God (Jon 4:3–4, 9; 3:7–10).

In his teaching, Jesus extends to his generation the shock waves that originate in the book of Jonah. To the self-righteous scribes and Pharisees, he presents the Ninevites as examplars of belief in God's word, resulting in genuine repentance, which brings people into the life of God's Kingdom (Mt 12:38–42; Lk 11:29–32; cf. Jon 3:1–10). For Jesus, the Ninevites of Jonah's day and the Queen of Sheba of Solomon's day are paradigms of gentile faith. These figures foreshadow the Gentiles who are more responsive to the Gospel than are those of the chosen people who remain entrenched in their legalism and resist Jesus' extension of God's mercy to all people (e.g., Mt 12:1–32).

Jesus focuses on a different element in the book when he refers to the "sign of Jonah" (Mt 12:39; cf. 16:4; Lk 11:30; cf. Jon 2:1, 11). There are few texts in the Old Testament that foreshadow the "three days" of Christ in the tomb between his death and Resurrection (1 Cor 15:4; cf. Hos 6:2). For Matthew, the duration of Jonah's abode in the belly of the fish prefigures the three days of Christ in the tomb (Mt 12:40). The significance of Jonah's plight is his spiritual agony, which allows us to consider the "sign of Jonah" as a reference not just to the time interval in the tomb but rather to the descent of Christ into the realm of death. The early evangelists declared that, at his death, Jesus entered into the ultimate depths of "Hades" (Sheol), and, from there, God raised him to a glorified life (Acts 2:24, 31; Rom 10:7; Heb 13:20). As we understand the "sign of Jonah", we realize that Jesus entered the depths of the netherworld in order to rescue once for all everyone imprisoned there (1 Pt 3:18–22). This gives us confidence that he will likewise rescue us at the hour of our death.

In the book of Jonah, we see the prophetic tradition ending on the theme where the Gospel begins, namely, with the proclamation of God's merciful grace extending to all peoples of the world. By its emphasis on salvation as an event of divine mercy, the book of Jonah foreshadows Paul's insistence that, because all have fallen short of the glory of God, everyone, Gentile as well as Jew, receives justification as a free unmerited gift through the event of the cross (Rom 3:9–31).

STUDY QUESTIONS

1. What were two trends affecting Judaism after Nehemiah's reforms until the time of Alexander the Great's conquests?
2. How does Zechariah 9–14 differ from Zechariah 1–8?
3. How is Deutero-Zechariah different than Deutero-Isaiah?
4. Describe the shepherds in Deutero-Zechariah.
5. What is the wonder of the new Jerusalem that Deutero-Zechariah foretold?
6. What texts in Deutero-Zechariah are prophetic of Jesus?
7. How is Jonah a literary parable?
8. How is Jonah's encounter with Gentiles in both halves of the book significant?
9. What is the message of the book of Jonah?
10. How does Jesus fulfill the "sign of Jonah"?
11. What modern metaphor would suit your concept of leadership that Zechariah used shepherds to express? Pilots? Directors? How do these metaphors fall short of what "shepherd" conveys to you in terms of leadership, concern, and community?
12. Discuss whether in your own life you have felt the Lord call you to do something that, like Jonah, you preferred not to do. How did your reactions correspond with those of Jonah? How has the Lord continued to show you his grace as he did to Jonah?

ZECHARIAH 9–14

I. The First Collection: Judgment before Salvation (9:1–11:17)
- A. Yahweh Overthrows Nations and Restores Judah (9:1–8)
- B. The King of Peace (9:9–10)
- C. Yahweh Frees the Captives and Gives Israel Victory (9:11–17)
- D. Abundant Crops from Yahweh, Not from Other Gods (10:1–2)
- E. The Regathering of Scattered Israel (10:3–12)
- F. The Destruction of Neighboring Foes (11:1–3)
- G. The Shepherd and His Broken Staffs (11:4–17)

II. The Second Collection: Salvation after Judgment (12:1–14:21)
- A. Jerusalem Withstands the Nations (12:1–8)
- B. The Pierced One and Repentance in Jerusalem (12:9–14)
- C. Jerusalem Cleansed of Idols and False Prophecy (13:1–6)
- D. Striking the Shepherd and Scattering the Sheep (13:7–9)
- E. The Final Combat: Holiness in Jerusalem (14:1–21)

JONAH

I. Jonah's First Mission (1:1–2:11)
- A. Jonah's Flight from His Call onto the Gentile Boat (1:1–16)
  1. Jonah Flees toward the City in the West (1:1–4)
  2. The Gentile Captain and Sailors Pray for Deliverance (1:5–16)
- B. His Prayer for Life and Deliverance from the Fish (2:1–11)

II. Jonah's Second Mission (3:1–4:11)
- A. Jonah Preaches and the Gentile City Repents (3:1–10)
  1. Jonah Preaches in the City in the East (3:1–4)
  2. The Gentile King and Citizens Repent (3:5–10)
- B. His Prayer for Death; Deliverance by the Tree (4:1–11).

WRITINGS

30

INTRODUCTION TO WISDOM LITERATURE

We need wisdom in order to live well. All of us who are raising a family, caring for friends, conducting business, or simply living in society make countless decisions every day that affect ourselves and others. In assuming their responsibilities, virtuous people are concerned about doing good and avoiding evil, attaining success and overcoming failure, growing in unity and healing divisions. Virtue produces life, and wisdom is the mother of virtue. Wisdom provides the foundational principles for living. At its deepest level, wisdom is a grace God gives to those who seek his will in all things. By examining the ideas, motives, attitudes, and judgments that underlie our manner of living, wisdom cultivates the proper use of reason, which in turn, through the exercise of personal discipline, leads to unity with God and with all other human beings.

The wisdom literature in the Bible is distinguished by its preoccupation with the perennial concerns of all people about how to live life well. While the Pentateuch draws our attention to observance of the Law, and the Prophets summon us to obey God's spoken word, the wisdom books show us the path to virtue by reflecting on existence. If the Law and the Prophets emphasize the supreme importance of God's revelation, the wisdom literature highlights the value of human reason. Certainly, we must not juxtapose revelation and reason, since they complement one another as the means by which God engages us in an interpersonal dialogue. At first, reason can take us to the frontier of understanding where we learn to pray for revelation, and, afterward, revelation can transform our minds so that we reason in a new way, in union with the mind of God.

Because of its preoccupation with the experience of life common to every human being, wisdom literature has the capacity to speak more directly than the Law and the Prophets to all people of our time. An adult who is doubtful about being able to understand the Old Testament would do well to begin by reading one book in the category of wisdom literature, since these texts offer guidance applicable to the life situations of everyone.

The nucleus of Old Testament wisdom literature consists of the books of

393

Proverbs, Job, Qoheleth (Ecclesiastes), Sirach (Ecclesiasticus), and Wisdom. All these books seek to interpret life by means of reason common to all people. (References to the distinctive salvation history of Israel become the focus of attention only in the last part of Sirach [Sir 44:1–50:29] and in the second half of the book of Wisdom [Wis 10:1–19:22].) To this core of texts, we should add the Song of Songs, the love poem that conveys the impression of divine grace suffusing spousal love while making only one direct reference to Yahweh (cf. Sg 8:6).

In addition to these books, which display an aspect of universality extending beyond the intellectual frontiers distinguishing Israel from the rest of the world, a variety of texts in the Bible express wisdom themes from a markedly Jewish viewpoint. Wisdom narratives unfold the engaging stories of heroes who deal shrewdly with foreigners. Wisdom elements captivate us in the historical narrative of Joseph (Gn 37:2–50:26) and in the idyllic stories of Daniel (Dn 1:1–6:29), Esther, and Judith. The narrative of Ruth and the prophetic story of Jonah hover on the frontiers between wisdom and history (Ruth), on the one hand, and wisdom and prophecy (Jonah) on the other. Furthermore, we find pieces of wisdom literature incorporated into other books: the wisdom psalms make up a distinct category of spiritual literature (Pss 1; 32; 34; 37; 49; 73; 91; 112; 119; 127; 128; 133; 139); Tobit's advice to his son takes the form of proverbs (Tb 4:3–21; 12:6–10); and Baruch's hymn extolling wisdom in Israel recalls the psalms (Bar 3:9–4:4).

Wisdom in the Ancient Near East

Israel's wisdom literature developed in dialogue with the reflections of sages in both Egypt and Mesopotamia. Egyptian writings spanning two millennia (c. 2500–500 B.C.) employ a diversity of literary forms to communicate insights on a variety of topics. The ancient *Instruction of Ptah-hotep* (c. 2400 B.C.) provides guidance on friendships, table manners, diplomacy, and a number of other topics that come up in old Israelite proverbs. *The Wisdom of Amenemophis* (c. 1000 B.C.) consists of thirty proverbs that almost match Proverbs 22:17–24:22. Literature of a more discursive type is represented by *A Dispute between a Man and His Soul* (whose theme touches upon the concerns expressed in Job and Qoheleth) and by *The Protests of the Eloquent Peasant* (which raises issues of justice for the poor).

In Mesopotamia, the ancient Sumerians were composing proverbs before the time of Abraham. The Akkadian poem *I Will Praise the Lord of Wisdom* wrestles with the relationship of the gods to human suffering, the theme taken up in Job. *The Dialogue about Human Misery* resembles Job insofar as it takes the form of a conversation between one who suffers and a friend who enters into dialogue with him. The Akkadian *A Pessimistic Dialogue between Master and Servant,* between a master and his slave on the meaning of life, concludes that death is the only absolute and thus calls to mind the reflections of Qoheleth.

The History of Wisdom in Israel

The pursuit of wisdom was an endeavor that crossed the boundaries of politics and cultures in the ancient Near East. To some extent, the reflections of Egyptian and Babylonian sages influenced the thinkers of Israel. Nevertheless, in order to find the roots of wisdom literature in the Bible, we must dig into the soil of tradition within Israel itself. We will study the development of Hebrew wisdom by asking two questions: Who were "the wise", and what settings in life produced the literature we have in the Bible?

Who Were the Wise? By the time of Jeremiah (c. 598 B.C.), public convention distinguished between three categories of ministers of the word in Judah: the priests who interpreted the Law, the prophets who announced the word, and the wise who offered counsel (Jer 18:18). The first two groups seem rather easy to identify: the priests were from clerical families and served at the Temple, while the prophets exercised a distinct role of announcing God's word in the royal court, the public square, or the Temple precincts. By comparison with our clearly defined understanding of priests and prophets, we have only a vague impression of who were "the wise" of ancient Israel.

At least in part, our relative unfamiliarity with the wise derives from the fact that the historical texts tell us the names of priests (e.g., Zadok and Abiathar/2 Sm 20:25) and prophets (e.g., Isaiah and Jeremiah) but rarely ·identify the wise by name. Considering the personnel who made up David's cabinet, we can surmise that the secretary of the administration probably qualified as one of the wise in Israel (Shiya/2 Sm 20:25). Ezekiel, Jeremiah's contemporary in Babylon throughout the decade prior to the fall of Jerusalem, apparently confirms this suggestion since he seems to identify "the wise" as "the elders" who offer counsel to the king (Ez 7:26; cf. Jer 18:18).

However, "the wise" was a designation that extended beyond the king's advisers and scribes (cf. Jer 8:8–9) to include a variety of people such as: the skilled men and women who designed and built the wilderness sanctuary (Ex 31:2–6; 35:10, 25–26; 35:30–36:1) and Solomon's Temple (1 Kgs 7:14); sailors and shipbuilders (Ez 27:8–9); judges (Dt 16:18–20); and especially parents (Prv 1:8; 31:1), teachers (Prv 1:4), and the aged (Jb 12:12).

What Environments Gave Rise to Wisdom in Israel? Wisdom originated in the home, with the instructions fathers and mothers gave to their children (Prv 4:3–4; 31:1–9). They passed on counsel in the form of proverbs that encouraged a moral life and in the form of stories that inspired virtue.

Once David (1010–970 B.C.) established the monarchy in Jerusalem, he developed a retinue of advisers who became skilled in the affairs of state. The example of his son Solomon (970–931 B.C.) established the bond between wisdom and kingship (1 Kgs 3:4–15, 16–28). Under Solomon, there was an outpouring of literary activity manifest in the work of the Yahwist and in composition of the Court History of David's reign (2 Sm 9–20; 1 Kgs 1–2). The composers might have crafted the nucleus of the Song of Songs to celebrate one of Solomon's marriages (Sg 3:6–11; cf. Ps 45). Solomon sponsored the development of wisdom expressed in proverbs (1 Kgs 5:9–14; Prv 10:1–22:16). It is quite possible that such instructions represent the pearls of teaching offered in an academy he founded to provide training in diplomacy and world affairs for the brightest youths of Israel. The court and the scribal academy now became centers of wisdom.

Throughout the period of kingship in Israel and Judah (931–587 B.C.), the formal development of wisdom took place at the royal court. For example, during the days of Hezekiah (716–687 B.C.), scholars edited a new collection of proverbs (see Prv 25:1–29:27). At the same time, we note that there were tensions between prophets and the wise at court. Isaiah strongly disputed the counsel offered by Hezekiah's advisers concerning alliances with foreign nations (Is 29:14, 15; 30:1–5). Less than a century later, Jeremiah severely admonished the "wise" elders in Jehoiakim's court (Jer 8:8–9; 9:22–23).

During the period of the Exile (587–538 B.C.), the people of Judah came into contact with Babylonian cosmology, which caused them to consider more deeply God's relationship to creation. Deutero-Isaiah developed an appreciation of the unity between God's work of redemption and creation (Is 42:5–9). At some point, the psalmists were calling attention to the God-given dignity of the individual (Ps 8; cf. Ps 139). After the end of the Exile, the Priestly editor was inspired to develop these reflections into the coherent exposition of the creation of the world and of mankind that stands at the beginning of the Pentateuch (Gn 1:1–2:3).

After the Exile, wisdom developed in the circles of priests at the Temple who pondered the Law of the Lord (Ps 119) and in the academies of scholars who reflected on the nature of existence from a more secular perspective. Creation provided the common ground for their reflections. One school tended to emphasize the union between creation and the Law (Ps 19), while the other contemplated the relationship between creation and divine wisdom (Prv 8:22–31). Obviously we must avoid making absolute distinctions between the Temple and the academy and between the Law and wisdom. At the same time, we recognize that Job's rejection of the admonitions of his pious friends and Qoheleth's suspicion of theological absolutes challenged the religious elders to engage the world in a dialogue founded on reason and revelation without appealing to religious tradition.

The final editions of all the wisdom literature in the Bible come from the postexilic period (538 B.C. to the Christian era). The introduction to Proverbs (Prv 1:1–9:18), with its discursive instructions (1:8–7:27), and meditations on wisdom personified as the divine agent at creation (Prv 8:22–31) come from the fifth century (500–400 B.C.). The book of Job was composed in the first half of the fifth century (500–450 B.C.). Qoheleth seems to fit better into the early Greek period (c. 300 B.C.). The tradition underlying the Song of Songs apparently originates in the days of Solomon (970–931 B.C.), and its final composition might come from the fourth century (400–300 B.C.)

Their defense of Jewish culture distinguishes the books of Sirach and Wisdom from the other texts of wisdom literature. Both these texts argue that the wisdom God has communicated to his people far surpasses the philosophies of other cultures in the world. Jesus Ben Sira composed and edited his reflections in Hebrew between 190 and 180 B.C., when he completed his teaching career in Jerusalem. Ben Sira's grandson translated his work into Greek in Alexandria, Egypt, perhaps in 117 B.C. The author of the book of Wisdom lived in the academic climate of Alexandria, Egypt, and defended his faith against the intellectual and even physical attacks of the adversaries of the Jews who lived there just after 30 B.C.

Characteristics of Wisdom in Israel

The postexilic dating of the wisdom literature causes us to reflect on the unique perspective of Israel's sages by comparison with the postexilic prophets and teachers of the Law. In our study of people such as Joel, Obadiah, and Deutero-Zechariah, we detected a tendency in them to be protective of Judah and suspicious of foreign nations. The wisdom literature of the time, represented in the books of Job and Qoheleth, offers a counterbalance, at least insofar as it poses questions to the common theology in Judah and implies an openness to life in other cultures. We note that Job's home is in the land of Uz beyond Israel's frontiers (Jb 1:1). This territory is the same as Edom, the country Obadiah denounced with the strongest vehemence (Ob vv. 1–21).

We can illustrate wisdom's dialogue with the Law and the Prophets by focusing on three topics central to the writings of Israel's sages: creation, human responsibility, and the personification of wisdom.

Creation: Wisdom literature presents a theology based on creation. It presumes that reality makes sense and has an internal structure based on discoverable laws and principles. In other words, the whole universe is a word from God and a source of divine revelation. God is not within creation, but he reigns over creation and reveals his wisdom through the laws inherent in all that exists. For the most part, wisdom literature does not refer to Yahweh's promises, salvific deeds, or covenants with Israel, elements central to the proclamation of the prophets and the interpretation of the Law. Nevertheless, we have noted that both the prophets (e.g., Is 40:12–31) and the Priestly editor (Gn 1:1–2:3; 9:1–17) point to creation as a source of revelation. Furthermore, the sages, like the prophets and the interpreters of the Law, call their people to repentance. The composer of wisdom directs our attention to the cosmos and allows us to hear the voice of God expose our ignorance of its mysteries (Jb 38:1–41:26) so that we will experience conversion in the presence of Yahweh its Creator (Jb 42:1–6).

Human Responsibility: The sages insisted that everyone must use reason in order to live well. The primary virtue essential for living a life of wisdom is fear of the Lord (Prv 1:7), a reverent acknowledgment that Yahweh is supreme over creation and over our personal existence. We note that the same virtue is commended in the Law (Ex 20:20) and the prophets (e.g., Is 11:2, 3).

Wisdom is not speculative but practical. The exemplary wise person is the woman who exhibits foresight, intelligence, and diligence in caring for her family (Prv 31:10–31). The young attain wisdom by "listening" to their parents and teachers, an exercise they fulfill only when they put into practice what they have been taught (Prv 1:8–19; 3:1–12). Gaining wisdom requires an exercise of the will in obedience to the truth. The wisdom tradition asserts that every person must take responsibility for his or her life by knowing the truth and exercising the discipline necessary to live by it.

Wisdom Personified: Ultimately, wisdom does not belong to man but to God. Wisdom was with God from before the creation of the cosmos (Prv 8:22–31; Sir 24:1–9; Wis 9:9–11). Wisdom was God's agent in bringing the cosmos into existence. It is through wisdom that God becomes present to mankind. Sirach achieves a synthesis between the traditions of wisdom, prophecy, and Torah by describing wisdom personified as the revelation God uniquely communicated to his people at the Temple in Jerusalem (Sir 24:1–31). The understanding of wisdom's relationship to God prior to creation offers a prelude to the fullness of revelation made manifest when the eternal Word becomes flesh in the Incarnation (Jn 1:1–18).

STUDY QUESTIONS

1. How does wisdom literature differ from the Law and the Prophets?
2. What are the books that make up wisdom literature?
3. Who were "the wise" in Israel?
4. What are three topics central to wisdom literature?
5. How does the personified wisdom foreshadow Jesus?
6. Discuss how you can seek wisdom from the Lord in your personal prayer time.
7. Discuss how obtaining wisdom from God is the appropriate corollary to prophecy because both build the church community.

THE PSALMS: SING TO THE LORD A NEW SONG

The book of Psalms (or Psalter) is the Bible's manual of inspired song and prayer. The wonder of the Psalms is that we cannot read them without praying. As soon as we glance at them, we become engaged in a personal discourse with God. Moreover, it is impossible for us to remain aloof and detached, since the words expose our hearts to the presence of God. Our discourse is immediate and direct, expressing wonder, praise, complaint, hope, fear, even anger, as well as love and faith. Because it contains both personal and communal prayers, the Psalter exposes the deepest motives of our hearts while bringing us into relationship with all God's people who join us in worship. This one collection demonstrates a capacity to offer us communion with all God's people and with God himself in the same act of worship. Their inclusion in the canon of inspired Scripture implies an amazing aspect of the psalms: human words addressed to God become God's word addressed to us.

We cannot fully interpret the psalms by simply reading these texts because, for the most part, they were composed to be sung aloud to the accompaniment of music. Our term "psalm" comes from the Greek word *psalmos,* which the translators of the Septuagint used to interpret the Hebrew word *mizmor,* the term that occurs most often (57 times; e.g., Pss 3; 48; 75) in the preliminary notations to each psalm. Other types are the "song" (*sur:* 30 times; e.g., Pss 38; 87; 92), the "poem" (*maskil:* 13 times; e.g., Pss 32; 46; 76), and the "hymn of praise" (*tehillah:* Ps 145). So convinced was the Jewish tradition about the choral dimension of these prayers that it designated the whole collection as the hymns of praise (*tehillim*), a designation that occurs only once in the preliminary notations (Ps 145) but which is found throughout a number of psalms (see Pss 65:1; 106:12; 147:1; 149:1). The preliminary notation "For the choirmaster" (e.g., Pss 81; 109; 140) and mention of musical instruments, such as strings (e.g., Pss 4; 55; 76) and flutes (Ps 5), further sustain our conviction that the psalms receive their fullest interpretation when a congregation sings them in faith-filled response to the revelation of God in the midst of the assembly.

The Psalter is distinctive in the Bible because it takes the form of an anthology of self-contained units each of which has its own unique history. The collection of 150 psalms represents the culmination of a long tradition that extends across almost the full span of the history of ancient Israel, from the Exodus (c. 1280 B.C.) until the last centuries of the Old Testament era (c. 200 B.C.). We will begin our study of the Psalms by considering their present arrangement in the final edition of the book. Then we will consider various categories of psalms by their classification according to theme. Thus, we will be able to interpret their meaning within the setting of Israel's worship and their significance when quoted in the New Testament.

The Book of Psalms

The final editors of the Psalter arranged the psalms into five books (perhaps recalling the Pentateuch): (I) Pss 1–41; (II) Pss 42–72; (III) Pss 73–89; (IV) Pss 90–106; and (V) Pss 107–150. Each of these books ends with a doxology or verse that gives glory to Yahweh (Pss 41:13; 72:18–20; 89:52; 106:48). Psalm 150 is the song of praise that provides the conclusion for the fifth book and for the Psalter as a whole. The wise and regal Psalms 1 and 2 stand at the beginning to serve as introductions to the Psalter. Their importance as a prelude to the whole collection is suggested by the fact that both of them lack the preliminary notation that identifies almost all the remaining prayers in Book I as psalms "of David" (Pss 3–41; except Ps 33). Furthermore, Psalm 2 ends on a refrain that echoes the beatitude announced at the beginning of Psalm 1.

It seems that the final editors preserved intact two other collections inherited from tradition. Psalms 42–83 seem to comprise an "Elohistic" corpus, since each of these psalms prefers the more generic title "God" (Hebrew: Elohim) to the specific name of "Yahweh". Psalms 120–134 comprise another subgroup in which each psalm is a "Song of Ascents". Do the collections in Book I (Pss 1–41) and Book V (Pss 107–150) originate in a consciously "Yahwistic" circle of the faithful at some point in Israel's history? The evidence of their extreme preference for "Yahweh" (more than 270 occurrences in Psalms 1–41; more than 300 occurrences in Psalms 107–150) over "Elohim" (under 20 occurrences in Psalms 1–41; 10 occurrences in Psalms 107–150) provides the basis for such a conjecture.

The editors of the Psalter probably broke up some preexisting collections when they gave the book its ultimate design. The preliminary notations relate some 73 psalms to David. In addition to the collection comprising the first book (Pss 3–41), it is likely that another "Davidic" collection (Pss 51–71; 138–145) circulated as a unit before being incorporated into its present setting.

The psalms of Korah (Pss 42–49; 84; 85; 87; 88), named after the levitical guild of singers at the Temple (2 Chr 20:19; cf. 1 Chr 9:19; 26:1, 19; 1 Chr 6:7), provided choral material suited to both individual and communal worship. The psalms of Asaph (Ps 50; 73–83) bore the name of David's renowned music minister (1 Chr 16:5, 7, 37), who was so proficient as to be called a prophet by the Chronicler (1 Chr 25:1–2). It seems that Asaph's name was synonymous with a tradition of vocal excellence at the Temple for centuries (2 Chr 35:15).

Finally, we note some groupings of psalms according to theme that might have been the work of the Psalter's final editors. Psalms 93–100 announce Yahweh's sovereign rule over his people and over all creation. The Psalter concludes with a succession of Alleluia psalms (Hebrew: *hallelu ya:* "Praise Yahweh"/Pss 146–150).

The complex process of gathering various preexisting collections at different times accounts for the duplicates in the final edition of the Psalter. Psalm 14 appears to be an earlier "Yahwistic" version of the "Elohistic" Psalm 53. Psalm 70 is practically a transcription of Psalm 40:13–17. Psalm 108 is a combination of Psalms 57:7–11 and 60:5–12. Psalms 71 and 31 begin with almost identical words (71:1–3; cf. 31:1–3).

In rare cases, there is room for disagreement about where one psalm ends and another begins. We see this most clearly when we compare the numbering of the psalms in the Septuagint with their identification in the Hebrew Masoretic text. Both versions agree that there are 150 psalms. (The Septuagint contains an apocryphal Psalm 151 but indicates in its title that it is "beyond the number" of the psalms.) However, the Greek numbering of the psalms differs from the Hebrew. Their discrepancies focus on Psalms 9 and 10, 114–16 and 147 (according to the Hebrew numbering system: see "Comparison of Hebrew and Greek Numbering" at the end of the chapter on page 416).

The Septuagint correctly identifies Psalms 9 and 10 as one psalm that follows an acrostic pattern in which the first word of each section begins with a successive letter in the Hebrew alphabet. In a more arbitrary decision, the Septuagint editors decided to view Psalms 114 and 115 as a unity they designate as Psalm 113. In a contrasting manner, they split Psalm 116 into two parts that make up their Psalms 114 (Ps 116:1–9) and 115 (Ps 116:10–19). Once more toward the end of the collection, they divide Psalm 147 into two parts that serve as their Psalms 146 (Ps 147:1–11) and 147 (Ps 147:12–20).

Finally, we note that while neither the Hebrew nor the Greek system takes account of it, Psalms 42 and 43 belong together as a single unit, since the same theme and refrain recur throughout both texts (Pss 42:5–6, 11; 43:5).

The Origins and Authorship of the Psalms

The preliminary notations or headings that introduce 116 of the psalms come from the hands of either composers or editors at various points in Israel's music history. The Hebrew textual tradition counts these titles as the first verse of these psalms, while the Greek tradition joins them to the lines that follow immediately and identifies the resulting combination as the first verse. While the headings provide intriguing indications about such details as psalm type (e.g., a "prayer"/Ps 102/or a "poem"/Ps 44), musical accompaniment (e.g., "on stringed instruments"/Ps 54), and festive occasions (e.g., "For the Sabbath"/Ps 92), the most pressing question they raise focuses on their mention of personal names.

How should we interpret the references to David (Hebrew: l^edavid) in the titles of 73 psalms? Is he their author ("of David")? Or is he mentioned as the patron of liturgical music ("for David")? Or does the reference to him simply indicate that the psalm belongs to a Davidic collection ("of David")? Furthermore, what should we think of the sub-headings that associate 14 psalms (Pss 3; 7; 18; 30; 34; 51; 52; 54; 56; 57; 59; 60; 63; 142) with particular incidents in his life, such as when he fled from his son Absalom (Ps 3; cf. 2 Sm 15:13–17:29) or when Nathan confronted him about his sin with Bathsheba (Ps 51; cf. 2 Sm 11:1–12:31)?

The historical record shows that from his youth David was a skilled musician (1 Sm 16:17–23), and, as king, he sang songs of praise before the ark of the Lord (2 Sm 6:5; cf. 23:1–7). Certainly, he was a patron of liturgical music (1 Chr 16:4–43). It seems very probable that David composed some psalms. However, we cannot be certain which, if any, of the collection in the book of Psalms might have come from his hand. Nevertheless, we can rest assured that David had a pervasive influence in the authorship of the Psalms. Their composers grew up in the tradition David inspired, and the final editors kept his name foremost throughout the collection by preserving it in the preliminary notations of more than half the total number of psalms. In the traditional culture of ancient Israel, where there was greater honor in being associated with the heritage of an ancient master than in seeking individual prominence, both the composers and the editors would have agreed that David was the true author of their work since he was the servant whose love of the Lord truly inspired them. The preliminary notations referring to specific incidents in his life (Ps 18; cf. 2 Sm 22) indicate that either the composer or a later editor was contemplating the character of David when he worked on the psalm.

We must date each of the psalms individually on the basis of indications not in the preliminary notations as much as within the body of the text. The only psalm whose setting in history we can ascertain without difficulty is Psalm 137, which manifestly comes from the period of exile in Babylon (see Ps 137:1–2, 7–9). It seems likely that the compendium of 150 psalms represents almost every era in the history of ancient Israel, from the days prior to the monarchy (c. 1100 B.C.) until the Greek era (c. 250 B.C.). We know that the final editors had to have completed the Psalter before the Septuagint translation was undertaken after 250 B.C.

Grouping the Psalms according to Thematic Types

Scholars generally study the Psalms by grouping together those that share common themes and structure. We will classify the songs and prayers of the Psalter according to four categories: (1) hymns of praise, (2) laments and songs of thanksgiving, (3) royal psalms, and (4) wisdom psalms. We will consider the characteristics that are typical of the psalms in each category and then reflect on the role they played in Israel's worship. After considering the revelation each category communicates, we will reflect on how psalms of each group point forward to Jesus Christ according to the inspired insight of the New Testament writers.

1. Hymns of Praise

The psalms of praise celebrate the majesty and power of Yahweh revealed in creation (e.g., Ps 104) and demonstrated in the saving deeds he has worked in Israel's history (e.g., Ps 105). The hymns of praise follow a basic three-part structure. The opening lines take the form of an invitation to worship the Lord with a song of praise (e.g., Ps 135:1–2). The leader of the assembly would have voiced such words to encourage the congregation to enter into the time of worship. The body of the psalm follows a motive clause (beginning with the words, "for . . ." or "because . . .": Hebrew: *ki* . . .) expressing the reason for acclaiming the Lord (e.g., Ps 135:3–6, 7–18). Here, the psalmist recounts the Lord's attributes manifest in the universe and in the mighty works by which he shows himself faithful to his people. Finally, the psalm comes to a conclusion in a recapitulation of the introduction that reinforces how appropriate it is to praise the Lord, now in light of all that the psalmist has said about him (e.g., Ps 135:19–21).

The hymns of praise can take the form of a personal meditation of the individual (e.g., Pss 8; 139), but most often they presume a setting in the gathering of the whole community for worship at the sanctuary or Temple.

Even when these psalms express their message in the first person singular, they presume that the individuals who are praying have a sense of joining their voices with all their brothers and sisters who similarly confess their faith (e.g., Ps 145).

Three psalms of praise in particular stand out as compositions intended for the celebration of the Temple liturgy. The choir or custodians at the Temple gate probably sang Psalms 15 and 24 to invite the people who approached the sacred precincts to reflect on their state of worthiness evident in acts of justice toward their neighbors (Pss 15:1–5; 24:3–5). Psalm 134, the last of the "Songs of Ascents", seems to be a blessing the priest announced over people as they entered the Temple area.

A subgrouping of the songs of praise extols God's election of Zion as the place he prefers above all others on the face of the earth (Pss 46; 48; 76; 84; 87; 122). The congregation would have voiced such words especially when people gathered from all parts of the country for the great feasts in Jerusalem. Perhaps during a celebration that focused on the presence of the Lord over the ark, the people would have acclaimed the protection of the Lord who is in their midst (Ps 46).

Another thematic category of the hymns proclaims Yahweh as king over the people (Pss 47; 93; 96–99). These psalms played a central role in the celebration at the Temple on the great feasts of Israel. They emphasize the sovereignty of Yahweh over the world (Pss 93; 97–99) and especially over his people (Pss 47; 96). The announcement of the Lord's reign motivates the members of his covenanted people to turn from their wickedness and also to find security in his presence (Pss 96; 97).

Toward the New Testament: The One Who Is over All Things

The hymns of praise offered the New Testament writers insight into the authority of Jesus over creation and over the Church. We will concentrate our attention on their manner of quoting Psalm 8 to illustrate the majesty of the risen Christ and the power of his redemption for those who believe in him.

In its original form, Psalm 8 provides a meditation on the primacy of human beings over all other creatures. Only the descendants of Adam bear the image of God and exercise stewardship over creation (Ps 8:5–6; cf. Gn 1:26–31). Both the author of Hebrews and Paul were forthright enough to acknowledge how reality challenges the psalmist's assertion that God has submitted all things to mankind's authority (Ps 8:6). In fact, when we look at the affliction of people and the state of our world, sometimes we have reason to question both the glory of individuals and their capacity to exercise authority over their situations.

The author of Hebrews frankly admits that, at the moment, man does not have the authority over the universe that the psalmist suggested (Heb 2:5–9). Therefore, the psalmist describes a divine promise that reaches fulfillment only in Christ. In fact, according to the inspired reading of the author of Hebrews, the whole psalm reveals Christ as the one who mediates the fulfillment of God's promise by his death and Resurrection. Hebrews quotes the Septuagint version of the psalm because it emphasizes that only "for a short while" did God make the child of Adam less than the angels. For Jesus, this "short while" comprised the days of his earthly life, but now, in virtue of his Resurrection, he is "crowned . . . with glory and honor" (Heb 2:7). Hebrews' exposure of the psalm's deeper meaning in the light of Christ functions on the principle of Jesus' solidarity with mankind. Christ is God's vision for humanity, and Jesus' death is the event that redeems mankind, enabling us to partake in the glorious life of Christ.

Paul alludes to Psalm 8 whenever he speaks about Christ subjecting all things to himself by means of his death and Resurrection (1 Cor 15:27; Phil 3:21; cf. Eph 1:22; 1 Pt 3:22; Ps 8:6). Whereas the psalmist was thinking of how mankind exercises dominion over the physical world by means of work, for example, by fishing and tending livestock (Ps 8:5–8), Paul saw more deeply into the text in light of Christ and realized that "all things" especially referred to the great enemies that oppress us, such as "every ruling force and power", including death itself (1 Cor 15:24–28). By the event of his cross, Christ has overcome all that separates humanity from God, and he promises a participation in his Resurrection to all who share in his life by faith (Phil 3:21).

In the Gospel of Matthew, Jesus quotes an earlier verse of the psalm (Ps 8:2) to indicate that the acclamations with which the crowds greeted him in the Temple constitute a fulfillment of Scripture (Mt 21:16, quoting the Septuagint). The manner in which Matthew employs the psalm in his Gospel accomplishes two functions: first, it provides an indirect scriptural support for the confession of the crowd that Jesus is the son of David (Mt 21:15), and, secondly, it describes the type of faith necessary to receive life from Christ. Only those who "change and become like little children . . . " can enter the Kingdom of heaven (Mt 18:1–4; cf. 21:16). The children who acclaim Jesus in the Temple provide the symbol of the Christian community that looks to the Lord with joy and humility in contrast to the indignant religious leaders who oppose him.

2. Psalms of Lament, Thanksgiving, and Faith

More than half the psalms in the Psalter focus on God's activity of delivering his people from affliction and death. Both the psalms of lament and those of thanksgiving appeal to Yahweh as the Redeemer, but they do so from differing perspectives: the psalms of lament express the sorrow of someone who is seeking deliverance, while the prayers of thanksgiving express the gratitude of someone who has recently experienced deliverance. The psalms of faith express confidence in Yahweh but lack the intensity that the immediacy of danger present or past generates in the prayers of either lament or gratitude.

The psalms of lament and thanksgiving share the same basic six-part structure: (a) an appeal to the Lord's name in the opening lines; (b) a description of suffering in the present (lament) or in the past (thanksgiving); (c) a plea for deliverance in the present (lament) or past (thanksgiving); (d) an exposition of the worthiness of the cause; (e) a vow to offer sacrifice in gratitude for the deliverance; and (f) a declaration of thanksgiving to the Lord.

The psalms of national or communal lament express the grief that issues from the heart of ancient Israel in the depths of affliction. While no other psalm contains the historical detail evident in Psalm 137 (which certainly comes from the Exile), nevertheless, we can estimate the general situations that prompted the composition of many psalms. For instance, we can be confident that the destruction of Jerusalem in 587 B.C. was the dominant topic of numerous laments (such as Pss 44; 74; 79; 80; cf. Lam 1:1–5:22). The end of the Exile brought with it an anticipation of a new era of peace in the Promised Land (Pss 85; 123). However, the hardship of restoration challenged the people's faith and caused them to review the former days prior to the Babylonian invasion when the Lord made Israel secure in the land (Ps 77). The harassment by foreigners at the time of Nehemiah might have caused the psalmists to express anger toward other nations and their rulers, similar in tone to the prospect of judgment that prophets such as Obadiah and Joel expressed (Pss 82; 83; cf. Ob vv. 1–21; Jl 4:1–17). Another most important source of Israel's grief was her sin, which the people confessed in a national liturgy of repentance (Ps 106; cf. Neh 9:5–37; Is 63:7–64:11).

Israel sang the psalms of faith and thanksgiving at harvest time to express gratitude for the abundant crops (Pss 65; 67). Deliverance from immediate danger (Ps 124) and from the threat of Zion's enemies (Ps 125) provided additional incentive to give thanks to God for his mighty deeds throughout Israel's history (Ps 68). The description of the new Exodus (Ps 66; cf. Is 44:27; 50:2) and the exhortation against idolatry (Ps 115; cf. Is 44:9–20) suggest the influence of Deutero-Isaiah's tradition in the development of postexilic psalmody. Composers formulated the great liturgical hymn of thanksgiving for the

Temple liturgy, which in the preexilic days would have been appropriate for a king celebrating a military triumph and, in the postexilic era, for celebrating the renewal of life at the Temple (Ps 118; cf. Neh 8:13–18).

The laments of individuals express the outcry of the afflicted (Hebrew: *'anawim*), who have only Yahweh as their source of healing and deliverance from sickness and oppression. These psalms proclaim that Yahweh is on the side of the abandoned, in contradiction to the popular wisdom that maintained that sickness and misfortune were indications of God's disfavor (Ps 69). When the poor cry out to the Lord, they pray for vindication in the sight of their wicked oppressors (Ps 28). Jeremiah's Confessions (e.g., Jer 20:7–18) and Deutero-Isaiah's Song of the Suffering Servant (Is 52:13–53:12) inspired the profound psalmody of the suffering of the Lord's faithful one (Ps 22). Another cause of personal affliction is individual sin that God heals in response to the confession of guilt expressed in the seven penitential psalms (Pss 6; 32; 38; 51; 102; 130; 143).

The psalms of personal faith express the confidence of individuals who renew their commitment to rely on Yahweh as their source of life and hope (Ps 16). The faithful person approaches the Lord in the vigor of life and prays for greater understanding and submission to the ways of the Lord (Ps 27). The person who trusts in the Lord decides not to fear the power of the wicked, because, in the past, he or she has experienced the Lord's mercy and faithfulness (Ps 116).

Toward the New Testament: The Rejected One Who Is the Cornerstone

In order to appreciate the wealth of revelation that issues from God's word in light of Christ, we will devote our attention to four psalms of lament and thanksgiving that find their fullest expression in the death and Resurrection of Jesus. Psalms 22 and 69 prefigure his death, Psalm 16 contains a suggestion of his Resurrection, while Psalm 118 indicates how rejection of the Messiah is part of God's design to establish Christ as the foundation of his redeemed people.

Psalm 22. Jesus' suffering and execution as a criminal was the greatest obstacle to believing that he was the Messiah. When he interpreted his messianic character to his disciples, Jesus referred to himself as the Lord's Suffering Servant prophesied by Deutero-Isaiah (Is 52:13–53:12; e.g., Mk 10:45; 14:24). Another text he highlighted was Psalm 22, a lament of an individual, which originally might have drawn its inspiration from the last Servant Song (Ps 22; cf. Is 52:13–53:12; Mk 15:34; Mt 27:46).

The fact that we have his native Aramaic words quoted in the Greek texts of Matthew and Mark substantiates the claim beyond doubt that Jesus actually quoted the first verse of Psalm 22 when he died on the cross (Mk 15:34; Mt 27:46; cf. Ps 22:1). While these words express to God a sense of absolute abandonment, they do not ultimately represent despair but faith. We must recall that, as the lament of the righteous one who suffers unjustly, Psalm 22 reaches a climax in its last third (Ps 22:22–31), which expresses the servant's confidence that God will rescue and vindicate him. In light of the mystery of Christ, the first two-thirds of Psalm 22 describe Jesus' death (Ps 22:1–21) and the last third, his Resurrection (Ps 22:22–31).

The evangelists who wrote the Gospels constantly allude to Psalm 22 in their description of Jesus' Passion since the details of the events correspond so closely to this text. Three episodes stand out: the soldiers gambling for his clothes (Mk 15:24; Mt 27:35; Lk 23:34; cf. Jn 19:24; Ps 22:18), the mannerisms of the crowd (Mk 15:29; Mt 27:39; Lk 23:35; cf. Ps 22:7), and their mocking him (Mt 27:43; cf. Ps 22:9). Furthermore, Psalm 22 takes us beyond Jesus' death to his Resurrection. When Jesus appears as the risen Lord and identifies his disciples as his "brothers", he is alluding to the victorious side of the psalm, which prefigures not just his own Resurrection but the new relationship that Jesus' followers have with their Lord by virtue of his death and Resurrection (Mt 28:10; Jn 20:17; Heb 2:12; cf. Ps 22:22, 25, 30).

Psalm 69. This is another psalm that reveals Jesus as the Christ precisely in the scandalous event of his death on the cross. As with Psalm 22, the evangelists discovered here a detail of Scripture that corresponded precisely with an incident that took place at the time of Jesus' death. The action of a bystander giving Jesus vinegar to drink in his last moment reveals Jesus as the Messiah insofar as the gesture fulfills what the Scripture had foretold (Mk 15:36; Mt 27:48; cf. Lk 23:36; cf. Ps 69:21). The account of Jesus' final moments in the Gospel of John draws our attention to both Psalms 22 and 69 when the evangelist tells us that Jesus says "I thirst" in order to fulfill the Scripture (Jn 19:28–29; cf. Pss 69:21; 22:15).

The New Testament writers perceived that Psalm 69 casts light on both the death of Jesus and the enmity of those who opposed him. The Gospel of John refers to another verse in the psalm to indicate that Jesus died because of his zeal for the Temple (Jn 2:17, 21; cf. Ps 69:9). In the same Gospel, Jesus quotes yet another line when he explains to his disciples that the world's hatred of him is unjustified but nevertheless conforms to the promise of God's word (Jn 15:25; cf. Ps 69:4). Furthermore, in the Acts of the Apostles, Luke quotes another verse about the destiny of the righteous one's oppressors in order to interpret the death of Judas (Acts 1:20; cf. Ps 69:25).

Psalm 16. In order to emphasize that Jesus is the Messiah by virtue of his Resurrection, Luke directs our attention to a psalm that expresses the trust of one who loves Yahweh. In relating the primary sermons of Peter (at Pentecost/ Acts 2:14–36) and Paul (in Pisidian Antioch/Acts 13:16–41), Acts appeals to Psalm 16 to demonstrate that Jesus' Resurrection reveals him to be even greater than David. In its original form, Psalm 16 expresses the conviction that Yahweh will not abandon his faithful one to Sheol (Ps 16:10). While the psalmist could simply be expressing the conviction that Yahweh will preserve him for a long time from physical death, it is also possible that he is suggesting a life with God beyond death. The final parts of Psalms 16 (16:9–11), 49 (49:15), and 73 (73:23–28) express a vague openness to life after death that becomes clearer in the later texts about resurrection (Dn 12:2; 2 Mc 7:9).

Peter quotes Psalm 16 in order to demonstrate that, in view of his Resurrection, Jesus surpasses the stature of even David, and therefore he is the promised Messiah (Acts 2:25–32; cf. Ps 16:8–11). First of all, by directly attributing the psalm to David, Peter gives the venerable king the role of prophet who foretells the Messiah (Acts 2:25). After quoting the psalm, Peter goes on to argue that the text cannot refer to David because his body lies in a tomb in Jerusalem. By contrast, Jesus' tomb is empty because he has experienced a bodily resurrection as the "holy one" whom God would not allow to undergo corruption (Acts 2:29–32). The psalm, which originally offered only a vague reference to life after death, now expresses a clear testimony to the uniqueness and power of Jesus' Resurrection from the dead. In this way, Psalm 16 offers scriptural support to the confession that, through his Resurrection, Jesus is Lord and Messiah (Acts 2:36).

Psalm 118. The Gospel proclaims as Messiah the one whom mankind has rejected. As the new people of God, the Christian community claims as its Lord the one whom most of the covenanted people had cast out from their midst. In order to gain deeper insight into the paradox Jesus poses to our minds, the New Testament writers turned to Psalm 118. Originally, the psalm acclaimed Yahweh's victory on behalf of the king and the people of Israel. If it originated in the preexilic period, it announced the Lord rescuing the king and his troops from almost certain military defeat. When sung in the postexilic period of restoration, the psalm probably celebrated the rebuilding or refurbishing of the Temple and, in the process, drew attention to the cornerstone (Ps 118:22–24).

The New Testament authors focused on two verses of the psalm in particular. The acclamation greeting the king or priest as he entered the Temple in the celebration now refers to Jesus, the Messiah, who comes to bring salvation as he fulfills his mission in Jerusalem (Mk 11:9–10; Mt 21:9; Lk

19:38; Jn 12:13; cf. Ps 118:25–26). Moreover, a prior verse in the psalm reflects upon Jesus as the one who brings salvation precisely in the event of his people's rejecting him. The New Testament evangelists and teachers realized that Scripture foreshadowed the Jewish authorities' rejection of Jesus (Mk 12:10–11; Mt 21:42; Lk 20:17; Acts 4:11; 1 Pt 2:7; cf. Ps 118:22). By the marvelous design of God, this rejection opened the way for him to provide the foundation for the universal Church, which would gather both Jew and Gentile into one body.

3. The Royal Psalms

God's covenant with David provided Israel with the assurance of enduring as an everlasting kingdom (2 Sm 7:4–17). Because the king was the servant of Yahweh, he was a prominent figure in the religious life of Israel. The royal psalms exhibit a common concern for the welfare of Israel's king. Together, they represent a diversity of prayer forms including: intercessions (Pss 20; 72; 144:1–11), confession of trust (Pss 18; 101), prophecies of victory (Ps 21), liturgies of enthronement (Pss 2; 110), commemoration of the covenant (Pss 89; 132), and a wedding song (Ps 45).

The "messianic" psalms (Pss 2; 110; 72; 89:19–37; 132) look for the coming of the future king who will fulfill the promises God made to David and through him to his people. The messianic prophecies influenced the development and interpretation of these psalms over the course of Israel's history (Is 9:5–6; 11:1–5; Mi 5:1–3; Jer 23:5–6; Ez 34:23–24; 37:24–28; Zec 3:8; 6:12; 9:9). In fact, some of the messianic psalms contain the oracles that Temple prophets announced at the liturgy of enthronement (e.g., Pss 2:7; 89:19–37; cf. 110:1–7).

Psalms 2 and 110 merit particular attention in light of their importance in the New Testament. Psalm 2 originated as a song that echoed through the Temple at the enthronement of the king. The text exalts the status of Zion as the mountain upon which Solomon built the Temple and where God had chosen to dwell (Ps 2:6; cf. 2 Sm 5:7–9; Is 2:1–3; 11:9). Yahweh has preferred Jerusalem to all other places and vows to protect her from the oppressive nations who threaten attack. The high point of the liturgy occurs when the king announces that he has heard the Lord call him his son and thus claim him as his own by virtue of adoption on the day of his coronation or enthronement (Ps 2:7; cf. 2 Sm 7:14). After the Exile, when Israel no longer had a king, this psalm of enthronement was interpreted as a prophecy of a future messianic king.

Psalm 110 might have originated in the very early days of the monarchy at the enthronement of either David or Solomon in Jerusalem. The psalm consists of two parts, each of which is a prophetic declaration to the king. In the first part (110:1–3), the prophet announces Yahweh's enthronement of the king at his "right hand", with authority to exercise dominion over the surrounding nations. In the second part (110:4–7), the prophet confers on Israel's king a priestly status like that of Melchizedek, the ancient king of Jerusalem, who blessed Abraham in the venerable days of the Patriarchs. In both parts of the psalm, Yahweh promises his king a dominion that will have worldwide extension.

Toward the New Testament: The Messianic King

The New Testament teachers announce that Jesus fulfills the messianic expectations contained in Psalms 2 and 110. They quote these psalms to reveal the identity of Jesus as the Son of God in a manner that would have been inconceivable to the original composers of these prophetic verses.

In the early proclamation of the Gospel, the evangelists first apply to Jesus the prophetic words of sonship by virtue of his Resurrection from the dead (Acts 13:33; Rom 1:4; cf. Ps 2:7). The same text of the psalm resonates in the Father's identification of Jesus as "my Son" at his baptism (Mk 1:11; Mt 3:17; Lk 3:22; cf. Jn 1:34). The texts in the Greek of the New Testament take on an exalted meaning that exceeds the boundaries of their original Semitic context. Whereas the king received an adoptive sonship conferred on him by the prophetic word, Jesus reveals a truly divine sonship since he participates in the life of God his Father. The words of the psalm as applied to Christ verify the truth that, as the Son of God, he has a dignity beyond that of the angels (Heb 1:4–5; cf. Ps 2:7).

Just as Psalm 2 reflects the divine sonship of Jesus, which the disciples first comprehended in light of his Resurrection, so Psalm 110 manifests the authority he exercises over the universe as the exalted Lord. Through his Resurrection and Ascension, Jesus has taken his place at "the right hand" of God (Acts 2:33–35; cf. Ps 110:1). By his Resurrection, Jesus has not simply overcome personal death; he has also established his reign as Lord over the cosmos.

Again when applied to Jesus, the inspired text surpasses the conceptual limitations of its original composer. While the prophet-psalmist used the image of sitting at the right hand of God to illustrate God's anointing of Israel's king to guarantee victory against the surrounding nations (Ps 110), the Christian evangelists perceived that the text speaks of Christ, who exercises God's authority over all the powers of darkness in the world (Rom 8:34; 1 Cor 15:24–25; Eph 1:20–21; cf. Col 3:1; cf. Ps 110:1). Jesus, the exalted Lord who now governs the world, will return to establish the fullness of God's reign over all things in the end time (Mk 14:62; Mt 26:64; Lk 22:69; cf. Ps 110:1).

The author of Hebrews develops a magnificent exposition of Jesus' priest-hood on the basis of the reference to Melchizedek in the same psalm (Heb 5:6, 10; 7:17, 21; cf. Ps 110:4). Jesus' sacrifice consists of the surrender of his life in obedience to the Father (Heb 5:6–10). Now he exercises a heavenly priesthood that has infinitely surpassed the old order because of the divine power and quality of Jesus' ministry in the heavenly sanctuary (Heb 7:1–10:18).

4. The Wisdom Psalms

The psalms that contain directions and admonitions about the proper conduct of one's life express the spirituality of Israel's wisdom tradition. Many of these psalms are not so much prayers as reflections that offer guiding principles for living in everyday circumstances. We can usually recognize wisdom psalms by their themes. These texts contrast the life of the virtuous with that of the wicked (Ps 37) and confront us with the decision of choosing between the pathway that leads to life and the one that leads to death (Ps 1). The wisdom tradition extols the Torah as the source of all righteousness (Ps 119) and upholds the fear of the Lord as the foremost of virtues (Pss 34; 112). Often the wisdom psalms exhibit a distinctive form, for instance, by following an acrostic pattern (Pss 34; 37; 111; 112; 119) or by formulating beatitudes (Pss 1:1; 32:1–2; 128:1) or by handing on proverbs (Ps 37:1, 5, 16, 23, 37–38).

Psalms that offer moral and religious exhortations seem to form a connec-tion between the schools of prophecy and of wisdom. One of these psalms sounds like the admonitions of Israel's earliest literary prophets, who decried the futility of ritual worship without social justice (Ps 50; cf. Am 5:21–27). A couple of them convey the Temple prophet's appeal to the assembled worship-pers that they would obey the Lord's word (Pss 81; 95). Other psalms offer personal advice typical of the wisdom schools, exposing the folly of those whose ignorance of God is manifest in their manner of living (Pss 14; 52–54).

Toward the New Testament: True Blessedness

The wisdom psalms provide an introduction to the Christian life. The concern for choosing the correct "way" of living (Pss 1:1–6; 119:1) provided the basis for designating the followers of Jesus as members of "the Way" (Acts 9:2; 18:25–26; 19:9, 23; 22:4; 24:14, 22; cf. Jn 14:6).

A brief summary of the quotations of some wisdom psalms in the New Testament provides a collage of principles that guide the life of the community. When Jesus declares the beatitude of the meek who will inherit the earth, he is quoting a wisdom psalm that identifies the afflicted (Hebrew: *'anawim*) as the ones whom God cherishes (Mt 5:4; cf. Ps 37:11). According to the charter for community that Jesus presents in the beatitudes, his disciples become the poor of the Lord (*'anawim*) in the world.

Paul quotes another wisdom psalm in order to cultivate the virtues of generosity and lack of material possessiveness among the Corinthians when he invites them to contribute to the collection for the impoverished church in Jerusalem (2 Cor 9:8–9; cf. Ps 112:9). Christians have received salvation as Christ's gift (2 Cor 8:9), which they could not merit because all humanity has fallen short of God's glory (Rom 3:10–12; cf. Ps 14:1–3). Having received new life through baptism into Christ, every Christian must respond to the admonition that originated with the Temple prophets, who exhorted the people not to harden their hearts but to respond to the Lord's voice and so enter into his rest (Heb 3:7–11; cf. Ps 95:7–11).

STUDY QUESTIONS

1. How were the psalms meant to be voiced?
2. What are four categories of psalms?
3. What historical events may underlie the psalms of lament?
4. How does Psalm 8 illustrate the majesty of the risen Christ?
5. How are Psalms 22 and 69 significant to the crucifixion of Jesus?
6. How are Psalms 16 and 118 relevant to Jesus as Messiah?
7. How are Psalms 2 and 110 interpreted in light of Jesus?
8. How do the wisdom psalms portray "the Way"?
9. Discuss how it is not possible to read the psalms without also praying them. Why do you think they have this effect?
10. How does the act of singing thanksgiving in the psalms differ from the way you normally pray to God?
11. Discuss in what way the psalmists seem to have an intimate relationship with God that we frequently miss in our formal prayer. How can we retrieve that sense of divine intimacy?
12. When do you most feel like singing to the Lord? In times of joy? of sorrow? Select the psalms you identify with most and consider praying them as part of your daily prayer.

PSALMS

Outline

Book I	Psalms 1–41
Book II	Psalms 42–72
Book III	Psalms 73–89
Book IV	Psalms 90–106
Book V	Psalms 107–50

Comparison of Hebrew and Greek Numbering

HEBREW	GREEK
1–8	1–8
9–10	9
11–113	10–112
114–15	113
116:1–9	114
116:10–19	115
117–46	116–45
147:1–11	146
147:12–20	147
148–50	148–50

A CLASSIFICATION OF THE PSALMS

I.   Hymns of Praise
      A.   Songs of the Community and of Individuals: Psalms 8, 19,
            29, 33, 78, 104, 105, 111, 113, 114, 117, 129, 134, 135, 136, 139,
            145, 146, 147, 148, 149, 150

      B.   Liturgical Psalms: Psalms 15, 24, 134

      C.   Songs of the Lord's Kingship: Psalms 47, 93, 95, 96, 97, 98,
            99, 100

      D.   The Songs of Zion: Psalms 46, 48, 76, 84, 87, 122

II.   Psalms of Lament and Prayers for Deliverance
      A.   Of the Community: Psalms 44, 60, 74, 77, 79, 80, 82, 83,
            85, 90, 94, 106, 108, 123, 126, 137

      B.   Of the Individual: Psalms 5, 7, 12, 13, 17, 22, 25, 26, 28, 31,
            35, 36, 39, 42–43, 54, 55, 56, 57, 58, 59, 61, 63, 64, 69, 70,
            71, 86, 88, 109, 120, 140, 141, 142
            Penitential Psalms: 6, 32, 38, 51, 102, 130, 143

III. Psalms of Thanksgiving and Trust
      A.   Of the Community: Psalms 65, 66, 67, 68, 103, 115, 118,
            124, 125, 129

      B.   Of the Individual: Psalms 3, 4, 9–10, 11, 16, 23, 27, 30, 34,
            40, 41, 62, 92, 107, 116, 121, 131, 138

IV.   Royal Psalms

      Psalms 2, 18, 20, 21, 45, 72, 89, 101, 110, 132, 144

V.   Wisdom Psalms

      Psalms 1, 32, 34, 37, 49, 73, 91, 112, 119, 127, 128, 133, 139

      Exhortations: Psalms 14 (=53), 50, 52, 75, 81, 95

(Adapted by permission from *The Psalms, Their Origin and Meaning*, by L. Sabourin
[New York: Alba House, 1969], 443.)

32

THE PROVERBS: WISDOM FOR LIVING

"A stitch in time saves nine." "A bird in the hand is worth two in the bush." "Better late than never." All of us use proverbs of some kind or other in our daily language. Generally we repeat these pithy sayings when we are explaining our behavior to others or when we are teaching the young how to make practical decisions.

What are proverbs? What purpose do they serve? Proverbs are traditional sayings that capture our attention because they are short, rhythmic, and wise. We use them, in part, because they help to relieve the stress of the moment by getting us out of ourselves. Proverbs have two wonderful qualities: they make us smile, and they temper our loneliness. They possess these qualities because proverbs are at once both witty and traditional. Their spriteful cadence humors us and helps to relieve us of the burden of self-concern. Because they communicate the wisdom of our forebears, proverbs connect us with our heritage and thereby moderate our sense of being all alone when facing moral dilemmas. Finally, proverbs can offer a sense of consistency in our lives, since we tend to employ our favorite ones to explain our behavior in a variety of situations.

In summary, proverbs reduce stress and improve our practical judgment in decision-making. A treasury of proverbs is an unparalleled asset to every parent, homemaker, business person, and student in today's world.

The Collection of Proverbs

The book of Proverbs is the Bible's compendium of practical wisdom. In fact, as we outline the book according to the titles embedded in the text, we realize that Proverbs is an anthology of ancient collections: (1) poems on wisdom (1:1–9:18); (2) "The Proverbs of Solomon" (10:1–22:16); (3) "Thirty Sayings of the Sages" (22:17–24:22); (4) "More Sayings of the Sages" (24:23–34); (5) "Proverbs of Solomon Transcribed under Hezekiah" (25:1–29:27); (6) "The Words of Agur" (30:1–14); (7) Numerical Proverbs (30:15–33); (8) "The Words of Lemuel" (31:1–9); and (9) an Ode to the Exemplary Wife (31:10–31). A preliminary observation of form highlights the fact that two poetic sections (1:1–9:18 and 31:10–31) frame a general collection of individual proverbs that makes up the body of the text (10:1–31:9).

Perusing Proverbs is like walking through a shop of fine antiques. We appreciate the value of the collection more when we identify its assorted portions according to the place and time of their origin. The proverbs come from outside as well as within Israel's borders. The notation that Agur and Lemuel both come from the tribe of Massa in northern Arabia attests to the book's international flavor (30:1; 31:1; Gn 25:14). We find further certification of Proverbs' cosmopolitan aspect when we discover that the "Thirty Sayings of the Sages" (22:17–24:22) derive from *The Wisdom of Amenemophis,* an Egyptian document of the eleventh century B.C. The material of domestic origin in Israel is gathered in two collections: (1) "The Proverbs of Solomon" (10:1–22:16) consist of elements that date back to the days of the patron-king himself, but these are indistinguishable from the elements of later tradition that accumulated during the period of the monarchy up to the time of the Exile (c. 970–587 B.C.); and (2) the second collection of "Solomon's Proverbs" (25:1–29:17), which, according to 25:1, was compiled after the fall of the northern kingdom but a century before the Exile during the reign of the reformer King Hezekiah (716–687 B.C.).

The two poetic sections (1:1–9:18; 31:10–31) that frame the anthology of ancient proverbs (10:1–31:9) are the latest compositions in the book. The ode to the exemplary wife (31:10–31), which concludes the book, is an acrostic or alphabetical poem (like Pss 9–10; 25; 34; 37; 111; 112; 119; 145, and the five psalms of Lamentations), dating perhaps from the fifth century B.C. The final editors of the book of Proverbs composed the opening nine chapters (1:1–9:18). They crafted these magnificent poems as the mature flowering of the seeds of the wisdom tradition that earlier generations had sown in the form of individual proverbs. The final authors gave the book of Proverbs its present definitive shape around 400 B.C., probably in the wake of the reforms of Ezra and Nehemiah.

The Origin of Proverbs

Biblical tradition ascribed the Law to Moses, the Psalms to David, and the wisdom books of Proverbs, Song of Songs, and Qoheleth (Ecclesiastes) to Solomon. Our survey of the book's contents indicates that Solomon was not the author of Proverbs. However, as David was a most qualified patron of the Psalms, so Solomon was a most qualified patron of the wisdom tradition. We recall that Solomon prayed only for wisdom when he ascended to the throne of his father David in 970 B.C. (1 Kgs 3:9). So pleased was the Lord with the king's request that he bestowed upon him unparalleled success in the history of Israel's monarchy (1 Kgs 3:10–14).

Solomon was responsible for creating the climate in Jerusalem that allowed the wisdom tradition to take root and to flourish. We detect his at least indirect influence on Proverbs in a three-fold manner. First, Solomon is the best witness to the practical dimension of wisdom underscored throughout Proverbs. The great king's genius did not consist in abstract reflection but in the exercise of practical judgment to govern his people and to strengthen their position in the world. His wisdom was manifest in the unprecedented extension of Israel's frontiers, the erection of fortifications, the reinforcement of the military, the establishment of a naval fleet, and the fine construction of the Lord's Temple and the king's palace in Jerusalem (1 Kgs 3:16–7:51). Solomon's reputation for proverbs and songs was matched by his genius as an administrator in the world of his day (1 Kgs 5:12). From him, we realize that wisdom in proverbs leads to action, not to idle speculation.

Second, by transforming Jerusalem into a cosmopolitan city, Solomon provided the conditions necessary for Israelite wisdom to take on a cosmopolitan aspect. His negotiations with Hiram brought craftsmen from Tyre to work on the Temple project (1 Kgs 5:15–30); his marriage to Pharaoh's daughter sealed an alliance with Egypt (1 Kgs 3:1); his opening up trade with Africa, Asia Minor, and points west as well as with Arabia and Mesopotamia to the east brought visitors from afar. The Queen of Sheba's adulation of Solomon is indicative of his international renown (1 Kgs 10:1–29). The influence of Arabia and Egypt evident in Proverbs derives from Solomon's initiative to open Jerusalem's gates to the whole ancient world.

Third, because Solomon understood the value of learning, it is most likely that Israel established schools under his patronage similar to institutions of learning in Egypt and Mesopotamia. Although we have no definite evidence of them in the Bible, these would have been diplomatic academies for training young men to serve in the royal court and to be ambassadors in foreign affairs. Such academies cultivated wisdom with an international flavor and assured its transmission from one generation to the next. The book of Proverbs is a compendium of Israelite wisdom spanning five or six centuries, from the time of Solomon (970–931 B.C.) until the era of Nehemiah, the great diplomat and organizer (445–c. 410 B.C.). In the successive stages of its development, Proverbs might have served as a textbook used in training well-born young men for diplomatic service in the royal court before the Exile and in the governing assembly after the Exile.

10:1–31:9: Instructions of the Ancients

Following the historical development of the book, we will peruse the more ancient collection of proverbs (10:1–31:9) before examining the poetic sections at the beginning and end of the book (1:1–9:18; 31:10–31).

The proverb is the basic literary form that dominates the whole compendium of ancient material (10:1–31:9). The Hebrew proverb is a self-contained pithy statement consisting of two parallel lines set in equilibrium with the purpose of communicating an insight for practical living. Because the proverb is an independent unit that does not rely on its context within the book for its meaning, each proverb stands by itself and demands that we evaluate it according to its unique capacity to crystallize truth. Only in rare instances do proverbs cluster around particular themes, such as the Lord's sovereignty over human affairs (16:1–9) or the qualities demanded of a king (16:10–15) or the treachery of an uncontrolled tongue (12:13–23; 10:18–21).

We must scan the whole collection in order to identify the primary issues in Proverbs. For the purpose of offering a brief thematic summary, we will assemble the material around three issues: (1) the nature of wisdom; (2) the virtues of the wise; and (3) the social implications of wisdom.

Wisdom is essential for a meaningful existence (13:14; 16:22). Life is a matter of continual decisions, and a person must have wisdom in order to make the right ones (14:16; 19:20; 23:19; 24:5–6; 28:26). This is why everyone should invest in wisdom rather than in material benefits (16:16; 19:8; 23:4, 23). Wisdom is practical, not theoretical. It is the quality that distinguishes a prudent homemaker (14:1), a shrewd warrior (24:5; 21:22), and a just ruler (31:1–9). In particular, wisdom provides adeptness in handling personal relationships. It is the practical capacity to work out our lives with others, beginning within the family (17:6; 23:22), extending to friendships (13:20) and even to proper comportment in the presence of the king (23:1–2).

Acquiring wisdom is an arduous task demanding long-term perseverance and commitment. From childhood, everyone has a tendency toward folly that leads to self-destruction (22:15; 29:17). Selfish desire rules the "fool", who therefore is lazy (24:30–34), deceptive (10:18), thoughtless (18:2), hot-tempered (12:16), quarrelsome (20:3), and unrestrained (14:16). The perversity goes very deep because folly is blind to its own existence and defies correction (12:15). Self-righteousness is the enemy of wisdom (26:12), for the mind is easily deceived (14:12; 28:26).

How, then, do we acquire wisdom? In a word, through discipline (12:1). "Reproof" and "admonition" coincide with "instruction" (10:17; 15:32). Gaining wisdom in the biblical sense is more a matter of desire and will than of intelligence. We must seek wisdom by accepting correction with a readiness to change our manner of life (15:5; 19:20). Since no one is born innately wise, everyone gains understanding by living with a master—a role filled first of all by mother and father (23:22; 31:1). "Whoever walks with the wise becomes wise . . . " (13:20).

Ultimately, wisdom consists in obeying the Lord, who accomplishes his purposes in our lives (19:21). The Lord mysteriously works out his plan in ways that are incomprehensible to the individual (20:24; 16:1, 9). We receive genuine wisdom by trusting in the Lord (16:20) who probes the innermost depths of the human spirit (16:2; 17:3; 20:27).

Virtue is the essential means of acquiring wisdom. Fear of the Lord is the primary virtue that undergirds all others. This virtue has nothing to do with being frightened of God. On the contrary, fear of the Lord is the capacity of being open to God so that we live in harmony with him as we become ever more conscious of his glory and goodness manifest in creation. This practice of submitting to God in all things constitutes in itself the school of wisdom (15:33). Fearing the Lord means reverencing his plan and order for all things, obeying his commandments, and allowing his truth to shape one's life. It is a personal orientation toward reality that has the practical effect of providing for and securing one's home life (19:23). This virtue is the pathway to life (14:27) and the only sure foundation for family life in the world (14:26).

Other allies of wisdom are humility and prudence, while its primary enemy is pride (11:2; 16:18; 18:12). Honesty and discretion are distinguishing marks of the wise (12:19; 17:24). Wisdom and righteousness are companions in life. The righteous person demonstrates wisdom in action (10:31). In Proverbs, just as the wise are contrasted with the foolish (10:8), so the righteous are counterpoised to the wicked (10:20). Righteousness defines the person who lives with integrity in relationship both to God and other human beings. The authors of Proverbs exhibit almost unqualified confidence that the righteous will attain success and longevity, while the wicked will perish in the end (14:32; 16:31; 21:21). Nevertheless, they refuse to consider achievement in materialistic terms: "Better have little and with it uprightness than great revenues with injustice" (16:8).

Social justice is the fruit of wisdom and righteousness. The righteous person is distinguished by a sensitivity for the just claims of the poor (19:17; 22:9; 29:7). Providence will always reward those who are generous toward the needy but will frustrate the negligent and miserly (28:8, 27). The justice a king brings to the oppressed will determine the quality of his reign (29:14; 31:8–9).

The inspired sages perceived that the afflicted belong to the Lord in a special way, and, therefore, serving their needs is an act of reverence for their Creator (14:31). Foreshadowing a sentiment of Job, they assert that the Lord is the "Redeemer" (*go'el*) of the afflicted, their nearest kin who will defend their rights and punish their oppressors (22:22–23; 23:10–11; Lv 25:23–25; cf. Jb 19:25–29).

1:1–9:18; 31:10–31: Wisdom's Personality

The poetic sections that form a parenthesis around the collections of individual proverbs represent the latest compositions in the whole book. The final editors placed them at the beginning (1:1–9:18) and at the end (31:10–31) of the text in order to highlight truths that were particularly central to the wisdom tradition in view of their life situation in postexilic Judah of the fifth century B.C.

We will focus our attention on the two spheres of wisdom's manifestation highlighted by the inspired authors in the introduction and conclusion of the book: first, in marriage, parenting, and family life; and, secondly, in creation. A brief reflection on what we have studied about the Priestly writers' completion of the Pentateuch, the late traditions of the prophets, and the reforms of Ezra and Nehemiah suggests that by focusing on these issues, the inspired authors of Proverbs were addressing pastoral and theological concerns of their day.

The weakened state of marriage was a primary concern, first for Malachi (Mal 2:10–16) and, later, for Ezra (Ezr 9:1–10:17) and Nehemiah (Neh 13:23–27) in the fifth century B.C. Admittedly, Proverbs does not address the specific issue of intermarriage with foreigners that preoccupied Ezra and Nehemiah. Nevertheless, Proverbs' long exposition in the form of parental guidance (1:1–9:18), with its counsel advocating fidelity in marriage (5:18–23), and the concluding poem in praise of the ideal wife (31:10–31) must have provided a model for marriage preparation and enrichment in the fifth century B.C. On a more theological plane, when they elaborated on wisdom's role in creation (8:22–31), the postexilic sages were taking up the theme of the world's origins that Deutero-Isaiah addressed in the Exile (Is 40:12–31) and that the Priestly writers further developed (before 400 B.C.) in their magnificent description of cosmogenesis, which introduces the Pentateuch (Gn 1:1–2:3). Let us take a closer look at the pastoral issue of family life and the theological issue of creation according to Proverbs.

Parents must get involved in the lives of their children as their primary teachers. We noted that Lemuel's instructions are a striking witness to a mother's role in educating her child (31:1–9). In corresponding fashion, the opening section of Proverbs (1:1–9:18) takes the form of a father's instruction to his son and so underscores the importance of fatherhood in the formation of children. As examples of instruction offered in the academy, these texts might also illustrate the rapport between teacher and student, which can strive only to approximate the foremost relationship of father and son.

The communication from father to son gives these poems a deeply personal aspect that distinguishes them from the rest of Proverbs. We must be sensitive to the texture as well as to the content of the discourse. Here, wisdom arises out of mature love, and admonition expresses personal concern. A father's primary interest is the formation of his child from his innermost personal depths. He expresses his dominant preoccupation when he says, "More than all else, keep watch over your heart, since here are the wellsprings of life" (4:23).

The wise parent teaches his child how to think. He draws upon his own formation to illustrate how correct reason, judgment, and action undergird an authentic and effective life (4:3–4). He teaches his son the virtue of self-knowledge and does not hesitate to warn him about his vulnerability to temptation and deception. Such a parent has the confidence to exhort his child to "listen", "take . . . to heart", "not forget", and "pay attention to" his instruction over and above the contrary voices of the world (1:8–19; 2:1; 3:1; 4:1; 5:1). This parent—himself disciplined in the ways of God—is fulfilling the mandate of the Torah to lead his child in the path of revelation (Dt 6:7, 20; Ex 12:26; 13:8).

The topics he covers are models for what parents must teach their children in every age. The foremost principle announced at the beginning and end of the section provides its overarching theme: "The first principle of wisdom is the fear of Yahweh" (9:10; cf. 1:7). The value of knowing God and receiving wisdom as the most precious of all gifts must surpass every desire for worldly wealth and power (2:1–9; 3:15).

Parents in our own day will note that their wise forebears in the faith directed their children's attention to two issues in particular: the need to make friends with reliable people and the need to avoid the temptation of illicit sexual activity. Lemuel's mother spoke to her son about sexuality in a straightforward manner (31:3). The wise father takes up the same issue with exemplary frankness by offering a description of how young men are allured into sexual sin and suffer the subsequent loss of their integrity and capacity for wisdom (2:16–19; 5:1–14, 20–23; 7:6–27). This instruction is part of his more general concern to offer his son a vision of married life that establishes fidelity as its cornerstone and incorporates a very positive view of sexuality in the relationship between husband and wife (5:15–19).

We can read the whole instruction as an essay on friendship. Turning away from bad company while associating with those who seek virtue keeps the heart aright to develop in accordance with God's designs (1:8–19; 4:14–19).

The sages present wisdom as a woman who is the first and best companion of youth (7:4). In the light of wisdom, a young man can discern the folly of the adulterous woman (5:1–14, 20–23; 7:6–27) and therefore highly esteem fidelity in marriage (5:15–19).

The authors placed the ode to the exemplary wife at the end of the book because she more than anyone else is the model of wisdom for all mankind (31:10–31). She is the antithesis of the adulterous woman, who exemplifies folly (5:1–14; 7:6–27). Furthermore, the manner in which she creates a home reflects the action of wisdom herself (31:10–31; cf. 9:1–6). This woman who is wife, mother, teacher, merchant, and advocate of the poor is the cornerstone of society and the primary witness to wisdom personified (31:10–31; cf. 8:1–36).

The personification of wisdom is the crown jewel of the book of Proverbs. For the anointed sages of God's people, wisdom is a person who desires to win our hearts from the allurements of worldly folly. She first introduces herself as a prophet, perhaps like Jeremiah, who cries out in the marketplace, calling everyone to repentance, warning against impending doom owing to our stubborn ignorance and lack of reverence for the Lord (1:20–33; cf. Jer 5:12–17; 11:1–14). Lady Wisdom is a noblewoman who opens her fine home and extends an invitation to everyone to come to the banquet she has prepared. One can feast at her table by turning from the world of selfish ignorance (9:1–6). By her manner of beckoning all people from the streets, this Lady Wisdom sets herself against the adulterous Dame Folly, who lures the imprudent into her chambers by seduction and deceit (7:6–27; cf. 8:1–36).

You can experience today what the holy sages were talking about. Just walk along a major downtown street in a big city. As you pass the theaters, the clubs, the cinemas, the churches, the libraries, the museums, and the book shops, do you not hear the conflicting voices of Lady Wisdom and Dame Folly inviting you to come into their contrasting environments?

Wisdom is much more than the prophetic voice of God speaking to the heart of every person. Wisdom is also the means by which the Lord created the universe (3:19–20). The inspired ancients, by contemplating God's revelation, perceived that Wisdom was the Lord's companion, who acted as his masterful artisan in creating all that exists (8:22–31). Wisdom, whom God intends as the foremost companion of every person, was first of all God's most intimate associate eternally delighting in the divine presence. God created the world in wisdom, and wisdom's special joy is to be in the midst of mankind (8:30–31; cf. 7:4).

Now we can appreciate something of how God inspired the sages who lived around 400 B.C. to penetrate deeply into the divine mystery that suffuses creation. Their presentation develops the theme of the Lord's sovereign work in creation that Deutero-Isaiah had brought to the forefront perhaps a century and a half earlier in Babylon (Is 40:12–31). The Priestly editors who completed the Pentateuch by 400 B.C. further developed the portrait of God as Creator of the universe by the power of his word (Gn 1:1–2:3). During the same era, Judah's sages personified wisdom as God's agent in bringing the universe into existence (Prv 8:22–31). By the fourth century B.C., the three major traditions representing the Law, the Prophets, and wisdom found common ground in contemplating God in view of creation. By discerning the unique role of wisdom as God's eternal agent, the inspired sages of Judah made an important advance in preparing us to understand fully Christ in the New Testament.

Toward the New Testament: Christ, the Wisdom of God

The portraits of creation in Genesis and Proverbs developed further (especially through Sirach 24:1–34 and Wisdom 7:22–8:1) to reach their climax in the revelation of Christ as the eternal Wisdom of God in whom and through whom all creation came into existence. The Prologue to the Fourth Gospel draws upon both the wisdom tradition (developing from Proverbs 8:22–31) and the Priestly account of creation (Gn 1:1–2:3) in revealing the divine Word of God through whom everything has come into being. This Word became flesh in the person of Jesus Christ (Jn 1:1–18). Likewise, the Pauline tradition alludes to Proverbs in proclaiming that Christ "is the image of the unseen God, the first-born of all creation . . ." (Col 1:15–20; cf. Prv 8:22–31).

Although we find relatively few actual quotations of Proverbs in the New Testament, Jesus and the inspired writers made allusions to a wide cross-section of material scattered throughout Proverbs. We detect the undertones of Proverbs in the content of Jesus' message, especially in the Gospel of Matthew, as well as in his manner of speech in the Gospel of John. Furthermore, echoes of Proverbs resonate throughout the Letter of James, and we find references dotting the letters of Paul and Peter as well as in the Letter to the Hebrews.

Jesus drew upon Proverbs as background for the Sermon on the Mount and for some parables of the Kingdom. The Beatitudes, which declare God's blessing on the pure of heart (Mt 5:8; cf. Prv 22:11), on those who strive for righteousness (Mt 5:6; cf. Prv 21:21), on the peacemakers (Mt 5:9; cf. Prv 12:20), and on the innocent, to whom he promises the earth as their inheritance (Mt 5:4; cf. Prv 2:21), all find their roots in Proverbs. Jesus' meditation on the book of Proverbs is apparent in his subsequent instructions: on loving one's enemies (Mt 5:43–48; cf. Prv 3:28), on practicing prayer, fasting, and almsgiving (Mt 6:2, 5, 16; cf. Prv 20:6), on living the Golden Rule (Mt 7:12; cf. Prv 3:27), and on forgiving debts (Mt 6:12, 14–15; cf. Prv 24:29). Jesus' admonition to "ask", "search", and "knock" refers to revelation that God will give to those who persevere in appealing for wisdom (Mt 7:7–11; cf. Prv 8:17). In the same vein, he draws upon a metaphor describing the search for wisdom when he describes the kingdom as a buried treasure for which one sells everything (Mt 13:44–46; cf. Prv 4:7). Furthermore, he alludes to the description of wisdom inviting people into her feast when he depicts the Kingdom of heaven as a banquet prepared by a king who sends out messengers into the streets to beckon guests to his table (Mt 22:1–14; Lk 14:15–24; cf. Prv 9:1–6).

In the Gospel of John, Jesus presents himself as the wisdom of God, who "crie[s] out" in Jerusalem, exhorting the people to renounce their ignorance and obstinacy in order to receive life from him (Jn 7:33–39; 8:12; cf. Prv 1:20–33; 8:3; 4:18). The stream of water that signifies the Spirit in John is a symbol of wisdom in Proverbs (Jn 7:38; cf. Prv 18:4). This water flowing from Jesus' side on the cross indicates that, in his death, he pours upon the Church the divine life and wisdom in the Spirit (Jn 19:34–35; cf. 7:37–39).

The Letter of James, which exhibits many affinities to the Sermon on the Mount, draws upon the treasure-house of Proverbs in offering pastoral guidance. James emphasizes that God is the one who gives wisdom to those who pray for it (Jas 1:5–8; cf. Prv 2:6). He admonishes his people to practical service, especially through care of the poor. He reinforces the proverbial assertion that material wealth will rot away, while a life of justice and generosity will provide an eternal inheritance (Jas 5:2–3; cf. Prv 11:4, 28). He devotes particular attention to the use of the tongue, which can destroy the community through malicious speech (Jas 3:2–12; cf. Prv 10:19; 18:21). Consistent with Proverbs, James advocates the value of listening over speaking (Jas 1:19; cf. Prv 14:17). From Proverbs, he draws his metaphor, which depicts the tongue as a firebrand capable of igniting an enormous blaze of hostility (Jas 3:6; cf. Prv 16:27; 26:18–21). Humility counteracts our inclination to worldliness, which feeds on selfish dominance of others. To support his admonition, James identifies a principle in the Septuagint version of Proverbs: "God opposes the proud but he accords his favor to the humble" (Jas 4:6; cf. Prv 3:34).

The First Letter of Peter quotes the same text to advocate reverent submission to God, who will raise up those who entrust themselves to his grace (1 Pt 5:5; cf. Prv 3:34). The community who received this letter was suffering persecution (1 Pt 4:12–19). The apostle encourages them to keep their minds on the judgment of God and the promise of his Kingdom. As part of his appeal, he quotes another Septuagint text of Proverbs, "If it is hard for the upright to be saved, what will happen to the wicked and to sinners?" (1 Pt 4:18; cf. Prv 11:31). By applying the text to God's judgment, the New

Testament author brings out a fullness of meaning that goes beyond the mind of the original author. Whereas the text in Proverbs originally spoke only about life within this world, 1 Peter highlights the solemnity of divine judgment beyond death.

In a similar vein, the author of Hebrews profiles a text from the poetic section of Proverbs to elaborate on how affliction resulting from persecution is not a contradiction but rather a confirmation of the Christian's identity as a "son of God" according to the pattern of Jesus in his suffering (Heb 12:5–13; cf. Prv 3:11–12). Appealing to the Septuagint text allows the author of Hebrews to describe God's work in the life of his faithful one as "correction" and "training" that, in their proper time, identify a person as a child of God just as graces of spiritual consolation do at other times.

In Romans, Paul uses a quotation from Proverbs to illustrate how Christians must practice deeds of love toward their enemies in order to overcome evil with good and perhaps open the way to repentance for the other person: "If your enemy is hungry, give him something to eat; if thirsty, something to drink. By this, you will be heaping red-hot coals on his head" (Rom 12:20; cf. Prv 25:21–22).

After a fashion, Proverbs has prepared us for an extended meditation on the relationship between God and the faithful one who is suffering. We find the classical presentation of the mystery of human affliction in the book of Job.

STUDY QUESTIONS

1. What is a proverb?
2. How did Solomon at least indirectly influence the book of Proverbs?
3. Contrast wisdom and folly.
4. What is the relationship of virtue to wisdom?
5. Define "fear of the Lord".
6. What does Proverbs have to say about social justice?
7. What are two major precepts that parents are to teach their children?
8. Describe wisdom's role in creation.
9. How is Christ the Wisdom of God?
10. How does the Sermon on the Mount reflect Proverbs?
11. How do the letters of Peter and of James and the letters to the Romans and to the Hebrews rely upon the book of Proverbs?
12. When have you experienced the revelation of God's wisdom? Consider the times you have contemplated the birth of a child, the beauty of creation, or the majesty of the sacred Liturgy.

PROVERBS

33

JOB: IN SEARCH OF GOD

Whenever we suffer, we instinctively ask, "Why?" We try to find the reason in the area of morality, that is, of right and wrong. We ask, both frightened and angry, "What have I done to deserve this?" Frantically, our minds race as we try to understand what is going on. We feel that we are the helpless victim of an injustice: "This should not be happening to me."

Very quickly, we pass from wondering "Who is doing this to me?" to fixing our accusations on God: "Why are you allowing this to happen to me?" Now the problem has become a theological one of the most personal kind. We speak our words directly to God: "How could you, my Creator, let me suffer so?" Our suffering draws us into relationship with God because we want to know why, and only he can tell us. Could it be that this is God's design so that, of necessity, at the crises in our lives, each one of us will interrelate to him personally?

The book of Job takes us through the experience of human suffering. It is not a textbook on "theodicy", which pretends to explain why a good God tolerates the existence of evil. In fact, its illustrations of Job's friends reveal the ineptitude of human beings to explain the depth of our misery. Job suggests to us that suffering remains a mystery and goes on further to indicate that we must enter into this mystery in order to understand both God and ourselves. Job leads us into its depths and, in the process, guides us toward the horizon of the Absolute Mystery who is God. In both style and content, Job is the Bible's source book for ministry to the suffering, speaking to both the giver and receiver of pastoral care.

The Dramatic Form of Job

The book of Job resembles more the form of drama than of historical narrative. We can think of it as a stage play, since its magnificent language and style distinguish it as the "Shakespearean" text of the Hebrew Bible.

The name of Job as well as the place names associated with him and his friends serve to enhance the dramatic rather than the historical character of the work. In biblical tradition, Job was one of the venerable ancients along with Noah and Danel (Ez 14:14, 20). Apparently these three figures were models of righteousness in ancient stories that circulated among the Canaanites (in the case of Danel) or Israelites (in the case of Job and Noah).

Uz, the land where Job lives, is an ancient and perhaps poetic reference to southern Edom on the far side of the Jordan (see Gn 36:28; Lam 4:21). Similarly, Teman, Shuah, and Naamath (the native territories of Eliphaz, Bildad, and Zophar, respectively) designate lesser-known locations beyond Israel's frontiers to the south and east in Edom and Arabia (Jb 2:11; cf. Ob vv. 8–9). The author was not so much interested in geographical precision as in the exotic quality of these names, which located Job and his friends in foreign regions that the popular mind likely associated with wisdom (cf. Prv 31:1–9). Job is one of the "Sons of the East", a title that conjures up images of the wise in the days of Solomon (1:3; 1 Kgs 5:10–11). The fact that Job inhabits gentile territory gives him a universal quality. Everyone can relate to Job because of his identification with the larger world beyond the Holy Land.

A closer look at the text confirms our intuition of its dramatic rather than historical character. The prologue (1:1–2:13) and epilogue (42:7–17) are in prose form, while the central body of the text is poetry. The prose sections at the beginning and the end of the book employ idyllic and stereotyped images of happiness, disaster, and restoration (1:1–2:13; 42:7–17). The first words of the book are the Hebrew equivalent of "Once upon a time . . ." (1:1). The opening section (1:1–2:13) consists of six carefully balanced scenes in which Job loses his property, family, and personal health in sequence. The story's perspective alternates between heaven and earth in order to show us that, unknown to Job, what happens to him on earth is a consequence of the debate between God and the Adversary (Satan) in heaven. The conclusion represents a reversal of the introduction. Whatever Job lost in terms of property, family, and well-being, the Lord restores in a surpassing abundance (42:7–17).

The main body of the text consists of extended dialogues between Job and his three friends (3:1–31:40), which precede the discourses of Elihu (32:1–37:24) and God's addresses to Job from the whirlwind (38:1–42:6). An artistic hand has arranged the poetic corpus. The section of the dialogues between Job and his friends (3:1–31:40) opens and closes with Job's splendid soliloquy (3:1–26; 29:1–31:40). The actual dialogues take the form of three cycles of speeches (4:1–14:22; 15:1–21:34; 22:1–27:23) in which each of the friends makes an extended address to which Job replies one by one (4:1–27:23). In the end, after Job has rebuffed the arguments of each of his friends, it remains for God alone to address Job directly (38:1–42:6). Job's declaration of repentance in response to the Lord's revelation provides the climax of the book (42:1–6).

The poetic sections give evidence of some editorial modifications in their present form. Because the text would flow easily from the end of Job's final soliloquy (31:35–37) to the beginning of the Lord's address (38:1–3), some commentators think that Elihu's speeches (32:1–37:24) are a later insertion. Job's meditation on the inscrutability of wisdom is a self-contained masterpiece (28:1–28; cf. Prv 8:22–31). Some commentators note that the third cycle of speeches (22:1–27:23) seems incomplete compared to the first two, since Bildad speaks only a few words (25:1–6) and Zophar is not mentioned. Some editors try to rearrange the material so that it conforms to the pattern of the first two cycles (for example, see Jb 24:18–27:23 in the *New Jerusalem Bible,* which relocates 26:1–4 after 26:5–14, and 24:18–24 after 27:23).

We will study the book of Job according to its format in the Hebrew text prior to the attempts at rearrangement of modern editions. All of these ingredients contribute to the dramatic tension of the book: the brevity of Bildad's final comments (25:1–6), the silence of Zophar at the end of the dialogues, the insertion of the poem on wisdom (28:1–28), and the intrusion of Elihu into the conversation (32:1–37:24). Because these passages enhance the power of the book, we consider its contents according to the unaltered numbering of chapters and verses.

The book of Job seems to represent a combination of two ingredients: an ancient traditional story in prose frames a more recent poetic composition. The original story of Job (1:1–2:13; 42:7–17) could have circulated in the days of the monarchy or earlier in the tenth or eleventh century B.C. Wisdom circles probably handed on the story across the centuries until an inspired scribe in the postexilic period composed the poetic sections. This author was familiar with Deuteronomic theology, some traditions of prophets such as Isaiah and Jeremiah, and the tenets of wisdom in a variety of psalms and proverbs. How did he know so much about suffering? His profound insight allows us to speculate that he might have written from firsthand experience of the trials of the people during the Exile (587–538 B.C.) or of his own personal ordeal entailing affliction, grief, and loss. Scholars have not determined how Job relates to the Confessions of Jeremiah (11:18–12:6; 15:10–21; 17:14–18; 18:18–23; 20:7–18) and to the Servant Songs (42:1–9; 49:1–7; 50:4–11; 52:13–53:12), the other two poetic collections in the Hebrew Bible that articulate the struggle of God's servant in the face of unmerited suffering. Although it is very difficult to date the work, we will suggest that a sage composed the book of Job in Judah not long after the Exile, perhaps during the first half of the fifth century B.C. (500–450 B.C.).

The Crucial Issues

The book of Job challenges the validity of a theology of retribution that interprets God's relationship to human beings solely in terms of moral conduct. Retributive justice rewards good and punishes evil. A theology based on this premise asserts that God acts in people's lives by bestowing prosperity on the virtuous and affliction on the wicked.

Retributive theology represents an aberration of the type of thinking we find in the Deuteronomic tradition and in the wisdom tradition of Proverbs. For example, we recall that the Deuteronomists explained the overthrow of kings and the fall of Jerusalem as the consequences of both personal and national sin (e.g., Dt 4:25–28; 28:63; 2 Kgs 23:26–27). In a similar vein, a number of Proverbs reinforce a single premise that the Lord rewards the righteous and punishes the wicked (e.g., Prv 10:3, 25, 27–32). Furthermore, certain psalms promise God's blessings on the faithful and his judgment on the impious (e.g., Pss 7:11–16; 34:11–22; 37:25–29). People mistakenly perceived God in terms of retributive justice by absolutizing elements such as these to the exclusion of others, such as God's love for the poor (Dt 7:7–8; 15:11; Prv 22:22–23; 23:10–11; Ps 37:10–11) and the mysterious nature of God and his plans (1 Kgs 19:9–13; Prv 16:9; 19:21; Ps 8). Furthermore, Ezekiel insists on individual responsibility (Ez 18:1–32; 33:10–20). Retributive justice becomes totally perverse when popular thought reverses the logic of biblical maxims. Although the just may receive reward and the unjust experience punishment on this earth, it surely does not follow that those who suffer are wicked and those who enjoy peace are virtuous!

The book of Job corrects the theological error of picturing God's relationship to mankind exclusively in terms of retributive justice, challenging the simplistic application of moral principles that we occasionally read in Proverbs and Deuteronomy. Consider, for instance, a rather fundamental proverb: "The fear of Yahweh adds length to life, the years of the wicked will be cut short" (Prv 10:27; cf. Ps 34:11–12). At face value, the saying is an observation on life. However, some may interpret the proverb as offering a motive for living a religious life, namely, in order to enjoy a long life span and to avoid the tragedy of premature death. Precisely here, we find the beginning of Job: Satan questions the self-serving nature of piety implied in such a proverb. He poses to God his rhetorical question: "Job is not God-fearing for nothing is he?" (Jb 1:9).

This is a primary issue in Job: "Can one worship God out of pure love and devotion?" Or, to phrase it in more critical terms analogous to Satan's: "Are not religious people motivated by self-interest, fulfilling their obligations out of the hope of reward and the fear of punishment from God?" (cf. 1:9; 2:5).

While the prose introduction questions the religious motives of human beings, the poetic dialogues debate the very justice of God in his dealings with someone who suffers. Job asks God, "Is it right for you to attack me, in contempt for what you yourself have made, thus abetting the schemes of the wicked?" (10:3). This question is intimately related to his doubt over the value of a painful existence: "Why give light to a man of grief?" (3:20); "Is not human life on earth just conscript service? Do we not live a hireling's life?" (7:1).

Satan and Job direct their primary questions to God. The dramatic tension builds throughout the book as we wonder whether the Lord will ever respond fully to such fundamental inquiries. In the end, God does respond to Job, not in theological syllogisms, but in personal revelation. The book demonstrates that encountering God is the most essential component in our search for meaning.

Job teaches us that divine truth becomes manifest through relationships. The book describes relationships of two kinds: between ourselves and our friends and between ourselves and God. The dynamics of the relationships influence our growth in wisdom. In order to appreciate the personal quality of truth in Job, we will first consider his conversations with his friends and then with God. In both cases, we will examine the content of the discourses and also the dynamics of the relationships in order to appreciate how knowledge of God grows out of personal encounter.

Job and His Friends: Suffering and Divine Justice (3:1–37:24)

The heart of the book consists of the dialogues between Job and his three friends Eliphaz, Bildad, and Zophar (3:1–31:40). Their speeches express more than ideas; they form the relationship between Job and each of his friends. Their words have an affective as well as an informational dimension. Indeed, the friends come to visit the afflicted Job precisely to offer him "sympathy and consolation" rather than a lesson in theology (2:11). We will evaluate how well they carry out their intention. Our study of the discourses will begin by focusing on the theological content of the addresses before considering the impact of their expression on the relationship between Job and his friends.

Theological Content: Job is preoccupied with God under the two rubrics of Creator and Judge. When contemplating creation, Job considers his own conception and birth (3:3–23; 10:10–11) as well as the origin of all things (9:5–13; cf. 28:1–28). When reflecting on his personal existence, Job sounds like Jeremiah as he curses the day of his birth and questions the reason for his miserable existence (3:3–23; cf. Jer 20:14–18). Job is familiar with the Yahwist's portrayal of the Lord exercising meticulous care in creating every human being (Gn 2:7). He is also well acquainted with the psalms that express awe at God's mysterious work in bringing each of us into existence from the time of our conception (10:8–12; cf. Pss 8:1–9; 139:13–15; Gn 2:7). However, Job debates the theme of the psalmists who thank the Lord for the gift of existence. Job suggests that life is a curse for the person who suffers and implies that he would prefer never having come into existence. From the beginning, he protests, "Why give life to those bitter of heart, who long for a death that never comes . . . ?" (3:20–21). Such words stand in marked contrast to the psalmist who praises God saying, "You created my inmost self, knit me together in my mother's womb . . . a wonder am I, and all your works are wonders" (Ps 139:13–14).

Job's affliction has jaundiced even his view of God's dominion over all creation. Prophets and psalmists had invited their people to contemplate the greatness of God by considering the magnificence of his creation (Is 40:12–31; Pss 19:1–6; 104:1–35). Job does not doubt the Lord's sovereignty over all that exists, but he suspects that God exercises his power for ends that are more destructive than constructive. Job's description associates violence with the divine activity whereby God casts down mountains in anger, shakes the pillars of the earth, and tramples down the sea (9:5–9; cf. Is 40:21–24; Ps 89:9–12).

Job's suspicions of God as Creator extend to his interpretation of God's providence. While the psalmists and prophets extolled the Lord as the God of history who overthrows the kingdoms of the proud and raises up his lowly people (Ps 107:40), Job concentrates on how God casts down human beings who have attained some prominence (12:13–25). From Job's perspective, the wicked prosper and attain success, while the prayers of the faithful have little effect (21:7–34).

Job's perception of God serves only to increase his affliction. God is elusive to him. In the same breath, while contradicting the psalmist, Job describes God as both unfindable and yet so present that he inspects every movement of the afflicted (23:8–10; cf. Ps 139:1–10). While the psalmist finds consolation in the fact that God knows his innermost depths, Job considers God's omniscience as a threat, since God will expose the most hidden of sins (7:17–21; cf. Pss 139; 144:1–8). Job's discomfort derives from his sense of living under the glaring light of divine scrutiny that will expose all his transgressions. Job's sense of condemnation has made him a slave (7:1–21). He perceives that his only path to freedom consists in entering into a lawsuit with God.

Job demands his day in court when he can demonstrate the injustice of God and his own innocence. Yet, going to court is a fearsome prospect, since Job conceives of God as both his Judge and his Prosecutor (9:14–35).

Nevertheless, he announces, "I am putting my flesh between my teeth, I am taking my life in my hands; let him kill me if he will; I have no other hope than to justify my conduct in his eyes" (13:14–16). Job requests only that God relieve him of his terror and expose his sins (13:17–27). Job's initial confidence in his own innocence wanes (6:10; cf. 9:21). Yet he knows that he will find a resolution in his existence only by encountering God face to face, even at the expense of his life (13:17–27).

While battling through his predicament in dealing with a God whom he conceives to be at once his Judge (9:14–15) and his Prosecutor (19:6), Job wishes there were an "arbiter" between himself and God (9:33). Later, he mentions his "defender", his "witness in heaven", who would express his side of the case in God's presence (16:19–21). Such figures serve as a prelude to his insistence that he has a "Defender" (go'el) who will take up the role of his nearest kin and defend his cause (19:23–27; cf. Lv 25:25; Dt 25:5–10; Ru 2:20). Through the Defender's mediation, Job asserts his confidence of fulfilling his desire to stand in the presence of God. Despite all his anxieties, nightmares, doubts, and terror, Job maintains an underlying conviction that his search for God will not be in vain.

True to the sentiments he expresses throughout his discourses to his friends, Job concludes his case by asserting his innocence and asking for a hearing in the presence of God (29:1–31:40). His final address recalls the stature he enjoyed as a person who exemplified righteousness and labored for justice on behalf of others (29:1–20). All of this provides a marked contrast to his present experience of affliction and derision (30:1–31). His reflections provoke him to call down oaths upon himself to protest his faultlessness and to plead for an appearance before God. Listen to his words: "Will no one give me a hearing? I have said my last word; now let Shaddai reply! . . . I shall give him an account of my every step and go as boldly as a prince to meet him" (31:35–37). Now, it remains for God to respond.

Earlier in the story, Eliphaz, Bildad, and Zophar offered predictable responses to Job's musings. The theology of retribution controls the reflections of all three of them. Each in his own way attempts to account for Job's predicament with the presupposition that his misery derives from his sinfulness. Eliphaz invites Job to search for the root of his troubles in his personal sin according to his conviction that "It is people who breed trouble for themselves" (5:7; cf. 4:1–5:27). When Job persists in his claims of innocence, Eliphaz asserts the basic iniquity of mankind as he challenges, "How can anyone be pure, anyone born of woman be upright?" (15:14, in 15:1–35; cf. 4:17–18). In ultimate exasperation at Job's lack of remorse, Eliphaz finally offers a list of accusations in which he charges Job with various forms of injustice toward the oppressed (22:5–11, in 22:1–30).

Bildad is vaguer and platitudinous. He piles up images to insist that everything that happens is a result of God's righteous order (8:1–22; 18:1–21; 25:1–6). He protests to Job, "Can God deflect the course of right or Shaddai falsify justice?" (8:3). When Job remains unmoved by Bildad's elaborate presentation of the wicked person's descent into oblivion, Bildad finally resorts to imitating Eliphaz's assertion of the basic corruption of mankind (25:4–6; cf. 4:17–21; 15:14–16).

Finally, Zophar adds a few sentences that assert that God sees through the basic deceit of human beings (11:11, in 11:1–20). Rather than dwell on the issue of Job's guilt, Zophar prefers elaborate descriptions of God's wrath coming upon the wicked (20:23, in 20:1–29). Each of Job's friends offers the identical solution to his problems: Job must undergo moral rehabilitation in order to experience the blessings of God in abundance (5:7–27; 8:20–22; 11:13–20). According to their mind set, everyone must merit God's favor.

The Dynamics of the Relationships: Along with doctrinal content, manner of speech is an important component of the discourses. Pastoral theology must flow from the heart as well as from the mind. The defensiveness of Job's friends in matters of doctrine effectively prevents them from extending to him the sympathy and compassion that motivated them to come to him in the first place (cf. 2:11).

The discourses of Eliphaz, Bildad, and Zophar are a study in misdirected communication. They always miss the point because they are unable to listen to Job's pain. Echoing Jeremiah's words concerning his compatriots in Anathoth, Job compares these brothers to a "deceptive" wadi (river bed) in the wilderness, which is full of water when it rains but quickly runs dry (6:15–17). He knows that his disfigured appearance is a scandal to them as he tells them, "And this is how you treat me, terrified at the sight of me, you take fright" (6:21, in 6:15–29; cf. Jer 15:10, 17–18). Far from offering consolation, Job's friends begin each of their discourses by reprimanding Job for his insolence and lack of contrition (e.g., 4:1–6; 8:2; 11:1–4).

Job's friends lack personality and creativity. Never do they break out of the confines of a warped retribution mentality in order to announce God's consolation based on his forgiveness and love (cf. Dt 7:7–8; Is 40:1–11; Ps 51). As the cycles of discourses wear on, the friends have less and less to say. Bildad's final speech consists of a mere few lines that denigrate man in the hope of exalting God (25:1–6). Job knows the line so well that he interrupts Bildad and finishes the speech with a parody of the way his friends would speak (26:5a–14). Zophar does not have a third speech simply because he has nothing more to say. Job provides the correct evaluation of his three friends: they are truly inept and pretentious defenders of God (13:3–13).

Precisely when his interlocutors exhibit the silence of spiritual burnout, Job becomes most eloquent. He moves beyond the discourse to offer his sublime meditation on the nature of wisdom, which transcends the heights and depths to which man's technology can reach (28:1–28; cf. Prv 8:22–31). Then, he provides a magnificent display of his life's history, past and present, as a prelude to his summary request to encounter the living God (29:1–31:40).

After such a magnificent oration by Job, Elihu's intrusion is aggravating, juvenile, and inappropriate. In other words, the youthful Elihu embodies all the bad traits of Job's three friends plus the inexperience of youth. Elihu's speeches are long-winded, self-serving, airy puffs of theological smoke that repeat the ideas of Eliphaz, Bildad, and Zophar (32:1–37:24). It is a relief just to reach the end of such rambling locutions. Yet Elihu has served a purpose. By now, we beg for deliverance from superficial theology. Along with Job, we look to God for an answer to life's questions.

God and Job: Revelation and Repentance

The Lord reveals himself to Job from the heart of the storm in a manner that recalls his great theophanies to the Israelites at the Sea of Reeds and at Mount Sinai and to Ezekiel in the land of Exile (38:1; 40:6; cf. Ex 13:22; 14:20; 19:16; Ez 1:4). His association with the powerful whirlwind indicates that this God will not exhibit the functional predictability that Job's friends expected of their Deity. The setting of the storm guarantees that the Lord is a mighty God, who acts in freedom and not in conformity with anyone's expectations. We will consider both the content of what he says and the dynamic development of his relationship with Job.

Theological Content: The Lord does not respond to Job's questions about either the justice of innocent suffering or about Job's personal virtue (cf. 3:11–23; 31:1–40). However, he does take up the challenge of debating with Job in a public hearing (38:3; cf. 31:35–37).

The Lord presents Job with a relentless barrage of questions that challenge Job to consider his place within the total scope of God's work in the universe (38:1–39:30). Creation provides the theme for his interrogation. By implication, the Lord's questions blow apart all of Job's negativity about God's power reigning over the cosmos (cf. 9:5–13; 12:15–25). The Lord exhibits the bearing of a masterful prosecuting attorney as he phrases questions so that Job, were he to answer them, would have to give brief, repetitive replies betraying his ignorance and powerlessness. For example, God asks, "Where were you when I laid the earth's foundations?" "Have you been right down to the sources of the sea . . . ?" "Have you an inkling of the extent of the earth . . . ?" "Can you fasten the harness of the Pleiades, or untie Orion's bands?" (38:4, 16, 18, 31). To each of these and other questions, Job would have to respond in the negative, admitting his human frailty and limitation. Then the Lord extends the subject matter of his inquiry from the realm of the cosmos (38:4–38) to the world of living creatures (38:39–39:30).

The Lord pauses to offer a direct challenge to Job, who responds with mute reverence (40:1–5). Then, the Lord proclaims his authority over all sinister powers. He confronts Job's insistence that he is justified in his protests by asking him, "Do you really want to reverse my judgment, put me in the wrong and yourself in the right?" (40:8; cf. 13:14–16). When the Lord illustrates his dominion over the great monsters of the sea, Behemoth and Leviathan, his case is complete (40:15–41:26): the Lord, Yahweh, is God over all.

The Dynamics of the Relationship: In the introductory prose section, we find an early portrait of Satan as a member of the heavenly court who is suspicious of human beings and literally the "Adversary" (*satan* in Hebrew) of God's servants (1:6–12; 2:1–6; cf. Zec 3:1–2). Satan's conversations with the Lord are the cause of Job's ordeal. Because we overhear these conversations, we perceive from the beginning that the Lord is really on Job's side and desires to prove him righteous. If his servant can maintain his integrity throughout his suffering, both Yahweh and Job will be vindicated against Satan.

However, as the discourses unfold, we realize that Job must find a new basis for his relationship to God. Although he refutes the narrow theological model of divine retribution that his friends uphold, Job still argues for a justification based on his own virtue and deeds (6:10; 13:14–16; 31:1–40). This whole schema of relating to God solely on the basis of morality and merit breaks down under the weight of human misery. The innocent do suffer and the wicked do experience success. Job is correct in protesting that the God of moralism is simply too small.

Job teaches us that the basis for our relationship to God is divine revelation. In other words, when we meet God, we relate to him and he to us in a personal manner. When the Lord discloses himself to Job, their relationship becomes immediate, direct, and genuine. The proper response to revelation is repentance and faith. Job's words to God provide the climax of the book: "Before, I knew you only by hearsay but now, having seen you with my own eyes, I retract what I have said, and repent in dust and ashes" (42:5–6).

In the end, God declares Job righteous because he came to ever-deeper repentance in response to divine revelation (cf. 42:7–9). By contrast, God chastises Job's friends for their lack of docility to genuine revelation. Insofar as

Job exemplifies faith, he recalls the first of the Patriarchs, of whom we read: "Abram put his faith in Yahweh and this was reckoned to him as uprightness" (Gn 15:6).

Toward the New Testament: The Suffering of the Virtuous

The Letter of James recommends the perseverance (not the "patience") of Job as a model for Christians who will have to suffer persecution (Jas 5:11). Our reading of Job underlines the fact that his perseverance exhibited an aspect of spiritual and mental toughness; he was not passively resigned to the force of powerful opposition. The Letter of James is consistent in stating that mental strength and agility that hunger for wisdom must undergird our perseverance (cf. Jas 1:5–8).

In the Pauline writings, Paul quotes a text of Job to support his warning against the folly of worldly wisdom (1 Cor 3:19; cf. Jb 5:13). While this text comes from Eliphaz rather than Job, nevertheless, it is a sound statement that expresses a truth basic to the whole book of Job: "He [God] traps the crafty in the snare of their own cunning." In Job, the statement has a certain irony, as Eliphaz is one of those whom the Lord reprimands in the end for his false speech about divine matters (Jb 42:7–9). Paul's use of the text suggests that Christians can learn from Job the importance of testing their thinking against the standard of divine revelation lest they distort the Gospel to conform with the mind set of the present age (1 Cor 2:6–16; cf. Jb 42:5–6).

Our study would not be complete unless we considered how Job foreshadows the fullness of life that is ours in Christ. The book of Job demonstrates that God is not impassive to the plight of the innocent who suffer. God demonstrates his solidarity with the afflicted most fully in the Passion and death of Jesus. The Letter to the Hebrews teaches us that the eternal Son is a merciful High Priest because he embraced the reality of our human condition and "learnt obedience . . . through his sufferings" (Heb 5:8). Therefore, he has become for those who obey him the source of eternal salvation (Heb 5:7–10). In the Passion of Jesus, God entered into the innermost recesses of human affliction and death to make even of them a sacred place for us to encounter his grace.

Finally, Job can teach us that we must receive the Gospel through revelation (cf. Gal 1:11–17; Mt 16:17; 1 Cor 2:7). Such revelation provides the basis for founding our lives on God and not on ourselves. Salvation is God's free gift of himself to us in Jesus Christ. Job teaches us that our personal virtue independent of God's life cannot accomplish salvation. Job prepares us to realize that "someone is reckoned as upright not by practicing the Law but by faith in Jesus Christ" (Gal 2:16; Rom 3:28; 4:5; Eph 2:8–9). We cannot merit salvation by our effort; however, every day we can receive it in faith as God's free gift to us in Christ. This faith is a trusting obedience to Christ, which bears fruit in the good works that flow from his indwelling in the Holy Spirit (see Rom 1:4–5; 16:26; Eph 2:9–10; Jas 2:14–26).

STUDY QUESTIONS

1. How does the book of Job seem like a stage production?
2. What is the attitude of Job's three friends to his suffering?
3. What are the two salutary effects of human suffering?
4. What is the effect on Job in beholding the majesty of God?
5. How does God address Job in the climactic scene of the book?
6. How does God view Job's three friends?
7. What does Job learn from his personal encounter with God?
8. How does the book of Job foreshadow Jesus?
9. Discuss how, in modern times, Job has come to mean innocent suffering. How does the theme of innocent suffering contrast with the ending of the book, when Job repents in dust and ashes because he realizes no one is innocent before God?
10. Discuss how suffering can bring a person to experience the revelation of God at a depth that would not be possible in other circumstances.
11. Are we prone to use arguments like those of Job's three friends to explain away the hard times in someone else's life? How does the book of Job correct our tendency to relate suffering to personal sin?
12. Discuss how you can understand innocent suffering in God's plan most clearly by meditating on the suffering of Jesus.

JOB

34

RUTH AND ESTHER:
STORIES OF GOD'S PROVIDENCE

We need to hear stories of God in order to know how he wants to work in our lives. Stories are interpretations of life. They give us a perspective on reality that helps us to make sense out of our own situation. By identifying or comparing ourselves with the main characters of a story, we have a chance to grasp the meaning of what has happened to us in the past and then decide on our goals for the future.

The books of Ruth and Esther are two insightful stories of God's providence. They both describe remarkable people who lived by faith through very trying circumstances. Interestingly enough, God remains in the background of both stories, and yet he is their primary character since they each unfold the working of his providence.

These stories are about remarkably different people who lived in distinctive historical settings but who bear witness to the same faith. The first is about a foreigner in Israelite territory, while the second is about a Jewess in foreign territory. Ruth is a foreigner, a poor Moabite widow, who becomes God's instrument in Bethlehem, the rural town of Judah in the days before the monarchy. Esther is a Jewess who serves God on foreign soil as the wife of a wealthy Persian king in the citadel of Susa after the Exile. Both these women are bereft of their parents and face life-threatening hardship, Ruth in her widowhood and Esther in her marriage to a gentile monarch. Each of them acts in union with a beloved elder who is an indirect relative. Ruth follows the counsel of her mother-in-law Naomi, and Esther receives guidance from Mordecai, her first cousin, who has been her guardian since the death of her parents. Ruth and Esther each exhibit wit and resourcefulness as the fruit of fidelity.

Both these stories illustrate God's covenant loyalty to his people. He blesses those who trust him above all else. The traditional telling of these two narratives on the Jewish feasts of Weeks or Pentecost (Ruth) and Purim (Esther) bears witness to their spiritual wealth.

RUTH

The story of Ruth unfolds against the background of life in Israel prior to the era of the monarchy, presumably around 1100 B.C. This literary masterpiece is a short story with a vivid historical setting that draws us into the environs of Bethlehem, eight miles south of Jerusalem (which was a Jebusite stronghold in those days). The author's craft introduces us to the closely knit townspeople who welcome back their bereaved sister Naomi (1:19), witness the business transactions of their esteemed Boaz (4:9), and eventually bestow their blessing on his new wife Ruth (4:11–12). Through the course of the story, we are taken to the important centers of village life: the fields (2:1–23), the threshing floor (3:1–18), and the city gate (4:1–12). It is early summer, time for harvesting the barley crop, some seven weeks after Passover, at the time we call Pentecost (Lv 23:15–22).

An outline of the book offers us an overview of the story's development: (1) Naomi and Ruth move from Moab to settle in Bethlehem (1:1–22); (2) Ruth gleans the barley left by the harvesters in Boaz's field (2:1–23); (3) Ruth encounters Boaz at the threshing floor (3:1–18); (4) Boaz marries Ruth, and they have a son, Obed (4:1–17); and (5) an appendix provides the genealogy of David, the grandson of Obed (4:18–22).

In order to date the composition, we must note the following elements in Ruth: allusions to the story of Tamar and Judah (4:12; cf. Gn 38:1–30; Ru 1:11), mention of Jacob's wives (4:11; cf. Gn 35:16–20, 23–26), as well as references to the law of levirate marriage (4:1–12; cf. Dt 25:5–10) and to the statutes governing the redemption of property (4:1–9; cf. Lv 25:25; Jer 32:6–10). Furthermore, at least in retrospect, we perceive a Davidic quality to the story insofar as it recounts the action of God in the lives of David's ancestors.

All of this evidence suggests that a scribe in Judah composed the story sometime after the reign of David, perhaps as early as the days of Solomon (970–931 B.C.) and probably no later than the time of Micah (740–701 B.C./Ru 1:2; cf. Mi 5:1). The refined quality of prose in Ruth invites us to recall the narrative art of David's Court History (2 Sm 9–20; 1 Kgs 1–2), which was representative of the literature composed in the Solomonic era. The story of Ruth (1:1–4:17) was composed sometime between the tenth and the eighth centuries B.C. A Priestly editor added the appendix (4:18–22) from a source like 1 Chronicles 2:9–15 sometime after the Exile, perhaps around 400 B.C.

In the preexilic period, the story illustrated God's providence in action both in the particular lives of its righteous protagonists and in the broader history of Israel, which culminated in the Davidic line of kings. In the postexilic period, the story of the union between Ruth the Moabitess and

Boaz, the great-grandfather of David, could have been a counterbalance to the injunctions of Ezra and Nehemiah against the marriages between Jews and foreigners (cf. Ezr 9:1–10:17; Neh 13:23–27). The story of Ruth is all the more astounding when we recall the Deuteronomic legislation that expressly forbids admission of a Moabite into the assembly of Yahweh (cf. Dt 23:4–7).

The Lord's Faithful Love (Hesed)

The story of Ruth begins with death and ends with birth. Tragedy overwhelms Naomi in the beginning as her husband and two sons die, leaving her in the company of her widowed daughters-in-law (1:1–7). However, blessing surrounds her in the end as she embraces the newborn Obed as her legal grandson (4:14–17). The famine mentioned in the beginning (1:1) gives way to the harvest in which Ruth meets Boaz (2:1–23). Naomi and Ruth, the despondent, isolated figures of the beginning, become the center of the joy-filled community in the end (1:15–22; cf. 4:13–17).

The book of Ruth is a story of God revealing his faithful love (*hesed*) to three unforgettable individuals and, through them, to his whole people. The lives of Naomi, Ruth, and Boaz undergo dramatic transformation as they experience the effects of the Lord's blessing. On five different occasions, significant figures in the story pronounce a blessing on either Ruth or Boaz (1:9; 2:12; 2:20; 3:10; 4:11). The story reaches its climax when the Lord unites them in marriage and gives them a son (4:13). The birth of Obed, a legal descendant in the line of Elimelech, demonstrates the Lord's faithful love (*hesed*) to Ruth, to Naomi (cf. 1:9), and to their deceased husbands (cf. 2:20).

Faithful love (*hesed*) characterizes the behavior of Ruth as well (3:10; cf. 1:8; 2:20). When Ruth abandons her land, she also leaves behind the god of the Moabites. Hers is a journey both into the land and into the faith of Israel (cf. 2:11). When she pledges herself to Naomi, she declares her loyalty to the people of Israel and to their God (1:16–17; cf. Dt 23:4–7). Unlike Orpah, who justifiably remains in her native Moab, Ruth maintains her allegiance to the heritage of her dead husband. Her identification with his family leads her into the relationship with Boaz.

Ruth's stature increases as her relationship to Boaz deepens. At first, in his eyes, she is an anonymous "young woman" and "Moabitess" (2:5–6). In their first meeting, which takes place in the field during the day, they have a master-servant relationship: he calls her "daughter", and Ruth calls him "my lord", while identifying herself as "a foreigner" (2:8–13). During their second meeting, which occurs at the threshing floor in the night, Ruth identifies herself as Boaz's servant, but he corrects her by declaring that, in the eyes of all the townspeople, she is "a woman of great worth" (3:6–15). Eventually, Ruth, the once-impoverished foreigner, becomes a woman whose standing recalls that of Rachel, Jacob's wife, whose tomb was the most famous site in Bethlehem (4:11; cf. 35:16–20).

Boaz is a figure of patriarchal stature who acts with uprightness and generosity. His servants gather his harvest according to the law, which requires that they leave some standing grain for the poor (2:1–7; cf. Lv 19:9–10; 23:22; Dt 24:19). He manifests compassion when he extends to Ruth hospitality and guarantees of security beyond the legal requirements (see 2:8–15). He demonstrates his reverence for the Law when he announces that Ruth has a kinsman whose right to marry her precedes his own (3:12).

When the righteous Boaz brings his case to the public square, he intertwines the laws of property redemption (Lv 25:25; cf. Jer 32:6–10) with the laws governing "levirate" marriage (from Latin *levir:* "a husband's brother"/Dt 25:5–10). According to the statutes on property, the nearest of kin (Hebrew *go'el:* "redeemer") had the responsibility (and privilege) of buying the property his relative was selling in order to pay off a debt (Lv 25:25). The marriage law prescribed that a man had to marry his widowed sister-in-law in order to provide a descendance for his deceased brother (Dt 25:5–10). When Boaz presents his case to the elders of Bethlehem, he extends the levirate obligation beyond the brother to the nearest kin, and he links the right of property redemption with the levirate obligation (Ru 4:1–8; Lv 25:25 and Dt 25:5–10). When the anonymous kinsman of Ruth's husband renounces his right to marry Ruth, he gives up his claim to Elimelech's property. The legally correct manner of Boaz wins him the acclaim of the elders. Furthermore, the townsfolk of Bethlehem welcome Ruth into their midst by pronouncing upon her the blessings of Rachel and Leah (the wives of Jacob) and by thinking of her in terms of Tamar (the daughter-in-law of Judah) (4:11–12; cf. Gn 35:19–20, 23–26; 38:1–30).

Ruth's son, Obed, provides the essential link in the genealogy extending forward from Judah to King David (4:12, 17, 18–22). Thus, the story of the Lord's faithful love (*hesed*) to Ruth is part of the broader biblical concern that reveals the providence of God extending from Judah to David (4:17–22).

Toward the New Testament: The Birth of Christ

By this marvelous working of God's providence, Ruth the Moabitess became the great-grandmother of David (4:17–22). The Gospel of Matthew mentions Ruth in the genealogy of Christ because her participation in the unfathomable plan of God foreshadows the vocation of Mary of Nazareth, who would be the mother of the ultimate Son of David (Mt 1:5, 16). Just as God intervened in an astonishing way to the Israelites by making a Moabitess the great-grandmother of David, so he defied human expectation by having his Son born of a virgin.

The Gospel of Luke provides another allusion connecting the narrative of Jesus' birth with the book of Ruth. As a woman bereft of offspring in her old age, Naomi resembles Mary's kinswoman Elizabeth. Just as the people of Judah blessed the Lord on behalf of Naomi when Ruth gave birth to a son, so they acclaim the Lord's mercy bestowed on Elizabeth when she gave birth to John the Baptist (Lk 1:58; Ru 4:14).

When considered from the standpoint of the New Testament, the story of God's action in the lives of Naomi, Ruth, and Boaz represents a stirring testimony to the truth that "God works with those who love him, those who have been called in accordance with his purpose, and turns everything to their good" (Rom 8:28).

ESTHER

The story of Esther is different from that of Ruth in character and tone. The narrative of Ruth unfolds within a precise historical setting, and its characters exhibit unique traits as individuals. By comparison, the Esther account lacks the specific details necessary to identify its historical circumstances with precision. Moreover, the characters in Esther are less defined as individuals; they tend to be rather generic figures whom the whole people should take as their models. While Ruth exhibits the qualities of a historical short story, Esther manifests the character of a heroic novella.

Esther exhibits a comparatively subdued spiritual texture. The narrative sections of Ruth contain only two references to the Lord (Ru 1:6; 4:13) but, in direct conversation, a variety of characters speak of him frequently (Ru 1:8–9, 13, 16–17; 21; 2:4, 12, 20; 3:10, 13; 4:11–12, 14). By contrast, the Esther narrative displays a rather secular bearing insofar as it does not mention God even once. The absence of any explicit reference to God accounts for the relative hesitancy of early Jewish and Christian tradition to admit the book of Esther to the canon of Sacred Scripture.

Although the narrative provides us with few particulars, we can locate the Esther story within a general historical context. Ahasuerus is the Hebrew name of the Persian King Xerxes I (486–465 B.C.). During his reign, the Persian Empire did, indeed, extend "from India to Ethiopia" (1:1; 8:9), and it had a remarkable communications system (cf. 3:13; 8:10). Archaeologists have uncovered an administrative list indicating that a certain *Marduka* (=

"Mordecai"?) was a court official in Susa at the beginning of his reign. Xerxes I was married to Amestris, and there is no mention of either Vashti or Esther in the annals of the royal court.

The story of Esther belongs to the Persian era (538–333 B.C.). The original Hebrew version dates from the fifth century B.C. We suggest that it fits best in the last half of the century (450–400 B.C.), during the era of Ezra and Nehemiah, the two Jewish leaders who won the favor of Persian kings for the benefit of the Jewish people (see Ezr 7:1–28; Neh 1:11–2:10).

Scribes in Jerusalem reshaped and transformed the story of Esther in light of the Maccabaean era of the second century B.C. In our study of Esther, we will consider the story in its original Hebrew form before examining the Deuterocanonical additions in the Greek text.

The story of Esther in Hebrew explains the origins of Purim (from Hebrew *pur* meaning "lot"/3:7; 9:24), a minor Jewish feast held in February or March. We do not find a reference to Purim elsewhere in the Bible. The feast must have developed among the Jews of the Diaspora during the Persian era. Purim is a two-day celebration with three objectives: (1) to cultivate a strong sense of identity among Jews living in the gentile world (cf. 9:1–17); (2) to provide a time of rest and joy (9:18–19); and (3) to encourage generosity in the community by exchanging gifts and giving to the poor (9:20–28).

In outline form, the book has three major sections. The first part describes how, through a remarkable sequence of events, the beautiful Esther replaces Vashti as Ahasuerus' Queen of Persia (1:1–2:23). The second part describes both Mordecai's conflict with Haman and Esther's intervention with the king to thwart the government's ill-conceived initiative to persecute the Jews (3:1–7:10). The third part describes how, through Mordecai's leadership, the Jews receive their civil rights to self-defense and free assembly, which enable them to attain victory over their oppressors (8:1–10:3).

Divine Providence and Personal Character

The book of Esther provides remarkable illustrations that invite us to ponder three issues: the ways of divine providence, the character strength of people who belong to the faith community, and the proper form of openness to the larger world, which they must demonstrate in order to advance the cause of God's people.

Without making any direct reference to God, the book of Esther is a story of divine providence. The drama of Esther bears striking similarities to the adventures of Joseph and Daniel insofar as it is an edifying tale that describes the success of a gifted young Jewish person who rises to prominence in a foreign court (Est 1–10; cf. Gn 37–50; Dn 1–6). Events unfold in an amazing sequence to the benefit of the oppressed Jews and to the detriment of their gentile oppressors. Esther, the orphaned child of refugees from Jerusalem, becomes Queen of Persia (2:1–18). Her foster father, Mordecai, emerges from death row to witness the hanging of his would-be executioner and to assume an exalted office in the royal court (3:1–7:10; 8:1–10:3). The Jewish people emerge from being under the threat of annihilation to destroy their enemies (3:7–15; 9:1–32). Events begin to turn in favor of the Jews when Mordecai sends his message to Esther implying that divine providence accounts for her rise to prominence exactly when her people are in greatest peril: "Who knows? Perhaps you have come to the throne for just such a time as this" (4:14).

The Jews exhibit character strength that distinguishes them from the Gentiles. Esther's confidence and acumen develop to the point that she eventually has the king offering her an equal share in his power (5:3–5). She does not fear to keep him waiting in anticipation of her request in defense of the Jews (5:6–14; 7:1–10). The patience and decisiveness of Esther stand in marked contrast to the impulsiveness and indecision of King Ahasuerus. The gentile monarch has to contradict himself by executing Haman, the very man whom he had endowed with royal authority to annihilate the Jews (3:7–13; cf. 7:1–10). Ironically, Ahasuerus had deposed Queen Vashti for insubordination only to marry Esther, who surpasses him in wit and initiative (1:9–22; cf. 5:1–14; 7:1–10; 8:1–12).

The contrast between Mordecai and Haman further emphasizes the character distinction between Jew and Gentile. Mordecai's self-composure and fearlessness are unnerving to Haman, whose vanity and insecurity produce delusions of grandeur (3:1–13). Every benefit Haman desired eventually falls to Mordecai (6:1–13; 8:1–12). And all the evil Haman intended against Mordecai turns back against himself. No one can miss the poetic justice contained in the fact that Haman was hanged upon the gallows that he had constructed for Mordecai (5:9–14; cf. 7:8–10). The contrasting destinies of Mordecai and Haman bear out the proverb, "Whoever strives for good obtains favor, whoever looks for evil will get an evil return" (Prv 11:27).

The examples of Esther and Mordecai suggest that partnership in faith produces sound character. Esther reaches maturity by following the counsel of Mordecai. When she first ascends the throne, she seems to defer to the Gentiles (2:8–18). However, once Mordecai communicates his admonition for her to act on behalf of her people (4:12–14), she sets aside any self-concern and fearlessly takes the initiative, acting like the king's adviser.

We can speculate that the figure of Esther must have provided a role model for young Jewish women, especially in the Diaspora. In some circles,

Esther might have been a feminine counterpart to Daniel, the heroic figure for young men. Diverse stories about Daniel (Dn 1–6) probably circulated in Diaspora communities before the Hasidim gave them their definitive form at the time of Judas Maccabaeus. Esther and Daniel exhibit some noteworthy similarities: both are exilic refugees whom the imperial monarch mandates for service at the royal court (Est 2:5–11; Dn 1:3–20); and both win their respective king's favor even as royal advisers persuade the king to initiate a persecution of the Jews for insubordination to the crown (Est 2:15–4:17; Dn 2:1–49; 3:1–23; 6:1–29).

The book of Esther illustrates how Jewish people can interact with the larger gentile world without compromising their traditional standards. The communities of the Diaspora required leaders like Esther and Mordecai who could rise to prominence in public office in order to protect the rights of the Jews (8:1–10:3).

Mordecai is the exemplary Diaspora Jew. He is primarily concerned for his adopted daughter and for the well-being of his own people (2:5–20; 4:1–17). Nevertheless, he respects the gentile king enough to intervene in order to protect him from assassination (2:21–23; 6:1–2). Yet he refuses to be subservient to his gentile rival, Haman (3:1–6). When facing the prospect of persecution of the Jews, he takes the initiative to eliminate the threat (3:7–4:17). The story assures the Diaspora communities that even a rather hapless gentile ruler will reward a person of such integrity (6:1–13). Ultimately, Mordecai draws up the bill of rights for the Jews in the gentile world (8:9–12). Through the determined efforts of such a leader, the Jews will be able to overcome their adversaries and to celebrate their feasts with the approval of the gentile authorities (9:1–10:3).

The Deuterocanonical Additions to Esther

A scribe named Lysimachus, who worked in Jerusalem, translated an expanded version of Esther into Greek during the reign of John Hyrcanus I (134–104 B.C.). A Levite by the name of Dositheus carried this text to the Jewish community in Alexandria in 114 B.C. (Esther 3[*l*]/presuming that the Ptolemy in "Ptolemy and Cleopatra" refers to Ptolemy VIII Soter II [116–107 B.C.]). Thus, the Greek text of Esther belongs to the same historical period as the Greek translation of Sirach (see Sir: translator's prologue, vv. 27–35) and the Greek history of Judas Maccabaeus in 2 Maccabees. These three texts (2 Maccabees, Sirach, and Greek Esther) were brought from Jerusalem to Alexandria, likely within a decade or two of one another.

Mention of the "Day of Mordecai" in 2 Maccabees indicates that its author was familiar with the Esther story (2 Mc 15:36; cf. Est 9:1–19). However, this evidence also suggests that, in the retelling of the story during the Maccabaean era, Mordecai overshadowed Esther in importance. Furthermore, Mordecai's destruction of the Gentiles became the most memorable episode in the story. The figure of Mordecai must have prompted the latter-day Jewish audience to think of their liberator Judas Maccabaeus (Est 9:1–19; cf. 2 Mc 15:1–36). The reference to Mordecai in 2 Maccabees is a preliminary indication that the expansions in the Greek text of Esther represent a recasting of the story in light of Jewish concerns in the post-Maccabaean period.

The Greek edition of Esther contains six additions to the Hebrew text: (A) the story begins with Mordecai's dream (1^{a-r} [11:2–12:6]); (B) a transcription of the king's edict follows mention of its distribution throughout the empire (13^{a-g} [13:1–7]); (C) the prayers of Mordecai and Esther follow Esther's decision to act on behalf of her people (17^{a-z} [13:8–14:19]); (D) a portrait of Esther's emotional state expands the description of her audience with the king ($1^{a}–2^{b}$ [15:4–19]); (E) a transcription of the king's new edict follows promulgation of Jewish civil rights (12^{a-v} [16:1–24]); and (F) an interpretation of Mordecai's dream in light of the story provides the conclusion (3^{a-k} [10:4–13]). An archivist wrote the final note as an identification tag for the Greek text (3^{l} [11:1]).

The different systems for numbering these insertions derive from the way the translators placed them respectively in the Greek (Septuagint) and Latin (Vulgate) versions. The Greek editions incorporated these passages into the original text but noted them as additions. Modern Catholic versions adapted this system of notation by letters and numbers (e.g., 1a, 1b, etc. [NJB]; A:1–17 [NAB]). By contrast, around A.D. 400, when St. Jerome translated the text into Latin in his Vulgate edition, he collected all the insertions and compiled them together at the end of the text. When editors numbered the verses of the Latin text centuries later, they simply counted the collection of these six insertions as sequential chapters and verses, beginning with 10:4, following the last of the verses in Hebrew. The King James Version in 1611 adopted this system, and this is the Protestant standard for identifying the additions (therefore, e.g., 11:2–12:6 [NRSV] = 1^{a-r}[NJB] = A:1–17 [NAB]).

The six additions do not come from the same hand. Although they are extant only in Greek, these six additions probably originated in different languages. The evidence of vocabulary and style indicates that the two edicts (B and E) were composed in Greek, while the remaining four sections (A, C, D, F) originated in either Hebrew or Aramaic and, subsequently, were translated into Greek. Perhaps the two Greek edicts originated in Alexandria, while the four Semitic texts came from Jerusalem.

Prayer and Allegiance to God

The additions transform the Esther story so that its audience cannot miss the moral and spiritual implications for their lives in the post-Maccabaean era. Three alterations in theme highlight the difference between the expanded Greek text and the primary Hebrew version: (1) God comes to the forefront of the story; (2) prayer and spirituality become explicit rather than implied in the lives of the heroes; and (3) the tension between Jew and Gentile revolves around the difference between the living God of Abraham and the dead idols of paganism.

The additions make up for the absence of explicit reference to God in the primary story of Esther. The Greek version shows that God is in control from the beginning as he reveals his plans to Mordecai in a dream (1^{a-l} [11:2–12]). The prayers of both Mordecai and Esther emphasize the majesty of the Lord as Creator of the universe and savior of Israel (4:17^{b-c} [13:9–11]; 4:17^{l-m} [14:4–5]). In the end, Mordecai declares that God is the one who saved his people from the threat of the other nations of the world (10:3^{e-f} [10:8–9]).

The Greek version emphasizes the spirituality of the heroes. From beginning to end, Mordecai ponders the revelation he has received from the Lord (1^{a-l} [11:2–12]; 10:3^{a-k} [10:4–13]). The prayers of Mordecai and Esther give them wisdom and strength to confront the king (17^{a-z} [13:8–14:19]). In particular, each of them addresses the Lord as "King" in order to correct any impression that they would allow a Gentile with that title to control their lives (17^{b} [13:9]; 17^{l} [14:4]). Esther accompanies her prayer with gestures of mortification and renunciation of material comforts (17^{k} [14:1–3]).

In her prayer, Esther makes plain her disdain for life with a gentile king and denounces his idols as she puts her faith in the "Lord, God of Abraham" (17^{y}, in 17^{o-z} [14:18, in 14:8–19]). She follows the lead of Mordecai, who refuses to "place the glory of a man above the glory of God" (17^{e} [13:14]). Mordecai's defeat of Haman is a victory of the true faith over the pretensions of paganism. God changes the heart of the gentile king (5:1^{e} [15:11]), who acknowledges the Jews as "sons of the Most High" and God as "Master of the Universe" (12^{q} and ^{s}, in 12^{p-u} [16:16 and 19, in 16:15–23]). Thus, the Greek edition of Esther insists that explicit reverence for the living God is the most essential component for social order in the world.

Toward the New Testament: The Astuteness of the Apostles

The oath of Herod Antipas to the daughter of his consort Herodias, "I will give you anything you ask, even half my kingdom" (Mk 6:23), seems to contain the only literal reference to the book of Esther in the New Testament. These words had first voiced the promise of King Ahasuerus to Queen Esther (Est 5:3, 6; 7:2). What had been a sincere promise of a gentile king to his Jewish wife in Esther becomes twisted into a vain pledge of a drunk monarch to a seductive teenager in the Gospels of Matthew and Mark (Mk 6:17–29; Mt 14:3–12).

The book of Esther depicts the world as an unstable environment for the people of God. Those who wield political power are unreliable insofar as they are ignorant of God and therefore enslaved to the passions of their own egos. That is why Mordecai and Esther must act astutely to protect God's people. The way Esther follows the guidance of Mordecai and uses her charm to win the favor of Ahasuerus for the Jews illustrates the kind of shrewdness that Jesus would recommend for "the children of light" (Lk 16:8; cf. Est 5:1–14; 7:1–10; 8:1–17). We suggest that Esther and Mordecai exhibit a foretaste of the wisdom Jesus expected of the disciples whom he sent out "in pairs" (cf. Lk 10:1). They exemplify the character traits Jesus requires of the disciples whom he sends out with the commission, "Look, I am sending you out like sheep among wolves; so be cunning as snakes and yet innocent as doves" (Mt 10:16).

Finally, we must note that the ironic end of the treacherous Haman, whom the Persians hang on the gallows that he had constructed for Mordecai, furnishes preliminary testimony to the truth of Jesus' assertion: "[T]he judgments you give are the judgments you will get, and the standard you use will be the standard used for you" (Mt 7:2; Est 7:10).

STUDY QUESTIONS

1. How do the books of Ruth and Esther illustrate God's covenantal loyalty?
2. What is a levirate marriage?
3. Where are echoes of the book of Ruth in the New Testament?
4. How does the book of Esther differ from the book of Ruth?
5. What are three messages of Esther?
6. Why were six Greek insertions made into the book of Esther?
7. How do Mordecai and Esther exemplify the character traits required of disciples in the New Testament?
8. What is the significance in the chronology of Jesus to Ruth's being one of Jesus' ancestors?
9. Compare Boaz's care for Ruth with Joseph's care for Mary in the New Testament.
10. Compare the generosity of Ruth with that of Mary, the mother of Jesus.
11. Compare the courage of Esther, Ruth, and Mary.
12. Discuss the relationship of flexibility and faith in living God's plan for your life based on the books of Esther and of Ruth.

RUTH

ESTHER

[*Italics* denote the Deuterocanonical additions.]

35

LAMENTATIONS, SONG OF SONGS, AND QOHELETH: REFLECTIONS ON LIFE

Our hearts search for the living God in all the experiences that shape our lives. Funerals and weddings stand out as occasions of special revelation to the community. In grief and in joy, everyone spontaneously enters into a dialogue with God in prayer. However, our search for God is not simply a reaction to momentous events. In the most ordinary and common circumstances, our hearts persistently long to know God. Especially when our best efforts seem futile and our days seem monotonous, we ache for the presence of God.

Scripture teaches us that our very capacity to yearn for God amid sorrow, joy, and even boredom is a grace. The books of Lamentations, Song of Songs, and Qoheleth teach us how to search for God in the diverse experiences that constitute our lives. Each of these books probes the meaning of human existence in a different existential situation.

In the classification of the writings, the Hebrew Bible groups together the five *megilloth* (scrolls) that Jews traditionally read on these feasts: Ruth (Weeks or Pentecost), the Song of Songs (Passover), Qoheleth (Tabernacles), Lamentations (the ninth of Ab), and Esther (Purim). We have noted how Ruth and Esther share a common literary form as inspiring stories. The remaining *megilloth* exhibit a diversity of literary forms. Lamentations and the Song of Songs are lyrics intended for chanting or singing, while Qoheleth is a source book for solitary reflection. Each of them focuses on a different horizon of relationship. Lamentations voices the prayers of the whole community, the Song of Songs celebrates the marriage relationship, and Qoheleth meditates on the experience of the individual.

LAMENTATIONS

Lamentations is a prayer book for the people of God who suffered the ravages of war. This collection of five psalms voices the victims' grief over the destruction of Jerusalem and its Temple by the Babylonian army of Nebuchad-nezzar in 587 B.C. (2 Kgs 24:18–25:26; cf. Jer 52:1–30).

The Septuagint translation ascribes Lamentations to Jeremiah, probably on the premise of the Chronicler's reference to a psalm the prophet composed on the occasion of Josiah's death (2 Chr 35:25). However, the "Lamentations" to which the Chronicler refers was not the biblical book but another, no longer extant, collection that included songs of lament for King Josiah. The content of the book of Lamentations rules out the possibility of Jeremiah being its author. The prophet whose words anticipated the destruction of the Temple would not have reeled in shock when his prophecy became reality (Lam 1:10; cf. Jer 7:12–15). The one who told Zedekiah about the futility of an alliance with Egypt would not have expressed disappointment that foreigners were unable to turn the Babylonians away from Jerusalem (Lam 4:17; cf. Jer 37:3–10). Moreover, Jeremiah could not have been surprised when the Babylonians captured King Zedekiah, since this episode corresponded to his blunt prediction to the king (Lam 4:20; cf. Jer 37:17; cf. 24:8–10).

We cannot be certain that a single author composed all five psalms in Lamentations. If all the psalms do not come from the same hand, at least they are the product of one particular school. The similarity in form and theme that characterizes the various pieces in the collection indicates that their composers worked in unison with each other. All the psalms express the viewpoint of someone who is standing amid the ruins of Jerusalem and its Temple (Lam 1:10–13; 2:1, 6–7; 4:11–12; 5:18; cf. 3:45).

After the destruction of the Temple, the Jews who remained in the land congregated at the sacred precincts for prayer and penitential liturgies (see Jer 41:4–5; cf. Zec 7:1–7; 8:19). The psalms of Lamentations were composed in Jerusalem, perhaps by priests, for recitation at the liturgical rites that were held in the Temple ruins. The psalms could have originated anytime after the destruction of the Temple (587 B.C.) and before its reconstruction (515 B.C.). We prefer a date at the earlier rather than at the later extremity of this time frame. The poignant quality of the prayers suggests that their authors actually lived through the horrors of the desolation they describe.

Each year for centuries, the people of Judah prayed the psalms of Lamenta-tions on the anniversary of the destruction of the Temple. The Babylonians demolished the Temple of Solomon on either the seventh (2 Kgs 25:8–9) or the tenth (Jer 52:12) day of the month of Ab (fifth month) (July/August) 587 B.C. Ironically, in A.D. 70, the Roman legions of Titus destroyed the refurbished second Temple at the same time of year, on the tenth of Ab. Furthermore, rabbinical tradition identifies the ninth of Ab as the day on which the Romans eradicated the last vestiges of Jewish resistance from Judaea. This event occurred in A.D. 135, when the legions of the Emperor Hadrian defeated Simeon Bar

Kocheba at Bether, six miles southwest of Jerusalem. Subsequent Jewish tradition designated the book of Lamentations as the official liturgical text for their memorial rites on the ninth of Ab, in which the Jewish people recall all three events at once. This religious tradition remains true to the purpose for which the original authors intended the collection when they composed it soon after the destruction of Jerusalem in 587 B.C.

Each psalm is a self-contained unit. The first four psalms are "acrostic" or "alphabetic" poems: the first word of each unit begins with a successive letter in the Hebrew alphabetical sequence from *aleph* to *tav* (our "A to Z") (see the acrostic psalms: Pss 9–10; 25; 34; 37; 111; 112; 119; 145; cf. Prv 31:10–31). Each of the five psalms in the book of Lamentations consists of twenty-two units that correspond to the number of characters in the Hebrew alphabet. Each of the twenty-two units in the first three psalms consists of three Hebrew lines (or six lines in English versions, since they take two lines to present the single Hebrew bi-colon line). Therefore, each of the first three psalms consists of sixty-six lines in Hebrew (1:1–22; 2:1–22; 3:1–66). By comparison, in the fourth psalm, each unit consists of two lines in Hebrew (or four lines in English translation), giving it a total of forty-four lines (4:1–22). The fifth psalm consists of twenty-two lines, equivalent to the number of letters in the Hebrew alphabet. But this last psalm is not an "acrostic" since the first letter of each successive line does not follow an alphabetical sequence (5:1–22).

The third psalm has the most elaborate design, which is appropriate for the centerpiece of the collection (3:1–66). Not only does each unit begin with a successive letter in the Hebrew alphabet, but each of the three lines within a particular unit begins with the same Hebrew letter. Apparently, the editor of the collection arranged the five psalms in such a manner as to highlight the third psalm as the heart of the book.

What is the purpose of such precision of appearance in Hebrew, with each psalm consisting of twenty-two units equivalent to the number of letters in the Hebrew alphabet? Surely this represents more than an intriguing scribal mannerism or a helpful means to aid memorization. In the book of Lamentations, the acrostic device establishes a sense of divine order amid emotional chaos. In content and cadence, these poems convulse with grief. By contrast, in structure, their mathematical precision bespeaks a dispassionate equilibrium. To the Hebrew mind, the twenty-two units provide a sense of totality and completion, as if to suggest that they examine the desolation from beginning to end ("from A to Z"). The psalm is comprehensive. It provides a thorough expression of anguish while, at the same time, enclosing and containing the grief so that it does not spill forth at random. Furthermore, the acrostic style alludes to the perfection of God's designs even in the midst of tragedy.

Although the five psalms exhibit a remarkable synchronism in appearance, they are distinct from one another in literary movement and content. The psalms follow one another in this order: (1) two speakers, the psalmist (1:1–11, 17) and Zion herself (1:12–16, 18–22), lament the desolation of Jerusalem (1:1–22); (2) two speakers, the psalmist (as an observer [2:1–10] and as a friend in conversation with Zion [2:11–19]) and Zion (2:20–22), describe the Day of the Lord that has occurred (2:1–22); (3) an individual expresses his grief and hope for salvation (3:1–66); (4) the people express a communal lament in which they survey the desolate city (4:1–22); and (5) the community voices its appeal to the Lord from its present state of ruin (5:1–22).

Although each of the five psalms is a self-contained unit, their configuration in book form calls attention to the third psalm, which is the most personal of the five. Dialogue between the psalmist and daughter Zion (who represents the community) characterizes the first two psalms, while the last two psalms express the communal prayer of the whole people. In the third psalm, one individual personalizes the anguish that the whole community expresses in the other four psalms.

The intensity of experience increases until it reaches a climax at the center of the book. We detect a similarity in scope in chapters 1 and 5, and 2 and 4, respectively. The first and last psalms survey a broad panorama of desolation (1:1–22; cf. 5:1–22). The second and fourth psalms are more specific meditations that take us on a tour of Jerusalem to witness closely the details of the tragedy that manifested the Lord's wrath in judgment (2:1–22; cf. 4:1–22). This type of parallelism gives the book a *chiasmus* structure, in which themes balance on two opposite sides in order to focus on the central text, which is the fulcrum of the work.

The intensity of grief wells up from the beginning until it reaches a crescendo in the third psalm and subsequently diminishes until the end of the book. The confession of faith in the middle of the third psalm provides the essential core of the book (3:22–29). The first two psalms tend to portray the Lord as sinful Zion's adversary (1:11–15, 17; 2:1–8, 22; cf. 4:11, 16), whereas the last two psalms provide indications that he is desolate Zion's only source of hope (4:22; 5:19, 21). The book of Lamentations invites us to ponder the deeply personal relationship between the Lord and Zion.

The Lord and Daughter Zion

The book of Lamentations implies that an intense relationship between the Lord and Judah remains after the devastation of the city. Even when Jerusalem lies in ruins, she remains "the young daughter" (1:15; 2:13), "daughter of Zion" (1:6), "daughter of Judah" (2:2, 5), "daughter of Jerusalem" (2:15), and "daughter of my people" (4:3, 6, 10; cf. 3:48). Here, Lamentations is using prophetic language. Such terms echo the Lord's designation of his people according to Isaiah (Is 10:32; 22:4; 37:22). Jeremiah uses the title in reference to Jerusalem, who is faithless and vulnerable to divine judgment, which will come in the form of the Babylonian invasion (Jer 6:2, 23, 26; 8:19–21). Deutero-Isaiah uses this designation for Jerusalem, which is undergoing restoration after the Exile (Is 52:2). By calling ruined Jerusalem "daughter", Lamentations maintains that the city never ceases to belong to the Lord.

Nevertheless, Yahweh is the one who has destroyed Jerusalem. The book of Lamentations never mentions Babylon by name, for Jerusalem was not the victim of another nation. Her destruction is a theological, not a political, event. The sins of the people provoked Yahweh to demolish the city (Lam 1:11–18; 3:40–45; 4:11–14). On this point, Lamentations shares the conviction of the Deuteronomists that the people brought about their own destruction (Lam 1:11, 14; 2:2; cf. Dt 28:47–68; 2 Kgs 23:26–27). In his "anger", the Lord demolished the city and its Temple in keeping with the curses of the Mosaic covenant (Lam 1:5; 2:9, 17; 3:14, 44; cf. Dt 28:15–46). God's "anger" is the revelation of his righteousness to annihilate sin. Furthermore, the destruction of Jerusalem reveals the Lord acting in accordance with his prophetic word concerning the "Day of Yahweh" (Lam 1:21; 2:1–10, 16, 21–22; cf. Am 5:18–20; Zep 1:2–18). Lamentations describes the desolation of Jerusalem in words that resonate with Jeremiah and Ezekiel (Lam 1:4; cf. Jer 14:2; Lam 2:7; cf. Ez 24:21). The destruction of Jerusalem has exposed the tragic deceit of the false prophets and also fulfilled the word of the authentic servants of the word (Lam 2:14; 4:13; cf. Jer 5:31; 6:13; Ez 13:8–16).

The destruction of Jerusalem vindicates Yahweh's righteousness and, paradoxically, therein resides the hope of the people. The Lord who afflicted Jerusalem in righteousness will by that same righteousness heal her and restore her to new life. At the very heart of the book, one man expresses the anguish of the whole community in terms that contain resonances of Jeremiah's Confessions and of psalms of trust (Lam 3:1–39; cf. Jer 15:10–21; Pss 16; 40; 73). From the depths of Israel's misery, the psalmist realizes that mercy (*hesed*) characterized the Lord in his revelation to Moses after the people had sinned at Mount Sinai (Lam 3:22–23; cf. Ex 34:6–7). He recalls that Ezekiel, who prophesied the fall of Jerusalem, also declared that the Lord does not delight in death but in the life of his people (Lam 3:31–33; cf. Ez 33:11, in 33:10–20). All the children of Zion, along with the psalmist, now realize that they must place their hope in the Lord alone, for he can bring them from death to life (Lam 3:24; cf. Pss 16:5–11; 73:23–28).

The communal lament of the people concludes with the declaration of forgiveness to Zion, which foreshadows the opening lines of Deutero-Isaiah

(Lam 4:22; cf. Is 40:2). The community's final prayer leads to a profession of faith that provides the only sure foundation for hope: "you, Yahweh, rule from eternity; your throne endures from age to age" (Lam 5:19; cf. Pss 145; 146). The people cannot force the Lord's hand, but they can wait on him with the assurance that comes from remembering his deeds of mercy.

Toward the New Testament: Jerusalem and the Cross

In the book of Lamentations, Jerusalem stands at the turning point of history. God has destroyed the old order of sin, and the repentant city looks to her Lord, awaiting the new order of his grace. Similarly, in the Gospel of Luke, Jerusalem exhibits two personalities that are in tension with each other. On the one hand, she is the locus of greatest opposition to God, for she rejects and kills the prophets and ultimately provides the locale for the execution of the Messiah (Lk 13:34–35; 19:41–44). On the other hand, Jerusalem is the place of fulfillment, where God actualizes all of his promises, especially in the Resurrection of Jesus and in the outpouring of the Holy Spirit at Pentecost (Lk 24:1–53; Acts 1:4; 2:1–47). Therefore, as the primary locale of God's action in the world, Jerusalem reflects the past era of opposition to God but also is the prophetic witness of the new age of grace, which Christ will extend to the whole world through the ministry of the Church (see Acts 1:8; 2:1–13).

Jesus identifies himself with the desolate city that Lamentations describes. When he hangs upon the cross, Jesus experiences the same reaction that the public gave to the ravaged daughter of Jerusalem. Those who pass by wag their heads in derision (Mk 15:29; Mt 27:39; cf. Lam 2:15). Yet in both cases, the event of divine judgment that so scandalized the world is the manifestation of God's righteousness to destroy the old order of sin so that he can raise his people from death to new life in the holy city (cf. Mt 27:51–54).

Christian tradition developed the custom of praying the psalms of Lamentations on Good Friday and Holy Saturday. These prayers of contrition and repentance expose the emptiness of our old life and beckon us to experience the new life of reconciliation with God through Christ crucified (see 2 Cor 5:19–21).

THE SONG OF SONGS

The Song of Songs is the Bible's ode to spousal love. By analogy to the expression "Holy of Holies" (meaning "the holiest place": 1 Kgs 8:6), the Hebrew title "Song of Songs" means "the most wonderful song". In fact, the book is a collection of lyrics and poetic fragments representing a tradition that spanned perhaps six centuries in Israel, from Solomon to the Chronicler.

The text is ascribed to Solomon, who was renowned for his lyrical wisdom (Sg 1:1; cf. 1 Kgs 5:12). Indeed, one of the poems may have been composed for Solomon's wedding (Sg 3:6–11). However, Solomon could not have authored and edited our final edition of the whole work, since its vocabulary suggests an Aramaic influence typical of postexilic Judaism. While some of its contents may date from the magnificent days of Jerusalem's royal house in the tenth century B.C., the text probably attained its completed form in Judah in the fourth century B.C., after the missions of Ezra and Nehemiah. We suggest a date around 350 B.C.

As scribes in the court of Solomon, the composers of the earliest elements in the Song of Songs were contemporaries of the Yahwist, whose creation account focuses on the institution of marriage (Gn 2:4–25). Therefore, we can read the songs as expressions of the love and delight that give rise to the unity between husband and wife that the Yahwist so emphasized (Gn 2:22–25). Furthermore, as a component of the wisdom tradition in Israel, the Song of Songs would have complemented the instructions parents gave their children about personal relationships, sexuality, and marriage (see Prv 5:18–23; 6:20–7:27; 31:10–31). These are songs that must have been sung at weddings (see Ps 45; cf. Jer 7:34; 16:9). Moreover, we can appreciate that the Song of Songs provided a positive reinforcement for the marriage reforms advocated by Ezra and Nehemiah (Ezr 9:1–10:44; Neh 13:23–27). The songs illustrate how love rather than law must animate the relationship between spouses who share in the faith of Judah.

The arrangement of the book is the foremost concern for any interpreter. When we peruse the text devoid of modern editorial aids, it reads like a random collection of poetic fragments. We note a lack of consistency in the discourse (see 3:3–6; 5:1–2; 8:8–14). A refrain that addresses the daughters of Jerusalem recurs throughout the work (2:7; 3:5; 5:8; 8:4). A number of questions punctuate the text (3:6; 5:9; 6:1; 8:5). Four different poems employ remarkable metaphors to describe the physique of man and of woman (4:1–15; 5:10–16; 6:4–12; 7:2–10). Moreover, a closer look at the Hebrew text reveals alternate units that employ either masculine or feminine endings in the second person pronouns and adjectives (for "you" and "your").

Such evidence has led many commentators to suggest that the text takes the form of a dialogue between a young man and a young woman who are betrothed to each other (see "my promised bride" four times in 4:9–12). A chorus, presumably of the "daughters of Jerusalem", interjects a variety of acclamations and questions into the couple's exchange with one another (1:8; 5:9; 6:1; 7:1; 8:5a). We can make only tentative suggestions on some critical issues that must remain open to question. Is it the chorus or the poet who voices the description of Solomon's wedding procession and the invitation to begin the wedding celebration (3:6–11; 5:1c/NJB: poet; cf. NAB: chorus)? Do the admonitions to the daughters of Jerusalem come from the young man or from the young woman (NJB: man [2:7; 3:5; 8:4], woman [5:8]; cf. NAB: woman [2:7; 3:5; 5:8; 8:4])?

We have divided the text into ten sections: (1) the title (1:1); (2) a prelude in which the young woman speaks of the one whom she loves (1:2–4); (3) a conversation between the young man and young woman, which ensues after she introduces herself to the daughters of Jerusalem (1:5–2:7); (4) her anticipation of their being together but also her description of her search for him in the city (2:8–3:5); (5) the poet's description of the great wedding procession (3:6–11); (6) the young man's description of the beauty of his betrothed (4:1–5:1); (7) her account of another search for him (5:2–6:3); (8) each of them speaking of commitment to the other (6:4–8:4); (9) the culmination of the series of discourses with her description of genuine love (8:5–7); and (10) a series of additional fragments providing an appendix for the work (8:8–14).

The Song invites a bi-focal interpretation. In its primary sense, the Song of Songs is a sublime testimony to the beauty and goodness of spousal love. At the same time, the Song describes the profound covenant love God shares with his people. We will contemplate both dimensions of revelation in the Song.

Spousal Love

The Song of Songs is at once sensual and sublime. In these poems, the natural becomes transparent to the spiritual. An abundance of nature metaphors illustrates the depths and movements of personalities, both masculine and feminine. Creation provides a plethora of symbols that expose the inner life of man and of woman. The vast array of creatures includes: (a) animals, both domestic (goats [6:5], ewes [6:6], and sheep [2:16; 6:3]) and wild (gazelles and does [2:7, 9, 17; 3:5; 4:5; 7:4], stags [2:9, 17], foxes [2:15], lions and leopards [4:8]), as well as birds (ravens [5:11] and doves [2:14; 5:12]); (b) flowers (henna [1:14], lily [2:1; 7:3], rose [2:1]); and (c) vines (2:13) and trees (apple [2:3]; fig [2:13]; palm [7:8]; pomegranate [4:13; 6:11; 7:13; 8:2]; cf. cedar and cypress [1:17]). The garden is the predominant metaphor for the young woman (4:12–15, 16; 5:1; 6:2, 3, 11; 8:12) while the image of shepherd represents the young man (1:7; 2:16; 6:2–3).

The Song invites the listener's total personal involvement as its metaphors appeal to the five senses: the eye beholds precious stones (1:11; 5:14–15), the ear hearkens to the voice of the beloved (2:8, 10), the nose smells the exotic aromatic spices (1:12–14; 4:12–15; 5:5, 13), the palate tastes the wine of the wedding feast (5:1); and the fingers touch the evidence of the beloved's visitation (5:5).

The metaphors are particularly striking in the four poems that describe the beauty of each spouse (4:1–7; 5:9–16; 6:4–7; 7:2–10). Each of these texts is a *wasf*, an Arabic poetic form that employs metaphors from nature to describe a person. By directing attention to the physique, the *wasf* emphasizes the essential unity between body and spirit. These poems contain no suggestion of dualism or opposition between the physical and the spiritual. On the contrary, they imply that beauty and love are incarnational. The body mediates and expresses the person.

The Song of Songs affirms the dignity of sexuality. From beginning to end, these poems celebrate the goodness and beauty of intimacy between husband and wife in marriage. Sexuality is never reduced to base eroticism, which, by definition, selfishly objectifies and depersonalizes the other. In the Song of Songs, sexuality provides the language for self-surrender and self-abandonment. This is the language of people who desire "to know" one another in the fullest Semitic sense of the term (see Gn 4:1). In their communication with each other, the spouses exhibit a freedom that illustrates their desire to be transparent and vulnerable to one another (cf. Sg 2:16; 6:3; 7:13). Nakedness defines not merely a physical condition but a personal state of truth and openness to the other in love (see Gn 2:25). Each of the spouses desires union with the other that is free of Eden's shame (Sg 7:11; cf. Gn 3:16; Sg 4:1–15; 5:10–16; 2:16; 6:3; cf. Gn 2:23–25; 3:7). The theme of the garden and the images of luxuriant produce throughout the Song recall the atmosphere of paradise prior to the Fall (4:1–5:1; cf. Gn 2:8–9; Ez 31:3–9).

The relationship leading toward marriage must mature through crises of separation. The union of the spouses is the fruit of their decision to search for each other. On two occasions, the young woman frantically seeks her beloved because she fears that he has become lost to her (3:1–4; 5:6–8). On the first occasion, she takes the risk of running through the streets in the dark of night and, on the second occasion, she receives a beating because the watchmen presume she is a prostitute. Understandably, she becomes wary of the reactions of the general populace (8:1–2).

The spousal relationship develops within the broader setting of the world and the community of faith. The couple's quest for unity takes place against the backdrop of all the environments of life in the land, including the city (3:1–4; 5:6–8), the village and country (7:12), and even the desert (3:6). While the general public is prone to misunderstand them (5:7; 8:1), the community of faith listens to them and provides them with counsel. The "daughters of Jerusalem" represent the people of God (1:5; 2:7; 3:5; 3:11; 5:8, 16; 8:4). They are the bridal attendants who nurture the relationship between the spouses (1:8; 5:9; 6:1; 7:1). Their role in the Song of Songs indicates that the relationship between couples grows to maturity as they interact with the community of faith.

We might detect another allusion to the faith of Israel in geographical references: (a) to regions beyond Israel (Kedar [1:5]; Lebanon [3:9; 4:8, 11, 15; 7:5]); (b) to the landscape within Israel's frontiers, including mountains or plateaus (Mount Gilead [4:1]; Senir, Hermon, Amanus [4:8]; cf. the mountains of Bether [2:17]), and plains (Sharon [2:1]), and (c) to cities or towns both within Israel and beyond its borders (Jerusalem, Tirzah [3:5; 5:8; 6:4]; Damascus [7:5]). These images convey an appreciation of living in the Promised Land that is the inheritance God provides through the covenant (see Dt 28:1–14; Nm 34:1–15; Ez 47:13–21).

The Song reaches its culmination in the young woman's declaration that the force of committed love is stronger than anything, including even the power of death and the netherworld (8:6–7). As a "seal" on his heart, she will always be present to him, she will secure his identity in the world, and she will share in his authority (8:6; cf. Gn 38:18; 41:42; Hg 2:23). The life-giving passion of love is more adamant, fierce, and intense than the great enemy that is death. In the Isaian tradition, the word for this passion (Hebrew: *qin'ah*) refers to the Lord's jealous love, which motivates him to rescue and restore his people (Is 9:6; 37:32; 42:13; 59:17). Most importantly, the image of fire suggests that spousal love is a participation in the life of the Lord. The flame of committed love finds its origin in Yahweh, who reveals himself as "a consuming fire" (Sg 8:6; cf. Dt 4:24). This is the only verse in the Song to mention God. Love exhibits the strength of the Lord insofar as it survives the ordeal of chaos symbolized by the flood in Hebrew literature (Sg 8:7; cf. 2 Sm 22:17 = Pss 18:16; 144:7; Is 43:2, 16; 51:10).

In the Song of Songs, harmony suffuses the relationship between man and woman. Their communication with each other is devoid of any trace of suspicion or rivalry. Husband and wife are equal in dignity, and their union is the fruit of mutual and reciprocal giving of themselves to each other (2:16; 6:3; 7:11). The Song reflects the divine plan for man and woman in creation (cf. Gn 1:27; 2:18, 22–25).

The Covenant Love between God and His People

The prophets used marriage as a symbol of the union between God and his people in the covenant (Hos 2:16–17; Jer 2:2; Is 62:4–5; cf. Is 1:21; Jer 2:19; 3:1, 6–13; Ez 16:1–63; 23:1–49; Is 50:1; 54:6–7). The spousal language of the Song of Songs alludes to the covenant relationship between God and Israel. The Hebrew text alludes to the sacramental aspect of marriage insofar as it presents the union between husband and wife as a symbol of the bond between God and his people.

The Song of Songs adverts to the relationship between Israel and God in general and perhaps to the coming of the Messiah in particular. We will consider both these possibilities since the fluidity of the poems defies any attempt to reduce them to a one-dimensional code.

Identifying the man as a "king" allows him to represent the Lord who governs the world and who reigns over his people as King (Sg 1:4, 12; 7:6; cf. Pss 10:16; 24:10). In a similar fashion, the image of shepherd in the Songs is consistent with the identification of the Lord as Israel's shepherd (Sg 1:8; 2:16; cf. Ez 34). The young woman typifies the people insofar as the "daughters of Jerusalem" are her attendants throughout the Song (1:5; 2:7; 3:5; 5:8, 16; 8:4; cf. 3:11; cf. Is 10:32; 52:2; 62:11). From another perspective, the vineyard is a symbol of Israel in the prophets (Sg 1:6, 14; 2:13, 15; 6:11; 7:9, 13; cf. Is 5:1–7; Jer 2:21; Ez 15:1–8; cf. Ps 80:8–16).

The theme of sleep and awakening recurs in the admonitions to the daughters of Jerusalem. If these admonitions issue from the young man, then they reflect the Lord's appeal to Jerusalem at the end of the Exile, "Awake, awake! To your feet Jerusalem!" (Is 51:17); "Awake, awake! Clothe yourself in strength, Zion" (Is 52:1; cf. Sg 2:7; 3:5; 8:4). Furthermore, the theme of separation and search is prominent in the prophets' description of Israel's relationship to the Lord (Sg 3:1–4; 5:2–6). When the young woman runs through the city looking for her beloved, she exemplifies Israel, who heeds the call of the prophets when they say, "Seek out Yahweh while he is still to be found, call to him while he is still near" (Is 55:6; Jer 29:13; cf. Hos 2:9; 3:5; 5:6, 15; Am 5:4–6).

The woman's reference to the "seal" on "the heart" hearkens back to a Deuteronomic symbol of the covenant between God and Israel (Sg 8:6; cf. Dt 6:4–8; 11:18; Jer 31:33). Finally, we recall that the passion shared between the spouses is the same as the Lord's jealous love for Israel, which derives from the covenant bond (Sg 8:6; cf. Zec 8:2; Jl 2:18). All of these are but a few indications of the Song's symbolic power to describe God's relationship to his people.

A specifically messianic interpretation of the Song begins with a serious consideration of its seven references to Solomon (1:1, 5; 3:7, 9, 11; 8:11, 12). Neither the Deuteronomists nor the prophets considered this hereditary son of David as a messianic figure. By contrast, the Chronicler exalted the status of Solomon and gave him a place alongside his father in the unfolding of God's plan for Israel (see 1 Chr 22:6–16; 28:4–7; 29:17–25). The very name of

Solomon suggests the messianic gift of peace (Hebrew: *shalom*/ 1 Chr 22:9; cf. Is 9:2–5; Mi 5:4). In the mind of the Chronicler, Solomon, the son of David, prefigures the Messiah who is to come (see 1 Chr 17:4–14; cf. 2 Sm 7:4–17).

More than any other book in the canon, the Song of Songs shares the Chronicler's esteem for Solomon. Possibly these works come from the same era, around 350 B.C. A messianic interpretation arises from perceiving a double meaning in the Song. On one level, the Song refers to Solomon's marriage to the daughter of Pharaoh (Sg 1:5–7; cf. 1 Kgs 3:1). However, this marriage in the ancient past serves as a symbol of the anticipated union between the Messiah, who is the new Solomon, and his people. According to this line of interpretation, the "king" in the Song is the Messiah, while the young woman symbolizes Jerusalem (1:4, 12; 3:9, 11; 7:5; cf. Pss 2:6–7; 45:1–17; 72:1–20). The Song expresses the longings of Jerusalem for the Messiah in the postexilic period after the Davidic line had expired.

History had proven to the composer of the Song that the "seal" of messiahship belongs, not to Zerubbabel, but to "the Branch", the son of David who will come in the future (Sg 8:6; cf. Hg 2:23; Zec 6:12–13; Jer 23:5). David's likeness is evident in "the shepherd" whom Israel claims as her own (Sg 2:16; 6:3; cf. 1 Sm 13:14; 16:11–12; 17:15; 2 Sm 7:8; cf. Ps 89:28).

The messianic interpretation of the Song requires that the young woman issue the admonitions to the daughters of Jerusalem (Sg 2:7; 3:5; 5:8; 8:4). She "awakens" the Messiah in the same way that the psalmist speaks of awakening the Lord, by crying out to him for deliverance (8:5; cf. Pss 7:7; 35:23; 44:24–26). The young woman's appeal to her beloved reflects the plea of prophet and psalmist that the Lord would come to visit his people, "Oh, that you would tear the heavens open and come down . . . " (Is 63:19; cf. Ps 101:2; cf. Sg 4:9–5:1). In the appendix, when the woman declares that she has found true "peace" (*shalom*), she foreshadows the experience of God's people who will receive the messianic gift symbolized in the name of Solomon (8:10).

Toward the New Testament: The Metaphor of God's Love

The Song of Songs alludes to a truth that is foundational for the Christian vision of life: "love is from God and everyone who loves is a child of God and knows God. Whoever fails to love does not know God, because God is love" (1 Jn 4:7–8). Pauline doctrine supports this lapidary assertion of the Johannine tradition. "The best way of all" is love, which must guide the manifestation of spiritual gifts within the community (1 Cor 12:31–13:13). The "beloved" who insists in the Song that "Love is as strong as Death" provides support in advance for Paul's claim, "Love never comes to an end" (1 Cor 13:8, 13; cf. Sg

8:6). Her declaration that "passion [is] relentless as Sheol" corresponds with Paul's assertion that "neither death . . . nor the heights nor the depths . . . will be able to come between us and the love of God, known to us in Christ Jesus our Lord" (Rom 8:38–39; cf. Sg 8:6).

Resonances of the Song of Songs enhance the personal quality of a variety of passages in the New Testament. An awareness of the motivation and intensity of the young woman's search for her beloved in the Song of Songs broadens our appreciation of Jesus' admonition and promise, "Ask, and it will be given to you; search, and you will find; knock, and the door will be opened to you" (Mt 7:7, in 7:7–11; Lk 11:9–13; cf. Sg 3:1–4; 5:2–6). The witness of the young woman teaches us that we are not seeking "something" (such as information or security) but "someone", namely, the Lord who loves us. Furthermore, by altering the last of these Gospel admonitions, the book of Revelation assures us that Jesus the Lord is the lover who knocks at the door, awaiting entrance to our community and to our hearts (Rv 3:20; cf. Sg 5:2).

In the post-Resurrection account in the Gospel of John, Mary Magdalene reflects the disposition of the beloved in her search for the Lord (Jn 20:11–18). Both her desperation at not finding him and her temptation to cling to him when Jesus reveals himself reflect the mannerisms of the spouse in the Song (Jn 20:13, 17; cf. Sg 3:1, 4). The Gospel of John suggests that love enables one to know Jesus in his risen life (see Jn 20:8 [the faith of the "beloved" disciple]; cf. 7:34). Jesus admonishes Mary Magdalene not to cling to him because he will reveal himself with greater intimacy when he breathes into his disciples the gift of his new life in the Holy Spirit (Jn 20:17; cf. 20:19–23; Gn 2:7).

The sacramental dimension of the Song of Songs provides a background for the Pauline reflection on marriage as the symbol of Christ's love for his Church (Eph 5:21–33). The metaphor of the Church as the woman clothed with the sun echoes the description of the young woman in the Song (Rv 12:1; cf. Sg 6:10).

Both Jewish and Christian interpreters have contemplated the Song of Songs as an exposition of the love God has for his people. For this reason, late Jewish tradition developed the custom of reading the Song of Songs on the Sabbath during Passover. Origen established the precedent for a whole tradition of Christian interpretation in his ten-volume commentary on the Song of Songs. He considered the Song to be an allegory both of God's relationship to the Church and of Christ's relationship to the individual believer.

Moving outside the boundaries of strict exegesis, great Christian mystics of later centuries found in the Song of Songs an unparalleled source of meditation on the union of the soul with God in divine love. St. Bernard of Clairvaux (A.D. 1091–1153) composed eighty-six sermons on the first two chapters to describe the process whereby God leads the soul to share ever more fully in his divine life. The Song of Songs inspired St. John of the Cross (A.D. 1542–1591) to write his *Spiritual Canticle,* portraying the longing of the soul for her Spouse, the divine Word and Son of God. At approximately the same time, his older Spanish contemporary, St. Teresa of Avila (A.D. 1515–1582), also formulated her reflections on divine love based on the selections from the Song of Songs in the Divine Office of her day. The witness of these saints testifies to the wealth of spiritual wisdom we can discover from the Song of Songs if we approach these poems with an attentive mind and a heart that seeks to know the love of God in prayer.

QOHELETH

Qoheleth is the biblical skeptic. He articulates the reflections of the ordinary person on matters pertaining to life and death and to the relationship between God and the individual. Qoheleth's skepticism prompted debate over the holiness of his text among rabbis until the end of the first century A.D. Nevertheless, the book of Qoheleth eventually became traditional reading on the third day of the Jewish feast of Tabernacles.

Is "Qoheleth" the name of a person or the designation of an office? Seven times throughout his work, this title identifies the author of a remarkable collection of personal wisdom (1:1, 2, 12; 7:27; 12:8, 9, 10). The word "Qoheleth" in Hebrew is a cognate of the term that refers to "the assembly" (*qahal*) of Israel (Dt 9:10; Ezr 2:64 = Neh 7:66). The fact that in Hebrew the definite article precedes "Qoheleth" on two occasions in the book (7:27; 12:8) strengthens the possibility that the word refers to the office of one who "assembles" the congregation. (*Qoheleth* is a participle of the verb *qahal,* "to assemble".) "Ecclesiastes", the alternate title for the book in English, represents a Greek translation of "Qoheleth" and is a cognate of the Greek word (*ekklesia*), meaning "congregation" or "church".

The title associates Qoheleth with Solomon by introducing the author as "son of David" (1:1) and by describing the splendor of his reign over Jerusalem in terms reminiscent of the era of the great king (1:12–2:26; cf. 1 Kgs 7:1–12; 9:15–25). However, the postexilic language of the book rules out any possibility of Solomon's direct influence on the work. Certainly, allusions to the patron of wisdom would have enhanced the credibility of this controversial text, which goes against the grain of Israel's traditional world view. Possibly, Qoheleth did "reign ... over Israel from Jerusalem" (1:12) as an important government official who administered regional affairs on behalf of foreign regents. He was an educator who extended his instruction beyond the confines of a private school to reach the general public (12:9).

Qoheleth exhibits affinities with international wisdom traditions in the ancient Near East. Both Mesopotamia and Egypt produced a variety of works that share Qoheleth's preoccupations with the remoteness of God, the inevitability of death, and the limitations of wisdom. The ancient Mesopotamian *The Gilgamesh Epic* dramatizes man's confrontation with his mortality. The ancient Akkadian poem *I Will Praise the Lord of Wisdom* reflects on the apparent apathy of God toward the plight of mortals (cf. Qo 3:11; 8:12–14, 17). The Akkadian *A Pessimistic Dialogue between Master and Servant* ponders the impact of a woman on a man's life (cf. Qo 7:26–29). *The Babylonian Theodicy* muses on the injustices of life that incite a person to question God's involvement in the world (cf. Qo 4:1; 10:5–7). *A Dispute between a Man and His Soul* is an early Egyptian text that expresses a preoccupation with death (cf. Qo 3:19–20). The *Papyrus Insinger* and *The Instructions of Onkysheshonky,* two Egyptian texts of the fourth or third century B.C., encourage the cultivation of joy and speak of good deeds as bread cast on the water (cf. Qo 2:24–25; 11:1).

The contents of Qoheleth provide sparse information about the date of composition. The Persian influence evident in the Hebrew words for "garden" (2:5) and "sentence" (8:11) establishes Qoheleth as a postexilic work. The book's concern about material comforts and the lack of references to national tragedy suggest an era of prosperity and stability in Judah. Qoheleth originated during a time of peace either in the Persian era (c. 350 B.C.) or in the Greek era (c. 250 B.C.). We suggest a date during the Greek era around 250 B.C. when the Ptolemies controlled Judah from Egypt.

While Qoheleth reflects a consciousness of the intellectual world beyond Israel's borders, his work remains a product of Judah. He adopts conventional Hebrew literary forms, such as the singular proverb (e.g., 1:15; 1:18; 5:2; 6:10; cf. Prv 10:1–22:16), the poetic instruction (e.g., Qo 9:7–12; cf. Prv 5:15–23), and the autobiographical exposition (Qo 1:12–2:26; cf. Prv 7:6–27). His references to protocol at the Temple (Qo 4:17), to weather conditions at seed time and harvest (11:4), and to vineyards, gardens, and orchards (2:4–5) correspond with a setting in Judah.

The book of Qoheleth is the collection of the sage's seminal thoughts. Qoheleth gave the book its present form when he organized his meditations at the end of his career. After his death, his students reedited the work and appended a few notations about their master and his teachings (12:9–14). We cannot be sure if these later disciples inserted any editorial notes into the text (e.g., 8:12b–13).

Certain scholars have discerned a harmonious structure in the book of Qoheleth. The text consists of halves of equal length (1:1–6:9; 6:10–12:14). Each half begins with a question that identifies its particular focus of concern (1:3; 6:11–12). The first half of the book reflects on the futility of human enterprise while declaring the imperative of enjoying life (1:1–6:9). The second half ponders the limitations of wisdom by considering two distinct issues: (a) the inadequacy of conventional reflections on topics such as emotions, achievement, women, and authority (7:1–8:17); and (b) the impotency of wisdom to estimate the future (9:1–11:6). The editorial addition (11:7–12:14) makes the conclusion precisely the same length as the introduction (1:1–18).

The sage announces his thesis at the beginning and at the end of his book: "Sheer futility, Qoheleth says, . . . everything is futile" (1:2; 12:8). Because time conditions life, no human achievement has absolute value. Qoheleth reflects on the question of God and the meaning of life in view of the certainty of death. His meditations focus on the issues of destiny and the attainment of personal happiness.

Time, Death, and Destiny

A preoccupation with time runs throughout Qoheleth. In his introduction, he speaks of the passing of generations and, in his conclusion, of the aging of the individual (1:4; 11:7–12:7). According to Qoheleth, time exhibits both a cyclical and a linear character. The cyclical aspect pertains to the cosmos, while the linear aspect belongs to the life experience of the individual. The regular movements of sun, wind, and sea suggest that events eventually fold back on themselves. Nothing is new or unique because the universe is a closed system. Tragically, an individual cannot do anything that is truly memorable because the universe follows a predetermined course (1:4–11). In contrast to the cosmic cycles, the individual experiences his or her "life time" as a line in which every point is unrepeatable. A person is always conscious of aging and of moving helplessly toward death (11:7–12:7).

Qoheleth advances the cause of individualism in the biblical tradition. He does not speak about society or tradition except in terms of their impact on individuals (see 4:1–16; 5:7–8). By comparison with traditional wisdom literature in Israel, Qoheleth devotes surprisingly little attention to parents and offspring (e.g., 6:3; cf. Prv 1:8–7:27; Jb 1:18–19; 42:13–15; Sir 3:1–16). Indeed, for Qoheleth, the injustice of leaving his property to another who did not earn it is a greater preoccupation than the formation of children (Qo 2:15–23; 6:1–3). Qoheleth speaks from an intensely subjective posture. The first-person pronouns ("I", "me", and "my") dominate the text.

The issue of personal destiny absorbs Qoheleth's attention. His search for the meaning of human existence demands that he focus on the ultimate end of everyone's life (cf. Ps 39). Tragically, death is the fate of all people. Qoheleth expresses no hope for a life beyond the tomb (see 9:5, 6, 10). Death practically renders life absurd. The specter of death calls into question the importance of moral distinctions between the virtuous and the wicked (9:2–3; cf. 8:12b–13), the wise and the foolish (2:14–16). Even the superiority of man over the animals is open to doubt insofar as death is their common fate (3:18–19).

Qoheleth believes in God as the One who acts from a distance to determine the destiny of the world and of the individual. While the individual mortal swiftly passes into oblivion, the works of God endure forever, yet they are inscrutable to human wisdom (3:11, 14; 8:17). Particularly disconcerting is the realization that a person cannot foresee the future, which belongs to God alone (11:5; cf. 9:11–12). God distributes the benefits of life to individuals as he sees fit (5:18–19; 6:2). And God judges the virtuous and the wicked according to his designs (3:17–18; 11:9). At death, God receives back the gift of life he had bestowed on the individual he had created (12:7; cf. 3:20–21; Gn 2:7).

Although God seems remote, Qoheleth subscribes to the traditional wisdom that asserts that the fear of God is the foremost of virtues (3:14; 5:6). Of all the sage's teachings, this instruction on reverence for God is the one his posthumous editors emphasized, thereby anchoring his book in the mainstream of traditional wisdom (12:13; 8:12b–13; cf. Prv 1:7; 9:10). Reverence for God consists in properly fulfilling one's religious obligations at the Temple and in taking care to discharge one's vows correctly (Qo 4:17–5:6). The person who respects God will take a reasonable risk with the expectation that his efforts will produce a beneficial result (11:1).

The virtue of fearing God enables one to act in accordance with time. Just as God gives each individual his or her "lot" in life (3:22; 5:18–19), so each one has an appropriate "time" (7:17). A person of wisdom lives according to God's design for a particular time (3:11). The variety of seasons in a lifetime demands that the individual cultivate an agile intellect and a well-rounded range of emotions (3:1–8, 9–11).

Work, Futility, and Joy

The fleeting nature of individual existence prompts Qoheleth to declare that everything is "sheer futility" (1:2; 12:8). The Hebrew word (*hebel*) connotes something unsubstantial, ephemeral, or evanescent, such as a "puff" of wind (Is 57:13). Qoheleth alludes to this precise sense of the term in the seven thematic refrains that he disperses throughout the first half of his book. "Futility" is the same as "chasing after the wind" (see 1:14; 2:11, 17, 26; 4:4, 16; 6:9).

Qoheleth undertakes and succeeds at a variety of enterprises only to declare each of them "futile". The pursuit of pleasure, wisdom, and wealth are all futile because they cannot preserve one from death (2:1, 11, 15; 5:9). Qoheleth's judgment on these matters leads him to an important conclusion: work and material gain alone are incapable of giving ultimate meaning to one's life. Eventually, even for the most successful people, work becomes a burden insofar as it is the expression of a fragile ego driven by envy and ambition (4:4).

Given the presupposition that everything ends in death, no human accomplishment by itself can give meaning to life (5:14). On six different occasions, Qoheleth announces his most essential insight: happiness is a gift one must receive from God (2:24–26; 3:12–13, 22; 5:17; 8:15; 9:7–8). When Qoheleth exhorts his students to enjoy life, he is not encouraging self-indulgence but rather an openness to God. Furthermore, by comparison with his solitary musings, these exhortations suggest a communal dimension that is essential to everyone's life. The gestures of eating and drinking suggest hospitality and the atmosphere of a banquet with friends. For all of his emphasis on the individual, Qoheleth insists that communion with one another in friendship and marriage are essential to a meaningful life (see 4:9–12; 9:7–9).

Toward the New Testament: The Priority of God's Kingdom

Qoheleth is the Bible's spokesman on behalf of all people who experience God as distant and who consider death to be the conclusion of human existence. The fact that the book of Qoheleth belongs in the biblical canon indicates that such people belong in the community of faith. The book of Qoheleth provides the necessary service of articulating the common experience of everyone who grows up in a culture marked by materialism and individualism. Qoheleth serves as a primer for the New Testament by realistically representing the mentality of pragmatists to whom Jesus desires to reveal the alternative of life in the Kingdom of God.

The Gospel of Luke in particular enters into dialogue with the meditations of Qoheleth. When Luke mentions Jesus' sending out the seventy-two "in pairs", he indicates that he shares the conviction of Qoheleth, "Better two than one alone, since thus their work is really rewarding" (Lk 10:1; cf. Qo 4:10).

However, Luke's parables about the distribution of wealth and the Kingdom of God represent a dramatic alternative to Qoheleth's vision of life. The parable of the Rich Man and Lazarus indicates that Jesus does not share Qoheleth's view that the "lot" of the poor and of the rich are somehow predetermined and unchangeable (cf. Qo 4:1; 5:7–8). To the contrary, Jesus insists that the rich are responsible for the redistribution of their wealth to the poor (Lk 16:19–31). Furthermore, the banquet that truly provides a foretaste of God's Kingdom has as its distinguished guests those who are the socially marginalized of the present world (Lk 14:7–14, 15–24; cf. Qo 2:24–26; 3:12–13).

The parable of the Rich Fool provides the most direct allusions to Qoheleth (Lk 12:13–21). The inquirer asks Jesus to arbitrate a dispute over inheritance, which is a major concern for Qoheleth (Lk 12:13–15; cf. Qo 2:18–23; 6:1–2). The wealthy farmer in the parable speaks words that recall Qoheleth's admonitions but without the sense of gratitude for God's favor that was prevalent in Qoheleth (Lk 12:19; cf. Qo 2:24; 3:12–13). In contrast to the rich fool of the parable, Qoheleth was very conscious of the possibility of a sudden, personal catastrophe (Lk 12:20; cf. Qo 9:12). Of course, Jesus uses the parable to illustrate that death is not the end of life as much as the moment of divine judgment (Lk 12:20; cf. Qo 9:5, 6, 10). Because the rich fool in Luke is not cognizant of the unpredictability of his "time" (see Qo 7:17; 3:1–11), the prospect of life beyond death becomes a source of sadness rather than of the unanticipated joy for which Qoheleth always yearned.

STUDY QUESTIONS

1. Describe the book of Lamentations. What is an acrostic psalm?
2. Why is Lamentations read on the ninth of Ab in the Jewish calendar?
3. Read Lamentations 3:1–66. What does this text teach you about how to pray for renewal in your own life and in the Church?
4. What are the two sides of Jerusalem in the Gospel of Luke?
5. What does the title "Song of Songs" mean?
6. What qualities of married love become evident in the Song of Songs?
7. How is the Song of Songs a metaphor for the love between God and his people?
8. The Song of Songs teaches us about the intimate love God desires to share with us. How would you encourage someone to recognize the love of God? How would you help that person to respond with a reciprocal love for God?
9. Why does Qoheleth deem everything "futile"? To what degree does Qoheleth reflect a modern outlook on life?
10. How does our culture view death? How does faith in the Resurrection of Christ affect one's outlook on death?
11. If we were to examine our world, we could find ample substitutes for the subject matter of Lamentations and support for the conclusions of Qoheleth. Discuss what is your world view and how you would answer someone who found that all that was in the world and in his or her life led inevitably to sorrow.
12. How does reading Lamentations, the Song of Songs, and Qoheleth broaden your appreciation of the way God is involved in various stages of one's religious life?

LAMENTATIONS

THE SONG OF SONGS

QOHELETH

36

DANIEL: FAITH UNDER FIRE

Would you die for your faith? Is your conviction about the priority of God's love and truth so strong that you would sacrifice your life in time of persecution? Those of us who live in comfort and security might dismiss such questions as being too impractical and sensational. We can look at the same question in practical and less dramatic terms. What have I actually sacrificed for my faith in the past day, week, or month? Answering such a question should afford us insight into whether we are moving more toward God or the world.

Martyrdom, which is demonstrated in small acts of self-denial as well as in the supreme sacrifice of one's life, is a fruit of wisdom and divine love. We must distinguish this genuine martyrdom from its counterfeits, which are belligerent acts of self-destruction that religious fanaticism generates. Authentic martyrs set the standard of life for the community of faith because they have attained the goal of dying to themselves out of love for God and his people.

The book of Daniel is a textbook on martyrdom in the highest sense of the term. It is a daring book because it is addressed especially to youth. We will find that it has a contemporary ring because its author was calling young people to a life of holiness and nonviolence precisely when other voices in the religious community were advocating either a religious militancy or a total secularization of the faith in the name of modernity.

Daniel's World: The Seleucid Empire

The empire of Alexander the Great could not remain intact after his death in 323 B.C. Its territory in the regions of the eastern Mediterranean and beyond was parceled out to two of his generals: (1) Ptolemy, son of Lagus, set up his kingdom in Egypt while (2) Seleucus took control of Syria, Babylon, and Persia. Practically the only thing they shared in common was a determination to propagate and enhance further the Hellenistic (Greek) culture that Alexander had introduced into their domains. These two men established rival dynasties that competed for control over Palestine—the territory in between them—until the Roman legions of Pompey took command of the whole region in 63 B.C. Antioch in Syria, the western capital of the Seleucids, and Alexandria, the capital of Egypt, came into prominence at this time as intellectual and political centers that were models of Greek-style cities.

The Ptolemaic dynasty exerted control over Palestine practically throughout the third century B.C. (300–200 B.C.). During these years, a significant Jewish population grew up in Alexandria and was responsible for the Septuagint translation. By this time, more Jews were living in "the Diaspora", beyond the borders of Palestine, than within its confines.

In order to understand the background for the book of Daniel, we must place ourselves within the walls of Jerusalem early in the second century B.C., when the power struggle between the Ptolemies and the Seleucids reached a turning point. Shortly after 200 B.C., the Seleucids wrested control of Palestine from the Ptolemies to the initial delight of Jerusalem's populace, who anticipated that this turn of events would bring them greater religious freedom. However, their hopes were dashed within a few years as the Seleucids proved themselves to be an unscrupulous second-rate power that cowered in the shadow of the emerging strength of Rome.

First and Second Maccabees (I Mc I:I–4:6I; 2 Mc 3:I–I0:8) provide a basic outline of the historical developments that gave rise to the book of Daniel. These texts direct our attention to Antiochus IV Epiphanes (175–164 B.C.), the erratic Seleucid tyrant who visited upon Jerusalem its greatest crisis since the Babylonian forces of Nebuchadnezzar destroyed it (587 B.C.). He contrived with unscrupulous elements within the Jewish populace to enforce a policy of transforming Jerusalem into a Greek city. Under the influence of Antiochus Epiphanes, corrupt Jewish leaders seized the office of high priest from one another by means of bribery and murder (2 Mc 4:7–9, 23–26, 33–38). The Hellenistic lifestyle and games, including their religious association with pagan deities, became fashionable for aristocratic Jews. Youth from ambitious families frequented the gymnasium and were taught to be ashamed of their "primitive" Jewish customs, such as circumcision (I Mc I:II–I5; 2 Mc 4:7–22).

All of these were comparatively peripheral changes that merely anticipated Antiochus' attack on the heart of Judaism when he desecrated the Temple. In 169 B.C., he pillaged the sacred precincts and confiscated its most precious vessels and ornaments (I Mc I:20–24; 2 Mc 5:15–2I). In 167 B.C., he decreed an official persecution of Judaism and outlawed its practice as a matter of treason. He ordered Jewish priests to propagate the doctrine that the Lord of Israel was the same as Zeus of the Greeks, whose earthly representative was the king himself. He climaxed his attempt to submerge Judaism in an ocean of

Hellenistic culture by erecting an altar to the Olympian Zeus within the Temple itself. The symbol of Zeus to whom Antiochus dedicated the Jerusalem Temple is "the appalling abomination" of which the book of Daniel speaks (1 Mc 1:41–64; 2 Mc 6:1–6; for "the appalling abomination" see Dn 9:27; 11:31; 12:11; 1 Mc 1:54).

Antiochus ordered his troops to make examples of anyone who refused to abandon the fundamentals of Judaism. In response to his orders, the Seleucids executed Jewish infants and hung them around their mothers' necks. They martyred the Jewish men, young and old alike, after severe ordeal and torture (1 Mc 1:60–61; 2 Mc 6:7–7:42).

The Jews who survived split into two opposing factions according to their predispositions toward the gentile manner of life. One side accepted and even welcomed the assimilation of Greek culture into their religion. This group, which was led by urbane aristocrats, congregated around the fortified gentile enclave in Jerusalem, which was called the Citadel or "Acra" (1 Mc 1:43, 52; 6:21–24; 11:21). On the opposite side were the Jewish loyalists who refused to give way to their gentile oppressors.

We can distinguish two broad subgroupings within this latter group of Jewish resistance: one being violent and the other nonviolent. The more renowned group consisted of the freedom fighters who took up arms against the Seleucids in the Maccabaean revolt. They eventually succeeded in regaining possession of the Temple and purifying it in 164 B.C. (1 Mc 2:1–4:61). In contrast to these militants, we can identify an alternate subgroup of the *Hasidim* ("devout ones"), who advocated nonviolent resistance to their oppressors. Someone in this circle of saints wrote the book of Daniel in 165 B.C., over a year after the desecration of the Temple but before the death of Antiochus IV Epiphanes. He addressed the others in his circle, who formed an underground society of nonviolent opposition to the Seleucids.

The Traditions of Daniel

The contents of Daniel fall into two distinct parts, the first six chapters comprising the stories of Daniel (1:1–6:29) and the last six presenting the visions of Daniel (7:1–12:13). The clearest points of contact between the two major sections are found in the relationship between chapters 2 and 7, both of which describe the same succession of empires (Babylonian, Median, Persian, and Greek) under the guise of symbols. In fact, a close reading of the text suggests that Daniel 7:1–28 is a later refinement and development of Daniel 2:1–49. Daniel 8:1–12:13, in turn, reflects back on Daniel 7 and fills in details that draw out the full implications of its contents. The particulars about

Antiochus IV Epiphanes in Daniel 11:21–45 provide us with the evidence for dating the book in the last years of his reign.

The two parts of the book developed differently. The stories (1:1–6:29) probably had a long tradition that might have originated in the Exile and developed throughout the following three centuries as people passed them on. The Hasidim in Jerusalem composed the present definitive version of the stories prior to the publication of the visions. For their part, the visions (7:1–12:13) were original compositions written by a holy visionary in the days of terror under Antiochus IV Epiphanes. The author of the visions edited the whole work and created its present arrangement.

The intriguing quality of the overall composition of the book is further enhanced by the fact that Daniel 1:1–2:4a and 8:1–12:13 are written in Hebrew, while the intervening section (2:4b–7:28) is written in Aramaic. Possibly the whole text was originally composed in Aramaic, the common Semitic language of the day. The Hebrew sections are translations from Aramaic into the more revered tongue of the Sacred Scriptures to enhance their authority.

The Stories: Models for Youth (1:1–6:29)

An initial perusal of the book offers scant indications of the Seleucid era but instead gives the impression of transporting us back in time to the days of the Exile (587–538 B.C.). Daniel enters our view as a brilliant Jewish youth serving under three kings in the Babylonian and Median (or Persian) courts during the sixth century B.C. In the stories, he has a heroic bearing that recalls the figures of Joseph (Gn 37–50) and Esther (Est 1:1–10:3) insofar as each of them was a Jewish figure of high standing in the court of a potentially hostile foreign monarch.

We note significant historical inaccuracies in the book: (a) contrary to the sequence of kingdoms symbolized in Nebuchadnezzar's dream, historians have no record of the Medes as a world power between the eras of the neo-Babylonians and the Persians (cf. Dn 2:31–45; cf. 7:1–7); (b) Belshazzar was never titled a king, and he was the son of Nabonidus (556–539 B.C.), not of Nebuchadnezzar (605–562 B.C.) (cf. 5:1–30; cf. 7:1–7, 17; 8:1–27); and (c) we hear of Darius the Mede nowhere else except in the book of Daniel (6:1–29; 9:1–19). Darius I (522–486 B.C.) was king of Persia in the late sixth and early fifth centuries B.C.

Such evident confusion over basic information suggests that the stories in Daniel are not presented as historical narratives. They are edifying lessons intended to cultivate a sense of identity and idealism in Jewish youth. The stories aim at strengthening the moral and spiritual fiber of young people.

Historical inaccuracies concern details that are peripheral to the main objective of the authors of these traditional narratives. The Daniel stories teach a lesson that is valid every time the chosen people face persecution: God will provide the means for his faithful ones to survive in a capricious and treacherous gentile world.

Outside of this book, we have no information about Daniel. His name resembles that of a venerated ancient whom Ezekiel associates with Noah and Job (Ez 14:14; cf. 28:3). However, no connection exists between these figures because the "Danel" (note the difference in spelling) of Ezekiel seems to be a legendary Canaanite figure mentioned in Ugaritic literature of the fourteenth century B.C.

The six stories comprising the first half of the book (1:1–6:29) are heroic accounts that describe the providential deliverance of courageous young Jews who were willing to die for their faith. People likely passed on these exciting narratives to succeeding generations for centuries as a means of cultivating a courageous faith in the young who had to face antagonism in the world. The Hasidim produced them in their present written form in order to provide heroic models for the Jewish youth, who were sorely tempted to give themselves over to the ways of the Gentiles so as to avoid the scourge of Antiochus IV Epiphanes.

The traditional setting of Daniel in Babylon during the Exile is integral to the message the stories convey. The witness of Daniel and his friends pictured in the courts of Nebuchadnezzar, Belshazzar, and Darius of centuries past demonstrates that the threat of persecution is not something new to young, faithful Jews. What happened under the Seleucids had already happened under the Babylonians and others. Most importantly, God revealed himself and worked through the lives of young people in a special way precisely when they were facing death as a consequence of religious persecution. By implication, he will act in a similar manner on behalf of the present generation of young people who are wise and heroic in their practice of the faith.

God works in the lives of his loved ones by giving them wisdom in the most oppressive circumstances. God endowed Daniel and his companions with understanding that far surpassed that of the foreign monarch and his counselors (1:4, 17–20; 5:11–14). Like Joseph of patriarchal times (Gn 40:1–41:38), Daniel had the gift of penetrating the mystery of God's plan for the world by interpreting the gentile king's dreams (Dn 2:1–49; 3:31–4:34).

Most importantly, the youths refused to defile themselves by following gentile practices (1:8–16). Their willingness to die rather than to worship the king's idol would have been particularly evocative for young men whom Antiochus was obliging to worship the Olympian Zeus in the Temple (3:16–18; cf. 1 Mc 1:54; 2 Mc 6:2). Likewise, Daniel's reprimand of the king for feasting with the precious vessels of the Temple would have readily called to mind the sacrilegious plundering Antiochus carried out (Dn 5:22–23; cf. 1 Mc 1:20–23). The rescues of the young men from the fiery furnace (Dn 3:1–30) and of Daniel from the lion's den (6:2–29) bear witness to the protection God extends to those who trust him in the crucible of persecution.

The Visions: Living for God's Kingdom (7:1–12:13)

The second half of the book of Daniel (7:1–12:13) is apocalyptic, a very different literary type compared to the first half (1:1–6:29) and, indeed, compared to almost all of the Old Testament. Apocalyptic literature uses symbols to present the unfolding of God's plan for the world in view of his final intervention, which takes the form of a universal judgment. Apocalyptic is a written, not an oral, form of communication. It is the offspring of the interaction between the prophetic and wisdom traditions.

We noted that Joel and Deutero-Zechariah were the last of the classical prophets, and they labored in the fourth century B.C. These visionaries contemplated history in view of its impending climax, which would take the form of a final battle between Yahweh and his enemies in the world (Jl 3:1–4:21; Zec 14:1–21). Their portraits developed around the traditional theme of the "Day of Yahweh" on which the Lord would execute his judgment (cf. Am 5:18–20; Zep 1:14–18). Other late prophetic texts that offered symbolic portraits of the end times comprise Ezekiel 38–39 and Isaiah 24–27. When such strands of exilic and postexilic prophecy became intertwined with threads of the wisdom tradition, they produced the basic fabric that made up the apocalyptic represented in Daniel.

From the prophets, the Hasidim who wrote Daniel developed an ability to discern the spiritual undercurrents that generate history. Furthermore, from their prophetic forebears, they cultivated a sense of urgency in calling their people to repentance and faith in view of the crisis in their times. From the wisdom tradition, the Hasidim learned that the first of all virtues is fear of the Lord (Prv 1:7; 9:10). They understood that the wicked, though they be powerful, will fail, while the righteous who are wise will attain victory (Dn 7:23–28; 11:32–35; 12:1–3; cf. Prv 16:5, 18; 21:21).

In the stories section, Daniel distinguishes himself by his insight into the mysteries of God's plan hidden in dreams (Dn 2:28, in 2:14–45; 4:16–34). Similarly, in the visions section, Daniel receives divine wisdom from the angel of God in order to understand the course of history under God's guidance (9:22; 10:12). Through their book, the Hasidim exhort all Jews to assimilate the character of "the wise" who will remain steadfast in persecution even to the point of death (11:32–35). Their victory will burst the bonds of death itself. The "wise" who remain faithful to the end will rise from the dead in triumph (12:3; 12:10).

The book of Daniel is resistance literature. Its Hasidic authors spoke to their compatriots in symbols only they could decipher as members of the underground society that was their audience. The centerpiece of the whole work is the vision of the four beasts representing the kingdoms of Babylon, Media, Persia, and Greece in succession (7:1–28). This seems to be a refinement of a prophecy presented much earlier in the traditions of the Jews, which they now saw coming to fulfillment (2:1–49).

More important than the symbolic description of successive earthly powers is the extensive vision of the Kingdom of God over and above this world (7:9–27). This is the first passage in Old Testament literature to portray the state of the redeemed transcending all history in the presence of God. The all-holy God reveals himself as the sovereign judge over the world. No one rules except by his permission. The earthly tyrants will pass away, but, in his divine counsels, the Almighty has already bequeathed his Kingdom to his holy ones in the person of their angelic representative, the son of man, who presents himself at the divine throne (7:13–14). The disciples of the Hasidim would have understood the meaning of the vision. The text was teaching them that the battle against Antiochus is a prelude to the final judgment, when God will overthrow the present world order and establish his saints as the regents of his everlasting Kingdom (7:21–27).

The visions of Daniel conclude with a landmark text in Old Testament tradition describing the fulfillment of all things in the resurrection of the body (12:2–3). The "wise" who have disciplined themselves in obedience to God's laws and have not surrendered their faith in affliction will be raised to the fullness of life beyond death (12:8–13). This text is the first clear assertion of bodily resurrection in the Old Testament. The Isaian apocalypse promised that the corpses of the chosen people would come back to life (Is 26:19). The Isaian author of the fifth century B.C. seems to have been drawing upon Ezekiel's earlier symbolic vision of the raising of God's people from death to life (Ez 37:1–14). However, the author of Daniel is the first actually to describe and prophesy an individual bodily resurrection.

The book of Daniel taught its readers not to live for this world but for the Kingdom of God. All earthly powers are provisional in light of God's sovereign authority. Faith is a matter of daily trust in God and obedience to his commandments regardless of the cost. The nonviolent Hasidim wrote the book of Daniel in order to uphold the ideal of martyrdom as the supreme value for God's elect who must confront the darkness of a godless world. This text asserts that the truth of God, not weapons, will change the world (Dn 11:33–35).

The Deuterocanonical Additions

The Greek version of Daniel includes three additions to the contents of the Hebrew-Aramaic text. The Song of Azariah and the Song of the Three Young Men (after 3:23) issue from the mouths of the youths who were cast into the furnace. Both the story of Susanna and the account of Daniel's dealings with Bel and the Dragon are appended to the last chapter of the book (after 12:13).

The Song of Azariah and the Song of the Three Young Men (3:24–90) are Greek translations of either Hebrew or Aramaic originals. These songs originated after the composition of the primary version of Daniel (165 B.C.) and before the completion of the Septuagint version of Daniel (c. 100 B.C.). The prose section (3:46–50) functions as an introduction to the Song of the Three Young Men (3:51–90). The prayer of Azariah might have been inserted into the text after the Song of the Three Young Men. The whole composition expresses the piety of the Hasidim, who were confident in God's power to work miracles on behalf of his chosen ones (see 3:46–50).

The prayers are Hasidic psalms. Just as Daniel was the model of prayer in confessing both his sin and that of the people to the Lord (9:3–19), so his compatriot Azariah (whose gentile name was Abed-Nego: 1:7) proclaims the righteousness of God and pleads for divine mercy for the chosen ones in view of the covenant (3:26–45). The Song of the Three Young Men (3:51–90) is a hymn of praise glorifying God as the Creator of all (in the manner of Psalm 148) that resounds with an identical acclamation of praise in every verse (in the manner of Psalm 136). Together, these psalms give us an appreciation of the Hasidic school of prayer. From them, we learn to set our minds on the glory of God, especially when hardships tempt us to become preoccupied with ourselves.

The additions to Daniel at the end of the Greek text are heroic tales that recall to our minds the stories in the first half of the book (Dn 13–14; cf. 1–6). The story of Susanna is an elaborate wisdom tale in Greek that was probably a translation of either a Hebrew or an Aramaic original. The standard text of the Susanna story comes, not from the Septuagint, but from another Greek translation of the Old Testament called the Theodotian version. The narrative illustrates how God protects the virtuous (such as Susanna) who trust him (13:23) against the connivances of the wicked (here, the elder judges) (13:61). Susanna is a model of truth and integrity for young women. The declaration of her innocence demonstrates that God hears the prayer of the faithful when they suffer unjust accusation. Furthermore, the story provides reassurance about the justice of Jewish legal proceedings. Daniel exhibits the wisdom of Solomon by the manner in which he exposes the corruption of the devious Jewish elders on the evidence of their own speech (13:52–59; cf. 1 Kgs 3:16–28). The Law of Moses provides the guidance for passing sentence on the miscreants (Dn 13:62). This is the only text in Daniel that portrays Jews (and Jewish authorities at that!) as the enemies of God's people. By means of this story, were the Hasidim suggesting a need for the purification of the Jewish leadership in their day?

The last additional chapter describes the wise Daniel exposing the deception inherent in pagan worship. The Greek text of this section seems to be a translation of a Semitic original composed in either Hebrew or Aramaic. The first story recounts how Daniel exposes the fraud in the cult of Bel (14:1–22), illustrating the deceit that undergirds pagan idolatry. The shrewdness of Daniel exposes the insincerity of the idolatrous priests. Acting like a master sleuth, he scatters ashes to gain evidence proving that people, not the god Bel, eat the food and drink offerings. Daniel thus proves that Bel is nothing but a lifeless stone object (14:1–22).

While the first part of the story demonstrates the futility of stone idols, the second part illustrates the folly of deifying any creature (14:23–30). By another form of ingenuity, this time by using food, Daniel puts to death the pagan dragon-god.

Because Daniel unmasked the folly of their idol-worship, the pagans cast him into the lion's den (14:31–42; cf. 6:17–25). This time, he survives by an intervention of the Lord's angel, who transports Habakkuk from Judaea to Babylon to provide him with food. Daniel survives the ordeal with the lions to witness the conversion of the gentile king and the destruction of his enemies by the same punishment they had wished to inflict on him. By following Daniel's example, those who entrust their lives to God will be able to say with him, "You have kept me in mind, O God; you have not deserted those who love you" (14:38).

In summary, the three scenes of the final story (14:1–42) depict Daniel as a wise Jewish apologist who defends the faith by fearlessly exposing the error of false religion and receives the Lord's protection in his labors. With its emphasis on a single-minded allegiance to God and his Kingdom at all costs, the book of Daniel offers a foreshadowing of Jesus' call to repentance and faith in response to his proclamation of God's Kingdom (see Mk 1:14–15).

Toward the New Testament: The Coming of the Son of Man

The book of Daniel introduced a number of ingredients into the biblical tradition that crystallized in the New Testament writings. Its apocalyptic perspective inaugurated a literary tradition that developed through an array of "intertestamental" works (such as I Enoch, the Book of Jubilees, the Sybilline Oracles, and the Testament of the XII Patriarchs) and climaxed among Christians in the book of Revelation, which was written at the end of the first century A.D. Among devout Jews, the book of Daniel helped to generate an apocalyptic consciousness that enabled people to understand that they were living in the last days under the shadow of God's final intervention. In this way, the text of Daniel prepared the spiritual climate that gave rise to John the Baptist, who issued a call to repentance in view of the impending judgment of God (Mt 3:7–10).

Jesus developed the concept of "the Kingdom of God" that the book of Daniel had introduced (Mk 1:15; Dn 2:44; 7:27) and made it a central theme of his ministry. Daniel perceived that the Kingdom was above and beyond history. What is unique to Jesus is that he revealed the inbreaking of that Kingdom into history in a definitive way in his own person and through his words and deeds. This event of Jesus of Nazareth is the essential core of the Good News: "The time is fulfilled, and the kingdom of God is close at hand. Repent and believe the Gospel" (Mk 1:15; cf. Dn 7:9–27).

Jesus' most well-known words about the Kingdom of God took the form of parables. The Kingdom of heaven is like "a man who sowed good seed in his field", "a mustard seed", "the yeast a woman took and mixed with three measures of flour", "treasure hidden in a field", "a merchant looking for fine pearls", "a dragnet that is cast in the sea" (Mt 13:24–50). Not only Jesus' parables but also his deeds communicate the reality of the Kingdom. The miracles, healings, and exorcisms he performed reveal the event of the Kingdom in power and, therefore, demonstrate what his words announce: "But if it is through the Spirit of God that I drive out devils, then be sure that the kingdom of God has caught you unawares" (Mt 12:28; cf. Mk 11:10).

Another concept Jesus developed from the book of Daniel was the title "Son of Man". He preferred this title above others as a means of self-designation. In part, it seems that he chose "Son of Man" precisely because its meaning was not as fixed in people's minds as terms like "the Messiah" and "Son of God" (see Mk 8:27–33; cf. Jn 6:15). Although the term "Son of Man" was less defined in the public mind, it had a rich, biblical tradition with two dimensions, one earthly, the other heavenly. On the one hand, God applied this title to his prophet Ezekiel to emphasize the weak and ephemeral aspect of human flesh in contrast to the abiding splendor of the divine glory (Ez 2:1, 3; 3:1; cf. Mt

8:20). On the other hand, in Daniel, the "Son of Man" is a heavenly figure who approaches the throne of God to receive the divine authority over the Kingdom on behalf of the holy ones of the Most High (Dn 7:13–14; cf. 7:18, 27). Jesus encompasses both these dimensions in his human and divine aspects as "Son of Man".

On two important occasions, Jesus quoted the vision in Daniel concerning "the Son of man coming in the clouds": first, at the climax of his apocalyptic discourse to his disciples concerning the end time; and, secondly, at his trial before the Sanhedrin, in response to the interrogation of the high priest (Mk 13:26; see 14:62; cf. Dn 7:13). When he quoted Daniel, Jesus made one significant adjustment to the text. In Daniel, the Son of Man comes to the throne of God (Dn 7:13); by contrast, in Jesus' preaching, the Son of Man comes into the world on the last day in order to execute God's judgment and to assemble the scattered people of God (Mk 13:27; 14:62). Jesus inaugurated the end time and established the Kingdom of God in the world through his ministry, culminating in his death and Resurrection. At his second coming in judgment as the glorious Son of Man, he will bring to completion what he definitively initiated at the cross, namely, the submission of all creation to the reign of God.

Daniel was also a vital resource for Paul's exposition of God's plan for the world. The Pauline concept of "mystery", which is so central to the apostle's teaching, has its roots in Daniel's interpretation of Nebuchadnezzar's dream (Dn 2:18, 28, 29). The "mystery" in Daniel is God's plan of salvation that is about to be fulfilled in history. The "mystery" is the hidden design God is about to reveal to his holy ones (Dn 2:21, 28). Paul builds on this foundational understanding of mystery when he announces that God has "revealed" the "mystery" in the Spirit to Christians (1 Cor 2:7). The "mystery" is the Gospel of salvation in Jesus Christ, which was hidden in ages past and which the apostle now proclaims to the world in obedience to God's command (Rom 16:25–27). Pauline tradition expresses this succinctly, teaching that the mystery is "Christ among you, the hope of glory" (Col 1:27). The Letter to the Ephesians identifies the mystery with the Church in which both Jew and Gentile form the one Body of Christ as the fruit of divine grace (Eph 3:3–6).

Both Jesus and Paul allude to the Danielic metaphor concerning "the wise" when they describe Christians as reflections of the light of God's new life to a world lost in its own darkness (Mt 5:14; Phil 2:15; cf. Dn 12:3).

The book of Daniel makes its ultimate contribution to the history of revelation by setting our hopes on the resurrection of the body (Dn 12:1–3). The New Testament authors appreciated the fullest implications of this text as no one else could—in light of the bodily Resurrection of Jesus, who is "the first-born from the dead" (Col 1:18; 1 Cor 15:1–58; Jn 5:28–29; cf. Rom 8:29).

The destiny of God's faithful ones is not death but a transformed and glorious life in God. In the revelation of Christ risen from the dead, the New Testament proclaims the victory of God and the source of our hope to which the book of Daniel has introduced us.

We will appreciate the significance of Daniel for its original audience as we study more closely the history of their times as presented in First and Second Maccabees.

STUDY QUESTIONS

1. What was the "appalling abomination"?
2. In what period was the book of Daniel written and by whom?
3. What is the difference between the first and second parts of the book of Daniel?
4. In what languages is the book of Daniel written?
5. What is the main point of the Daniel stories?
6. What is apocalyptic literature?
7. What are Daniel's two salient characteristics?
8. How is the book of Daniel resistance literature?
9. What are the Song of Azariah and the Song of the Three Young Men?
10. In what way does Jesus use concepts from Daniel such as the Kingdom of God and the Son of Man?
11. How does the New Testament expand upon the book of Daniel's concept of the resurrection of the dead?
12. Discuss how Daniel's quiet belief in God and the principles of his faith affected every choice he made, brought him honor, and ultimately saved him.

DANIEL

[*Italics* denote the Deuterocanonical additions.]

DEUTEROCANONICAL BOOKS

37

1 AND 2 MACCABEES: DEFENDERS OF THE FAITH

Sometimes faithfulness to the Lord requires civil disobedience. When a governing power encroaches on its citizens' right to religious liberty, the community of believers must voice its protest and refuse to comply with malicious legislation. Far from being a threat to faith, persecution can provide the necessary opportunity for faith to become strong and genuine. The necessity of professing faith in the face of opposition is approached from alternate perspectives in 1 and 2 Maccabees, respectively. Reading both of these texts affords us the opportunity to evaluate the quality of our commitment to defend religious values in the public square.

First and Second Maccabees do not follow one another sequentially as do the first and second books of Samuel, Kings, and Chronicles. Rather, they overlap in the material they cover. Each book presents the history of the movement we call the Maccabaean revolt from a different theological perspective. Therefore, we should read these texts in parallel, similar to the way we compared the accounts of Chronicles with the narratives in Samuel and Kings.

History from Two Perspectives

First Maccabees narrates the history of the Jewish people from the enthronement of the Seleucid ruler Antiochus IV Epiphanes (175 B.C.) until the installation of John Hyrcanus I as the high priest in Jerusalem (134 B.C.). Second Maccabees focuses on only a portion of this era, covering a span of less than twenty years. It takes up the narrative earlier, in the last years of Seleucus IV (187–175 B.C.), and concludes with the Maccabaean victory over the Seleucid general Nicanor (160 B.C.). While 1 Maccabees spans the careers of all the Maccabees (Mattathias, Judas, Jonathan, and Simon), 2 Maccabees concentrates exclusively on the career of Judas Maccabaeus (the span covered in 1 Maccabees 1:10–7:50).

1. 1 Maccabees

A scribe living in Jerusalem originally wrote 1 Maccabees in Hebrew, but we have received the text only in its Greek translation. The Hebrew text originated around 100 B.C., shortly after the death of John Hyrcanus I (134–104 B.C./1 Mc 16:23–24), and our Greek version was completed sometime later in the first century B.C. Indications within the text suggest that the author could have been an official scribe who composed this book under the auspices of the early Hasmonaeans. He must have had ready access to the government archives in order to quote some thirteen different pieces of diplomatic correspondence, international treaties, and national legislation (e.g., 1 Mc 8:23–32; 12:6–18; 15:2–9). The official mandate granting Simon and his descendants power to reign over the Jewish state constitutes the climax of the political developments outlined in the book (14:27–49). The book concludes by portraying John Hyrcanus I, the first of the Hasmonaean rulers, as the worthy successor to the Maccabees (16:1–24).

The author of 1 Maccabees portrays the exploits of the Maccabees in terms reminiscent of the glorious campaigns of Moses, Joshua, Saul, and David. The book applauds the Maccabaean armed resistance against the Seleucids and their guerrilla attacks on the Syrian forces occupying Palestine. True to its contents, which defend the integrity of Judaism, the style of writing, although in Greek, exhibits a thoroughly Jewish quality. The translator provides a literal rendering of the Hebrew as if to force his audience to think as Palestinian Jews even as they read the translation in the tongue of the Hellenistic world.

2. 2 Maccabees

In contrast to 1 Maccabees, 2 Maccabees provides us with an alternate perspective that subordinates militarism to martyrdom. The heroes of this text are not the freedom fighters but the ordinary Jews who remained faithful to the Law in the face of the Seleucid persecution. Of all the Maccabees, only Judas merits attention, since he surpasses the rest as defender and advocate of the faithful. By focusing on the martyrs, 2 Maccabees suggests the primacy of spiritual protest over the call to arms. The author interprets events from a distinctly religious viewpoint, more precisely, from the standpoint of the Hasidim, who countered religious persecution with spiritual resistance. The author of 2 Maccabees stands in the tradition of the Hasidim who produced the book of Daniel.

The book of 2 Maccabees is a digest of an earlier five-volume history that a certain Jason of Cyrene had written in Greek (2 Mc 2:19–32). Although Jason was a North African Jew, his text indicates that he possessed a remarkable knowledge of the geography of Palestine. Jason of Cyrene seems to have completed his work—which is no longer extant—within a decade or two of the last events he describes, perhaps around 150 B.C.

The author who has provided us with the abridgment of Jason's work that we call 2 Maccabees was also a Hellenistic Jew. If the letters introducing the book come from his hand and were not added at a later date, then we can surmise that he was an important figure in the Jewish community of Alexandria, Egypt (2 Mc 1:1–9; 1:10–2:18). He finished his digest of Jason's work before the feast of Dedication in December of 124 B.C. (2 Mc 1:9). According to this estimation, 2 Maccabees reached completion during the high priesthood of John Hyrcanus I (134–104 B.C.), some twenty years before the original Hebrew edition of 1 Maccabees.

The Seleucids, Maccabees, and Hasmonaeans

In order to appreciate the unique perspectives of 1 and 2 Maccabees, we must chronicle the events that provide the raw material of these history texts. We follow a convention that distinguishes between the Maccabaean era (spanning the times of Mattathias, Judas, Jonathan, and Simon [166–134 B.C.]) and the subsequent Hasmonaean era (extending from the rise to power of Simon's son, John Hyrcanus I, until the invasion of Palestine by the Roman armies under Pompey [63 B.C.]). We will begin our survey of the period from the same starting point as 1 and 2 Maccabees, with a reflection on the historical roots of the Seleucid king, Antiochus IV Epiphanes.

1. The Seleucid Empire

Antiochus IV Epiphanes (1 Mc 1:1–2:70; 2 Mc 3:1–7:42): After the death of Alexander the Great (323 B.C.), one of his generals, Ptolemy (323–285 B.C.), took over Egypt. Seleucus (312–281 B.C.), the son of another of Alexander's generals (whose name was Antiochus), gained control, first of Babylon and eastern regions of the empire and, then, of Syria and most of Asia Minor. Ptolemy and Seleucus, who started out as allies, became archrivals in competition for control of Palestine. For more than a century (301–198 B.C.), the Ptolemies maintained their regency over Palestine from their capital in Alexandria. However, in 198 B.C., when Antiochus III the Great (223–187 B.C.) defeated the forces of Ptolemy at Panias (Caesarea Philippi of the Roman era/Mk 8:27), Palestine fell under the dominion of the Seleucids, who ruled from their capital in Antioch.

In 189 B.C., the Romans made their presence felt in the region by pushing the Seleucid troops back from Greece and then by issuing a stinging defeat to Antiochus III the Great at Magnesia on the Maeander River some distance north of Ephesus. The Romans dispossessed the Syrians of all their territory in Asia Minor and transferred it to the aegis of Rhodes and Pergamum. To signify their victory, the Romans took captive Antiochus IV, the youngest son of Antiochus III. He remained a hostage in Rome for fourteen years, while his older brother succeeded his father to the throne as Seleucus IV (187–175 B.C.). Shortly after the Romans released Antiochus IV, his brother Seleucus IV was assassinated by a government official, and the former prisoner of Rome seized power under the name of Antiochus IV Epiphanes (175–164 B.C.).

The external struggle between the Ptolemies and the Seleucids accentuated the internal polarization between factions inside the borders of Palestine. The power struggle centered around the office of high priest in particular. Simon II (220–195 B.C.) was a noble high priest whose integrity became almost legendary throughout the generations after his death insofar as the quality of his tenure represented a marked contrast to the intrigue and corruption associated with those who succeeded him in office (see Sir 50:1–24). The disturbances began with Onias III (196–175 B.C.), who inherited the high priesthood from his father. Onias III's pro-Ptolemaic sympathies provoked the suspicion of the Seleucid regents. Antiochus IV deposed Onias III from office and allowed Jason, another son of Simon II, to purchase the office of high priest. Jason (175–172 B.C.) promoted the transformation of Jerusalem into a Hellenistic city complete with a new name, "Antiochia", and a gymnasium. The high priest himself advocated suspension of rigorous observance of the Law in favor of Greek games and other forms of culture. However, Jason could not maintain the confidence of Antiochus IV, who replaced him with Menelaus, a man who offered the king large sums of money and who also had the support of the Tobiad family in Jerusalem. A fundamental change of mentality had occurred among the Jewish leaders: the high priest was more preoccupied with his role as the official representative of the Seleucid king than with his role as the religious leader of the Jewish people.

Menelaus drove Jason from Jerusalem by force of arms. However, the public rejected as illegitimate Menelaus' claim to the high priesthood. In 169 B.C., Antiochus IV made an incursion into Egypt (cf. Dn 11:25–28). On his way back to Antioch, he entered Jerusalem and plundered the Temple treasury. The following year, Antiochus IV returned to Egypt and attained some success until the Roman ambassador in Alexandria provoked his retreat by simply telling him, on behalf of the Senate in Rome, to restore whatever he had captured and then to get out of the land (cf. Dn 11:29). Antiochus IV, stinging from this humiliating reprimand, again passed through Jerusalem on his way back to Antioch. This time, he slaughtered the Jews who had risen up against Menelaus when Jason returned to Jerusalem in the misbelief that Antiochus IV had been killed in Egypt.

In an attempt to eliminate potential Jewish rebellion in the future, Antiochus IV imposed the Seleucid stamp on Jerusalem. His general Apollonius constructed the walled Citadel (the *Acra*) for the Syrian officials and the Jewish elite who supported the Hellenistic reforms. The most blatant affront to Judaism occurred at the Temple. In December 167 B.C., the Hellenizers inaugurated the cult of the Olympian Zeus and the Syrian Baal-Shamem, whom they equated with Yahweh (see 1 Mc 1:54—"the appalling abomination"). Now, devotees came to the Temple to worship a variety of Hellenistic deities and to participate in orgiastic rites. Antiochus IV issued edicts that propagated the pagan rituals throughout the land while prohibiting the observance of the Jewish religion. He forbade the Jews, under pain of death, to practice the Law by observing the Sabbath, performing circumcision, or adhering to dietary prescriptions (1 Mc 1:41–64; 2 Mc 6:1–11).

2. The Maccabees

Judas Maccabaeus (1 Mc 2:1–9:22; 2 Mc 8:1–15:36): The ruthless persecution of Judaism produced a significant number of martyrs from the beginning and drove all faithful Jews out of Jerusalem. The forces of Jewish resistance regrouped in the countryside. When Mattathias, the priest of Modein, defied the Syrians, the Jews rallied together in the Judaean hills and initiated the Maccabaean revolt. The son of Mattathias, Judas Maccabaeus, emerged as the true leader who developed the military skills necessary to carry on guerrilla warfare that lasted some three years.

Judas continually outwitted the Syrian forces until he controlled the rural territories. Aware that Judas was going to advance on Jerusalem, the Syrian officials and Hellenistic Jews in the city persuaded Antiochus IV to repeal the proscription against Judaism (2 Mc 11:13–21). However, the king's decree in the spring of 164 B.C., which reinstated Jewish religious freedom (2 Mc 11:27–32), did nothing to stop the Maccabaean advance. In December 164 B.C., Judas seized control of the city and reclaimed the Temple for the Jews (1 Mc 4:28–61; 2 Mc 11:1–12; 10:1–8). The feast of Hanukkah celebrates the dedication of the Temple following the Maccabaean victory.

Meanwhile, Antiochus IV Epiphanes had died in battle against the Parthians on his northern frontier. While the Seleucids were in a state of transition, Judas intensified his campaign against the Gentiles in Galilee and expanded it beyond the Jordan to the east against Gilead, further to the south against Ammon and Idumaea, and to the west against Philistia (1 Mc 5:1–68; 2 Mc

12:1–16, 20–31). In 162 B.C., Antiochus V Eupator (164–162 B.C.), the son of Antiochus IV, issued a decree that guaranteed the Jews exclusive possession of the Temple (2 Mc 11:22–26). The Syrians executed Menelaus and installed as high priest Alcimus, who was, on the one hand, a Seleucid sympathizer but, on the other, a descendant of the legitimate Oniad priestly line. For protection against Judas, Alcimus turned to Demetrius I Soter (161–150 B.C.), who had seized the Seleucid throne after assassinating his cousin Antiochus V. Under orders from Demetrius I, the Syrian forces of general Bacchides killed Judas at the battle of Beer-Zaith in the spring of 160 B.C. (1 Mc 9:1–22).

Jonathan (1 Mc 9:23–12:53): Judas' brother, Jonathan, assumed the Jewish command, and, in 157 B.C., he negotiated a settlement with Bacchides that effectively ended the Maccabaean revolt (1 Mc 9:71–73). The treaty allowed Jonathan to exercise power as "judge" over the countryside from his residence in Michmash but excluded him from power in Jerusalem. Alcimus died in 159 B.C., and the office of high priest remained vacant for seven years. In 152 B.C., Alexander Balas (152–150, 150–145 B.C.) overthrew Demetrius I as ruler of the Seleucid empire. Alexander Balas immediately installed Jonathan as high priest in Jerusalem and governor of Judaea (1 Mc 10:1–21).

In 145 B.C., Demetrius II (145–140, 129–125 B.C.), the son of Demetrius I, deposed Alexander Balas in Antioch. By shrewd foresight, Jonathan managed to ally himself with Demetrius II and thereby extended his rule throughout Samaria and then through Galilee to Damascus. A Syrian official, Diodotus Trypho, undermined the rule of Demetrius II in favor of Antiochus VI, the son of Alexander Balas. Then Trypho deposed Antiochus VI and took the throne for himself. By a ruse, Trypho lured Jonathan to Ptolemais and imprisoned him there.

Simon (1 Mc 13:1–16:17): When Jonathan was captured and then murdered in 143 B.C., his brother Simon took over the rule of Judaea. Simon formed an alliance with Demetrius II against Trypho. When Demetrius II returned to power, Simon was able to expel the Syrians from the citadel in Jerusalem. On the international front, he established bonds with both Rome and Sparta. Simon's popularity reached a climax in 140 B.C., when the elders in Jerusalem and leaders in the countryside acclaimed him and his descendants as their high priest, commander-in-chief, and ruler (1 Mc 14:41; 13:41). This public endorsement provided the foundation for the Hasmonaean dynasty, which exercised control over Palestine until the advent of the Romans in 63 B.C.

Eventually, Simon had to turn back the troops of Antiochus VII Sidetes (139–129 B.C.), the replacement for Demetrius II on the Seleucid throne. In 134 B.C. Simon's death came at the hands, not of the Syrians, but of his own family as his son-in-law, Ptolemy, murdered Simon, his wife, and two sons.

3. The Hasmonaeans

John Hyrcanus I (1 Mc 16:11–24): However, another son of Simon survived because he was outside Jerusalem when his parents were murdered. He was John Hyrcanus I (134–104 B.C.), whose rule marks the inauguration of the Hasmonaean era in the strict sense.

After 129 B.C., when Antiochus VII Sidetes died in battle against the Parthians, John Hyrcanus had a relatively free hand extending control over Palestine. He took command of Samaria in the central highlands, Idumaea in the Negeb, and Medeba in the Transjordan. He imposed circumcision and the observance of the Law on the people of each of these regions.

The Successors of John Hyrcanus I: At the death of John Hyrcanus I, his son Aristobulus (104–103 B.C.) seized power but only for a year until he died. His wife Salome Alexandra married Alexander Jannaeus, who then assumed the roles of high priest, ruler, and military commander for more than twenty-five years (103–76 B.C.). This man waged battles throughout the region against both foreigners (such as the reigning Ptolemies, Seleucids, and Nabataean monarchs) and Jewish rebels (eight hundred of whom he crucified at one time). When her husband died, Salome Alexandra (76–67 B.C.) took over the political and military leadership and installed her son Hyrcanus II as high priest. When she died, Salome Alexandra's other son Aristobulus II (67–63 B.C.) expelled his brother Hyrcanus II and ruled Jerusalem. However, Hyrcanus II fled southward to the Nabataeans at Petra with whom he made an alliance in order to depose his brother from power. In 63 B.C., the Roman general Pompey resolved the dispute by seizing Jerusalem and bestowing his approval on Hyrcanus II. A new era began as the Romans incorporated Palestine into its province of Syria.

The Essenes, Pharisees, and Sadducees

The Hasmonaean era provided the conditions for the emergence of three traditions that would deeply affect the shape of Palestinian Judaism until A.D. 70, when the Roman legions of Titus destroyed the Temple in Jerusalem. The Essenes, the Pharisees, and the Sadducees all originated within the ethos of life during the era of the Maccabees and the Hasmonaeans. The Essenes and the Pharisees developed out of the circles of Hasidim, who, on religious grounds, generally opposed the thrust of Hasmonaean policy. The Sadducees, on the other hand, grew out of the upper class Jewish families associated with the high priesthood, who were sympathetic to the Hasmonaean rulers.

The Sadducees were "the sons of Zadok", descendants of the preexilic family of priests (1 Kgs 1:26; Ez 40:46). We might expect that people who claimed such a priestly lineage would take exception to the Hasmonaean seizure of the high priestly office under the auspices of the Seleucids. However, as members of the Jerusalem aristocracy, the Sadducees preferred the privileges and security of association with the Hasmonaean high priests. They were political survivors who were distinguished from the Hasidim for their tolerance of the Hellenistic culture imposed on Jerusalem by the Seleucids. Their cautious bent in religious matters is evident in their acceptance of only the written Torah and in their denial of angels, resurrection, and an afterlife (Mk 12:18; Acts 23:8).

The Pharisees were the "separatists" (from the Hebrew verb *paras:* "to divide"), so-named for their concern to cut themselves off from everyone and everything that was not holy according to the prescriptions of the Law. They emerged from the ranks of the Hasidim of Maccabaean times, who resisted the imposition of gentile manners on Jewish society. The Pharisees' opposition to Hellenistic culture in Palestine brought them into periodic confrontation with the Hasmonaeans and the Sadducees. Undoubtedly, Pharisees comprised a significant portion of those whom Alexander Jannaeus crucified. The Pharisees wanted to teach ordinary Jews how they could live every day according to the Law and free of gentile influence. They collected and subscribed to the "sayings of the Fathers", which applied the Law to life situations (Mk 7:3). Furthermore, they were convinced of the existence of angels and the resurrection of the body (Acts 23:8).

The Essenes bore a Greek name that echoed the Hebrew title Hasidim. They were successors to the faithful who, from the earliest days of the Maccabaean revolt, resisted the Seleucid persecution of Judaism (1 Mc 2:42). This group practiced a more radical form of separation from the Gentiles than the Pharisees, who continued to inhabit cities, towns, and villages. The Essenes retired to the Judaean desert by the Dead Sea and established a community at Qumran. They made their retreat shortly after 150 B.C. in reaction to the high priesthood of both Jonathan and Simon, which they deemed to be illegitimate. The Essenes gathered around the "Teacher of Righteousness" with the vision of forming a faithful remnant in anticipation of the end times. Their community at Qumran endured until the Romans destroyed it in A.D. 68, two years before sacking Jerusalem.

A preliminary comparison between 1 and 2 Maccabees indicates that the differences in these texts follows the lines of doctrinal distinctions between the Hasmonaeans and Sadducees, on one hand, and the Hasidim and Pharisees, on the other. First Maccabees remains faithful to the beliefs of the Sadducees by emphasizing the importance of prayer, recalling the witness of scriptural heroes, preferring the indirect term "Heaven" to any direct reference to God, and avoiding any suggestion of a possible resurrection. By contrast, the doctrines of the Hasidim and Pharisees surface throughout 2 Maccabees in references to acts of divine intervention, miracles, martyrdom, and the life of the resurrected after death.

I MACCABEES: THE JEWISH CRUSADES

The Maccabaean revolt aimed at reclaiming the Holy Land from foreign occupation. The presentation of this crusade in I Maccabees follows a chronological outline that begins with an introduction of the oppressor, Antiochus IV Epiphanes (1:1–64), and continues with a narration of the succession of Maccabees who opposed him: Mattathias (2:1–70), Judas (3:1–9:22), Jonathan (9:23–12:53), and Simon (13:1–16:24). This is a story of liberation: the Jews, who were oppressed by a foreign overlord in the beginning, appoint one of their own as ruler in the end (1:10–64; cf. 14:27–49). Nevertheless, the text still conveys the necessity of courageous leadership because the Jewish struggle continues in a treacherous world (15:1–16:24).

At first reading, I Maccabees strikes us as a rather secular work, preoccupied with the complexities of international politics, the intrigue of national power struggles, and the treachery of guerrilla warfare. However, even at this level, the merit of its inclusion among the Deuterocanonical books rests in its insistence that the people of God must live out their faith within the political tensions of the real world. A closer reading of the language of I Maccabees leads us to a better appreciation of the theological and spiritual dimensions of the book. In summary fashion, we will consider three components that convey the deeper message of the text: (a) its vision of sacred history; (b) its insistence on prayer and spiritual discipline; and (c) its overriding reverence for religious institutions, such as the Temple, the priesthood, and the Holy City.

1. Sacred History Experienced in the Present

The author of I Maccabees studied "the holy books" (12:9). He adopts the style of the Deuteronomists to describe the adventures of the Maccabees and, in particular, he imitates the books of Samuel. He wants to demonstrate that God is at work in the times of the Maccabees as he had been in the golden age of David. While he narrates the exploits of the Maccabees, his language recalls the great events of the Exodus and the conquest and establishment of the kingdom of Israel in the era from Moses to David. His pen illustrates how the Maccabaean revolt and the establishment of independent rule in Palestine literally "represent" the history of salvation.

Mattathias, the priest of Modein, is a new Phinehas who begins a purification of the people by punishing them for worshipping the gods of foreigners (2:26; cf. Nm 25:6–15). Alternatively, Mattathias resembles David when he goes into the desert and assembles a force that will eventually take control of Israel (1 Mc 2:29–30, 42–44; cf. 1 Sm 22:1–2). This patriarch of the Maccabees is a hero of the faith in the line of the ancients, whom he extols in a list extending from Abraham to David to Elijah to Daniel (1 Mc 2:51–64).

Judas Maccabaeus reflects the character of God's anointed servants: he is like Moses and his people are like the Israelites when he leads them through the hostile territory of ancient Bashan (5:45–54 ["Beth-Shean"]; cf. Nm 20:14–21; 21:21–22:1); he is a new Joshua who reconquers the land by executing the curse of destruction on the strongholds of foreigners (1 Mc 5:5, 28, 51; cf. Jos 6:17). He prepares his people for the conquest with instructions that reflect Moses' exhortations on the plains of Moab. At the same time, he recalls the examples of Jonathan and David when he leads his small army against the superior strength of the Syrian Goliaths (1 Mc 3:17–26; 4:30–34; cf. Dt. 1:29–33; 3:18–22; cf. 1 Sm 14:1–23; 17:45).

The people who followed the Maccabaean leaders relived the ancient experiences of renewal and deliverance. Like the ancients of Samuel's day, they gathered at Mizpah to repent, pray, and unite with their leader (1 Mc 3:46–54; cf. 1 Sm 7:5–6; 10:17). Like the citizens of Jerusalem who witnessed the Lord defeat Sennacherib's troops, the people of Adasa see the ultimate destruction of the Syrian general Nicanor and his forces (1 Mc 7:39–50; cf. Is 36:1–37:38). Finally, under Simon, they begin to enter an era of peace that seems to have had messianic qualities, according to the words of Zechariah (1 Mc 14:4–15; cf. Zec 3:10; 8:4–5, 12).

The Maccabaean violence recalls the campaigns of Joshua. The author illustrates how the insurrection is sparked by reverence for the first commandment, which prohibits idolatry (1 Mc 1:43; 2:15–18; cf. Dt 13:7–19; 5:6–10; 6:7). As a latter-day Joshua, Judas Maccabaeus carries on a holy war in accordance with the legislation in the Torah (1 Mc 3:55–60; cf. Dt 20:1–20). He destroys the gentile strongholds with their temples and altars in order to purify the land and reclaim the Temple as the unique dwelling place of the Lord (1 Mc 5:44, 51, 68). The author attributes the success of the Maccabees to their spirituality.

2. Prayer, Spiritual Discipline, and Worship

The achievements of the Maccabees are the fruit of prayer and reverence for the Law. These two components provide the foundation for the initial formation of the troops by Judas at Mizpah (3:46–60). Before the battle at Emmaus, the people pray and then witness a victory over impossible odds (4:10). They resemble Joshua's expedition against Jericho insofar as they attack the foe in the Transjordan with prayer (5:31, 33; cf. Jos 6:1–16). Through prayer, Jonathan and his troops experience deliverance from the Syrians at the Jordan (1 Mc 9:46). Later, at Hazor, he turns defeat into victory through prayer and repentance (11:71). Even in his official correspondence with Rome, Jonathan announces that "the holy books" are the consolation of his people, and prayer is their greatest defense against their foes (12:9, 15).

After battle, the triumphant forces sing psalms in thanksgiving for the mercy God has extended to them (4:24; cf. Ps 118). All the efforts of Judas and his forces culminate in praise and adoration when they rededicate the Temple (1 Mc 4:36–59). Similarly, Simon and his people take control of the Citadel in Jerusalem with a liturgical procession of song and music (13:51).

The name of the Lord is too holy to be uttered in 1 Maccabees. Out of reverence, the author employs the indirect appellation "Heaven" when referring to God (e.g., 2:21; 3:18, 19, 50, 60; 4:10, 24, 40, 55; 12:15; 16:3). Whenever the people cry out to "Heaven", their prayers bring deliverance and victory.

Obedience must accompany prayer. Dedication to the Law unites and energizes the Jewish resistance. The insurrection begins because Mattathias burns with zeal for the Law and beckons all Jews to do the same (2:26–27, 64, 67–68). The apostates are identified as those who forgot the Law because of fear of persecution or attraction to gentile manners (1:52). The company of Judas are distinguished by adopting the Law as their guide (3:48). When they rededicate the sanctuary, they follow the prescriptions of the Law, and Judas handpicks as ministers at the Temple those priests who gave their lives to the study of the sacred precepts (4:42, 47, 53). Victory results from observance of the Law and is manifest in the right of the Jewish people to live in accordance with the Law (6:58–59; 13:40).

3. Reverence for Institutions: The Temple and the Holy City

The Maccabees fought on behalf of the Temple and the Law (14:29) against the oppression of the Gentiles (5:1, 9) and the apostasy of the Jews, especially those who had moved into the Citadel, the enclave of Hellenism in Jerusalem (1:52; 2:43; 3:23; 6:18; 11:20; 13:50–53). The author of 1 Maccabees communicates to us a salutary reverence for religious institutions through the manner in which he focuses our attention on the Temple.

The Temple is worth more than one's life: this conviction motivates Judas and his forces to sacrifice themselves in battle (3:58–59). His campaign across the whole of Palestine reaches its climax in the recapture and rededication of the Temple (4:36–61). The Maccabaean hopes come to fulfillment when Simon receives the authority to govern the sanctuary and guarantee its sacredness (14:42).

Because of the Lord's presence in the Temple, Jerusalem is the "Holy City" (2:7). The author of 1 Maccabees suggests that any attack on Jerusalem eventually brings about the downfall of the attacker. The mighty Antiochus IV Epiphanes, as he lies dying, attributes his forthcoming death, not to the Parthians who defeated him, but to divine justice in retribution for his invasion of Jerusalem (6:12–13). Similarly, Alcimus, the corrupt high priest, suffers an agonizing death for dismantling one of the Temple walls (9:54–57).

On the side of the Jewish advocates, Jonathan's career reaches its apex when he repairs the damage and then fortifies Jerusalem by strengthening its walls and isolating the Citadel in his last years (10:10–11; 12:35–36). Ultimately, Simon completes the Maccabaean mission to Jerusalem when he breaks into the Citadel and sanctifies it for the Jewish people (13:50–53).

Even when the Maccabees attain their goal of ruling Jerusalem, history remains incomplete according to the vision of 1 Maccabees. The people of God still await the coming of the prophet who will bring the history of Jerusalem to fulfillment (4:46; 9:27; 14:40).

Toward the New Testament: Endurance to the End

The messianic expectation suggested in 1 Maccabees developed over the next century to become a significant element in the spiritual ethos of Palestine in the time of Jesus. During his Galilean ministry, people wondered whether or not he was "the one who is to come" (Mt 11:3; cf. Mal 3:1; Dt 18:15, 18).

However, by his words and deeds, Jesus of Nazareth demonstrates that the Kingdom of God consists in much more than a new national or political order, which the Maccabees had attempted to realize. Jesus teaches his disciples that the Kingdom will break into the world, not by a military victory, but by the complete surrender of his life on the cross to defeat the power of Satan (Mk 8:31–33; Jn 12:31–36).

The Gospels (especially Luke) and 1 Maccabees both highlight the importance of Jerusalem. The author of 1 Maccabees accentuates the actions of Judas Maccabaeus to possess and purify the Temple. Similarly, in the Gospel of Luke, Jesus' ministry reaches its climax when he casts out the worldly elements and takes possession of the sacred precincts by his preaching (Lk 19:45–21:38; cf. 1 Mc 4:36–59). At the end of 1 Maccabees, Simon receives full power over Jerusalem. In an analogous manner in Luke, the resurrected Jesus appears to his disciples within the holy city or in its immediate vicinity (Lk 24:1–53). Both texts describe victory for God's people centered in Jerusalem.

Although the Gospels and 1 Maccabees share a concern for Jerusalem and the Temple, they differ over whether to use violence to achieve God's victory. The Maccabees take control by means of war and violence against the occupation forces of the Gentiles (Syrians) and the apostate Jews. Jesus, on the other hand, takes control by his surrender to death at the hands of the gentile (Roman) occupation forces and of the Jewish authorities. In his ministry, Jesus' actions distance him from his Maccabaean forebears. As Messiah, Jesus renounces the violence of the Maccabees. He demands that his disciples love their enemies, bless their persecutors, and renounce the sword (Mt 5:43–48; 26:51–52; Lk 22:49–52). In fact, one of the twelve, Simon, is a convert from the Zealot party in Galilee who were the ideological descendants of the Maccabees insofar as they sought to drive the Gentiles from the land by guerrilla warfare (Lk 6:15; Acts 1:13; cf. Acts 5:37). Jesus demonstrates love for the Gentiles who occupy the land when he praises the Roman centurion for his faith and heals his servant (Lk 7:1–10).

Jesus shares with the Maccabaeans a conviction about the necessity of responding with action when the Temple is desecrated. Jesus admonishes his disciples to escape to the mountains, whereas the Maccabaeans resorted to the use of violence to overthrow the foreign occupation. In his prophecy concerning the destruction of Jerusalem, Jesus refers to the "appalling abomination" (Mk 13:14; Mt 24:15). In 1 Maccabees, this object was the statue and altar of Zeus Olympus that Antiochus IV Epiphanes erected in the Jerusalem Temple in 167 B.C. (1 Mc 1:54; 6:7; cf. Dn 9:27; 11:31; 12:11). For Jesus, "the appalling abomination" is a symbol of pagan sacrilege that foreshadows the destruction of the Temple. His prophecy of the Temple's end was fulfilled when the Roman armies of Titus overran the holy city and destroyed the Temple in A.D. 70.

In his discourse, Jesus did not simply predict the future; he instructed every generation of Christians about the necessity of facing trials with perseverance in order for their faith to reach maturity. While shunning the violent methods of their Maccabaean forebears, the disciples of Jesus had to confront the world's hostility to the holiness of God and bear witness to the Gospel in the face of adversity (Mk 13:3–23).

2 MACCABEES: THE VICTORY OF FAITH

Because God constantly oversees the course of history, faith brings victory to his people in all circumstances. Second Maccabees communicates this message by illustrating God's interventions to restore Jerusalem and the Temple to his people through the career of Judas Maccabaeus.

While 1 Maccabees presents history "from below" in the form of a chronicle of observable events, 2 Maccabees describes history "from above" in descriptions of God's direct actions within history through visions, miracles, and angelic visitations. While 1 Maccabees concentrates on the interplay of political forces between the Syrians and the Jews, 2 Maccabees penetrates to the interior life by exposing the thoughts, motives, prayers, and even dreams of the main characters on the stage of history. While the author of 1 Maccabees makes observations that are rather prosaic and mundane (1 Mc 6:61–62), Jason of Cyrene forthrightly expresses his discernment of the spiritual and moral lessons contained in the history he narrates (2 Mc 5:17–20; 6:12–17; 12:38–45).

Second Maccabees opens with an unusual preface composed of three parts: (a) a letter to the Jews of Alexandria in 124 B.C., encouraging them to celebrate the feast of Hanukkah (1:1–9); (b) a letter interpreting the importance of Hanukkah to the Jewish scholar Aristobulus, who resided in Alexandria (1:10–2:18); and (c) a foreword by the anonymous abridger of the five-volume history authored by Jason of Cyrene (2:19–32). The condensation of Jason's history actually consists of three parts: (1) the introductory episode of the miraculous conversion of Heliodorus in the Temple during the reign of Seleucus IV Philopator (3:1–40); (2) the description of the desecration of the Temple by the Syrians and its purification by Judas Maccabaeus during the reign of Antiochus IV Epiphanes (4:1–10:8); and (3) the narration of the campaigns of Judas Maccabaeus during the subsequent reigns of Antiochus V Eupator and Demetrius I Soter (10:9–15:36). The book concludes with an afterword by the summarizer of Jason's work (15:37–39).

From a thematic perspective, the history is composed of two halves, each of which concludes with a mention of a feast that is celebrated to commemorate the events described (3:1–10:8; 10:9–15:36). The first half ends with an explanation of the feast of Hanukkah (10:5–8), and the second half concludes with a reference to the Day of Mordecai ([15:36], the feast of Purim in Esther [Est 9:20–32]). The first half of the history opens and closes with a scene in the Temple: the introduction being the conversion of Heliodorus in the Treasury (2 Mc 3:1–40) and the conclusion being the purification of the sanctuary by Judas Maccabaeus (10:1–8). The second half of the history reaches a climax when Judas defeats Nicanor, thus preserving the Temple from defilement and liberating the holy city (15:25–36).

Jason of Cyrene intended to provide doctrinal instruction as he recounted the history of Judas Maccabaeus. In 2 Maccabees, we can detect three of his primary concerns: (1) to analyze God's interaction with his people in history; (2) to present a spirituality based on prayer and inspired by the Temple and the Law; and (3) to furnish illustrations of holiness by offering character portraits of God's servants.

1. God's Interaction with His People

God exercises judgment upon his people within history so that he can bring them to salvation in the end (6:12–17). The afflictions suffered by the Jews at the hands of their Seleucid oppressors were punishments for their sins and severe forms of discipline to prevent them from trespassing the divine commandments ever again (7:18, 32–33; 10:4). However, his people always live in hope because, just as sin provokes God's judgment, so repentance evokes his mercy (6:16; 7:6, 29; 8:5, 27, 29). When God's people live in obedience to his commands, he gives them victory over the pagans (10:28, 38; 12:15–16; 13:15–17). Indeed, the cases of Heliodorus and Antiochus IV Epiphanes indicate that the Lord can bring to conversion even the most powerful opponents who have hardened themselves against his people (3:24–40; 9:11–17).

The Lord intervenes in history by effecting life-changing apparitions designed to terrify the heathen and strengthen the believer (14:15): (1) the vision of horse, fearsome rider, and two disciplinarians brings the contemptuous Heliodorus to the ground in the Temple (3:25–28); (2) the citizens of the holy city experience apparitions of the heavenly army who come to defend Jerusalem (5:1–4); (3) the adversaries of Judas are thrown into confusion outside Gezer when they see five heavenly horsemen leading the Jewish army (10:29–30); (4) Judas and his companions are encouraged to go into battle at Beth-Zur when a rider clothed in white appears to lead them (11:8); (5) at Carnaim, in the eyes of the enemy, the cohort of Judas seem to take on an aspect of the Divinity (12:22); and (6) Judas is strengthened for the final battle against Nicanor when, in a dream-like vision, he encounters Onias the priest who introduces him to Jeremiah the prophet from whom he receives the golden sword (15:11–16).

In view of such interventions, Judas' prayer to "the Lord who works miracles" (15:21) seems highly appropriate. However, 2 Maccabees presents God not only as the one who intervenes within history but also as the one who is sovereign over both the beginning and end of history. At once, he is both the Creator of the world and the Author of every life from the moment of its mysterious conception in its mother's womb (7:23, 27–28; 13:14). The mother of the seven brothers shows herself to be the model theologian in the book when she presents her meditations linking the mystery of conception with the mystery of resurrection from the dead (7:23, 27–29). Her sons exhibit the fruit of her wisdom when they declare that the God who creates each person is the one who will raise his faithful people from death to life (7:9, 11,

14). Later, the witness of the noble Razis reinforces his people's confidence in experiencing a bodily resurrection (14:46).

Furthermore, 2 Maccabees provides important insights into the nature of life after death. The prayers of the living can be efficacious on behalf of those who have died even in some condition of sin. The text implies this when it describes Judas and his brethren offering sacrifices for the Jews who had been massacred at Adullam (12:41–45). As the living pray for those who died in human imperfection, so the dead saints intercede for the living. In his apparition to Judas, Jeremiah is introduced as the prophet who makes supplication for his people (15:14).

2. Prayer, the Temple, the Law

Prayer is always victorious. According to 2 Maccabees, Judas experiences success more because he marshals a campaign of prayer than because he wages a military crusade against the infidels (8:2–4). Before the battle, his people commit their lives to the Lord in humility, trust, and adoration (8:14–15; 10:16; 12:28; 15:22–24). Sometimes their prayer is accompanied by fasting and acts of repentance (10:25–26; 13:9–17; 14:15). The momentum changes in their favor when Judas and his companions proclaim the praises of God in the midst of the battle (12:36–37; 15:27). After the battle, the whole army expresses its gratitude in songs of praise and thanksgiving (8:27; 10:38; 15:29).

The people pray not so much for their own survival as for the preservation of the Temple and observance of the Law in the land (13:10–11). The Temple in Jerusalem distinguishes God's people from all other nations. This is the greatest and most holy Temple in all the earth (2:19, 22; 5:15; 14:31). The beginning of the book illustrates how the Lord defeats the enemies of his people because he desires to protect the Temple, and the end of the book shows Judas and his people giving their lives for the same purpose (3:39; 15:17–24). The Lord allows the infidels to defile the Temple only as a means of disciplining his people (5:17; 6:12). However, he restores his people by teaching Judas and his followers how to recapture, purify, and rededicate the Temple (10:1–8).

As important as the Temple is in the eyes of God, it is not more important than the people. Jason of Cyrene announces an essential principle of the theology of election when he asserts, "The Lord, however, had not chosen the people for the sake of the holy place, but the holy place for the sake of the people" (5:19). God forms his people by means of his sacred commandments. Obedience to the Law makes the people invincible against their adversaries (8:36; 10:26, 38). However, trespassing the divine precepts brings disaster

(6:9). Observance of the Sabbath is a distinguishing mark of Judas and his companions in 2 Maccabees (8:27; 15:1–4; cf. 1 Mc 2:41).

In summary, 2 Maccabees illustrates how obedience to the word of God must animate prayer in order to shape the life of the people. Judas insists that his delegate read the "Holy Book" aloud to his forces (8:23). As leader, he prepares his troops by quoting from the various sacred texts that made up "the Law and the Prophets" in his day (15:9).

3. The Character Portraits of Faith

Second Maccabees illustrates how faith produces authenticity. Prayer and trusting obedience to God's word form character that is capable of overcoming every fear and even death itself. Jason of Cyrene highlights the exemplary qualities of the heroes and heroines of faith so that we can incorporate their virtues into our lives.

Judas Maccabaeus is the model of leadership and courage (10:33). We have just noted his commitment to prayer, his reverence for the Temple, and his allegiance to God's word (13:9–17; 15:6–16). We cannot dismiss Judas as a religious zealot when we appreciate that he is eventually presented to us as a normal family man (14:25).

By no means is Judas an isolated model of faith in the text. In fact, he is overshadowed in virtue by the martyrs who are ordinary people ·of all ages and stations in life. The witness of the venerable Eleazar suggests that the elderly among God's people are the first to exemplify the wisdom and dignity of unconditional faith in God (6:18–31). Eleazar is an official teacher of the Law, while the mother of the seven brothers is a pastoral theologian who establishes the substance of faith as the foundation for her sons' lives. As a mother, this woman is a model of integrity and truth who dies for her convictions (7:1–42). Her seven sons are exemplars of faith as it should be experienced in brotherhood among young people. Finally, the death of Razis, the elder of Jerusalem who personifies kindness, demonstrates self-sacrificing allegiance to the Lord (14:37–46).

What God's people lack in worldly power, they make up for in strength of character. By contrast, the impious, who have at their disposal enormous forces of arms, suffer defeat because of their character defects, all of which stem from lack of faith. Jason, the apostate high priest, is driven by personal ambition (4:7–20; 5:6). The equally corrupt Menelaus who deposes Jason exhibits astonishing cruelty in his actions toward his own people (4:23–29, 34–35, 50). Antiochus IV Epiphanes is a caricature of ruthless pride (5:17; 9:11–12). Each of these men dies in forms of torment and disgrace that correspond to their vices (5:9–10; 9:18; 13:7–8). God's justice permeates the contrast between the horror that accompanies the death of the impious and the serenity stemming from the promise of resurrection that marks the martyrdom of God's faithful ones.

Toward the New Testament: The Witness of Martyrdom

Second Maccabees sensitizes us to matters of faith, martyrdom, and divine judgment that are fully elaborated in the New Testament writings.

Just as Jason of Cyrene stated, "The Lord, however, had not chosen the people for the sake of the holy place, but the holy place for the sake of the people", so Jesus announces, "The Sabbath was made for man, not man for the Sabbath" (Mk 2:27; cf. 2 Mc 5:19). The phraseology in Jesus' pronouncement recalls the literary balance in Jason of Cyrene's statement. Possibly Jesus was alluding to 2 Maccabees in order to reinforce the impact of his statement on the Pharisees, who revered the abridged text of Jason's work.

The graphic portraits of martyrdom in 2 Maccabees established a standard of witnessing to the faith that inflamed the hearts of Christians who faced persecution two centuries later (Heb 11:35–38; 12:1–4). Events such as the stoning of Stephen and the beheading of James the apostle must have encouraged the community in Jerusalem to recall the accounts of martyrdom in 2 Maccabees (Acts 7:54–8:1; 12:1–2). Indeed, Acts uses terms reminiscent of the portrayal of Antiochus' death in 2 Maccabees to describe the demise of Herod Agrippa I, the executioner of James (Acts 12:20–23; cf. 2 Mc 9:5–28). Furthermore, the inspiration of 2 Maccabees, with its esteem for martyrdom and conviction about the resurrection, might undergird some passages in the book of Revelation that describe the glorious state of the Christian martyrs, who "even in the face of death . . . did not cling to life" as they suffered persecution at the hands of the Roman emperor, Domitian (A.D. 81–96/Rv 12:11).

The martyrdom of Christians produced life, not death, in the Christian communities because their members recognized in their executed leaders the reflection of Christ crucified (Acts 7:54–8:1; 12:1–2; Rv 7:13–17). The assurance of God's power to raise the dead to life that the mother in 2 Maccabees voiced to her seven sons facing martyrdom is eternally authenticated in the Resurrection of the crucified Christ (Acts 2:33, 36; cf. 2 Mc 7:22–23, 28–29). Might we not see in this woman a foreshadowing of the mother of Jesus at the foot of the cross (Jn 19:25–27; Lk 2:34–35; cf. 2 Mc 7:5–41)? In Jesus our risen Lord, all of us are called to share in the confidence of Paul: "The temporary, light burden of our hardships is earning us forever an utterly incomparable, eternal weight of glory" (2 Cor 4:17; cf. 2 Mc 7:36).

Second Maccabees directs our attention to the prospect of God's final judgment when he will vindicate his people (2 Mc 7:9; 12:38–45). According to this perspective, the impious will suffer annihilation in death, while the righteous will ultimately experience bodily resurrection (2 Mc 7:36; cf. 14:46; cf. 6:14). Christ offers a complete picture of the final judgment when he describes the resurrection of all the dead, in which the virtuous will enter eternal life, while the wicked will experience ultimate separation from God (Jn 5:29). While contemplating the prospect of divine judgment, Paul echoes a theme of 2 Maccabees in his description of God's bringing to light the hidden counsels of everyone's heart (1 Cor 4:5; cf. 2 Mc 12:41–42).

STUDY QUESTIONS

1. What is the background of 1 and 2 Maccabees?
2. Compare 1 and 2 Maccabees as to authorship, content, and purpose.
3. What does the feast of Hanukkah celebrate?
4. How did 1 Maccabees contribute to messianic expectancy?
5. How was Maccabaean resistance instructional for Jesus' disciples?
6. What is the importance of the Temple to 2 Maccabees and to the Gospels?
7. What elements in 2 Maccabees and Daniel are similar?
8. How were 2 Maccabaean concepts of martyrdom and resurrection important to the early Church?
9. How do Maccabaean and Jesus' views toward resisting gentile corruption differ?
10. Describe the role of suffering in bringing God's people to holiness.
11. Compare the difference between the Maccabaean hope in a Messiah and Jesus' fulfillment of that hope and instruction on how to live in the Kingdom.
12. Discuss how you deal with the idols of modern culture—the overemphasis on sex, fancy cars, high-tech toys—when you or your family may yearn for them against your better judgment.

I MACCABEES

I. Antiochus IV Epiphanes: Suppression of Judaism (1:1–64) (175–164 B.C.)
   A. Alexander the Great and His Successors (1:1–9)
   B. The Hellenization of Jerusalem (1:10–64)

II. Mattathias: Priest, Initiator of the Revolt (2:1–70) (166 B.C.)
   A. The Crucial Act of Defiance in Modein (2:1–28)
   B. Early Organization of Resistance (2:29–48)
   C. The Legacy of Mattathias (2:49–70)

III. Judas Maccabaeus: Commander of the Holy War (3:1–9:22) (166–160 B.C.)
   A. The Ode to Judas (3:1–9)
   B. Initial Victories of Judas (3:10–26)
   C. Judas Defeats the Syrian Generals (3:27–4:35)
   D. The Purification and Dedication of the Temple (4:36–61)
   E. Judas Fights the Surrounding Peoples (5:1–68)
   F. The Death of Antiochus IV Epiphanes (6:1–17)
   G. The Battle for the Citadel in Jerusalem (6:18–63)
   H. The Defeat of Nicanor (7:1–50)
   I. The Alliance between the Jews and the Romans (8:1–32)
   J. The Death of Judas in the Battle of Beer-Zaith (9:1–22)

IV. Jonathan: High Priest and Statesman (9:23–12:53) (160–143 B.C.)
   A. Jonathan Battles the Syrian General Bacchides (9:23–73)
   B. Jonathan, High Priest under Alexander Balas (10:1–66)
   C. Jonathan, Ally and Foe of Demetrius II (10:67–11:74)
   D. Jonathan's Alliances with Rome and Sparta (12:1–23)
   E. Trypho Captures Jonathan at Ptolemais (12:24–53)

V. Simon: High Priest and Architect of the Dynasty (13:1–16:24) (143–134 B.C.)
   A. Simon's Agenda as Leader (13:1–11)
   B. Simon Defeats Trypho (13:12–24)
   C. The Family Monument at Jonathan's Tomb (13:25–30)
   D. Simon Takes the Citadel in Jerusalem (13:31–53)
   E. The Ode to Simon (14:1–15)

2 MACCABEES

38

SIRACH: WISDOM IN THE LAW

Each one of us thinks about God within the framework of the world view provided by our culture, that is, our language, customs, social institutions, art forms, and sporting activities. In order for faith to become foundational in our lives, it has to enter into dialogue with our culture. Otherwise, faith apart from culture is reduced to a set of rituals and principles of a bygone era to which we adhere through habit or religious nostalgia. Reflection on faith becomes acutely necessary in times like ours, when popular culture treats belief in God as if it were an unreasonable fantasy. God's people need gifted teachers who can unveil the depth and breadth of wisdom that comes from faith. Such masters will illustrate how God's revelation can transform our world view and, thereby, provide the foundation for a culture that enhances human dignity.

In his own time, Jeshua ben Eleazar ben Sira (literally, Jesus son of Eleazar son of Sira [50:27; 51:30]) was this kind of teacher. He was the master of an academy in Jerusalem who devoted his life to drawing out the implications of faith for the culture of his people. At the end of a long and distinguished academic career, he arranged his lecture notes and personal reflections into the form of a book modeled after Proverbs. The title of the book in Greek is "Sirach", the Hellenized version of its author's name. The Latin Vulgate called it "Ecclesiasticus" or "the Church's text". We will use the term "Sirach" when referring to the book and "Ben Sira" when referring to its author.

Internal evidence embedded within the text suggests that Ben Sira completed his work in Hebrew after 190 B.C. but before 175 B.C. He wrote the tribute to the high priest Simon II (220–195 B.C./50:1–24) some years after the great religious leader's death. His prayer for the Lord to deliver Jerusalem from servitude to foreign powers corresponds to the situation of Jerusalem after 190 B.C. (36:1–17). In 189 B.C., at Magnesia (north of Ephesus), the Romans defeated the Seleucid army of Antiochus III ("the Great") (223–187 B.C.) (see Dn 11:18). In response to the defeat, the Syrian overlord rescinded favorable concessions he had previously extended to Jerusalem. However, Ben Sira gives no indication of writing during the reign of terror perpetrated by

Antiochus IV Epiphanes (175–164 B.C.). In summary, all indications point to 180 B.C. as the approximate date when Ben Sira completed his work.

Ben Sira wrote the original in Hebrew as a resident of Jerusalem. However, we have received the book primarily in its Greek translation, which his grandson rendered after moving to Egypt in 132 B.C. (the "thirty-eighth year of the late King [Ptolemy VII] Euergetes" [170–164; 145–117 B.C.]: see translator's prologue, v. 27). It is quite possible that Ben Sira's grandson finished the translation sometime after the death of "King Euergetes" in 117 B.C. The Hebrew text gradually receded from public view after A.D. 100 and became lost over the next centuries, probably because Sirach was not counted among the sacred books of the Jewish canon of Scripture. However, within the last century, almost three-quarters of the Hebrew original has been recovered in discoveries of manuscripts in Cairo and fragments at Masada and Qumran in Israel.

Judaism and Hellenism

In Ben Sira's time, Hellenism—the ascendance of Greek thought and culture across the world—was creating a crisis of faith within Judaism. Since the Ptolemies controlled the territory of Judah for more than a century (301–198 B.C.) following the death of Alexander the Great, the Jews initially experienced the impact of Hellenism under the auspices of their Egyptian-based rulers. Throughout the third century B.C., the Jewish population increased in various parts of Egypt and established a dynamic community in the great city of Alexandria. Around 250 B.C., this community undertook the Greek translation of the Hebrew Scriptures that eventually would become known as the Septuagint. By 200 B.C., more Jews were living outside the Holy Land than within its boundaries. In 198 B.C., the Seleucid ruler Antiochus III the Great (223–187 B.C.) defeated the Ptolemies at Panion (later called Caesarea Philippi: Mt 16:13) and took control of Palestine. Although Antiochus III was tolerant of Jewish customs, Hellenistic influence continued to infiltrate Jewish society under the Syrians as it had under the Egyptians.

Particularly in Jerusalem, the sophisticated upper classes were tempted to dismiss Jewish tradition as provincial and Hebrew literature as lacking in the speculative flair of Greek drama, poetry, and philosophy. It is within this atmosphere of increasing Hellenization that Ben Sira composed his book. However, his text is neither an attack on Greek culture nor a defense of Jewish tradition. It is, rather, a personal handbook for practical living in accord with divine wisdom. In the course of his exposition, Ben Sira leaves no doubt that the Lord mediates the subtleties and depths of wisdom in an unparalleled fashion through the Scriptures, prayer, and the Temple liturgy distinctive of Judaism. While Ben Sira professes to address a universal audience of all who seek instruction, we can surmise that his primary concern was for the brightest young Jewish minds of his day who were falling under the spell of Hellenism because they did not appreciate the greater richness of wisdom that was contained in their own traditions of faith.

Although he did not openly engage in polemics, Ben Sira indirectly helped to provide the intellectual and spiritual foundation for the Jewish response to the imposition of Hellenism on Jerusalem by Antiochus IV Epiphanes. Our study of the books of Daniel and of 1 and 2 Maccabees informed us that, just over a decade after Ben Sira, the cultural friction between Judaism and Hellenism would ignite a revolution and civil war in Judah through the uprising of the Maccabees against the repressive attempts of the Seleucids to hellenize Jerusalem. It is quite possible that, among the students in Ben Sira's classroom of later years, there were some who would be immortalized as "the wise"—the Hasidic martyrs eventually acclaimed as the great witnesses to faith in the book of Daniel (Dn 11:33–35; 12:3).

Ben Sira and His Traditions

Ben Sira cultivated for his own times the wisdom tradition so magnificently represented in the book of Proverbs. Insofar as he was an elder of an academy that trained promising Jewish youth in the traditions of their faith for life in the world (51:23–30), he resembles the author of Proverbs 1–9, who predated him by more than two centuries. Ben Sira thought of himself as a teacher with a mission that extended beyond his own generation into the future. He considered his instruction to be "like prophecy" that could shape the consciousness of his people for the times that lay ahead (24:30–34). He demands one requirement for entrance into his classes (and therefore for reading his book!): a person must be "seeking instruction", that is, desiring to grow in wisdom through a change of heart (24:34; 33:18).

Apparently, Ben Sira was a well-traveled man whose acquaintance with cultures beyond the boundaries of Palestine came from firsthand experience (34:9–14; 51:13; cf. 39:4; 8:15). His writings suggest a familiarity with elements of both Greek and Egyptian literature. For example, he reflects Homer's *Iliad* when he likens the passing of generations to the seasonal falling and budding of leaves (14:18). His wariness of involvement with others who can damage one's good name reflects the maxims of an Egyptian sage named Phibis who probably lived in the third century B.C. (13:1–14:2; 41:11–13). However, Ben

Sira is never indebted to foreign wisdom for the final product of his work. He adapts the source material so as to make the wisdom of the Greeks and Egyptians serve the cause of Judaism.

For the primary sources of his meditations, Ben Sira turned to the sacred scrolls of the Law, the Prophets, and the wisdom literature (39:1; translator's prologue, vv. 1, 7–11). His hymn in praise of the inspired ancients indicates the breadth of his familiarity with the Scriptures of his day (see 44:1–49:29; the translator's prologue, vv. 1, 7–11). He alludes to all the books written before his time that would eventually comprise the canon of Sacred Scripture, with the exception of Ruth, Ezra, and Esther. His mention of the twelve minor prophets suggests that, by his day, these texts comprised a distinctive collection (49:10).

Sirach: The New Proverbs

In both style and content, Sirach imitates Proverbs. The rhythmic, balanced proverb remains a constant element throughout his work (e.g., 3:26; 20:7; 32:10). These pithy statements exhibit a variety of forms, such as: (a) the comparative ("better than") proverb ("Wine and music cheer the heart; better than either, the love of wisdom"—40:20, in 40:18–26; cf. 30:15–17); (b) the admonition ("Do not abandon yourself to sorrow, do not torment yourself with brooding"—30:21; cf. 31:12–24); (c) the observation on life ("There is a person who is prevented from sinning by poverty; no qualms of conscience disturb that person's rest"—20:21, in 20:1–23); and (d) the beatitude ("Blessed is anyone who meditates on wisdom and reasons with intelligence . . . "—14:20; cf. 14:1–2; 26:1; 34:17).

Nevertheless, Sirach demonstrates stylistic developments beyond Proverbs. In contrast to the lack of topical coherence in Proverbs (Prv 10:1–31:9), Ben Sira collected his maxims into groups around particular themes, such as: discretion in speech (20:1–8, 18–23), the distinction between wisdom and folly (21:11–28; 22:9–18), and the development of friendship (22:19–26). In most of his book, the singular proverbial statement gives way to longer didactic poems that reflect the style of the final editor of Proverbs. The early chapters of Sirach resemble Proverbs 1–9 both in forms of address ("My child" [Sir 2:1; 3:17; 6:18; cf. Prv 1:8; 2:1]) and subject matter (on wisdom and the fear of the Lord [Sir 1:1–10, 11–20; cf. Prv 1:20–33; 1:7; 9:10] and on obedience to parents [Sir 3:1–16; Prv 6:20–22]). However, compared to his forebear who edited Proverbs, Ben Sira covers a much more wide-ranging spectrum of topics, including: virtues (especially humility, charity, and discretion in speech), vices (pride, anger, and greed), relationships (with parents, children, women, friends, and even doctors), financial management, etiquette at table, travel, and general prescriptions for a satisfying life.

Ben Sira surpasses the theological boundaries of Proverbs by bringing his teaching to a crescendo in hymns and prayers. Nowhere in Proverbs do we find the sage addressing God in direct speech. However, Ben Sira encourages his disciples to contemplate the greatness of God in his creation and rule over all people (16:24–17:14; cf. 17:15–18:14) so as to offer the Lord praise beyond measure as the culmination of their study (39:12–35; 43:27–33). Ben Sira is more than a sage in the traditional sense of the term. He is a spiritual father who shows his followers how to pray, on their own behalf, for deliverance from prideful ignorance (22:27–23:6) and, on behalf of Jerusalem, for deliverance from the power of foreign (Seleucid) governors (36:1–17). Ben Sira's unabashed love for the Temple liturgy (see 50:1–24) and concern for personal prayer distinguish him from the sages who authored the book of Proverbs.

Ben Sira breaks through the barriers that had separated the traditions of wisdom from the Law and the Prophets (cf. Jer 18:18). We recall that sages such as Qoheleth and the composers of Proverbs did not quote the Torah or the prophets, nor did they allude to Israel's history of salvation. Creation and natural reason provided the raw material for their reflections. In contrast to such predecessors in the wisdom tradition, Ben Sira brings his text to a climax by acclaiming the heroism of the great figures whose exploits are narrated in the Scriptures (44:1–49:16). Furthermore, sometimes his instructions draw their inspiration directly from the Scriptures and take the form of penetrating expositions of the Law. For example, his teaching on the respect children owe their parents is really a commentary on the commandment to honor one's father and mother and contains allusions to both Genesis and Proverbs (3:1–16; cf. Ex 20:12; cf. Gn 49:2–7; Prv 17:6). Reading Sirach affords us the opportunity of reviewing a panorama of biblical texts through the mind of a scholar who faced the pastoral challenge of teaching his people the practical application of Scripture to their lives.

A survey of Sirach's contents reveals the author's wide-ranging concern for all matters of practical living, including, for instance: the cultivation of personal virtues (4:20–6:4; 10:6–31), the rearing of children (3:1–16; 30:1–13), the establishment of good friendships (6:5–17; 12:8–18), the management of finances (29:1–20), and the etiquette of entertaining (31:12–32:13). For the most part, his treatment of this kaleidoscope of topics follows little discernible order. Nevertheless, we note that the book reaches its spiritual heights at the beginning, middle, and end: first, in the opening meditations on the nature of wisdom and the virtue of fearing God (1:1–2:18); then, in the poem describing wisdom's dramatic decision to dwell in Jerusalem (24:1–34); and, finally, in the odes to the perfection of God reflected in his creation, in Israel's leaders in the faith, and in the model High Priest (42:15–43:33; 44:1–49:16; 50:1–24). The poem on wisdom's dramatic movement from God to Jerusalem provides the spiritual acme of the book (24:1–22, 23–34), rising from fragmentary meditations on the specifics of wise practical living (3:1–23:27; 25:1–42:14). Standing out in the midst of the general expanse of material are the periodic reflections on wisdom (1:1–10; 4:12–19; 14:20–15:10; 16:24–18:14; 37:16–26; cf. 51:13–30), trust in God (1:11–2:18; 11:12–28; 15:11–16:23; 32:14–33:18), and worship (34:18–35:24). Ben Sira's hymns and prayers illustrate the master's conviction that genuine instruction leads to adoration of God (36:1–17; 39:12–35; 42:15–43:33; 51:1–12).

We will highlight Ben Sira's contribution to the biblical tradition by focusing on his distinctive instruction about three issues in particular: (a) the relationships among wisdom, creation, and the Law; (b) the fear of the Lord and other virtues required for gaining wisdom; and (c) the importance of prayer and liturgy.

Wisdom, Creation, and the Law

The cultivation of wisdom is Ben Sira's expressed concern from beginning to end (1:1; 50:27). True to his strength as a traditional rather than innovative thinker, he relies heavily on Proverbs to provide the foundation for his exposition of wisdom (see Prv 1:20–33; 8:1–36; 9:1–6). He reasserts the conventional doctrines of wisdom's preexistence (Sir 1:4; 24:3, 9; cf. Prv 8:22–26), origin in God (Sir 1:1; 24:3; cf. Prv 2:6), and supremacy over creation (Sir 24:3–6; Prv 8:27–31). Following the lead of Proverbs, he personifies wisdom as a woman who is at the same time mother, sister, teacher, and beloved spouse (Sir 1:16–17; 4:11–19; 14:20–15:10; 51:13–21; cf. Prv 1:20–33; 7:4; 8:1–9:6).

Wisdom suffuses all creation (Sir 42:21). The celestial dance of sun, moon, and stars and the transfiguration of nature under alternating conditions of heat and cold reflect the wisdom of their Creator (42:15–43:33). Human nature in all its grandeur and pathos points beyond itself to the Lord who brought everyone into existence (16:24–17:14; cf. 18:8–14). Everything owes its being to the Lord and subsists in the delicate balance wrought by divine providence. Like a master potter, the Lord molds human clay into unique vessels capable of serving his intentions (33:7–15). Because all things originate in God's intention, everything has a purpose proper to its own time (39:12–35). In summary, every aspect of creation owes its meaning to wisdom, which is God's power to establish order in existence.

In his meditation on the creation account that begins the Pentateuch, Ben

Sira makes a significant advance beyond his forebears by highlighting the role of God's word. He makes explicit what the Priestly author implied throughout his description, namely, that God created by the power of his word (42:15; cf. Gn 1:1–2:3; cf. Ps 33:6). Furthermore, the decrees of the Lord now govern all the elements of creation (Sir 43:10, 13; cf. 16:26). Most significant is the case of mankind. Ben Sira perceives that the reign of God's word penetrates to the core of every individual by the very fact of his or her existence. When God created human beings, he bestowed intelligence upon them, "put his own light in their hearts", and "he endowed them with the law of life" (17:7–11). All people possess the inner governing principle of this law that directs them in search of wisdom.

Ben Sira's appreciation of the power of God's word in creation provides the basis for his conviction that God reveals wisdom to mankind not only in creation but also, most especially, in the Law. His poetic masterpiece on wisdom's preexistence and activity within history advances beyond the theology of Proverbs by forging a synthesis between God's work in creation and in revelation (24:1–34; cf. Prv 8:1–36). Wisdom personified as the word issues from the mouth of God to create the universe (Sir 24:3–6; cf. Prv 8:22–31). She is both the primeval mist that hovered over the abyss at creation and the pillar of cloud that overshadowed the Israelites and led them through the sea (Sir 24:3–5; cf. Ex 13:21–22; cf. Gn 1:2). Although wisdom reigns over all nations, her encampment in the desert Tabernacle among the Israelites is unprecedented and unique in human history (Sir 24:6–8; cf. Ex 25:8–9; 40:34–35). This was but a foreshadowing of her taking up permanent residence in the Temple in Jerusalem, where she fills the atmosphere like the aroma of sacrificial incense in the liturgical rites (Sir 24:9–12, 15; 1 Kgs 8:10–11). Divine wisdom grows and spreads out like a fruitful vine from her roots in the Temple precincts (Sir 24:13–22). Furthermore, wisdom not only manifests herself in the Temple worship but also speaks through the Law. She pours forth the life-giving water of instruction upon an arid world from her reservoir in the Book of the Covenant (24:23–29).

For Ben Sira, the Mosaic Torah represents the interior revelation of divine order to mankind. Creation and Scripture are not two independent sources of revelation in Sirach. The scriptural Law represents the self-disclosure of wisdom subsisting throughout creation. Far from being an external set of rules, the Law is a deeply spiritual reality. Indeed, the Law is the manifestation of the mind of God, which brought all things into being and now governs their existence with providential care. The Law acquaints individuals with the divine order inherent in all creation. By allowing the Law to govern our actions, each of us develops a personal order that puts our lives in harmony with the rhythm of the divine symphony that resonates throughout creation.

Virtues in the Pursuit of Wisdom

The life of wisdom is a life lived in conformity with the Law. However, such adherence to the Law consists in something more than scrupulous observance of external precepts. The Law leads one into the depths of wisdom by cultivating virtue in the heart. The foremost of all virtues is fear of the Lord, which, in Sirach, is almost synonymous with wisdom. For Ben Sira, wisdom, which objectively subsists in the Law, takes up residence within the heart through the practice of fear of the Lord. "Wisdom consists entirely in fearing the Lord, and wisdom is entirely constituted by the fulfilling of the Law" (19:20).

Sirach takes up the proverbial maxim, "The first principle of wisdom is the fear of Yahweh" (Prv 9:10; cf. 1:7) and proceeds to illustrate the interior and personal aspects of the virtue. Fear of the Lord is a disposition of positive reverential love marked by an eagerness to please God in deed and humbly to venerate his presence in worship (Sir 2:15–18). One who fears the Lord trusts his mercy, forgiveness, and providence (2:1–9). Fear of the Lord bears the fruits of joy, happiness, and longevity (1:11–20).

We acquire the virtue of fear of the Lord by confessing our sins and by persevering through times of trial and adversity (2:1–18). We are challenged to develop this virtue especially when making decisions that demand public courage. Fear of the Lord would prohibit Ben Sira's students from trying to live according to both Jewish and Hellenistic ways. "Woe to faint hearts . . . and to the sinner who treads two paths" (2:12; cf. 4:21). Thus, fear of the Lord creates purity of heart born out of affliction. "My child, if you aspire to serve the Lord, prepare yourself for an ordeal" (2:1). Consider the new and deeper meaning given to such an assertion by those who would lay down their lives in martyrdom at the hands of Antiochus Epiphanes a little more than a decade after Sirach (Dn 11:32–35).

Fear of the Lord provides the foundation for other virtues that are integral to a life of wisdom. Humility, discretion, and generosity to the poor distinguish the disciple who will mature in the ways of God (Sir 3:17–24; 3:30–4:10; 4:20–31). One grows in wisdom more through the exercise of practical judgment and discipline than by theoretical reflection. Each situation, encounter, and moment offers the possibility of transformation and new growth in harmony with God's designs. Therefore, one must be reflective, prudent, and circumspect but also deliberate, straightforward, and courageous (5:9–6:4; 8:1–19; 32:14–33:6). Pride, anger, and intemperance in speech will shipwreck one's life (10:6–18; 27:22–28:11; 28:12–26). However, increasing acquaintance with wisdom cultivates personal stability and nurtures sound relationships in family, community, and business (6:5–17, 18–37; 9:1–18;

30:1–13). An ever-deepening trust in God based on familiarity with his ways constitutes an unshakable foundation for meeting any eventuality in life.

Prayer and the Temple

Prayer constitutes the beginning and the end of the pursuit of wisdom. Because wisdom is a gift that God bestows on those who revere him, we must pray in order to receive it (43:33; cf. 1:10, 26). Ben Sira alludes to three basic types of prayer: the petition for forgiveness of sins, the request for enlightenment, and the utterance of divine praises.

The wise scribe begins each day seeking the Lord with his heart, asking forgiveness of his sins, and pleading for enlightenment (39:5–7). Ben Sira teaches each of his disciples to address God as Father when praying for purification of mind and deliverance from erroneous impulses (23:1–6). The disciple must pray as one who has the personal relationship to God that a child has to his father, who provides instruction throughout the day (23:1, 4; cf. 3:1). Self-examination is essential because sin breeds deception and ignorance that give birth to folly. No one can grow in wisdom by turning a blind eye to sin, but everyone who repents will experience divine encouragement (5:4–7; 17:24). Because the condition of the heart is all-important, the humble who set their minds on the Lord's service will receive an immediate hearing when they offer their prayers (35:16–17; cf. 21:5). Ben Sira's psalm of thanksgiving testifies to his personal experience of salvation from life-threatening peril in response to prayer (51:1–12).

The hymn of praise exercises a primary role in Ben Sira's spirituality. All reflection should begin and end with acclamations of praise. As an introduction to study, praise will afford us the correct perspective for considering the vexing issues of life. When we are prone to question God's benevolence and ask "What is this?" or "Why is that?", we must voice a hymn in praise of all God's works. This exercise will broaden the horizon of our minds so that we can contemplate the matters at hand with overriding conviction of the goodness of all the Lord's works (39:12–35). The study of the wise person will end as it began: in praise of God. Ben Sira provides the outline of a spirituality for, among others, scientists when he points out that observation of natural phenomena will reach its climax with acclamations in praise of the Creator (43:27–33; cf. 42:15–43:26).

The Temple in Jerusalem is the focus and source of spiritual life. Ben Sira's own example indicates that anyone who desires wisdom should first seek her out in the holy precincts (51:13–14). The sacrifices and offerings one renders to the Lord in the Temple should express a life of service and dedication to the

Lord in daily works of charity and justice (34:18–35:24). For Ben Sira, the Temple liturgy celebrates and reflects the fullness of wisdom dwelling among the people of God. His love for the priesthood reflects his conviction that caring for the Temple and ministering before the Lord in the sanctuary are the most essential of ministries for the well-being of the people. Nowhere else in wisdom literature do we find instructions comparable to Ben Sira's insistence on honoring the priesthood (7:29–31) and his glowing portraits of the great priests Aaron, Phinehas, and Simon II (45:6–22; 45:23–26; 50:1–24). For Ben Sira, the Temple bore witness to the Lord's faithfulness to his people even as they lived under the shadow of the Seleucid ruler Antiochus III (223–187 B.C.). The Lord's presence in the sanctuary gave Ben Sira the vision to pray for the deliverance of Zion from foreign domination and the return to Jerusalem of all the Jews scattered throughout the world in the Diaspora. The sage lived in anticipation of the messianic era when God would reveal the fullness of salvation in accordance with his ancient promises (36:1–17).

Toward the New Testament: The Incarnation of Wisdom

We detect diverse resonances of Sirach in the teaching of Jesus. In the Gospels, Christ transforms a variety of Ben Sira's instructions into principles of the life characteristic of God's Kingdom. We will contemplate Sirach's contribution to the message of the New Testament by noting its influence on themes of wisdom, ethics, and prayer in the Gospels and in the Letter of James.

Ben Sira's poem on wisdom's activity in creation and eventual indwelling in Judah represents a dramatic advance in sacred tradition in preparation for the revelation of the Word in the Prologue to the Gospel of John (Jn 1:1–18; cf. Sir 24:1–34). Sirach describes divine wisdom's movement from hidden communion with God to her continual manifestation in the world through the Temple liturgy and in the Law. The evangelist, who knew the risen Christ by the grace of the Holy Spirit, realized that the text in Sirach only foreshadowed the fullness of truth that God now reveals in the Incarnation of the Word (cf. Jn 2:21–22; 12:16; 14:26).

The Prologue to John follows Sirach in charting the trajectory of the divine Word from primal union with God to residence in the world. However, the Gospel reworks the earlier wisdom poem in order to express depths of reality and truth that Ben Sira could not have imagined. In John, the Word is eternally with God, and is God, not the first of his creations (Jn 1:1; cf. Sir 24:3, 8). Furthermore, in Christ, the dwelling of the Word in human flesh mediates an intimacy and solidarity impossible for the Law to realize (cf. Sir 24:23–34). As the incarnate Word, Jesus Christ communicates to us "grace and truth" that the Mosaic Law could only foreshadow (Jn 1:16–17; cf. Sir 24:13–22). The final lines of the Prologue indicate that the divine Son reveals God in a manner that was unfathomable to previous generations (Jn 1:18; cf. Sir 43:31). In retrospect, by noting its influence on texts such as the Johannine Prologue, we can appreciate Sirach's contribution to the eventual development of the theology of the Incarnation and the Trinity in the New Testament and in the writings of the Fathers of the Church.

In the body of John's Gospel, Jesus speaks as divine wisdom. He will give the bread and water of divine revelation to everyone who believes in him (Jn 4:10, 13–14; 6:35; cf. Sir 15:3; 24:23–29). He reflects the demand of wisdom when he tells his disciples that the demonstration of their love for him will be obedience to his commandments (Jn 14:15, 21, 23; cf. Sir 2:15). Similarly, on one noteworthy occurrence in the Gospel of Matthew, Jesus assumes the role of wisdom, when he invites his disciples to take his yoke upon their shoulders with the promise that, through this exercise, they will attain spiritual rest (Mt 11:29; cf. Sir 6:23–30; 51:26).

Some of Jesus' instructions in the Sermon on the Mount bring to maturity certain injunctions of Ben Sira. Christ's prohibition of making oaths and his demand for straightforward speech recall the sage's admonitions, "Be steady in your convictions, and be a person of your word" and "Do not get into the habit of swearing, do not make a habit of naming the Holy One ... " (Sir 5:10; 23:9; cf. Mt 5:34, 37). Jesus' precept that forgiving others is a condition for receiving forgiveness from God is rooted in Ben Sira's exhortation, "Pardon your neighbor any wrongs done to you and when you pray, your sins will be forgiven" (Sir 28:2; cf. Mk 11:25; Mt 6:14–15; cf. Mt 5:23–24; 18:21–35).

At this point, we must note that Jesus supersedes the constraints of Sirach by demanding a new depth of personal dispossession and the extension of generosity to all, not just to members of the holy people. Whereas Sirach advocates almsgiving to impoverished "friends and brothers" in the faith, Jesus exhorts his disciples to renounce the pursuit of wealth and to give their possessions without discrimination to anyone who is poor (Sir 29:8–13; cf. Mt 6:19–21; 19:21; Lk 16:9). The radical thrust of Jesus' teaching beyond the tradition is most evident in his counsel on good works. Sirach encourages acts of kindness toward "the right person", namely, "the devout" and "the humble", but not toward "the godless" and "the sinner" (Sir 12:1–7). Jesus flatly contradicts and supersedes Ben Sira on this point when he commands his disciples to love their enemies (Mt 5:43–48; Lk 6:27–36). Whereas Sirach bases his counsel on the premise that "the Most High himself detests sinners ... ", Jesus insists "[your Father] causes his sun to rise on the bad as well as the good ... " (Sir 12:6; cf. Mt 5:45).

Since the Letter of James exhibits numerous points of contact with the

Sermon on the Mount, we are not surprised to detect resonances of Sirach also in this apostolic letter. James follows Ben Sira when he corrects those who blame God for temptation and sin rather than assume personal responsibility for their sinful tendencies (Jas 1:13–15; cf. Sir 15:11–20). The extensive discourse on the ruination wrought by misuse of the tongue echoes a recurrent theme in Sirach (Jas 3:1–12; cf. Sir 28:13–26; 5:9–15).

The prayer of Ben Sira offers a remarkable advancement toward the spirituality of the Gospels. The one element that stands out among all others is Ben Sira's invocation of God as "Father" (Sir 23:1, 4; 51:10). Nowhere else in the Old Testament do we find an individual actually calling upon God as "my Father" (cf. Tb 13:4: "our Father"). In the prophets, we hear of the whole people petitioning God as their Father (Is 63:15–16; 64:7; cf. Jer 3:4, 19; 31:9; cf. Mal 2:10; Dt 32:6), and we are told indirectly that the Davidic king could pray in this manner (Ps 89:26). When he invokes God as "Father", Ben Sira personalizes this tradition by making uniquely his own as an individual the form of address voiced by the whole assembly.

Nevertheless, Ben Sira's appellation lacks the radical intimacy of Jesus' distinctive expression, "Abba, Father" (Mk 14:36; cf. Mt 6:9; 11:25–26; Lk 11:2). In the culture of Palestinian Judaism, the Aramaic word "Abba" was a term of endearment suggestive of the home, not of the Temple. "Abba" was reserved exclusively for the address of a child to his or her actual father, and it bore the connotation of filial love, trust, honor, and deference. Ben Sira's expression did not correspond to "Abba" but maintained the formality of traditional Temple piety. On the lips of Jesus, "Abba" expresses such an unprecedented relationship to God as son to father that it provoked the religious officials to charge him with blasphemy (e.g., Mk 14:61–64; Mt 26:63–65; Lk 22:67–71; cf. Jn 5:17–38). In virtue of his death and Resurrection, Jesus the risen Lord communicates the Spirit of Sonship to those who believe in him, thus forging in them a new filial relationship to God that is manifest in their unique capacity to pray "Abba, Father" (Rom 8:14–17; Gal 4:4–6; Lk 11:1–4, 13).

STUDY QUESTIONS

1. When and by whom was Sirach written?
2. What is the purpose of the book of Sirach?
3. What was the danger of Hellenism?
4. How is wisdom acquired?
5. How does Sirach further develop the concept of personified wisdom?
6. What is the greatest form of prayer?
7. How is Sirach 24 a preparation for the Prologue to the Gospel of John?
8. How does Jesus' calling the Father "Abba" expand upon Sirach's calling God "Father"?
9. Discuss how faith and reason reinforce one another in the decisions you make each day at home and at work.
10. How does Sirach provide a model for the religious education of young people and adults? Consider his apprehension of global wisdom and his practical guidance.
11. Read Sirach 24. Discuss how belief in God, daily worship, and reading Scripture lead to wisdom.
12. Discuss the relationship of common sense to wisdom, and contrast both of them to emotion and impulse.

SIRACH

39

TOBIT, JUDITH, BARUCH: THE LAW IN LIFE

God's word communicates life and wisdom to his people. The word produces life because it reveals the presence of God. At the same time, the word expresses wisdom because it manifests God's will. Faith is the only response we can make that allows God's word to produce its life-giving effects. This faith consists of both trust and obedience. By faith, we acknowledge the presence of God who speaks and turn to him with trust in his love. Furthermore, by faith, we assent to the truth of what God says and respond in obedience to the divine commandments. God renews and raises us to new life when we receive his word into our hearts through faith. Tobit, Judith, and Baruch provide biblical illustrations of this kind of renewal arising from the response of ordinary people to God.

The books of Tobit, Judith, and Baruch express the devotion of the Hasidim in the second century B.C. Probably Pharisees wrote them in order to provide models of spirituality for Jews who lived under gentile influence both within the Holy Land and in the Diaspora.

Tobit and Judith are edifying and entertaining stories that are similar to Daniel and Esther. All these texts describe humble, faithful people (in Hebrew: 'anawim) acting with wisdom as they strive to serve the Lord while suffering persecution at the hands of Gentiles. These four texts form a distinct category of biblical literature as Hasidic stories designed to illustrate the unparalleled wisdom and authority God bestows on his people when they observe his Law.

The text of Baruch is a collection of poetry, prayers, and sermons that indirectly complements the stories of Tobit and Judith. All these texts demonstrate a profound reverence for God's word contained in the Law. His word comes to life when people listen and respond in prayer. Hearing the word produces repentance expressed in confession of sin and accompanied by fasting and mortification. The word motivates the believer to act in charity (Tobit) and in defense of the faith (Judith). Ultimately, the word leads to adoration, calling the people to worship the Lord at the Temple in Jerusalem, thereby fulfilling the deepest longings in every believer's heart.

TOBIT

The book of Tobit originated in either Hebrew or Aramaic. In the excavations at Qumran, scholars discovered a portion of the text in Hebrew and segments of four texts written in Aramaic. However, we have received the book in its entirety only in Greek, in two recensions that contain significant variations from each other. The version in the Codex Sinaiticus is the preferred one because it is longer and more representative of a Hebrew mentality than the version that recurs in both the Codex Alexandrinus and the Codex Vaticanus.

Evidence within the text suggests that the book of Tobit was composed in Jerusalem for an audience in the Diaspora prior to 180 B.C. Jerusalem provided the most conducive environment for producing a work in Hebrew or Aramaic. Furthermore, the author's devotion to the holy city is evident throughout the story. The narrative setting in Mesopotamia and Persia would have captured the attention of Jews living in Syria or regions farther east. Because the book offers no suggestion of the tensions that gave rise to the Maccabaean revolt, we suppose that it was written in a time of relative peace, perhaps around 200 B.C.

Tobit presents a model for Jewish life in the Diaspora. This story illustrates God's providential activity within the setting of marriage and family life beyond the borders of the Holy Land. The personal witness of Tobit demonstrates how God blesses someone who is devout, charitable, and faithful to the Law even when suffering under great duress. The divine provision for the marriage between Tobit's son, Tobias, and Sarah advocates the importance of finding a spouse within Judaism, thus avoiding intermarriage with Gentiles. Prayer for the return to Jerusalem of all the Jews scattered throughout the world summarizes the reverent hope of God's people.

The story of Tobit unfolds against the background of Assyria's conquest of the northern ten tribes that had comprised the kingdom of Israel (2 Kgs 17:5–23). The author is not concerned with chronological or geographical details. For example, he allows Tobit to convey the impression of growing up in the region of Naphtali prior to Jeroboam's rebellion in 921 B.C. (Tb 1:4–5; cf. 1 Kgs 12:1–14:31). Subsequently, we read that the Assyrians deported Tobit and his wife Anna into exile in Nineveh during the reign of Shalmaneser V (726–722 B.C.) (Tb 1:1–2, 10–14; cf. 2 Kgs 15:29; 17:5–23). Finally, we hear that Tobias lived to see the destruction of Nineveh that took place in 612 B.C. (Tb 14:15; cf. Na 1–3). There are geographical discrepancies as well. For instance, contrary to the estimation in the text, the 200-mile journey between Ecbatana and Rhages would have taken considerably more than two days (Tb 5:6). Indications such as these lead us to surmise that the author did not intend to present a history but rather an artistic composition that provides a model of spirituality for Jews in the Diaspora.

The drama of Tobit takes place in four acts. After a brief superscription (1:1–2), the first act contains two scenes, one that draws our attention to the affliction of Tobit in Nineveh (1:3–3:6) and the other that introduces us to the plight of Sarah in Ecbatana (3:7–17). Unknown to one another, Tobit and Sarah simultaneously pray for death as a release from their sorrows. The second act describes how Tobit puts his affairs in order by commissioning his son Tobias to make a journey to Rhages in Media in order to collect a deposit of money that will serve as his inheritance. The angel Raphael, disguised as a kinsman named Azarias, volunteers to accompany the lad in his travels (4:1–6:1). The third act recounts Tobias' journey from Nineveh to Ecbatana and back (6:2–11:18). A fish that Tobias catches and uses according to Raphael's instructions heals both Sarah and Tobit of their afflictions. The marriage of Tobias to Sarah is a blessing of divine providence that transcends the distance between Ecbatana and Nineveh to join the two Diaspora families. The fourth act encourages the audience to look to the future with faith in God's power to protect his people and to fulfill his promise of restoring them to their own land (12:1–14:15).

The story of Tobit illustrates how God blesses families who exercise their faith while living in the pagan world. We can summarize the message of the book by considering three of its themes: (1) God blesses a faith that is expressed in acts of love; (2) divine providence will overcome the obstacles that faithful couples face in marriage and family life; and (3) all people of faith look forward in hope to the time when God will gather his scattered children together in Jerusalem.

Faith Expressed in Love

Tobit is a latter-day Job whose sufferings begin early in life. Orphaned as a child, exiled to Nineveh as a young man, and stricken with blindness in his mature years, Tobit, nevertheless, remains devoted to God (1:8, 16–18; 2:10). As a youth in the Holy Land, he made pilgrimages to Jerusalem for the great feasts and, as a mature man in Nineveh, he spends himself caring for the poor and risking his life to bury his brethren who were victims of persecution (1:18–19; 2:2–8). Such acts of charity bring upon him death threats, the confiscation of his property, the ridicule of his neighbors, and, as in the case of Job, the scorn of his wife (1:19–20; 2:8, 14; cf. Jb 2:9). He loses his eyesight as a consequence of observing the Law, because it required him to sleep outside after burying the dead, and he was exposed there to bird droppings in his eyes (Tb 2:10).

By word and example, Tobit insists that faith must become evident in concrete acts of charity. This is a textbook on the importance of works of mercy, especially caring for the poor and burying the dead (2:2–10; 4:7–11, 16–17). Tobit highlights one form of generosity above all others when he declares, "almsgiving delivers from death and saves people from passing down to darkness. Almsgiving is a most effective offering for all those who do it in the presence of the Most High" (4:10–11; cf. 1:3; 12:8–9; 14:2, 8, 10–11). The book's concern for the concrete expression of faith in action is evident both in the collection of proverbs that serves as a preliminary testament of father to son and in the final words of Tobit to Tobias (4:1–21; 14:2–11).

Prayer animates the generosity of Tobit. The book illustrates the harmony between prayer and action. Tobit's pilgrimages to Jerusalem while living in the Holy Land and his observance of major feasts while in exile provide the setting for his charitable activities (1:1–2:8). True, the first time we hear him pray, he is a blind but contrite Job who utters a psalm of lament asking for the mercy of death (3:1–6; cf. Jb 3:1–26). Concurrently, hundreds of miles away, the maiden Sarah likewise prays for an early end after witnessing seven spouses die at the hands of the demon Asmodeus (3:7–15). When righteous servants of God such as these pray for death, the Lord hastens to respond by blessing them with healing and life (3:16–17). After Tobit's cure, his psalm of lament gives way to a hymn of thanksgiving and expression of confidence that the Lord will restore all his people to the environs of the Temple in the holy city (13:1–17). Similarly, after her deliverance from the power of the demon, Sarah's anguished plea gives way to her and her new husband's song of praise for the blessing of their marriage (8:5–7).

The Blessings of Marriage and Family Life

God responds to the prayers of Tobit and Sarah by putting his angel Raphael (Hebrew: "God heals") in the path of Tobias (5:1–6:1). Raphael teaches Tobias how to use the fish he catches to heal both Sarah and Tobit. Cooking the heart and liver on incense drives away the demon from Sarah, and applying the gall to Tobit's eyes restores his sight (6:2–9; 8:3; 11:7–13). These miraculous healings indicate God's blessing on marriage and family life for those who devote themselves to his Law.

The betrothal of Sarah to Tobias has an elegant bearing that recalls the marriage of Rebekah to Isaac: a long journey to the home of a kinsman, then a request for a decision from the parents, followed by the meal, which climaxes in the father's giving his daughter in marriage (7:1–16; cf. Gn 24:1–67). Sarah's parents, Raguel and Edna, share a common concern with Tobias' parents, Tobit and Anna, that the marriage take place according to stipulations of the Mosaic Law (4:12–13; 7:11–13). While the marriage perfectly meets the legal requirements, its inspiration comes from the revelation of God's will. Tobias falls in love with his bride-to-be, not when he sees her, but when Raphael teaches him that this is God's plan (6:18). Their marriage drawing life from prayer is celebrated as God's consolation for both of their families (8:4–6, 14–18; 9:1–12:21).

The Promise of a Future for God's People

The Lord's action in the life of one family contains the promise of life for all his people in the future. The fortunes of Jerusalem and Nineveh are reversed from the beginning to the end of the book. In the introduction, the Assyrians take control over Jerusalem, and, in the conclusion, Nineveh is destroyed while Jerusalem becomes the city of promise (1:3–9; 14:2–15).

Jerusalem and its Temple provide the focal point of unity for God's faithful people. Tobit's preexilic pilgrimages to the Temple in the holy city only foreshadow the final days when God will gather together in Jerusalem all the faithful who are scattered throughout the world (1:3–9; 13:5–6).

Tobit's hymn is a profession of faith in God, who is the hope of his people (13:1–17). Just as the dispersion took place as a consequence of unbelief, so the assembly of God's people in Jerusalem will be the fruit of repentance and faith. Tobit's final testament gives a universal extension to this vision by describing the conversion of the Gentiles in terms reminiscent of the major prophets (14:4–7; cf. Is 18:7; 56:8; Jer 16:19).

Toward the New Testament: Solidarity with the Poor

Tobit exemplifies the manner of life typical of "the lowly ones" (in Hebrew: the 'anawim), who depend on the Lord to meet all their needs. As such, he is a precursor in faith for the holy people who surround Jesus at his birth, notably Zechariah and Elizabeth as well as the prophets Simeon and Anna (Lk 1:5–80; 2:22–38). Like Tobit, these elders turn to the Lord and bless his name in expectant prayer for the redemption of God's people (Lk 1:67–79; 2:29–32; cf. Tb 13:1–17). The simplicity and holy poverty that characterize Tobit become necessary virtues of an apostle in the Pauline tradition (1 Tm 6:6–8; cf. Tb 4:21).

Tobit's instructions to Tobias before sending him off to the east are a compendium of proverbial wisdom that includes a number of items that Jesus' teaching brings into full light (Tb 4:1–21). While material possessions tarnish and corrode, practicing the virtue of charity builds an incorruptible treasure and is capable of overcoming death itself (Tb 4:9–11; cf. Mt 6:19–20). Almsgiving, care for the poor, and giving without counting the cost are the hallmarks of Tobit. Jesus fully develops Tobit's counsel to feed the hungry and clothe the naked in his description of the final judgment (Mt 25:35–36, in 25:31–46; cf. Tb 4:16). Tobit initiates the tradition that develops into the Golden Rule with the dictum, "Do to no one what you would not want done to you" (4:15; cf. Mt 7:12; Lk 6:31). Raphael's counsel capsulizes the maxims of Tobit and, at the same time, provides an introduction to the spirituality of the Sermon on the Mount: "Prayer with fasting and alms with uprightness are better than riches with iniquity" (Tb 12:8; cf. Mt 6:1–18).

Tobit's example indicates that almsgiving consists in more than a contribution of funds to the poor, who remain distant and unknown to the giver. Tobit invites the poor to his own table and thus provides a model in support of Jesus' vision for the kind of banquet that reflects life in the Kingdom of God (Tb 2:1–2; cf. Lk 14:12–24). In summary, Tobit's humble dependence on the Lord in all circumstances and his wise fatherly guidance about the primacy of spiritual values can inspire men in our own day to lead their families in the ways of faith.

JUDITH

Like Tobit, the book of Judith is a dramatic story that illustrates how devotion to the Lord brings deliverance to his people. Both texts highlight the importance of Jerusalem, the Temple, the Law, and prayer. However, Judith approaches faith from a different perspective from Tobit. Tobit is a story about Jews in the Diaspora, while Judith concerns those who live in the Holy Land. Tobit exemplifies faith lived out within the setting of family life, while Judith exhibits faith that provides leadership to the whole community. The witness of Tobit illuminates the value of nonviolent endurance of affliction, while the witness of Judith suggests the importance of aggressive action in defense of the faith. In their manner of confronting Gentiles, the man Tobit is a pacifist, while the woman Judith is a militant. However, each of them in a unique way represents the lowly (Hebrew: 'anawim) who trust in the Lord alone for vindication.

We have received the text of Judith only in Greek. However, a close examination of the language has led many scholars to suggest that this Greek represents a translation from a Hebrew original. While acknowledging the sparsity of evidence, we suggest that the author of the book was a Palestinian Jew who composed the work around 100 B.C., either in the last years of John Hyrcanus I (134–104 B.C.) or in the first years of Alexander Jannaeus (103–76 B.C.). Late in his reign, John Hyrcanus incorporated Samaria into the Jewish territory. The author of Judith looks favorably on Samaria since he describes it as the setting in which the Jews repelled the Assyrian invasion and thus preserved Jerusalem and the Temple (14:1–15:7; cf. 4:4–8). His untainted esteem for the region suggests that he wrote the book some years after the annexation of Samaria.

The Story of Judith

The book of Judith is a drama in two parts. The first part describes Nebuchadnezzar's troops, under the command of his general Holofernes, sweeping into Palestine and laying siege to the town of Bethulia in Samaria (1:1–7:32). The second part recounts how Judith, the saintly woman of the town, delivers Bethulia and all Israel from the Assyrian invasion (8:1–16:25).

This is a story like David and Goliath depicted in the global terms of international political history (cf. 1 Sm 17:1–54). Goliath, in this case, is the Assyrian military machine of the god-king Nebuchadnezzar, which first routed the forces of the Median king Arphaxad and then rolled over every nation west of Nineveh as far as the Mediterranean (1:1–3:10). David, in this case, is the Jewish people represented by the unknown town of Bethulia in Samaria, which provides the last line of defense protecting Jerusalem. The Assyrian force simply dwarfs the Jewish settlement that it surrounds with an infantry of 120,000, a calvary of 12,000, and an auxiliary brigade of 5,000 (7:2, 17).

The author describes the siege by shifting the scene between Bethulia and the Assyrian camp (4:1–7:32). Defying the impossible odds as no other nation, Judaea mounts its resistance, but the people in the town find no hope except in prayer (4:1–15). The desperation in the town stands in marked contrast to the powerful self-assurance that reigns in the military camp. Holofernes marshals his troops and those of the surrounding nations with disdain for his opposition. However, Achior, the leader of the neighboring Ammonites, dares to express his admiration for the Jews in a discourse that amounts to a recitation of Israel's profession of faith (5:1–21). Because such a creed denies that Nebuchadnezzar is a god, Holofernes punishes Achior by sending him to Bethulia to die there with the doomed citizenry. The Jewish populace welcomes Achior and again prays that God will defeat the Assyrian pride (5:22–6:21). Desperation mounts as the Assyrians cut off supplies to Bethulia, which can hold out only five more days before capitulating to the enemy (7:1–32).

The entire first half of the book provides a preliminary setting for the more important second half, which focuses on the character of Judith (8:1–16:25). A widow, bereft of her husband for more than three years, she is renowned both for her great beauty and her meticulous observance of the Law. Emerging from the seclusion of her widowhood, she steps into the public eye by convoking a meeting of the city elders. As one who knows the experience of grief, she takes up the theme of faith and admonishes the elders for putting the Lord to the test by invoking a deadline after which they will surrender to the infidels. Judith will take action to deliver the city from its oppressors (8:1–36).

As in the first half, so here the scene shifts between the town and the Assyrian camp as we follow Judith's movements. After her time of prayer in Bethulia (9:1–14), Judith dresses herself in her most attractive finery and leaves the city to enter the enemy's enclave. Following a course that is the reverse of Achior's, she charms her way into the midst of the Assyrians under the pretext of abandoning her people (10:1–23). During their first conference, Holofernes becomes infatuated with Judith's beauty (11:1–12:9). Subsequently, he extends to her an invitation to attend an intimate banquet, which happens to fall on the night before the date the Jews had determined for their surrender (the "fourth" day/12:10; cf. "five days"/7:30). After dismissing his servants, Holofernes falls into a drunken stupor that affords Judith the opportunity of cutting off his head with his own sword (12:10–13:10). Judith returns to the city to display the general's head and to announce an impending victory for the Jews (13:11–14:10). Since the enemy is literally headless, the Jews mount an attack against their oppressors and drive them from the land (14:11–15:7). Finally, Judith wins the blessing of Jerusalem and the acclaim of the people and offers a magnificent song of praise to God (15:8–16:20). The book concludes with a description of Judith's death and burial in the manner of the great Patriarchs and their wives (16:21–25; cf. Gn 23:1, 19; 35:28; 49:29–33).

The Literary Form of Judith

The book of Judith is a short story composed with remarkable artistic skill. The author goes to some lengths in order to indicate that he is not writing history as he communicates a lesson that is both edifying and entertaining. He mixes up a variety of personalities and nations who were Israel's adversaries in the past so as to make of them a collage of the gentile world that had been hostile to Israel throughout her history. Chronological and political inaccuracies abound throughout the story. Nebuchadnezzar (605–562 B.C.) was king of Babylon, not of Assyria; his armies never suffered defeat in Judah; he did, in fact, destroy the Temple; and he died while the Jews were in exile, not after they had returned to Judah (cf. 1:1; 4:3; 5:19). Arphaxad never ruled the Medes; this name belonged to a grandson of Noah through Shem (cf. Gn 10:22, 24). Holofernes and Bagoas were not Assyrian but Persian military commanders under Artaxerxes III (358–338 B.C.) (cf. 2:4; 12:11). Furthermore, government by the high priest and a council of elders in Jerusalem defined Judaea's political system in the second century B.C. but not in the days of the Assyrian and Babylonian empires prior to the Exile (4:8; 15:8). The Jewish concern that the Temple not be desecrated by the gentile monarch who declares himself to be a god describes their preoccupation with the Seleucid monarch, Antiochus IV Epiphanes (175–164 B.C.), during the Maccabaean era (3:8; 4:12: cf. 1 Mc 1:10–2:26).

As they listened to the story of Judith, the original audience would have identified the foes with Israel's most recent enemies: the Assyrians were the Seleucids to the north; Nebuchadnezzar was Antiochus IV Epiphanes; and Holofernes was a caricature of the Syrian Nicanor, a general whose head the Jews cut off and put on display (cf. 1 Mc 7:25–50). However, because it alludes to the whole chronological span of Israel's northern enemies (including the Assyrians, the Babylonians, and the Persians), the story is not confined to a particular period in history. The tale of Judith has universal appeal because it dramatizes the confrontation between Judah and the world in every age. This is an adventure story that fires the heart with zeal for the Lord.

The very name "Judith" identifies our heroine with "Judah". She personifies the dignity and virtue of Judaism. Just as the enemies display the vices of all Israel's foes throughout history, so Judith exhibits the virtues of her ancestors who founded the kingdom of Israel. When she provides military leadership beyond that of Uzziah and intones liturgical songs, she recalls Deborah, who delivered the people when Barak was captive to his fears at the time of the Judges (Jdt 8:1–16:20; Jgs 4:1–5:31). She dispatches Holofernes just as Jael disposed of the enemy commander Sisera and thereby saved her people (Jdt 13:4–11: cf. Jgs 4:17–22). When she cuts off Holofernes' head with his own sword, she even reflects the prowess of David when he delivered his final blow to Goliath (Jdt 13:6–8; cf. 1 Sm 17:51). Furthermore, as a widow who refuses to take another spouse, Judith typifies the people of God who feel bereft of their Lord but remain faithful to him even as they face trials in the world (Jdt 8:1–8; 16:21–25; cf. Is 52:1–6; 49:18).

The story of Judith communicates a number of lessons about faith that we will consider under three thematic principles: (1) the authority of faith in the living God will always triumph over the power of worldly despots; (2) prayer and observance of the commandments provide the strength for God's people; and (3) wisdom and beauty are distinguishing qualities of people of faith.

The Triumph of Orthodox Faith

A conflict of creeds lies at the root of the military confrontation in Judith. The story invites us to ponder the question, "Who is the God that rules history?" Public consensus suggests that the most powerful leader on earth is the one who really determines the fate of nations and peoples. The same consensus looks at the insignificance and misery of the people who call upon the Lord and concludes that their God cannot possibly be the One who reigns over history. The story of Judith contradicts worldly opinion by showing how the true and living God shapes history by acting through his humble people.

Holofernes declares that Nebuchadnezzar is a god (3:8; 6:2). He is "king of the whole world" (11:1, 7). (Note the similarities between the portraits of Nebuchadnezzar in Judith and in Daniel [Jdt 11:1, 7; cf. Dn 2:37–38; Jdt 6:2–3; cf. Dn 3:14–18]). This arrogant potentate issues commands and utters promises to Holofernes in a manner that resembles the Lord's address to his great prophets (Jdt 2:11; cf. Ez 9:5, 10; Jdt 2:12; cf. Is 46:11). As his armies surge across the world, they carry out a religious purge that mimics the one the Lord mandated at Mount Sinai (Jdt 3:8; cf. Ex 34:13–16). Holofernes speaks of Nebuchadnezzar in words that echo the prophets' assertions concerning the Lord, the Redeemer of Judah (Jdt 6:2–4; cf. Is 44:6–8; 46:9). The cult of Nebuchadnezzar represents the perennial heresy of the human race to worship man as God (cf. Gn 3:5).

Judith's destruction of Holofernes symbolizes the triumph of orthodox faith over human religion. In contrast to her adversary, Judith prays to the "Master of heaven and earth, Creator of the waters, King of your whole creation" (Jdt 9:12; cf. 11:1, 7). She professes her belief in the transcendent God, who brought all things into existence and who has acted in the history of her people in such a manner that she can also call him, "God of my father, God of the heritage of Israel" (9:12). While Holofernes trusts in the despot who rules by military force, Judith says to the Lord, "Your strength does not lie in numbers, nor your might in strong men; since you are the God of the humble, the help of the oppressed, the support of the weak, the refuge of the forsaken, the Savior of the despairing" (9:11; cf. 6:2–4).

Gentiles as well as Jews can learn the truth and come to faith in the living God whom Judith proclaims. Achior the Ammonite provides an illustration of conversion that testifies to the authenticity of Judaism over the religion of the world. He is the first person to teach Holofernes about the revelation of God to the Israelites. His instruction amounts to a proclamation of Judah's creed (5:5–21; cf. Dt 26:5–10). When Achior journeys from the camp of the infidels to the city of God's people, he makes his own Exodus out of slavery into freedom in keeping with the words he spoke (Jdt 6:1–21). His pilgrimage reaches completion after he witnesses the way in which God acts through Judith to overcome Holofernes. He professes faith in the God of Israel and receives admission into the holy people (14:10). The infidels do not have to die like Holofernes; they can enter into the new life of faith like Achior.

Spiritual Authority: Prayer and Obedience to the Law

Judith, the lowly widow, has the power to overcome the commander of legions because she is orthodox in her profession and practice of the faith. Just as Holofernes held a council of his officers to demand that they profess faith in Nebuchadnezzar, so Judith convenes a meeting of the elders in Bethulia to teach them the foundations of their faith (5:1–6:9; cf. 8:9–36). She reprimands them for testing the Lord by setting a date for surrender when, in fact, they should have appreciated their trial as the means by which the Lord was testing them in order to make them more mature in faith (8:9–31).

Both Achior and Judith assert that Israel's capacity to resist the most powerful of foes derives from its obedience to the Law. History demonstrates that no worldly oppressor but only sin can bring about the downfall of God's people (5:17–21; 11:10; cf. 7:28). However, even though they have fallen, the chosen people will experience restoration through repentance (5:19).

Judith demonstrates that the virtue of fearing God provides the spiritual strength to overcome the greatest adversity (8:8). Prayer achieves victory over the enemy forces (see Ps 20:7). When the adversary advances on Jerusalem and surrounds Bethulia, the people worship God in prayer accompanied by fasting and penitential gestures (4:9–15; 6:18–21). Similarly, Judith entrusts her life and the whole people to God in her psalm of intercession. Exactly when time is at a premium as the deadline for surrender approaches, Judith spends a considerable period devoted to this lengthy prayer (9:1–14; 10:9). Her plea for deliverance will give way to her hymn of thanksgiving, in which she praises the Lord as Savior of his people and Creator of the universe (16:1–17). Especially when she is in the camp of the enemy, Judith is concerned to purify herself and to pray at regular intervals (11:17). Her consistency in this practice enables her to escape from the Assyrian camp with the head of Holofernes without provoking suspicion (12:6–9; 13:3, 10).

In Judith, personal prayer unites with the communal worship of the whole people. The Temple in Jerusalem provides the source of unity: the citizens of Jerusalem prostrate themselves in front of the Temple (4:9–12); Judith prays at the hour of the evening incense (9:1); after the victory, the high priest blesses her (15:9–10); and, finally, the whole people celebrate their deliverance in a magnificent Temple liturgy that lasts for three months (16:18–20).

The Beauty and Wisdom of Faith

Judith overcomes Holofernes with her beauty and wisdom. Her unparalleled glamour captivates the successive lines of Assyrian guards to the point that they escort her into the presence of Holofernes, who completely falls under her charm (10:4, 7, 14, 23). Subsequently, her wisdom in conversation holds the general and his attendants spellbound (11:21, 23).

The reader must not commit the error of Holofernes, who cannot go beyond the sensual. The discerning audience realizes that Judith's qualities have a spiritual origin. The reactions of the infidels to Judith suggest that the authentic believer is fascinating and attractive to everyone, even the most worldly of people. Her wisdom and beauty are the distinguishing marks of a person who lives by faith. Judith has a unique bearing because, unlike people of the surrounding nations (and even her own people!), she does not fear man but God and lives by faith in him (8:8, 20, 27; 10:1; cf. 2:28). She stands out among her frightened people as the authentic witness to Judaism, thus exemplifying the Jerusalem of faith (10:7–8; cf. 4:2; 7:4).

Judith uses her beauty and wisdom to defeat Holofernes. In the process, she exposes the decadence of man-centered religion. The description of Judith's encounters with Holofernes is filled with irony. Beauty disarms power, and wisdom defeats pride. Boasting in the forces under his command, Holofernes prophesies correctly that, by entering into his camp, Judith will survive to enjoy a long life. But, in reality, her salvation will be the result of Nebuchadnezzar's defeat rather than his victory (11:1–4; cf. 16:21–25)! Judith plays on Holofernes' vanity, mesmerizing him with her charm, as she draws him out of his depth in theological discourse. After she speaks of weighty matters pertaining to the Law, sin, and Jewish authority, he responds with comments on her attractiveness that at once betray his infatuation and his ignorance (11:5–23). We know that Judith has taken control when Holofernes contemplates the possibility of his own conversion by telling her, "if you do as you have promised, your God shall be my God . . . " (11:23; cf. Ru 1:16).

Judith exhibits her shrewdness through irony. Her words mean the opposite of what Holofernes imagines. When she speaks of her "lord", she looks at Holofernes but really addresses the God of Israel in her heart with confessions of faith and obedience: "I shall speak no word of a lie to my lord tonight"; "in what my lord undertakes, he will not fail"; "Who am I . . . to resist my lord? I shall not hesitate to do whatever he wishes, and doing this will be my joy to my dying day" (11:5, 6; 12:14). Holofernes envisions a conquest when her words decree his defeat: "God has sent me to do things with you at which the world will be astonished when it hears" (11:16). When she speaks of the Lord's plan and her life's purpose, he thinks it will all serve his own gratification (12:4, 12, 18). Holofernes comes to an end that suits the irony of the story. In fact, he had lost his head over Judith well before she administered the final blow with his sword (13:1–10; 14:15).

Judith's wisdom derives from her determination to submit her life to God in every circumstance. Her strength comes through faith and obedience. Thus, her story demonstrates how God uses the weak in this world to overcome the mighty (see 13:15).

Toward the New Testament: A Woman's Victorious Faith

A Christian reading the book of Judith should reinterpret the violent deed of its heroine in light of Jesus' admonition to love one's enemies (Mt 5:43–48). The text does not advocate injuring or killing another person; rather, it illustrates the conquest of faith over the evil powers that threaten God's people in the world. As a model of faith, Judith foreshadows Mary insofar as she does the will of God on behalf of her people.

Uzziah's blessing on Judith foreshadows Elizabeth's pronouncement that Mary is "Of all women . . . the most blessed" (Lk 1:42; cf. Jdt 13:18). As Judith reverences the wisdom of God more than her contemporaries, so Mary is noted for pondering God's revelation manifest to the world in her son (Lk 2:19, 51; Jdt 8:14). Judith's prayerful disposition and declaration of God's vindication of the lowly over the mighty foreshadow Mary's acclamation of praise for God's work of deliverance on behalf of the humble (Lk 1:46–55; cf. Jdt 9:11–12; 16:2–17).

Judith is a symbol of Judaism at the time. In similar fashion, especially in the Johannine tradition, the mother of Jesus represents the Church (see Jn 2:1–10; 19:25–27). By her resplendent beauty and wisdom, Judith defeats the powers who were forcing the world to worship a mere man instead of God. As a personification of God's people, Judith foreshadows "a woman robed with the sun" in the book of Revelation (Rv 12:1–17). For the original audience of John the Presbyter, this "woman" exemplified the Church, which experienced persecution for refusing to worship the Emperor Domitian (A.D. 81–96) at the end of the first century (see Rv 13:1–10, 16; cf. 1:4–8; 2:1–3:22). As the perennial symbol of God's people, she communicates the assurance of victory to all who remain faithful to God as they confront the worldly powers of darkness.

BARUCH

Baruch shares with Tobit and Judith a concern for prayer, Jerusalem, the Temple, and the integrity of Judaism in a gentile world. However, this is an entirely different type of literature from the stories of faith. Baruch is not a unified text but a collection of diverse material that includes poetry, prayers, and exhortations.

The book of Baruch is a composite of five distinct literary units: (1) a narrative introduction that mentions Baruch and refers to the days of the Exile (1:1–14); (2) an extensive prayer that voices the people's repentance in light of their exile (1:15–3:8); (3) a wisdom poem that ponders the uniqueness of God's revelation to Israel (3:9–4:4); (4) a psalm of encouragement that expresses the current desolation and future aspiration of Jerusalem (4:5–5:9); and (5) a document that purports to be a letter of Jeremiah but is, in fact, a discourse against idolatry (6:1–72).

This letter of Jeremiah (6:1–72) was originally independent of the other two sections, for it stands by itself in two major Greek manuscripts, the Codex Vaticanus and the Codex Alexandrinus. It comes at the end of the book of Baruch in the Latin Vulgate and in some minor Greek versions.

The Origins of Baruch

The book receives its name from Jeremiah's intimate associate and scribe, who transmitted the prophet's words to King Jehoiakim in 605 B.C. and who composed some of the biographical sections in the book of Jeremiah (see Jer 36:1–32; 32:11–15; 45:1–5). In spite of its claim to a historical setting either in 582 B.C. (Bar 1:1–2) or in the interval between 597 and 587 B.C. (1:3–14), the text could not have come from the hand of Baruch, the secretary of Jeremiah.

Evidence throughout the text indicates that the book originated well after the death of the revered scribe. Historical incongruities abound: the book of Jeremiah states that Baruch went to Egypt, not to Babylon, after the destruction of Jerusalem in 587 B.C. (1:1–4; cf. Jer 43:4–7); the opening lines presume that the Babylonians had destroyed the Temple five years earlier, while the following section presumes a date in the interval between the first invasion and the ultimate destruction of the sanctuary (Bar 1:1–2; cf. 1:4–14; see 2 Kgs 24:8–17); during the Exile, the Temple site was a heap of ruins, and the priests would not have offered sacrifice there for its destroyer, Nebuchadnezzar (Bar 1:10–14; cf. Jer 41:4–5; Ezr 3:1–13); and the Persians, not the Babylonians, sanctioned the return of furnishings to the Temple (Bar 1:5–9; cf. Ezr 1:2–4, 7–11). Furthermore, various components of the text derive their inspiration from literature composed after Baruch's lifetime: the exiles' prayer reflects Daniel 9 (Bar 1:15–3:8; cf. Dn 9:1–19); the wisdom poem alludes to Job 28 (Bar 3:9–4:4; cf. Jb 28:1–28); and the psalm about Jerusalem reflects the sentiments of Deutero- and Trito-Isaiah (Bar 4:5–5:9; cf. Is 40–66).

Although some scholars have dated the text as late as the first century B.C. or even the first century A.D., we agree with others who suggest that a scribe in Jerusalem compiled the text sometime after the Maccabaean revolt late in the second century B.C. This scribal editor probably authored the introduction (Bar 1:1–14). One historical inaccuracy in the introduction corresponds with that in the book of Daniel: in fact, the father of Belshazzar was Nabonidus (556–539 B.C.), not Nebuchadnezzar (605–562 B.C.) (1:10–14; cf. Dn 5:1–2). Moreover, some sections of Baruch exhibit affinities with documents originating just before or during the Maccabaean era, notably Daniel (Bar 2:15–3:8; cf. Dn 9:1–19), and Sirach (Bar 3:9–4:4; cf. Sir 24:1–34). The scribe who wrote the prefatory letter in 2 Maccabees mentions the epistle of Jeremiah and thereby testifies to its circulation before 100 B.C. (2 Mc 2:1–3; cf. Bar 6:1–72).

In summary, diverse indications suggest that the various literary pieces in Baruch originated in a variety of periods before and after the Maccabaean revolt. Four different writers authored the respective compositions that follow each other after the introduction (1:15–3:8; 3:9–4:4; 4:5–5:9; 6:1–72). These literary units existed independently of each other until the scribal editor provided for their present arrangement within the setting of the introduction he composed (1:1–14). Although we possess the text only in Greek, the vocabulary and style provide substantial indications that this version is a translation of a Hebrew original.

The scribal editor of Baruch compiled the texts in order to call his people to conversion and faith. By describing the situations of both Jerusalem and Babylon in his introduction, he allows the book to address all Jews, both those in Palestine and those scattered throughout the world in the Diaspora. He employs Baruch as the venerable figure who expresses what the ancient prophets would say to the present generation. His inspiration for casting his whole collection of texts in the form of an address to the king and people in exile seems to derive from the story of Baruch's scroll and the transcription of Jeremiah's letter to the exiles in the book of Jeremiah (1:1–14; cf. Jer 36:1–32; 29:1–32).

All the texts in Baruch share the common presupposition that the Jewish people are spiritual exiles in the world. Their sin in the past produced this present state of alienation from God and dispersal from their land. Now they must repent, come to a new appreciation of the Lord's revelation and promises, and renounce all forms of idolatry. Each of the various texts making up Baruch exhibits a distinctive theology. We will consider the central theme in each of the four sections that follow the introduction: repentance in light of the Scriptures (prayer) (1:15–3:8); wisdom (poem) (3:9–4:4); God's promises (psalm) (4:5–5:9); and the denunciation of idolatry (Jeremiah's letter) (6:1–72).

The Penitential Prayer (1:15–3:8)

The extensive prayer (1:15–3:8) consists of two parts: a confession of guilt, which speaks of God in the third person (1:15–2:10), and a plea for mercy, which addresses God directly in the second person (2:11–3:8). The prayer is so closely modeled on Daniel's supplication that, in certain places, it employs the same vocabulary (Dn 9:4–19/Bar 1:19–22; cf. Dn 9:11/Bar 2:1–2; cf. Dn 9:12–13/Bar 2:11; cf. Dn 9:15). The author of the prayer meditated on the covenant stipulations in Deuteronomy and on Jeremiah's prophesies concerning the destruction and restoration of Jerusalem (Dt 28:1–68; Jer 7:1–8:3; 29:4–23; 31:31–34).

This invocation of the Lord's mercy demonstrates that God's word should provide the substance for his people's prayer. The Scriptures reveal both the justice of God and the unrighteousness of his people, the two doctrinal standards of their confession (1:15–2:10). The people can praise the Lord on the basis of his mercy (he is faithful to his promises), not on the basis of their righteousness or merit (2:19–3:8). The Lord will deliver Israel because, even as a dispersed remnant, she alone bears his name and exists to give him glory (2:13–18). Although disobedience brought about the downfall of the holy city, the Lord has not abandoned his own, and he never ceases to reveal his mercy and compassion to them (2:27). In the Exile and dispersion, the Lord purifies the people and brings them to conversion by forming in them a heart that desires to obey him (2:30–31; 3:7). In the fullness of time, the Lord will gather together his scattered people into the land of their inheritance (2:34–35).

The Poem of Wisdom in the Law (3:9–4:4)

The centerpiece of Baruch is the poem (3:9–4:4) that extols wisdom as the unique gift that the Lord has bestowed upon his people. This text draws together the two qualities of wisdom that seem to be poles apart in the scriptural tradition. On the one hand, Job illustrates that wisdom is unfathomable (Jb 28:1–28), while, on the other hand, Ben Sira asserts that wisdom is accessible in the Law (Sir 24:1–34).

Baruch draws upon both of these texts to demonstrate that these qualities are not incompatible. He alludes to Job 28 when he asserts that no one has been able to seize control of wisdom, since only God knows her (Bar 3:15–23, 24–35). But he also relates to Sirach 24 when he declares that God has condescended to reveal this fathomless wisdom to Israel in the Law (Bar 3:36–4:4). Baruch is even more evocative than Ben Sira when he describes the Law as an incarnation of wisdom in these terms: "[God] has uncovered the whole way of knowledge and shown it to his servant Jacob, to Israel his well-beloved; only then did she appear on earth and live among human beings" (3:36–37). Whereas the nations who carried out their futile search perished for lack of wisdom, Israel can live by conforming itself to the wisdom of the Law (4:1–4; cf. 3:9–14).

The Psalm of Jerusalem's Consolation (4:5–5:9)

The psalm in Baruch is a hymn of consolation for Jerusalem as the mother of God's people (4:5–5:9). After the preface explaining the dispersion as the consequence of sin (4:5–9a), Jerusalem addresses her children and invites them to place their trust in the mercy that God soon will reveal to them (4:9b–29). The present trials are the means by which God is chastening his people so that they will be able to receive complete joy from him in due time (4:21–29). The psalmist draws upon Deutero- and Trito-Isaiah (Is 40–55; 56–66) to provide the vision for the fullness of time when God will reveal his glory by gathering all his people to Jerusalem from the four corners of the earth (4:30–5:9).

The Sermon against Idolatry (6:1–72)

The purported "Letter of Jeremiah" (6:1–72) lacks any literary or structural indications typical of an epistle. This is not a letter but rather a sermon that ridicules idolatry and paganism. If we take seriously the mention of seven generations after the first deportation to Babylon, we must date the text around 317 B.C. (by counting forty years for each generation, beginning in 597 B.C.: 6:2; cf. Nm 32:13; 2 Kgs 24:10–17). A date in the third century B.C. would identify this text as the oldest in the collection of Baruch (6:2).

The diatribe draws upon Jeremiah 10 and other texts, especially in Deutero-Isaiah and the Psalms, that dismiss idolatry (see Jer 10:1–16; Is 44:9–20; 46:1–7; Pss 115:3–8; 135:15–18). The whole exposition may be a sermon on the only Aramaic verse in the book of Jeremiah: "The gods who did not make the heavens and the earth will vanish from the earth and from under these heavens" (Jer 10:11).

The sermon consists of ten parts, each of which belittles the worship of idols and warns the audience to resist the cultural intimidation that paganism exercised. The homilist punctuates his sermon by repeating variations of the same refrain nine times throughout the text: "they are not gods; do not be afraid of them" (6:14, 22, 28, 64, 68; cf. 39, 44, 51, 56). The dullness of the sermon helps convey to the audience the shallowness of the pagan worship propagated by the world's superpowers.

Toward the New Testament: A Resonance of the Incarnation

The poem describing wisdom's descent to earth in the form of the Law provides the structural center of the book of Baruch (3:9–4:4). This reference to wisdom revealed through the Law foreshadows the description of the Incarnation of the Word of God in Jesus Christ (Jn 1:1–18). Baruch's declaration of the nations' ignorance of wisdom prefigures the Gospel of John's lament that the world did not receive the Word who brought it into existence (Bar 3:19–23, 31; cf. Jn 1:9–11). Baruch's portrait of wisdom making her abode with Judah in the Law prepares for John's announcement of the Word taking flesh in Jesus Christ and dwelling in our midst (Bar 3:37–38; cf. Jn 1:14). In Baruch, the Law guaranteed life for the obedient, while, in John, the Father brings to new birth every person who receives his incarnate Word (Bar 4:1; cf. Jn 1:12–13). Therefore, as the divine Son who has come from the Father, Jesus is the revelation who fulfills the Law by surpassing it in glory: "for the Law was given through Moses, grace and truth have come through Jesus Christ" (Jn 1:17).

STUDY QUESTIONS

1. What are three themes of Tobit?
2. How does Tobit exemplify the *'anawim?*
3. How does Jesus fully develop Tobit's counsel to feed the hungry and clothe the naked?
4. How does Tobit resemble Daniel and 2 Maccabees while Judith resembles 1 Maccabees?
5. What are three themes of Judith?
6. How does Judith represent the best of Judaic tradition?
7. In what manner does Mary embody Judith's virtues?
8. What are the major sections of Baruch?
9. Discuss how perseverance in faith was the mainstay of Tobit and Judith when faced with what seemed insurmountable obstacles.
10. Describe the heroism exemplified by Tobit and Anna and by Raguel and Edna.
11. Judith embodies the more dashing aspects of heroism. Yet, can you see how her quiet life of faith prepared her for the heroic deed she performed?
12. Can you relate repentance to a prayer of thanksgiving based on the prayers and psalm in Baruch? Have you ever viewed a trying time as a time of grace and revelation? Can you think back now to times of distress and discern the Lord's particular action in your life?

TOBIT

JUDITH

BARUCH

40

WISDOM: RIGHTEOUSNESS AND ETERNAL LIFE

Why do many young people lose their faith when they go to a university or move from small towns to large metropolitan centers? Within these environments, youths have a firsthand encounter with a cosmopolitan world of people and ideas that reshapes their minds. Their studies, personal experiences, and contacts with others contribute to a new world view that replaces their former outlook on life. A crisis of faith arises when their religious understanding does not keep pace with their intellectual development. For the undiscerning mind, the glamour of the latest ideas obscures the significance of religious practice. Insofar as secular education dismisses reflection on God to the periphery of intellectual concern, it persuades young people that belief is alien to sound reason and borders on superstition.

What is the remedy for the crisis of faith generated by secular thinking? Evangelization, catechesis, prayer, and worship are all important. Undergirding such initiatives must be a presentation of the faith that speaks to the mind by exposing the meaning of doctrine for the present-day world. Genuine instruction illustrates the dynamic interaction between human reason and divine revelation. Sound teaching will demonstrate the surpassing quality of wisdom we receive by allowing God's word to nourish our intellects and guide us to the fullness of truth.

The book of Wisdom provides a model for the kind of teaching that can address the crisis of faith that many experience today. A teacher in Alexandria wrote the text for bright young Jews who were in danger of losing their faith in the big city. He wanted to rescue the best young minds of the community from the seductive influence of various new forms of religious consciousness that were proliferating in the metropolis. He had to confront public opinion, which considered traditional Judaism to be primitive, unsophisticated, and overly moralistic. In some cases, the opposition coalesced into demonstrations of prejudice and discrimination against Jewish believers. We will be able to appreciate the book of Wisdom as a fine example of biblical apologetics when we understand it within the historical setting of Judaism in the era of the Roman Empire.

The Roman Empire

The Roman Empire in Palestine and the eastern Mediterranean began with the victorious campaign of Pompey. In 67 B.C., he took command of the Mediterranean coastline by searching for and destroying the fleets of pirates who controlled the seas by means of terrorism. In subsequent years, he brought all of Asia Minor under Roman control by defeating Mithridates, the king of Pontus, and by forcing into submission Tirganes, the king of Armenia. Pompey's campaign reached completion in 63 B.C., when he moved southward and secured his possession of Syria and Palestine. In the process, he entered Jerusalem, killing more than a thousand Jewish partisans in the Temple precincts before barging his way right into the Holy of Holies. Thus the Holy Land was incorporated into the Roman Empire as a subdivision of the Roman province of Syria.

After 63 B.C., political developments in Rome had a direct impact on the Jews living in Palestine and scattered beyond its borders in the Diaspora. A brief survey of Roman history up to the birth of Christ introduces us to an array of classical leaders whose interaction reshaped the political order of the world.

Pompey returned to Rome and formed a powerful triumvirate with Julius Caesar and Marcus Licinius Crassus. This alliance eventually turned into a rivalry for absolute power between Pompey and Caesar. In 49 B.C., Caesar crossed the Rubicon (which separated Gaul from Italy) in order to challenge Pompey, who commanded the army of the Republic. After losing the decisive battle at Pharsalus in northeastern Greece, Pompey escaped to Egypt, where he was assassinated in September 48 B.C. During the next four years, Julius Caesar dreamed of building a worldwide empire. In the process of consolidating his influence in the eastern Mediterranean, he entered into a liaison with Cleopatra VII, the queen of Egypt (51–30 B.C.). She claimed that their union produced a son, Ptolemy XV Caesar (nicknamed "Caesarion"). Once he had returned to Rome, Caesar spent the next few years amassing such power that he gained a regal stature. Caesar's Pompeian rivals (led by Marcus Brutus and Gaius Cassius) reacted to his machinations by assassinating him on the ides (15th) of March 44 B.C.

Six months before his assassination, Caesar had adopted his great-nephew Octavian as his son and heir. When he was twenty years old, Octavian formed a triumvirate with two of his uncle's army commanders, Mark Antony and Marcus Lepidus. In 42 B.C., Octavian and Antony consolidated their authority when their combined forces defeated the troops of Brutus and Cassius at Philippi in Macedonia. In 36 B.C., Lepidus retired to private life, leaving Octavian and Antony to carry on a power struggle.

In general terms, throughout the era of the triumvirate, Octavian exercised authority over the western provinces, while Antony directed his attention eastward. Antony's career reached a turning point in 41 B.C., when, in seeking an alliance with Egypt, he provided a splendid reception for Cleopatra at Tarsus in Cilicia and then passed the winter months with her in Egypt. Subsequently Antony went back to Rome, where he married and then abandoned Octavian's sister, only to return to Egypt in 37 B.C. in order to live with Cleopatra. Antony and Cleopatra exhibited a divine bearing in the eyes of the populace who lived in Egypt and the eastern provinces. While Antony presented himself as the god Dionysius (Greek) or Osiris (Egyptian), Cleopatra appeared as the goddess Isis (the wife of Osiris in classical mythology). At Alexandria in 34 B.C., with Antony's consent, Cleopatra received the title "Queen of Kings", while her son Ptolemy XV Caesar ("Caesarion") became "King of Kings". Moreover, the twin children of Antony and Cleopatra received nominal claims to far-flung territories: their son, Alexander, was to rule east of the Euphrates, while their daughter, Cleopatra, was to reign over Cyraenica in north Africa.

The pretensions of Antony and Cleopatra to establish a worldwide empire provoked Octavian to enter into war against Egypt. In September 31 B.C., at Actium on the western coast of Greece, the Roman navy of Octavian defeated the Egyptian fleet commanded by Antony. Antony escaped to Egypt, where he and Cleopatra committed suicide sometime before Octavian reached Alexandria almost a year later. In August 30 B.C., Octavian took control of Egypt and made it a Roman province. In the process, he executed Cleopatra's son, Caesarion, the only man in the world who could dispute his claim as the rightful heir of Caesar. Three years later, in 27 B.C., the Senate in Rome conferred upon Octavian the title "Augustus". In the subsequent decades of his long tenure as Emperor "Caesar Augustus" (27 B.C.–A.D. 14), Octavian expanded the frontiers of Roman rule while laying the foundations for an extended period of international peace in the Mediterranean.

Palestine under Roman Rule: Herod the Great

Palestine always experienced repercussions stemming from the various transitions in the power structure of Rome. By exercising diplomacy with Roman powerbrokers and treachery with their domestic rivals, the Herodians were able to replace the Hasmonaeans as the local dynastic force that controlled Judaea. Palestine's history in the last half century before Christ focused on its two most important elements: the office of the high priest and the family of Herod.

The Herodians came from Idumaea, a territory south and west of Judaea whose southernmost city was Beersheba. Ethnically, the Idumaeans were distinct from the Jews. They probably descended from the Edomites (who became extinct sometime after the Exile [cf. Mal 1:1–4; Ez 35:1–15]) and were related to the Nabataeans (1 Mc 5:25; 9:35). Spiritually, they exhibited only a veneer of Jewish religion that had been forced upon them by John Hyrcanus I (134–104 B.C.).

Antipater II, Herod's father, brought his family into prominence in Judaea by allying himself with Hyrcanus II, who became high priest after winning the approval of Pompey. Eventually Antipater, the Idumaean commander, and Hyrcanus, the Hasmonaean high priest, worked together to support the interests of Julius Caesar, especially in Egypt. Caesar rewarded each of them with power in Judaea: Hyrcanus became the ethnarch, an office which gave him authority over all the Jews in the region; and Antipater became a Roman citizen and the procurator, the administrative agent who protected Rome's interests in the region.

Herod stepped into public office for the first time when his father designated him as governor of Galilee at the same time as he appointed another son, Phaesal, as governor of Judaea and Perea. Herod became the most powerful native figure in Palestine by cultivating friendships with the succession of Roman leaders. He managed to curry the favor of Caesar, Cassius, Mark Antony, and Octavian, each of whom deposed his predecessor by assassination or war. The major crisis for Herod occurred in 40 B.C., when Antigonus, the son of Aristobulus II (the fraternal rival of Hyrcanus II), assumed the position of high priest and king of Jerusalem. Herod escaped to Rome, where the Senate conferred on him the title "King of the Jews" after he won the support of both Antony and Octavian. He returned to Judaea, where he deposed Antigonus. When Herod established himself as king in 37 B.C., the Hasmonaean era came to an end and the Herodian family began its dynastic control over Judaea, which was destined to endure for almost a hundred years.

Judaea lived under Herod's ruthless hand for more than thirty years (37 B.C.–A.D. 4). From the beginning, Herod eliminated any rivals or even loved ones who provoked his suspicions, including one of his wives, his mother-in-law, at least two of his sons, and a high priest. He was a friend of Antony but a rival of Cleopatra, who wanted to rule Judaea from Egypt. After Octavian defeated Antony, the Emperor bestowed on Herod an increase of his power in Judaea. Herod bequeathed to Palestine a legacy of magnificent building projects, including: a splendid reconstruction of the Temple (which was eventually finished in A.D. 63/cf. Mk 13:1–2), the erection of fortresses, such as Herodium and Masada, the establishment of the seaport of Caesarea Maritima, and the construction of the town of Sebaste on the site of the ancient capital of

Samaria. Caesar Augustus (Octavian) allowed Herodian power to continue for generations when, after the death of Herod the Great, he distributed the kingdom among his three sons: Archelaus (ethnarch of Judaea, Samaria, and Idumaea: 4 B.C.–A.D. 6); Philip (tetrarch of Gaulanitis, Batanaea, Trachonitus, Auranitis, and Ituraea: 4 B.C.–A.D. 34); and Herod Antipas (tetrarch of Galilee and Peraea: 4 B.C.–A.D. 39). These figures shaped the world of Jesus' birth and ministry (cf. Lk 2:1–2; 3:1–2; 13:31; Mk 6:17–29).

Diaspora Jews in Alexandria

By 31 B.C., when Octavian brought Egypt under Roman control, its capital, Alexandria, was a metropolis of perhaps a million inhabitants. Situated on the Mediterranean some fifteen miles west of the Nile Delta, the city was the prime international port and meeting place of East and West in the ancient world. Only its reputation as the intellectual center without parallel anywhere superseded its commercial prominence. As the assembly point of Greek scholarship, this city was Harvard and Oxford combined into one. All the classical texts of Greek philosophy, literature, and drama were collected in its libraries and studied in its classrooms. The empirical and natural sciences of mathematics, geography, biology, and anatomy stimulated bright minds with new discoveries.

Alexandria also boasted the largest Jewish population of any city in the Diaspora. By popular account, the Great Synagogue of Alexandria was so large that some members at the back of the congregation were unable to follow the services by eye and ear; they had to receive a signal indicating the appropriate moment for them to respond to the prayers. In the first century B.C., synagogue buildings were only beginning to come into vogue both in Palestine and in the Diaspora. Alexandria, like Rome, boasted a Jewish population large enough to merit a number of synagogues in the city.

Strong political and religious ties linked Alexandria to Jerusalem. Our historical survey mentioned some episodes in the sphere of politics: the high priest, Hyrcanus II, guaranteed the loyalty of Egyptian Jews to Julius Caesar; Herod rose to power in Judaea on the premise of his friendship with Antony, who lived in Alexandria; yet Cleopatra coveted Judaea as a region over which she desired to rule from Egypt. In the religious sphere, we recall the literary developments that suggest a strong interaction between the Jews of Alexandria and their peers in Palestine: Ben Sira wrote a Hebrew text in Jerusalem, which his grandson translated into Greek in Alexandria (Sir: translator's prologue, vv. 1–35); the scribe who wrote about events in Palestine in 2 Maccabees introduced his work with two letters addressed to the Jews of Alexandria (2

Mc 1:1–9; 1:10–2:18); and Lysimachus of Jerusalem provided the Jews in Alexandria with the Greek version of the book of Esther (Est 10:3^l).

By the first century B.C., Alexandria had become the major center of Hellenistic Judaism—the culture of Greek-speaking Jews living outside Palestine. We have already noted that, beginning in the reign of Ptolemy II Philadelphus (285–246 B.C.), scholars in Alexandria set about translating the Hebrew Scriptures into Greek in the version we call the Septuagint. (Of course, the Alexandrian Jews completed the full Septuagint corpus sometime after the book of Wisdom.) Alexandria's climate eventually gave birth to a brilliant and prolific Jewish scholar, Philo of Alexandria (20 B.C.–A.D. 50), who would attempt to form an intellectual synthesis of Greek philosophy and Hebrew revelation.

Alexandria and the Book of Wisdom

Another Jewish scholar who worked in Alexandria wrote the last book of the Old Testament, perhaps a decade before the birth of Philo. The author of the book of Wisdom did not leave us his name, for he was content to communicate God's word to his people in the persona of Solomon (see Wis 6:22–9:18; cf. 1 Kgs 3:4–15; 5:9–14). He stands in the tradition of Ben Sira as a theologian who demonstrates how faith illuminates understanding to provide the most truthful, profound, and comprehensive vision of reality.

The vocabulary of the text suggests that its author was an Alexandrian Jew who completed the book of Wisdom shortly after 30 B.C., perhaps at the beginning of Octavian's imperial rule as Caesar Augustus (27 B.C.–A.D. 14). The author composed the book in Greek. He uses a number of terms that began to occur in texts of science, religion, and philosophy early in the Augustinian period. That the author comes from a thoroughly Jewish background is evident from the constant references to Scripture that suffuse his book from beginning to end. The sage who wrote the book of Wisdom exhibits an encyclopedic intellectual range. He demonstrates a familiarity with the philosophical traditions of Platonism and Stoicism, the religious traditions of the Isis cult, and the scientific developments in astronomy and botany. He possessed the erudition of a genuine Alexandrian scholar. However, he was most deeply a Jewish theologian, for Sacred Scripture remained the field of his expertise because it was the nutrition for his soul.

He composed his book for Jewish students and intellectuals who were abandoning their faith as they embraced Hellenistic philosophy and religion. His work is an apologia that demonstrates how Judaism surpasses Greek systems of thought as the ultimate embodiment of wisdom in the world. He challenges the self-indulgent agnosticism of the Epicureans (cf. 1:16–2:9); and he implies that the biblical revelation of wisdom already contains the best insights of Stoicism and Platonism (cf. 7:22–26; 8:7). Furthermore, his book represents a vehement polemic against the popular Hellenistic mystery cults that were alluring fashion-sensitive Jews away from the synagogue. Pastoral concern motivated him to provide a chastising analysis of idolatry (13:1–15:19) designed to win back those of his people who had begun partaking in the rites of Isis and Dionysius (cf. 12:5; 14:22–31).

The book of Wisdom takes the form of an exhortation by King Solomon to all world rulers (see 1:1–2; 6:1–11; 7:1–14; 8:2–9:18; cf. 1 Kgs 3:6–9). By means of this literary device, the book represents the authoritative voice of Judaism instructing all peoples and cultures. Under the pretext of speaking to nobility, the author actually directs his attention to Jewish intellectuals who have succumbed to the spell of gentile potentates and trendsetters. His mention of God's judgment on great leaders must have provoked the Alexandrians to recall the latter-day turbulence in Rome and Judaea, which most recently had culminated in the suicides of their previously deified sovereigns, Antony and Cleopatra (cf. 6:4).

The situation of his people demanded that the author provide a defense of Judaism that was pastoral as well as intellectual. Rationally, he had to demonstrate the superiority of scriptural revelation over Greek philosophy in understanding the nature of wisdom. Pastorally, he needed to explain why the people of God suffer affliction at the hands of the mighty who dismiss them as weak and inferior.

To accomplish his task, he produced a work in three parts that are remarkably distinct in form from each other. The first part (1:1–5:23) is an instruction that points out the direct relationship between righteousness and immortality. The second part (6:1–9:18) is a first-person testimony concerning wisdom given under the persona of Solomon. The third part (10:1–19:22) is a biblical reflection on the Exodus that illustrates how God's wisdom has been at work within the history of Israel. We will peruse the contents of the book by focusing on three themes that are central to the successive parts of the text: (1) immortality is the fruit of righteousness; (2) wisdom is a gift God bestows in answer to prayer; and (3) the Lord alone is God; therefore, worshipping idols is tragic foolishness.

Righteousness and Eternal Life

The book of Wisdom exhibits a greater preoccupation with life after death than any other text in the Old Testament. Existence in the present world is but a preparation for eternity. Because God created every person to be immortal, life beyond the grave provides the standard for estimating the value of the present moment.

The author of Wisdom developed this conviction by reading Sacred Scripture with a mind that appreciated the legitimate insights of Hellenistic reflection. He discerned a universal truth underlying a prophecy in Ezekiel: "God did not make Death" (1:13; cf. Ez 18:32; 33:11). According to his reading of Genesis, the divine "image" in human beings is God's immortal nature (Wis 2:23; cf. Gn 1:26–27). Furthermore, he is the first author to equate the Yahwist's serpent with the devil and to identify him as the source of death (Wis 2:24; cf. Gn 3:1–24).

Death, in this case, is spiritual as well as physical. It is the annihilation that the godless experience as the effect of their wickedness. This death stands in absolute contrast to the immortal life God intends when he creates human beings and endows each of them with a "soul" (see Wis 3:1; 4:14; 9:15). Here, the author borrows a term from Hellenistic philosophy but adapts its meaning to conform with scriptural theology. Whereas Plato asserted that the soul by itself is the source of immortality, the author of Wisdom insists that immortality is a gift that everyone must receive from God, who alone has "power over life and death" (16:13; 3:4; 4:1). According to the book of Wisdom, God endows the virtuous soul with immortality. Eternal life is the fruit of righteousness. "Uprightness is immortal" because righteousness defines a life lived in harmony with God and therefore free of sin, the harbinger of death (1:14–15; 3:1; 15:3; cf. 1:16; 14:31).

The author's preoccupation with righteousness extends throughout the text from the very first line (see "uprightness:" 1:1; 4:7; 5:15; 8:7; 10:10; 16:17). In most instances, he contrasts "the righteous" (who enter life) with "the godless" (who fall into death) (1:16–2:24; 3:1–12; 3:13–4:6; 4:7–19; 4:20–5:23). The righteous are those who reverence and obey God in all they do. The godless are the people—especially apostate Jews—who subscribe to the philosophies of the day and arrogantly dismiss God and his Law from their lives (see 2:12). In the present life, the godless have the upper hand and persecute the righteous (2:10–20).

How is it possible for a God of justice to allow his righteous ones to suffer at the hands of the godless who enjoy prosperity and comfort? The book of Wisdom provides a two-fold response to this dilemma based on the premise that earthly evaluations are erroneous because they take no account of God's eternal Kingdom. First, God's judgment will reverse the present order of fortunes. Even in the present moment, the cynicism of the godless produces despair, which they try to escape by practicing debauchery and oppression (2:1–5, 6–9, 10–20). However, in the end, they will behold the vindication of the righteous even as they themselves disintegrate into the void of eternal death (2:21-24; 3:10-12; 4:20-5:14; 5:17-23). The righteous, by contrast, will experience eternal peace in God's presence as they exercise authority in his Kingdom (3:1-9; 5:15-16).

Secondly, the sufferings of the righteous prepare them for eternal life. Texts such as the Confessions of Jeremiah (e.g., 11:18-12:6), the Song of the Suffering Servant (Is 52:13-53:12) and the psalm of the innocent in anguish (Ps 22) inspired the author of Wisdom to perceive that God identifies himself most closely with the righteous one whom the world despises (2:10-20). "The upright man is God's son"; he can "boast ... of having God for his father" (2:16-20; cf. 16:10, 26; 18:4, 13). If physical death should overtake the youth who obeys the Lord, it acts more as a servant than as an adversary insofar as it rescues him from the peril of evil and brings him into the safety of God's eternal embrace (4:7-19). The first-person confession of the adversaries in the Song of the Suffering Servant (Is 53:1-10) echoes in the words of the godless who acknowledge the victory of the righteous whom they had afflicted (Wis 4:20-5:14).

In summary, we note that the book of Wisdom stands in the tradition of Daniel and 2 Maccabees insofar as it proclaims a life after death as God's reward for the righteous individual, especially the one who suffers persecution and martyrdom (Wis 3:1-9; 4:7-19; 5:15-16; cf. Dn 12:1-2; 2 Mc 7:11, 23, 36). However, the book of Wisdom incorporates a Hellenistic dimension into the biblical tradition by describing life beyond the grave in terms of immortality of the soul rather than in terms of resurrection from the dead.

Wisdom and Prayer

Immortality comes from wisdom as well as righteousness (6:17-19; 8:13, 17). These two principles are inseparable: wisdom, being the mother of virtue, gives birth to righteousness, which, in turn, leads to eternal life (8:7; 9:11). But where does wisdom originate, and how can one attain it? Wisdom resides with God and is a gift that everyone must receive through prayer (8:21).

Wisdom is personified as God's beloved consort who stands by his heavenly throne yet, at the same time, suffuses his creation (8:2-3; 9:4, 9; 7:17-21). This portrait of Lady Wisdom (Greek: *Sophia*) represents a development of the traditional poetic descriptions of wisdom's activity: in creation (Prv 8:22-31; cf. Jb 28:1-28); in everyday life (Prv 1:20-33; 8:1-21; 9:1-6); and in the Law (Sir 24:23-34; cf. Bar 3:9-4:4). While basing his reflection on scriptural tradition, the author of the book incorporates into his portrait of wisdom touches of Hellenistic religion and philosophy. We may detect allusions to the cult of Isis in the description of Lady Wisdom as the spouse of God (Wis 9:4), the source of eternal life (8:13), the one who can do all things (7:27). Mention of her communicating "the secrets of God's knowledge" reflects the language of the Hellenistic mystery religions (8:4, in 8:2–16). The twenty-one qualities of Wisdom suggest an absolute perfection (7×3) reminiscent of the cosmic soul in Greek philosophy (7:22–23, 24–26). Furthermore, wisdom produces the four virtues most esteemed by the philosophical tradition (8:7). By clothing scriptural wisdom in the terminology of the Greek world, the author demonstrates that whatever his audience might be seeking in the cult of Isis or in Hellenistic philosophy is most genuinely available to them in their own religious tradition.

In the most basic terms, Wisdom is God's providence (8:1). She was his agent at creation (9:1–2, 9), and she guides history according to the divine plan (8:1). Because of her association with God, Wisdom exhibits divine qualities of radiance and goodness (7:24–26). Being the object of God's love, she is, in turn, the lover of mankind (Greek: *philanthropos:* 1:6; 7:23). Only someone who loves Wisdom can truly know her (cf. 8:2).

Solomon testifies that one gains wisdom through prayer that accompanies intellectual endeavor (8:17–21; 6:14–20). The goal of prayer is revelation rather than information. Through prayer, one enters into a life-changing dialogue with God (see 9:1–18). When God pours forth wisdom, he draws people into relationship with himself as his "friends", like Abraham, Moses, and the prophets (7:14, 27; 8:21; cf. Is 41:8; Ex 33:11).

The Benevolence of God and the Foolishness of Idolatry

Wisdom is not only an agent of creation but also of salvation (9:18). Wisdom's activity in history is the subject of the final section of the book (10:1–19:22). Here, the author provides an extended commentary on the Exodus in order to illustrate the manner in which wisdom guided the formation of Israel. However, his presentation is not so much a history lesson as a theological and pastoral exposition for his contemporaries. In the author's retelling of the story, the Israelites become metaphors of the local Diaspora Jews, and the Egyptians represent their gentile contemporaries in Alexandria. Egyptian idolatry takes the form of the orgiastic rites of Dionysius and various mystery cults in the first century B.C. (see 12:5; 14:15–16, 22–26).

The tension between the righteous and the godless that suffused the first part of the book (1:1–5:23) now resurfaces under the guise of the conflict between the Israelites and the Egyptians. The righteous Jews worship the living God even as they experience severe oppression under the godless

Gentiles who venerate their hand-crafted idols (15:1-6; 18:9; cf. 13:10-19; 15:7-13). Scripture (in the form of the Exodus narrative) reinforces the promise of a reversal of fortunes that had been announced earlier in the book (3:1-5:23). The godless Egyptians prospered for only a brief moment before suffering the judgment of God and witnessing the deliverance of righteous Israel (10:15-11:3; 11:4-14; 16:1-19:17).

In order to highlight the saving activity of Wisdom, the expository analysis illustrates seven contrasts between Egypt and Israel in the Exodus (11:4-14; 16:1-19:17). Each of these contrasts supports the principle about divine providence that the author articulates in conversation with God, "by the very vengeance that you exacted on our adversaries, you glorified us by calling us to you" (18:8). God saves the righteous by the same means he uses to punish the godless. The first couple of instances are typical of each of the seven contrasts: while the Israelites received water from the rock, the Egyptians saw their river turn to blood (11:4-14); the Egyptians lost their appetites at the sight of the frogs, while the Israelites relished the quail after being a short time without food (16:1-4).

The miracles of the Exodus demonstrate the unity of God's activity in creation and in salvation. Earlier, the author noted how the discoveries of natural science reveal wisdom's designs in the material universe (7:17-21). Now he points out that the cosmos is not a closed system but is always open to transformation in accordance with God's saving activity. In his address to God, the author articulates this principle that the seven contrasts illustrate: "the creation being at the service of you, its Creator, tautens to punish the wicked and slackens for the benefit of those who trust in you" (16:24). His words suggest that salvation brings with it the prospect of a new creation (19:18-21).

The author interrupts his exposition between the first and second contrasts to provide two extended reflections, the first in defense of God's goodness (11:15-12:27) and the second in opposition to idolatry (13:1-15:19). He defends the fundamental thesis that God loves everything he has created and desires to extend his mercy to all people (11:21-12:2). Scripture makes evident the Lord's forbearance toward the Egyptians and Canaanites (11:15-12:18). He carried out his sanctions on them in a gradual fashion in an attempt to bring them to conversion (12:10). The Alexandrian Jews should imitate their Lord by acknowledging the divine mercy shown to them and by extending that mercy to their enemies (12:22).

A society becomes dissolute by alienating itself from the living God. Idolatry is the root cause of social disintegration (see 14:12, 22-31). All forms of paganism originate in ignorance of God and consist in worshipping creatures instead of their Creator (13:1-9). When people venerate anything other than the true God, they lose their dignity because they submit to something inferior to themselves (15:16–17). The rites of paganism provide their own punishment: as people surrender to unsanctified passion, they necessarily extinguish any instinct for holiness that might call them to redemption and to a higher life with God (14:22–31). Only by worshipping God does one become aware of one's own worth and open to the prospect of eternal life (cf. 15:11).

Eternal life consists in personal knowledge of the living God. "To know you is indeed the perfect virtue, and to know your power is the root of immortality" (15:3). We know God by experiencing his mercy through the gift of repentance (15:1–2). From Adam to Moses, the forebears of the Israelites came to know God as wisdom brought them through trials and ordeals (10:1–14). As they hold fast to wisdom in the face of persecution, God's people are revealed to the world as his son (see 18:13; cf. Ex 4:22; Dt 1:31; Hos 11:1).

Toward the New Testament: Christ, the Righteous Son of God

The book of Wisdom acquaints us with the mentality of the Hellenistic world just before the time of Christ. The fact that the sacred authors composed the New Testament documents in Greek rather than in Aramaic indicates that, for the most part, they were addressing Hellenistic Jews and Gentiles beyond the frontiers of Palestine. They had to proclaim the Gospel in the terminology that spoke to the mind sets of their audience. When speaking of Christ to Greek-speaking Jews, Paul and the evangelists found it most advantageous to employ some of the conceptual framework we have discovered in the book of Wisdom. Therefore, the book of Wisdom attunes our minds to detect some of the deeper theological nuances contained in the New Testament writings.

The book of Wisdom enriches our appreciation of the early Church's teaching concerning both sin and salvation. Two themes in particular merit our attention: (1) the Pauline analysis of man's alienation from God, and (2) the portrait of Christ both as the righteous Son of God and as the Wisdom of God.

Paul's doctrine of justification by grace and faith stands on the premise that "all have sinned and lack God's glory" (Rom 3:23–24; cf. 3:9, 20). He establishes this premise at the beginning of the Letter to the Romans by analyzing mankind's alienation from God, first in the case of the Gentiles (1:18–32) and then in the case of the Jews (2:1–3:8). His description of the state of the Gentiles echoes the discourse on idolatry in the book of Wisdom (see especially Rom 1:24–32; cf. Wis 14:22–31). Like the author of Wisdom, Paul discerns that idolatry is the root source of immorality. Disordered sexual behavior and injustice toward others are the primary characteristics of a society that makes and worships its own gods (Rom 1:25–27, 29–31; Wis 14:12, 27).

Idolatry is an offense against wisdom. People worship idols because they refuse to seek out the living God (Rom 1:19–20; cf. Wis 13:1–2). Thus they deify the creature instead of worshipping the Creator (Rom 1:23, 25; cf. Wis 11:15; 12:24; 13:10). Like the author of Wisdom (Wis 11:15–16; 12:23–27), Paul discerns that God's judgment consists in allowing idolatry to provide its own punishment. However, Paul is more perceptive about the devastating consequences on the interior life. Step by step, God concedes to the wishes of men and women by abandoning them to degrading passions, which, in turn, rule their minds and make them less and less capable of knowing God (Rom 1:24, 26, 28). The penalty consists in attaining the goal of their desire, namely, separation from God. Such independence constitutes a tragic state of alienation from their Creator and of enmity toward others (Rom 1:28–32; cf. Wis 14:23–29).

The author of Wisdom studied the narrative of the Fall in search of the origin of death (Wis 2:24; cf. Gn 3:1–24). He identified the serpent in Eden with the devil. Thus, he was able to determine the spiritual source (Satan) who had sufficient power to produce the effect of spiritual death. When Paul considered the roots of death, he followed the lead of this learned Hellenistic Jew and directed his attention to the story of the Fall (Rom 5:12–21; Gn 3:1–24; cf. Wis 2:23–24; cf. 10:1–2). However, for Paul, sin is the primary agent of death. In Wisdom we read, "Death came into the world only through the Devil's envy ... " (Wis 2:24), whereas, in Romans, we read, "it was through one man that sin came into the world, and through sin death" (Rom 5:12). Sin in Romans acts like the devil in Wisdom and like the serpent in Genesis. In Wisdom, we discover the basis for Paul's personification of sin as a primeval, intelligent, demonic power that holds mankind in captivity. Paul's theology of sin provides the context for his theology of salvation, which focuses on Christ's triumph over sin and death in the event of his cross (Rom 5:12–21; 8:3).

The Passion narratives of Matthew and Luke reveal Jesus as the righteous Son of God. The meditation on the suffering of the just man in the book of Wisdom acquires a prophetic tenor when read in light of the Gospels (see Wis 2:10–20). The religious authorities in Jerusalem plot to destroy Jesus because of his opposition to their teaching and style of life (Mt 26:3–5; see 23:1–36; cf. Wis 2:12). After condemning him, they ridicule and abuse him and ask for the death sentence (Mt 26:67–68; 27:12, 22–23; cf. Wis 2:19). When he hangs upon the cross, they deride him for claiming to be the Son of God (Mt 27:43; cf. Wis 2:18). In spite of all this opposition, the wife of the gentile governor Pilate identifies him correctly as "that upright man" (Mt 27:19; cf. Wis 2:19).

According to the account in Luke, when Jesus dies, his executioner confesses, "Truly, this was an upright man" (Lk 23:47). This Gentile echoes the convictions of the repentant criminal (Lk 23:41) and of Pilate, who three times declares Jesus' innocence (Lk 23:4, 14–15, 22). As in Matthew, so in Luke, the Sanhedrin's condemnation of Jesus as the Son of God only proves the validity of his claim, since their behavior corresponds to that of the wicked toward the righteous man in the book of Wisdom (Lk 22:70; cf. Wis 2:13). For anyone familiar with the book of Wisdom, the events of the Passion verify rather than refute that Jesus is the Son of God (cf. Wis 2:10–20). Therefore, in the Acts of the Apostles, Peter, Stephen, and Ananias each declare that Jesus is the "Upright One" whom everyone rejected (Acts 3:14; 7:52; 22:14).

Among the New Testament documents, the Pauline letters, the Gospel of John, and the Letter to the Hebrews reveal Christ most completely as the divine Word and Son of God (1 Cor 8:6; Col 1:15–20; Jn 1:1–18; Heb 1:1–4). At least in part, the revelation of the full identity of Christ developed in light of the traditions of Hellenistic Judaism concerning Wisdom. The description of eternal Wisdom's perfection elaborated in the exposition of her twenty-one (3 × 7) qualities, her diverse movements, and her activity in the cosmos foreshadows the revelation of Christ glorified (Wis 7:22–8:1).

The Johannine Prologue brings into clear definition the divine status and activity of God's Word in creation: "He was with God in the beginning. Through him all things came into being, not one thing came into being except through him" (Jn 1:2–3; cf. Wis 9:1). Light characterizes the divine Word and signifies his power to overcome spiritual darkness (Jn 1:5; cf. Wis 7:29–8:1).

When Paul addresses the Greek-speaking world, he rejects the Hellenistic pantheon of gods and announces, instead, that "for us there is only one God, the Father from whom all things come and for whom we exist, and one Lord, Jesus Christ, through whom all things come and through whom we exist" (1 Cor 8:6). Here, he speaks of Christ in language that recalls the portrait of divine wisdom in Hellenistic Judaism (cf. Wis 7:21; 7:22–8:1). Thus, the tradition of wisdom that developed in the Jewish Diaspora prepared the Church to contemplate Christ's preexistence and role as mediator in creation.

The Letter to the Colossians describes Christ as the "image of the unseen God" who is before all things and who reigns throughout the cosmos (Col 1:15–20). Two streams of tradition converge in the acclamation of Christ as the "image of God". First, in light of Genesis, he is the new Adam who restores man to his original dignity as the "image of God" (cf. Gn 1:27). Secondly, in light of Hellenistic Judaism, Christ is the divine Wisdom who is the "image of [God's] goodness" (cf. Wis 7:26). Therefore, as the "image of

God", Christ is the revelation both of man and of God at one and the same time.

The Letter to the Hebrews introduces Christ by concentrating on his uniqueness in relationship to God. The author of Hebrews borrows a term from Wisdom when describing Christ as the "reflection [Greek: *apaugasma*] of God's glory" (Heb 1:3; cf. Wis 7:25–26). The word indicates not only that Christ reflects the awesome radiance of God (cf. Ex 24:16–18) but also that he shares in the very nature of the Father as the divine Son (Heb 1:1–2). When the author of Hebrews declares that Christ "bears the impress of God's own being", he is probably alluding to the divine attributes mentioned in Wisdom (Heb 1:3; cf. Wis 7:15–16). Christ shares in God's power, eternity, and goodness.

The eternal union between the Father and the Son constitutes the summit of divine revelation. The Son partakes of the same divine nature as the Father but as a distinct person. Christ is the Son who has come into our midst to open for us the way to the Father. As our great High Priest, he has cleansed us from sin so that we can enter the heavenly sanctuary where he abides at the right hand of the divine Majesty (Heb 1:3; 4:14–5:10; 5:11–10:18; 12:1–13).

In summary, all Scripture leads us to Christ, who is the source and the center of the Father's plan for the whole cosmos. Reading the Old Testament from beginning to end causes us to marvel at the faithfulness of God and to appreciate the present hour as a crucial time of grace and revelation.

"At many moments in the past and by many means, God spoke to our ancestors through the prophets; but in our time, the final days, he has spoken to us in the person of his Son, whom he appointed heir of all things and through whom he made the ages" (Heb 1:1–2).

STUDY QUESTIONS

1. What is the purpose of the book of Wisdom?
2. What is the unifying theme of the book of Wisdom?
3. How does wisdom lead us to God?
4. What is at the root of all sin?
5. How did the book of Wisdom influence Paul's understanding of sin?
6. How does the book of Wisdom presage the afflictions of Christ?
7. How does pondering the word of God through Scripture and the teachings of the Church lead to wisdom?
8. Discuss some of the actions in your life that appear to you to be wiser than others. What characteristics of your decision show that you were wise?
9. Discuss how our modern culture with its emphasis on the instant— sound bytes on the televised news, fast-food restaurants, purchases today on credit cards paid off some time in the future—conflicts with the cultivation of wisdom.
10. How does Mary's pondering in her heart all the events of Jesus' life show that she had wisdom?
11. Read John 1:1–18; Colossians 1:15–20; Hebrews 1:1–4. How do these texts reveal Christ as the Wisdom of God?
12. Read 2 Corinthians 13:13 and reflect on how God invites you to share in the life of the Trinity.

WISDOM

AFTERWORD

The outcome or the fruit of reading holy Scripture is by no means negligible: it is the fullness of eternal happiness. For these are the books which tell us of eternal life, which were written not only that we might believe but also that we might have everlasting life. When we do live that life we shall understand fully, we shall love completely, and our desires will be totally satisfied. Then, with all our needs fulfilled, we shall truly know *the love that surpasses understanding* and so *be filled with the fullness of God.* The purpose of the Scriptures, which come to us from God, is to lead us to this fullness according to the truths contained in th[e] sayings of the apostles.... In order to achieve this, we must study holy Scripture carefully, and teach it and listen to it in the same way.

If we are to attain the ultimate goal of eternal happiness by the path of virtue described in the Scriptures, we have to begin at the very beginning. We must come with a pure faith to the Father of Light and acknowledge him in our hearts. We must ask him to give us, through his Son and in the Holy Spirit, a true knowledge of Jesus Christ, and along with that knowledge a love of him. Knowing and loving him in this way, confirmed in our faith and grounded in our love, we can know *the length and the breadth and height and depth* of his sacred Scripture. Through that knowledge we can come at last to know perfectly and love completely the most blessed Trinity, whom the saints desire to know and love and in whom all that is good and true finds its meaning and fulfillment.

Excerpt from the Prologue to *The Breviloquium* by Saint Bonaventure (A.D. 1221–74), from the English translation of *The Liturgy of the Hours. Office of Readings,* vol. III (International Committee on English in the Liturgy, Inc., © 1974, all rights reserved), 175 (Monday of the Fifth Week of Ordinary Time).

A CHRONOLOGY OF THE OLD TESTAMENT ERA

YEAR	ISRAEL'S HISTORY	RELATED EVENTS OF OTHER NATIONS
	I *Prior to Abraham*	
7000	A Settlement at Jericho (c. 7000)	
3000		Old Kingdom of Egypt: Pyramids (c. 3000) Cities of Sumer (c. 3000) State of Akkad (c. 2500) Ebla Tablets (c. 2400)
2000		Middle Kingdom of Egypt (2030–1720)
	II *The Patriarchs and the Egyptian Era* (c. 1850–1280 B.C.)	
2000		Middle Kingdom in Egypt (2030–1720)
1900	Abraham's Call (1850)	
1800		
1700		The Code of Hammurabi
1600	Joseph in Egypt	Hyksos Rule in Egypt (1720–1552)
1500		
1400		The Founding of Ugarit (1400) Nuzi Tablets 18th Dynasty in Egypt (1552–1304)
	III *The Exodus and Settlement* (1280–1200 B.C.)	
1300		Egypt: 19th Dynasty (1304–1184) Pharaoh Rameses II (1290–1224)
	The Exodus under Moses (c. 1280) The Wilderness Journey (1280–1240) Israel Enters Canaan under Joshua (c. 1240)	Pharaoh Merneptah (1224–1211) Merneptah Stele (1220)
1200	Invasion of Sea Peoples (c. 1200)	Ugarit Destroyed (1200)

585

YEAR	ISRAEL'S HISTORY	RELATED EVENTS OF OTHER NATIONS

	IV *The Judges* (1200–1050 B.C.)	

1100	Deborah's Victory at Tanaach (c. 1125) Eli's Death: Philistines Defeat Israel (1050)	

	V *The United Kingdom* (1050–931 B.C.)	

	Samuel at Shiloh (1040–1020) Saul (c. 1030–1010)	
1000	Jerusalem the Capital (1000) David (c. 1010–970) Solomon (c. 970–931)	

	VI *The Divided Kingdom* (931–721 B.C.)	

	Judah	*Israel*	
900	Rehoboam (931–913)	Jeroboam (931–910)	Sheshonk I of Egypt
	Abijah (913–911)	Nadab (910–909)	Invades Judah and
	Asa (911–870)	Baasha (909–886)	Israel (c. 925)
		Elah (886–885)	
		Zimri (885)	
		Omri (885–874)	
	Jehoshaphat (870–848)	Ahab (874–853)	853 Shalmaneser III of
		Ahaziah (853–852)	Assyria (858–824);
	Jehoram (848–841)	Jehoram (852–841)	Battle of Kharkah
	Ahaziah (841)	Jehu (841–814)	against Ahab
	Athaliah (841–835)		
800	Jehoash (Joash) (835–796)	Jehoahaz (814–798)	
	Amaziah (796–781)	Jehoash (Joash) (798–783)	
	Uzziah (781–740)	Jeroboam II (783–743)	Weakness in Assyria
		Zechariah (743)	(783–745)
		Shallum (743)	
	Jotham (740–736)	Menahem (743–738)	
		Pekahiah (738–737)	

YEAR ISRAEL'S HISTORY	RELATED EVENTS OF OTHER NATIONS
Ahaz (736–716) 735–734: War between Israel-Damascus and Judah	Pekah (737–732) 734: Assyria Takes Galilee

Hoshea (732–724)

                             732: Assyria Takes
                                 Damascus
                                 Shalmaneser V of
724: Assyria Besieges   Assyria (726–721)
Samaria
721: Assyria Captures
Samaria and Ends
Northern Kingdom of
Israel

VII   *The Kingdom of Judah* (721–587 B.C.)

716–687 Hezekiah	Sargon II of Assyria (721–705) 711: Sargon II Invades Philistia
701: Assyria Surrounds Jerusalem Then Withdraws	Sennacherib of Assyria (704–681)

700 Manasseh (687–642)   Escharhaddon of Assyria (680–669)
     Amon (642–640)
     Josiah (640–609)   Ashurbanipal (669–630)
        Zephaniah (635–630) 626: Babylon Takes Asshur
        Jeremiah (627–585)   Nebupolassar of Babylon (626–605)
        Nahum (612)   612: Nineveh Falls to Babylon
        Habakkuk (c. 604–599) 609: Babylon Repels Assyria at Haran
                               609–05: Necho of Egypt Controls Judah
                               605–562: Nebuchadnezzar of Babylon

600 March 597: Babylon's First
     Invasion of Jerusalem
     Jan 588–Aug 587:
     Babylon's Second
     Invasion of Jerusalem:
     –Jan 588:

YEAR ISRAEL'S HISTORY   RELATED EVENTS OF OTHER NATIONS

Babylon Surrounds
Jerusalem
–Jun–Jul 587:
Babylon Breaks
through the Walls
–Aug 587:
Babylon Destroys
Temple and City:
Exile Begins

VIII   *The Babylonian Exile* (587–538 B.C.)

Sep/Oct 587: Gedaliah
Assassinated
582–581:
Fresh Deportations
561: Evil-Merodach   562–560: Evil-Merodach
Pardons Jehoiachin   560–556: Neriglissar
                            556–539: Nabonidus
                            c. 555–530: Cyrus II

IX   *Restoring the Temple and the Persian Era* (538–332 B.C.)

                            539: Cyrus Takes Babylon
538: Edict of Cyrus:
End of Exile
537: Restoration of Worship
at Temple Site

                            529–522: Cambyses II
                            522–486: Darius I
                            520–515: Zerubbabel, Joshua, Haggai,
                            Zechariah

500   486–465: Xerxes I
458: Ezra's Mission
445–433: First Mission of
Nehemiah
428: Second Mission of
Nehemiah

                            423: Xerxes II
                            423–404: Darius II Nothus

YEAR	ISRAEL'S HISTORY	RELATED EVENTS OF OTHER NATIONS
400		404–358: Artaxerxes II Mnemon
		359/8–338/7: Artaxerxes III Ochus
		342: Reconquest of Egypt

X *Greek (Hellenistic) Rule* (332–63 B.C.)

		336–323: Alexander the Great
		The Seleucids
		323–285: Ptolemy I Soter
		305/4–281: Seleucus I Nicator
300		223–187: Antiochus III the Great
		202–200: Antiochus Reconquers Palestine
200	200–142: Judaea Ruled by Seleucids	
	167–164: The Great Persecution. In the Temple, Sacrifices Made to Olympian Zeus. Revolt of Mattathias	175–164: Antiochus IV Epiphanes
	166–160: Judas Maccabaeus	164–162: Antiochus V Eupator
	Dec 164: Purification of the Temple (Hanukkah)	
	160–143: Jonathan	161–150: Demetrius I Soter
		150–145: Alexander II Balas
	143–134: Simon	145–140: Demetrius II Nicator against Trypho and Antiochus VI
	134–104: John Hyrcanus I	139–128: Antiochus VII Sidetes
	104–103: Aristobulus I	
	103–76: Alexander Jannaeus	
	76–67: Alexandra	
	76–67: Hyrcanus II—High Priest	
	67–63: Aristobulus II— King and High Priest	

XI   *Roman Rule* (63 B.C. and Beyond)

	63: Pompey Takes Control of Eastern Mediterranean and Seizes Jerusalem	63–48: Pompey-Julius Caesar-Crassus

YEAR	ISRAEL'S HISTORY	RELATED EVENTS OF OTHER NATIONS
	63–40: Hyrcanus II & Antipater	48–44: Julius Caesar
	40–37: Antigonus—King and High Priest	44–31: Octavian-Mark Antony-Lepidus
	37 B.C.–A.D. 4: Herod the Great	37–31 B.C. Antony & Cleopatra in Egypt
		36–31 B.C. Octavian-Mark Antony
		31 B.C.–A.D. 14: Octavian: Emperor Caesar Augustus

Herod Archelaus	Herod Antipas	Herod Philip
Judaea, Samaria, Idumaea	Galilee, Peraea	Batanaea, Trachonitus, Auranitis, Ituraea, Gaulanitis
4 B.C.–A.D. 6	4 B.C.–A.D. 39	4 B.C.–A.D. 34

(From *The New Jerusalem Bible,* © 1985 by Darton, Longman & Todd and Doubleday, a division of Bantam Doubleday Dell Publishing Group. Adapted from Chronological Table, 2055–74, and reprinted by permission.)

A CHRONOLOGY OF THE OLD TESTAMENT WRITINGS

Period	The Pentateuch	The Former Prophets	The Later Prophets	The Writings	Deuterocanonicals
1. The Patriarchs 1850–1550 B.C. and The Egyptian Era 1550–1280 B.C.	Primitive oral traditions about the Patriarchs				
2. The Exodus 1280–1240 B.C.	Oral traditions: —Moses' teaching —Laws & customs for nomads —Songs of redemption				
3. The Conquest and Settlement of the Land 1240–1030 B.C.	Written traditions: —Early law codes —Songs of victory (Ex 15)	Oral and early written traditions: —Conquest and settlement in Canaan —Stories of Judges —Songs of victory (Jgs 5)			

Period	The Pentateuch	The Former Prophets	The Latter Prophets	The Writings	Deuterocanonicals
4. *The United Kingdom* 1030–931 B.C.	Written text of the Yahwist (J)	Traditions of Samuel and Saul Text of David's family at court (2 Sm 9–20; 1 Kgs 1–2) Stories of David Stories of Solomon		Writing under Solomon's Patronage: —Proverbs (Prv 10–22) —Songs of love & marriage —Psalms for the Temple Ruth (first edition)	
5. *The Divided Kingdom:* Israel (N) & Judah (S) 931–721 B.C.	Elohist (E) tradition in Israel Deuteronomic circles develop in Israel	Royal Court and Temple records of Israel&Judah (1–2 Kgs; 1–2 Chr) Stories of Elijah and Elisha in Israel (1 Kgs 17 to 2 Kgs 10)			

Period	The Pentateuch	The Former Prophets	The Latter Prophets	The Writings	Deuterocanonicals
			Amos & Hosea in Israel		
			Isaiah & Micah in Judah		
6. The Kingdom of Judah 721–587 B.C.	Elohist (E) account is blended into the Yahwist's (J) text Edition of Dt discovered in Temple storeroom: the basis of Josiah's reform (622 B.C.) The Holiness Code (Lv 17–26)	Royal Court and Temple records of Judah Edition of Deuteronomic History written during Josiah's reign	Zephaniah Nahum Jeremiah's early work (written by Baruch [Jer 36]) Habakkuk	Under Hezekiah's patronage: –Proverbs (Prv 25–29)	
7. The Exile in Babylon 587–538 B.C.	Priestly (P) traditions		Ezekiel	Lamentations	

Period	The Pentateuch	The Former Prophets	The Latter Prophets	The Writings	Deuterocanonicals
	Deuteronomy: final edition (D)	Deuteronomic History (Jos, Jgs, 1–2 Sm, 1–2 Kgs): final edition	Deuteronomists edit the text of Jeremiah Texts of Preexilic prophets Deutero-Isaiah (Is 40–55)		
8. The Persian Era 538–332 B.C.			Haggai and Zechariah (Zec 1–8) Trito-Isaiah (Is 56–66) Malachi Obadiah Isaian Apocalypse (Is 24–27) Final edition of Isaiah	Mission of Zerubbabel and Joshua the Priest	
	Priestly editors complete the Pentateuch (c. 400 B.C.)			Memoirs of Ezra & Nehemiah Esther Ruth Job Proverbs: final edition The Chronicler's History Ezra & Nehemiah Song of Songs	
			Joel		

Period	The Pentateuch	The Former Prophets	The Latter Prophets	The Writings	Deuterocanonicals
			Deutero-Zechariah (Zec 9–14)	Psalms: final edition	
			Jonah		
9. The Greek Era 332–63 B.C.				Qoheleth	Septuagint translation (LXX) Tobit Sirach
				Daniel	1 Maccabees 2 Maccabees Judith Esther additions Daniel additions Baruch
10. The Roman Era 63 B.C. and beyond					Wisdom of Solomon

(R. E. Brown and R. F. Collins, "Canonicity", in *The New Jerome Biblical Commentary*, edited by Brown, Fitzmyer, Murphy [© 1990], 1038. Adapted by permission of Prentice Hall, Englewood Cliffs, New Jersey.)

MAPS

The following maps indicate the position of various sites relative to one another. However, they do not always provide a precise indication of distances between sites. Therefore, no scale is provided.

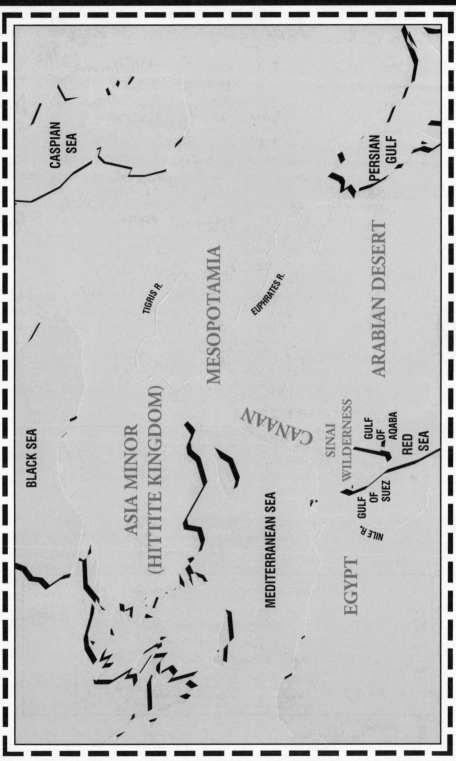

MAP 1: The Ancient Near East

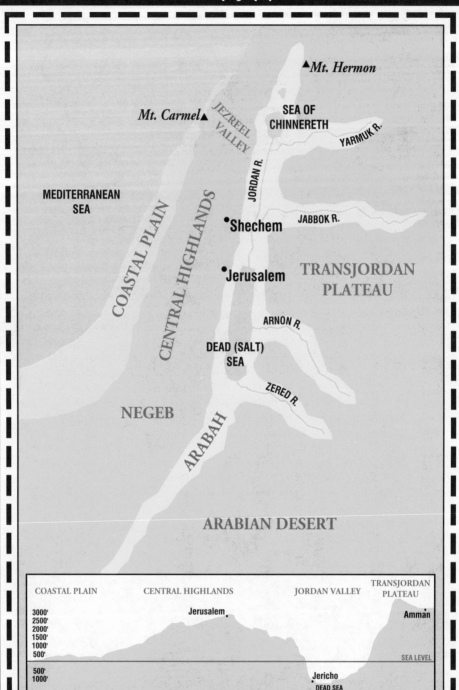

MAP 2: The Topography of Israel

▲*Mt. Hermon*

Mt. Carmel▲

JEZREEL VALLEY

SEA OF CHINNERETH

YARMUK R.

JORDAN R.

MEDITERRANEAN SEA

COASTAL PLAIN

CENTRAL HIGHLANDS

JABBOK R.

•Shechem

•Jerusalem

TRANSJORDAN PLATEAU

ARNON R.

DEAD (SALT) SEA

ZERED R.

NEGEB

ARABAH

ARABIAN DESERT

| COASTAL PLAIN | CENTRAL HIGHLANDS | JORDAN VALLEY | TRANSJORDAN PLATEAU |

3000'
2500'
2000'
1500'
1000'
500'

Jerusalem.

Amman

SEA LEVEL

500'
1000'

Jericho.
DEAD SEA

Cross-section adapted from ATLAS OF THE BIBLE,
by permission of Andromeda Oxford Ltd.

MAP 3: The World of the Patriarchs

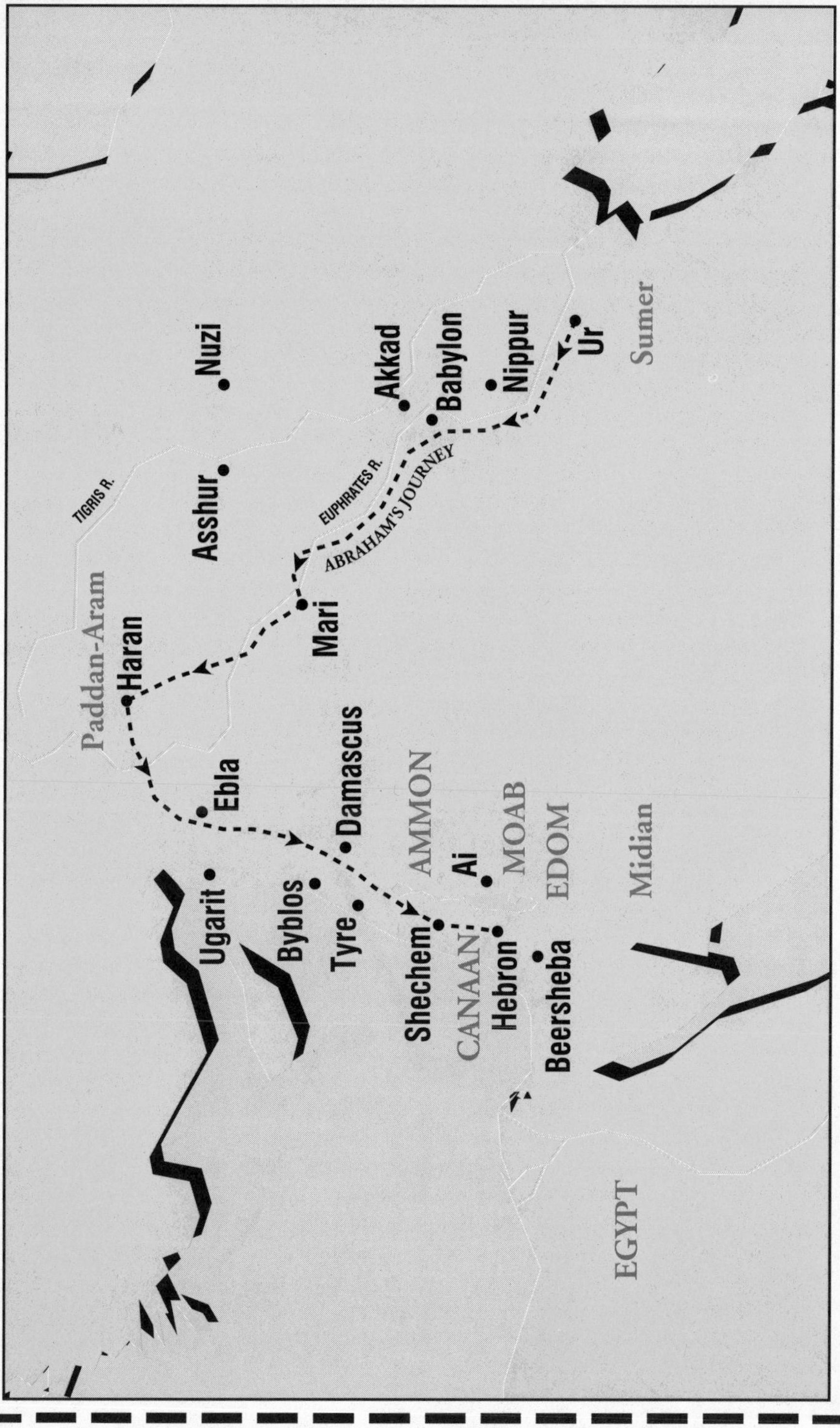

Sumer

Nuzi

Akkad

Babylon

Nippur

Ur

Asshur

TIGRIS R.

EUPHRATES R.

ABRAHAM'S JOURNEY

Paddan-Aram

Mari

Haran

Ebla

Damascus

AMMON

Ugarit

Byblos

Tyre

Shechem

Ai

MOAB

EDOM

Midian

CANAAN

Hebron

Beersheba

EGYPT

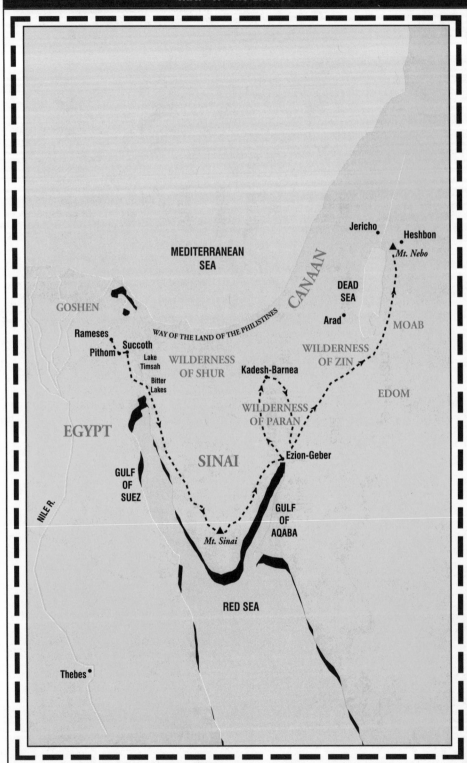

MAP 4: The Exodus

MEDITERRANEAN SEA

CANAAN

Jericho

Heshbon

Mt. Nebo

DEAD SEA

GOSHEN

Arad

MOAB

Rameses

Succoth

Pithom

WAY OF THE LAND OF THE PHILISTINES

Lake Timsah

WILDERNESS OF SHUR

Kadesh-Barnea

WILDERNESS OF ZIN

Bitter Lakes

EDOM

WILDERNESS OF PARAN

EGYPT

SINAI

Ezion-Geber

GULF OF SUEZ

GULF OF AQABA

NILE R.

Mt. Sinai

RED SEA

Thebes

MAP 5: The Settlement in Canaan (c.1200-1010 B.C.)

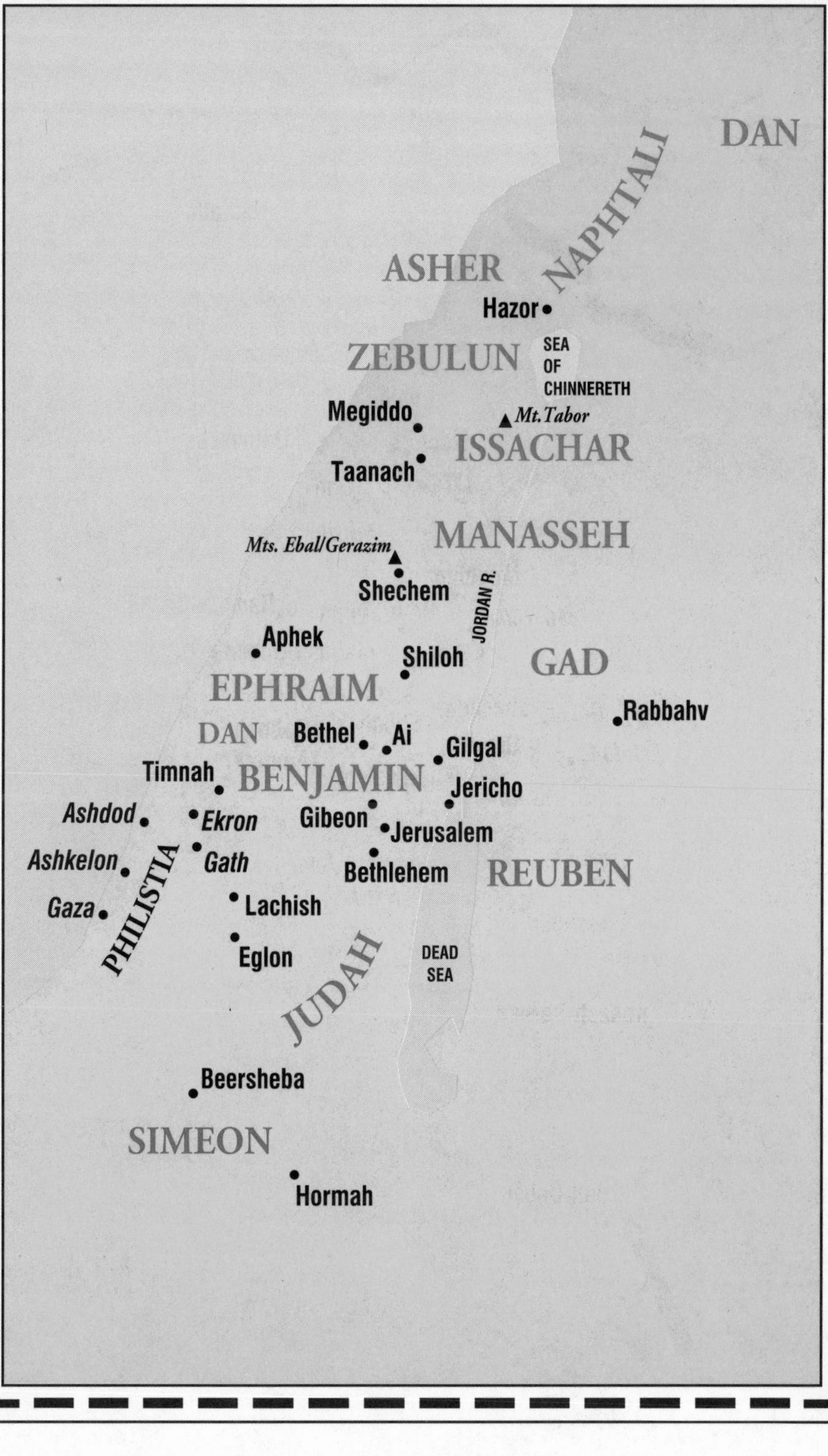

DAN

NAPHTALI

ASHER

Hazor •

ZEBULUN

SEA OF CHINNERETH

Megiddo •

▲ Mt. Tabor

ISSACHAR

Taanach •

MANASSEH

Mts. Ebal/Gerazim ▲

Shechem •

JORDAN R.

Aphek •

Shiloh •

GAD

EPHRAIM

Rabbahv •

DAN

Bethel • Ai •

Gilgal •

Timnah •

BENJAMIN

Jericho •

Ashdod •

Ekron •

Gibeon •

Jerusalem •

Ashkelon •

PHILISTIA

Gath •

Bethlehem •

REUBEN

Gaza •

Lachish •

Eglon •

DEAD SEA

JUDAH

Beersheba •

SIMEON

Hormah •

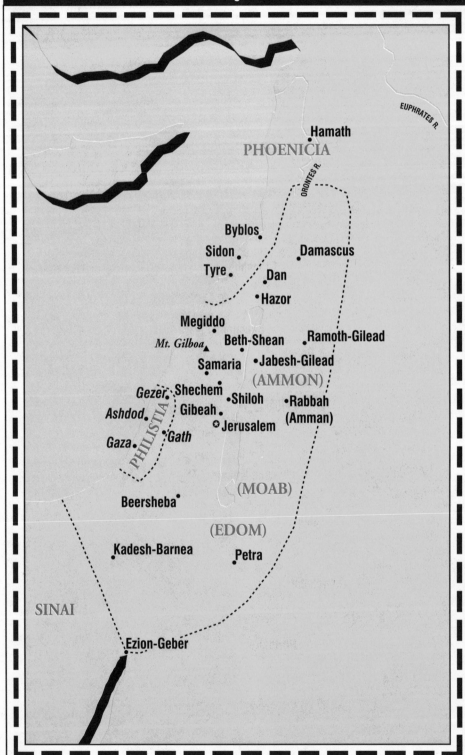

MAP 6: The United Kingdom (c.1030-931 B.C.)

EUPHRATES R.

ORONTES R.

• Hamath

PHOENICIA

Byblos •

Sidon •   • Damascus
Tyre •
                • Dan
                • Hazor

Megiddo •
Mt. Gilboa ▲   • Beth-Shean   • Ramoth-Gilead
          • Samaria   • Jabesh-Gilead
                    (AMMON)
Gezer •   • Shechem
Ashdod •   • Gibeah • Shiloh   • Rabbah
                ✡ Jerusalem   (Amman)
Gaza •   • Gath
PHILISTIA

            (MOAB)

Beersheba •

        (EDOM)

Kadesh-Barnea •   • Petra

SINAI

Ezion-Geber •

MAP 7: Design of Solomon's Temple

I. VIEW FROM ABOVE

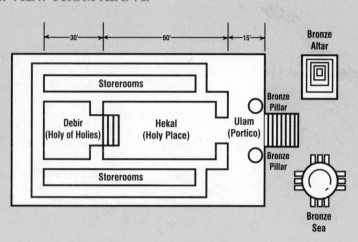

II. FRONTAL VIEW

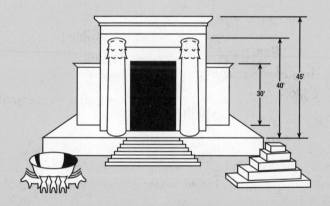

Text References: 1 Kings 6-8; 2 Chronicles 2-4; cf. Ezekiel 40-46

Brown/Fitzmyer/Murphy, THE NEW JEROME BIBLICAL COMMENTARY ©1990, p.1263.
Adapted by permission of Prentice Hall, Englewood Cliffs, New Jersey.

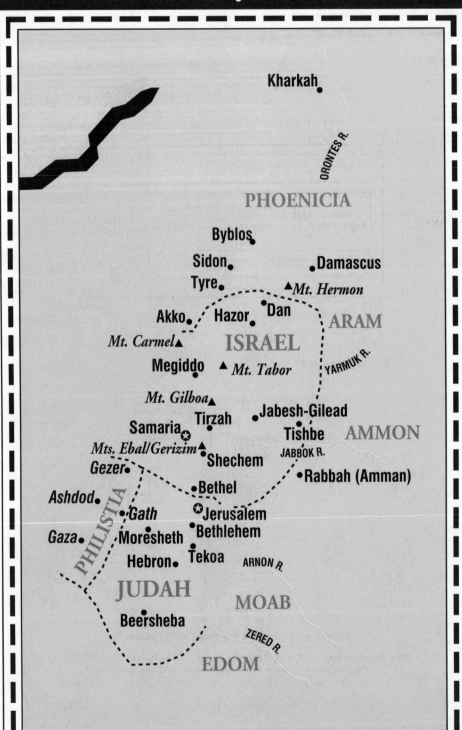

MAP 8: The Divided Kingdom (c.973-721 B.C.)

Kharkah

ORONTES R.

PHOENICIA

Byblos

Sidon

Damascus

Tyre

▲Mt. Hermon

Akko Hazor Dan ARAM

Mt. Carmel▲ ISRAEL

Megiddo ▲ Mt. Tabor YARMUK R.

Mt. Gilboa▲

Tirzah Jabesh-Gilead

Samaria✪ Tishbe AMMON

Mts. Ebal/Gerizim▲ JABBOK R.

Shechem

Gezer Rabbah (Amman)

Bethel

Ashdod PHILISTIA

Gath ✪Jerusalem

Gaza Moresheth Bethlehem

Hebron Tekoa ARNON R.

JUDAH MOAB

Beersheba

ZERED R.

EDOM

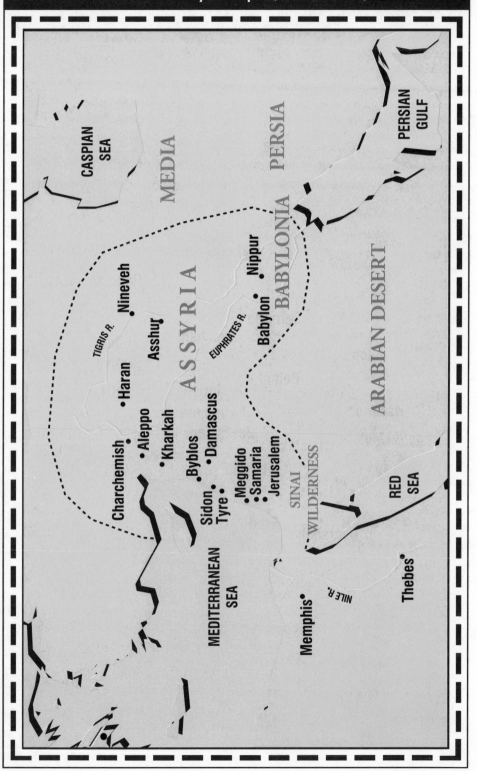

MAP 9: The Assyrian Empire (c.850-612 B.C.)

CASPIAN SEA

MEDIA

PERSIA

PERSIAN GULF

BABYLONIA

Nippur

ASSYRIA

Nineveh

TIGRIS R.

Asshur

Haran

EUPHRATES R.

Babylon

ARABIAN DESERT

Charchemish

Aleppo

Kharkah

Byblos

Damascus

Meggido

Samaria

Jerusalem

Sidon

Tyre

SINAI

WILDERNESS

RED SEA

MEDITERRANEAN SEA

NILE R.

Memphis

Thebes

MAP 10: Judah (721-587 B.C.)

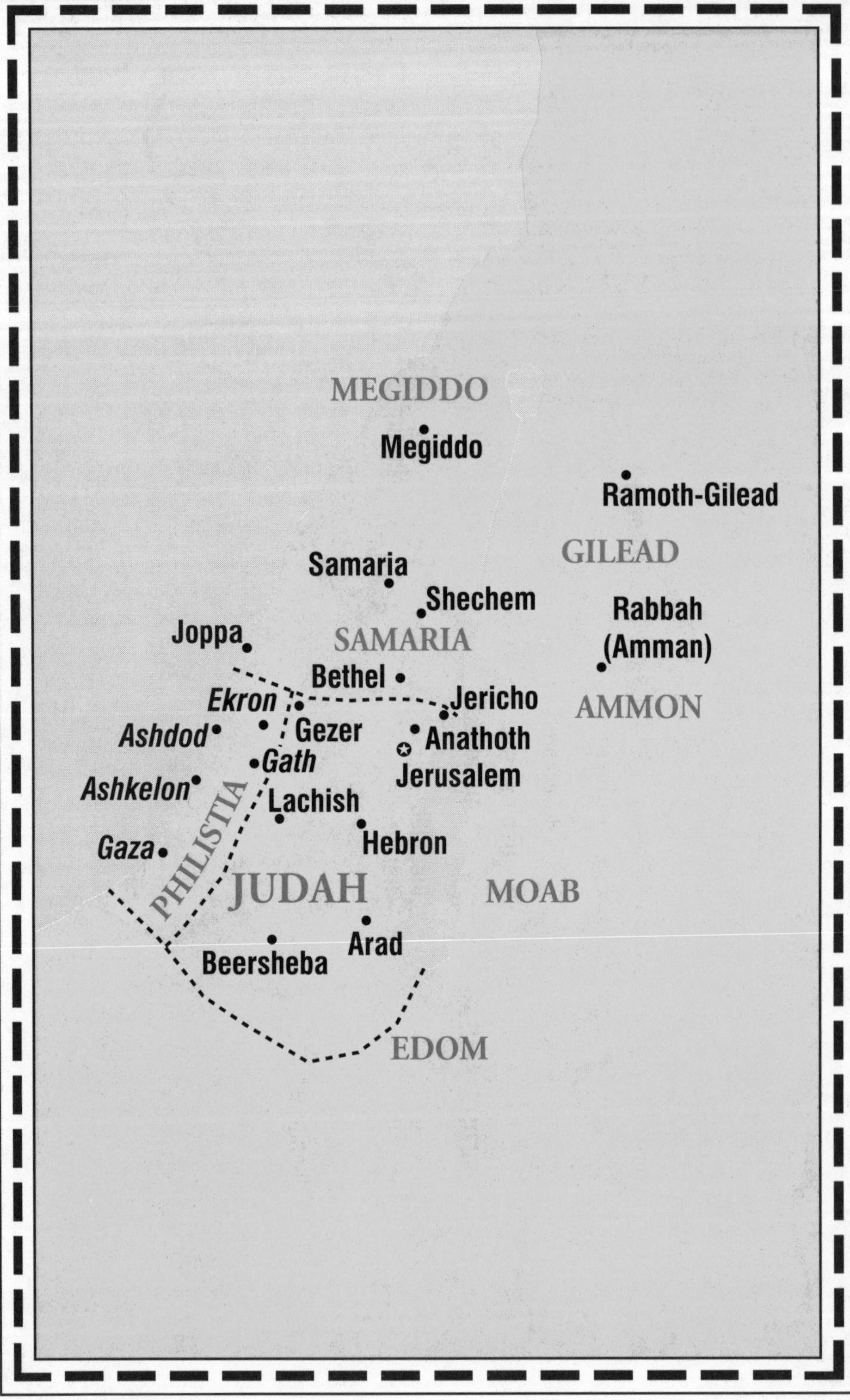

MEGIDDO

Megiddo

Ramoth-Gilead

GILEAD

Samaria

Shechem

Rabbah
(Amman)

Joppa

SAMARIA

Bethel

Jericho

AMMON

Ekron

Gezer

Anathoth

Ashdod

Jerusalem

Gath

Ashkelon

Lachish

PHILISTIA

Hebron

Gaza

JUDAH

MOAB

Beersheba

Arad

EDOM

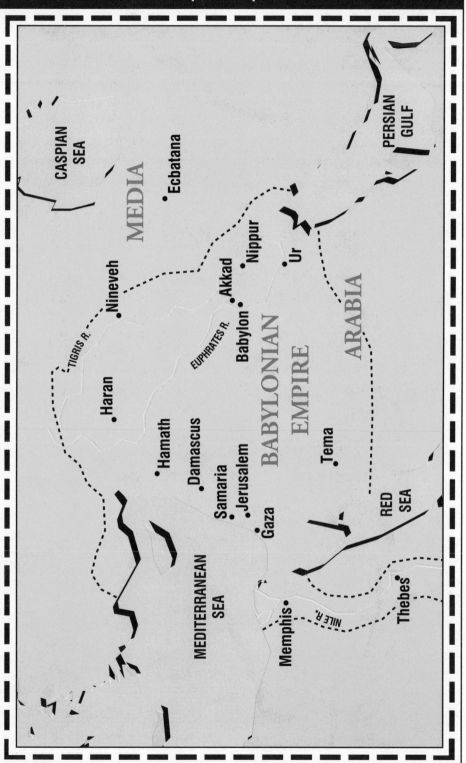

MAP 11: The Babylonian Empire (c.612-538 B.C.)

CASPIAN
SEA

MEDIA

• Ecbatana

PERSIAN
GULF

• Nippur

• Ur

Nineveh •

Akkad •

ARABIA

EUPHRATES R.

Babylon •

TIGRIS R.

Haran •

BABYLONIAN

EMPIRE

• Hamath

• Damascus

Samaria •

Jerusalem •

• Tema

Gaza •

RED
SEA

MEDITERRANEAN
SEA

Memphis •

NILE R.

Thebes •

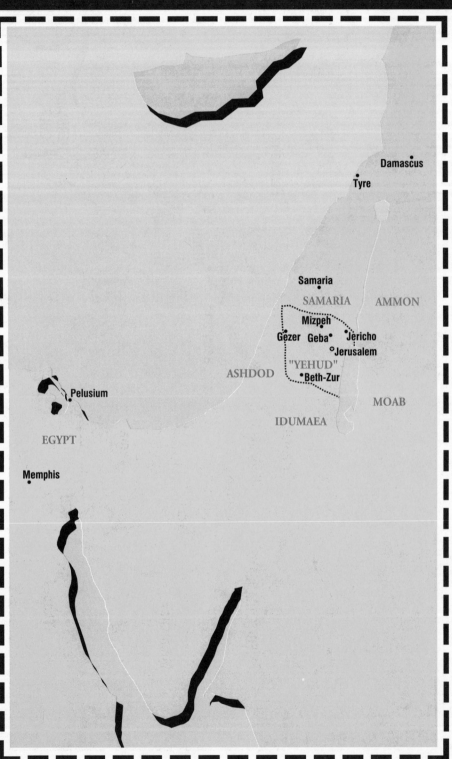

MAP 12: Post -Exilic Judea (460-400 B.C.)

Damascus

Tyre

Samaria

SAMARIA

AMMON

Mizpeh

Gezer   Geba   Jericho

Jerusalem

"YEHUD"

ASHDOD   Beth-Zur

MOAB

IDUMAEA

Pelusium

EGYPT

Memphis

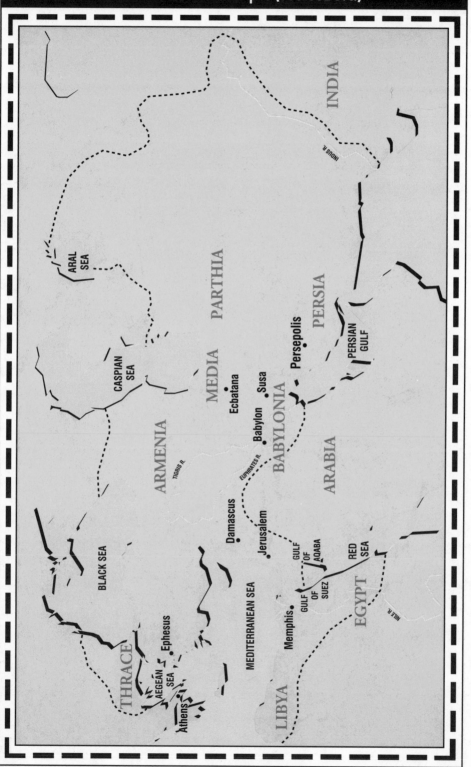

MAP 13: The Persian Empire (538-332 B.C.)

INDIA

INDUS R.

ARAL SEA

PARTHIA

PERSIA

MEDIA

PERSIAN GULF

CASPIAN SEA

Ecbatana

Susa

Babylon

Persepolis

ARMENIA

BABYLONIA

TIGRIS R.

EUPHRATES R.

ARABIA

Damascus

Jerusalem

GULF OF AQABA

RED SEA

BLACK SEA

MEDITERRANEAN SEA

GULF OF SUEZ

Memphis

EGYPT

NILE R.

THRACE

AEGEAN SEA

Ephesus

Athens

LIBYA

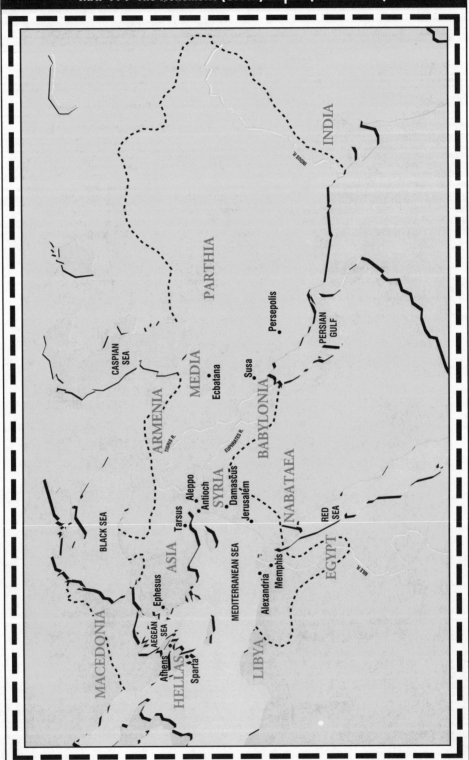

MAP 14 : The Hellenistic (Greek) Empire (323-63 B.C.)

INDIA

INDUS R.

PARTHIA

Persepolis

PERSIAN GULF

CASPIAN SEA

MEDIA

Ecbatana

Susa

ARMENIA

BABYLONIA

TIGRIS R.

EUPHRATES R.

SYRIA

NABATAEA

Aleppo

Antioch

Damascus

Jerusalem

RED SEA

Tarsus

BLACK SEA

ASIA

MEDITERRANEAN SEA

EGYPT

NILE R.

MACEDONIA

Ephesus

AEGEAN SEA

Alexandria

Memphis

Athens

HELLAS

Sparta

LIBYA

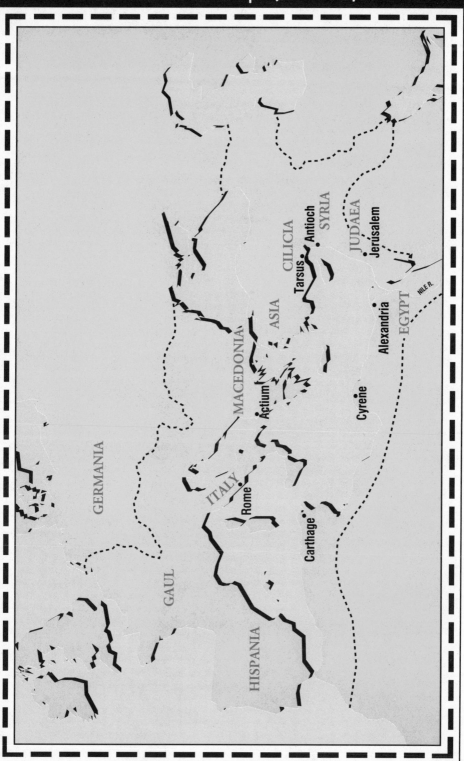

MAP 15 : The Roman Empire (after 63 B.C.)

GERMANIA

GAUL

HISPANIA

ITALY

Rome

Carthage

MACEDONIA

Actium

Cyrene

ASIA

CILICIA

Tarsus

Antioch

SYRIA

JUDAEA

Jerusalem

Alexandria

EGYPT

NILE R.

BIBLIOGRAPHY

GENERAL BIBLIOGRAPHY

Bibles:

Biblia Hebraica Stuttgartensia. Stuttgart: Deutsche Bibelgesellschaft, 1983.
The Catholic Study Bible. New American Bible. Edited by Donald Senior. New York: Oxford University Press, 1990.
The Greek New Testament. 3d ed. Edited by Kurt Aland, et al. New York: United Bible Societies, 1975.
Holy Bible: New Revised Standard Version with Apocrypha. Edited by Bruce M. Metzger. New York and Oxford: Oxford University Press, 1989.
New Jerusalem Bible. Edited by Henry Wansbrough, et al. Garden City, NY: Doubleday & Co., 1985.
The Revised English Bible with the Apocrypha. Edited by Donald Coggan. Oxford University Press and Cambridge University Press, 1989.
Septuaginta I and II. Edited by Alfred Rahlfs. Stuttgart: Württembergische Bibelanstalt, 1971.

Dictionaries of the Bible:

Achtemeier, Paul J., ed. *Harper's Bible Dictionary.* San Francisco: Harper and Row, 1985.
Botterweck, G. Johannes, and Ringgren, Helmer, eds. *Theological Dictionary of the Old Testament.* Translated by John T. Willis. 6 vols. Grand Rapids, MI: William B. Eerdmans Publishing Co., 1974, 1975, 1978, 1980, 1986, 1990.
Buttrick, George Arthur, et al., eds. *The Interpreter's Dictionary of the Bible.* 4 vols. Nashville and New York: Abingdon Press, 1962.
Crim, Keith, et al., eds. *The Interpreter's Dictionary of the Bible. Supp. Vol.* Nashville: Abingdon Press, 1976.
Léon-Dufour, Xavier, ed. *Dictionary of Biblical Theology.* 2d ed., rev. Translated by P. J. Cahill. New York: Seabury Press, 1973.
McKenzie, John L. *Dictionary of the Bible.* New York: Macmillan Publishing Co., 1965; London: Geoffrey Chapman, 1968.

One-Volume Commentaries on the Bible:

Bergant, Dianne, and Karris, Robert J., eds. *The Collegeville Bible Commentary.* Collegeville, MN: The Liturgical Press, 1989.

Brown, R. E.; Fitzmyer, J. A.; and Murphy, R. E., eds. *The Jerome Biblical Commentary.* Englewood Cliffs, NJ: Prentice-Hall, 1968.

Brown, R. E.; Fitzmyer, J. A.; and Murphy, R. E., eds. *The New Jerome Biblical Commentary.* Englewood Cliffs, NJ: Prentice Hall, 1990.

Mays, James L., ed. *Harper's Bible Commentary.* San Francisco: Harper and Row, 1988.

Biblical History and Archaeology:

Albright, William Foxwell. *From the Stone Age to Christianity: Monotheism and the Historical Process.* 2d ed. Garden City, NY: Doubleday, Anchor Books, 1957.

Bright, John. *A History of Israel.* 3d ed. Philadelphia: Westminster Press, 1981.

Cornfeld, Gaalyah, and Freedman, David Noel. *Archaeology of the Bible: Book by Book.* Peabody, MA: Hendrickson Publishers, 1989.

De Vaux, Roland. *Ancient Israel: Its Life and Institutions.* Translated by John McHugh. London: Darton, Longman & Todd, 1973.

Filson, Floyd V. *A New Testament History.* London: SCM Press, 1974.

Finegan, Jack. *Archaeological History of the Ancient Middle East.* New York: Dorset Press, 1979.

Hammond, N. G. L., and Scullard, H. H., eds. *The Oxford Classical Dictionary.* 2d ed. Oxford: Oxford University Press, Clarendon, 1987.

Kraft, Robert A., and Nickelsburg, George W. E., eds. *Early Judaism and Its Modern Interpreters.* Atlanta: Scholars Press, 1986.

Leaney, A. R. C. *The Jewish & Christian World 200 B.C. to A.D. 200.* Cambridge Commentaries on Writings of the Jewish & Christian World 200 BC to AD 200, vol. 7. New York: Cambridge University Press, 1984.

Lohse, Eduard. *The New Testament Environment.* Translated by John E. Steely. Nashville: Abingdon Press, 1976.

North, Robert, and King, Philip J. "Biblical Archaeology". *NJBC,* 1196–1218.

Olmstead, A. T. *History of the Persian Empire.* Chicago and London: University of Chicago Press, 1948.

Orlinsky, Harry M. *Understanding the Bible through History and Archaeology.* New York: KTAV Publishing House, 1972.

Reicke, Bo. *The New Testament Era: The World of the Bible from 500 B.C. to A.D. 100.* Translated by David E. Green. Philadelphia: Fortress Press, 5th printing, 1985.

Safrai, S., and Stern, M., eds. *The Jewish People in the First Century.* 2 vols. Philadelphia: Fortress Press, 2d printing, 1974, 1987.

Saggs, H. W. F. *Everyday Life in Babylonia & Assyria.* New York: Dorset Press, 1987.

Wright, Addison G.; Murphy, Roland E.; and Fitzmyer, Joseph A. "A History of Israel". *NJBC,* 1219–52.

Würthwein, Ernst. *The Text of the Old Testament: An Introduction to the Biblia Hebraica.* Translated by Erroll F. Rhodes. Reprint. Grand Rapids, MI: William B. Eerdmans Publishing Co., 1985.

Extrabiblical Texts:

Charles, R. H., ed. *The Apocrypha and Pseudepigrapha of the Old Testament in English.* Vol. 2: *Pseudepigrapha.* Oxford: Clarendon Press, 1973.
Charlesworth, James H., ed. *The Old Testament Pseudepigrapha.* 2 vols. Garden City, NY: Doubleday & Co., 1983, 1985.
Gaster, Theodor H. *The Dead Sea Scriptures.* 3d ed., rev. and enl. English trans. Garden City, NY: Anchor Books (Anchor Press, Doubleday), 1976.
Heidel, Alexander, trans. *The Babylonian Genesis: The Story of Creation.* 2d ed. Chicago and London: University of Chicago Press, 8th impression, 1974.
Heidel, Alexander, trans. *The Gilgamesh Epic and Old Testament Parallels.* Chicago and London: University of Chicago Press, 9th impression, 1973.
Pritchard, James B., ed. *Ancient Near Eastern Texts Relating to the Old Testament.* 3d ed. with supp. Princeton, NJ: Princeton University Press, 1969.
Whiston, William, trans. *The Works of Flavius Josephus.* 4 vols. Grand Rapids, MI: Baker Book House, 12th printing, 1985.

Introductions to the Old Testament:

Anderson, Bernard W. *Understanding the Old Testament.* 3d ed. Englewood Cliffs, NJ: Prentice-Hall, 1975.
Boadt, Lawrence E. *Reading the Old Testament: An Introduction.* New York: Paulist Press, 1984.
Eissfeldt, Otto. *The Old Testament: An Introduction.* Translated by Peter R. Ackroyd. Oxford: Basil Blackwell, 1966.
Fohrer, Georg. *Introduction to the Old Testament.* Translated by David Green. London: S. P. C. K., 1968.
Jensen, Joseph. *God's Word to Israel.* Rev. ed. Wilmington, DE: Michael Glazier, 4th printing, 1988.

Theologies of the Old Testament:

Eichrodt, Walther. *Theology of the Old Testament.* 2 vols. Translated by John A. Baker. London: SCM Press, 1961, 1967.
Von Rad, Gerhard. *Old Testament Theology. I. The Theology of Israel's Historical Traditions. II. The Theology of Israel's Prophetic Traditions.* Translated by D. M. G. Stalker. Edinburgh-London: Oliver and Boyd, 1962, 1965.

Specific Issues in Old Testament Theology:

Collins, John J. *The Apocalyptic Imagination: An Introduction to the Jewish Matrix of Christianity.* New York: Crossroad, 1987.

Craigie, Peter C. *The Problem of War in the Old Testament.* Grand Rapids, MI: William B. Eerdmans Publishing Co., 1978.

Hanson, Paul D. *The Dawn of Apocalyptic: The Historical and Sociological Roots of Jewish Apocalyptic Eschatology.* Rev. ed. Philadelphia: Fortress Press, 2d printing, 1983.

Koch, Klaus. *The Prophets. I. The Assyrian Period, II. The Babylonian and Persian Periods.* Translated by Margaret Kohl. Philadelphia: Fortress Press, 1982; pap. 2d printing, 1985, 1986.

Koch, Klaus. *The Rediscovery of Apocalyptic.* Translated by Margaret Kohl. London: SCM Press, 2d impression, 1981.

McCarthy, Dennis J. *Treaty and Covenant.* Analecta Biblica, 21. Rome: Pontifical Biblical Institute, 1963.

Mowinckel, Sigmund. *He That Cometh: The Messiah Concept in the Old Testament and Later Judaism.* Translated by G. W. Anderson. Nashville and New York: Abingdon Press, 1954.

Rowley, H. H. *Faith in Israel: Aspects of Old Testament Thought.* London: SCM Press, 6th impression, 1974.

Rowley, H. H. *The Servant of the Lord and Other Essays on the Old Testament.* 2d ed., rev. Oxford: Basil Blackwell, 1965.

Von Rad, Gerhard. *Wisdom in Israel.* Translated by James D. Martin. London, SCM Press, 2d impression, 1975.

Westermann, Claus. *What Does the Old Testament Say about God?* Edited by Friedemann W. Golka. Atlanta: John Knox Press, 1979.

Wolff, Hans Walter. *Anthropology of the Old Testament.* Translated by Margaret Kohl. Philadelphia: Fortress Press, 1974.

Literary Approaches to the Old Testament:

Ackroyd, P. R., and Evans, C. F., eds. *The Cambridge History of the Bible. I. From the Beginnings to Jerome;* Lampe, G. W. H., ed. *II. The West from the Fathers to the Reformation;* Greenslade, S. L., ed. *III. The West from the Reformation to the Present Day.* Reprint. Cambridge: Cambridge University Press, 1976.

Alter, Robert, and Kermode, Frank, eds. *The Literary Guide to the Bible.* Cambridge, MA: Belknap Press of Harvard University Press, 1987.

Childs, Brevard S. *Introduction to the Old Testament as Scripture.* Philadelphia: Fortress Press, 2d printing, 1980.

Childs, Brevard S. *Old Testament Theology in a Canonical Context.* Philadelphia: Fortress Press, 1986.

SPECIFIC BIBLIOGRAPHY

I. THE OLD TESTAMENT:

In keeping with the popular tone of this introduction to the Old Testament, I have limited the scholarly apparatus to a minimum. Obviously, I am indebted to all the sources I studied. The following are the major works I consulted in the composition of each chapter.

Edition of the Biblical Text:

New Jerusalem Bible, edited by Henry Wansbrough, et al. (Garden City, NY: Doubleday & Co., 1985). In composing every chapter of this book, I drew upon the wealth of reference material in the *NJB,* including: the essays that introduce each book, the outline of each book, the footnotes to specific verses and themes, the cross-references to various biblical texts, the chronological chart, the table of measures, and the maps.

Abbreviations

AI = *Ancient Israel: Its Life and Institutions.* By Roland de Vaux. Translated by John McHugh. London: Darton, Longman & Todd, 1973.

AB = Anchor Bible. Garden City, NY: Doubleday & Co.

GWI = *God's Word to Israel.* Rev. ed. By Joseph Jensen. Wilmington, DE: Michael Glazier, 4th printing, 1988.

HBA = *Harper's Atlas of the Bible.* Edited by James B. Pritchard, et al. New York: Harper & Row, 1987.

HBC = *Harper's Bible Commentary.* Edited by James L. Mays. San Francisco: Harper and Row, 1988.

HBD = *Harper's Bible Dictionary.* Edited by Paul J. Achtemeier. San Francisco: Harper and Row, 1985.

HI = *A History of Israel.* 3d ed. By John Bright. Philadelphia: Westminster Press, 1981.

IDB = *The Interpreter's Dictionary of the Bible.* 4 vols. Edited by George Arthur Buttrick, et al. Nashville and New York: Abingdon Press, 1962.

IDBsv = *The Interpreter's Dictionary of the Bible Supplementary Volume.* Edited by Keith Crim, et al. Nashville: Abingdon, 1976.

IOTS = *Introduction to the Old Testament as Scripture.* By Brevard S. Childs. Philadelphia: Fortress Press, 2d printing, 1980.

JBC = *The Jerome Biblical Commentary*. Edited by R. E. Brown, J. A. Fitzmyer, and R. E. Murphy. Englewood Cliffs, NJ: Prentice-Hall, 1968.

LGB = *The Literary Guide to the Bible*. Edited by Robert Alter and Frank Kermode. Cambridge, MA: Belknap Press of Harvard University Press, 1987.

NJB = *The New Jerusalem Bible*. Edited by Henry Wansbrough et al. Garden City, NY: Doubleday & Co., 1985.

NJBC = *The New Jerome Biblical Commentary*. Edited by R. E. Brown, J. A. Fitzmyer, and R. E. Murphy. Englewood Cliffs, NJ: Prentice Hall, 1990.

OTL = *The Old Testament Library*. London: SCM Press.

OTT = *Old Testament Theology. I. The Theology of Israel's Historical Traditions. II. The Theology of Israel's Prophetic Traditions*. By Gerhard von Rad. Translated by D. M. G. Stalker. Edinburgh and London: Oliver and Boyd, 1962, 1965.

PRPH = *The Prophets. I. The Assyrian Period* and *II. The Babylonian and Persian Periods*. By Klaus Koch, translated by Margaret Kohl. Philadelphia: Fortress Press, 1982; pap. 2d printing, 1985, 1986.

ROTI = *Reading the Old Testament: An Introduction*. By Lawrence Boadt. New York: Paulist Press, 1984.

TDOT = *Theological Dictionary of the Old Testament*. 6 vols. Edited by Johannes G. Botterweck and Helmer Ringgren. Translated by John T. Willis. Grand Rapids, MI: Eerdmans Publishing Co., 1974, 1975, 1978, 1980, 1986, 1990.

WBC = *Word Biblical Commentary*. Waco, TX: Word Books.

WI = *Wisdom in Israel*. By Gerhard von Rad. Translated by James D. Martin. London: SCM Press, 2d impression, 1975.

General Introduction

"Dogmatic Constitution on Divine Revelation [*Dei Verbum*]". Austin P. Flannery, ed. *Documents of Vatican II*. Grand Rapids, MI: William B. Eerdmans Publishing Co., 1978, 750–65.

Ratzinger, J.; Grillmeier, A.; and Rigaux, B. "Dogmatic Constitution on Divine Revelation". *Commentary on the Documents of Vatican II*. Vol. III. Edited by Herbert Vorgrimler. London: Burns and Oates; New York: Herder and Herder, 1968.

Chapter 1: The Old Testament Library

Boadt, Lawrence. "Introducing the Old Testament". *ROTI,* 11–27.
Brown, Raymond E., and Collins, Raymond F. "Canonicity". *NJBC,* 1034–54.
Brown, Raymond E.; Johnson, D. W.; and O'Connell, Kevin G. "Texts and Versions". *NJBC,* 1083–112.
Bruce, F. F. *The Canon of Scripture.* Downers Grove, IL: InterVarsity Press, 1988.
Freedman, D. N. "Canon of the OT". *IDBsv,* 130–36.
Pfeiffer, R. H., "Canon of the OT". *IDB* I, 498–520.
Würthein, Ernst. *The Text of the Old Testament.* Translated by Erroll F. Rhodes. Grand Rapids, MI: William B. Eerdmans Publishing Co., 1979.

Chapter 2: People, Places, and Events

Archaeology:

Hoade, Eugene. *Guide to the Holy Land.* 7th ed. Jerusalem: Franciscan Printing Press, 1974.
Orlinsky, Harry M. *Understanding the Bible through History and Archaeology.* New York: KTAV Publishing House, 1972.
North, Robert, and King, Philip J. "Biblical Archaeology". *NJBC,* 1196–218.

Geography:

Aharoni, Yohanan, and Avi-Yonah, Michael. *The Macmillan Bible Atlas.* Rev. ed. New York: Macmillan Publishing Co., 1977.
Baly, Denis. *The Geography of the Bible.* New York-Evanston-London: Harper and Row, 1957.
Beitzel, Barry J. *The Moody Atlas of Bible Lands.* Chicago: Moody Press, 1985.
Boadt, Lawrence. "The People and Lands of the Old Testament". *ROTI,* 28–51.
Brown, Raymond E., and North, Robert. "Biblical Geography". *NJBC,* 1175–95.
Hoade, Eugene. *Guide to the Holy Land.* Jerusalem: Franciscan Printing Press, 1975.
Hunt, Ignatius. "Israel and Her Neighbors". *JBC* I, 210–22.
Jensen, Joseph. "Panorama". *GWI,* 22–28.
Pritchard, James B., ed. *The Harper Atlas of the Bible.* New York: Harper & Row, 1987.

History:

Bright, John. *A History of Israel.* 3d ed. Philadelphia: Westminster Press, 1981.

Chapter 3: The History of Writing the Old Testament

Brown, Raymond E., and Collins, Raymond F., "Canonicity". *NJBC,* 1034–54.
Freedman, D. N.. "Canon of the OT". *IDBsv,* 130–36.
Wansbrough, Henry, ed. *NJB:*
    "Introduction to the Pentateuch". 5–16;
    "Introduction to the Books of Joshua, Judges, Ruth, Samuel and Kings".
       273–83;
    "Introduction to Tobit, Judith and Esther". 621–24;
    "Introduction to the Books of Maccabees". 674–77;
    "Introduction to the Wisdom Books". 749–52;
    "Introduction to the Book of Job". 753–56;
    "Introduction to the Psalms". 809–15;
    "Introduction to the Proverbs". 964–65;
    "Introduction to Ecclesiastes". 1012–13;
    "Introduction to the Song of Songs". 1027–29;
    "Introduction to the Book of Wisdom". 1042–44;
    "Introduction to Ecclesiasticus". 1076–78;
    "Introduction to the Prophets". 1157–89.

Chapter 4. The Pentateuch: Its Structure

Freedman, D. N. "Pentateuch". *IDB* III, 711–27.

Chapter 5: The Pentateuch: Its Outline and Historical Setting

Bright, John. "The Age of the Patriarchs". *HI,* 45–104.
    "Exodus and Conquest: The Formation of the People Israel". *HI,* 107–43.
Cornfeld, Gaalyah, and Freedman, David Noel. *Archaeology of the Bible: Book by Book.* Peabody, MA: Hendrickson Publishers, 1989. 5–66.
Haran, M. "The Exodus". *IDBsv,* 304–10.
Murphy, Roland E. "From Abraham to Pompey". In "A History of Israel". *NJBC,* 1224–26.
Pritchard, James B., et al., *HBA:*

"Ramesses II of Egypt in Contest with the Hittite Empire". 48–49.
"The Campaign of Pharaoh Merneptah". 51.
"Exodus and the Wanderings". 56–57.

Chapter 6: The Pentateuch: Its Sources and Formation

Boadt, Lawrence. "The Pentateuch". *ROTI,* 89–108.
Brueggemann, W. "Yahwist". *IDBsv,* 971–75.
Eissfeldt, Otto. "The Pentateuch". *The Old Testament. An Introduction.* Translated by Peter R. Ackroyd. Oxford: Basil Blackwell, 1966. 155–241.
Fohrer, Georg. "The Pentateuch". *Introduction to the Old Testament.* Translated by David Green. London: S. P. C. K., 2d impression, 1974. 103–95.
Freedman, D. N. "Pentateuch". *IDB* III, 711–27.
Fretheim, T. E. "Elohist". *IDBsv,* 259–63.
Jensen, Joseph. "The Composition of the Pentateuch". *GWI,* 29–42.
Lohfink, N. "Deuteronomy". *IDBsv,* 229–32.
Maly, Eugene H. "Introduction to the Pentateuch". *JBC* I, 1–6.
Murphy, Roland E. "Introduction to the Pentateuch". *NJBC,* 3–7.
Von Rad, Gerhard. "A History of Jahwism and of the Sacral Institutions in Israel in Outline". "The Theology of Israel's Historical Traditions". *OTT* I, 1–102, 103–305.

Chapters 7–8: Genesis

Boadt, Lawrence. "Genesis 1–11: The Preface to Israel's Story". "Genesis 12–50: The Patriarchs". *ROTI,* 109–32, 133–54.
Childs, Brevard S. "Genesis". *IOTS,* 136–60.
De Vaux, Roland. "The Family". "Marriage". *AI,* 19–23, 24–38.
Eissfeldt, O. "Genesis". *IDB* II, 366–80.
Fokkelmann, J. P. "Genesis". *LGB,* 36–55.
Jensen, Joseph. "Primeval History". "A Wandering Aramean". *GWI,* 43–64, 65–93.
Kselman, John S. "Genesis". *HBC,* 85–128.
Maly, E. H. "Genesis". *JBC* I, 7–46.
Vawter, Bruce. *On Genesis. A New Reading.* Garden City, NY: Doubleday & Company, 1977.
Von Rad, Gerhard. *Genesis: A Commentary.* Rev. ed. (OTL) Translated by John H. Marks. London: SCM Press, 1972.
Wenham, G. J. *Genesis 1–15.* (WBC, 1) 1987.

Westermann, Claus. *Genesis I–II: A Commentary.* Translated by John J. Scullion. Minneapolis: Augsburg Publishing House, 1984.

Westermann, C., and Albertz, R. "Genesis". *IDBsv,* 356–61.

Chapter 9: Exodus

Boadt, Lawrence. "The Exodus from Egypt". "The Covenant and Journey to Canaan". *ROTI,* 155–72, 173–94.

Childs, Brevard S. *The Book of Exodus: A Critical, Theological Commentary.* (OTL) Philadelphia: The Westminster Press, 1974.

Childs, Brevard S. "Exodus". *IOTS,* 161–79.

Durham, John I. *Exodus.* (WBC, 3) 1987.

Fokkelman, J. P. "Exodus". *LGB,* 56–65.

Huesman, John E. "Exodus". *JBC* I, 47–66.

Jensen, Joseph. " 'Out of Egypt I Called My Son' ". *GWI,* 74–93.

McCarter, P. Kyle, Jr. "Exodus". *HBC,* 129–56.

McKenzie, John L. "Aspects of Old Testament Thought: The God of Israel". "Israel—God's Covenant People". *NJBC,* 1285–94, 1295–301.

Mendenhall, G. E. "Covenant". *IDB* I, 714–23.

Riemann, P. A. "Covenant, Mosaic". *IDBsv,* 192–97.

Weinfeld, M. "Bᵉrîth". *TDOT* II, 253–79.

Chapter 10: Leviticus

Castelot, John J., and Cody, Aelred. "The Priesthood". "Altars and Sacrifices". *NJBC,* 1254–59, 1266–75.

Childs, Brevard S. "Leviticus". *IOTS,* 180–89.

Damrosch, David. "Leviticus". *LGB,* 66–77.

De Vaux, Roland. "The Ritual of Sacrifice". "The History of Sacrifice in Israel". "The Origin of Israelite Ritual". "The Religious Significance of Sacrifice". *AI,* 415–23, 424–32, 433–46, 447–56.

Faley, Roland J. "Leviticus". *JBC* I, 67–85.

Hayes, John H. "Leviticus". *HBC,* 157–81.

Milgrom, J. "Leviticus". "Sacrifices and Offerings, OT". *IDBsv,* 541–45, 763–71.

Noth, Martin. *Leviticus: A Commentary.* Rev. ed. (OTL) Translated by J. E. Anderson. Philadelphia: Westminster Press, 1977.

Wenham, G. J. *The Book of Leviticus.* The New International Commentary on the Old Testament. Reprint. Grand Rapids, MI: William B. Eerdmans Publishing Co., 1988.

Chapter 11: Numbers

Ackerman, James S. "Numbers". *LGB,* 78–91.
Budd, Philip J. *Numbers.* (WBC, 5) 1984.
Childs, Brevard S. "Numbers". *IOTS,* 190–201.
Moriarty, Frederick L. "Numbers". *JBC* I, 86–100.
Noth, Martin. *Numbers: A Commentary.* (OTL) Translated by James D. Martin. Philadelphia: Westminster Press, 1968.
Olson, Dennis T. "Numbers". *HBC,* 182–208.

Chapter 12: Deuteronomy

Blenkinsopp, Joseph. "Deuteronomy". *JBC* I, 101–22.
Childs, Brevard S. "Deuteronomy". *IOTS,* 202–25.
Craigie, Peter C. *The Book of Deuteronomy.* The New International Commentary on the Old Testament. Grand Rapids, MI: William B. Eerdmans Publishing Co., 1976.
Jensen, Joseph. "Deuteronomy and the Deuteronomic School". *GWI,* 100–109.
Lohfink, N. "Deuteronomy". *IDBsv,* 229–32.
McCarthy, Dennis J. *Treaty and Covenant.* Analecta Biblica, 21. Rome: Pontifical Biblical Institute Press, 1963.
Nelson, Richard D. "Deuteronomy". *HBC,* 209–34.
Polzin, Robert. "Deuteronomy". *LGB,* 92–101.
Von Rad, G. "Deuteronomy". *IDB* I, 831–38.
Von Rad, Gerhard. *Deuteronomy: A Commentary.* (OTL) Translated by Dorothea Barton. Philadelphia: Westminster Press, 1966.

Chapter 13: The Deuteronomic History

Boadt, Lawrence. "The Deuteronomist's History". *ROTI,* 374–82.
Childs, Brevard S. "Introduction to the Former Prophets". *IOTS,* 229–38.
Freedman, D. N. "The Deuteronomic History". *IDBsv,* 226–28.
Jensen, Joseph. "Deuteronomy and the Deuteronomic School". "Redemptive Themes in Deuteronomic History". *GWI,* 100–109, 144–47.

Von Rad, Gerhard. "The Granting of the Land of Canaan". "Israel's Anointed".
    OTT I, 296–305, 306–47.

Chapter 14: Joshua and Judges

Joshua:

Boadt, Lawrence. "The Israelite Possession of Canaan: The Books of Joshua
    and Judges". "Canaanite Religion and Culture". *ROTI,* 195–212, 213–26.
Bright, John. "Part Two: The Formative Period". *HI,* 105–82.
Childs, Brevard S. "Joshua". *IOTS,* 239–53.
Coogan, Michael David. "Joshua". *NJBC,* 110–31.
De Moor, J. C. "Ugarit". *IDBsv,* 928–31.
De Vaux, Roland. "War". "The Holy War". *AI,* 247–57, 258–67.
Gunn, David M. "Joshua and Judges". *LGB,* 102–21.
Jensen, Joseph. " 'He Gave Them the Lands of the Nations' ". *GWI,* 110–22.
Kearney, Peter J. "Joshua". *JBC* I, 123–48.
Pritchard, James B., et al. *HBA:*
    "Ugarit—A Centre of Trade and Influence". 44–45.
    "Conquests of Joshua in Canaan". 62–63.
    "Occupation of the Land". 64–65.
    "The Philistines". 66–67.
    "The Heroic Age of the Judges". 68–69.
Rast, Walter E. "Joshua". *HBC,* 235–44.
Soggin, J. Alberto. *Joshua: A Commentary.* (OTL) Translated by R. A. Wilson.
    Philadelphia: Westminster Press, 1972.
Trent, C. Butler. *Joshua.* (WBC, 7) 1983.
Weippert, M. "Canaan, Conquest and Settlement of". *IDBsv,* 125–30.

Judges:

Childs, Brevard S. "Judges". *IOTS,* 254–62.
Crossan, Dominic M. "Judges". *JBC* I, 149–62.
Exum, J. Cheryl. "Judges". *HBC,* 245–61.
O'Connor, M. "Judges". *NJBC,* 132–44.
Soggin, J. Alberto. *Judges: A Commentary.* (OTL) Translated by John Bowden.
    Philadelphia: Westminster Press, 1981.

Chapter 15: 1 and 2 Samuel

Anderson, A. A. "2 Samuel". (WBC, 11) 1989.
Boadt, Lawrence. " 'A King Like Those of Other Nations': The Books of
    Samuel and Kings". *ROTI,* 227–44.

Bright, John. "From Tribal Confederacy to Dynastic State". *HI*, 184–228.
Campbell, Antony F., and Flanagan, James W. "1–2 Samuel". *NJBC*, 145–59.
Childs, Brevard S. "Samuel". *IOTS*, 263–80.
Cohn, Robert L. "1 Samuel". *HBC*, 268–86.
De Vaux, Roland, *AI:*
    "Marriage". 24–38.
    "The Israelite Concept of the State". 91–99.
    "The Person of the King". 100–114.
    "The Royal Household". 115–26.
    "The Administration of the Kingdom". 133–38.
    "Finance and Public Works". 139–42.
Gunn, David M. "2 Samuel". *HBC*, 287–304.
Hertzberg, Hans Wilhelm. *I and II Samuel: A Commentary.* (OTL) Translated by J. S. Bowden. Philadelphia: Westminster Press, 4th printing, 1976.
Klein, Ralph W. *1 Samuel.* (WBC, 10) 1983.
Rosenberg, Joel. "1 and 2 Samuel". *LGB*, 122–45.
Turro, James C. "1–2 Samuel". *JBC* I, 163–78.
Weinfeld, M. "Covenant, Davidic". *IDBsv*, 188–92.

Chapter 16: 1 and 2 Kings

Barré, Lloyd M. *The Rhetoric of Political Persuasion: The Narrative Artistry and Political Intentions of 2 Kings 9–11.* The Catholic Biblical Quarterly Monograph Series, 20. Washington, DC: Catholic Biblical Association of America, 1988.
Boadt, Lawrence. "The Kingdom Split into Two". *ROTI*, 292–308.
Bright, John. "The Independent Kingdoms of Israel and Judah". "The Monarchy: Crisis and Downfall". "Tragedy and Beyond". *HI*, 229–66, 267–339, 341–402.
Castelot, John J., and Cody, Aelred. "The Temple of Jerusalem". *NJBC*, 1262–66.
Childs, Brevard S. "Kings". *IOTS*, 281–301.
De Vaux, Roland. "The Temple at Jerusalem". "The Centralization of the Cult". *AI*, 312–30, 331–44.
De Vries, Simon J. *1 Kings.* (WBC, 12) 1985.
Ellis, Peter F. "1–2 Kings". *JBC* I, 179–209.
Gray, John. *I and II Kings: A Commentary.* 2d rev. ed. (OTL) Philadelphia: Westminster Press, 4th printing, 1976.
Hobbs, T. R. *2 Kings.* (WBC, 13) 1985.
Meyers, Carol L. "The Temple". *HBD*, 1021–29.
Savran, George. "1 and 2 Kings". *LGB*, 146–64.

Walsh, Jerome T., and Begg, Christopher T. "1–2 Kings". *NJBC*, 160–85.

Chapter 17: 1 & 2 Chronicles

Ackroyd, P. R. "Chronicles, I and II". *IDBsv*, 156–58.
Boadt, Lawrence. "Life in the Post-Exilic Community". *ROTI*, 449–71.
Braun, Roddy. *1 Chronicles*. (WBC, 14) 1986.
Bright, John. "The Jewish Community of the Fifth Century: The Reforms of Nehemiah and Ezra". *HI*, 373–402.
Childs, Brevard S. "Chronicles". *IOTS*, 639–55.
De Vaux, Roland. "The Levites". "The Priesthood after the Exile". *AI*, 358–71, 387–405.
Dillard, Raymond B. *2 Chronicles*. (WBC, 15) 1987.
Myers, Jacob M. *I Chronicles; II Chronicles* (AB, 12, 13) 2d ed., 8th printing, 1983.
North, Robert. "The Chronicler: 1–2 Chronicles, Ezra, Nehemiah". *NJBC*, 362–98.
Pfeiffer, R. H. "Chronicles, I and II". *IDB* I, 572–80.
Talmon, Shemaryahu. "1 and 2 Chronicles". *LGB*, 365–72.
Von Rad, Gerhard. "The Historical Work of the Chronicler". *OTT* I, 347–54.

Chapter 18: Ezra and Nehemiah

Bright, John. "The Jewish Community of the Fifth Century: The Reforms of Ezra and Nehemiah". *HI*, 373–402.
Childs, Brevard S. "Ezra and Nehemiah". *IOTS*, 624–38.
Jensen, Joseph. "Ezra and Nehemiah: The Work of the Chronicler". *GWI*, 212–18.
Myers, Jacob M. *Ezra-Nehemiah*. (AB, 14) 9th printing, 1983.
North, Robert. "The Chronicler: 1–2 Chronicles, Ezra, Nehemiah". *NJBC*, 362–98.
Talmon, Shemaryahu. "Ezra and Nehemiah". *LGB*, 357–64.
Williamson, H. G. M. *Ezra-Nehemiah*. (WBC, 16) 1985.

Chapter 19: Introduction to the Prophets

Buss, M. J. "Prophecy in Ancient Israel". *IDBsv*, 694–97.
Childs, Brevard S. "Introduction to the Latter Prophets". *IOTS*, 305–10.

Jensen, Joseph. "Spokesmen for God". *GWI*, 148–57.

Koch, Klaus. *PRPH* I and II.

Napier, B. D. "Prophet, Prophetism". *IDB* III, 896–919.

Vawter, Bruce. "Introduction to Prophetic Literature". *NJBC*, 186–200.

Von Rad, Gerhard. "General Considerations in Prophecy". *OTT* II, 3–125.

Chapter 20: Amos and Hosea

Amos:

Barré, Michael L. "Amos". *NJBC*, 209–16.

Bright, John. "The Internal Sickness of Israel: The First of the Classical Prophets". *HI*, 259–66.

Childs, Brevard S. "Amos". *IOTS*, 395–410.

Jensen, Joseph. "The Pre-Exilic Prophets". *GWI*, 158–86.

King, Philip J. "Amos". *JBC* I, 245–52.

Koch, Klaus. "Unconditional Prophecy of Doom at the Beginning of the Assyrian Period". *PRPH* I, 36–76.

May, James Luther. *Amos: A Commentary.* (OTL) Philadelphia: Westminster Press, 4th printing, 1976.

Smart, J. D. "Amos". *IDB* I, 116–21.

Stuart, Douglas. "Amos". In *Hosea-Jonah.* (WBC, 31) 1987. 274–400.

Von Rad, Gerhard. "Amos and Hosea". *OTT* II, 129–46.

Ward, J. M. "Amos". *IDBsv,* 21–23.

Wolff, Hans Walter. "Amos". In *Joel and Amos* (Hermeneia). Edited by S. Dean McBride, Jr. Translated by Waldemar Janzen, S. Dean McBride, Jr., and Charles A. Muenchow. Philadelphia: Fortress Press, 1977. 87–355.

Hosea:

Andersen, Francis I., and Freedman, David Noel. *Hosea.* (AB, 24) 1st ed., 4th printing, 1985.

Childs, Brevard S. "Hosea". *IOTS,* 373–84.

Koch, Klaus. "Hosea". *PRPH* I, 76–93.

Mays, James Luther. *Hosea. A Commentary.* (OTL) Philadelphia: Westminster Press, 4th printing, 1976.

McCarthy, Dennis J. "Hosea". *JBC* I, 253–64.

Stuart, Douglas. "Hosea". In *Hosea-Jonah.* (WBC, 31) 1987. 2–220.

Von Rad, Gerhard. "The New Element in Eighth-Century Prophecy". *OTT* II, 176–87.

Chapter 21: Isaiah and Micah

Isaiah:

Alonso Schökel, Luis. "Isaiah". *LGB,* 165–83.

Bright, John. "The Period of Assyrian Conquest: From the Mid-Eighth Century to the Death of Hezekiah". *HI,* 269–309.

Childs, Brevard S. "Isaiah". *IOTS,* 311–38.

Jensen, Joseph, and Irwin, William H. "Isaiah 1–39". *NJBC,* 229–48.

Kaiser, Otto. *Isaiah 1–12.* (OTL) Translated by R. A. Wilson. Philadelphia: Westminster Press, 1972.

Koch, Klaus. "Isaiah". *PRPH* I, 105–55.

Millar, William R. *Isaiah 24–27 and the Origin of Apocalyptic.* Harvard Semitic Museum. Harvard Semitic Monograph Series, 11. Missoula, MT: Scholars Press, 1976.

Moriarty, Frederick L. "Isaiah 1–39". *JBC* I, 265–82.

North, C. R. "Isaiah". *IDB* II, 731–44.

Ward, J. M.. "Isaiah". *IDBsv,* 456–61.

Watts, John D. W. *Isaiah 1–33; 34–66.* (WBC, 24 and 25) 1985, 1987.

Von Rad, Gerhard. "Isaiah and Micah". *OTT* II, 147–75.

Micah:

Childs, Brevard S. "Micah". *IOTS,* 428–39.

King, Philip J. "Micah". *JBC* I, 283–89.

Koch, Klaus. "Micah of Moresheth". *PRPH* I, 94–105.

Mays, James Luther. *Micah: A Commentary.* (OTL) Philadelphia: Westminster Press, 1976.

Smith, Ralph L. "Micah". In *Micah-Malachi.* (WBC, 32) 1984. 2–60.

Chapter 22: Zephaniah, Nahum, Habakkuk

Zephaniah:

Bright, John. "The Kingdom of Judah: The Last Century". *HI,* 310–39.

Childs, Brevard S. "Zephaniah". *IOTS,* 457–62.

Koch, Klaus. "The End of Assyria and the Growing Hope for the Day of Yahweh: Joel, Nahum, Zephaniah". *PRPH* I, 157–63.

Smith, Ralph L. "Zephaniah". In *Micah-Malachi.* (WBC, 32) 1984. 120–44.

Wahl, Thomas P. "Zephaniah". *NJBC,* 255–58.

Nahum:

Childs, Brevard S. "Nahum". *IOTS,* 440–46.

Christensen, Duane L. "Nahum". *HBC,* 736–38.

Koch, Klaus. "The End of Assyria and the Growing Hope for the Day of Yahweh: Joel, Nahum, Zephaniah". *PRPH* I, 157–63.

Nowell, Irene. "Nahum". *NJBC,* 258–61.

Smith, Ralph L. "Nahum". In *Micah-Malachi.* (WBC, 32) 1984. 61–90.

Habakkuk:

Ceresko, Anthony R. "Habakkuk". *NJBC,* 261–64.

Childs, Brevard S. "Habakkuk". *IOTS,* 447–56.

Koch, Klaus. "Habakkuk". *PRPH* II, 80–83.

Murphy, Richard T. A. "Habakkuk". *JBC* I, 296–99.

Smith, Ralph L. "Habakkuk". In *Micah-Malachi.* (WBC, 32) 1984. 92–117.

Sweeney, Marvin A. "Habakkuk". *HBC,* 739–41.

Chapter 23: Jeremiah

Boadt, Lawrence. "Jeremiah and the Deuteronomistic History". *ROTI,* 360–82.

Bright, John. *Jeremiah.* (AB, 21) 1965.

Bright, John. "The Kingdom of Judah: The Last Century". *HI,* 310–39.

Childs, Brevard S. "Jeremiah". *IOTS,* 339–54.

Couturier, Guy P. "Jeremiah". *NJBC,* 265–97.

Koch, Klaus. "Jeremiah ben Hilkiah". *PRPH* II, 13–80.

Muilenburg, J. "Jeremiah the Prophet". *IDB* II, 823–35.

O'Connor, Kathleen M. *The Confessions of Jeremiah: Their Interpretation and Role in Chapters 1–25.* SBL Dissertation Series, 94. Atlanta, GA: Scholars Press, 1988.

Rosenberg, Joel. "Jeremiah and Ezekiel". *LGB,* 184–206.

Thompson, J. A. *The Book of Jeremiah.* The New International Commentary on the Old Testament. Grand Rapids, MI: William B. Eerdmans Publishing Co., 1980.

Von Rad, Gerhard. "The Age of Jeremiah". *OTT* II, 188–219.

Chapter 24: Ezekiel

Boadt, Lawrence. "Ezekiel". *NJBC,* 305–28.

Boadt, Lawrence. "Prophecy during the Babylonian Exile". *ROTI,* 383–404.

Childs, Brevard S. "Ezekiel". *IOTS*, 355–72.
Eichrodt, Walther. *Ezekiel: A Commentary.* (OTL) Translated by Cosslett Quin. Philadelphia: Westminster Press, 1970.
Greenberg, Moshe. *Ezekiel 1–20.* (AB, 22) 1983.
Howie, C. G. "Ezekiel". *IDB* II, 203–13.
Jensen, Joseph. "Ezekiel". *GWI*, 189–94.
Koch, Klaus. "Ezekiel ben Buzi". *PRPH* II, 84–118.
Von Rad, Gerhard. "Ezekiel". *OTT* II, 220–37.
Wilson, Robert R. "Ezekiel". *HBC*, 652–94.
Zimmerli, W. "Ezekiel". *IDBsv*, 314–17.
Zimmerli, Walther. *Ezekiel 1; Ezekiel 2.* (Hermeneia) Translated by Ronald E. Clements. Philadelphia: Fortress Press, 1979, 1983.

Chapter 25: Deutero-Isaiah

Bright, John. "Exile and Restoration". *HI*, 343–72.
Clifford, Richard J. "Isaiah 40–66". *HBC*, 571–96.
Koch, Klaus. "Deutero-Isaiah". *PRPH* II, 118–51.
North, Christopher R. *The Second Isaiah: Introduction, Translation and Commentary to Chapters XL–LV.* Oxford: Clarendon Press, 1972.
North, C. R. "The Servant of the Lord". *IDB* IV, 292–94.
Rowley, H. H. "The Servant of the Lord in the Light of Three Decades of Criticism". "The Suffering Servant and the Davidic Messiah". In *The Servant of the Lord and Other Essays on the Old Testament.* 2d ed., rev. Oxford: Basil Blackwell, 1965. 1–60, 61–93.
Stuhlmueller, Carroll. "Deutero-Isaiah". *JBC* I, 366–86.
Stuhlmueller, Carroll. "Deutero-Isaiah and Trito-Isaiah". *NJBC*, 329–48.
Von Rad, Gerhard. "Deutero-Isaiah". *OTT* II, 238–62.
Westermann, Claus. *Isaiah 40–66.* (OTL) Translated by David M. G. Stalker. London: SCM Press, 1969.

Chapter 26: Haggai and Zechariah

Haggai:

Ackroyd, Peter R. "Haggai". *HBC*, 745–46.
Bright, John. "Tragedy and Beyond: The Exilic and Postexilic Periods". *HI*, 341–402.
Childs, Brevard S. "Haggai". *IOTS*, 463–71.
Cody, Aelred. "Haggai". *NJBC*, 349–51.

Koch, Klaus. "Haggai and Zechariah ben Berechiah". *PRPH* II, 159–75.
Neil, W. "Haggai". *IDB* II, 509–11.
Petersen, David L. "Haggai". In *Haggai and Zechariah 1–8. A Commentary.* (OTL) Philadelphia: Westminster Press, 1984. 17–106.
Smith, Ralph L. "Haggai". In *Micah-Malachi.* (WBC, 32) 1984. 146–63.
Stuhlmueller, Carroll. "Haggai". *JBC* I, 387–89.

Zechariah:

Childs, Brevard S. "Zechariah". *IOTS,* 472–87.
Cody, Aelred. "Zechariah". *NJBC,* 352–59.
Hanson, P. D. "Book of Zechariah". *IDBsv,* 982–83.
Neil, W. "Book of Zechariah". *IDB* IV, 943–47.
Petersen, David L. "Zechariah". *HBC,* 747–52.
Petersen, David L. "Zechariah 1–8". *Haggai and Zechariah 1–8. A Commentary.* (OTL) Philadelphia: Westminster Press, 1984. 109–320.
Smith, Ralph L. "Zechariah". In *Micah-Malachi.* (WBC, 32) 1984. 166–241.
Stuhlmueller, Carroll. "Zechariah". *JBC* I, 389–98.

Chapter 27: Trito-Isaiah and Malachi

Trito-Isaiah:

Clifford, Richard J. "Isaiah 40–66". *HBC,* 571–96.
Hanson, Paul D. "Isaiah 56–66 and the Visionary Disciples of Second Isaiah". "The Redactional Framework of Third Isaiah (56:1–8 and 66:17–24)". *The Dawn of Apocalyptic: The Historical and Sociological Roots of Jewish Apocalyptic Eschatology.* Rev. ed. Philadelphia: Fortress Press, 2nd printing, 1983. 32–208, 388–401.
Koch, Klaus. "Trito-Isaiah". *PRPH* II, 152–59.
Stuhlmueller, Carroll. "Deutero-Isaiah". *JBC* I, 366–86.
Stuhlmueller, Carroll. "Deutero-Isaiah and Trito-Isaiah". *NJBC,* 329–48.

Malachi:

Cody, Aelred. "Malachi". *NJBC,* 359–61.
Childs, Brevard S. "Malachi". *IOTS,* 488–98.
Hanson, Paul D. "Malachi". *HBC,* 753–56.
Koch, Klaus. "Malachi". *PRPH* II, 175–82.
Neil, W. "Malachi". *IDB* III, 228–32.
Smith, Ralph L. "Malachi". In *Micah-Malachi.* (WBC, 32) 1984. 296–342.
Stuhlmueller, Carroll. "Malachi". *JBC* I, 398–401.

Chapter 28: Obadiah and Joel

Obadiah:

Bright, John. "Tragedy and Beyond: The Exilic and Postexilic Periods". *HI,* 341–402.
Childs, Brevard S. "Obadiah". *IOTS,* 411–16.
Floyd, Michael H. "Obadiah". *HBC,* 726–27.
Koch, Klaus. "Obadiah". *PRPH* II, 83–84.
Mallon, Elias D. "Obadiah". *NJBC,* 403–5.
Muilenberg, J. "Obadiah". *IDB* III, 578–79.
Stuart, Douglas. "Obadiah". In *Hosea-Jonah.* (WBC, 31) 1987. 402–22.
Wolff, Hans Walter. *Obadiah and Jonah: A Commentary.* Translated by Margaret Kohl. Minneapolis: Augsburg Publishing House, 1986.
Wood, Geoffrey F. "Obadiah". *JBC* I, 443–45.

Joel:

Childs, Brevard S. "Joel". *IOTS,* 385–94.
Mallon, Elias D. "Joel". *NJBC,* 399–403.
Neil, W. "Book of Joel". *IDB* II, 926–29.
Stuart, Douglas. "Joel". In *Hosea-Jonah.* (WBC, 31) 1987. 222–71.
Whedbee, J. William. "Joel". *HBC,* 716–19.
Wolff, Hans Walter. "Joel". In *Joel and Amos.* (Hermeneia) Edited by S. Dean McBride, Jr. Translated by Waldemar Janzen, S. Dean McBride, Jr., and Charles A. Muenchow. Philadelphia: Fortress Press, 1977. 3–86.
Wood, Geoffrey F. "Joel". *JBC* I, 439–43.

Chapter 29: Deutero-Zechariah and Jonah

Deutero-Zechariah:

Cody, Aelred. "Zechariah". *NJBC,* 352–59.
Hanson, P. D. "Book of Zechariah". *IDBsv,* 982–83.
Hanson, Paul D. "Zechariah 9–14 and the Development of the Apocalyptic Eschatology of the Visionaries". In *The Dawn of Apocalyptic: The Historical and Sociological Roots of Jewish Apocalyptic Eschatology.* Rev. ed. Philadelphia: Fortress Press, 2nd printing, 1983. 280–401.
Neil, W. "Book of Zechariah". *IDB* IV, 943–47.
Petersen, David L. "Zechariah". *HBC,* 749–52.
Smith, Ralph L. "Zechariah 9–14". In *Micah-Malachi.* (WBC, 32) 1984. 242–93.
Stuhlmueller, Carroll. "Zechariah". *JBC* I, 389–98.

Jonah:

Ceresko, Anthony R. "Jonah". *NJBC,* 580–84.

Childs, Brevard S. "Jonah". *IOTS,* 417–27.

Koch, Klaus. "The Story of Jonah". *PRPH* II, 182–84.

Landes, G. M. "Book of Jonah". *IDBsv,* 488–91.

McGowan, Jean C. "Jonah". *JBC* I, 633–37.

Stuart, Douglas. "Jonah". In *Hosea-Jonah.* (WBC, 31) 1987. 424–510.

Wolff, Hans Walter. "Jonah". In *Obadiah and Jonah: A Commentary.* Translated by Margaret Kohl. Minneapolis: Augsburg Publishing House, 1986. 75–177.

Chapter 30: Introduction to Wisdom Literature

Blank, S. H. "Wisdom". *IDB* IV, 852–61.

Boadt, Lawrence. "The Cultivation of Wisdom". *ROTI,* 472–91.

Boadt, Lawrence E. "An Introduction to the Wisdom Literature of Israel". *The Collegeville Bible Commentary.* Edited by Dianne Bergant and Robert J. Karris. Collegeville, MN: Liturgical Press, 1989. 634–43.

Childs, Brevard S. "Introduction to the Writings". *IOTS,* 501–3.

Cox, Dermot. "Introduction to Sapiential Literature". In *Proverbs.* Wilmington, DE: Michael Glazier, 1982. 1–79.

Crenshaw, J. L. "Wisdom in the OT". *IDBsv,* 952–56.

Jensen, Joseph. "God's Wisdom in Israel". *GWI,* 232–48.

Murphy, Roland E. "Introduction to Wisdom Literature". *NJBC,* 447–52.

Von Rad, Gerhard, *WI.*

Chapter 31: The Psalms

Childs, Brevard S. "The Psalms". *IOTS,* 504–25.

Dahood, Mitchell. *Psalms. I. 1–50; II. 51–100; III. 101–150.* (AB, 16, 17, 17A) 1966, 1968, 1970.

De Vaux, Roland. "The Person of the King". *AI,* 100–114.

Fitzgerald, Aloysius. "Hebrew Poetry". *NJBC,* 201–8.

Mowinckel, Sigmund. *The Psalms in Israel's Worship.* Translated by D. R. Ap-Thomas. Nashville: Abingdon, 6th printing, 1977.

Murphy, Roland E. "Psalms". *JBC* I, 569–602.

Sabourin, Leopold. *The Psalms: Their Origin and Meaning.* New York: Alba House, 1974.

Weiser, Artur. *The Psalms: A Commentary.* (OTL) Translated by Herbert Hartwell. Philadelphia: Westminster Press, 1962.
Westermann, C. "Book of Psalms". *IDBsv,* 705–10.

Chapter 32: The Proverbs

Blank, S. H. "Book of Proverbs". *IDB* III, 936–40.
Childs, Brevard S. "Proverbs". *IOTS,* 545–59.
Cox, Dermot. *Proverbs.* Wilmington, DE: Michael Glazier, 1982.
De Vaux, Roland. "Marriage". "The Position of Women: Widows". "Children". *AI,* 24–38, 39–40, 41–52.
McCreesh, Thomas P. "Proverbs". *NJBC,* 453–61.
McKane, William. *Proverbs: A New Approach.* (OTL) Philadelphia: Westminster Press, 1970.
Von Rad, Gerhard. "The Self-Revelation of Creation". *WI,* 144–76.
Whybray, R. N. "Book of Proverbs". *IDBsv,* 702–4.
Whybray, R. N. *Wisdom in Proverbs: The Concept of Wisdom in Proverbs 1–9.45.* Studies in Biblical Theology, 45. London: SCM Press, 2nd impression, 1967.
Williams, James G. "Proverbs and Ecclesiastes". *LGB,* 263–82.

Chapter 33: Job

Childs, Brevard S. "Job". *IOTS,* 526–44.
Good, Edwin M. "Job". *HBC,* 407–32.
Greenberg, Moshe. "Job". *LGB,* 283–304.
MacKenzie, R. A. F., and Murphy, Roland E. "Job". *NJBC,* 466–88.
Pope, Marvin H. *Job.* (AB, 15) 1965.
Pope, M. H. "Book of Job". *IDB* II, 911–25.
Rowley, H. H. *Job.* New Century Bible, New Series. Great Britain: Thomas Nelson and Sons, 1970.
Von Rad, Gerhard. "The Book of Job". *WI,* 206–26.
Zuckerman, B. "Book of Job". *IDBsv,* 479–81.

Chapter 34: Ruth and Esther

Ruth:

Berlin, Adele. "Ruth". *HBC,* 262–67.
Campbell, Edward F., Jr. *Ruth.* (AB, 7) 8th printing, 1985.
Childs, Brevard S. "Ruth". *IOTS,* 560–68.
De Vaux, Roland. "The Levirate". "Family Solidarity. The Go'el". *AI,* 37–38, 21–22.
Hals, R. M. "Book of Ruth". *IDBsv,* 758–59.
Hubbard, Robert L., Jr. *The Book of Ruth.* New International Commentary on the Old Testament. Grand Rapids, MI: William B. Eerdmans Publishing Co., 1988.
Laffey, Alice L. "Ruth". *NJBC,* 553–57.
Sasson, Jack M. "Ruth". *LGB,* 320–28.

Esther:

Childs, Brevard S. "Esther". *IOTS,* 598–607.
Clines, David J. A. "The Additions to Esther". *HBC,* 815–19.
Clines, David J. A. "Esther". *HBC,* 387–94.
Dumm, Demetrius. "Esther". *NJBC,* 576–79.
Harvey, D. "Book of Esther". *IDB* II, 149–51.
Humphreys, W. L. "Book of Esther". *IDBsv,* 279–81.
Moore, Carey A. *Daniel, Esther and Jeremiah, The Additions.* (AB, 44) 7th printing, 1987.
Moore, Carey A. *Esther.* (AB, 7B) 8th printing, 1988.

Chapter 35: Lamentations, Song of Songs, Qoheleth

Lamentations:

Childs, Brevard S. "Lamentations". *IOTS,* 590–97.
De Vaux, Roland, "The Ancient Feasts of Israel". "The Later Feasts." *AI,* 484–506, 507–17.
Gottwald, Norman K. "Lamentations". *HBC,* 646–51.
Gottwald, N. K. "Book of Lamentations". *IDB* III, 61–63.
Guinan, Michael D. "Lamentations". *NJBC,* 558–62.
Hillers, Delbert R. *Lamentations.* (AB, 7A) 1972.

Song of Songs:

Childs, Brevard S. "Song of Songs". *IOTS,* 569–79.
Falk, Marcia. "Song of Songs". *HBC,* 525–28.

Gottwald, N. K. "Song of Songs". *IDB* IV, 420–26.
Murphy, Roland E. "Canticle of Canticles". *NJBC,* 462–65.
Murphy, R. E. "Song of Songs". *IDBsv,* 836–38.
Pope, Marvin H. *Song of Songs.* (AB, 7C) 6th printing, 1985.
Tournay, Raymond Jacques. *Word of God, Song of Love. A Commentary on the Song of Songs.* Translated by J. Edward Crowley. New York: Paulist Press, 1988.

Qoheleth:

Blank, S. H. "Ecclesiastes". *IDB* II, 7–13.
Childs, Brevard S. "Ecclesiastes". *IOTS,* 580–89.
Crenshaw, James L. "Ecclesiastes". *HBC,* 518–24.
Crenshaw, James L. *Ecclesiastes.* (OTL) Philadelphia: Westminster Press, 1987.
Gordis, Robert. *Koheleth, the Man and His World: A Study of Ecclesiastes.* 3d ed. New York: Schocken Books, 1968.
Priest, J. F. "Ecclesiastes". *IDBsv,* 249–50.
Von Rad, Gerhard. "The Doctrine of the Proper Time". "Ecclesiastes". "Epilogue to Job and Ecclesiastes". *WI,* 138–43, 226–37, 237–39.
Wright, Addison G. "Ecclesiastes (Qoheleth)". *NJBC,* 489–95.

Chapter 36: Daniel

Bright, John. "The Formative Period of Judaism". *HI,* 403–57.
Childs, Brevard S. "Daniel". *IOTS,* 608–23.
Collins, John J. "Daniel". In *The Apocalyptic Imagination: An Introduction to the Jewish Matrix of Christianity.* New York: Crossroad, 1987. 68–92.
Collins, John J. *Daniel, First Maccabees, Second Maccabees with an Excursus on the Apocalyptic Genre.* Old Testament Message, 16. Wilmington, DE: Michael Glazier, 1981.
Di Lella, A. A. "Daniel". *IDBsv,* 205–7.
Doran, Robert. "The Additions to Daniel". *HBC,* 863–71.
Frost, S. B. "Daniel". *IDB* I, 761–68.
Goldingay, John E. *Daniel.* (WBC, 30) 1989.
Hartman, Louis F., and Di Lella, Alexander A. *The Book of Daniel.* (AB, 23) 3d printing, 1983.
Hartman, Louis F., and Di Lella, Alexander A. "Daniel". *NJBC,* 406–20.
Jensen, Joseph. "The Fourth Beast and the Son of Man". *GWI,* 249–58.
Moore, Carey A. *Daniel, Esther and Jeremiah: The Additions.* (AB, 44) 7th printing, 1987.

Porteous, Norman W. *Daniel: A Commentary.* (OTL) Philadelphia: Westminster Press, 3d printing, 1976.

Chapter 37: 1 and 2 Maccabees

Doran, Robert. *Temple Propaganda: The Purpose and Character of 2 Maccabees.* The Catholic Biblical Quarterly Monograph Series, 12. Washington, DC: The Catholic Biblical Association of America, 1981.

Fitzmyer, Joseph A. "From Pompey to Bar Cochba". In "A History of Israel". *NJBC,* 1243–52.

Goldstein, Jonathan A. *I Maccabees; II Maccabees.* (AB, 41, 41A) 1976, 1984.

Koester, Helmut. "Historical Survey". "Judaism in the Hellenistic Period". *Introduction to the New Testament* I. *History, Culture and Religion of the Hellenistic Age.* New York and Berlin: Walter de Gruyter & Co., 1987. 1–31, 205–80.

Leaney, A. R. C. *The Jewish and Christian World 200 B.C. to A.D. 200.* Cambridge Commentaries on Writings of the Jewish and Christian World 200 B.C. to A.D. 200, vol. 7. New York: Cambridge University Press, 1984.

Lohse, Eduard. "The Political History of Judaism in the Hellenistic Period". "Religious Movements and Intellectual Currents in Judaism in the Time of the New Testament". *The New Testament Environment.* Translated by John E. Steely. Nashville: Abingdon Press, 1976. 15–54, 55–145.

McEleney, Neil J. "1–2 Maccabees". *NJBC,* 421–46.

Murphy, Roland E. "The Greek Era (333–63 B.C.)". *NJBC,* 1239–43.

Pritchard, James B., et al. "The Seleucid Empire". "Seleucid Rule and Jewish Reaction—The Maccabaean Fight for Religion and Country". *HBA,* 144–45, 146–47.

Reicke, Bo. "Judea under Hellenistic Rule 332–142 B.C.". "The Hasmonean Rule 142–63 B.C.". In *The New Testament Era: The World of the Bible from 500 B.C. to A.D. 100.* Translated by David E. Green. Philadelphia: Fortress Press, 5th printing, 1985. 35–62, 63–75.

Schiffman, Lawrence H. "1 Maccabees". "2 Maccabees". *HBC,* 875–97, 898–915.

Chapter 38: Sirach

Burkill, T. A. "Ecclesiasticus". *IDB* II, 13–21.

Crenshaw, James L. "Sirach". *HBC,* 836–54.

Di Lella, Alexander A. "Sirach". *NJBC,* 496–509.

Sanders, Jack T. *Ben Sira and Demotic Wisdom*. SBL Monograph Ser., No. 28. Chico, CA: Scholars Press, 1983.

Skehan, P. W. "Ecclesiasticus". *IDBsv*, 250–51.

Skehan, Patrick W. *The Wisdom of Ben Sira*. Introduction. Alexander A. Di Lella. (AB, 39) 1987.

Von Rad, Gerhard. "The Wisdom of Jesus Sirach". *WI*, 240–62.

Chapter 39: Tobit, Judith, Baruch

Tobit:

Nickelsburg, George W. E. "Tobit". *HBC*, 791–803.

Nowell, Irene. "Tobit". *NJBC*, 568–71.

Wikgren, A. "Book of Tobit". *IDB* IV, 658–62.

Judith:

Alonso-Schökel, Luis. "Judith". *HBC*, 804–14.

Craven, Toni. "Judith". *NJBC*, 572–75.

Moore, Carey A. *Judith*. (AB, 40) 1985.

Winter, P. "Book of Judith". *IDB* II, 1023–26.

Baruch:

Fitzgerald, Aloysius. "Baruch". *NJBC*, 563–67.

Harrington, Daniel J. "Baruch". "Letter of Jeremiah". *HBC*, 855–60, 861–62.

Moore, Carey A. *Daniel, Esther and Jeremiah: The Additions*. (AB, 44) 1977.

Tedesche, S. "Book of Baruch". *IDB* I, 362–63.

Chapter 40: Wisdom

Fitzmyer, Joseph A. "From Pompey to Bar Cochba". In "A History of Israel". *NJBC*, 1243–52.

Garcia-Treto, Francisco O. "Herod". *HBD*, 385–88.

Hadas, M. "Wisdom of Solomon". *IDB* IV, 861–63.

Hammond, N. G. L., and Scullard, H. H., eds. *The Oxford Classical Dictionary*. 2d ed. Reprint. Oxford: Clarendon Press, 1987:

"Pompeius, Gnaeus (Pompey)". 857–58 (G. E. F. Chilver).

"Caesar, Gaius Julius". 189–90 (G. E. F. Chilver).

"Antonius, Marcus". 77–78 (G. W. Richardson and T. J. Cadoux).

"Augustus, C. Octavius". 149–51 (A. Momigliano).

"Egypt under the Greeks and Romans". 373–75 (J. G. Milne).

"Cleopatra VII". 251–55 (T. J. Cadoux).

Koester, Helmut. "Judaism in the Hellenistic Period". "The Roman Empire as the Heir of Hellenism". *Introduction to the New Testament* I. *History, Culture and Religion of the Hellenistic Age*. New York and Berlin: Walter de Gruyter & Co., 1987. 205–80, 281–412.

Leaney, A. R. C. *The Jewish and Christian World 200 B.C. to A.D. 200*. Cambridge Commentaries on Writings of the Jewish and Christian World 200 B.C. to A.D. 200, vol. 7. New York: Cambridge University Press, 1984.

Pritchard, James B., et al. "The Development of the Synagogue". *HBA*, 152.

Reese, James M. "Wisdom of Solomon". *HBC*, 820–35.

Safrai, S. "The Synagogue". In *The Jewish People in the First Century, Historical Geography, Political History, Social, Cultural and Religious Life and Institutions* II. Edited by S. Safrai and M. Stern. Philadelphia: Fortress Press, 2d printing, 1987. 908–44.

Sandmel, S. "Herod (Family)". *IDB* II, 585–94.

Willoughby, H. R. "Alexandria". *IDB* I, 79–81.

Winston, David. *The Wisdom of Solomon*. (AB, 43) 1979.

Wright, Addison G. "Wisdom". *NJBC*, 510–22.

II. THE NEW TESTAMENT:

The commentaries on the individual New Testament books are the major references that were consulted for the section entitled "Toward the New Testament", which concludes our reflection in each book of the Old Testament. The reader is encouraged to study the commentaries for a deeper appreciation of the manner in which the New Testament authors read the Old Testament texts in light of their fulfillment in Christ. I frequently consulted one text in particular that I recommend to the reader for its ground-breaking study of Old Testament citations in the New Testament: Lindars, Barnabas. *New Testament Apologetic: The Doctrinal Significance of the Old Testament Quotations*. London: SCM Press, 2d impression, 1973.

Studies on Old Testament Citations in the New Testament:

Bruce, F. F. *This Is That. The New Testament Development of Some Old Testament Themes*. Exeter: Paternoster Press, 1968.

Lindars, Barnabas. *New Testament Apologetic: The Doctrinal Significance of the Old Testament Quotations*. London: SCM Press, 2d impression, 1973.

Background to the New Testament:

Collins, Raymond F. *Introduction to the New Testament.* Garden City, NY: Image Books (Doubleday & Co.), 1987.

Hengel, Martin. *Judaism and Hellenism: Studies in Their Encounter in Palestine during the Early Hellenistic Period.* 2 vols. Translated by John Bowden. Philadelphia: Fortress Press, 1974; one-vol. ed., 1981.

Koester, Helmut. *Introduction to the New Testament.* Vol. I. *History, Culture and Religion of the Hellenistic Age;* Vol. II. *History and Literature of Early Christianity.* New York and Berlin: Walter de Gruyter & Co., 1987.

Kümmel, W. G. *Introduction to the New Testament.* Rev. ed. Translated by Howard Clark Kee. London: SCM Press, 1977.

Commentaries and Studies on Individual Books:

Matthew:

Brown, Raymond E. *The Birth of the Messiah.* Garden City, NY: Doubleday & Co., 1977.

Beare, F. W. *The Gospel according to Matthew.* San Francisco: Harper & Row, 1981.

Davies, W. D. *The Setting of the Sermon on the Mount.* Cambridge: University Press, 1964.

Filson, Floyd V. *The Gospel according to St. Matthew.* Harper's New Testament Commentaries. San Francisco: Harper & Row, 1960.

Luz, Ulrich. *Matthew 1–7: A Commentary.* Translated by Wilhelm C. Linss. Minneapolis: Augsburg Press, 1989.

Viviano, Benedict T. "The Gospel according to Matthew". *NJBC,* 630–74.

Mark:

Harrington, Daniel J. "The Gospel according to Mark". *NJBC,* 596–629.

Mann, C. S. *Mark* (AB, 27) 1986.

Stock, Augustine. *The Method and Message of Mark.* Wilmington, DE: Michael Glazier, 1989.

Taylor, Vincent. *The Gospel according to St. Mark.* 2d ed. Reprint. London: Macmillan, St. Martin's Press, 1969.

Luke:

Brown, Raymond E. *The Birth of the Messiah.* Garden City, NY: Doubleday & Co., 1977.

Fitzmyer, Joseph A. *The Gospel according to Luke. I–IX* and *X–XXIV.* (AB, 28 and 28A) 1981, 1985.

Fitzmyer, Joseph A. *Luke the Theologian: Aspects of His Teaching.* NY and Mahwah: Paulist Press, 1989.

Karris, Robert J. "The Gospel according to Luke". *NJBC,* 675–721.

Marshall, I. Howard. *Commentary on Luke.* New International Greek Testament Commentary. Grand Rapids, MI: William B. Eerdmans Publishing Co., 1978.

Neyrey, Jerome. *The Passion according to Luke: A Redaction Study of Luke's Soteriology.* NY and Mahwah: Paulist Press, 1985.

John:

Brown, Raymond E. *The Gospel according to John. I–XII* and *XIII–XXI.* (AB, 29 and 29A) 1966, 1970.

Schnackenburg, Rudolf. *The Gospel according to St. John* I, II, and III. New York: Crossroad, 1987.

Acts of the Apostles:

Conzelmann, Hans. *Acts of the Apostles.* (Hermeneia) Philadelphia: Fortress Press, 1987.

Dillon, Richard J. "Acts of the Apostles". *NJBC,* 722–67.

Haenchen, Ernst. *The Acts of the Apostles: A Commentary.* Oxford: Basil Blackwell, 1971.

Romans:

Black, Matthew. *Romans.* The New Century Bible Commentary. Grand Rapids, MI: William B. Eerdmans Publishing Co., 1981.

Cranfield, C. E. B. *The Epistle to the Romans* I and II. Reprint. Edinburgh: T. & T. Clark, 1987, 1986.

Fitzmyer, Joseph A. "The Letter to the Romans". *NJBC,* 830–68.

Käsemann, Ernst. *Commentary on Romans.* Translated and edited by Geoffrey W. Bromiley. Grand Rapids, MI: William B. Eerdmans Publishing Co., 1980.

First Corinthians:

Barrett, C. K. *The First Epistle to the Corinthians.* Harper's New Testament Commentaries. Peabody, MA: Hendrickson Publishers, 1987.

Conzelmann, Hans. *1 Corinthians.* (Hermeneia) Philadelphia: Fortress Press, 1975.

Fee, Gordon D. *The First Epistle to the Corinthians.* New International Commentary on the New Testament. Reprint. Grand Rapids, MI: William B. Eerdmans Publishing Co., 1988.

Murphy-O'Connor, Jerome. "The First Letter to the Corinthians". *NJBC,* 798–815.

Second Corinthians:

Barrett, C. K. *The Second Epistle to the Corinthians.* Harper's New Testament Commentaries. Peabody, MA: Hendrickson Publishers, 1987.

Hughes, Philip E. *The Second Epistle to the Corinthians.* New International Commentary on the New Testament. Reprint. Grand Rapids, MI: William B. Eerdmans Publishing Co., 1986.

Martin, Ralph P. *2 Corinthians.* (WBC, 40) 1986.

Murphy-O'Connor, Jerome. "The Second Letter to the Corinthians". *NJBC,* 816–29.

Galatians:

Bruce, F. F. *Commentary on Galatians.* New International Greek Testament Commentary. Grand Rapids, MI: William B. Eerdmans Publishing Co., 1982.

Fitzmyer, Joseph A. "The Letter to the Galatians". *NJBC,* 780–90.

Ephesians:

Barth, Marcus. *Ephesians. 1–3 and 4–6.* (AB, 34 and 34A) 1974.

Kobelski, Paul J. "The Letter to the Ephesians". *NJBC,* 883–90.

Philippians:

Beare, F. W. *The Epistle to the Philippians.* Harper's New Testament Commentaries. San Francisco: Harper & Row, 1959.

Byrne, Brendan. "The Letter to the Philippians". *NJBC,* 791–97.

Martin, Ralph P. *Carmen Christi: Philippians 2:5–11 in Recent Interpretation and in the Setting of Early Christian Worship.* Rev. ed. Grand Rapids, MI: William B. Eerdmans Publishing Co., 1983.

Müller, Jac J. *The Epistles of Paul to the Philippians and to Philemon.* The New International Commentary on the New Testament. Reprint. Grand Rapids, MI: William B. Eerdmans Publishing Co., 1978.

Colossians:

Horgan, Maurya P. "The Letter to the Colossians". *NJBC,* 876–82.

Lohse, Eduard. *Colossians and Philemon.* Edited by Helmut Koester. (Hermeneia) Philadelphia: Fortress Press, 3d printing, 1982.

First Thessalonians:

Bruce, F. F. *1 & 2 Thessalonians.* (WBC, 45) 1982.

Collins, Raymond F. "The First Letter to the Thessalonians". *NJBC,* 772–79.

Pastoral Letters:

Dibelius, Martin, and Conzelmann, Hans. *The Pastoral Epistles.* (Hermeneia) Philadelphia: Fortress Press, 3d printing, 1983.
Kelly, J. N. D. *The Pastoral Epistles, Timothy I and II, Titus.* Harper's New Testament Commentaries. San Francisco: Harper & Row, 1960.
Wild, Robert A. "The Pastoral Letters". *NJBC,* 891–902.

Hebrews:

Bourke, Myles M. "The Epistle to the Hebrews". *NJBC,* 920–41.
Bruce, F. F. *The Epistle to the Hebrews.* New International Commentary on the New Testament. Reprint. Grand Rapids, MI: William B. Eerdmans Publishing Co., 1981.
Buchanan, George Wesley. *To the Hebrews.* (AB, 36) 1972.
Hughes, Philip E. *A Commentary on the Epistle to the Hebrews.* Reprint. Grand Rapids, MI: William B. Eerdmans Publishing Co., 1983.

James:

Davids, Peter H. *Commentary on James.* New International Greek Testament Commentary. Grand Rapids, MI: William B. Eerdmans Publishing Co., 1982.
Leahey, Thomas W. "The Epistle of James". *NJBC,* 909–16.

First Peter:

Dalton, William J. "The First Epistle of Peter". *NJBC,* 903–8.
Kelly, J. N. D. *A Commentary on the Epistles of Peter and Jude.* Thornapple Commentaries. Grand Rapids, MI: Baker Book House, 2d printing, 1982.
Selwyn, Edward Gordon. *The First Epistle of St. Peter.* 2d ed. Thornapple Commentaries. Grand Rapids, MI: Baker Book House, 2d printing, 1983.

First John:

Brown, Raymond E. *The Epistles of John.* (AB, 30) 1982.
Marshall, I. Howard. *The Epistles of John.* New International Commentary on the New Testament. Grand Rapids, MI: William B. Eerdmans Publishing Co., 3d printing, 1981.
Perkins, Pheme. "The Johannine Epistles". *NJBC,* 986–95.

Revelation:

Beasley-Murray, G. R. *The Book of Revelation.* Rev. ed. New Century Bible. London: Oliphants (Marshall, Morgan and Scott), 1978.
Collins, Adela Yarbro. *The Apocalypse.* New Testament Message, 22. Wilmington, DE: Michael Glazier, 1985.
Collins, Adela Yarbro. "The Apocalypse (Revelation)". *NJBC,* 996–1016.

INDEX OF PROPER NAMES

647

INDEX OF THEMES

This index identifies the occurrences of major themes which we noted principally in the Old Testament (OT) but also in citations and allusions in the New Testament (NT). We designed it to help the reader trace important theological and pastoral currents throughout the Bible. Parentheticals following page references indicate the biblical books in which the reader will find these themes.

INDEX OF NEW TESTAMENT CITATIONS